# DATA STRUCTURES & PROGRAM DESIGN IN

# C

## *Second Edition*

# 数据结构与程序设计
# （C 语言描述）

## 第 2 版

**Robert L. Kruse**
*St . Mary's University Halifax , Nova Scotia Canada*

**Clovis L. Tondo**
*T&T TechWorks , Inc . Coral Springs , Florida U . S . A .*

**Bruce P. Leung**
*Connected Components Corp . Cambridge , Massachusetts U . S . A*

2000/11

清华大学出版社
**Prentice-Hall International, Inc.**

(京) 新登字 158 号

Data structures & program design in C 2nd ed./Robert L. Kruse, Clovis. L. Tondo, Bruce P. Leung

**图书在版编目(CIP)数据**

数据结构与程序设计(C语言描述)第 2 版:英文/克鲁泽(Kruse,R.)等著. — 影印版. — 北京:清华大学出版社,1998.7
(大学计算机教育丛书)
ISBN 7-302-02943-1

Ⅰ.数… Ⅱ.克… Ⅲ.C语言-数据结构-程序设计-教材-英文
Ⅳ.TP311.12

中国版本图书馆 CIP 数据核字(98)第 09273 号

出版者:清华大学出版社(北京清华大学校内,邮编 100084)
　　　　因特网地址:www.tup.tsinghua.edu.cn
印刷者:清华大学印刷厂
发行者:新华书店总店北京科技发行所
开　本: 850×1168 1/32　印张: 21.625
版　次: 1998 年 7 月第 1 版　1998 年 7 月第 1 次印刷
书　号: ISBN 7-302-02943-1/TP·1555
印　数: 0001~5000
定　价: 32.00 元

# 出 版 前 言

　　我们的大学生、研究生毕业后,面临的将是一个国际化的信息时代。他们将需要随时查阅大量的外文资料;会有更多的机会参加国际性学术交流活动;接待外国学者;走上国际会议的讲坛。作为科技工作者,他们不仅应有与国外同行进行口头和书面交流的能力,更为重要的是,他们必须具备极强的查阅外文资料获取信息的能力。有鉴于此,在国家教委所颁布的"大学英语教学大纲"中有一条规定:专业阅读应作为必修课程开设。同时,在大纲中还规定了这门课程的学时和教学要求。有些高校除开设"专业阅读"课之外,还在某些专业课拟进行英语授课。但教、学双方都苦于没有一定数量的合适的英文原版教材作为教学参考书。为满足这方面的需要,我们挑选了 7 本计算机科学方面最新版本的教材,进行影印出版。首批影印出版的 6 本书受到广大读者的热情欢迎,我们深受鼓舞,今后还将陆续推出新书。希望读者继续给予大力支持。Prentice Hall 公司和清华大学出版社这次合作将国际先进水平的教材引入我国高等学校,为师生们提供了教学用书,相信会对高校教材改革产生积极的影响。

清华大学出版社

Prentice Hall 公司

1997.11

# Contents

# Preface

An apprentice carpenter may want only a hammer and a saw, but a master craftsman employs many precision tools. Computer programming likewise requires sophisticated tools to cope with the complexity of real applications, and only practice with these tools will build skill in their use. This book treats structured problem solving, data abstraction, software engineering principles, and the comparative analysis of algorithms as fundamental tools of program design. Several case studies of substantial size are worked out in detail, to show how all the tools are used together to build complete programs.

Many of the algorithms and data structures we study possess an intrinsic elegance, a simplicity that cloaks the range and power of their applicability. Before long the student discovers that vast improvements can be made over the naïve methods usually used in introductory courses. Yet this elegance of method is tempered with uncertainty. The student soon finds that it can be far from obvious which of several approaches will prove best in particular applications. Hence comes an early opportunity to introduce truly difficult problems of both intrinsic interest and practical importance and to exhibit the applicability of mathematical methods to algorithm verification and analysis.

Many students find difficulty in translating abstract ideas into practice. This book, therefore, takes special care in the formulation of ideas into algorithms and in the refinement of algorithms into concrete programs that can be applied to practical problems. The process of data specification and abstraction, similarly, comes before the selection of data structures and their implementations.

We believe in progressing from the concrete to the abstract, in the careful development of motivating examples, followed by the presentation of ideas in a more general form. At an early stage of their careers most students need reinforcement from seeing the immediate application of the ideas that they study, and they require the practice of writing and running programs to illustrate each important concept that they learn. This book therefore contains many sample programs, both short functions and complete programs of substantial length. The exercises and programming projects, moreover, constitute an indispensable part of the book. Many of these are immediate applications of the topic under study, often requesting that programs be written and run, so that algorithms may be tested and compared. Some are larger projects, and a few are suitable for use by a small group of students working together.

# Synopsis

By working through the first large project (CONWAY's game of Life), Chapter 1 expounds principles of top-down refinement, program design, review, and testing, principles that the student will see demonstrated and is expected to follow throughout the sequel. At the same time, this project provides an opportunity for the student to review the syntax of C, the programming language used throughout the book.

Chapter 2 introduces a few of the basic concerns of software engineering, including problem specification and analysis, prototyping, data abstraction, algorithm design, refinement, verification, and analysis. The chapter applies these principles to the development of a second program for the Life game, one based on an algorithm that is sufficiently subtle as to show the need for precise specifications and verification, and one that shows why care must be taken in the choice of data structures.

Chapter 3 continues to elucidate data abstraction and algorithm design by studying stacks as an abstract data type, recursion as a problem-solving method, and the intimate connections among stacks, recursion, and certain trees.

Queues and lists are the central topics of the next two chapters. The chapters expound several different implementations of each abstract data type, develop large application programs showing the relative advantages of different implementations, and introduce algorithm analysis in a very informal way. A major goal of these chapters is to bring the student to appreciate data abstraction and to apply methods of top-down design to data as well as to algorithms.

Chapters 6, 7, and 8 present algorithms for searching, sorting, and table access (including hashing). These chapters illustrate the interplay between algorithms and the associated abstract data types, data structures, and implementations. The text introduces the "big O" notation for elementary algorithm analysis and highlights the crucial choices to be made regarding best use of space, time, and programming effort.

These choices require that we find analytical methods to assess algorithms, and producing such analyses is a battle for which combinatorial mathematics must provide the arsenal. At an elementary level we can expect students neither to be well armed nor to possess the mathematical maturity needed to hone their skills to perfection. Our goal, therefore, is to help students recognize the importance of such skills in anticipation of later chances to study mathematics.

Binary trees are surely among the most elegant and useful of data structures. Their study, which occupies Chapter 9, ties together concepts from lists, searching, and sorting. As recursively defined data structures, binary trees afford an excellent opportunity for the student to become comfortable with recursion applied both to data structures and algorithms. The chapter begins with elementary topics and progresses as far as splay trees and amortized algorithm analysis.

Chapter 10 continues the study of more sophisticated data structures, including tries, B-trees, and red-black trees. The next chapter introduces graphs as more general structures useful for problem solving.

The case study in Chapter 12 examines the Polish notation in considerable detail, exploring the interplay of recursion, trees, and stacks as vehicles for problem solving and algorithm development. Some of the questions addressed can serve as an informal introduction to compiler design. As usual, the algorithms are fully developed within a functioning C program. This program accepts as input an expression in ordinary (infix) form, translates the expression into postfix form, and evaluates the expression for specified values of the variable(s).

The appendices discuss several topics that are not properly part of the book's subject but that are often missing from the student's preparation.

*A. Mathematical Methods*

Appendix A presents several topics from discrete mathematics. Its final two sections, on Fibonacci and Catalan numbers, are more advanced and not needed for any vital purpose in the text, but are included to encourage combinatorial interest in the more mathematically inclined.

Removal of recursion is a topic that most programmers should no longer need to study. But at present some important work must still be done in contexts (like FORTRAN or COBOL) disallowing recursion. Methods for manual recursion removal

*B. Removal of Recursion*

are therefore sometimes required, and are collected for reference as Appendix B. Some instructors will wish to include the study of threaded binary trees with Chapter 9; this section is therefore written so that it can be read independently of the remainder of Appendix B.

*C. An Introduction to C*

Appendix C, finally, is a brief introduction to the C programming language. This is not a thorough treatment of the language, but it is intended to serve as a review of C syntax and as a reference for the student.

## Changes in the Second Edition

In this edition, the entire text has been carefully reviewed and revised to update its presentation and to reflect the ideas of many readers who have communicated their experiences in studying the book. The principal changes are summarized as follows.

- All the programs have been rewritten, revised, and polished to emphasize data abstraction, to develop and employ reusable code, and to strengthen uniformity and elegance of style.

- The documentation has been strengthened by including informal specifications (pre- and postconditions) with all subprograms.

- Recursion is treated much earlier in the text and then emphasized by repeated use thereafter.

- The coverage of more advanced, modern topics has been extended by the inclusion of several new sections, including splay trees, red-black trees, and amortized algorithm analysis.

- The text highlights new case studies, such as the miniature text editor in Chapter 5.

- New exercises and programming projects have been added, including continuing projects on information retrieval that request the student to compare the performance of several different data structures and algorithms.

- The material on graph theory and graph algorithms has now been collected as a separate chapter.
- The treatment of lists has been streamlined.
- The source code for all the programs and program extracts printed in the book will be available on the internet. To reach this software under `ftp`, log in as user anonymous on the `ftp` site `prenhall.com` and change to the directory

  `pub/esm/computer_science.s-041/kruse/dspdc2`

- Instructors teaching from this book may obtain, at no charge, the *Instructor's Resource Manual*, which includes:

  - Brief teaching notes on each chapter;
  - Full solutions to all exercises in the textbook;
  - Transparency masters;
  - A PC disk containing both the software mentioned previously and the full source code for all programming projects from the textbook.

## Course Structure

*prerequisite*

The prerequisite for this book is a first course in programming, with experience using the elementary features of C. Appendix C presents several advanced aspects of C programming that are often omitted from introductory courses. A good knowledge of high school mathematics will suffice for almost all the algorithm analyses, but further (perhaps concurrent) preparation in discrete mathematics will prove valuable. Appendix A reviews all required mathematics.

*content*

This book is intended for courses such as the ACM Course CS2 (*Program Design and Implementation*), ACM Course CS7 (*Data Structures and Algorithm Analysis*), or a course combining these. Thorough coverage is given to most of the ACM/IEEE knowledge units[1] on data structures and algorithms. These include:

AL1 Basic data structures, such as arrays, tables, stacks, queues, trees, and graphs;

AL2 Abstract data types;

AL3 Recursion and recursive algorithms;

AL4 Complexity analysis using the big O notation;

AL6 Sorting and searching; and

AL8 Practical problem-solving strategies, with large case studies.

The three most advanced knowledge units, AL5 (complexity classes, NP-complete problems), AL7 (computability and undecidability), and AL9 (parallel and distributed algorithms) are not treated in this book.

Most chapters of this book are structured so that the core topics are presented first, followed by examples, applications, and larger case studies. Hence, if time allows only a brief study of a topic, it is possible, with no loss of continuity, to move

---

[1] See *Computing Curricula 1991: Report of the ACM/IEEE-CS Joint Curriculum Task Force*, ACM Press, New York, 1990.

rapidly from chapter to chapter covering only the core topics. When time permits, however, both students and instructor will enjoy the occasional excursion into the supplementary topics and worked-out projects.

*two-term course*
A two-term course can cover nearly the entire book, thereby attaining a satisfying integration of many topics from the areas of problem solving, data structures, program development, and algorithm analysis. Students need time and practice to understand general methods. By combining the studies of data abstraction, data structures, and algorithms with their implementations in projects of realistic size, an integrated course can build a solid foundation on which, later, more theoretical courses can be built.

Even if this book is not covered in its entirety, it will provide enough depth to enable interested students to continue using it as a reference in later work. It is important in any case to assign major programming projects and to allow adequate time for their completion.

## Book Production

This book and its supplements were written and produced with the first author's software called PreTEX, a preprocessor and macro package for the TEX typesetting system.[2] PreTEX, by exploiting context dependency, automatically supplies much of the typesetting markup required by TEX. PreTEX also supplies several tools useful to the author, such as a powerful cross-reference system, greatly simplified typesetting of mathematics and computer-program listings, and automatic generation of the index and table of contents, while allowing the processing of the book in conveniently small files at every stage. Solutions, placed with exercises and projects, are automatically removed from the text and placed in a separate manual. In conjunction with the POSTSCRIPT page-description language, PreTEX provides convenient facilities for color separation, halftone screens, and other special results.

For a book such as this, PreTEX's treatment of computer programs is its most important feature. Computer programs are not included with the main body of the text; instead, they are placed in separate, secondary files, along with any desired explanatory text, and with any desired typesetting markup in place. By placing tags at appropriate places in the secondary files, PreTEX can extract arbitrary parts of a secondary file, in any desired order, for typesetting with the text. Another utility (called *StripTEX*) can be used on the same file to remove all the tags, text, and markup, with output that is a program ready to be compiled. The same input file thus automatically produces both typeset program listings and compiled program code. In this way, the reader gains increased confidence in the accuracy of the computer program listings appearing in the text.

For this edition, all the diagrams and artwork have been produced as POSTSCRIPT code in Adobe Illustrator. This allows the automatic inclusion of all figures in the preliminary drafts of the manuscript and shortens the final stages of production by removing any need for manual processing of camera copy.

---

[2] TEX was developed by DONALD E. KNUTH, who has also made many important contributions to our knowledge of data structures and algorithms. (See the entries under his name in the index.)

## Acknowledgments ─────────────────────────────────────

Over the years, this book and its Pascal antecedents have benefitted greatly from the contributions of many people: family, friends, colleagues, and students. The first edition lists some of the people whose contributions are especially noteworthy. Since the publication of the first edition, translations into several languages have also appeared, and many more people have kindly forwarded their comments and suggestions to us. In particular, it is a pleasure to acknowledge the suggestions of the reviewers for the current edition: ALEX RYBA (Marquette University), RICHARD SAUNDERS (University of Arizona), DAVID STRAIGHT (University of Tennessee, Knoxville), CARLOS CUNHA (Boston University), and GREG CAMERON (Ricks College).

C. L. TONDO also acknowledges the help of GEORGE EDMUNDS, TOM HORTON, SAM HSU, MARIA PETRIE (all of Florida Atlantic University), ROLIE GUILD (Nova Southeastern University), LOUIS VOSLOO (Y&Y, Inc.), NELSON FELIPPE DA SILVA (Polydata, Inc.), LUIZ BIAVATTI, A. CARLOS TONDO (T&T TechWorks, Inc.), ED HAUGHNEY, ANDREW NATHANSON, RED VISCUSO, and CAREN E. TONDO.

The editorial staff of Prentice Hall, especially ALAN APT, Publisher, and LAURA STEELE, Managing Editor, have displayed much patience, interest, and helpfulness in bringing this project to a successful conclusion.

JIM COOPER of PreT̸EX, Inc., has expedited the appearance of this book and its supplements by checking all the C programs, solving many problems of page makeup, and by completing all the solutions to exercises and reworking the programming projects.

Finally, let us note that this book is an adaptation into C, by the second and third authors, of the Pascal-based *Data Structures and Program Design*, third edition, by the first author. The first author is responsible for the language-independent discussion and the other authors for the C programs and language-specific exposition.

ROBERT L. KRUSE
CLOVIS L. TONDO
BRUCE P. LEUNG

# 1

# Programming Principles

THIS CHAPTER summarizes important principles of good programming, especially as applied to large projects, and illustrates methods for discovering effective algorithms. In the process we raise questions in program design that we shall address in later chapters, and review many of the special features of the language C by using them to write programs.

## 1.1 Introduction

The greatest difficulties of writing large computer programs are not in deciding what the goals of the program should be, nor even in finding methods that can be used to reach these goals. The president of a business might say, "Let's get a computer to keep track of all our inventory information, accounting records, and personnel files, and let it tell us when inventories need to be reordered and budget lines are overspent, and let it handle the payroll." With enough time and effort, a staff of systems analysts and programmers might be able to determine how various staff members are now doing these tasks and write programs to do the work in the same way.

*problems of large programs*

This approach, however, is almost certain to be a disastrous failure. While interviewing employees, the systems analysts will find some tasks that can be put on the computer easily and will proceed to do so. Then, as they move other work to the computer, they will find that it depends on the first tasks. The output from these, unfortunately, will not be quite in the proper form. Hence they need more programming to convert the data from the form given for one task to the form needed for another. The programming project begins to resemble a patchwork quilt. Some of the pieces are stronger, some weaker. Some of the pieces are carefully sewn onto the adjacent ones, some are barely tacked together. If the programmers are lucky, their creation may hold together well enough to do most of the routine work most of the time. But if any change must be made, it will have unpredictable consequences throughout the system. Later, a new request will come along, or an unexpected problem, perhaps even an emergency, and the programmers' efforts will prove as effective as using a patchwork quilt as a safety net for people jumping from a tall building.

*purpose of book*

The main purpose of this book is to describe programming methods and tools that will prove effective for projects of realistic size, programs much larger than those ordinarily used to illustrate features of elementary programming. Since a piecemeal approach to large problems is doomed to fail, we must first of all adopt a consistent, unified, and logical approach, and we must also be careful to observe important principles of program design, principles that are sometimes ignored in writing small programs, but whose neglect will prove disastrous for large projects.

*problem specification*

The first major hurdle in attacking a large problem is deciding exactly what the problem is. It is necessary to translate vague goals, contradictory requests, and perhaps unstated desires into a precisely formulated project that can be programmed. And the methods or divisions of work that people have previously used are not necessarily the best for use in a machine. Hence our approach must be to determine overall goals, but precise ones, and then slowly divide the work into smaller problems until they become of manageable size.

*program design*

The maxim that many programmers observe, "First make your program work, then make it pretty," may be effective for small programs, but not for large ones. Each part of a large program must be well organized, clearly written, and thoroughly understood, or else its structure will have been forgotten, and it can no longer be tied to the other parts of the project at some much later time, perhaps by another programmer. Hence we do not separate style from other parts of program design, but from the beginning we must be careful to form good habits.

Even with very large projects, difficulties usually arise not from the inability to find a solution but, rather, from the fact that there can be so many different methods and algorithms that might work that it can be hard to decide which is best, which may lead to programming difficulties, or which may be hopelessly inefficient. The

*data structures*

greatest room for variability in algorithm design is generally in the way in which the data of the program are stored:

- How they are arranged in relation to each other.
- Which data are kept in memory.
- Which are calculated when needed.
- Which are kept in files, and how the files are arranged.

A second goal of this book, therefore, is to present several elegant, yet fundamentally simple ideas for the organization and manipulation of data. Lists, stacks, and queues are the first three such methods that we study. Later, we shall develop several powerful algorithms for important tasks within data processing, such as sorting and searching.

When there are several different ways to organize data and devise algorithms it becomes important to develop criteria to recommend a choice. Hence we devote

*analysis*

attention to analyzing the behavior of algorithms under various conditions.

The difficulty of debugging a program increases much faster than its size. That is, if one program is twice the size of another, then it will likely not take twice as

*testing and verification*

long to debug, but perhaps four times as long. Many very large programs (such as operating systems) are put into use still containing errors that the programmers have despaired of finding, because the difficulties seem insurmountable. Sometimes projects that have consumed years of effort must be discarded because it is impossible to discover why they will not work. If we do not wish such a fate for our own projects, then we must use methods that will

*program correctness*

- Reduce the number of errors, making it easier to spot those that remain.
- Enable us to verify in advance that our algorithms are correct.
- Provide us with ways to test our programs so that we can be reasonably confident that they will not misbehave.

Development of such methods is another of our goals, but one that cannot yet be fully within our grasp.

Informal surveys show that, once a large and important program is fully debugged and in use, less than half of the programming effort that will be invested

*maintenance*

altogether in the project will have been completed. *Maintenance* of programs, that is, modifications needed to meet new requests and new operating environments, takes, on average, more than half of the programming investment. For this reason, it is essential that a large project be written to make it as easy to understand and modify as possible.

*C*

The programming language C has several features that make it an appropriate choice to express the algorithms we shall develop. C has been carefully designed to facilitate the discipline of writing carefully structured programs, with requirements implementing principles of program design. It contains relatively few features, in comparison with most high-level languages, so that it can be mastered quickly, and yet it contains powerful features for handling data which ease the translation from general algorithms to specific programs.

Several sections of this and later chapters mention features of C informally as they appear while we write programs. For the precise details of C syntax (grammar), consult Appendix C or a textbook on C programming.

# 1.2 The Game of Life

If we may take the liberty to abuse an old proverb,

*One concrete problem is worth a thousand unapplied abstractions.*

*case study*

Throughout this chapter and the next we shall concentrate on one case study that, while not large by realistic standards, illustrates both the methods of program design and the pitfalls that we should learn to avoid. Sometimes the example motivates general principles; sometimes the general discussion comes first; always it is with the view of discovering general methods that will prove their value in a range of practical applications. In later chapters we shall employ similar methods for larger projects. The example we shall use is the game called *Life*, which was introduced by the British mathematician J. H. CONWAY in 1970.

## 1.2.1 RULES FOR THE GAME OF LIFE

*definitions*

Life is really a simulation, not a game with players. It takes place on an unbounded rectangular grid in which each cell can either be occupied by an organism or not. Occupied cells are called *alive*; unoccupied cells are called *dead*. Which cells are alive changes from generation to generation according to the number of neighboring cells that are alive, as follows:

*transition rules*

1. The neighbors of a given cell are the eight cells that touch it vertically, horizontally, or diagonally.

2. If a cell is alive but either has no neighboring cells alive or only one alive, then in the next generation the cell dies of loneliness.

3. If a cell is alive and has four or more neighboring cells also alive, then in the next generation the cell dies of overcrowding.

4. A living cell with either two or three living neighbors remains alive in the next generation.

5. If a cell is dead, then in the next generation it will become alive if it has exactly three neighboring cells, no more or fewer, that are already alive. All other dead cells remain dead in the next generation.

6. All births and deaths take place at exactly the same time, so that dying cells can help to give birth to another, but cannot prevent the death of others by reducing overcrowding, nor can cells being born either preserve or kill cells living in the previous generation.

### 1.2.2 EXAMPLES

As a first example, consider the community

| | | | | |
|---|---|---|---|---|
| | | | | |
| | | • | • | |
| | | | | |

The counts of living neighbors for the cells are as follows:

| 0 | 0 | 0 | 0 | 0 | 0 |
|---|---|---|---|---|---|
| 0 | 1 | 2 | 2 | 1 | 0 |
| 0 | 1 | •1 | •1 | 1 | 0 |
| 0 | 1 | 2 | 2 | 1 | 0 |
| 0 | 0 | 0 | 0 | 0 | 0 |

*moribund example*

By rule 2 both the living cells will die in the coming generation, and rule 5 shows that no cells will become alive, so the community dies out.

On the other hand, the community

| 0 | 0 | 0 | 0 | 0 | 0 |
|---|---|---|---|---|---|
| 0 | 1 | 2 | 2 | 1 | 0 |
| 0 | 2 | •3 | •3 | 2 | 0 |
| 0 | 2 | •3 | •3 | 2 | 0 |
| 0 | 1 | 2 | 2 | 1 | 0 |
| 0 | 0 | 0 | 0 | 0 | 0 |

*stability*

has the neighbor counts as shown. Each of the living cells has a neighbor count of three, and hence remains alive, but the dead cells all have neighbor counts of two or less, and hence none of them becomes alive.

The two communities

| 0 | 0 | 0 | 0 | 0 |
|---|---|---|---|---|
| 1 | 2 | 3 | 2 | 1 |
| 1 | •1 | •2 | •1 | 1 |
| 1 | 2 | 3 | 2 | 1 |
| 0 | 0 | 0 | 0 | 0 |

and

| 0 | 1 | 1 | 1 | 0 |
|---|---|---|---|---|
| 0 | 2 | •1 | 2 | 0 |
| 0 | 3 | •2 | 3 | 0 |
| 0 | 2 | •1 | 2 | 0 |
| 0 | 1 | 1 | 1 | 0 |

*alternation*

continue to alternate from generation to generation, as indicated by the neighbor counts shown.

It is a surprising fact that, from very simple initial configurations, quite complicated progressions of Life communities can develop, lasting many generations, and it is usually not obvious what changes will happen as generations progress.

*variety*

Some very small initial configurations will grow into large communities; others will slowly die out; many will reach a state where they do not change, or where they go through a repeating pattern every few generations.

*popularity*

Not long after its invention, MARTIN GARDNER discussed the Life game in his column in *Scientific American*, and, from that time on, it has fascinated many people, so that for several years there was even a quarterly newsletter devoted to related topics. It makes an ideal display for home microcomputers.

Our first goal, of course, is to write a program that will show how an initial community will change from generation to generation.

### 1.2.3 THE SOLUTION

At most a few minutes' thought will show that the solution to the Life problem is so simple that it would be a good exercise for the members of a beginning programming class who had just learned about arrays. All we need to do is to set up a large rectangular array[1] whose entries correspond to the Life cells and will

*method*

be marked with the status of the cell, either alive or dead. To determine what happens from one generation to the next, we then need only count the number of living neighbors of each cell and apply the rules. Since, however, we shall be using loops to go through the rectangular array, we must be careful not to violate rule 6 by allowing changes made earlier to affect the count of neighbors for cells studied later. The easiest way to avoid this pitfall is to set up a second rectangular array that will represent the community at the next generation and, after it has been completely calculated, then make the generation change by copying it to the original rectangular array.

Next let us rewrite this method as the steps of an informal algorithm.

*algorithm*

Initialize a rectangular array called map to contain the initial configuration of living cells.

Repeat the following steps for as long as desired:

For each cell in the rectangular array do the following:

Count the number of living neighbors of the cell.

If the count is 0, 1, 4, 5, 6, 7, or 8, then set the corresponding cell in another rectangular array called newmap to be dead; if the count is 3, then set the corresponding cell to be alive; and if the count is 2, then set the corresponding cell to be the same as the cell in the rectangular array map (since the status of a cell with count 2 does not change).

Copy the rectangular array newmap into the rectangular array map.

Print the rectangular array map for the user.

---

[1] An array with two indices is called *rectangular*. The first index determines the *row* in the array and the second the *column*.

### 1.2.4 LIFE: THE MAIN PROGRAM

```
/* Simulation of Conway's game of Life on a bounded grid
   Pre:  The user must supply an initial configuration of living cells.
   Post: The program prints a sequence of maps showing the changes in the configu-
         ration of living cells according to the rules for the game of Life.
   Uses: functions Initialize, WriteMap, NeighborCount, and UserSaysYes */
#include "common.h"        /* common include files and definitions          */
#include "life.h"          /* Life's defines, typedefs, and prototypes       */
void main(void)
{
    int row, col;
    Grid map;              /* current generation                            */
    Grid newmap;           /* next generation                               */
    Initialize(map);
    WriteMap(map);
    printf("This is the initial configuration you have chosen.\n"
        "Press < Enter > to continue.\n");
    while(getchar( ) != '\n')
        ;
    do {
        for (row = 1;  row <= MAXROW;  row++)
            for (col = 1;  col <= MAXCOL;  col++)
                switch(NeighborCount(map, row, col)) {
                case 0 :
                case 1 :
                    newmap[row] [col] = DEAD;
                    break;
                case 2 :
                    newmap[row] [col] = map[row] [col];
                    break;
                case 3 :
                    newmap[row] [col] = ALIVE;
                    break;
                case 4 :
                case 5 :
                case 6 :
                case 7 :
                case 8 :
                    newmap[row] [col] = DEAD;
                    break;
                }
        CopyMap(map, newmap);
        WriteMap(map);
        printf("Do you wish to continue viewing the new generations");
    } while (UserSaysYes( ));
}
```

*initialization*

*calculate changes*

*advance generation*

Before we discuss the preceding C program we need to establish what is included with the #include preprocessor command. There are two files: common.h and life.h.

The file common.h contains the definitions and #include statements for the standard files that appear in many programs and will be used throughout this book. The file includes

```
#include <stdio.h>
#include <stdlib.h>
typedef enum boolean { FALSE, TRUE } Boolean;

void Error(char *);

void Warning(char *);
```

The function Error is a simple function we use throughout the book. Error displays an error message and terminates execution. Here is the function, which we discuss further in Chapter 2.

```
/* Error: report program error.
   Pre:  s points to the message to be printed.
   Post: The function prints the message and terminates the program. */
void Error(char *s)
{
    fprintf(stderr, "%s\n", s);
    exit(1);
}
```

*functions*

The file life.h contains the definitions and the function prototypes for the Life program:

```
#define MAXROW 20          /* maximum row range         */
#define MAXCOL 60          /* maximum column range      */
typedef enum state { DEAD, ALIVE } State;

typedef State Grid[MAXROW + 2][MAXCOL + 2];

void CopyMap(Grid map, Grid newmap);
Boolean UserSaysYes(void);
void Initialize(Grid map);
int NeighborCount(Grid map, int row, int column);
void WriteMap(Grid map);
```

*program specifications* The documentation for this program begins with its *specifications*, that is, precise statements of the conditions required to hold when the program begins and the conditions that will hold after it finishes. These are called, respectively, the *preconditions* and *postconditions* for the program. Including precise preconditions and postconditions for each function not only clearly explains the purpose of the function but helps us avoid errors in the interface between functions. Including specifications is so helpful that we single it out as our first programming precept:

---

**Programming Precept**

*Include precise preconditions and postconditions
with every function that you write.*

---

*functions*

A third part of the specifications for our program is a list of the functions that it uses. Such a list should also be included with every function.

In the Life program we still must write the functions:

- Initialize(map) will initialize the grid and input the initial configuration.

- WriteMap(map) will do the output.

- NeighborCount(map, row, col) will count the number of cells neighboring the one in row, col that are occupied in the rectangular array map.

- CopyMap(map, newmap) will copy the updated grid, newmap, into map.

- UserSaysYes( ) will ask the user whether or not to go on to the next generation.

*action of the program*

The action of the program Life is entirely straightforward. First, we read in the initial situation to establish the first configuration of occupied cells. Then we commence a loop that makes one pass for each generation. Within this loop we first have a nested pair of loops on row and col that will run over all entries in the rectangular array map. The body of these nested loops consists of the multiway selection statement

switch { ... }

In the present application the function NeighborCount(map, row, col) will return one of the values 0, 1, ..., 8, and for each of these cases we can take a separate action, or, as in our program, some of the cases may lead to the same action. You should check that the action prescribed in each case corresponds correctly to the rules 2, 3, 4, and 5 of Section 1.2.1. Finally, after using the nested loops and switch statement to set up the rectangular array newmap, the function CopyMap(map, newmap) copies array newmap into array map, and the function WriteMap(map) writes out the result.

**Exercises 1.2**    Determine by hand calculation what will happen to each of the communities shown in Figure 1.1 over the course of five generations. [*Suggestion*: Set up the Life configuration on a checkerboard. Use one color of checkers for living cells in the current generation and a second color to mark those that will be born or die in the next generation.]

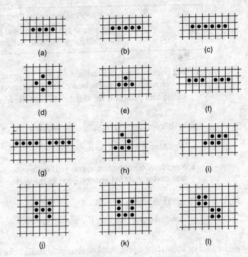

Figure 1.1. Simple Life configurations

## 1.3 Programming Style

Before we turn to writing the functions for the Life game, let us pause to consider several principles that we should be careful to employ in programming.

### 1.3.1 NAMES

In the story of creation (GENESIS 2:19), the LORD brought all the animals to ADAM to see what names he would give them. According to an old Jewish tradition, it was only when ADAM had named an animal that it sprang to life. This story brings an important moral to computer programming: Even if data and algorithms previously exist, it is only when they are given meaningful names that their places in the program can be properly recognized and appreciated, that they first acquire a life of their own.

*purpose of careful
naming*

For a program to work properly it is of the utmost importance to know exactly what each variable represents and what each function does. Documentation explaining the variables and functions should therefore always be included. The names of variables and functions should be chosen with care so as to identify their meanings clearly and succinctly. Finding good names is not always an easy task, but is important enough to be singled out as our second programming precept:

---

**Programming Precept**

*Always name your variables and functions
with the greatest care, and explain them thoroughly.*

---

C goes some distance toward enforcing this precept by requiring a section to declare variables. C also allows a more extensive use of names than most languages. Constants used in different places should be given names, and so should different data types, so that the compiler can catch errors that might otherwise be difficult to spot.

The careful choice of names can go a long way in clarifying a program and in helping to avoid misprints and common errors. Some guidelines are:

*guidelines*

1. Give special care to the choice of names for functions, constants, and all global variables and types used in different parts of the program. These names should be meaningful and should suggest clearly the purpose of the function, variable, and the like.

2. Keep the names simple for variables used only briefly and locally. Mathematicians usually use a single letter to stand for a variable, and sometimes, when writing mathematical programs, it may be permissible to use a single-letter name for a mathematical variable. However, even for the variable controlling a for loop, it is usually possible to find a short but meaningful word that better describes the use of the variable.

3. Use common prefixes or suffixes to associate names of the same general category. The files used in a program, for example, might be called

    InputFile   TransactionFile   TotalFile   OutFile   RejectFile

4. Avoid deliberate misspellings and meaningless suffixes to obtain different names. Of all the names

    index   indx   ndex   indexx   index2   index3

only one (the first) should normally be used. When you are tempted to introduce multiple names of this sort, take it as a sign that you should think harder and devise names that better describe the intended use.

5. Avoid choosing cute names whose meaning has little or nothing to do with the problem. The statements

```
while (tv == HOCK)
    Study( );
if (!sleepy)
    Play( );
else
    Nap( );
```

may be funny but they are bad programming!

6. Avoid choosing names that are close to each other in spelling or otherwise easy to confuse.

7. Be careful in the use of the letter "l" (small ell), "O" (capital oh) and "0" (zero). Within words or numbers these usually can be recognized from the context and cause no problem, but "l" and "O" should never be used alone as names. Consider the examples

```
l = 1;    x = 1;    x = l;    x = O;    O = 0;
```

## 1.3.2 DOCUMENTATION AND FORMAT

*the purpose of documentation*

Most students initially regard documentation as a chore that must be endured after a program is finished, to ensure that the marker and instructor can read it, so that no credit will be lost for obscurity. The author of a small program indeed can keep all the details in mind, and so needs documentation only to explain the program to someone else. With large programs (and with small ones after some months have elapsed), it becomes impossible to remember how every detail relates to every other, and therefore to write large programs, it is essential that appropriate documentation be prepared along with each small part of the program. A good habit is to prepare documentation as the program is being written, and an even better one, as we shall see later, is to prepare part of the documentation before starting to write the program.

Not all documentation is appropriate. Almost as common as programs with little documentation or only cryptic comments are programs with verbose documentation that adds little to understanding the program. Hence our third programming precept:

---

**Programming Precept**
*Keep your documentation concise but descriptive.*

---

The style of documentation, as with all writing styles, is highly personal, and many different styles can prove effective. There are, nonetheless, some commonly accepted guidelines that should be respected:

*guidelines*

1. Place a prologue at the beginning of each function, including

    (a) Identification (programmer's name, date, version number).[2]
    (b) Statement of the purpose of the function and method used.
    (c) The changes the function makes and what data it uses.
    (d) Reference to further documentation external to the program.

2. When each variable, constant, or type is declared, explain what it is and how it is used. Better still, make this information evident from the name.

3. Introduce each significant section (paragraph or function) of the program with a comment briefly stating its purpose or action.

4. Indicate the end of each significant section if it is not otherwise obvious.

5. Avoid comments that parrot what the code does, such as

    count++;                    /* Increase counter by 1 */

    or that are meaningless jargon, such as

    /* horse string length into correctitude */

    (This example was taken directly from a systems program.)

6. Explain any statement that employs a trick or whose meaning is unclear. Better still, avoid such statements.

7. The code itself should explain *how* the program works. The documentation should explain *why* it works and *what* it does.

8. Whenever a program is modified, be sure that the documentation is correspondingly modified.

*format*

Spaces, blank lines, and indentation in a program are an important form of documentation. They make the program easy to read, allow you to tell at a glance which parts of the program relate to each other, where the major breaks occur, and precisely which statements are contained in each loop or each alternative of a conditional statement. There are many systems (some automated) for indentation and spacing, all with the goal of making it easier to determine the structure of the program.

*prettyprinting*

A **prettyprinter** is a system utility that reads a C program, moving the text between lines and adjusting the indentation so as to improve the appearance of

---

[2] To save space, programs printed in this book do not include identification lines or some other parts of the prologue, since the surrounding text gives the necessary information.

the program and make its structure more obvious. If a prettyprinter is available on your system, you might experiment with it to see if it helps the appearance of your programs.

*consistency*

Because of the importance of good format for programs, you should settle on some reasonable rules for spacing and indentation and use your rules consistently in all the programs you write. Consistency is essential if the system is to be useful in reading programs. Many professional programming groups decide on a uniform system and insist that all the programs they write conform. Some classes or student programming teams do likewise. In this way, it becomes much easier for one programmer to read and understand the work of another.

---

**Programming Precept**

*The reading time for programs is much more than the writing time.*
*Make reading easy to do.*

---

### 1.3.3 REFINEMENT AND MODULARITY

*problem solving*

Computers do not solve problems; people do. Usually the most important part of the process is dividing the problem into smaller problems that can be understood in more detail. If these are still too difficult, then they are subdivided again, and so on. In any large organization the top management cannot worry about every detail of every activity; the top managers must concentrate on general goals and problems and delegate specific responsibilities to their subordinates. Again, middle-level managers cannot do everything: They must subdivide the work and send it to

*subdivision*

other people. So it is with computer programming. Even when a project is small enough that one person can take it from start to finish, it is most important to divide the work, starting with an overall understanding of the problem, dividing it into subproblems, and attacking each of these in turn without worrying about the others.

Let us restate this principle with a classic proverb:

---

**Programming Precept**

*Don't lose sight of the forest for its trees.*

---

*top-down refinement*

This principle, called **top-down refinement**, is the real key to writing large programs that work. The principle implies the postponement of detailed consideration, but not the postponement of precision and rigor. It does not mean that the main program becomes some vague entity whose task can hardly be described. On the contrary, the main program will send almost all the work out to various functions,

*specifications*

and as we write the main program (which we should do first), we decide *exactly* how the work will be divided among them. Then, as we later work on a particular function, we shall know before starting exactly what it is expected to do.

It is often not easy to decide exactly how to divide the work into functions, and sometimes a decision once made must later be modified. Even so, two guidelines can help in deciding how to divide the work:

---

**Programming Precept**
*Each function should do only one task, but do it well.*

---

That is, we should be able to describe the purpose of a function succinctly. If you find yourself writing a long paragraph to specify the preconditions or postconditions for a function, then either you are giving too much detail (that is, you are writing the function before it is time to do so) or you should rethink the division of work. The function itself will undoubtedly contain many details, but they should not appear until the next stage of refinement.

---

**Programming Precept**
*Each function should hide something.*

---

A middle-level manager in a large company does not pass on everything he receives from his departments to his superior; he summarizes, collates, and weeds out the information, handles many requests himself, and sends on only what is needed at the upper levels. Similarly, he does not transmit everything he learns from higher management to his subordinates. He transmits to each person only what he needs to do his job. The functions we write should do likewise.

One of the most important parts of the refinement process is deciding exactly what the task of each function is, specifying precisely what its preconditions and postconditions will be, that is, what its input will be and what result it will produce. Errors in these specifications are among the most frequent program bugs and are among the hardest to find. First, the data used in the function must be precisely specified. These data are of five kinds:

*parameters*

- *Input parameters* are used by the function but are not changed by the function. In C, input parameters are usually value parameters. (Exception: arrays are always passed by reference; that is, the address of the array is passed to the function.)

- *Output parameters* contain the results of the calculations from the function. In C, output parameters must be passed by reference.

- *Inout parameters* are used for both input and output; the initial value of the parameter is used and then modified by the function. In C, inout parameters must be passed by reference.

*variables*

- *Local variables* are declared in the function and exist only while the function is being executed. They are not initialized before the function begins and are discarded when the function ends.

- *Global variables* are used in the function but not declared in the function. It can be quite dangerous to use global variables in a function, since after the function is written its author may forget exactly what global variables were used and how. If the main program is later changed, then the function may mysteriously begin to misbehave. If a function alters the value of a global variable it is said to cause a *side effect*. Side effects are even more dangerous than using global variables as input to the function because side effects may alter the performance of other functions, thereby misdirecting the programmer's debugging efforts to a part of the program that is already correct.

*side effects*

---

**Programming Precept**

*Keep your connections simple. Avoid global variables whenever possible.*

---

---

**Programming Precept**

*Never cause side effects if you can avoid it.*
*If you must use global variables as input, document them thoroughly.*

---

For functions the definition of *side effect* is expanded to include changes made to parameters as well as global variables. A function typically returns one result. When a function does not return a result the function should be of type void. When the function returns a result then the function should have a type qualifier that indicates the type of the result being returned. If a function needs to produce more than one result, then some of the parameters should be passed by reference.

While all these principles of top-down design may seem almost self-evident, the only way to learn them thoroughly is by practice. Hence throughout this book we shall be careful to apply them to the large programs that we write, and in a moment it will be appropriate to return to our first example project.

---

**Exercises 1.3**   E1. Rewrite the following function so that it accomplishes the same result in a less tricky way.

```
void DoesSomething(int *first, int *second)
{
    *first = *second - *first;
    *second = *second - *first;
    *first = *second + *first;
}
```

**E2.** Determine what each of the following functions does. Rewrite each function with meaningful variable names, with better format, and without unnecessary variables and statements.

(a) 
```
#define MAXINT 100
int Calculate(int apple, int orange)
{ int peach, lemon;
peach = 0; lemon = 0; if (apple < orange) {
peach = orange; } else if (orange <= apple) {
peach = apple; } else { peach = MAXINT; lemon = MAXINT;
} if (lemon != MAXINT) { return(peach); } }
```

(b) 
```
double Figure(double vector1 [ ], int n)
{ int loop1; double loop2; double loop3; int loop4;
loop1 = 0; loop2 = vector1 [loop1]; loop3 = 0.0;
loop4 = loop1; for (loop4 = 0; loop4 < n; loop4 = loop4 + 1)
{ loop1 = loop1 + 1; loop2 = vector1 [loop1 – 1];
loop3 = loop2 + loop3; } loop2 = loop1;
loop2 = loop3/loop2; return(loop2); }
```

(c) 
```
void Question(int *a17, int *stuff)
{ int another, yetanother, stillonemore;
another = yetanother; stillonemore = *a17;
yetanother = *stuff; another = stillonemore; *a17 = yetanother;
stillonemore = yetanother;
*stuff = another; another = yetanother; yetanother = *stuff; }
```

(d) 
```
int Mystery(int apple, int orange, int peach)
{ if (apple >orange) if (apple > peach) if
(peach > orange) return(peach); else if (apple < orange)
return(apple); else return(orange); else return(apple); else
if (peach > apple) if (peach > orange) return(orange); else
return(peach); else return(apple); }
```

**E3.** The following statement is designed to check the relative sizes of three integers, which you may assume to be different from each other:

```
if (x < z) if (x < y) if (y < z) c = 1; else c = 2; else
if (y < z) c = 3; else c = 4; else if (x < y)
if (x < z) c = 5; else c = 6; else if (y < z) c = 7; else
if (z < x) if (z < y) c = 8; else c = 9; else c = 10;
```

(a) Rewrite this statement in a form that is easier to read.

(b) Since there are only six possible orderings for the three integers, only six of the ten cases can actually occur. Find those that can never occur, and eliminate the redundant checks.

(c) Write a simpler, shorter statement that accomplishes the same result.

**E4.** The following C function calculates the cube root of a real number (by the NEWTON approximation), using the fact that, if $y$ is one approximation to the cube root of $x$, then

$$z = \frac{2y + x/y^2}{3}$$

is a closer approximation.

```
double Fcn(double stuff)
{ double april, tim, tiny, shadow, tom, tam, square;
Boolean flag;
tim = stuff; tam = stuff; tiny = 0.00001;
if (stuff != 0) do { shadow = tim + tim;
square = tim * tim;
tom = (shadow + stuff/square);
april = tom/3;
if (april * april * april - tam > -tiny)
if (april * april * april - tam < tiny) flag = TRUE;
else flag = FALSE; else flag = FALSE;
if (flag == FALSE) tim = april; else tim = tam; }
while (flag == FALSE);
if (stuff == 0) return(stuff); else return(april); }
```

(a) Rewrite this function with meaningful variable names, without the extra variables that contribute nothing to the understanding, with a better layout, and without the redundant and useless statements.

(b) Write a function for calculating the cube root of x directly from the mathematical formula, by starting with the assignment y = x and then repeating

$$y = (2 * y + x/(y * y))/3$$

until fabs(y * y * y - x) <= 0.00001.

(c) Which of these tasks is easier?

**E5.** The *mean* of a sequence of real numbers is their sum divided by the count of numbers in the sequence. The (population) *variance* of the sequence is the mean of the squares of all numbers in the sequence, minus the square of the mean of the numbers in the sequence. The *standard deviation* is the square root of the variance. Write a well-structured C function to calculate the standard deviation of a sequence of $n$ numbers, where $n$ is a constant and the numbers are in an array indexed from 0 to $n - 1$, where $n$ is a parameter to the function. Write, then use, subsidiary functions to calculate the mean and variance.

*plotting*

**E6.** Design a program that will plot a given set of points on a graph. The input to the program will be a text file, each line of which contains two numbers that are the $x$ and $y$ coordinates of a point to be plotted. The program will use a routine to plot one such pair of coordinates. The details of the routine involve the specific method of plotting and cannot be written since they depend on the requirements of the plotting equipment, which we do not know. Before plotting the points the program needs to know the maximum and minimum values of $x$ and $y$ that appear in its input file. The program should therefore use another routine Bounds that will read the whole file and determine these four maxima and minima. Afterward, another routine is used to draw and label the axes; then the file can be reset and the individual points plotted.

(a) Write the main program, not including the routines.

(b) Write the function Bounds.

(c) Write the header lines for the remaining functions together with appropriate documentation showing their purposes and their requirements.

# 1.4 Coding, Testing, and Further Refinement

The three processes in the title above go hand-in-hand and must be done together. Yet it is important to keep them separate in our thinking, since each requires its own approach and method. *Coding*, of course, is the process of writing an algorithm in the correct syntax (grammar) of a computer language like C, and *testing* is the process of running the program on sample data chosen to find errors if they are present. For further refinement, we turn to the functions not yet written and repeat these steps.

## 1.4.1 STUBS

*early debugging and testing*

After coding the main program, most programmers will wish to complete the writing and coding of the functions as soon as possible, to see if the whole project will work. For a project as small as the Life game, this approach may work, but for larger projects, writing and coding all the functions will be such a large job that, by the time it is complete, many of the details of the main program and functions that were written early will have been forgotten. In fact, different people may be writing different functions, and some of those who started the project may have left it before all functions are written. It is much easier to understand and debug a program when it is fresh in your mind. Hence, for larger projects, it is much more efficient to debug and test each function as soon as it is written than it is to wait until the project has been completely coded.

Even for smaller projects, there are good reasons for debugging functions one at a time. We might, for example, be unsure of some point of C syntax that will appear in several places through the program. If we can compile each function separately, then we shall quickly learn to avoid errors in syntax in later functions. As a second example, suppose that we have decided that the major steps of the program should be done in a certain order. If we test the main program as soon as it is written, then we may find that sometimes the major steps are done in the wrong order, and we can quickly correct the problem, doing so more easily than if we waited until the major steps were perhaps obscured by the many details contained in each of them.

*stubs*

To compile the program correctly, there must be something in the place of each function that is used, and hence we must put in short, dummy functions, called **stubs**. The simplest stubs are those that do nothing at all:

```
/* Initialize: initialize grid map. */
void Initialize(Grid map)
{
}
/* WriteMap: write grid map. */
void WriteMap(Grid map)
{
}
/* NeighborCount: count neighbors of row,col. */
int NeighborCount(Grid map, int row, int col)
{
    return 1;
}
```

Even with these stubs we can at least compile the program and make sure that the declarations of types and variables are syntactically correct. Normally, however, each stub should print a message stating that the function was invoked. When we execute the program, we find that some variables are used without initialization, and hence, to avoid these errors, we can add code to function Initialize. Hence the stub can slowly grow and be refined into the final form of the function. For a small project like the Life game, we can simply write each function in turn, substitute it for its stub, and observe the effect on program execution.

## 1.4.2 COUNTING NEIGHBORS

*function NeighborCount*

*hedge*

*sentinel*

Let us now refine our program further. The function that counts neighbors of the cell in row, col requires that we look in the eight adjoining positions. We shall use a pair of for loops to do this, one running from row − 1 to row + 1 and the other from col − 1 to col + 1. We need only be careful, when row, col is on a boundary of the grid, that we look only at legitimate positions in the grid. Rather than using tests to make sure that we do not go outside the grid, we introduce a **hedge** around the grid: We should enlarge the grid by adding two extra rows, one before the first real row of the grid and one after the last, and two extra columns, one before the first column and one after the last. The cells in these hedge rows and columns will always be dead, so they will not affect the counts of living neighbors at all. Their presence, however, means that the for loops counting neighbors need make no distinction between rows or columns on the boundary of the grid and any other rows or columns. See the examples in Figure 1.2.

Another term often used instead of hedge is **sentinel**: A sentinel is an extra entry put into a data structure so that boundary conditions need not be treated as a special case.

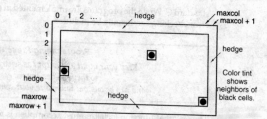

Figure 1.2. Life grid with a hedge

```
/* NeighborCount: count neighbors of row,col.
   Pre:   The pair row, col is a valid cell in a Life configuration.
   Post:  The function returns the number of living neighbors of the living cell. */
int NeighborCount(Grid map, int row, int col)
{
   int i;                      /* row of a neighbor of the cell (row, col)       */
   int j;                      /* column of a neighbor of the cell (row, col)    */
   int count = 0;              /* counter of living neighbors                    */
   for (i = row - 1; i <= row + 1; i++)
      for (j = col - 1; j <= col + 1; j++)
         if (map[i][j] == ALIVE)
            count++;
   if (map[row][col] == ALIVE)
      count--;
   return count;
}
```

### 1.4.3 INPUT AND OUTPUT

*careful input and output*

It now remains only to write the functions Initialize, WriteMap, and UserSaysYes that do the input and output. In computer programs designed to be used by many people, the functions performing input and output are often the longest. Input to the program must be fully checked to be certain that it is valid and consistent, and errors in input must be processed in ways to avoid catastrophic failure or production of ridiculous results. The output must be carefully organized and formatted, with considerable thought to what should or should not be printed, and with provision of various alternatives to suit differing circumstances.

The programming tools needed to design comprehensive input and output functions, unfortunately, still differ considerably from one computer system to another, and in any case are more concerned with the details of the language and the problem at hand than with general ideas. It is therefore impossible to include as much error checking as we would wish, working only within the provisions of standard C. When the programs are implemented in a particular system, additional error checking can usually be included.

> **Programming Precept**
> *Keep your input and output as separate functions,*
> *so they can be changed easily*
> *and can be custom-tailored to your computing system.*

*initialization*

The task that function Initialize must accomplish is to set the map to its initial configuration. To initialize the map, we could consider each possible coordinate pair separately and request the user to indicate whether the cell is to be occupied or not.

*input method*

This method would require the user to type in

$$\text{MAXROW} * \text{MAXCOL} = 10 * 30 = 300$$

entries, which is prohibitive. Hence, instead, we input only those coordinate pairs corresponding to initially occupied cells.

```c
/* Initialize: initialize grid map.
   Pre:  None.
   Post: All the cells in the grid map have been set to initial configuration of living cells. */
void Initialize(Grid map)
{
    int row, col;                /* coordinates of a cell                              */
    printf("This program is a simulation of the game of Life.\n"
           "The grid has a size of %d rows and "
           " %d columns.\n", MAXROW, MAXCOL);
    for (row = 0; row <= MAXROW + 1; row++)
        for (col = 0; col <= MAXCOL + 1; col++)
            map[row][col] = DEAD;    /* Set all cells empty, including the hedge.     */
    printf("On each line give a pair of coordinates for a living cell.\n"
           "Terminate the list with the special pair 0 0.\n");
    scanf("%d %d", &row, &col);
    while (row != 0 || col != 0) {   /* Check termination condition.                  */
        if (row >= 1 && row <= MAXROW && col >= 1 && col <= MAXCOL)
            map[row][col] = ALIVE;
        else
            printf("Values are not within range.\n");
        scanf("%d %d", &row, &col);
    }
    while (getchar() != '\n')    /* Discard remaining characters.                     */
        ;
}
```

*output*

For the output function WriteMap we adopt the simple method of writing out the entire rectangular array at each generation, with occupied cells denoted by `'*'` and empty cells by `'-'`.

```
/* WriteMap: display grid map.
   Pre:   The rectangular array map contains the current Life configuration.
   Post:  The current Life configuration is written for the user. */
void WriteMap(Grid map)
{
   int row, col;
   putchar('\n');
   putchar('\n');
   for (row = 1;  row <= MAXROW;  row++) {
      for (col = 1;  col <= MAXCOL;  col++)
         if (map[row][col] == ALIVE)
               putchar('*');
         else
               putchar('-');
      putchar('\n');
   }
}
```

The function CopyMap copies newmap into map.

```
/* CopyMap: copy newmap into map.
   Pre:   The grid newmap has the current Life configuration.
   Post:  The grid map has a copy of newmap. */
void CopyMap(Grid map, Grid newmap)
{
   int row, col;
   for (row = 0;  row <= MAXROW + 1;  row++)
      for (col = 0;  col <= MAXCOL + 1;  col++)
         map[row][col] = newmap[row][col];
}
```

*response from user*

Finally comes the function UserSaysYes that determines whether the user wishes to go on to calculate the next generation. The task of UserSaysYes is to ask the user to respond yes or no. To make the program more tolerant of mistakes in input, this request is placed in a loop that repeats until the user's response is acceptable.

```
/* UserSaysYes: TRUE if the user wants to continue execution.
   Pre:  None.
   Post: Returns TRUE if the user's answer begins with either y or Y, FALSE if the user
         responds with any response beginning with either n or N. */
Boolean UserSaysYes(void)
{
    int c;
    printf(" (y,n)? ");
    do {
        while ((c = getchar()) == '\n')
            ;                        /* Ignore new line character.          */
        if (c == 'y' || c == 'Y' || c == 'n' || c == 'N')
            return (c == 'y' || c == 'Y');
        printf("Please respond by typing one of the letters y or n\n");
    } while (1);
}
```

We shall find that the UserSaysYes function is useful not just for the Life game, but for many programs that we write. That is, we shall consider it a *utility* function that we have available whenever we need it.

At this point, we have all the functions for the Life simulation. It is time to pause and check that it works.

### 1.4.4 DRIVERS

*separate debugging*

For small projects, each function is usually inserted in its proper place as soon as it is written, and the resulting program can then be debugged and tested as far as possible. For large projects, however, compilation of the entire project can overwhelm that of a new function being debugged, and it can be difficult to tell, looking only at the way the whole program runs, whether a particular function is working correctly or not. Even in small projects the output of one function may be used by another in ways that do not immediately reveal whether the information transmitted is correct.

One way to debug and test a single function is to write a short auxiliary program whose purpose is to provide the necessary input for the function, call it, and evaluate the result. Such an auxiliary program is called a *driver* for the function. By using drivers, each function can be isolated and studied by itself, and thereby errors can often be spotted quickly.

*driver program*

As an example, let us write drivers for the functions of the Life project. First, we consider the function NeighborCount. In the main program its output is used, but has not been directly displayed for our inspection, so we should have little confidence that it is correct. To test NeighborCount we shall supply it with the rectangular array map, call it for each entry of the rectangular array, and write out the results. The resulting driver hence uses function Initialize to set up the rectangular array and bears some resemblance to the original main program.

```
/* Driver: test NeighborCount( ).
   Pre:  The user must supply an initial configuration of living cells.
   Post: The program repeatedly invokes NeighborCount and displays the values re-
         turned. */
int main(void)
{
    Grid map;
    int i, j;
    Initialize(map);
    for (i = 0;  i < MAXROW;  i++) {
        for (j = 0;  j < MAXCOL;  j++)
            printf("%3d", NeighborCount(map, i, j));
        printf("\n");
    }
    return 0;
}
```

Sometimes two functions can be used to check each other. The easiest way, for example, to check functions Initialize and WriteMap is to use a driver whose declarations are those of the main program, and whose action part is

```
Initialize(map);
WriteMap(map);
```

Both functions can be tested by running this driver and making sure that the configuration printed is the same as that given as input.

## 1.4.5 PROGRAM TRACING

After the functions have been assembled into a complete program, it is time to check out the completed whole. One of the most effective ways to uncover hidden defects is called a *structured walkthrough*. In this the programmer shows the completed program to another programmer or a small group of programmers and explains exactly what happens, beginning with an explanation of the main program followed by the functions, one by one. Structured walkthroughs are helpful for three reasons. First, programmers who are not familiar with the actual code can often spot bugs or conceptual errors that the original programmer overlooked. Second, the questions that other people ask can help you to clarify your own thinking and discover your own mistakes. Third, the structured walkthrough often suggests tests that prove useful in later stages of software production.

*group discussion*

It is unusual for a large program to run correctly the first time it is executed as a whole, and if it does not, it may not be easy to determine exactly where the errors are. On many systems sophisticated *trace tools* are available to keep track of function calls, changes of variables, and so on. A simple and effective debugging tool, however, is to take *snapshots* of program execution by inserting printf statements at key points in the main program. A message can be printed each time a function is called, and the values of important variables can be printed before and after each function is called. Such snapshots can help the programmer converge quickly on the particular location where an error is occurring.

printf *statements for debugging*

*temporary scaffolding*

*Scaffolding* is another term frequently used to describe code inserted into a program to help with debugging. Never hesitate to put scaffolding into your programs as you write them; it will be easy to recompile the code without the printf statements by not defining certain flags at compile time, and it may save you much grief during debugging.

When your program has a mysterious error that you cannot localize at all, then it is very useful to put scaffolding into the main program to print the values of important variables. This scaffolding should be put at one or two of the major dividing points in the main program. (If you have written a program of any significant size that does not subdivide its work into several major sections, then you have already made serious errors in the design and structure of your program that you should correct.) With printouts at the major dividing points, you should be able to determine which section of the program is misbehaving, and you can then concentrate on that section, introducing scaffolding into its subdivisions.

*defensive programming*

Another important method for detecting errors is to practice *defensive* programming. Put if statements at the beginning of functions to check that the preconditions do in fact hold. If not, print an error message. In this way, you will be alerted as soon as a supposedly impossible situation arises, and if it does not arise, the error checking will be completely invisible to the user. It is, of course, particularly important to check that the preconditions hold when the input to a function comes from the user, or from a file, or from some other source outside the program itself. It is, however, surprising how often checking preconditions will reveal errors even in places where you are sure everything is correct.

*static analyzer*

For very large programs yet another tool is sometimes used. This is a *static analyzer*, a program that examines the source program (as written in C, for example) looking for uninitialized or unused variables, sections of the code that can never be reached, and other occurrences that are probably incorrect. One example is the UNIX utility lint. This utility finds portability problems, performs type checking more strictly than the compiler, and finds problems that are difficult to see. If a version of lint is available on your system you might want to run your code through it and check the warnings it may give.

## 1.4.6 PRINCIPLES OF PROGRAM TESTING

*choosing test data*

So far we have said nothing about the choice of data to be used to test programs and functions. This choice, of course, depends intimately on the project under development, so we can make only some general remarks. First we should note:

---

**Programming Precept**
*The quality of test data is more important than its quantity.*

---

Many sample runs that do the same calculations in the same cases provide no more effective a test than one run.

> **Programming Precept**
> *Program testing can be used to show the presence of bugs,*
> *but never their absence.*

It is possible that other cases remain that have never been tested even after many sample runs. For any program of substantial complexity, it is impossible to perform exhaustive tests, yet the careful choice of test data can provide substantial confidence in the program. Everyone, for example, has great confidence that the typical computer can add two floating-point numbers correctly, but this confidence is certainly not based on testing the computer by having it add all possible floating-point numbers and checking the results. If a double-precision floating-point number takes 64 bits, then there are $2^{128}$ distinct pairs of numbers that could be added. This number is astronomically large: all computers manufactured to date have performed altogether but a tiny fraction of this number of additions. Our confidence that computers add correctly is based on tests of each component separately, that is, by checking that each of the 64 digits is added correctly, and that carrying from one place to another is done correctly.

*testing methods*         There are at least three general philosophies that are used in the choice of test data.

### 1. The Black-Box Method

Most users of a large program are not interested in the details of its functioning; they only wish to obtain answers. That is, they wish to treat the program as a black box; hence the name of this method. Similarly, test data should be chosen according to the specifications of the problem, without regard to the internal details of the program, to check that the program operates correctly. At a minimum the test data should be selected in the following ways:

*data selection*

1. *Easy values.* The program should be debugged with data that are easy to check. More than one student who tried a program only for complicated data, and thought it worked properly, has been embarrassed when the instructor tried a trivial example.

2. *Typical, realistic values.* Always try a program on data chosen to represent how the program will be used. These data should be sufficiently simple so that the results can be checked by hand.

3. *Extreme values.* Many programs err at the limits of their range of applications. It is very easy for counters or array bounds to be off by one.

4. *Illegal values.* "Garbage in, garbage out" is an old saying in computer circles that should not be respected. When a good program has garbage coming in, then its output should at least be a sensible error message. Indeed, the program should provide some indication of the likely errors in input and perform any calculations that remain possible after disregarding the erroneous input.

## 2. The Glass-Box Method

The second approach to choosing test data begins with the observation that a program can hardly be regarded as thoroughly tested if there are some parts of its code that, in fact, have never been executed. In the *glass-box* method of testing, the logical structure of the program is examined, and for each alternative that may occur, test data are devised that will lead to that alternative. Thus care is taken to choose data to check each possibility in every case statement, each clause of every if statement, and the termination condition of each loop. If the program has several selection or iteration statements then it will require different combinations of test data to check all the paths that are possible. Figure 1.3 shows a short program segment with its possible execution paths.

*path testing*

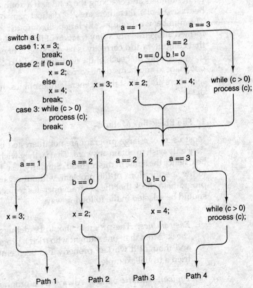

```
switch a {
  case 1: x = 3;
          break;
  case 2: if (b == 0)
              x = 2;
          else
              x = 4;
          break;
  case 3: while (c > 0)
              process (c);
          break;
}
```

Figure 1.3. The execution paths through a program segment

For a large program the glass-box approach is clearly not practicable, but for a single small module, it is an excellent debugging and testing method. In a well-designed program, each module will involve few loops and alternatives. Hence only a few well-chosen test cases will suffice to test each module on its own.

*modular testing*

In glass-box testing, the advantages of modular program design become evident. Let us consider a typical example of a project involving 50 functions, each of which can involve 5 different cases or alternatives. If we were to test the whole program as one, we would need $5^{50}$ test cases to be sure that each alternative was tested. Each module separately requires only 5 (easier) test cases, for a total of $5 \times 50 = 250$. Hence a problem of impossible size has been reduced to one that, for a large program, is of quite modest size.

*comparison*

Before you conclude that glass-box testing is always the preferable method, we should comment that, in practice, black-box testing is usually more effective in uncovering errors. Perhaps one reason is that the most subtle programming errors often occur not within a function but in the interface between functions, in misunderstanding of the exact conditions and standards of information interchange between functions. It would therefore appear that a reasonable testing philosophy for a large project would be to apply glass-box methods to each small module as it is written and use black-box test data to test larger sections of the program when they are complete.

*interface errors*

### 3. The Ticking-Box Method

To conclude this section, let us mention one further philosophy of program testing, a philosophy that is, unfortunately, quite widely used. This might be called the *ticking-box* method. It consists of doing no testing at all after the project is fairly well debugged, but instead turning it over to the customer for trial and acceptance. The result, of course, is a time bomb.

---

**Exercises 1.4**

**E1.** If you suspected that the Life program contained errors, where would be a good place to insert scaffolding into the main program? What information should be printed out?

**E2.** Take your solution to Exercise E6 of Section 1.3 (designing a program to plot a set of points), and indicate good places to insert scaffolding if needed.

**E3.** Find suitable black-box test data for each of the following:

   **(a)** A function that returns the largest of its three parameters, which are real numbers.

   **(b)** A function that returns the square root of a real number.

   **(c)** A function that returns the least common multiple of its two parameters, which must be positive integers. (The *least common multiple* is the smallest integer that is a multiple of both parameters. Examples: The least common multiple of 4 and 6 is 12, of 3 and 9 is 9, and of 5 and 7 is 35.)

   **(d)** A function that sorts three integers, given as its parameters, into ascending order.

   **(e)** A function that sorts an array a of integers indexed from 0 to a variable $n - 1$ into ascending order, where a and n are both parameters.

**E4.** Find suitable glass-box test data for each of the following:

   **(a)** The statement

```
if (a < b) if (c > d) x = 1;  else if (c == d) x = 2;
else x = 3;  else if (a == b) x = 4;  else if (c == d) x = 5;
else x = 6;
```

   **(b)** The function NeighborCount(map, row, col).

**Programming Projects 1.4**

P1. Enter the Life program of this chapter on your computer and make sure that it works correctly.

P2. Test the Life program with the examples shown in Figure 1.1.

P3. Run the Life program with the initial configurations shown in Figure 1.4. Several of these go through many changes before reaching a configuration that remains the same or has predictable behavior.

# Pointers and Pitfalls

1. Be sure you understand your problem before you decide how to solve it.

2. Be sure you understand the algorithmic method before you start to program.

3. In case of difficulty, divide the problem into pieces and think of each part separately.

4. Keep your functions short and simple; rarely should a single function be more than a page long.

5. Include careful documentation (as presented in Section 1.3.2) with each function as you write it.

6. Be careful to write down precise preconditions and postconditions for every function.

7. Include error checking at the beginning of functions to check that the preconditions actually hold.

8. Every time a function is used, ask yourself why you know that its preconditions will be satisfied.

9. Use stubs and drivers, black-box and glass-box testing to simplify debugging.

10. Use plenty of scaffolding to help localize errors.

11. In programming with arrays, be wary of index values that are off by 1. Always use extreme-value testing to check programs that use arrays.

12. Keep your programs well-formatted as you write them—it will make debugging much easier.

13. Keep your documentation consistent with your code, and when reading a program make sure that you debug the code and not just the comments.

14. Explain your program to somebody else: Doing so will help you understand it better yourself.

15. Remember the Programming Precepts!

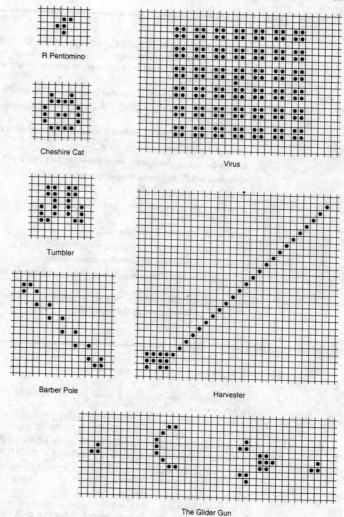

Figure 1.4. Life configurations

# Review Questions

Most chapters of this book conclude with a set of questions designed to help you review the main ideas of the chapter. These questions can all be answered directly from the discussion in the book; if you are unsure of any answer, refer to the appropriate section.

*1.3*
1. When is it appropriate to use one-letter variable names?
2. Name four kinds of information that should be included in program documentation.
3. What is the difference between *external* and *internal* documentation?
4. What are pre- and postconditions?
5. Name three kinds of parameters. How are they processed in C?
6. Why should side effects of functions be avoided?

*1.4*
7. What is a program stub?
8. What is the difference between stubs and drivers, and when should each be used?
9. What is a structured walkthrough?
10. What is *scaffolding* in a program, and when is it used?
11. Name a way to practice *defensive* programming.
12. Name two methods for testing a program, and discuss when each should be used.
13. If you cannot immediately picture all details needed for solving a problem, what should you do with the problem?

# References for Further Study

C

The C programming language was devised by DENNIS M. RITCHIE. The standard reference is

BRIAN W. KERNIGHAN and DENNIS M. RITCHIE, *The C Programming Language*, second edition, Prentice Hall, Englewood Cliffs, N.J., 1988, 272 pages.

This book contains many examples and exercises. For the solutions to the exercises in Kernighan and Ritchie, together with a chance to study C code, see

CLOVIS L. TONDO and SCOTT E. GIMPEL, *The C Answer Book*, second edition, Prentice Hall, Englewood Cliffs, N.J., 1989, 208 pages.

Many good textbooks provide a more leisurely description of C, too many books to list here. These textbooks also provide many examples and applications. Some books designed for introductory courses, however, omit important "advanced" features of C that will be used often in this book. Be sure that any textbook you select covers the full syntax of ANSI C.

## PROGRAMMING PRINCIPLES

Three books that contain many helpful hints on programming style and correctness, as well as examples of good and bad practices, are

BRIAN KERNIGHAN and P. J. PLAUGER, *The Elements of Programming Style*, second edition, McGraw–Hill, New York, 1978, 168 pages.

HENRY F. LEDGARD, PAUL A. NAGIN, and JOHN F. HUERAS, *C with Style: Programming Proverbs*, Hayden Book Company, Hasbrouk Heights, N.J., 1979, 210 pages.

DENNIE VAN TASSEL, *Program Style, Design, Efficiency, Debugging, and Testing*, second edition, Prentice-Hall, Englewood Cliffs, N.J., 1978, 323 pages.

EDSGER W. DIJKSTRA pioneered the movement known as structured programming, which insists on taking a carefully organized top-down approach to the design and writing of programs, when in March 1968 he caused some consternation by publishing a letter entitled "Go To Statement Considered Harmful" in the *Communications of the ACM* (vol. 11, pages 147–148). DIJKSTRA has since published several papers and books that are most instructive in programming method. One book of special interest is

EDSGER W. DIJKSTRA, *A Discipline of Programming*, Prentice-Hall, Englewood Cliffs, N.J., 1976, 217 pages.

## THE GAME OF LIFE

The prominent British mathematician J. H. CONWAY has made many original contributions to subjects as diverse as the theory of finite simple groups, logic, and combinatorics. He devised the game of Life by starting with previous, technical studies of cellular automata and devising reproduction rules that would make it difficult for a configuration to grow without bound, but for which many configurations would go through interesting progressions. CONWAY, however, did not publish his observations, but communicated them to MARTIN GARDNER. The popularity of the game skyrocketed when it was discussed in

MARTIN GARDNER, "Mathematical Games" (regular column), *Scientific American* 223, no. 4 (October 1970), 120–123; 224, no. 2 (February 1971), 112–117.

The examples at the end of Sections 1.2 and 1.4 are taken from these columns. These columns have been reprinted with further results in

MARTIN GARDNER, *Wheels, Life and Other Mathematical Amusements*, W. H. Freeman, New York, 1983, pp. 214–257.

This book also contains a bibliography of articles on Life. A quarterly newsletter, entitled *Lifeline*, was even published for a few years to keep the real devotees up to date on current developments in Life and related topics.

**2**

# Introduction
# to Software
# Engineering

THIS CHAPTER *continues to expound
the principles of good program design,
with special emphasis on techniques
required for the production of large
software systems. These techniques
include problem specification, algorithm
development, verification, and analysis, as
well as program testing and maintenance.
These general principles are introduced
in the context of developing a second
program for the Life game, one based on
more sophisticated methods than those of
the last chapter.*

*Software engineering* is the discipline within computer science concerned with techniques needed for the production and maintenance of large software systems. Our goal in introducing some of these techniques is to demonstrate their importance in problems of practical size. Although much of the discussion in this chapter is motivated by the Life game and applied specifically to its program, the discussion is always intended to illustrate more general methods that can be applied to a much broader range of problems of practical importance.

# 2.1 Program Maintenance

Small programs written as exercises or demonstrations are usually run a few times and then discarded, but the disposition of large practical programs is quite different. A program of practical value will be run many times, usually by many different people, and its writing and debugging mark only the beginning of its use. They also mark only the beginning of the work required to make and keep the program useful. It is necessary to *review* and *analyze* the program to ensure that it meets the requirements specified for it, *adapt* it to changing environments, and *modify* it to make it better meet the needs of its users.

Let us illustrate these activities by reconsidering the program for the Life game written and tested in Chapter 1. We shall rework this project completely. Doing so, in one sense, is really overkill, since a toy project like the Life game is not, in itself, worth the effort we shall invest. In the process, however, we shall develop programming methods important for many other applications.

## 2.1.1 REVIEW OF THE LIFE PROGRAM

*problems*

In running the Life program, the major problem you will have likely found is the poor method for input of the initial configuration. It is unnatural for a person to calculate and type in the numerical coordinates of each living cell. The form of

*poor input*

input should instead reflect the same visual imagery as the way the map is printed.

There is also a second problem that you may have found if you ran the program on a very slow machine or on a busy time-sharing system: You may have found the program's speed somewhat disappointing. There can be a noticeable pause

*poor speed*

between printing one generation and starting to print the next.

Our goal is to improve the program so that it will run really efficiently on a small microcomputer. The problem of improving the form of input is addressed as an exercise; the text discusses the problem of improving the speed.

### 1. Analysis of the Life Program

We must first find out where the program is spending most of its computation time. If we examine the program, we can first note that the trouble cannot be in the function Initialize, since this is done only once, before the main loop is started. Within the loop that counts generations, we have a pair of nested loops that, together, will

*operation counts*

iterate

$$\text{MAXROW} \times \text{MAXCOL} = 20 \times 60 = 1200$$

times. Hence program lines within these loops will contribute substantially to the time used.

Within the loops, we first invoke the function NeighborCount(map, row, col). The function itself includes a pair of nested loops (note that we are now nested to a total depth of 5), which do their inner statement 9 times. The function also does 3 statements outside the loops, for a total of 12.

Within the nested loops of the main program there are, along with the call to the function, only the comparison to find which case to do and the appropriate assignment statement. That is, there are only 2 statements additional to the 12 in the function. Outside of the nested loops there is the function call Copy-Map(map, newmap), which, in copying 1200 entries, is about equivalent to 1 more statement within the loops. There is also a call to the function WriteMap, some variation of which is needed in any case so that the user can see what the program is doing. Our primary concern is with the computation, however, so let us not worry about the time that WriteMap may need. We thus see that for each generation, the computation involves about $1200 \times 15 = 18,000$ statements, of which about $1200 \times 12 = 14,400$ are done in the function.

On a slow microcomputer or a tiny share of a busy time-sharing system, each statement can easily require 100 to 500 microseconds for execution, so the time to calculate a generation may easily range as high as 15 seconds, a delay that most users will find unacceptable. On the other hand, with a faster computer, all the calculations can easily be done so quickly that the user will notice no delay between printing one generation and the next.

Since by far the greatest amount of time is used in the function calculating the number of occupied neighbors of a cell, to speed up the program we should concentrate our attention on doing this job more efficiently. Before starting to develop some ideas, however, let us pause momentarily to pontificate:

---

**Programming Precept**

*Most programs spend 90 percent of their time doing 10 percent of their instructions.*
*Find this 10 percent, and concentrate your efforts for efficiency there.*

---

It takes much practice and experience to decide what is important and what may be neglected in analyzing algorithms for efficiency, but it is a skill that you should carefully develop to enable you to choose alternative methods or to concentrate your programming efforts where they will do the most good.

### 2. Problem-solving Alternatives

Once we know where a program is doing most of its work, we can begin to consider alternative methods in the hope of improving its efficiency. In the case of the Life game, let us ask ourselves how we can reduce the amount of work needed to keep *use of array*

track of the number of occupied neighbors of each Life cell. Is it necessary for us to calculate the number of neighbors of every cell at every generation? Clearly not, if we use some way (such as an array) to remember the number of neighbors, and if this number does not change from one generation to the next. If you have spent some time experimenting with the Life program, then you will certainly have noticed that in many interesting configurations, the number of occupied cells at any time is far below the total number of positions available. Out of 1200 positions, typically fewer than 40 are occupied. Our program is spending much of its time laboriously calculating the obvious facts that cells isolated from the living cells indeed have no occupied neighbors and will not become occupied. If we can prevent or substantially reduce such useless calculation, we shall obtain a much better program.

As a first approach, let us consider trying to limit the calculations to cells in a limited area around those that are occupied. If this occupied area (which we would have to define precisely) is roughly rectangular, then we can implement this scheme easily by replacing the limits in the loops by other variables that would bound the occupied area. But this scheme would be very inefficient if the occupied area were shaped like a large ring, or, indeed, if there were only two small occupied areas in opposite corners of a very large rectangle. To try to carry out this plan for occupied areas not at all rectangular in shape would probably require us to do so many comparisons, as well as the loops, as to obviate any saving of time.

### 2.1.2 A FRESH START AND A NEW METHOD FOR LIFE

*arrays and functions*

Let us back up for a moment. If we can now decide to keep an array to remember the number of occupied neighbors of each cell, then the only counts in the array that will change from generation to generation will be those that correspond to immediate neighbors of cells that die or are born.

We can substantially improve the running time of our program if we convert the function NeighborCount into an array and add appropriate statements to update the array while we are doing the changes from one generation to the next embodied in the switch statement, or, if we prefer (what is perhaps conceptually easier), while we are copying newmap into map we can note where the births and deaths have occurred and at that time update the array.

To emphasize that we are now using an array instead of the function Neighbor-Count, we shall change the name and write numbernbrs for the array.

The method we have now developed still involves scanning at least once through the full array map at every generation, which likely means much useless work. By being slightly more careful, we can avoid the need ever to look at unoccupied areas.

*algorithm development*

As a cell is born or dies it changes the value of numbernbrs for each of its immediate neighbors. While making these changes we can note when we find a cell whose count becomes such that it will be born or die in the next generation.

Thus we should keep track of the cells that, so to speak, are moribund or are expecting in the coming generation. In this way, once we have finished making the changes of the current generation and printing the map, we will have waiting for us all the cells that will become alive or will die in the coming generation.

It should now be clear that we really need two structures to hold the births and two for the deaths, one each for the changes being made now and one each (which are being added to) containing the changes for the next generation. When the changes for the current generation are complete, we print the map and then determine the changes that will be needed for the coming generation. This process is illustrated in Figure 2.1.

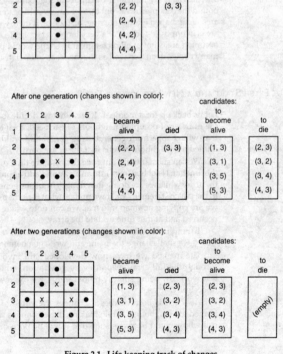

Figure 2.1. Life keeping track of changes

Let us now summarize our decisions by writing down an informal outline of the program we shall develop.

*initialization*

Get the initial configuration of living cells and use it to calculate an array holding the neighbor counts of all cells. Determine the cells that will become alive and that will become dead in the first generation;

*main loop*

Repeat the following steps as long as desired:

Vivify[1] each cell that is ready to become alive;

Kill each cell that is ready to die;

Write out the map for the user;

*prepare for next generation*

Increase the neighbor counts for each neighbor of each cell that has become alive; If a neighbor count reaches the appropriate value, then keep track of the cell as a candidate to be made alive or dead in the next generation;

Decrease the neighbor counts for each neighbor of each cell that has become dead; If a neighbor count reaches the appropriate value, then keep track of the cell as a candidate to be made alive or dead in the next generation;

Clearly a great many details remain to be specified in this outline. We shall turn to these details in the next section, beginning with a careful specification of the data structure used to keep track of cells, followed by the specifications for each of the functions.

---

**Exercises 2.1**

**E1.** Sometimes the user might wish to run the Life game (from the last chapter) on a grid smaller than $20 \times 60$. Determine how it is possible to make MAXROW and MAXCOL into variables that the user can set when the program is run. Try to make as few changes in the program as possible.

**E2.** One idea for speeding up the function NeighborCount(map, row, col) is to delete the *hedge* (the extra rows and columns that are always dead) from the grids map and newmap. Then, when a cell is on the boundary, NeighborCount will look at fewer than the eight neighboring cells, since some of these are outside the bounds of the grid. To do this, the function will need to determine whether or not the cell (row, col) is on the boundary, but this can be done outside the loops. How would this change affect the count of statements executed in Neighbor-Count?

**Programming Projects 2.1**

**P1.** Rewrite the function Initialize so that it accepts the occupied positions as a sequence of blanks and x's in appropriate rows, rather than requiring the occupied positions to be entered as numerical coordinate pairs.

---

[1] The word *vivify* means *make alive*.

**P2.** Add a feature to the function Initialize so that it can read the initial configuration from a file. The first line of the file will be a comment giving the name of the configuration. Each remaining line of the file will correspond to a row of the configuration. Each line will contain x in each living position and a blank in each dead position.

**P3.** On a slow-speed terminal writing out the entire map at every generation will be quite slow. If you have access to a video terminal for which the cursor can be controlled by the program (direct cursor addressing), rewrite WriteMap so that it updates the map instead of completely rewriting it at each generation.

# 2.2 Algorithm Development: A Second Version of Life ▬▬▬▬

After deciding on the basic method and the overall outline of the data structures needed for solving a problem, it is time to commence the process of algorithm development, beginning with careful specifications for the data structures, then the main program, and then slowly introducing refinements until all the subprograms are specified and the whole project is formulated in a computer language.

## 2.2.1 LISTS: SPECIFICATIONS FOR A DATA STRUCTURE

### 1. Lists and Arrays
Soon after the introduction of loops and arrays, every elementary programming class attempts some programming exercise like the following:

*Read an integer $n$, which will be at most 25, then read a list of $n$ numbers, and print the list in reverse order.*

This simple exercise will probably cause difficulty for some students. Most will realize that they need to use an array, but some will attempt to set up the array to have $n$ entries and will be confused by the error message resulting from attempting to use a variable rather than a constant to declare the size of the array. Other students will say, "I could solve the problem if I knew that there were 25 numbers, but I don't see how to handle fewer." Or "Tell me before I write the program how large $n$ is, and then I can do it."

*lists and arrays*

The difficulties of these students come not from stupidity, but from thinking logically. A beginning course sometimes does not draw enough distinction between two quite different concepts. First is the concept of a *list* of $n$ numbers, a list whose size is variable, that is, a list for which numbers can be inserted or deleted, so that, if $n = 3$, then the list contains only 3 numbers, and if $n = 19$, then it contains 19 numbers. Second is the programming feature called an *array* or a vector, which contains a constant number of positions, that is, whose size is fixed when the program is compiled. A list is a *dynamic* data structure because its size can change, while an array is a *static* data structure because it has a fixed size.

*implementation*

The concepts of a list and an array are, of course, related in that a list of variable size can be implemented in a computer as occupying part of an array of fixed size, with some of the entries in the array remaining unused. We shall later find, however, that there are several different ways to implement lists, and therefore we should not confuse implementation decisions with more fundamental decisions on choosing and specifying data structures.

## 2. Basic List Operations

For the sake of processing cells in the Life game, it is appropriate to use lists, since the number of cells waiting to be processed changes from one generation to the next.

By checking the outline of the new Life algorithm in Section 2.1.2, we can find what operations are needed for the lists we use. First, we shall need to *create* a list, and we shall need to *clear* a list to make it empty. We may need status operations to determine if a list is *empty* or is *full*, or a function giving the *size* of a list. We need a function to *add* a new entry to the end of a list. Finally, we need to *traverse* a list: *Traversal* means going through a list and performing a specified operation on every entry in the list.

*simple lists*    Although many other operations are possible for lists, these seven are all that are needed not only for the Life game but for a surprising variety of other applications. Let us therefore now give precise specifications for lists, simplified to allow only these seven operations.

## 3. Type Declarations

*entry type*    To write down the specifications precisely, we need to decide on names for the types involved. To keep as much generality as we can, let us use ListEntry for the type of entries in our list. For one application, ListEntry might be int; for another it might be char. For the Life project, we wish the list entries to be coordinates of cells, so we shall include the declaration

typedef Cell ListEntry;

in our program. (We will see the definition of Cell later in this chapter.) By keeping the type ListEntry general, we can use the same collection of functions for many different applications.

*generics*    The ability to use the same underlying data structure and operations for different entry types is called *generics*. Some programming languages (Ada and C++, for example), but not C, allow the programmer to declare data structures and functions generically and then use them, unchanged, for many different entry types. C does not allow this practice, so we must work harder to achieve declarations that can be used in many different applications. In this book, we shall illustrate two methods for achieving this goal. When the entry type is one of C's standard types, we shall construct a set of header files and function definitions that we can use without modification in any application we wish. When the entry type is non-standard, such as the cells used in the Life project, we shall make modifications as appropriate and use the new version with just the application for which it was customized.

Thus, for the Life project, the primary header file will include the type declaration

typedef Cell ListEntry;

and will then include a compiler directive to copy in the list header file, as follows:

#include "list.h"

If, on the other hand, we were working with a list of characters, then, so that we could reuse the same files whenever we needed a list of characters, we would construct a header file, charlist.h, and a source file, charlist.c. In charlist.h we would include the type definition

typedef char ListEntry;

An application wishing to use a list of characters would include the header file and link with the source file.

To simplify writing our programs, we shall develop several different sets of header files for various purposes.

### 4. First Operations for Simple Lists

The first operation is required before a simple list can be used:

*initialization*

void CreateList(List *list);
*precondition:*  None.
*postcondition:*  The list list has been created and is initialized to be empty.

The next operation takes a list that already exists and makes it empty.

*reinitialization*

void ClearList(List *list);
*precondition:*  The list list has been created.
*postcondition:*  All entries in list have been removed; list is empty.

Next come the operations for checking the status of a list.

*status operations*

Boolean ListEmpty(const List *list);
*precondition:*  The list list has been created.
*postcondition:*  The function returns true or false according as list is empty or not.

> Boolean ListFull(const List *list);
>
> *precondition*:  The list list has been created.
>
> *postcondition*:  The function returns true or false according as list is full or not.

> int ListSize(const List *list);
>
> *precondition*:  The list list has been created.
>
> *postcondition*:  The function returns the number of entries in list.

Note that, in these specifications, some of the functions for these simple lists show list with a const type qualifier while others show list without the qualifier. When the const type qualifier is not present, such as in the function ClearList, the function may be changing the list. When there is a const, such as in ListSize, absolutely no changes may be made to the list.

*parameters and efficiency*

**NOTE**

In giving specifications for the operations on any data type, we shall generally be careful to use reference parameters exactly when a subprogram may change the parameter. When we come to the implementation details of actually writing the subprograms, however, we shall usually take a different point of view, in order to avoid a very wasteful inefficiency: When a value parameter appears in C, a new copy of the parameter is made whenever the subprogram is started. If we are working with a large data structure, then it takes a great deal of time and space to make a new copy of the data structure. Hence we adhere to the convention discussed in Section 1.3.3, and in the actual implementation of simple lists we will use list as a reference parameter for all subprograms. In the future, for similar data structures we will also use reference parameters for the same reason.

## 5. Further Operations for Simple Lists

For our simplified lists, we will insert new entries only at the end:

> void AddList(ListEntry x, List *list);
>
> *precondition*:  The list list has been created and is not full; x is an element of
>                  type ListEntry.
>
> *postcondition*:  The element x has been inserted as the last element of list.

*traverse and visit*

One more action is commonly done with lists, called *traversal* of the list. *Traversal* means to start at the beginning of the list and do some action for each entry in the list in turn, finishing with the last entry in the list. What action is done for each entry depends on the application. For generality, we say that we *visit* each entry in the list. Hence we have the final function for list processing:

---

void TraverseList(List *list, void (*Visit)(ListEntry));

*precondition:*    The list list has been created. Visit is a function that processes elements of type ListEntry, but Visit cannot make insertions or deletions in list.

*postcondition:*    The action specified by function Visit has been performed on every entry of list, beginning at the first entry and doing each in turn.

---

*pointers to functions*    Yes, this function declaration is standard C; pointers to functions are allowed as formal parameters for other functions, although this feature is not often used in elementary programming. This particular use is declaring Visit as a pointer to a function that takes one parameter of type ListEntry and returns void. As with all parameters, the parameter Visit is only a formal name that is replaced by another function, the actual parameter, when the TraverseList operation is used. Visit itself does not necessarily exist in its own right; the name Visit stands for the function that will be used during traversal to process each entry in the list. If, for example, we had two functions void Update(ListEntry x) and void Modify(ListEntry x) and list is of type List, then the application program could include the commands TraverseList(list, Update) or TraverseList(list, Modify) to perform either of these operations on every entry of the list. If, as scaffolding, it is desired to print out all the entries of a list, then all that is needed is to write TraverseList(list, Print); where void Print(ListEntry x) prints a single entry of a list.

We shall find several applications for the traverse operation in the Life program under development.

The use of pointers to functions introduces one more complication into our programming. For the formal parameter Visit we specified only one parameter, the list entry currently being processed. It may well be, however, that the actual function used in place of Visit needs additional variables that would normally be specified as further parameters. Since what these are depends on the application, it is impossible for us to specify them as part of the declaration of TraverseList and its formal parameter Visit. Hence we are forced to use only the one (ListEntry) parameter both in Visit and in the actual function that replaces it. This actual function must then use global variables in place of additional parameters. Sometimes it must even cause side effects by changing these global variables.

---

**Programming Precept**

*When the use of global variables and side effects is unavoidable,*
*be sure to document them carefully both in the specifications*
*and in the use of the subprogram.*

---

## MAIN PROGRAM

With the data structures specified for the Life project, we can take the outline of the method given in Section 2.1.2, thereby translating the outline into a main program written in C. With few exceptions, the declarations of constants, types, and variables follow the discussion in Section 2.1 and Section 2.2 along with the corresponding declarations for the first version of the Life game. The lists maylive and maydie contain the cells that are candidates to become alive or dead in the current generation. Some of these cells, however, may be on the lists incorrectly. Hence, after the correct cells have been made alive or dead, the lists newlive and newdie hold the cells that were actually vivified (that is, *made alive*) or killed.

The declarations in life2.h are:

```
#define MAXROW 20          /* maximum size of grid                                  */
#define MAXCOL 60          /* dependent on the size of the screen output            */
#define MAXLIST 300        /* maximum size allowed for each of the four lists       */
typedef enum state { DEAD, ALIVE } State;  /* cell status                           */
typedef State Grid[MAXROW + 2][MAXCOL + 2];
typedef int Gridcount[MAXROW + 2][MAXCOL + 2];  /* number of neighbors              */
typedef struct cell {
        int row, col;      /* grid coordinate                                       */
} Cell;
typedef Cell ListEntry;
#include "simplist.h"
Boolean UserSaysYes(void);
void WriteMap(Grid);
void FindSize(int *, int *);
void ReadMap(List *, Grid);
void Vivify(ListEntry);
void Kill(ListEntry);
void AddNeighbors(ListEntry);
void SubtractNeighbors(ListEntry);
void Initialize (Grid, Gridcount, List *, List *, List *, List *);
```

Note that ListEntry is defined just before we include simplist.h. The header file simplist.h contains the declarations for simple lists:

```
typedef struct list {
        int count;
        ListEntry entry[MAXLIST];
} List;
void CreateList(List *);
void ClearList(List *);
Boolean ListEmpty(const List *);
Boolean ListFull(const List *);
int ListSize(const List *);
void AddList(ListEntry, List *);
void TraverseList(List *, void (*)(ListEntry));
void CopyList(List *, const List *);
```

The main program is as follows:

*Life2, main program*

```
/* Life2: Second version of Life program
   Pre:   The user supplies an initial configuration of living cells.
   Post:  The program prints a sequence of maps showing the changes in the configu-
          ration of living cells according to the rules for the game of Life. */
#include "common.h"
#include "life2.h"
Grid map;                       /* global: square array holding cells                      */
Gridcount numbernbrs;           /* global: square array holding neighbor counts            */
List newlive,                   /* global: the cells that have just been vivified          */
     newdie,                    /* global: the cells that have just died                   */
     maylive,                   /* global: candidates to vivify in the next generation     */
     maydie;                    /* global: candidates to kill in the next generation       */
int maxrow, maxcol;             /* global: user defined grid size                          */
int main(void)
{
```

*initialization*

```
   Initialize(map, numbernbrs, &newlive, &newdie, &maylive, &maydie);
   WriteMap(map);
   printf("Proceed with the demonstration");
   while (UserSaysYes( )) {
```

*main loop*

```
       TraverseList( &maylive, Vivify);
                               /* uses numbernbrs, changes map and newlive    */
       TraverseList( &maydie, Kill);
                               /* uses numbernbrs, changes map and newdie     */
       WriteMap(map);
       ClearList( &maylive);
       ClearList( &maydie);
       TraverseList( &newlive, AddNeighbors);
                               /* changes numbernbrs, maylive, maydie         */
       TraverseList( &newdie, SubtractNeighbors);
       ClearList( &newlive);
       ClearList( &newdie);
       printf("Do you want to continue viewing new generations");
   }
   return 0;
}
```

*description*

Most of the action of the program is postponed to various functions. After initializing all the lists and arrays, the program begins its main loop. At each generation
we first go through the cells waiting in lists maylive and maydie in order to update
the array map, which, as in the first version of Life, keeps track of which cells are
alive. This work is done in the functions Vivify and Kill. After writing the revised
configuration, we update the count of neighbors for each cell that has been born
or has died, using the functions AddNeighbors and SubtractNeighbors and the array
numbernbrs. As part of the same functions, when the neighbor count reaches an
appropriate value, a cell is added to the list maylive or maydie to indicate that it will

be born or die in the coming generation. After we use the entries from a list, we clear it in preparation for the next generation.

Note especially the use of the function TraverseList, called four times to move through a list and perform one of the actions Vivify, Kill, AddNeighbors, or Subtract-Neighbors on each entry of the list. Each of these four functions, in turn, is the

*pointers to functions*  actual parameter that replaces the dummy parameter Visit that was specified in the declaration of TraverseList.

Note also that each of these four functions not only uses an entry from the list being traversed, but it also changes (adds to) one or more of the other lists. Vivify, for example, uses an entry from maylive and adds the vivified cells to newlive. The function declarations in life2.h show that all four functions have the *same* parameters as the dummy function Visit, and Visit was specified to have only one parameter, the list entry that it processes. Hence, each of the four functions Vivify,

**NOTE**  Kill, AddNeighbors, and SubtractNeighbors is allowed to have only this one parameter, even though it will change other lists besides. In other words, we are *forced* by the original declaration of Visit to write these four functions to use and change lists as global variables, that is, we are forced into the poor programming practice of causing side effects. When such a practice is necessary, it becomes doubly important to document what we are doing, especially by writing the specifications for each function with the greatest care.

## 2.2.3 INFORMATION HIDING

Notice that we have been able to write our main program for the Life project and use the list-processing functions, even though we have not yet considered how the lists will actually be implemented in storage and before we write the details of

*use of functions*  the various functions. In this way, we have an example of *information hiding*: If someone else had already written the functions and functions for handling lists, then we could use them without needing to know the details of how lists are kept in memory or of how the list operations are actually done.

As a matter of fact, we have already practiced information hiding in our previous programs without thinking about it. Whenever we have written a program using an array or a structure, we have been content to use the operations on these structures without considering how the C compiler actually represents them in terms of bits or bytes in the computer memory or the machine-language steps it

*built-in structures*  follows to look up an index or select a field. The only real difference between practicing information hiding with regard to arrays and structures and practicing information hiding with regard to lists is that C provides built-in operations for arrays and structures but not for lists.

Some computer languages, such as LISP or Scheme, do provide lists as a built-in data type. If we were using one of these languages, we would be performing operations on lists as readily as we do on arrays or structures. There is a good reason, however, why C does not provide lists as a built-in data type. In the coming

*alternative*  chapters, we shall see that for lists (as for almost all the data types we shall study)
*implementations*  there are several different ways to represent the data in the computer memory, and there are several different ways to do the operations.

In some applications, one method is better, while in other applications another method proves superior. In C we can choose whichever method is best for our application and then include the appropriate functions and functions that implement our choice.

Even in a single large program, we may first decide to represent lists one way and then, as we gain experience with the program, we may decide that another way

*change of implementation*

is better. If the instructions for manipulating a list have been written out every time a list is used, then every occurrence of these instructions will need to be changed. If we have practiced information hiding by using separate functions and functions for manipulating lists, then only the declarations will need to be changed.

*clarity of program*

One more advantage of information hiding for lists is that the very appearance of words like AddList and ListEmpty will immediately alert a person reading the program to what is being done, whereas the instructions themselves might be more obscure.

*top-down design*

A final advantage we shall find is that separating the use of data structures from their implementation will help us improve the top-down design of both our data structures and our programs.

## 2.2.4 REFINEMENT: DEVELOPMENT OF THE SUBPROGRAMS

After the solution to a problem has been outlined, it is time to turn to the various parts of the outline, to include more details and thereby specify the solution exactly. While making these refinements, however, the programmer often discovers that the task of each subprogram was not specified as carefully as necessary, that the in-

*specifications and problem solving*

terface between different subprograms must be reworked and spelled out in more detail, so that the different subprograms accomplish all necessary tasks, and so that they do so without duplication or contradictory requirements. In a real sense, therefore, the process of refinement requires going back to the problem-solving phase to find the best way to split the required tasks among the various subprograms. Ideally, this process of refinement and specification should be completed before any coding is done.

Let us illustrate this activity by working through the requirements for the various subprograms for the Life game.

### 1. The Task for AddNeighbors

Much of the work of our program will be done in the functions AddNeighbors and SubtractNeighbors. We shall develop the first of these, leaving the second as an exercise. The function AddNeighbors is given (as its parameter) one entry from the list newlive. AddNeighbors then finds the immediate neighbors of this cell (as done in the original function NeighborCount), increases the count in numbernbrs for each of these neighbors, and must put some of the neighbors into the lists maylive and maydie. To determine which, let us denote by $n$ the updated count for one of the neighbors and consider cases.

*cases for*
AddNeighbors

1. It is impossible that $n = 0$, since we have just increased $n$ by 1.

2. If $n = 1$ or $n = 2$, then the cell is already dead and it should remain dead in the next generation. We need do nothing.

3. If $n = 3$, then a previously living cell still lives; a previously dead cell must be added to the list maylive.

4. If $n = 4$, then a previously living cell dies; add it to maydie. If the cell is dead, it remains so.

5. if $n > 4$, then the cell is already dead (or is already on list maydie) and remains dead.

## 2. Problems

One subtle problem arises with this function. When the neighbor count for a dead cell reaches 3, we add it to the list maylive, but it may well be that later in function

*spurious entries*

AddNeighbors, its neighbor count will again be increased (beyond 3) so that it should not be vivified in the next generation after all. Similarly when the neighbor count for a living cell reaches 4, we add it to maydie, but the function SubtractNeighbors may well reduce its neighbor count below 4, so that it should be removed from maydie. Thus the final determination of lists maylive and maydie cannot be made until the array numbernbrs has been fully updated, but yet, as we proceed, we must tentatively add entries to the lists.

*postpone difficulty*

It turns out that, if we postpone this problem, it becomes much easier. In the functions AddNeighbors and SubtractNeighbors, let us add cells to maylive and maydie without worrying whether they will later be removed. Then when we use maylive and maydie while performing Vivify and Kill, respectively, we can check that the neighbor counts are correct (in maylive, for example, only dead cells with a neighbor count of exactly 3 should appear) and ignore the erroneous entries with no difficulty.

*duplicate entries*

After doing this, however, an even more subtle error remains. It is possible that the same cell may appear in list maylive (or maydie) more than once. A dead cell, for example, may initially have a count of 2, which, when increased, adds the cell to maylive. Its count may then be increased further, and in SubtractNeighbors decreased one or more times, perhaps ending at 3, so that SubtractNeighbors again adds it to maylive. Then, when neighbor counts are updated in the next generation, this birth will incorrectly contribute 2 rather than 1 to the neighbor counts. We could solve this problem by searching the lists for duplicates before using them, but to do so would be slow, and we can again solve the problem more easily by postponing it. When, in the next generation, we wish to vivify a cell, we shall first check whether it is already alive. If so, then we know that its entry is a duplicate of one earlier on list maylive, and so, again, we shall ignore the entry.

Figure 2.2 shows the trace of Life2 for one small configuration and exhibits the appearance and deletion of spurious and duplicate entries in the various lists. The behavior of this configuration depends on the fact that the grid has only four rows in this example.

---

**Programming Precept**

*Sometimes postponing problems simplifies their solution.*

---

With these decisions made, we can now give precise specifications for the four key functions. Specifications for SubtractNeighbors and for Kill are left as exercises. For AddNeighbors and Vivify we obtain:

---

void AddNeighbors(ListEntry cell);

*precondition:*   cell has just become alive.

*postcondition:*   Array numbernbrs has increased counts for all cells neighboring cell. If the increased neighbor count makes the cell a candidate to be vivified [*resp.* killed] then the cell has been added to list maylive [*resp.* maydie].

*uses:*   Function AddList; changes array numbernbrs and lists maylive and maydie as global variables (side effects).

---

void Vivify(ListEntry cell);

*precondition:*   The cell is a candidate to become alive.

*postcondition:*   Checks that cell meets all requirements to become alive. If not, no change is made. If so, then cell is added to the list newlive, and array map is updated.

*uses:*   Function AddList, array numbernbrs, changes array map and list newlive as global variables (side effects).

---

## 2.2.5 VERIFICATION OF ALGORITHMS

Another important aspect of the design of large programs is algorithm verification, that is, a *proof* that the algorithm accomplishes its task. This kind of proof is usually formulated by looking at the specifications for the subprograms and then arguing that these specifications combine properly to accomplish the task of the whole

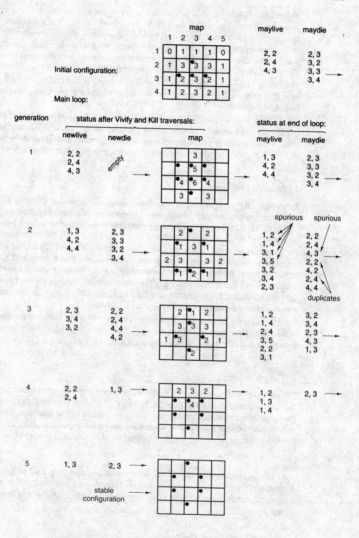

Figure 2.2. A trace of program Life2

algorithm. While constructing such a proof we may find that the specifications must be changed to enable us to infer the correctness of the algorithm, and, in doing so, the proof itself helps us formulate the specifications for each subprogram with greater precision. Hence algorithm verification and algorithm design can go hand-in-hand, and sometimes the verification can even lead the way. In any case, algorithm verification should precede coding.

Let us again illustrate these concepts by turning to the Life program, first to be sure that its algorithm is correct and second to assist us in designing the remaining function, Initialize.

Indeed, the fact that there were subtle difficulties in our initial attempts to organize the work done in functions Vivify, Kill, AddNeighbors, and SubtractNeighbors should alert us to the possible presence of further errors, or at least to the necessity of exercising considerably more care to be sure that our algorithms are correct.

*caution*

### 1. Possible Problems

By postponing the checking of neighbor counts, we were able to avoid difficulties with both the problems of duplicate and of erroneous entries. But, for example, is it still possible that the same cell might erroneously be included in both lists maylive and maydie? If so, then it might first be vivified and then killed immediately in the same generation (clearly an illegal happening). The answer to this particular question is *no* since the main program uses both functions Vivify and Kill before either function AddNeighbors or SubtractNeighbors. Thus the cell keeps the same status (alive or dead) from the end of the traversal with Kill until the next generation, and the functions AddNeighbors and SubtractNeighbors check that only dead cells are added to maylive and only living cells to maydie.

How can we be sure that there are not more subtle questions of this sort, some of which might not be so easy to answer? The only way we can really be confident is to *prove* that our program does the right action in each case.

### 2. The Main Loop

The difficulty with our program is that what happens in one generation might affect the next generation in some unexpected way. Therefore we focus our attention on the large loop in the main program. At the beginning of the loop it is the contents of lists maylive and maydie that determine everything that happens later. Let us therefore summarize what we know about these lists from our previous study.

*At the beginning of the main loop, list maylive contains only dead cells, and list maydie contains only living cells, but the lists may contain duplicate entries, or spurious entries whose neighbor counts are wrong. The lists newlive and newdie are empty.*

At the very start of the program, it is one task of function Initialize to ensure that the four lists are set up properly, so that the preceding statements are correct at the start of the first generation. What we must prove, then, is that if the statements are true at the start of any one generation, then after the nine function calls within the loop, they will again be true for the next generation.

### 3. Proof by Mathematical Induction

At this point, you should note that what we are really doing is using the method of ***mathematical induction*** to establish that the program is correct. In this method

*initial case*

of proof, we begin by establishing the result for an initial case. Next we prove the result for a later case, say case $n$, by using the result for earlier cases (those between the initial case and case $n - 1$). For the Life program, we use the generation number for the induction.

Verification of the initial case amounts to a verification that Initialize works properly. This part of the proof amounts to writing down correct specifications for Initialize.

*induction step*

For the second part of the proof, the induction step, let us examine the actions in the main loop, assuming that the statements are correct at its beginning. The traversal with Vivify uses only list maylive and, according to the specifications for Vivify, carefully checks each entry before it vivifies a cell, putting only those properly vivified onto list newlive. Hence, at the conclusion of the first traversal, list newlive contains only those cells that were properly vivified, and no duplicates.

The traversal with function Kill similarly uses list maydie and sets newdie to contain exactly those cells that were just killed. Since maylive and maydie originally had no cells in common, and none has been added to either list, no cells have been improperly both vivified and killed.

Next, function WriteMap is called, but does not change the lists.

Function AddNeighbors works only from list newlive and puts only dead cells on list maylive, and only living ones on list maydie. Similarly, function Subtract-Neighbors keeps the dead and living cells properly separated. Together these two functions add all the cells whose status should change in the next generation to the lists, but may add duplicate or spurious entries.

*end of proof*

Finally, newlive and newdie are cleared, as required to show that all conditions in our statements are again true at the beginning of the next generation. The logic of our program is therefore correct.

### 4. Invariants and Assertions

Statements such as the one we established in the preceding proof are called *loop invariants*. In general, a loop invariant is a statement that is true at the beginning of every iteration of the loop. The statements we made about the status of various lists at different points of the loop are called *assertions*.

### 5. Initialization

Our informal verification of the main loop of the Life program has one more benefit: The loop invariant that we wrote down leads easily to the specifications for the initialization function, the last remaining major function of the project:

---

void Initialize (Grid map, Gridcount numbernbrs,
               List *newlive, List *newdie, List *maylive, List *maydie);

*precondition*:   None.

*postcondition*:  Array map contains the initial configuration of living and dead cells. Array numbernbrs contains counts of living neighbors corresponding to the configuration in array map. List maylive contains only dead cells and includes all candidates that may be vivified in the first generation. List maydie contains only living cells and contains all candidates that may die in the first generation. Lists newlive and newdie are empty.

*uses*:           Simple list package, functions FindSize, ReadMap, AddNeighbors.

---

### 6. Conclusion

*simplification*

The purpose of loop invariants and assertions is to capture the essence of the dynamic process. It is not always easy to find loop invariants and assertions that will lead to a proof that a program is correct, but it is a very useful exercise. Attempting to find invariants and assertions sometimes leads to simplifications in design of the algorithm, which make its correctness more obvious. Our goal should always be to make our algorithms so straightforward and clear that their logic is obviously correct, and the use of loop invariants can help in this process.

Algorithm verification is a subject under active research, in which many important questions remain to be answered. Correctness proofs have not yet been supplied for a large number of important algorithms that are in constant use. Sometimes exceptional cases appear that cause an algorithm to misbehave; correctness proofs would provide a consistent means to delineate these exceptions and provide for their processing.

One of the most important uses of these formal methods is in deriving how an algorithm should operate by determining precise specifications, just as we have done for the Initialization function.

---

**Exercises 2.2**     Write down preconditions and postconditions for each of the following functions.

E1. float SquareRoot(float x);   returns the square root of x

E2. float Mean(List *A);   calculates the mean (average) value in a list of floating point numbers (that is, ListEntry is float)

E3. void Kill(Cell current);

E4. void SubtractNeighbors(Cell current);

E5. void WriteMap(Grid map);

E6. void ReadMap(List *newlive, Grid map);

# 2.3 Coding

Now that we have spelled out completely and precisely the specifications for each function, it is time to code them into our programming language. In a large software project it is necessary to do the coding at the right time, not too soon and not too late. Most programmers err by starting to code too soon. If coding is

*specifications complete* begun before the specifications are made precise, then unwarranted assumptions about the specifications will inevitably be made while coding, and these assumptions may render different subprograms incompatible with each other or make the programming task much more difficult than it need be.

---

**Programming Precept**

*Never code until the specifications are precise and complete.*

---

*top-down coding* It is possible but unlikely, on the other hand, to delay coding too long. Just as we design from the top down, we should code from the top down. Once the specifications at the top levels are complete and precise, we should code the subprograms at these levels and test them by including appropriate stubs. If we then find that our design is flawed, we can modify it without paying an exorbitant price in low-level functions that have been rendered useless. In this section, we program the simple list functions, and in the next section we shall complete the Life project.

## 2.3.1 THE LIST FUNCTIONS

Note that, even though we have been using list operations for some time, we have not yet needed to consider how the list routines will be implemented. There are, in fact, two standard implementations for lists, either of which would work well for the Life project. In this section, we shall develop the *contiguous* implementation, in which the entries in the list are stored next to each other within an array. The *linked* implementation uses C pointers and dynamic memory in place of an array. Simple linked lists are studied in Chapter 5.

### 1. Data Storage

In the contiguous implementation of lists, we set up an array to hold the entries, and we need to keep a separate counter to indicate how many of the array positions are occupied. We combine these into a single structure[2] by declaring:

```
typedef struct list {
        int count;
        ListEntry entry[MAXLIST];
} List;
```

---

[2]  C structures are studied in Appendix C.

### 2. Sample Operations

Coding the operations for simple lists is now straightforward, and most of them will be left as exercises. Here is the function to insert an additional entry.

```
/* AddList:
    Pre:   The list list has been created and is not full; x is an element of type ListEntry.
    Post:  The element x has been inserted as the last element of list. */
void AddList(ListEntry x, List *list)
{
    if (ListFull(list))
        Warning("Attempt to insert at the end of a full list.");
    else
        list->entry[list->count++] = x;
}
```

The function for traversing a list uses the function pointer Visit.

```
/* TraverseList:
    Pre:   The list list has been created.
    Post:  The action specified by function Visit has been performed on every entry of
           list, beginning at the first entry and doing each in turn. */
void TraverseList(List *list, void (*Visit)(ListEntry))
{
    int i;
    for (i = 0;  i < list->count;  i++)
        (*Visit)(list->entry[i]);
}
```

## 2.3.2 ERROR PROCESSING

Note that the AddList function invokes another function called Warning in the case when it cannot do its work because the list is full. This provides us with a first example of error processing, an important safeguard that we should build into our programs whenever possible.

There are two different ways that we could handle errors. In production programs that have been thoroughly debugged, the occurrence of an error usually indicates that something serious has gone wrong, and so errors are usually fatal to the execution of the program. That is, the program would print an error message and terminate. While we are developing and debugging a program, however, errors are quite likely to occur. We shall therefore adopt two different methods of error handling, *warnings* and *errors*. An error indicates a more serious problem and behaves as above. A warning, instead of terminating the program, will make the program write an informative message indicating what went wrong. The

NOTE

program will then skip the affected operation and continue. In this way we can continue to study the program and learn more of what went wrong. The programmer is responsible, of course, for correcting the program so that, eventually, it will run without any of the warning messages. After this, the implementation subprograms can be changed to production versions in which the occurrence of an error will terminate the program.

We shall consistently refer warnings and errors to two functions (Warning and Error) that will accept a string as their one parameter, print an error message, and then return to the calling program or exit the program. We shall therefore use these functions throughout the book and include declarations in our common.h include file.

```
/* Warning: display a warning message
   Pre:    message is the warning message to display.
   Post:   The warning message has been printed to stderr. */
void Warning(char *message)
{
    fprintf(stderr, "Warning: %s\n", message);
}


/* Error: display an error message
   Pre:    message is the error message to display.
   Post:   The error message has been printed to stderr and the program terminates. */
void Error(char *message)
{
    fprintf(stderr, "Error: %s\n", message);
    exit(1);
}
```

### 2.3.3 DEMONSTRATION AND TESTING

*menu-driven demonstration*

After we have written a collection of header files and functions for processing a data structure, we should immediately test the implementation to make sure that every part of it works correctly. One of the best ways to do this is to write a **menu-driven demonstration program** that will set up the data structure and allow the user to perform all possible operations on the data structure in any desired order, printing out the results whenever the user wishes. Let us now develop such a program for the simple list routines. This program will then serve as the basis for similar programs for further data structures throughout the book.

We can make the entries in the list have any type we wish, so for simplicity let us use a list of characters. Hence the entries will be single letters, digits, punctuation marks, and such.

At each iteration of its main loop, the program will ask the user to choose an operation. It will then (if possible) perform that operation on the data structure and print the results.

Hence the main program is:

```
/* Simple List Driver
   Pre:   None.
   Post:  Acts as a menu-driven demonstration program for simple lists. */

#include "common.h"
#include <ctype.h>              /* Used for converting uppercase to lowercase.    */
#include "simplist.h"

void Print(ListEntry);
void Introduction(void);
void Help(void);
char GetCommand(void);
void DoCommand(char, List *);


int main(void)
{
    List list;

    Introduction( );
    CreateList( &list);

    /* endless loop; DoCommand( ) will call exit( ) to end the program. */
    while (TRUE)
        DoCommand(GetCommand( ), &list);
    return 1;                   /* This statement should never be executed.       */

}
```

In this program, we use single characters to select commands. The meanings of these commands are explained by the Help function:

```
/* Help:
   Pre:   None.
   Post:  A help screen for the program has been printed. */

void Help(void)
{
    printf("\nThis program allows one command to be entered on each line.\n"
           "For example, if the command I is entered at the command line\n"
           "then the program will ask for a string of characters and\n"
           "insert them one at a time into the simple list.\n");
```

```
        printf("Valid commands are:\n"
            "\tI - Insert values into the simple list\n"
            "\tP - Print the simple list\n"
            "\tT - Traverse the simple list (same as print)\n"
            "\tS - The current size of the simple list\n"
            "\tD - Delete the simple list\n"
            "\tC - Clear the simple list (same as delete)\n"
            "\tH - This help screen\n"
            "\tQ - Quit\n"
            "Press < Enter> to continue.");
        while (getchar( ) != '\n')
            ;
}
```

There is also an Introduction function used only once at the start of the program. This function explains briefly what the program does and shows the user how to begin. Further instructions come either from Help or from ReadCommand.

The function GetCommand prints the menu, obtains a command from the user, checking that it is valid and converting it to lowercase by using a macro declared in the standard header file ctype.h.

```
/* GetCommand:
    Pre:   None.
    Post:  Gets a valid command from the terminal and returns it through command. */
char GetCommand(void)
{
    char command;
    printf("\n\t[I]nsert entry\t[P]rint list\t[S]ize of list\n"
        "\t[D]elete list\t[C]lear list\t[H]elp\n"
        "\t[T]raverse the list\t\t[Q]uit.\n"
        "Select command and press < Enter > :");
    while (TRUE) {
        while ((command = getchar( )) == '\n')
            ;
        command = tolower(command);  /* changes case if necessary      */
        if (   command == 'i' || command == 'p' || command == 't' ||
            command == 's' || command == 'd' || command == 'c' ||
            command == 'h' || command == 'q') {
            while (getchar( ) != '\n')
                ;
            return command;
        }
        printf("Please enter a valid command or H for help:");
    }
}
```

The work of selecting and performing commands, finally, is performed by DoCommand. It is often desirable to make several insertions, one after the next, and therefore DoCommand is written with a loop permitting multiple insertions.

```
/* DoCommand:
   Pre:   command contains a valid command.
   Post:  Performs command on list. */
void DoCommand(char command, List *list)
{
    ListEntry x;              /* used to insert a new entry              */
    switch (command) {
    case 'i' :                /* insert new entries                     */
        if (ListFull(list))
            Warning("Sorry, list is full.");
        else {
            printf("Enter new key(s) to insert:");
            while ((x = getchar()) != '\n' && !ListFull(list))
                AddList(x, list);
            if (x != '\n') {
                Warning("The list is full, cannot insert any more entries.");
                while ((x = getchar()) != '\n')
                    ;
            }
        }
        break;
    case 'd' :                /* deleting the entries                   */
    case 'c' :
        ClearList(list);
        printf("List is cleared.\n");
        break;
    case 'p' :                /* printing the entries                   */
    case 't' :
        if (ListEmpty(list))
            printf("List is empty.\n");
        else {
            printf("\nTraversing the list; it contains:\n");
            TraverseList(list, Print);   /* function as a parameter     */
        }
        break;
    case 's' :
        printf("The size of the list is %d\n", ListSize(list));
        break;
    case 'h' :
        Help();
        break;
    case 'q' :
        printf("Simple list demonstration finished.\n");
        exit(0);
    }
}
```

Finally, in traversing a list to print it, we must have a function in the correct form to serve as the formal parameter Visit:

```
/* Print: display a ListEntry.
   Pre:   x contains a valid list entry (a character).
   Post:  Prints out the value of x. */
void Print(ListEntry x)
{
   printf(" %c", x);
}
```

You should note that, in all these functions, we have been careful to maintain the principles of data abstraction. We have used the list functions as a separately compiled file, so, if we wish, we can replace this implementation with another, and the program will work with no further change. We have also written the other functions so we can use the program to test other data structures later, changing almost nothing other than the valid operations and the Introduction and Help screens.

---

**Exercises 2.3**

**E1.** Write code for the contiguous implementation of the remaining operations for simple lists, following the specifications in Section 2.2.1:

  (a) CreateList

  (b) ClearList

  (c) ListEmpty

  (d) ListFull

  (e) ListSize

**E2.** Describe the changes needed to the simple list functions and to the menu-driven demonstration program to make it work with integers in place of characters as list entries.

**E3.** Start with the simple list routines, and write a function CopyList with the following specifications:

---

void CopyList(List *dest, const List *source);

*precondition*:  Lists source and dest have been created.

*postcondition*: List dest has become an exact copy of list source; source is unchanged.

---

Write two versions of your function:

  (a) Use the functions in the list implementation to traverse the source list and add each entry onto the end of the dest list.

**(b)** Use the implementation details and write a loop that copies entries from source to dest.

Which of these is easiest to write? Which will run most quickly if the list is nearly full? Which will run most quickly if the list is nearly empty? Which would be the best method if the implementation might be changed?

**Programming Projects 2.3**

**P1.** Complete the simple list demonstration program by supplying any missing functions and declarations, and testing the program.

**P2.** Write an implementation of the simple list functions that uses linked lists in place of the contiguous implementation developed in the text. Test the project by using your implementation in the menu-driven demonstration program. [Linked lists are introduced in Chapter 5, where most of the functions for this project are fully developed.]

## 2.4 Coding the Life Functions

With the specifications in hand for the Life subprograms, we can easily embody our decisions into functions coded in C.

**1. Function Vivify**

The function Vivify takes an entry from the list maylive and vivifies the cell, provided that it was previously dead and had a neighbor count of exactly 3. Otherwise, the cell is one of the spurious entries, and Vivify ignores it. If the cell is actually vivified, then it is added to list newlive, so, at the conclusion of the traversal, newlive contains exactly those cells that were vivified and whose neighbor counts must therefore be updated by AddNeighbors.

```
/* Vivify: vivify cell if applicable.
   Pre:   The cell is a candidate to become alive.
   Post:  Checks that cell meets all requirements to become alive. If not, no change is
          made. If so, then cell is added to the list newlive, and array map is updated.
   Uses:  Function AddList, array numbernbrs, changes array map and list newlive as
          global variables (side effects). */
```

*make cells alive*
```
void Vivify(ListEntry cell)
{
    if (map[cell.row][cell.col] == DEAD &&
        numbernbrs[cell.row][cell.col] == 3)
        if (cell.row >= 1 && cell.row <= maxrow &&    /* not on hedge            */
            cell.col >= 1 && cell.col <= maxcol) {
            map[cell.row][cell.col] = ALIVE;
            AddList(cell, &newlive);
        }
}
```

## 2. Function AddNeighbors

At the conclusion of the traversal with Vivify, list newlive contains the cells that were actually vivified. Hence the function AddNeighbors can update all the related neighbor counts without problem. This function has the following form.

```
/* AddNeighbors: adjust neighbor counts of vivified cell.
   Pre:   cell has just become alive.
   Post:  Array numbernbrs has increased counts for all cells neighboring cell. If the
          increased neighbor count makes the cell a candidate to be vivified [resp. killed]
          then the cell has been added to list maylive [resp. maydie].
   Uses:  Function AddList; changes array numbernbrs and lists maylive and maydie as
          global variables (side effects). */
```

*update neighbor counts*

```c
void AddNeighbors(ListEntry cell)
{
    int nbrrow,                       /* loop index for row of neighbor loops       */
        nbrcol;                       /* column loop index                          */
    Cell neighbor;                    /* structure form of a neighbor               */
```

*bounds for loop*

```c
    for (nbrrow = cell.row − 1; nbrrow <= cell.row + 1; nbrrow++)
        for (nbrcol = cell.col − 1; nbrcol <= cell.col + 1; nbrcol++)
```

*find a neighbor*

```c
            if (nbrrow != cell.row || nbrcol != cell.col) {  /* Skip cell itself.    */
                numbernbrs [nbrrow] [nbrcol] ++;
                switch (numbernbrs [nbrrow] [nbrcol]) {
```

*put cells into lists*

```c
                case 0:
                    Error("Impossible case in AddNeighbors.");
                    break;

                case 3:
                    if (map [nbrrow] [nbrcol] == DEAD) {
                        neighbor.row = nbrrow;   /* Set up a coordinate record.      */
                        neighbor.col = nbrcol;
                        AddList(neighbor, &maylive);
                    }
                    break;

                case 4:
                    if (map [nbrrow] [nbrcol] == ALIVE) {
                        neighbor.row = nbrrow;   /* Set up a coordinate record.      */
                        neighbor.col = nbrcol;
                        AddList(neighbor, &maydie);
                    }
                    break;
                }                       /* switch statement                          */
            }
}
```

### 3. Miscellaneous Functions

The functions Kill and SubtractNeighbors are similar to Vivify and AddNeighbors; they will be left as exercises. The function WriteMap can be used without change from the first version, but a more efficient version is possible that uses the lists newlive and newdie to update the screen rather than rewriting it at each generation.

### 4. Initialization

*design of* Initialize

As we turn, finally, to the function Initialize, let us use the postconditions for the function to help in its composition. The first postcondition states that the array map is to be initialized with the starting configuration of living and dead cells. This task is similar to the initialization of the first version of the program, and we leave the resulting function ReadMap as an exercise. We shall, however, need the list of initially living cells for calculating the neighbor counts, so we shall also require ReadMap to put this list into list newlive. As one of its postconditions ReadMap will be required to make sure that there are no duplicates in this list. (This can be achieved easily if the reading is done properly.)

The second task is to initialize the neighbor counts in array numbernbrs. But we have required ReadMap to set up list newlive so that it contains exactly the information needed for function AddNeighbors to set the neighbor counts properly for all neighbors of living cells, provided that before calling AddNeighbors, we first set all entries in numbernbrs to 0. As well as initializing numbernbrs, function AddNeighbors will locate all dead cells that will become alive in the following generation and add them to list maylive. Hence by setting maylive to be empty before calling AddNeighbors, we accomplish another of the postconditions of Initialize.

The final postcondition is that list maydie contain all living cells that should die in the next generation. Some, but perhaps not all, of these may be found by AddNeighbors (in the main loop, the remainder would be found by SubtractNeighbors, which we have no way to use in Initialize). We can accomplish the postcondition more easily, however, by simply putting *all* the living cells into list newdie: Recall that function Kill allows spurious entries on its input list. Hence, on the first pass only, we allow Kill to look at all living cells to see which should die.

In this way, the postconditions lead to the following function:

```
/* Initialize: initialize Life game.
   Pre:   None.
   Post:  Array map contains the initial configuration of living and dead cells. Array num-
          bernbrs contains counts of living neighbors corresponding to the configuration
          in array map. List maylive contains only dead cells and includes all candidates
          that may be vivified in the first generation. List maydie contains only living cells
          and contains all candidates that may die in the first generation. Lists newlive
          and newdie are empty.
   Uses:  Simple list package, functions FindSize, ReadMap, AddNeighbors. */
```

```
void Initialize (Grid map, Gridcount numbernbrs,
                 List *newlive, List *newdie, List *maylive, List *maydie)
```

*initialization*

```
{
        /* The following variables are used to set all entries in numbernbrs to 0. */
        int row, col;

        CreateList(newlive);
        CreateList(newdie);
        CreateList(maylive);
        CreateList(maydie);

        /* Put out an initial message and establish the bounds for the grid. */
        FindSize( &maxrow,  &maxcol);

        /* Obtain the initial configuration. */
        ReadMap(newlive, map);

        /* Set all the entries in numbernbrs to 0. */
        for (row = 0;  row <= maxrow + 1;  row++)
           for (col = 0;  col <= maxcol + 1;  col++)
              numbernbrs[row][col] = 0;

        /* Put the candidates to live into maylive. */
        TraverseList(newlive, AddNeighbors);

        /* Check all the living cells to see which may die. */
        CopyList(maydie, newlive);

        ClearList(newlive);
}
```

---

**Programming Projects 2.4**

**P1.** Write the missing functions for the second version of Life:

    **(a)** Kill                       **(c)** FindSize

    **(b)** SubtractNeighbors       **(d)** ReadMap

**P2.** Write a driver program for ReadMap to verify that it works.

**P3.** Write driver programs for the functions

    **(a)** Kill and

    **(b)** SubtractNeighbors,

and devise appropriate test data to check the performance of these functions.

## 2.5 Program Analysis and Comparison ━━━━━━

In designing algorithms, we need methods to separate bad algorithms fr
ones. We need methods to help us decide, when we have several possible
which to proceed, which way will prove the most effective for our prob
this reason the analysis of algorithms and the comparison of alternative
constitute an important part of software engineering.

### 1. Statement Counts

Let us now see about how much more quickly the program Life2 should
the previous version. As we did for the first version, let us ignore the tim
for input and output in the main program, and look only at the statemen
the principal loop counting generations. Almost all this work occurs in
statements that each traverses a list. Thus the key improvement of Li
the original program is that the amount of computation is no longer pro
to the size of the grid but to the number of changes being made. For
configuration, there might be about 50 occupied cells, with likely no mor
dying or being born in a single generation. With these assumptions, we
each traversal of a list will make about 25 calls to the function it uses.

Since almost all the work of Life2 is done within the four functions usec
traversals, we must analyze each in turn. In Vivify there are about 4 state
do (two if statements, one assignment, one call to AddList). Within AddN
there are nested loops iterating 9 times. Within the loops, there are an if st
an assignment, and the switch statement, which may include 4 other sta
We thus get a total count of about 54 for AddNeighbors. The counts for
*count for* Life2    SubtractNeighbors are similar; thus we obtain for each generation about

$$25 \times (4 + 54 + 4 + 54) = 2900$$

statements. The number of statements executed outside the loops is insi
(it is less than 10), so 2900 is a reasonable estimate of the statement count
generation.
*count for* Life1    Our first version of the Life program had a count of 18,000 statem
generation. Thus our revised program should run as much as 6 times f
a slow computer this would constitute a significant improvement, partic
view of the fact that when program Life2 slows down, it is because many
are being made, not because it is repeating the same predictable calculati

### 2. Comparisons

From other points of view, however, our second program is not as good as
*programming effort*    The first of these is the point of view of programming effort. The first
was short and easy to write, simple to understand, and easy to debug. Th
program is longer, entailed subtle problems, and required sophisticated r

to establish its correctness. Whether this additional work is worthwhile depends on the application and the number of times the program will be used. If a simple method works well enough, then we should not go out of our way to find a more sophisticated approach. Only when simple methods fail do we need to try further devices.

---

**Programming Precept**

*Keep your algorithms as simple as you can.*
*When in doubt, choose the simple way.*

---

*space requirements*

The second point of view is that of storage requirements. Our first program used very little memory (apart from that for the instructions) except for the two arrays map and newmap. These arrays have entries that, in assuming only the two values alive and dead, can be packed so that each entry takes only a single bit. In a typical computer with word size of 32 or 16 bits, and if we take a grid size of 20 by 60, then the two arrays need occupy no more than 75 or 150 words, respectively. On the other hand, program Life2 requires, along with the space for its instructions, space for one such array, plus 1200 words for the array numbernbrs and 300 words for each of its four lists, giving a total of about 2500 words.

## 3. Time and Space Trade-offs

We have just seen the first of many examples illustrating the substantial trade-offs that can occur between time and space in computer algorithms. Which to choose depends on available equipment. If the storage space is available and otherwise unused, it is obviously preferable to use the algorithm requiring more space and less time. If not, then time may have to be sacrificed. Finally, for an important problem, by far the best approach may be to sit back and rethink the whole problem: you will have learned much from your first efforts and may very well be able to find another approach that will save both time and space.

---

**Programming Precept**

*Consider time and space trade-offs in deciding on your algorithm.*

---

**Programming Precept**

*Never be afraid to start over.*
*Next time it may be both shorter and easier.*

---

**Exercises 2.5**

E1. We could save the space needed for the array map by making a slight modification in how we keep information in the array numbernbrs. We could use positive entries in numbernbrs to denote living cells and negative entries to denote dead cells. However, we could then not tell whether an entry of 0 meant a dead cell or a living cell with no living neighbors. We could easily overcome that problem by changing the definition of neighbor so that a cell is considered its own neighbor (so the neighbor count for a dead cell would range from 0 to 8, stored in numbernbrs as 0 to −8, and that for a living cell from 1 to 9).

(a) With this change of definition, write down the revised rules (from Section 1.2.1) for the game of Life.

(b) Do you think that implementing the changes to eliminate array map is worth the effort? Why or why not?

(c) If you answered the last question positively, describe exactly what changes are needed in the program.

**Programming Projects 2.5**

P1. If you use a video terminal with direct cursor addressing, write a version of the function WriteMap that takes advantage of the lists newlive and newdie to update the map rather than completely rewriting it at each generation.

P2. Modify the function ReadMap so it gives the user a choice between reading the initial configuration from the terminal or from a file. The first line of the file is to be a comment describing the configuration; the remaining lines are to contain a pattern of blanks for dead cells and non-blanks for living cells.

P3. Run the complete program Life2 and compare timings with those of Life1.

# 2.6 Conclusions and Preview

This chapter has surveyed a great deal of ground, but mainly from a bird's-eye view. Some themes we shall treat in much greater depth in later chapters; others must be postponed to more advanced courses; still others are best learned by practice.

## 2.6.1 THE GAME OF LIFE

### 1. Future Directions

We are not yet finished with the game of Life, although we next shall turn to other topics. When we return to the Life game (in Section 8.9), we shall find an algorithm that does not require us to keep a large rectangular grid in memory.

### 2. Problem specification

For the moment, however, let us make only one observation, one that you may well have already made and, if so, one that has likely been bothering you. What we have done throughout this chapter and the previous one has been, in fact, incorrect, in that we have not been solving the Life game as it was originally described in

Section 1.2. The rules make no mention of the boundaries of the grid containing the cells. In our programs, when a moving colony gets sufficiently close to a boundary, then room for neighbors disappears, and the colony will be distorted by the very presence of the boundary. That is not supposed to be.

It is of course true that in any computer simulation there are absolute bounds on the values that may appear, but certainly our use of a 20 by 60 grid is highly restrictive and arbitrary. Writing a more realistic program must be one of our goals when we return to this problem. But on a first try, restrictions are often reasonable. Nevertheless,

---

**Programming Precept**

*Be sure you understand your problem completely.*
*If you must change its terms, explain exactly what you have done.*

---

When we started in Section 1.4, we did nothing of the sort, but plunged right in with an approach leaving much to be desired. Almost every programmer learns this experience the hard way and can sympathize with the following:

---

**Programming Precept**

*Act in haste and repent at leisure.*
*Program in haste and debug forever.*

---

The same thought can be expressed somewhat more positively:

---

**Programming Precept**

*Starting afresh is usually easier than patching an old program.*

---

A good rule of thumb is that, if more than ten percent of a program must be modified, then it is time to rewrite the program completely. With repeated patches to a large program, the number of bugs tends to remain constant. That is, the patches become so complicated that each new patch tends to introduce as many new errors as it corrects.

## 3. Prototyping

An excellent way to avoid having to rewrite a large project from scratch is to plan from the beginning to write two versions. Before a program is running, it is often impossible to know what parts of the design will cause difficulty or what features need to be changed to meet the needs of the users. Engineers have known for many years that it is not possible to build a large project directly from the drawing board. For large projects engineers always build *prototypes*, that is, scaled-down models that can be studied, tested, and sometimes even used for limited purposes. Models of bridges are built and tested in wind tunnels; pilot plants are constructed before attempting to use new technology on the assembly line.

*software prototypes*    Prototyping is especially helpful for computer software, since it eases communication between users and designers early in the project, thereby reducing misunderstandings and helping to settle the design to everyone's satisfaction. In building a software prototype the designer can use programs that are already written for input-output, for sorting, or for other common requirements. The building blocks can be assembled with as little new programming as possible to make a working model that can do some of the intended tasks. Even though the prototype may not function efficiently or do everything that the final system will, it provides an excellent laboratory for the user and designer to experiment with alternative ideas for the final design.

---

**Programming Precept**

*Always plan to build a prototype and throw it away.*
*You'll do so whether you plan to or not.*

---

## 2.6.2 PROGRAM DESIGN

### 1. Criteria for Programs

A major goal of this book is to evaluate algorithms and data structures that purport to solve a problem. Amongst the many criteria by which we can judge a program, the following are some of the most important:

1. Does it solve the problem that is requested, according to the given specifications?

2. Does it work correctly under all conditions?

3. Does it include clear and sufficient information for its user, in the form of instructions and documentation?

4. Is it logically and clearly written, with short modules and subprograms as appropriate to do logical tasks?

5. Does it make efficient use of time and of space?

Some of these criteria will be closely studied for the programs we write. Others will not be mentioned explicitly, but not because of any lack of importance. These criteria, rather, can be met automatically if sufficient thought and effort are invested in every stage of program design. I hope that the examples we study will reveal such care.

## 2. Software Engineering

*Software engineering* is the study and practice of methods helpful for the construction and maintenance of large software systems. Although small by realistic standards, the program we have studied in this chapter illustrates many aspects of software engineering.

Software engineering begins with the realization that it is a very long process to obtain good software. It begins before any programs are coded and continues maintenance for years after the programs are put into use. This continuing process is known as the *life cycle* of software. This life cycle can be divided into phases as follows:

*phases of life cycle*

1. *Analyze* the problem precisely and completely. Be sure to *specify* all necessary user interface with care.

2. *Build* a prototype and *experiment* with it until all specifications can be finalized.

3. *Design* the algorithm, using the tools of data structures and of other algorithms whose function is already known.

4. *Verify* that the algorithm is correct, or make it so simple that its correctness is self-evident.

5. *Analyze* the algorithm to determine its requirements and make sure that it meets the specifications.

6. *Code* the algorithm into the appropriate programming language.

7. *Test* and *evaluate* the program on carefully chosen test data.

8. *Refine* and *repeat* the foregoing steps as needed for additional subprograms until the software is complete and fully functional.

9. *Optimize* the code to improve performance, but only if necessary.

10. *Maintain* the program so that it will meet the changing needs of its users.

Most of these topics have been discussed and illustrated in various sections of this and the preceding chapter, but a few further remarks on the first phase, problem analysis and specification, are in order.

## 3. Problem Analysis

Analysis of the problem is often the most difficult phase of the software life cycle. This is not because practical problems are conceptually more difficult than are computing science exercises—the reverse is often the case—but because users and programmers tend to speak different languages. Here are some questions on which the analyst and user must reach an understanding:

*specifications*

1. What form will the input and output data take? How much data will there be?

2. Are there any special requirements for the processing? What special occurrences will require separate treatment?

3. Will these requirements change? If so, how? How fast will the demands on the system grow?

4. What parts of the system are the most important? Which must run most efficiently?

5. How should erroneous data be treated? What other error processing is needed?

6. What kinds of people will use the software? What kind of training will they have? What kind of user interface will be best?

7. How portable must the software be, to move to new kinds of equipment? With what other software and hardware systems must the project be compatible?

8. What extensions or other maintenance are anticipated? What is the history of previous changes to software and hardware?

### 4. Requirements Specification

The problem analysis and experimentation for a large project finally lead to a formal statement of the requirements for the project. This statement becomes the primary way in which the user and the software engineer attempt to understand each other and establishes the standard by which the final project will be judged. Among the contents of this specification will be the following:

1. *Functional requirements* for the system: what it will do and what commands will be available to the user.

2. *Assumptions* and *limitations* on the system: what hardware will be used for the system, what form the input must take, the maximum size of input, the largest number of users, and so on.

3. *Maintenance requirements*: anticipated extensions or growth of the system, changes in hardware, changes in user interface.

4. *Documentation requirements*: what kind of explanatory material is required for what kinds of users.

The requirements specifications state *what* the software will do, not *how* it will be done. These specifications should be understandable both to the user and to the programmer. If carefully prepared, they will form the basis for the subsequent phases of design, coding, testing, and maintenance.

**2.6.3  C**

In this chapter and the previous one, we have used many features of C. No attempt has been made to present an orderly or complete description of C features. A concise summary of C appears in Appendix C, to which you should refer with questions of C syntax. For further examples and discussion, consult a C textbook.

*data types*

One of the more powerful features of C is the flexibility of its data types. We have hardly scratched the surface in uncovering these resources. As occasions arise, we shall use the other C tools in making data types: files and pointer types. The ability to combine the type definitions in flexible ways (arrays of file pointers, structures containing arrays, arrays of structures, and the like) gives almost endless ways to organize our data structures.

---

**Programming Projects 2.6**

**P1.** A *magic square* is a square array of integers such that the sum of every row, the sum of every column, and sum of each of the two diagonals are all equal. Two magic squares are shown in Figure 2.3.[3]

  **(a)** Write a program that reads a square array of integers and determines whether or not it is a magic square.

  **(b)** Write a program that generates a magic square by the following method. This method works only when the size of the square is an odd number. Start by placing 1 in the middle of the top row. Write down successive integers 2, 3, ... along a diagonal going upward and to the right. When you reach the top row (as you do immediately since 1 is in the top row), continue to the bottom row as though the bottom row were immediately above the top row. When you reach the rightmost column, continue to the leftmost column as though it were immediately to the right of the rightmost one. When you reach a position that is already occupied, instead drop straight down one position from the previous number to insert the new one. The $5 \times 5$ magic square constructed by this method is shown in Figure 2.3.

sum = 34        sum = 65

Figure 2.3. Two magic squares

---

[3] The magic square on the left appears as shown here in the etching *Melancolia* by Albrecht Dürer. Note the inclusion of the date of the etching, 1514.

**P2.** *One-dimensional Life* takes place on a straight line instead of a rectangular grid. Each cell has four neighboring positions: those at distance one or two from it on each side. The rules are similar to those of two-dimensional Life except (1) a dead cell with either two or three living neighbors will become alive in the next generation, and (2) a living cell dies if it has zero, one, or three living neighbors. (Hence a dead cell with zero, one, or four living neighbors stays dead; a living cell with two or four living neighbors stays alive.) The progress of sample communities is shown in Figure 2.4. Design, write, and test a program for one-dimensional Life.

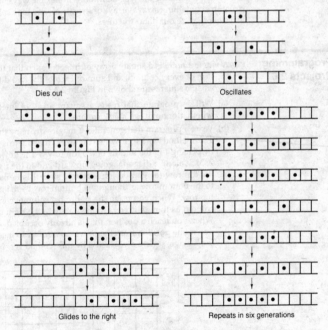

Figure 2.4. One-dimensional Life configurations

**P3.** **(a)** Write a program that will print the calendar of the current year.

**(b)** Modify the program so that it will read a year number and print the calendar for that year. A year is a leap year (that is, February has 29 instead of 28 days) if it is a multiple of 4, except that century years (multiple of 100) are leap years only when the year is divisible by 400. Hence the year 1900 is not a leap year, but the year 2000 is a leap year.

(c) Modify the program so that it will accept any date (day, month, year) and print the day of the week for that date.

(d) Modify the program so that it will read two dates and print the number of days from one to the other.

(e) Using the rules on leap years, show that the sequence of calendars repeats exactly every 400 years.

(f) What is the probability (over a 400-year period) that the 13th of a month is a Friday? Why is the 13th of the month more likely to be a Friday than any other day of the week? Write a program to calculate how many Friday the 13ths occur in this century.

## Pointers and Pitfalls

1. To improve your program, review the logic. Don't optimize code based on a poor algorithm.

2. Never optimize a program until it is correct and working.

3. Don't optimize code unless it is absolutely necessary.

4. Use structures to clarify the logic of your programs.

5. Keep your functions short; rarely should any function be more than a page long.

6. Be sure your algorithm is correct before starting to code.

7. Verify the intricate parts of your algorithm.

8. Keep your logic simple.

9. Review the Programming Precepts!

## Review Questions

2.1     1. What is program maintenance?

2.2     2. What is mathematical induction?

     3. What is a loop invariant?

     4. What are preconditions and postconditions of a subprogram?

2.3     5. When should allocation of tasks among functions be made?

     6. How long should coding be delayed?

2.5     7. What is a time-space tradeoff?

2.6     8. What is a prototype?

     9. Name at least six phases of the software life cycle and state what each is.

     10. Define software engineering.

     11. What are requirements specifications for a program?

## References for Further Study ━━━━━━━━━━━━━━━━

*software engineering*    A thorough discussion of many aspects of structured programming is:

> EDWARD YOURDON, *Techniques of Program Structure and Design*, Prentice-Hall, Englewood Cliffs, N. J., 1975, 364 pages.

A perceptive discussion (in a book that is also enjoyable reading) of the many problems that arise in the construction of large software systems is:

> FREDERICK P. BROOKS, JR., *The Mythical Man–Month: Essays on Software Engineering*, Addison-Wesley, Reading, Mass., 1975, 195 pages.

A good textbook on software engineering is:

> IAN SOMMERVILLE, *Software Engineering*, Addison-Wesley, Wokingham, England, 1985, 334 pages.

Program testing has been developed to the point where its methods can fill a large book:

> WILLIAM E. PERRY, *A Structured Approach to Systems Testing*, Prentice-Hall, Englewood Cliffs, N. J., 1983, 451 pages.

*algorithm verification*    Two books concerned with proving programs and using assertions and invariants to develop algorithms are

> DAVID GRIES, *The Science of Programming*, Springer-Verlag, New York, 1981, 366 pages.

> SUAD ALAGIĆ and MICHAEL A. ARBIB, *The Design of Well–Structured and Correct Programs*, Springer-Verlag, New York, 1978, 292 pages.

Keeping programs so simple in design that they can be proved to be correct is not easy, but is very important. C. A. R. HOARE (who invented the quicksort algorithm that we shall study in Chapter 7) writes: "There are two ways of constructing a software design: One way is to make it so simple that there are obviously no deficiencies, and the other way is to make it so complicated that there are no obvious deficiencies. The first method is far more difficult." This quotation is from the 1980 Turing Award Lecture: "The emperor's old clothes," *Communications of the ACM* 24 (1981), 75–83.

Two books concerned with methods of problem solving are

*problem solving*    GEORGE PÓLYA, *How to Solve It*, second edition, Doubleday, Garden City, N.Y., 1957, 253 pages.

> WAYNE A. WICKELGREN, *How to Solve Problems*, W. H. Freeman, San Francisco, 1974, 262 pages.

The programming project on one-dimensional Life is taken from

> JONATHAN K. MILLER, "One-dimensional Life," *Byte* 3 (December, 1978), 68–74.

# 3

# Stacks and Recursion

THIS CHAPTER *introduces the study of stacks, one of the simplest but most important of all data structures. We shall find that stacks relate closely to recursion, the method in which a problem is solved by reducing it to smaller cases of the same problem. To illustrate recursion we shall study some applications and sample programs. Later in the chapter we analyze how recursion is usually implemented on a computer. In the process, we shall obtain guidelines regarding good and bad uses of recursion, when it is appropriate, and when it should best be avoided.*

## 3.1 Stacks

### 3.1.1 INTRODUCTION

*stacks*

A *stack* is a data structure in which all insertions and deletions of entries are made at one end, called the *top* of the stack. A helpful analogy (see Figure 3.1) is to think of a stack of trays or of plates sitting on the counter in a busy cafeteria. Throughout the lunch hour, customers take trays off the top of the stack, and employees place returned trays back on top of the stack. The tray most recently put on the stack is the first one taken off. The bottom tray is the first one put on, and the last one to be used.

Figure 3.1. Stacks

Sometimes this picture is described with plates or trays on a spring-loaded device so that the top of the stack stays near the same height. This imagery is poor and should be avoided. If we were to implement a computer stack in this way, it would mean moving every item in the stack whenever one item was inserted or deleted. It is far better to think of the stack as resting on a firm counter or floor, so that only the top item is moved when it is added or deleted. The spring-loaded imagery, however, has contributed a pair of colorful words that are firmly embedded in computer jargon, and which we shall use to name the fundamental operations on a stack. When we add an item to a stack, we say that we *push* it onto the stack, and when we remove an item, we say that we *pop* it from the stack. See Figure 3.2. Note that the last item pushed onto a stack is always the first that will be popped from the stack. This property is called *last in, first out,* or *LIFO* for short.

*push and pop*

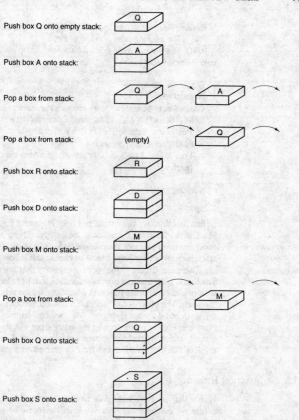

Push box Q onto empty stack:

Push box A onto stack:

Pop a box from stack:

Pop a box from stack:          (empty)

Push box R onto stack:

Push box D onto stack:

Push box M onto stack:

Pop a box from stack:

Push box Q onto stack:

Push box S onto stack:

Figure 3.2. Pushing and popping a stack

## 3.1.2 FIRST EXAMPLE: REVERSING A LINE

As a simple example of using stacks, let us suppose that we wish to make a function that will read a line of input and will then write it out backward. We can accomplish this task by pushing each character onto a stack as it is read. When the line is finished, we then pop characters off the stack, and they will come off in the reverse order. Hence our function takes the following form:

```
/* ReverseRead: read one line of input and write it backward.
  Pre:   The user supplies one line of input.
  Post:  The line has been printed backward, using a stack. */
void ReverseRead(void)
{
  StackEntry item;
  Stack stack;
  CreateStack( &stack);           /* Initialize the stack to be empty.        */
  while (!StackFull( &stack) && (item = getchar( )) != '\n')
      Push(item, &stack);         /* Push each item onto the stack.           */
  while (!StackEmpty( &stack)) {
      Pop( &item, &stack);        /* Pop an item from the stack.              */
      putchar(item);
  }
  putchar('\n');
}
```

In this function, we have used not only Push and Pop, but also a function Create-Stack that initializes the stack to be empty. There are also two Boolean-valued functions used to check the current status of a stack: StackEmpty checks whether a stack is empty or not, and StackFull checks if it is completely full.

*reinitialization*

*stack size*

*top of stack*

There are, finally, three more operations that are sometimes useful for stacks. The first is ClearStack, which takes a stack that has already been created and makes it empty. Second is the function StackSize, which returns the number of entries in the stack. The other is the function StackTop, which returns the entry on the top of the stack but does not change it. We could, of course, construct this function from Push and Pop by first popping the entry from the stack, retaining its value as the output, and then pushing it back onto the stack. Usually, however, it is better to think of StackTop as a fundamental operation on a stack.

### 3.1.3 INFORMATION HIDING

*use of functions*

Notice that we have been able to write our function for reversing a line of input before we consider how the stack will actually be implemented in storage and before we write the details of the various functions. In this way, we have one more example of *information hiding*: If someone else had already written the functions for handling stacks, then we could use them without needing to know the details of how stacks are kept in memory or of how the stack operations are actually done.

*alternative implementations*

In the coming chapters, we shall see that for stacks (as for almost all the data types we shall study) there are several different ways to represent the data in the computer memory, and there are several different ways to do the operations. In some applications, one method is better, while in other applications another method proves superior.

*change of implementation*

Even in a single large program, we may first decide to represent stacks one way and then, as we gain experience with the program, we may decide that another way is better. If the instructions for manipulating a stack have been written out every time a stack is used, then every occurrence of these instructions will need to be changed. If we have practiced information hiding by using separate functions for manipulating stacks, then only the declarations will need to be changed.

*clarity of program*

One more advantage of information hiding for stacks is that the very appearance of the words *Push* and *Pop* will immediately alert a person reading the program to what is being done, whereas the instructions themselves might be more obscure.

*top-down design*

A final advantage we shall find is that separating the use of data structures from their implementation will help us improve the top-down design of both our data structures and our programs.

### 3.1.4 SPECIFICATIONS FOR A STACK

To conclude this section, let us consider the precise specifications for a stack in terms of the preconditions and postconditions for each function and function that we have introduced. In these declarations, we shall use the type Stack for the stack. In accordance with the principles of information hiding and top-down design, we shall leave this type unspecified until we consider the implementation of stacks in the next section. The entries that are stored in a stack will have a type that we call StackEntry, which will change according to the application. For reversing the line of input, we need the definition typedef char StackEntry; . For other applications, we shall define the type StackEntry in different ways.

The first step we must perform in working with any stack is to initialize it:

*initialization*

---

void CreateStack(Stack *s);

*precondition*:   None.

*postcondition*:   The stack s has been created and is initialized to be empty.

---

*status*

Next come the operations for checking the status of a stack.

---

Boolean StackEmpty(Stack *s);

*precondition*:   The stack exists and it has been initialized.

*postcondition*:   Return TRUE if the stack is empty, FALSE otherwise.

---

Boolean StackFull(Stack *s);

*precondition*:   The stack exists and it has been initialized.

*postcondition*:   Return TRUE if the stack is full, FALSE otherwise.

---

*basic operations*   The declarations for the fundamental operations on a stack come next.

---

void Push(StackEntry item, Stack ∗s);

*precondition*:   The stack exists and it is not full.

*postcondition*:  The argument item has been stored at the top of the stack.

---

void Pop(StackEntry ∗item, Stack ∗s);

*precondition*:   The stack exists and it is not empty.

*postcondition*:  The top of the stack has been removed and returned in ∗item.

---

Note from the preconditions that it is an error to attempt to push an item onto a full stack or to pop an entry from an empty stack. If we write the functions Push and Pop carefully, then they should return error messages if they are used incorrectly. From the declarations, however, there is no guarantee that the functions will catch the errors, and, if they do not, then they may produce spurious and unpredictable results. Hence the careful programmer should always make sure, whenever invoking a subprogram, that its preconditions are guaranteed to be satisfied.

There remain three more stack operations that are sometimes useful.

*other operations*

---

void ClearStack(Stack ∗s);

*precondition*:   The stack exists and it has been initialized.

*postcondition*:  All entries in the stack have been deleted; the stack is empty.

---

int StackSize(Stack ∗s);

*precondition*:   The stack exists and it has been initialized.

*postcondition*:  The function returns the number of entries in the stack.

---

void StackTop(StackEntry ∗item, Stack ∗s);

*precondition*:   The stack exists and it is not empty.

*postcondition*:  The item at the top of the stack is returned (in ∗item) without being removed; the stack remains unchanged.

---

*traversable stack*   In a ***traversable stack*** there is one more operation, in addition to all the standard operations for a stack: It is also permissible to move through all the entries of the stack, looking at each entry but not changing any entries. (The only way to change the traversable stack is by using Push and Pop, whereby all changes are made at its top.) As we did for the traversal of lists, we shall use a *pointer* to a function called Visit to denote the operation that is to be done at each entry of the stack. For further discussion of pointers to functions, see Appendix C.

The specifications for stack traversal are:

```
void TraverseStack(Stack *s, void (*Visit)());
```
*precondition*:  The stack exists and it has been initialized.

*postcondition*:  The function that Visit points to, has been invoked for each entry
                  in the stack, beginning with the entry at the top and proceeding
                  toward the bottom of stack.

Strictly speaking, traversable stacks are a different data type from ordinary stacks,
and, for most applications, there is no need for the TraverseStack operation. For
demonstration purposes and for debugging, however, traversal is quite useful, and
hence we shall assume the availability of traversal whenever it is convenient, both
for stacks and for most other data types that we later define.

To conclude the details of the preceding specifications, let us recall from Section 2.2.1 our convention that, when specifying any data type, we use a call by
reference when a subprogram may change the parameter, and we use a call by
value otherwise. When we come to the implementation details of actually writing
the functions, however, we usually improve efficiency by using a call by reference,
whether or not the data structure is changed by the function.

### 3.1.5 IMPLEMENTATION OF STACKS

Now that we have specified all the operations on stacks, we can consider the programming details needed for their implementation. We shall begin with the *contiguous* implementation, where the stack entries are stored in an array. Afterwards,
we shall study the *linked* implementation using dynamic memory.

### 1. Declarations

For the contiguous implementation, we shall set up an array that will hold the
entries in the stack and a counter that will indicate how many entries there are.
In C we shall make the following declarations for a stack containing items of type
char, where the value of MAXSTACK will be changed to suit the application:

*stack type*

```
#define MAXSTACK 10
typedef char StackEntry;
typedef struct stack {
    int top;
    StackEntry entry[MAXSTACK];
} Stack;
```

### 2. Pushing and Popping

Pushing and popping the stack are then implemented as follows. We must be
careful of the extreme cases: We might attempt to pop an entry from an empty stack
or to push an entry onto a full stack. These conditions are errors. According to
the specifications, it is not necessary that the stack functions recognize these errors,
since they are violations of the preconditions for the functions. It is, nevertheless,
good practice of defensive programming always to include as many checks as

practical to ensure that the preconditions are met. Hence we use the Error function to inform the user when a condition is violated.

```
/* Push: push an item onto the stack.
   Pre:   The stack exists and it is not full.
   Post:  The argument item has been stored at the top of the stack. */
void Push(StackEntry item, Stack *s)
{
   if (StackFull(s))
       Error("Stack is full");
   else
       s->entry[s->top++] = item;
}
```

```
/* Pop: pop an item from the stack.
   Pre:   The stack exists and it is not empty.
   Post:  The item at the top of stack has been removed and returned in *item. */
void Pop(StackEntry *item, Stack *s)
{
   if (StackEmpty(s))
       Error("Stack is empty");
   else
       *item = s->entry[--s->top];
}
```

### 3. Other Operations

```
/* StackEmpty: returns non-zero if the stack is empty.
   Pre:   The stack exists and it has been initialized.
   Post:  Return non-zero if the stack is empty; return zero, otherwise. */
Boolean StackEmpty(Stack *s)
{
   return s->top <= 0;
}
```

```
/* StackFull: returns non-zero if the stack is full.
   Pre:   The stack exists and it has been initialized.
   Post:  Return non-zero if the stack is full; return zero, otherwise. */
Boolean StackFull(Stack *s)
{
   return s->top >= MAXSTACK;
}
```

Note that we have used a pointer to the stack in these two functions (call by reference), even though it is used only as an input parameter. The reason is that of efficiency: If we used a call by value, we would pass a complete copy of the stack every time the function was called.

One more function is needed to initialize a stack before it is first used in a program:

```
/* CreateStack: initialize the stack to be empty.
   Pre:  None.
   Post: The stack has been initialized to be empty. */
void CreateStack(Stack *s)
{
    s->top = 0;
}
```

We shall leave the functions StackTop, ClearStack, TraverseStack, and StackSize as exercises.

### 3.1.6 LINKED STACKS

It is equally easy to implement stacks as linked structures in dynamic memory.[1] To do so, we first need declarations establishing the structure of a node:

```
typedef struct node {
    StackEntry entry;
    struct node *next;
} Node;
```

As with the entries of contiguous stacks, we shall *push* and *pop* nodes from one end of a linked stack, called its *top*. If we have an item item that we wish to push onto a linked stack, we must first make a new node and put item into the node, and then push the node onto the stack. We make a new node with MakeNode:

```
/* MakeNode: make a new node and insert item.
   Pre:  None.
   Post: Create a new node and insert item in it. */
Node *MakeNode(StackEntry item)
{
    Node *nodepointer;
    if ((nodepointer = malloc(sizeof(Node))) == NULL)
        Error("Exhausted memory.");
    else {
        nodepointer->entry = item;
        nodepointer->next = NULL;
    }
    return nodepointer;
}
```

---

[1] This section requires familiarity with the concepts of dynamic memory in C. See Section 4.5 or a textbook on C programming (references at the end of Chapter 1). These concepts will also be developed in connection with linked queues in the following chapter. The material in this section is not used in the remainder of this chapter, but will be needed in future chapters. Hence its study can be postponed to be combined with that of linked queues.

*node processing*

Before we push the node on the stack, we must consider some more details of how a linked stack will be implemented.

The first question to settle is to determine whether the beginning or the end of the linked structure will be the top of the stack. At first glance, it may appear that (as for contiguous stacks) it might be easier to add a node at the end, but this method makes popping the stack difficult: There is no quick way to find the node immediately before a given one in a linked structure, since the pointers stored in the structure give only one-way directions. Thus, after we remove the last element, finding the element now at the end of the linked structure might require tracing all the way from its head. To pop our linked stack, it is much better to make all additions and deletions at the beginning of the structure. Hence the top of the stack will always be the *first* node of the linked structure.

Each linked list has a header variable that points to its first node; for a linked stack this header variable will always point to the top of the stack. Since each node of a linked list points to the next one, the only information needed to keep track of a linked stack is the location of its top. We shall therefore declare a linked stack by setting up a structure having the top of the stack and nothing else:

*declaration of type*
Stack

```
typedef struct stack {
    Node *top;
} Stack;
```

Since this structure contains only one field, we could dispense with the structure and refer to the top by the same name that we assign to the stack itself.

There are three reasons, however, for using the structure we have introduced. The most important is to maintain the logical distinction between the stack itself, which is made up of all of its entries (each in a node), and the top of the stack, which points to a single node. The fact that we need only keep track of the top of the stack to find all its entries is irrelevant to this logical structure. The second reason is to maintain consistency with other data structures and other implementations, where structures are needed to collect several pieces of information. Thirdly, keeping a stack and a pointer to its top as incompatible data types helps with debugging by allowing the compiler to perform better type checking.

*empty stack*

Let us start with an empty stack, which now means s->top == NULL, and add the first node. We shall assume that this node has already been made somewhere in dynamic memory, and we shall locate this node by using a pointer variable np (a node pointer). Pushing np onto the stack consists of the instructions

$$\text{s->top = np;} \qquad \text{np->next = NULL;}$$

As we continue, let us suppose that we already have a nonempty stack and that we wish to push a node np onto it. The required adjustments of pointers are shown in Figure 3.3. First, we must set the pointer coming from the new node np to the old top of the stack, and then we must change the top to become the new node. The order of these two assignments is important: If we attempted to do them in the reverse order, the change of the top from its previous value would mean that we would lose track of the old part of the list. We thus obtain the following function:

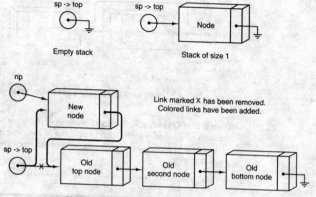

Figure 3.3. Pushing a node onto a linked stack

*item processing*

```
/* Push: make a new node with item and push it onto stack.
    Pre:   The stack exists and has been initialized.
    Post:  The argument item has been stored at the top of the stack. */
void Push(StackEntry item, Stack *s)
{
    Node *np = MakeNode(item);
    if (np == NULL)
        Error("Attempted to push a non-existing node.");
    else {
        np->next = s->top;
        s->top = np;
    }
}
```

In all our functions, it is important to include error checking and to consider extreme cases. Hence it is an error to attempt to push a nonexistent node onto the stack.

One extreme case for the function is that of an empty stack, which means s->top == NULL. Note that, in this case, the function works just as well to push the first node onto an empty stack as to push an additional node onto a nonempty stack.

*popping a linked stack*

It is equally simple to pop a node from a linked stack. This process is illustrated in Figure 3.4, with the details left as an exercise.

The remaining operations for linked stacks are all quite simple and will be left as exercises. Note, however, that to clear a linked stack, we wish not only to set the header variable to NULL, but we wish to dispose of all the nodes in the stack so that the system may reclaim their space. This action, therefore, is quite different

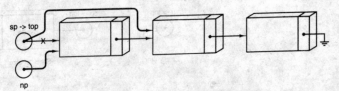

Figure 3.4. **Popping a node from a linked stack**

from that of CreateStack. To program this operation, we shall need a loop that runs through all the nodes in the stack, disposing of each one in turn. The simplest way to do this is to continue popping a node from the stack and disposing of it until the stack is empty.

**Exercises 3.1**    **E1.** Draw a sequence of stack frames like Figure 3.2 showing the progress of each of the following segments of code. (s is a pointer to a stack of characters, and x, y, z are character variables.)

    **(a)** CreateStack(s);
        Push('a', s);
        Push('b', s);
        Push('c', s);
        Pop( &x, s);
        Pop( &y, s);
        Pop( &z, s);

    **(b)** CreateStack(s);
        Push('a', s);
        Push('b', s);
        Push('c', s);
        Pop( &x, s);
        Pop( &y, s);
        Push(x, s);
        Push(y, s);
        Pop( &z, s);

    **(c)** CreateStack(s);
        Push('a', s);
        Push('b', s);
        ClearStack(s);
        Push('c', s);
        Pop( &x, s);
        Push('a', s);
        Pop( &y, s);
        Push('b', s);
        Pop( &z, s);

    **(d)** CreateStack(s);
        Push('a', s);
        Push('b', s);
        Push('c', s);
        while (! StackEmpty(s))
          Pop( &x, s);

**E2.** Let stack be a stack of integers and x be an integer variable. Use the functions Push, Pop, CreateStack, StackEmpty, and StackFull to write a function that sets x to the top element of the stack stack and leaves the top element of stack unchanged. If stack is empty, the function sets x to maxint.

**E3.** A stack may be regarded as a railway switching network like the one in Figure 3.5. Cars numbered 1, 2, ..., $n$ are on the line at the left, and it is desired to

*stack permutations*

rearrange (permute) the cars as they leave on the right-hand track. A car that is on the spur (stack) can be left there or sent on its way down the right track, but it can never be sent back to the incoming track. For example, if $n = 3$, and we have the cars 1, 2, 3 on the left track, then 3 first goes to the spur. We could then send 2 to the spur, then on its way to the right, then send 3 on the way, then 1, obtaining the new order 1, 3, 2.

**(a)** For $n = 3$, find all possible permutations that can be obtained.

**(b)** For $n = 4$, find all possible permutations that can be obtained.

**(c)** [Challenging] For general $n$, find how many permutations can be obtained by using this stack.

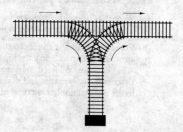

Figure 3.5. Switching network for stack permutations

**E4.** Write the function StackSize for the contiguous implementation developed in this section.

**E5.** **(a)** Write the function ClearStack that reinitializes a stack to become empty. Use the contiguous implementation.

**(b)** In view of the similarity between this function and CreateStack, why is it still a good idea to keep ClearStack as a separate function?

**E6.** Write the function void StackTop(StackEntry *item, Stack *s).

**(a)** Use the functions Push and Pop to construct StackTop. Your function should use only the basic functions that manipulate stacks; it should not rely on the method of implementation.

**(b)** Write the function StackTop on the lower level of looking directly inside the array, using the contiguous implementation developed in this section.

**(c)** What are the advantages and disadvantages of each of these ways to construct StackTop?

**E7.** **(a)** Write the function TraverseStack for the contiguous implementation.

**(b)** Is it possible to write TraverseStack using only the basic operations on a stack, without either using the details of implementation or some auxiliary storage (such as a separate array or another stack)?

**E8.** Write the following C functions for linked stacks.

**(a)** CreateStack            **(e)** PopNode
**(b)** ClearStack             **(f)** Pop
**(c)** StackEmpty          **(g)** StackTop
**(d)** StackFull             **(h)** TraverseStack

**E9.** For a linked stack, the function StackSize requires a loop that moves through the entire stack to count the entries, since the number of entries in the stack is not kept as a separate field in the stack record.

**(a)** Write the C function StackSize for a linked stack by using a loop that moves a pointer variable from node to node through the stack.

**(b)** Consider modifying the declaration of a linked stack to make a stack into a structure with two fields, the top of the stack and a counter giving its size. What changes will need to be made to all the functions for linked stacks? Discuss the advantages and disadvantages of this modification compared to the original implementation of linked stacks.

**Programming Project 3.1**

**P1.** **(a)** Write declarations and functions for processing contiguous stacks, suitable for use by an application program. Develop stack units that use characters, real numbers, and integers. For the sake of demonstration programs, include the function TraverseStack.

**(b)** Write declarations and functions for processing linked stacks, suitable for use by an application program.

**(c)** Write a demonstration program that can be used to check the functions written in this section for manipulating stacks. Model your program on the one developed in Section 2.3.3 and use as much of that code as possible. The entries in your stack should be characters. Your program should write a one-line menu from which the user can select any of the stack operations. After your program does the requested operation, it should inform the user of the result and ask for the next request. When the user wishes to push a character onto the stack, your program will need to ask what character to push. Use the contiguous implementation of stacks, and be careful to maintain the principles of information hiding.

**(d)** Replace the functions for contiguous stack operations with the equivalent functions for linked stacks. Make no other change, and verify that the program works correctly.

## 3.2 Introduction to Recursion

### 3.2.1 STACK FRAMES FOR SUBPROGRAMS

As one important application of stacks, consider what happens within the computer system when subprograms are called. The system (or the program) must remember the place where the call was made, so that it can return there after the subprogram is complete. It must also remember all the local variables, processor registers, and the like, so that information will not be lost while the subprogram is working. We can think of all this information as one large record, a temporary storage area for each subprogram.

*subprogram data storage*

Suppose now that we have three subprograms called $A$, $B$, and $C$, and suppose that $A$ invokes $B$ and $B$ invokes $C$. Then $B$ will not have finished its work until $C$ has finished and returned. Similarly $A$ is the first to start work, but it is the last to be finished, not until sometime after $B$ has finished and returned. Thus the sequence by which subprogram activity proceeds is summed up as the property *last in, first out*. If we consider the machine's task of assigning temporary storage areas for use by subprograms, then these areas would be allocated in a list with this same property, that is, in a stack (see Figure 3.6). Hence a stack plays a key role in invoking subprograms in a computer system.

*definition: recursion*

Notice from Figure 3.6 that it makes no difference whether the temporary storage areas pushed on the stack come from different subprograms or from repeated occurrences of the same subprogram. *Recursion* is the name for the case when a subprogram invokes itself or invokes a series of other subprograms that eventually invokes the first subprogram again. In regard to stack frames for subprogram calls, recursion is no different from any other subprogram calls.

### 3.2.2 TREE OF SUBPROGRAM CALLS

One more method elucidates the connection between stacks and subprogram calls. This is to draw a *tree* diagram showing the order in which the subprograms are

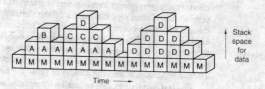

Figure 3.6. Stack frames for subprogram calls

invoked. Such a tree diagram appears in Figure 3.7, corresponding to the stack frames shown in Figure 3.6. The main program is shown as the root of the tree, and all the calls that the main program makes directly are shown as the vertices directly below the root. Each of these subprograms may, of course, call other subprograms, which are shown as further vertices on lower levels. In this way, the tree grows into a form like the one in Figure 3.7. We shall call such a tree a *tree of subprogram calls.*

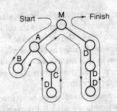

Figure 3.7. Tree of subprogram calls

We start at the top of the tree, which is called its *root* and corresponds to the main program, and move around it as shown by the colored path. This colored path is called a *traversal* of the tree. Each circle (called a *vertex* or a *node*) corresponds to a call to a subprogram. When we come to a vertex while moving downward we invoke the subprogram. After we traverse the part of the tree below the vertex, we reach it again on the way up, and this represents termination and return from the subprogram.

*recursion tree*

We are especially interested in recursion, so that often we draw only the part of the tree showing the recursive calls, and call it a *recursion tree.*

You should first notice from the diagram that there is no difference in the way a recursive call appears and the way any other subprogram call occurs. Different recursive calls appear simply as different vertices that happen to have the same name of subprogram attached. Second, note carefully that the tree shows the *calls* to subprograms. Hence a subprogram called from only one place, but within a loop executed more than once, will appear several times in the tree, once for each execution of the loop. Similarly, if a subprogram is called from a conditional statement that is not executed, then the call will not appear in the tree.

*execution trace*

*stack frames*

The stack frames like Figure 3.6 show the nesting of recursive calls and also illustrate the storage requirements for recursion. If a function calls itself recursively several times, then separate copies of the variables declared in the function are created for each recursive call. In the usual implementation of recursion, these are kept on a stack. Note that the amount of space needed for this stack is proportional to the height of the recursion tree, *not* to the total number of nodes in the tree. That is, the amount of space needed to implement a recursive function depends on the *depth* of recursion, not on the *number* of times the function is invoked.

*space requirement*

The last two figures can, in fact, be interpreted in a broader context than as the process of invoking subprograms. They thereby elucidate an easy but important observation, providing an intimate connection between arbitrary trees and stacks:

**Theorem 3.1**   *During the traversal of any tree, vertices are added to or deleted from the path back to the root in the fashion of a stack. Given any stack, conversely, a tree can be drawn to portray the life history of the stack, as items are pushed onto or popped from it.*

We now turn to the study of several simple examples of recursion. We next analyze how recursion is usually implemented on a computer. In the process, we shall obtain guidelines regarding good and bad uses of recursion, when it is appropriate, and when it should best be avoided.

### 3.2.3 FACTORIALS: A RECURSIVE DEFINITION

In mathematics, the *factorial* function of a nonnegative integer is usually defined by the formula

*informal definition*

$$n! = n \times (n-1) \times \cdots \times 1.$$

The ellipsis (three dots) in this formula means "continue in the same way." This notation is not precise, since there can be more than one sensible way to fill in the ellipsis. To calculate factorials, we need a more precise definition, such as the following:

*formal definition*

$$n! = \begin{cases} 1 & \text{if } n = 0 \\ n \times (n-1)! & \text{if } n > 0. \end{cases}$$

This definition tells us exactly how to calculate a factorial, provided we follow the rules carefully and use a piece of paper to help us remember where we are.

*example*

Suppose that we wish to calculate 4!. Since 4 > 0, the definition tells us that 4! = 4 × 3!. This may be some help, but not enough, since we do not know what 3! is. Since 3 > 0, the definition again gives us 3! = 3 × 2!. Again, we do not know the value of 2!, but the definition gives us 2! = 2 × 1!. We still do not know 1!, but, since 1 > 0, we have 1! = 1 × 0!. The definition, finally, treats the case $n = 0$ separately, so we know that 0! = 1. We can substitute this answer into the expression for 1! and obtain 1! = 1 × 0! = 1 × 1 = 1. Now comes the reason for using a piece of paper to keep track of partial results. Unless we write the computation down in an organized fashion, by the time we work our way through a definition several times we will have forgotten the early steps of the process before we reach the lowest level and begin to use the results to complete the earlier calculation. For the factorial calculation, it is of course easy to write out all the steps in an organized way:

$$
\begin{aligned}
4! &= 4 \times 3! \\
&= 4 \times (3 \times 2!) \\
&= 4 \times (3 \times (2 \times 1!)) \\
&= 4 \times (3 \times (2 \times (1 \times 0!))) \\
&= 4 \times (3 \times (2 \times (1 \times 1))) \\
&= 4 \times (3 \times (2 \times 1)) \\
&= 4 \times (3 \times 2) \\
&= 4 \times 6 \\
&= 24.
\end{aligned}
$$

*problem reduction*

This calculation illustrates the essence of the way recursion works. To obtain the answer to a large problem, a general method is used that reduces the large problem to one or more problems of a similar nature but a smaller size. The same general method is then used for these subproblems, and so recursion continues until the size of the subproblems is reduced to some smallest, base case, where the solution is given directly without using further recursion. In other words:

*Every recursive process consists of two parts:*

1. *A smallest, base case that is processed without recursion; and*

2. *A general method that reduces a particular case to one or more of the smaller cases, thereby making progress toward eventually reducing the problem all the way to the base case.*

C, like most modern computer languages, provides easy access to recursion. The factorial calculation in C becomes the following function.

*recursive program*

```
/* Factorial: compute n!
   Pre:   n is a nonnegative integer.
   Post:  The function value is the factorial of n. */
int Factorial(int n)
{
    if (n == 0)
        return 1;
    else
        return n * Factorial(n – 1);
}
```

As you can see from this example of factorials, the recursive definition and recursive solution of a problem can be both concise and elegant, but the computational details can require keeping track of many partial computations before the process is complete.

*remembering partial computations*

Computers are very good at keeping track of such partial computations; the human mind is not at all good for such tasks. It is exceedingly difficult to remember a long chain of partial results and then go back through it to complete the work. When we use recursion, therefore, it is necessary for us to think in somewhat different terms than with other programming methods. Programmers must look at the big picture and leave the detailed computations to the computer.

We must specify in our algorithm the precise form of the general step in reducing a large problem to smaller cases; we must determine the stopping rule (the smallest case) and how it is processed. On the other hand, except for a few simple and small examples, we should generally *not* try to understand a recursive algorithm by working the general case all the way down to the stopping rule or by tracing the action the computer will take on a good-sized case. We would quickly become so confused by all the postponed tasks that we would lose track of the complete problem and the overall method used for its solution.

There are good general methods and tools that allow us to concentrate on the general methods and key steps while at the same time analyzing the amount of work that the computer will do in carrying out all the details. We now turn to an example that illustrates some of these methods and tools.

### 3.2.4 DIVIDE AND CONQUER: THE TOWERS OF HANOI

**1. The Problem**

*the story*

In the nineteenth century, a game called the ***Towers of Hanoi*** appeared in Europe, together with promotional material (undoubtedly apocryphal) explaining that the game represented a task underway in the Temple of Brahma. At the creation of the world, the priests were given a brass platform on which were 3 diamond needles. On the first needle were stacked 64 golden disks, each one slightly smaller than the one under it. (The less exotic version sold in Europe had 8 cardboard disks and 3 wooden posts.) The priests were assigned the task of moving all the golden disks from the first needle to the third, subject to the conditions that only one disk can be moved at a time, and that no disk is ever allowed to be placed on top of a smaller disk. The priests were told that when they had finished moving the 64 disks, it would signify the end of the world. See Figure 3.8.

Our task, of course, is to write a computer program that will type out a list of instructions for the priests. We can summarize our task by the instruction

Move(64, 1, 3, 2)

which means

*Move 64 disks from tower 1 to tower 3 using tower 2 as temporary storage.*

**2. The Solution**

The idea that gives a solution is to concentrate our attention not on the first step (which must be to move the top disk somewhere), but rather on the hardest step: moving the bottom disk. There is no way to reach the bottom disk until the top 63 disks have been moved, and, furthermore, they must all be on tower 2 so that we can move the bottom disk from tower 1 to tower 3. This is because only one disk

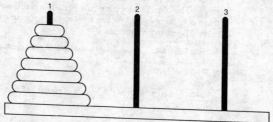

**Figure 3.8. The Towers of Hanoi**

can be moved at a time and the bottom (largest) one can never be on top of any other, so that when we move the bottom one, there can be no other disks on towers 1 or 3. Thus we can summarize the steps of our algorithm for the Towers of Hanoi as

        Move(63, 1, 2, 3);
        printf("Move disk 64 from tower 1 to tower 3.\n");
        Move(63, 2, 3, 1)

*general reduction*

We now have a small step toward the solution, only a very small one since we must still describe how to move the 63 disks two times. It is a significant step nonetheless, since there is no reason why we cannot move the 63 remaining disks in the same way. (In fact, we must do so in the same way since there is again a largest disk that must be moved last.)

*divide and conquer*

This is exactly the idea of recursion. We have described how to do the key step and asserted that the rest of the problem is done in essentially the same way. This is also the idea of *divide and conquer*: To solve a problem, we split the work into smaller and smaller parts, each of which is easier to solve than the original problem.

### 3. Refinement

To write the algorithm formally, we shall need to know at each step which tower may be used for temporary storage, and thus we will invoke the function with specifications as follows:

---

int Move(int count, int start, int finish, int temp);

*precondition*:   There are at least count disks on the tower start. The top disk (if any) on each of towers temp and finish is larger than any of the top count disks on tower start.

*postcondition*:  The top count disks on start have been moved to finish; temp (used for temporary storage) has been returned to its starting position.

---

*stopping rule*

Supposedly our task is to be finished in a finite number of steps (even if it does mark the end of the world!), and thus there must be some way that the recursion stops. The obvious stopping rule is that, when there are no disks to be moved, there is nothing to do. We can now write the complete program to embody these rules. The main program is:

```
#define DISKS 64              /* Number of disks on the first tower.          */

/* Towers of Hanoi
   Pre:   None.
   Post:  The simulation of the Towers of Hanoi has terminated. */
int main(void)
{
    Move(DISKS, 1, 3, 2);
    return 0;
}
```

The recursive function that does the work is:

*recursive function*

```
/* Move: moves count disks from start to finish using temp for temporary storage. */
void Move(int count, int start, int finish, int temp)
{
    if (count > 0) {
        Move(count - 1, start, temp, finish);
        printf("Move a disk from %d to %d.\n", start, finish);
        Move(count - 1, temp, finish, start);
    }
}
```

### 4. Program Tracing

One useful tool in studying a recursive function when applied to a very small example is to construct a trace of its action. Such a trace is shown in Figure 3.9 for the Towers of Hanoi in the case when the number of disks, DISKS, is 2. Each box in the diagram shows what happens in one of the calls. The outermost call Move(2, 1, 3, 2) (the call made by the main program) results essentially in the execution of the following three statements, shown as the statements in the outer box (colored gray) of the diagram.

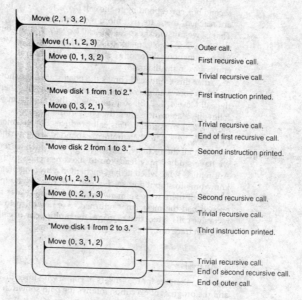

Figure 3.9. Trace of Hanoi for DISKS == 2

```
Move(1, 1, 2, 3);              /* Move 1 disk from tower 1 to tower 2 using tower 3. */
printf("Move disk 2 from tower 1 to tower 3.\n");
Move(1, 2, 3, 1);              /* Move 1 disk from tower 2 to tower 3 using tower 1. */
```

Doing the first and third of these statements requires recursive calls. The statement Move(1, 1, 2, 3) means to start the function Move over again from the top, but now with the new parameters. Hence this statement results essentially in the execution of the following three statements, shown as the statements in the first inner box (shown in color):

```
Move(0, 1, 3, 2);              /* Move 0 disks.                             */
printf("Move disk 1 from tower 1 to tower 2.\n");
Move(0, 3, 2, 1);              /* Move 0 disks.                             */
```

If you wish, you may think of these three statements as written out in place of the call Move(1, 1, 2, 3), but think of them as having a different color from the statements of the outer call, since they constitute a new and different call to the function. These statements are shown as colored print in the figure.

After the box corresponding to this call comes the printf statement and then a second box corresponding to the call Move(1, 2, 3, 1). But before these statements are reached, there are two more recursive calls coming from the first inner box. That is, we must next expand the call Move(0, 1, 3, 2). But the function Move does nothing when its parameter count is 0; hence this call Move(0, 1, 3, 2) executes no further function calls or other statements. We show it as corresponding to the first empty box in the diagram.

After this empty call comes the printf statement shown in the first inner box, and then comes another call that does nothing. This then completes the work for the call Move(1, 1, 2, 3), so it returns to the place from which it was called. The following statement is then the printf in the outer box, and finally the statement Move(1, 2, 3, 1) is done. This call produces the statements shown in the second inner box, which are then, in turn, expanded as the further empty boxes shown.

*sorcerer's apprentice*

With all the recursive calls through which we worked our way, the example we have studied may lead you to liken recursion to the fable of the Sorcerer's Apprentice, who, when he had enchanted a broom to fetch water for him, did not know how to stop it and so chopped it in two, whereupon it started duplicating itself until there were so many brooms fetching water that disaster would have ensued had the master not returned. We now turn to another tool to visualize recursive calls, a tool that manages the multiplicity of calls more effectively than a program trace can. This tool is the recursion tree.

### 5. Analysis

The recursion tree for the Towers of Hanoi with three disks appears as Figure 3.10, and the progress of execution follows the path shown in color.

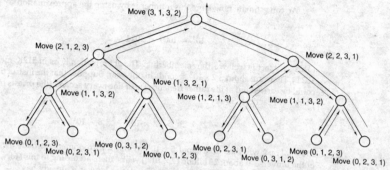

Figure 3.10. Recursion tree for three disks

Note that our program for the Towers of Hanoi not only produces a complete solution to the task, but it produces the best possible solution, and, in fact, the only solution that can be found except for the possible inclusion of redundant and useless sequences of instructions such as

Move disk 5 from tower 1 to tower 2.
Move disk 5 from tower 2 to tower 3.
Move disk 5 from tower 3 to tower 1.

To show the uniqueness of the irreducible solution, note that, at every stage, the task to be done can be summarized as to move a certain number of disks from one tower to another. There is no way to do this task except to move all the disks except the bottom one first, then perhaps make some redundant moves, then move the bottom one again, possibly make more redundant moves, and finally move the upper disks again.

Next, let us find out how many times the recursion will proceed before starting to return and back out. The first time function Move is called, it is with n == 64, and each recursive call reduces the value of n by 1. Thus, if we exclude the calls with n == 0, which do nothing, we have a total depth of recursion of 64. That is, if we were to draw the tree of recursive calls for the program, it would have 64 levels above its leaves. Except for the leaves, each vertex results in two recursive calls (as well as in writing out one instruction), and so the number of vertices on each level is exactly double that of the level above.

*depth of recursion*

From thinking about its recursion tree (even if it is much too large to draw), we can easily calculate how many instructions are needed to move 64 disks. One instruction is printed for each vertex in the tree, except for the leaves (which are calls with n == 0). The number of non-leaves is

*total number of moves*

$$1 + 2 + 4 + \cdots + 2^{63} = 2^0 + 2^1 + 2^2 + \cdots + 2^{63} = 2^{64} - 1,$$

and this is the number of moves required altogether for 64 disks.

We can estimate how large this number is by using the approximation

$$10^3 = 1000 < 1024 = 2^{10}.$$

(This easy fact is well worth remembering: The abbreviation K, as in 512K, means 1024.) There are about $3.2 \times 10^7$ seconds in one year. Suppose that the instructions could be carried out at the rather frenetic rate of one every second (the priests have plenty of practice). Since

$$2^{64} = 2^4 \times 2^{60} > 2^4 \times 10^{18} = 1.6 \times 10^{19},$$

the total task will then take about $5 \times 10^{11}$ years. If astronomers estimate the age of the universe at about 20 billion ($2 \times 10^{10}$) years, then, according to this story, the world will indeed endure a long time—25 times as long as it already has!

*time and space*

You should note carefully that, although no computer could ever carry out the full Towers of Hanoi, it would fail for lack of *time*, and certainly not for lack of *space*. The space needed is only that to keep track of 64 recursive calls, but the time needed is that required for $2^{64}$ calculations.

---

**Exercises 3.2**

**E1.** Consider the function $f(n)$ defined as follows, where $n$ is a nonnegative integer:

$$f(n) = \begin{cases} 0 & \text{if } n = 0; \\ f(\frac{1}{2}n) & \text{if } n \text{ is even, } n > 0; \\ 1 + f(n-1) & \text{if } n \text{ is odd, } n > 0. \end{cases}$$

Calculate the value of $f(n)$ for the following values of $n$.

(a) $n = 1$.   (c) $n = 3$.   (e) $n = 100$.
(b) $n = 2$.   (d) $n = 99$.  (f) $n = 128$.

**E2.** Consider the function $f(n)$ defined as follows, where $n$ is a nonnegative integer:

$$f(n) = \begin{cases} n & \text{if } n \le 1; \\ n + f(\frac{1}{2}n) & \text{if } n \text{ is even, } n > 1; \\ f(\frac{1}{2}(n+1)) + f(\frac{1}{2}(n-1)) & \text{if } n \text{ is odd, } n > 1. \end{cases}$$

For each of the following values of $n$, draw the recursion tree and calculate the value of $f(n)$.

(a) $n = 1$.   (c) $n = 3$.   (e) $n = 5$.
(b) $n = 2$.   (d) $n = 4$.   (f) $n = 6$.

**Programming Projects 3.2**

**P1.** Compare the running times for the recursive factorial function written in this section with a nonrecursive function obtained by initializing a local variable to 1 and using a loop to calculate the product $n! = 1 \times 2 \times \cdots \times n$. To obtain meaningful comparisons of the CPU time required, you will probably need to write a loop in your driver program that will repeat the same calculation of a factorial several hundred times. Integer overflow will occur if you attempt to calculate the factorial of a large number. To prevent this from happening, you may declare $n$ and the function value to have type float instead of integer.

**P2.** Confirm that the running time for the program Hanoi increases approximately like a constant multiple of $2^n$, where $n$ is the number of disks moved. To do this, make DISKS a variable, comment out the line that writes a message to the user, and run the program for several successive values of DISKS, such as 10, 11, ..., 15. How does the CPU time change from one value of DISKS to the next?

## 3.3 Backtracking: Postponing the Work

We have already seen some of the usefulness of recursion both as a problem-solving tool and a programming method. In this section, we study an example that demonstrates one of the variety of problems to which recursion may fruitfully be applied.

Let us consider the puzzle of how to place eight queens on a chessboard so that no queen can take another. Recall that in the rules for chess a queen can take another piece that lies on the same row, the same column, or the same diagonal (either direction) as the queen. The chessboard has eight rows and eight columns.

It is by no means obvious how to solve this puzzle, and its complete solution defied even the great C. F. GAUSS, who attempted it in 1850. It is typical of puzzles that do not seem suitable for analytic solutions, but require either luck coupled with trial and error, or else much exhaustive (and exhausting) computation. To convince you that solutions to this problem really do exist, two of them are shown in Figure 3.11.

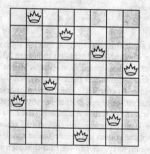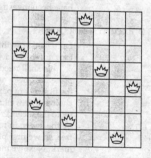

Figure 3.11. Two configurations showing eight nonattacking queens

### 3.3.1 SOLVING THE EIGHT-QUEENS PUZZLE

A person attempting to solve the eight-queens problem will usually soon abandon attempts to find all (or even one) of the solutions by being clever and will start to put queens on the board, perhaps randomly or perhaps in some logical order, but always making sure that no queen placed can take another already on the board. If the person is lucky enough to place eight queens on the board by proceeding in this way, then this is a solution; if not, then one or more of the queens must be removed and placed elsewhere to continue the search for a solution. To start formulating a program, let us sketch this method in algorithmic form. We denote the number of queens on the board by $n$; initially, $n = 0$. The key step is described as follows.

*outline*

```
void AddQueen(void)
{
    for (every unguarded position p on the board) {
        Place a queen in position p;
        n++;
        if (n == 8)
            Print the configuration;
        else
            AddQueen();
        Remove the queen from position p;
        n--;
    }
}
```

This sketch illustrates the use of recursion to mean "Continue to the next stage and repeat the task." Placing a queen in position p is only tentative; we leave it there only if we can continue adding queens until we have eight. Whether we reach eight or not, the function will return when it finds that it has finished or there are no further possibilities to investigate. After the inner call has returned, then, it is time to remove the queen from position p, because all possibilities with it there have been investigated.

### 3.3.2 EXAMPLE: FOUR QUEENS

Let us see how this algorithm works for a much simpler problem, that of placing four queens on a $4 \times 4$ board, as illustrated in Figure 3.12.

We shall need to put one queen in each row of the board. Let us first try to place the queen as far to the left in the row as we can. Such a choice is shown in the first row of part (a) of Figure 3.11. The question marks indicate other legitimate choices that we have not yet tried. Before we investigate these choices, we move on to the second row and try to insert a queen. The first two columns are guarded by the queen in row 1, as shown by the crossed-off squares. Columns 3 and 4 are free, so we first place the queen in column 3 and mark column 4 with a question mark. Next we move on to row 3, but we find that all four squares are guarded by one of the queens in the first two rows. We have now reached a dead end.

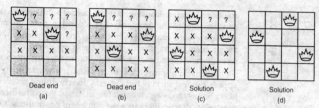

Figure 3.12. Solution to the Four-Queens problem

When we reach a dead end, we must *backtrack* by going back to the most recent choice we have made and trying another possibility. This situation is shown in part (b) of Figure 3.12, which shows the queen in row 1 unchanged, but the queen in row 2 moved to the second possible position (and the previously occupied position crossed off as no longer possible). Now we find that column 2 is the only possible position for a queen in row 3, but all four positions in row 4 are guarded. Hence we have again reached a point where no other queens can be added, and must backtrack.

At this point, we no longer have another choice for row 2, so we must move all the way back to row 1 and move the queen to the next possible position, column 2. This situation is shown in part (c) of Figure 3.12. Now we find that, in row 2, only column 4 is unguarded, so a queen must go there. In row 3, then, column 1 is the only possibility, and, in row 4, only column 3 is possible. This placement of queens, however, leads to a solution to the problem of four non attacking queens on the same $4 \times 4$ board.

If we wish to find *all* the solutions, we can continue in the same way, backtracking to the last choice we made and changing the queen to the next possible move. In part (c) we had no choice in rows 4, 3, or 2, so we now back up to row 1 and move the queen to column 3. This choice leads to the unique solution shown in part (d).

Finally, we should investigate the possibilities with a queen in column 4 of row 1, but, as in part (a), there will be no solution in this case. In fact, the configurations with a queen in either column 3 or column 4 of row 1 are just the mirror images of those with a queen in column 2 or column 1. If you do a left-right reflection of the board shown in part (c), you will obtain the board shown in (d), and the boards with a queen in column 4, row 1, are just the reflections of those shown in parts (a) and (b).

### 3.3.3 BACKTRACKING

This function is typical of a broad class called *backtracking algorithms*, which attempt to complete a search for a solution to a problem by constructing partial solutions, always ensuring that the partial solutions remain consistent with the requirements of the problem. The algorithm then attempts to extend a partial solution toward completion, but when an inconsistency with the requirements of the problem occurs, the algorithm backs up (*backtracks*) by removing the most recently constructed part of the solution and trying another possibility.

Backtracking proves useful in situations where many possibilities may first appear, but few survive further tests. In scheduling problems, for example, it will likely be easy to assign the first few matches, but as further matches are made, the constraints drastically reduce the number of possibilities. Or consider the problem of designing a compiler. In some languages (but not C), it is impossible to determine the meaning of a statement until almost all of it has been read. Consider, for example, the pair of FORTRAN statements

$$\text{DO 17 K = 1, 6}$$
$$\text{DO 17 K = 1. 6}$$

Both of these are legal: The first starts a loop, and the second assigns the number 1.6 to the variable DO17K, since FORTRAN ignores blanks, even those in the middle of identifiers. In such cases where the meaning cannot be deduced immediately, *parsing* — backtracking is a useful method in *parsing* (that is, splitting apart to decipher) the text of a program.

### 3.3.4 REFINEMENT: CHOOSING THE DATA STRUCTURES

To fill in the details of our algorithm for the eight-queens problem, we must first decide how we will determine which positions are unguarded at each stage and how we will loop through the unguarded positions. This amounts to reaching some decisions about the representation of data in the program.

A person working on the eight-queens puzzle with an actual chessboard will probably proceed to put queens into the squares one at a time. We can do the same *square Boolean array* — in a computer by introducing an $8 \times 8$ array with Boolean entries and by defining an entry to be true if a queen is there and false if not. To determine if a position is guarded, the person would scan the board to see if a queen is guarding the position, and we could do the same, but doing so would involve considerable searching.

A person working the puzzle on paper or on a blackboard often observes that when a queen is put on the board, time will be saved in the next stage if all the squares that the new queen guards are marked off, so that it is only necessary to look for an unmarked square to find an unguarded position for the next queen. Again, we could do the same by defining each entry of our array to be true if it is free and false if it is guarded.

A problem now arises, however, when we wish to remove a queen. We should not necessarily change a position that she has guarded from false to true, since it may well be that some other queen still guards that position. We can solve this *square integer array*     problem by making the entries of our array integers rather than Boolean, each entry denoting the number of queens guarding the position. Thus, to add a queen, we increase the count by 1 for each position on the same row, column, or diagonal as the queen, and, to remove a queen, we reduce the appropriate counts by 1. A position is unguarded if and only if it has a count of 0.

In spite of its obvious advantages over the previous attempt, this method still involves some searching to find unguarded positions and some calculation to change all the counts at each stage. The algorithm will be adding and removing queens a great many times, so that this calculation and searching may prove expensive. A person working on this puzzle soon makes another observation that saves even more work.

Once a queen has been put in the first row, no person would waste time searching to find a place to put another queen in the same row, since the row is fully guarded by the first queen. There can never be more than one queen in each row. But our goal is to put eight queens on the board, and there are only eight rows. It follows that there must be a queen, exactly one queen, in every one of the rows.

*pigeonhole principle*     (This is called the *pigeonhole principle*: If you have $n$ pigeons and $n$ pigeonholes, and no more than one pigeon ever goes in the same hole, then there must be a pigeon in every hole.)

*array of locations*     Thus, we can proceed by placing the queens on the board one row at a time, starting with the first, and we can keep track of where they are with a single array

int col[8];

where col[i] gives the column containing the queen in row i. To make sure that no two queens are on the same column or the same diagonal, we need not keep and search through an $8 \times 8$ array, but we need only keep track of whether each

*guards*     column is free or guarded, and whether each diagonal is likewise. We can do this with three Boolean arrays: colfree, upfree, and downfree, where diagonals from the lower left to the upper right are considered upward and those from the upper left to lower right are considered downward.

How do we identify the positions along a single diagonal? Along the main (downward) diagonal, the entries are

$$(0,0), \ (1,1), \ \ldots, \ (7,7).$$

These have the property that the row and column indices are equal; that, is, their *difference* is 0. It turns out that, along any downward diagonal, the row and column indices will have a constant difference. This difference is 0 for the main diagonal, and ranges from $0 - 7 = -7$ for the downward diagonal of length 1 in the upper right corner, to $7 - 0 = 7$ for the one in the lower left corner. Similarly, along upward diagonals, the *sum* of the row and column indices is constant, ranging from $0 + 0 = 0$ to $7 + 7 = 14$.

After making all these decisions, we can now define all our data structures formally, and, at the same time, we can write the main program. Since C does not allow negative bounds in arrays we must use an offset of 7 when accessing downfree.

*main program*

```
/* Queen: Eight-queens program.
   Pre:   None.
   Post:  All solutions to the eight-queens problem are printed.
   Uses:  Function AddQueen performs the recursive backtracking; WriteBoard prints
          the solutions. */
#include "common.h"

#define BOARDSIZE 8
#define DIAGONAL (2*BOARDSIZE – 1)
#define DOWNOFFSET 7
void WriteBoard(void);
void AddQueen(void);
int queencol[BOARDSIZE];        /* column with the queen           */
Boolean colfree[BOARDSIZE];     /* Is the column free?             */
Boolean upfree[DIAGONAL];       /* Is the upward diagonal free?    */
Boolean downfree[DIAGONAL];     /* Is the downward diagonal free?  */
int queencount = – 1,           /* row whose queen is currently placed */
    numsol = 0;                 /* number of solutions found so far    */


int main(void)
{
    int i;
    for (i = 0; i < BOARDSIZE; i++)
        colfree[i] = TRUE;
    for (i = 0; i < DIAGONAL; i++) {
        upfree[i] = TRUE;
        downfree[i] = TRUE;
    }
    AddQueen();
    return 0;
}
```

The recursive function is:

```
/* AddQueen: add a queen to the board.
   Pre:   Queens have been properly placed in rows 0 through queencount (provided
          queencount >= 0) and the information recorded in the above arrays.
   Post:  All solutions beginning with this configuration have been printed. queencount,
          and values in all arrays have been returned to their original values.
   Uses:  Global variable queencount, global arrays queencol, colfree, upfree, and down-
          free, and function WriteBoard. */
```

*recursive procedure*

```
void AddQueen(void)
{
    int col;                          /* column being tried for the queen      */
    queencount++;
    for (col = 0;  col < BOARDSIZE;  col++)
        if (colfree[col] && upfree[queencount + col] &&
            downfree[queencount - col + DOWNOFFSET]) {
            /* Put a queen in position (queencount, col). */
            queencol[queencount] = col;
            colfree[col] = FALSE;
            upfree[queencount + col] = FALSE;
            downfree[queencount - col + DOWNOFFSET] = FALSE;
            if (queencount == BOARDSIZE - 1) /* termination condition        */
                WriteBoard();
            else
                AddQueen();    /* Proceed recursively.                        */
            colfree[col] = TRUE;  /* Now backtrack by removing the queen.     */
            upfree[queencount + col] = TRUE;
            downfree[queencount - col + DOWNOFFSET] = TRUE;
        }
    queencount--;
}
```

Note that, in the eight-queens program, almost all the variables and arrays are declared globally, whereas, in the Towers of Hanoi program of Section 3.2.4, the variables were declared in the recursive function. If variables are declared within a function, then they are local to the function and not available outside it. In particular, variables declared in a recursive function are local to a single occurrence of the function, so that if the function is called again recursively, the variables are new and different, and the original variables will be remembered after the function returns. The copies of variables set up in an outer call are not available to the function during an inner recursive call. In the eight-queens program, we want the same information about guarded rows, columns, and diagonals to be available to all the recursive occurrences of the function, and to do this, the appropriate arrays are declared not in the function but as global variables.

The only reason for the array col[ ] is to communicate the positions of the queens to the function WriteBoard. The information in this array is also preserved in the eight local copies of the variable col set up during the recursive calls, but only one of these local copies is available to the program at a given time.

## 3.3.5 Analysis of Backtracking

Finally, let us estimate the amount of work that our program will do. If we had taken the naïve approach by writing a program that first placed all eight queens on the board and then rejected the illegal configurations, we would be investigating as many configurations as choosing eight places out of sixty-four, which is

$$\binom{64}{8} = 4{,}426{,}165{,}368.$$

The observation that there can be only one queen in each row immediately cuts this number to

$$8^8 = 16{,}777{,}216.$$

This number is still large, but our program will not investigate nearly this many positions. Instead, it rejects positions whose column or diagonals are guarded. The requirement that there be only one queen in each column reduces the number to

*reduced count*

$$8! = 40{,}320$$

which is quite manageable by computer, and the actual number of cases the program considers will be much less than this (see Project P1), since positions with guarded diagonals in the early rows will be rejected immediately, with no need to make the fruitless attempt to fill the later rows.

*effectiveness of backtracking*

This behavior summarizes the effectiveness of backtracking: positions that are discovered to be impossible prevent the later investigation of fruitless paths.

Another way to express this behavior of backtracking is to consider the tree of recursive calls to function AddQueen, part of which is shown in Figure 3.13. The two solutions shown in this tree are the same as the solutions shown in Figure 3.11. It appears formally that each node in the tree might have up to eight children

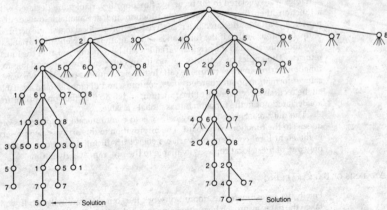

Figure 3.13. Part of the recursion tree, eight-queens problem

corresponding to the recursive calls to AddQueen for the eight possible values of col. Even at levels near the root, however, most of these branches are found to be impossible, and the removal of one node on an upper level removes a multitude of its descendents. Backtracking is a most effective tool to prune a recursion tree to manageable size.

**Exercises 3.3**

**E1.** What is the maximum depth of recursion in the eight-queens program?

**E2.** Starting with the following partial configuration of five queens on the board, construct the recursion tree of all situations that the eight-queens program will consider in trying to add the remaining three queens. Stop drawing the tree at the point where the program will backtrack and remove one of the original five queens.

**E3.** By performing backtracking by hand, find all solutions to the problem of placing five queens on a $5 \times 5$ board. You may use the left-right symmetry of the first row by considering only the possibilities when the queen in row 0 is in one of columns 0, 1, or 2.

**Programming Projects 3.3**

**P1.** Run the eight-queens program on your computer. You will need to write function WriteBoard to do the output. In addition, find out exactly how many positions are investigated by including a counter that is incremented every time function AddQueen is started. [Note that a method that placed all eight queens before checking for guarded squares would be equivalent to eight calls to AddQueen.]

**P2.** Describe a rectangular maze by indicating its paths and walls within an array. Write a backtracking program to find a way through the maze.

**P3.** Another chessboard puzzle (this one reputedly solved by GAUSS at the age of four) is to find a sequence of moves by a knight that will visit every square of the board exactly once. Recall that a knight's move is to jump two positions either vertically or horizontally and one position in the perpendicular direction. Such a move can be accomplished by setting $x$ to either 1 or 2, setting $y$ to $3 - x$, and then changing the first coordinate by $\pm x$ and the second by $\pm y$ (providing the resulting position is still on the board). Write a backtracking program that will input an initial position and search for a knight's tour starting at the given position and going to every square once and no square more than once. If you find that the program runs too slowly, a good method is to order the list of squares to which it can move from a given position so that it will first try to go to the squares with the least accessibility, that is, to the squares from which there are the fewest knight's moves to squares not yet visited.

## 3.4 Principles of Recursion

### 3.4.1 DESIGNING RECURSIVE ALGORITHMS

Recursion is a tool to allow the programmer to concentrate on the key step of an algorithm, without having initially to worry about coupling that step with all the others. As usual with problem solving, the first approach should usually be to consider several simple examples, and as these become better understood, to attempt to formulate a method that will work more generally. Some of the important parts of designing algorithms with recursion are:

- **Find the key step.**   Begin by asking yourself, "How can this problem be divided into parts?" or "How will the key step in the middle be done?" Be sure to keep your answer simple but generally applicable. Do not come up with a multitude of special cases that work only for small problems or at the beginning and end of large ones. Once you have a simple, small step toward the solution, ask whether the remainder of the problem can be done in the same or a similar way, and modify your method, if necessary, so that it will be sufficiently general.

- **Find a stopping rule.**   The stopping rule indicates that the problem or a suitable part of it is done. This stopping rule is usually the small, special case that is trivial or easy to handle without recursion.

- **Outline your algorithm.**   Combine the stopping rule and the key step, using an if statement to select between them. You should now be able to write the main program and a recursive function that will describe how to carry the key step through until the stopping rule applies.

- **Check termination.**   Next, and of great importance, is a verification that the recursion will always terminate. Start with a general situation and check that, in a finite number of steps, the stopping rule will be satisfied and the recursion will terminate. Be sure also that your algorithm correctly handles extreme cases. When called on to do nothing, any algorithm should be able to return gracefully, but it is especially important that recursive algorithms do so, since a call to do nothing is often the stopping rule.

- **Draw a recursion tree.**   The key tool for the analysis of recursive algorithms is the recursion tree. As we have seen for the Towers of Hanoi, the height of the tree is closely related to the amount of memory that the program will require, and the total size of the tree reflects the number of times the key step will be done, and hence the total time the program will use. It is usually highly instructive to draw the recursion tree for one or two simple examples appropriate to your problem.

## 3.4.2 How Recursion Works

*design versus implementation*

The question of how recursion is actually done in a computer should be carefully separated in our minds from the question of using recursion in designing algorithms. In the design phase, we should use all problem-solving methods that prove to be appropriate, and recursion is one of the most flexible and powerful of these tools. In the implementation phase, we may need to ask which of several methods is the best under the circumstances. There are at least two ways to accomplish recursion in computer systems. The first of these, at present, is only available in some large systems, but with changing costs and capabilities of computer equipment, it may soon be more common. Our major point in considering two different implementations is that, although restrictions in space and time do need to be considered, they should be considered separately from the process of algorithm design, since different kinds of computer equipment in the future may lead to different capabilities and restrictions.

### 1. Multiple Processors: Concurrency

Perhaps the most natural way to think of implementing recursion is to think of each subprogram not as occupying a different part of the same computer, but to think of each subprogram as running on a separate machine. In that way, when one subprogram invokes another, it starts the corresponding machine going, and when the other machine completes its work, it sends the answer back to the first machine, which can then continue its task. If a function makes two recursive calls to itself, then it will simply start two other machines working with the same instructions that it is using. When these machines complete their work, they will send the answers back to the one that started them going. If they, in turn, make recursive calls, then they will simply start still more machines working.

*costs*

At one time, the central processor was the most expensive component of a computer system, and any thought of a system including more than one processor would have been considered extravagant. The price of processing power compared to other computing costs has now dropped radically, and in all likelihood we shall, before long, see large computer systems that will include hundreds, if not thousands, of identical microprocessors among their components. When this occurs, implementation of recursion via multiple processors will become commonplace if not inevitable.

*parallel processing*

*concurrency*

With multiple processors, programmers should no longer consider algorithms solely as a linear sequence of actions, but should instead realize that some parts of the algorithm can often be done in parallel (at the same time) as other parts. Processes that take place simultaneously are called *concurrent*. The study of concurrent processes and the methods for communication between them is, at present, an active subject for research in computing science, one in which important developments will undoubtedly improve the ways in which algorithms will be described and implemented in coming years.

## 2. Single-Processor Implementation: Storage Areas

In order to determine how recursion can be efficiently implemented in a system with only one processor, let us first for the moment leave recursion to consider the question of what steps are needed to call a subprogram, on the primitive level of machine-language instructions in a simple computer.

The hardware of any computer has a limited range of instructions that includes (amongst other instructions) doing arithmetic on specified words of storage or on special locations within the CPU called *registers*, moving data to and from the memory and registers, and branching (jumping) to a specified address. When a calling program branches to the beginning of a subprogram, the address of the place whence the call was made must be stored in memory, or else the subprogram could not remember where to return. The addresses or values of the calling parameters

*return address*    must also be stored where the subprogram can find them, and where the answers can in turn be found by the calling program after the subprogram returns. When the subprogram starts, it will do various calculations on its local variables and

*local variables*    storage areas. Once the subprogram finishes, however, these local variables are lost, since they are not available outside the subprogram. The subprogram will, of course, have used the registers within the CPU for its calculations, so normally these would have different values after the subprogram finishes than before it is called. It is traditional, however, to expect that a subprogram will change nothing except its calling parameters or global variables (side effects). Thus it is customary that the subprogram will save all the registers it will use and restore their values before it returns.

In summary, when a subprogram is called, it must have a storage area (per-

*storage area*    haps scattered as several areas); it must save the registers or whatever else it will change, using the storage area also for its return address, calling parameters, and local variables. As it returns, it will restore the registers and the other storage that it was expected to restore. After the return, it no longer needs anything in its local storage area.

In this way, we implement subprogram calls by changing storage areas, an action that takes the place of changing processors that we considered before. In these considerations, it really makes no difference whether the subprogram is called recursively or not, providing that, in the recursive case, we are careful to regard two recursive calls as being different, so that we do not mix the storage areas for one call with those of another, any more than we would mix storage areas for different subprograms, one called from within the other. For a nonrecursive subprogram, the storage area can be one fixed area, permanently reserved, since we know that one call to the subprogram will have returned before another one is made, and after the first one returns, the information stored is no longer needed. For recursive subprograms, however, the information stored must be preserved until the outer call returns, so an inner call must use a different area for its temporary storage.

Note that the once-common practice of reserving a permanent storage area for a nonrecursive subprogram can in fact be quite wasteful, since a considerable amount of memory may be consumed in this way, memory that might be useful for other purposes while the subprogram is not active. This is, nevertheless, the way that storage was allocated for subprograms in older languages like FORTRAN and COBOL, and this is one reason why these languages did not allow recursion.

### 3. Re-Entrant Programs

Essentially the same problem of multiple storage areas arises in a quite different context, that of *re-entrant* programs. In a large time-sharing system, there may be many users simultaneously using the BASIC interpreter or the text-editing system. These systems programs are quite large, and it would be very wasteful of high-speed memory to keep thirty or forty copies of exactly the same large set of instructions in memory at once, one for each user. What is generally done instead is to write large systems programs like the text editor with the instructions in one area, but the addresses of all variables or other data kept in a separate area. Then, in the memory of the time-sharing system, there will be only one copy of the instructions, but a separate data area for each user.

This situation is somewhat analogous to students writing a test in a room where the questions are written on the blackboard. There is then only one set of questions that all students can read, but each student separately writes answers on different pieces of paper. There is no difficulty for different students to be reading the same or different questions at the same time, and with different pieces of paper, their answers will not be mixed with each other. See Figure 3.14.

**Figure 3.14. Example of re-entrant processes**

### 4. Data Structures: Stacks and Trees

We have yet to specify the data structure that will keep track of all these storage areas for subprograms; to do so, let us look at the tree of subprogram calls. So that an inner subprogram can access variables declared in an outer block, and so that we can return properly to the calling program, we must, at every point in the tree, remember all vertices on the path from the given point back to the root. As we move through the tree, vertices are added to and deleted from one end of this path; the other end (at the root) remains fixed. Hence the vertices on the path form a stack; the storage areas for subprograms likewise are to be kept as a stack. This process is illustrated in Figure 3.15.

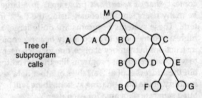

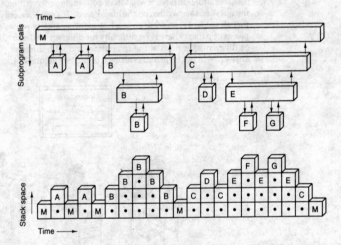

**Figure 3.15. A tree of subprogram calls and the associated stack frames**

From Figure 3.15 and our discussion, we can immediately conclude that the amount of space needed to implement recursion (which, of course, is related to the number of storage areas in current use) is directly proportional to the height of the recursion tree. Programmers who have not carefully studied recursion sometimes *time and space* mistakenly think that the space requirement relates to the total number of vertices *requirements* in the tree. The *time* requirement of the program is related to the number of times subprograms are done, and therefore to the total number of vertices in the tree, but the *space* requirement is only that of the storage areas on the path from a single vertex back to the root. Thus the space requirement is reflected in the height of the tree. A well-balanced, bushy recursion tree hence signifies a recursive process that can do much work with little need for extra space.

### 3.4.3 TAIL RECURSION

*discarding stack entries*

Suppose that the very last action of a function is to make a recursive call to itself. In the stack implementation of recursion, as we have seen, the local variables of the function will be pushed onto the stack as the recursive call is initiated. When the recursive call terminates, these local variables will be popped from the stack and thereby restored to their former values. But doing this step is pointless, because the recursive call was the last action of the function, so that the function now terminates and the just-restored local variables are immediately discarded.

When the very last action of a function is a recursive call to itself, it is thus pointless to use the stack, as we have seen, since no local variables need to be preserved. All that we need to do is to set the dummy calling parameters to their new values and branch to the beginning of the function. We summarize this principle for future reference.

*If the last-executed statement of a function is a recursive call to the function itself, then this call can be eliminated by reassigning the calling parameters to the values specified in the recursive call, and then repeating the whole function.*

The process of this transformation is shown in Figure 3.16. Part (a) shows the storage areas used by the calling program M and several copies of the recursive function P, each invoked by the previous one. The colored arrows show the flow of control from one subprogram call to the next and the blocks show the storage areas maintained by the system. Since each call by P to itself is its last action, there is no need to maintain the storage areas after returning from the call. The reduced storage areas are shown in part (b). Part (c), finally, shows the calls to P as repeated in iterative fashion on the same level of the diagram.

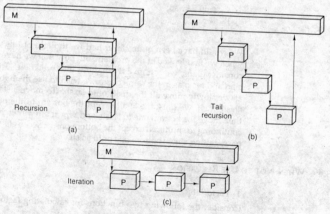

Figure 3.16. Tail recursion

*tail recursion*

This special case when a recursive call is the last-executed statement of the function is especially important because it frequently occurs. It is called **tail recursion**. You should carefully note that tail recursion means that the *last-executed* statement is a recursive call, not necessarily that the recursive call is the last statement appearing in the function. Tail recursion may appear, for example, within one clause of a switch statement or an if statement where other program lines appear later.

*time and space*

With most compilers, there will be little difference in execution *time* whether tail recursion is left in a program or is removed. If *space* considerations are important, however, then tail recursion should often be removed. By rearranging the termination condition, if needed, it is usually possible to repeat the function using a do while or a while statement.

Consider, for example, a divide-and-conquer algorithm like the Towers of Hanoi. By removing tail recursion, function Move of the original recursive program can be expressed as

```
/* Move: iterative version.
   Pre:   Disk count is a valid disk to be moved.
   Post:  Moves count disks from start to finish using temp for temporary storage. */
void Move(int count, int start, int finish, int temp)
```

*Hanoi without tail recursion*

```
{
    int swap;                    /* temporary storage to swap towers     */
    while (count > 0) {
        Move(count - 1, start, temp, finish);
        printf("Move disk %d from %d to %d.\n", count, start, finish);
        count--;
        swap = start;
        start = temp;
        temp = swap;
    }
}
```

We would have been quite clever had we thought of this version of the function when we first looked at the problem, but now that we have discovered it via other considerations, we can give it a natural interpretation. Think of the two towers start and temp as in the same class: we wish to use them for intermediate storage as we slowly move all the disks onto finish. To move a stack of count disks onto finish, then, we must move all except the bottom to the other one of start, finish, then move the bottom one to finish, and repeat after interchanging start and temp, continuing to shuffle all except the bottom one between start and temp, and, at each pass, getting a new bottom one onto finish.

## 3.4.4 WHEN NOT TO USE RECURSION

### 1. Factorials

Consider the following two functions for calculating factorials. We have already seen the recursive one:

```
/* Factorial: recursive version.
    Pre:  n is a nonnegative integer.
    Post:  The function value is the factorial of n. */
int Factorial(int n)
{
    if (n == 0)
        return 1;
    else
        return n * Factorial(n – 1);
}
```

There is an almost equally simple iterative version:

```
/* Function: iterative version.
    Pre:  n is a nonnegative integer.
    Post:  The function value is the factorial of n. */
int Factorial(int n)
{
    int count, product;
    for (product = 1, count = 2;  count <= n;  count + +)
        product *= count;
    return product;
}
```

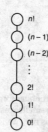

Which of these programs uses less storage space? At first glance, it might appear that the recursive one does, since it has no local variables, and the iterative program has two. But actually (see Figure 3.17), the recursive program will set up a stack and fill it with the $n$ numbers

$$n, \ n-1, \ n-2, \ \ldots, \ 2, \ 1$$

that are its calling parameters before each recursion and will then, as it works its way out of the recursion, multiply these numbers in the same order as does the second program. The progress of execution for the recursive function applied with $n = 5$ is as follows:

**Figure 3.17.**
**Recursion tree for**
**calculating**
**factorials**

$$
\begin{aligned}
\text{Factorial(5)} &= 5 * \text{Factorial(4)} \\
&= 5 * (4 * \text{Factorial(3)}) \\
&= 5 * (4 * (3 * \text{Factorial(2)})) \\
&= 5 * (4 * (3 * (2 * \text{Factorial(1)}))) \\
&= 5 * (4 * (3 * (2 * (1 * \text{Factorial(0)})))) \\
&= 5 * (4 * (3 * (2 * (1 * 1)))) \\
&= 5 * (4 * (3 * (2 * 1))) \\
&= 5 * (4 * (3 * 2)) \\
&= 5 * (4 * 6) \\
&= 5 * 24 \\
&= 120
\end{aligned}
$$

Thus the recursive program keeps more storage than the nonrecursive version, and it will take more time as well, since it must store and retrieve each number for the recursive call, as well as multiply all the numbers together.

### 2. Fibonacci Numbers

A far more wasteful example than factorials (that also appears as an apparently recommended program in some textbooks) is the computation of the *Fibonacci numbers*, which are defined by the recurrence relation

$$F_0 = 0,$$
$$F_1 = 1,$$
$$F_n = F_{n-1} + F_{n-2} \text{ for } n \geq 2.$$

The recursive program closely follows the definition:

```
/* Fibonacci: recursive version.
   Pre:   The parameter n is a nonnegative integer.
   Post:  The function returns the nth Fibonacci number. */
int Fibonacci(int n)
{
   if (n <= 0)
      return 0;
   else if (n == 1)
      return 1;
   else
      return Fibonacci(n - 1) + Fibonacci(n - 2);
}
```

In fact, this program is quite attractive, since it is of the divide-and-conquer form: Except for the initial cases, the answer is obtained by calculating two smaller cases of the same problem. As we shall see, however, in this example it is not "divide and conquer," but "divide and complicate."

To assess this algorithm, let us consider, as an example, the calculation of $F_7$, whose recursion tree is shown in Figure 3.18. The function will first have to obtain $F_6$ and $F_5$. To get $F_6$ requires $F_5$ and $F_4$, and so on. But after $F_5$ is calculated on the way to $F_6$, then it will be lost and unavailable when it is later needed to get $F_7$. Hence, as the recursion tree shows, the recursive program needlessly repeats the same calculations over and over. Further analysis appears as an exercise. It turns out that the amount of time used by the recursive function to calculate $F_n$ grows exponentially with $n$.

As with factorials, we can produce a simple iterative program by noting that we can start at 0 and keep only three variables, the current Fibonacci number and its two predecessors.

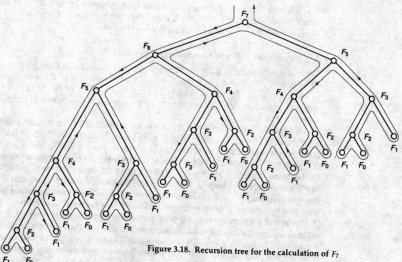

**Figure 3.18. Recursion tree for the calculation of $F_7$**

```
/* Fibonacci: iterative version.
   Pre:    The parameter n is a nonnegative integer.
   Post:   The function returns the nth Fibonacci number. */
int Fibonacci(int n)
{
    int i;
    int twoback;              /* second previous number, F_{i-2}   */
    int oneback;              /* previous number, F_{i-1}          */
    int current; .            /* current number, F_i               */
    if (n <= 0)
        return 0;
    else if (n ==  1)
        return 1;
    else {
        twoback = 0;
        oneback = 1;
        for (i = 2;  i <= n;  i++) {
            current = twoback + oneback;
            twoback = oneback;
            oneback = current;
        }
        return current;
    }
}
```

The iterative function obviously uses time that increases linearly in (that is, in direct proportion with) $n$, so that the time difference between this function and the exponential time of the recursive function will be vast.

### 3. Comparisons between Recursion and Iteration

What is fundamentally different between this last example and the proper uses of recursion? To answer this question, we shall again turn to the examination of recursion trees. It should already be clear that a study of the recursion tree will provide much useful information to help us decide when recursion should or should not be used.

*chain*

If a function makes only one recursive call to itself, then its recursion tree has a very simple form: It is a chain; that is, each vertex has only one child. This child corresponds to the single recursive call that occurs. Such a simple tree is easy to comprehend. For the factorial function, it is simply the list of requests to calculate the factorials from $(n - 1)!$ down to 1!. By reading the recursion tree from bottom to top instead of top to bottom, we immediately obtain the iterative program from the recursive one. When the tree does reduce to a chain, then transformation from recursion to iteration is often easy, and will likely save both space and time.

Note that a function's making only one recursive call to itself is not at all the same as having the recursive call made only one place in the function, since this place might be inside a loop. It is also possible to have two places that issue a recursive call (such as both the then and else clauses of an if statement) where only one call can actually occur.

*duplicate tasks*

The recursion tree for calculating Fibonacci numbers is not a chain, but contains a great many vertices signifying duplicate tasks. When a recursive program is run, it sets up a stack to use while traversing the tree, but if the results stored on the stack are discarded rather than kept in some other data structure for future use, then a great deal of duplication of work may occur, as in the recursive calculation of Fibonacci numbers.

*change data structures*

In such cases, it is preferable to substitute another data structure for the stack, one that allows references to locations other than the top. For the Fibonacci numbers, we needed only two additional temporary variables to hold the information required for calculating the current number.

*recursion removal*

Finally, by setting up an explicit stack, it is possible to take any recursive program and rearrange it into nonrecursive form. Appendix B describes methods for doing do. The resulting program, however, is almost always more complicated and harder to understand than is the recursive version. The only reason for translating a program to remove recursion is if you are forced to program in a language that does not support recursion, and fewer and fewer programs are written in such languages.

## 3.4.5 GUIDELINES AND CONCLUSIONS

In making a decision, then, about whether to write a particular algorithm in recursive or nonrecursive form, a good starting point is to consider the recursion tree.

- If the recursion tree has a simple form, the iterative version may be better.

- If the recursion tree involves duplicate tasks, then data structures other than stacks will be appropriate, and the need for recursion may disappear.

- If the recursion tree appears quite bushy, with little duplication of tasks, then recursion is likely the natural method.

*top-down design*

The stack used to resolve recursion can be regarded as a list of postponed obligations for the program. If this list can be easily constructed in advance, then iteration is probably better; if not, recursion may be. Recursion is something of a top-down approach to problem solving; it divides the problem into pieces or selects out one key step, postponing the rest. Iteration is more of a bottom-up approach; it begins with what is known and from this constructs the solution step by step.

*stacks or recursion*

It is always true that recursion can be replaced by iteration and stacks. It is also true, conversely (see the references for the proof), that any (iterative) program that manipulates a stack can be replaced by a recursive program with no stack. Thus the careful programmer should not only ask whether recursion should be removed, but should also ask, when a program involves stacks, whether the introduction of recursion might produce a more natural and understandable program that could lead to improvements in the approach and in the results.

**Exercises 3.4**

**E1.** In the recursive calculation of $F_n$, determine exactly how many times each smaller Fibonacci number will be calculated. From this, determine the order-of-magnitude time and space requirements of the recursive function. [You may find out either by setting up and solving a recurrence relation (top-down approach), or by finding the answer in simple cases and proving it more generally by mathematical induction (bottom-up approach).]

**E2.** The *greatest common divisor* (GCD) of two positive integers is the largest integer that divides both of them. Thus, for example, the GCD of 8 and 12 is 4, the GCD of 9 and 18 is 9, and the GCD of 16 and 25 is 1. **(a)** Write a recursive function GCD(x, y : integer) : integer that implements the *division algorithm*: If y = 0, then the GCD of x and y is x; otherwise the GCD of x and y is the same as the GCD of y and x % y. **(b)** Rewrite the function in iterative form.

**E3.** *Ackermann's function*, defined as follows, is a standard device to determine how well recursion is implemented on a computer.

$$A(0, n) = n + 1 \qquad \text{for } n \geq 0.$$
$$A(m, 0) = A(m - 1, 1) \qquad \text{for } m > 0.$$
$$A(m, n) = A(m - 1, A(m, n - 1)) \qquad \text{for } m > 0 \text{ and } n > 0.$$

**(a)** Calculate the following values:

$$A(0,0) \qquad A(0,9) \qquad A(1,8) \qquad A(2,2) \qquad A(2,0)$$
$$A(2,3) \qquad A(3,2) \qquad A(4,2) \qquad A(4,3) \qquad A(4,0)$$

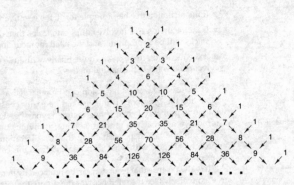

Figure 3.19. The top of Pascal's triangle of binomial coefficients

**E4.** The binomial coefficients may be defined by the following recurrence relation, which is the idea of *Pascal's triangle*. The top of Pascal's triangle is shown in Figure 3.19.

$$C(n,0) = 1 \quad \text{and} \quad C(n,n) = 1 \quad \text{for } n \geq 0.$$
$$C(n,k) = C(n-1,k) + C(n-1,k-1) \quad \text{for } n > k > 0.$$

(a) Write a recursive function to generate $C(n,k)$ by the foregoing formula.
(b) Draw the recursion tree for calculating $C(6,4)$.
(c) Use a square array, and write a nonrecursive program to generate Pascal's triangle in the lower left half of the array.
(d) Write a nonrecursive program that uses neither an array nor a stack to calculate $C(n,k)$ for arbitrary $n \geq k \geq 0$.
(e) Determine the approximate space and time requirements for each of the algorithms devised in parts (a), (c), and (d).

# Pointers and Pitfalls

1. Practice information hiding: Use functions to access your data structures, and keep these in packages separate from your application program.

2. Postpone decisions on the details of implementing your data structures as long as you can.

3. Stacks are among the simplest kind of data structures; use stacks when possible.

4. Avoid tricky ways of storing your data; tricks usually will not generalize to new situations.

5. Be sure to initialize your data structures.

6. In designing algorithms, always be careful about the extreme cases and handle them gracefully. Trace through your algorithm to determine what happens in extreme cases, particularly when a data structure is empty or full.

7. Recursion should be used freely in the initial design of algorithms. It is especially appropriate where the main step toward solution consists of reducing a problem to one or more smaller cases.

8. Study several simple examples to see whether recursion should be used and how it will work.

9. Attempt to formulate a method that will work more generally. Ask, "How can this problem be divided into parts?" or "How will the key step in the middle be done?"

10. Ask whether the remainder of the problem can be done in the same or a similar way, and modify your method if necessary so that it will be sufficiently general.

11. Find a stopping rule that will indicate that the problem or a suitable part of it is done.

12. Be very careful that your algorithm always terminates and handles trivial cases correctly.

13. The key tool for the analysis of recursive algorithms is the recursion tree. Draw the recursion tree for one or two simple examples appropriate to your problem.

14. The recursion tree should be studied to see whether the recursion is needlessly repeating work, or if the tree represents an efficient division of the work into pieces.

15. Recursive functions and iterative functions using stacks can accomplish exactly the same tasks. Consider carefully whether recursion or iteration will lead to a clearer program and give more insight into the problem.

16. Tail recursion may be removed if space considerations are important.

17. Recursion can always be translated into iteration, but the general rules will often produce a result that greatly obscures the structure of the program. Such obscurity should be tolerated only when the programming language makes it unavoidable, and even then it should be well documented.

18. Study your problem to see if it fits one of the standard paradigms for recursive algorithms, such as divide and conquer or backtracking.

19. Let the use of recursion fit the structure of the problem. When the conditions of the problem are thoroughly understood, the structure of the required algorithm will be easier to see.

20. Always be careful of the extreme cases. Be sure that your algorithm terminates gracefully when it reaches the end of its task.

21. Do as thorough error checking as possible. Be sure that every condition that a subprogram requires is stated in its preconditions, and, even so, defend your subprogram from as many violations of its preconditions as conveniently possible.

# Review Questions

1. What are the operations that can be done on a stack?
2. What are stack frames for subprograms? What do they show?
3. What are the advantages of writing the operations on a data structure as functions?

4. Define the term *divide and conquer*.

5. Name two different ways to implement recursion.
6. What is a *re-entrant* program?
7. How does the time requirement for a recursive function relate to its recursion tree?
8. How does the space requirement for a recursive function relate to its recursion tree?
9. What is *tail* recursion?
10. Describe the relationship between the shape of the recursion tree and the efficiency of the corresponding recursive algorithm.
11. What are the major phases of designing recursive algorithms?
12. What is *concurrency*?
13. What important kinds of information does the computer system need to keep while implementing a recursive function call?
14. Is the removal of tail recursion more important for saving time or for saving space?

15. Describe *backtracking* as a problem-solving method.
16. State the *pigeonhole* principle.

# References for Further Study

For many topics concerning data structures, such as stacks, the best source for additional information, historical notes, and mathematical analysis is the following series of books, which can be regarded almost like an encyclopædia for the aspects of computing science that they discuss:

*encyclopædic reference: KNUTH*

DONALD E. KNUTH, *The Art of Computer Programming*, published by Addison-Wesley, Reading, Mass.

Three volumes have appeared to date:

1. *Fundamental Algorithms*, second edition, 1973, 634 pages.
2. *Seminumerical Algorithms*, second edition, 1980, 700 pages.
3. *Sorting and Searching*, 1973, 722 pages.

In future chapters we shall often give references to this series of books, and for convenience we shall do so by specifying only the name KNUTH together with the volume and page numbers. The algorithms are written both in English and in an assembler language, where KNUTH calculates detailed counts of operations to compare various algorithms.

Two books giving thorough introductions to recursion, with many examples, and serving as excellent supplements to this book are:

ERIC S. ROBERTS, *Thinking Recursively*, John Wiley & Sons, New York, 1986, 179 pages.

J. S. ROHL, *Recursion via Pascal*, Cambridge University Press, 1984, 192 pages.

The Towers of Hanoi is quite well known and appears in many textbooks. A survey of related papers is

D. WOOD, "The Towers of Brahma and Hanoi revisited," *Journal of Recreational Math* 14 (1981–92), 17–24.

The proof that stacks may be eliminated by the introduction of recursion appears in

S. BROWN, D. GRIES and T. SZYMANSKI, "Program schemes with pushdown stores," *SIAM Journal on Computing* 1 (1972), 242–268.

Our treatment of the eight-queens problem especially follows that given in

N. WIRTH, *Algorithms + Data Structures = Programs*, Prentice-Hall, Englewood Cliffs, N.J., 1976, pp. 143–147.

This book by WIRTH also contains solutions of the Knight's Tour problem (pp. 137–142), as well as a chapter (pp. 280–349) on compiling and parsing.

Many other applications of recursion appear in books such as

E. HOROWITZ and S. SAHNI, *Fundamentals of Computer Algorithms*, Computer Science Press, 1978, 626 pages.

The general theory of recursion forms a research topic. A readable presentation from a theoretical approach is

R. S. BIRD, *Programs and Machines*, John Wiley, New York, 1976.

# 4

# Queues and Linked Lists

A QUEUE is a data structure modeled
after a line of people waiting to be
served. Along with stacks, queues are one
of the simplest kinds of data structures.
This chapter develops properties of
queues, studies how they are applied, and
examines different implementations. In
the process, we shall develop the ideas of
dynamic memory and linked lists and their
implementation in C.

# 4.1 Definitions

In ordinary English, a queue is defined as a waiting line, like a line of people waiting to purchase tickets, where the first person in line is the first person served. For computer applications, we similarly define a *queue* to be a list in which all additions to the list are made at one end, and all deletions from the list are made at the other end. Queues are also called *first-in, first-out lists*, or *FIFO* for short. See Figure 4.1.

**Figure 4.1. A queue**

*applications*

Applications of queues are, if anything, even more common than are applications of stacks, since in performing tasks by computer, as in all parts of life, it is so often necessary to wait one's turn before having access to something. Within a computer system there may be queues of tasks waiting for the printer, for access to disk storage, or even, in a time-sharing system, for use of the CPU. Within a single program, there may be multiple requests to be kept in a queue, or one task may create other tasks, which must be done in turn by keeping them in a queue.

*front and rear*

The entry in a queue ready to be served, that is, the first entry that will be removed from the queue, we call the *front* of the queue (or, sometimes, the *head* of the queue). Similarly, the last entry in the queue, that is, the one most recently added, we call the *rear* (or the *tail*) of the queue.

*operations*

To complete the definition of a queue, we must specify all the operations that it permits. We shall do so by listing the function name for each operation, together with the preconditions and postconditions that complete its specifications. As you read these specifications, you should note the similarity with the corresponding operations for a stack.

The first step we must perform in working with any queue is to use the function CreateQueue to initialize it for further use:

---

void CreateQueue(Queue *q);

*precondition*:   None.

*postcondition*:  The queue q has been initialized to be empty.

---

Next come the operations for checking the status of a queue.

---

Boolean QueueEmpty(Queue *q);

*precondition*:   The queue q has been created.

*postcondition*:  The function returns true or false according as queue q is empty or not.

---

Boolean QueueFull(Queue *q);

*precondition*:   The queue q has been created.

*postcondition*:  The function returns true or false according as queue q is full or not.

---

The declarations for the fundamental operations on a queue come next.

---

void Append(QueueEntry x, Queue *q);

*precondition*:   The queue q has been created and is not full.

*postcondition*:  The entry x has been stored in the queue as its last entry.

---

void Serve(QueueEntry *x, Queue *q);

*precondition*:   The queue q has been created and is not empty.

*postcondition*:  The first entry in the queue has been removed and returned as the value of x.

---

The names *Append* and *Serve* are used for the fundamental operations on a queue to indicate clearly what actions are performed and to avoid confusion with the terms we shall use for other data types. Other names, however, are very frequently used for these operations, terms such as *Insert* and *Delete* or the coined words *Enqueue* and *Dequeue*.

Note from the preconditions that it is an error to attempt to append an entry onto a full queue or to serve an entry from an empty queue. If we write the functions Append and Serve carefully, then they should return error messages when they are used incorrectly. The declarations, however, do not guarantee that the functions will catch the errors, and, if they do not, then they may produce spurious and unpredictable results. Hence the careful programmer should always make sure, whenever invoking a subprogram, that its preconditions are guaranteed to be satisfied.

There remain four more queue operations that are sometimes useful.

---

int QueueSize(Queue *q);

*precondition*:   The queue q has been created.

*postcondition*:   The function returns the number of entries in the queue q.

---

void ClearQueue(Queue *q);

*precondition*:   The queue q has previously been created.

*postcondition*:   All entries have been removed from q and it is now empty.

---

void QueueFront(QueueEntry *x, Queue *q);

*precondition*:   The queue q has been created and is not empty.

*postcondition*:   The variable x is a copy of the first entry in q; the queue q remains unchanged.

---

The final operation is not part of the strict definition of a queue, but it remains quite useful for debugging and demonstration.

---

void TraverseQueue(Queue *q, void (*Visit)(QueueEntry x));

*precondition*:   The queue q has been created.

*postcondition*:   The function Visit(QueueEntry x) has been performed for each entry in the queue, beginning with the entry at the front and proceeding toward the rear of q.

---

**Exercises 4.1**    E1. Suppose that q is a pointer to a queue that holds characters and that x, y, z are character variables. Show the contents of the queue at each step of the following code segments.

(a) CreateQueue(q);
    Append('a', q);
    Serve( &x, q);
    Append('b', q);
    Serve( &y, q);
    Append('c', q);
    Append('d', q);
    Serve( &z, q);

(b) CreateQueue(q);
    Append('a', q);
    Append('b', q);
    Serve( &x, q);
    Append('c', q);
    Append(x, q);
    Serve( &y, q);
    Serve( &z, q);

(c) CreateQueue(q);
    Append('a', q);
    x = 'b';
    Append('x', q);
    Serve( &y, q);
    Append(x, q);
    Serve( &z, q);
    Append(y, q);

*accounting*

E2. Suppose that you are a financier and purchase 100 shares of stock in Company $X$ in each of January, April, and September and sell 100 shares in each of June and November. The prices per share in these months were

| | Jan | Apr | Jun | Sep | Nov |
|---|---|---|---|---|---|
| | $10 | $30 | $20 | $50 | $30 |

Determine the total amount of your capital gain or loss using (a) FIFO (first-in, first-out) accounting and (b) LIFO (last-in, first-out) accounting (that is, assuming that you keep your stock certificates in (a) a queue or (b) a stack). The 100 shares you still own at the end of the year do not enter the calculation.

E3. Use the functions developed in the text to write other functions that will do the following tasks. In writing each function be sure to check for empty and full structures as appropriate.

(a) Move all the entries from a stack into a queue.

(b) Move all the entries from a queue onto a stack.

(c) Empty one stack onto the top of another stack in such a way that the entries that were in the first stack keep the same relative order.

(d) Empty one stack onto the top of another stack in such a way that the entries that were in the first stack are in the reverse of their original order.

(e) Start with a queue and an empty stack, and use the stack to reverse the order of all the entries in the queue.

(f) Start with a stack and an empty queue, and use the queue to reverse the order of all the entries in the stack.

## 4.2 Implementations of Queues

Now that we have considered how queues are defined and the operations they admit, let us change our point of view and consider how queues can be implemented with computer storage and C functions.

### 1. The Physical Model

As we did for stacks, we can create a queue in computer storage easily by setting up an ordinary array to hold the entries. Now, however, we must keep track of both the front and the rear of the queue. One method would be to keep the front of the queue always in the first location of the array. Then an entry could be appended to the queue simply by increasing the counter showing the rear, in exactly the same way as we added an entry to a stack. To delete an entry from the queue, however, would be very expensive indeed, since after the first entry was served, all the remaining entries would need to be moved one position up the queue to fill in the vacancy. With a long queue, this process would be prohibitively slow. Although this method of storage closely models a queue of people waiting to be served, it is a poor choice for use in computers.

### 2. Linear Implementation

For efficient processing of queues, we shall therefore need two indices so that we can keep track of both the front and the rear of the queue without moving any entries. To append an entry to the queue, we simply increase the rear by one and put the entry in that position. To serve an entry, we take it from the position at the front and then increase the front by one. This method, however, still has a major defect. Both the front and rear indices are increased but never decreased. Even if there are never more than two entries in the queue, an unbounded amount of storage will be needed for the queue if the sequence of operations is

*defect*

Append, Append, Serve, Append, Serve, Append, ....

The problem, of course, is that, as the queue moves down the array, the storage space at the beginning of the array is discarded and never used again. Perhaps the queue can be likened to a snake crawling through storage. Sometimes the snake is longer, sometimes shorter, but if it always keeps crawling in a straight line, then it will soon reach the end of the storage space.

*advantage*

Note, however, that for applications where the queue is regularly emptied (such as when a series of requests is allowed to build up to a certain point, and then a task is initiated that clears all the requests before returning), at a time when the queue is empty, the front and rear can both be reset to the beginning of the array, and the simple scheme of using two indices and straight-line storage becomes a very efficient implementation.

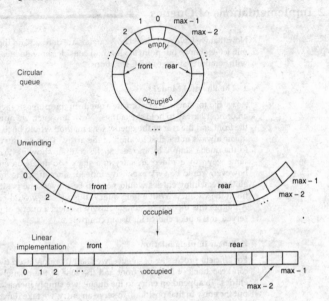

Figure 4.2. Queue in a circular array

### 3. Circular Arrays

In concept, we can overcome the inefficient use of space simply by thinking of the array as a circle rather than a straight line. See Figure 4.2. In this way, as entries are added and removed from the queue, the head will continually chase the tail around the array, so that the snake can keep crawling indefinitely but stay in a confined circuit. At different times, the queue will occupy different parts of the array, but we never need worry about running out of space unless the array is fully occupied, in which case we truly have overflow.

### 4. Implementation of Circular Arrays

Our next problem is to implement a circular array as an ordinary linear (that is, straight-line) array. To do so, we think of the positions around the circle as numbered from 0 to MAX − 1, where MAX is the total number of entries in the circular array, and to implement the circular array, we use the same-numbered entries of a linear array. Then moving the indices is just the same as doing modular arithmetic:

*modular arithmetic*    When we increase an index past MAX − 1, we start over again at 0. This is like doing arithmetic on a circular clock face; the hours are numbered from 1 to 12, and if we add four hours to ten o'clock, we obtain two o'clock.

Perhaps a good human analogy of this linear representation is that of a priest serving communion to people kneeling at the front of a church. The communicants do not move until the priest comes by and serves them. When the priest reaches the end of the row, he returns to the beginning and starts again, since by this time a new row of people have come forward.

### 5. Circular Arrays in C

In C, we can increase an index i by 1 in a circular array by writing

```
if (i >= MAX – 1)
    i = 0;
else
    i++;
```

or even more easily (but perhaps less efficiently at run time since it uses division) by using the % operator:

```
i = (i + 1) % MAX;
```

### 6. Boundary Conditions

Before writing formal algorithms to add to and delete from a queue, let us consider the boundary conditions, that is, the indicators that a queue is empty or full. If there is exactly one entry in the queue, then the front index will equal the rear index. When this one entry is removed, then the front will be increased by 1, so that an empty queue is indicated when the rear is one position before the front. Now suppose that the queue is nearly full. Then the rear will have moved well away from the front, all the way around the circle, and when the array is full the rear will be exactly one position before the front. Thus we have another difficulty:

*empty or full?*

The front and rear indices are in exactly the same relative positions for an empty queue and for a full queue! There is no way, by looking at the indices alone, to tell a full queue from an empty one. This situation is illustrated in Figure 4.3.

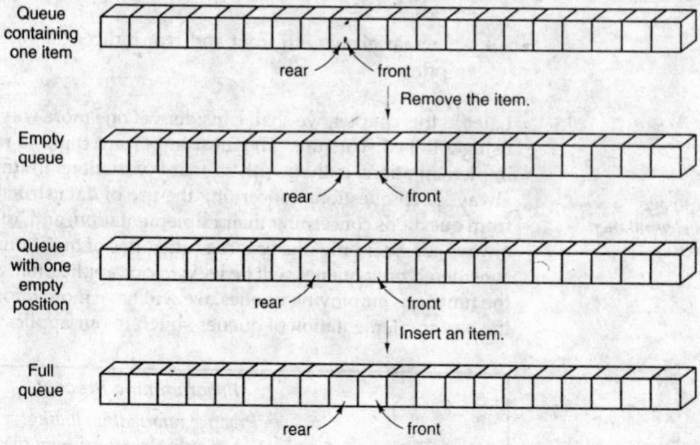

Figure 4.3. Empty and full queues

### 7. Possible Solutions

*1. empty position*

There are at least three essentially different ways to resolve this problem. One is to insist on leaving one empty position in the array, so that the queue is considered full when the rear index has moved within two positions of the front. A second method is to introduce a new variable. This can be a Boolean variable that will be used when the rear comes just before the front to indicate whether the queue is full or not (a Boolean variable to check emptiness would be just as good) or an integer variable that counts the number of entries in the queue. The third method is to set one or both of the indices to some value(s) that would otherwise never occur in order to indicate an empty (or full) queue. If, for example, the array entries are indexed from 0 to MAX − 1, then an empty queue could be indicated by setting the rear index to − 1.

*2. flag*

*3. special values*

### 8. Summary of Implementations

To summarize the discussion of queues, let us list all the methods we have discussed for implementing queues.

- The physical model: a linear array with the front always in the first position and all entries moved up the array whenever the front is deleted. This is generally a poor method for use in computers.

- A linear array with two indices always increasing. This is a good method if the queue can be emptied all at once.

- A circular array with front and rear indices and one position left vacant.

- A circular array with front and rear indices and a Boolean variable to indicate fullness (or emptiness).

- A circular array with front and rear indices and an integer variable counting entries.

- A circular array with front and rear indices taking special values to indicate emptiness.

*postpone implementation decisions*

Later in this chapter, we shall consider yet one more way to implement queues, by using a linked structure. The most important thing to remember from this list of implementations is that, with so many variations in implementation, we should always keep questions concerning the use of data structures like queues separate from questions concerning their implementation; and, in programming we should always consider only one of these categories of questions at a time. After we have considered how queues will be used in our application, and after we have written the functions employing queues, we will have more information to help us choose the best implementation of queues suited to our application.

---

**Programming Precept**

*Practice information hiding:*
*Separate the application of data structures from their implementation.*

---

# 4.3 Circular Queues in C

Next let us write C functions for implementation of a queue. It is clear from the last section that a great many implementations are possible, some of which are but slight variations on others. Let us therefore concentrate on only one implementation, leaving the others as exercises. The implementation in a circular array which uses a counter to keep track of the number of entries in the queue both illustrates techniques for handling circular arrays and simplifies the programming of some of the operations. Let us therefore work only with this implementation.

We shall take the queue as stored in an array indexed with the range

$$0 \quad \text{to} \quad \text{MAXQUEUE} - 1$$

*type queue*

and containing entries of a type QueueEntry. The variables front and rear will point to appropriate positions in the array. The variable count is used to keep track of the number of entries in the queue. The file queue.h contains the structure declaration for a queue and the prototypes associated with queues:

```
typedef struct queue {
    int count;
    int front;
    int rear;
    QueueEntry entry[MAXQUEUE];
} Queue;
void Append(QueueEntry, Queue *);
void CreateQueue(Queue *);
void Serve(QueueEntry *, Queue *);
int QueueSize(Queue *);
Boolean QueueEmpty(Queue *);
Boolean QueueFull(Queue *);
```

The definitions for MAXQUEUE and QueueEntry are application-program dependent. For example, for our test case they are

```
#define MAXQUEUE 3 /* small value for testing */
typedef char QueueEntry;
```

The first function we need will initialize the queue to be empty.

```
/* CreateQueue: create the queue.
Pre:    None.
Post:   The queue q has been initialized to be empty. */
void CreateQueue(Queue *q)
{
    q->count = 0;
    q->front = 0;
    q->rear = -1;
}
```

The functions for adding to and deleting from a queue follow our preceding discussion closely. Notice that we guard against a violation of the preconditions and invoke the Error function when necessary.

```
/* Append: append an entry to the queue.
    Pre:   The queue q has been created and is not full.
    Post:  The entry x has been stored in the queue as its last entry.
    Uses: QueueFull, Error. */
void Append(QueueEntry x, Queue *q)
{
    if (QueueFull(q))
        Error("Cannot append an entry to a full queue.");
    else {
        q->count++;
        q->rear = (q->rear + 1) % MAXQUEUE;
        q->entry[q->rear] = x;
    }
}
```

```
/* Serve: remove the first entry in the queue.
    Pre:   The queue q has been created and is not empty.
    Post:  The first entry in the queue has been removed and returned as the value of x.
    Uses: QueueEmpty, Error. */
void Serve(QueueEntry *x, Queue *q)
{
    if (QueueEmpty(q))
        Error("Cannot serve from an empty queue.");
    else {
        q->count--;
        *x = q->entry[q->front];
        q->front = (q->front + 1) % MAXQUEUE;
    }
}
```

The three functions concerning the size of the queue are all easy to write in this implementation.

```
/* QueueSize: return the number of entries in the queue.
    Pre:   The queue q has been created.
    Post:  The function returns the number of entries in the queue q. */
int QueueSize(Queue *q)
{
    return q->count;
}
```

```
/* QueueEmpty: returns non-zero if the queue is empty.
   Pre:   The queue q has been created.
   Post:  The function returns non-zero if the queue q is empty, zero otherwise. */
Boolean QueueEmpty(Queue *q)
{
    return q->count <= 0;
}


/* QueueFull: returns non-zero if the queue is full.
   Pre:   The queue q has been created.
   Post:  The function returns non-zero if the queue is full, zero otherwise. */
Boolean QueueFull(Queue *q)
{
    return q->count >= MAXQUEUE;
}
```

Note that the queue is specified as a pointer in each of these functions, even though it is not modified by any of them. This is a concession to efficiency that saves the time required to make a new local copy of the entire queue each time one of the functions is evaluated.

The functions ClearQueue, QueueFront, and TraverseQueue will be left as exercises.

---

**Exercises 4.3**

**E1.** Write the remaining functions for queues as implemented in this section.

    **(a)** ClearQueue      **(b)** QueueFront      **(c)** TraverseQueue

**E2.** Write the functions needed for the implementation of queues in a linear array when it can be assumed that the queue can be emptied when necessary. Write a function Append that will add an entry if there is room and, if not, will call another function (ServeAll) that will empty the queue. While writing this second function, you may assume the existence of an auxiliary function Service(QueueEntry x) that will process a single entry that you have just removed from the queue.

**E3.** Write C functions to implement queues by the simple but slow method of keeping the front of the queue always in the first position of a linear array.

**E4.** Write C functions to implement queues in a linear array with two indices front and rear, such that, when rear reaches the end of the array, all the entries are moved to the front positions of the array.

**E5.** Write the functions for processing a queue, where the implementation does not keep a count of the entries in the queue but instead uses the special conditions

$$rear = -1 \quad \text{and} \quad front = 0$$

to indicate an empty queue.

(a) CreateQueue    (d) QueueFull     (g) Serve
(b) ClearQueue     (e) QueueSize     (h) QueueFront
(c) QueueEmpty     (f) Append        (i) TraverseQueue

**E6.** Rewrite the C functions for queue processing from the text, using a Boolean variable Full instead of a counter of entries in the queue.

**E7.** Write C functions to implement queues in a circular array with one unused entry in the array. That is, we consider that the array is full when the rear is two positions before the front; when the rear is one position before, it will always indicate an empty queue.

*deque*    The word ***deque*** (pronounced either "deck" or "DQ") is a shortened form of ***double-ended queue*** and denotes a list in which entries can be added or deleted from either the first or the last position of the list, but no changes can be made elsewhere in the list. Thus a deque is a generalization of both a stack and a queue.

**E8.** Write the functions needed to implement a deque in a linear array.

**E9.** Write the functions needed to implement a deque in a circular array.

**E10.** Is it more appropriate to implement a deque in a linear array or in a circular array? Why?

**E11.** Write a menu-driven demonstration program for manipulating a deque of characters, similar to the stack demonstration program in Exercise E1(c) of Section 3.1.

**E12.** Note from Figure 3.5 that a stack can be represented pictorially as a spur track on a straight railway line. A queue can, of course, be represented simply as a straight track. Devise and draw a railway switching network that will represent a deque. The network should have only one entrance and one exit.

**E13.** Suppose that data items numbered 1, 2, 3, 4, 5, 6 come in the input stream in this order. That is, 1 comes first, then 2, and so on. By using (1) a queue and (2) a deque, which of the following rearrangements can be obtained in the output order? The entries also leave the deque in left-to-right order.

(a) 1 2 3 4 5 6    (b) 2 4 3 6 5 1    (c) 1 5 2 4 3 6
(d) 4 2 1 3 5 6    (e) 1 2 6 4 5 3    (f) 5 2 6 3 4 1

**Programming Projects 4.3**

**P1.** Write a demonstration program for manipulating queues. This program should have a form similar to that written to demonstrate stacks in Exercise E1(c) of Section 3.1 or simple lists in Section 2.3.3. The entries in your queue should be characters. Your demonstration program should write a menu from which the user can select any of the queue operations. After your program does the requested operation, it should inform the user of the result and ask for the next request. When the user wishes to append a character onto the queue, your program will need to ask what character to use.

**P2.** Write a function that will read one line of input from the terminal. The input is supposed to consist of two parts separated by a colon ':'. As its result, your function should produce a single character as follows:

| | |
|---|---|
| N | No colon on the line. |
| L | The left part (before the colon) is longer than the right. |
| R | The right part (after the colon) is longer than the left. |
| D | The left and right parts have the same length but are different. |
| S | The left and right parts are exactly the same. |

*Examples*:

| Input | Output |
|---|---|
| Sample Sample | N |
| Short:Long | L |
| Sample:Sample | S |

Use a queue to keep track of the left part of the line while reading the right part.

# 4.4 Application of Queues: Simulation

## 4.4.1 INTRODUCTION

*Simulation* is the use of one system to imitate the behavior of another system. Simulations are often used when it would be too expensive or dangerous to experiment with the real system. There are physical simulations, such as wind tunnels used to experiment with designs for car bodies and flight simulators used to train airline pilots. Mathematical simulations are systems of equations used to describe some system, and computer simulations use the steps of a program to imitate the behavior of the system under study.

*computer simulation*  In a computer simulation, the objects being studied are usually represented as data, often as data structures like records whose entries describe the properties of the objects. Actions being studied are represented as operations on the data, and the rules describing these actions are translated into computer algorithms. By changing the values of the data or by modifying these algorithms, we can observe the changes in the computer simulation, and then, we can draw worthwhile inferences concerning the behavior of the actual system.

While one object in a system is involved in some action, other objects and actions will often need to be kept waiting. Hence queues are important data structures for use in computer simulations. We shall study one of the most common and useful kinds of computer simulations, one that concentrates on queues as its basic data structure. These simulations imitate the behavior of systems (often, in fact, called *queueing systems*) in which there are queues of objects waiting to be served by various processes.

### 4.4.2 SIMULATION OF AN AIRPORT

As a specific example, let us consider a small but busy airport with only one runway (see Figure 4.4). In each unit of time, one plane can land or one plane can take off, but not both. Planes arrive ready to land or to take off at random times, so at any given unit of time, the runway may be idle or a plane may be landing or taking off, and there may be several planes waiting either to land or take off. We therefore

*rules*

need two queues, called landing and takeoff, to hold these planes. It is better to keep a plane waiting on the ground than in the air, so a small airport allows a plane to take off only if there are no planes waiting to land. Hence, after receiving requests from new planes to land or take off, our simulation will first service the head of the queue of planes waiting to land, and only if the landing queue is empty will it allow a plane to take off. We shall wish to run the simulation through many units of time, and, therefore, we embed the main action of the program in a loop that runs for curtime (denoting *current time*) from 1 to a variable endtime. With this notation, we can write an outline of the main program.

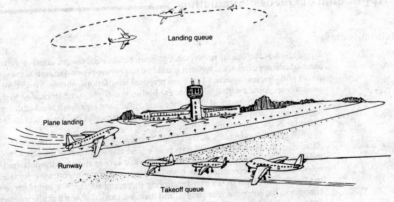

Figure 4.4. An airport

```
#include "common.h"
#include "simdefs.h"

/* simulation of an airport */
/* This is an outline only; not ready to compile. */
int main(void)
{
    Queue landing, takeoff;
    Queue *pl = &landing;
    Queue *pt = &takeoff;
    Plane plane;

    int curtime;            /* current time unit                 */
    int endtime;            /* total number of time units to run */
    int i;                  /* loop control variable             */
    CreateQueue(pl);        /* Initialize landing queue.         */
    CreateQueue(pt);        /* Initialize takeoff queue.         */
    for (curtime = 1;  curtime <= endtime;  curtime++) {
        for (i = 1;  i <= RandomNumber();  i++) {  /* landing queue   */
            NewPlane( &plane);
            if (QueueFull(pl))
                Refuse(plane);     /* Refuse plane if full.     */
            else
                Append(plane, pl);   /* Add to landing queue.   */
        }
        for (i = 1;  i <= RandomNumber();  i++) {  /* takeoff queue   */
            NewPlane( &plane);
            if (QueueFull(pt))
                Refuse(plane);
            else
                Append(plane, pt);
        }
        if (!QueueEmpty(pl)) {  /* Bring plane to land.          */
            Serve( &plane, pl);
            Land(plane);
        } else if (!QueueEmpty(pt)) {  /* Allow plane take off.  */
            Serve( &plane, pt);
            Fly(plane);
        } else
            Idle();
    }
    Conclude();
    return 0;
}
```

*first outline* (margin)

*new plane ready to land* (margin)

*new plane ready to take off* (margin)

*plane landing* (margin)

*plane taking off* (margin)

*idle runway* (margin)

### 4.4.3 THE MAIN PROGRAM

The preceding outline shows the use of queues in the airport simulation, but we need more detail to keep track of all the interesting statistics for the problem, such as the number of planes processed, the average time spent waiting, and the number of planes (if any) refused service. These details are reflected in the declarations of symbolic constants, typedefs, and variables to be included in the main program. We shall then need to write the functions to specify how this information is processed.

*declarations*

```
#define MAXQUEUE 5              /* use a small value for testing              */

typedef enum action { ARRIVE, DEPART } Action;

typedef struct plane {
    int id;                     /* identification number of airplane          */
    int tm;                     /* time of arrival in queue                   */
} Plane;
typedef Plane QueueEntry;

typedef struct queue {
    int count;                  /* number of airplanes in the queue           */
    int front;                  /* front of the queue                         */
    int rear;                   /* rear of the queue                          */
    QueueEntry entry[MAXQUEUE];
} Queue;
```

The version of the main program in C differs little from the preceding outline except for the inclusion of the many parameters used to update all the variables just declared:

```
/* simulation of an airport */

int main(void)
{
    Queue landing, takeoff;
    Queue *pl = &landing;
    Queue *pt = &takeoff;
    Plane plane;

    int curtime;                /* current time; one unit = time for take off or landing */
    int endtime;                /* total number of time units to run          */
    double expectarrive;        /* number of planes arriving in one unit      */
    double expectdepart;        /* number of planes newly ready to take off   */
```

```
                    int i;                    /* loop control variable                         */
                    int idletime;             /* number of units when runway is idle           */
                    int landwait;             /* total waiting time for planes landed          */
                    int nland;                /* number of planes landed                       */
                    int nplanes;              /* number of planes processed so far             */
                    int nrefuse;              /* number of planes refused use of airport       */
                    int ntakeoff;             /* number of planes taken off                    */
                    int pri;                  /* pseudo-random integer                         */
                    int takeoffwait;          /* total waiting time for take off               */
initialize          CreateQueue(pl);
                    CreateQueue(pt);
                    nplanes = nland = ntakeoff = nrefuse = 0;
                    landwait = takeoffwait = idletime = 0;
                    Start( &endtime, &expectarrive, &expectdepart);
                    for (curtime = 1;  curtime <= endtime;  curtime++) {
new plane(s) ready to     pri = PoissonRandom(expectarrive);
land                      for (i = 1;  i <= pri;  i++) { /* Add to landing queue.          */
                              NewPlane( &plane, &nplanes, curtime, ARRIVE);
                              if (QueueFull(pl))
                                  Refuse(plane, &nrefuse, ARRIVE);
                              else
                                  Append(plane, pl);
                          }
new plane(s) ready to     pri = PoissonRandom(expectdepart);
take off                  for (i = 1;  i <= pri;  i++) { /* Add to takeoff queue.          */
                              NewPlane( &plane, &nplanes, curtime, DEPART);
                              if (QueueFull(pt))
                                  Refuse(plane, &nrefuse, DEPART);
                              else
                                  Append(plane, pt);
                          }
plane landing             if (!QueueEmpty(pl)) { /* Bring plane to land.                   */
                              Serve( &plane, pl);
                              Land(plane, curtime, &nland, &landwait);
plane taking off          } else if (!QueueEmpty(pt)) { /* Allow plane to take off.         */
                              Serve( &plane, pt);
                              Fly(plane, curtime, &ntakeoff, &takeoffwait);
runway idle               } else
                              Idle(curtime, &idletime);
                    }
finish simulation   Conclude(nplanes, nland, ntakeoff, nrefuse, landwait,
                            takeoffwait, idletime, endtime, pt, pl);
                    return 0;
                }
```

### 4.4.4 STEPS OF THE SIMULATION

The actions of the functions for doing the steps of the simulation are generally straightforward, so we proceed to write each in turn, with comments only as needed for clarity.

#### 1. Initialization

```
#include "common.h"
#include "simdefs.h"

/* Start: print messages and initialize the parameters.
   Pre:  None.
   Post: Asks user for responses and initializes all variables specified as parameters.
   Uses: UserSaysYes. */
void Start(int *endtime, double *expectarrive, double *expectdepart)
{
    Boolean ok;
    printf("This program simulates an airport with only one runway.\n"
           "One plane can land or depart in each unit of time.\n"
           "Up to %d planes can be waiting to land or take off "
           "at any time.\n", MAXQUEUE);
    printf("How many units of time will the simulation run? ");
    scanf("%d", endtime);
    Randomize();                   /* Initialize random number generation.        */
    do {
        printf("Expected number of arrivals per unit time "
               "(real number)? ");
        scanf("%lf", expectarrive);
        printf("Expected number of departures per unit time? ");
        scanf("%lf", expectdepart);
        if (*expectarrive < 0.0 || *expectdepart < 0.0) {
            printf("These numbers must be nonnegative.\n");
            ok = FALSE;
        } else if (*expectarrive + *expectdepart > 1.0) {
            printf("The airport will become saturated. "
                   "Read new numbers? ");
            ok = !UserSaysYes();   /* If user says yes, repeat loop.               */
        } else
            ok = TRUE;
    } while (ok == FALSE);
}
```

*instruct user*

*input parameter*

*error checking*

#### 2. Accepting a New Plane

```
/* NewPlane: make a new record for a plane, update nplanes.
   Pre:  None.
   Post: Makes a new structure for a plane and updates nplanes. */
```

```
void NewPlane(Plane *p, int *nplanes, int curtime, Action kind)
{
    (*nplanes)++;
    p->id = *nplanes;
    p->tm = curtime;
    switch(kind) {
    case ARRIVE :
        printf("    Plane %3d ready to land.\n", *nplanes);
        break;
    case DEPART :
        printf("    Plane %3d ready to take off.\n", *nplanes);
        break;
    }
}
```

## 3. Handling a Full Queue

```
/* Refuse: processes a plane when the queue is full.
   Pre:  None.
   Post: Processes a plane wanting to use runway, but the queue is full. */
void Refuse(Plane p, int *nrefuse, Action kind)
{
    switch(kind) {
    case ARRIVE :
        printf("    Plane %3d directed to another airport.\n", p.id);
        break;
    case DEPART :
        printf("    Plane %3d told to try later.\n", p.id);
        break;
    }
    (*nrefuse)++;
}
```

## 4. Processing an Arriving Plane

```
/* Land: process a plane that is actually landing.
   Pre:  None.
   Post: Processes a plane p that is actually landing. */
void Land(Plane p, int curtime, int *nland, int *landwait)
{
    int wait;
    wait = curtime - p.tm;
    printf("%3d : Plane %3d landed; in queue %d units.\n",
           curtime, p.id, wait);
    (*nland)++;
    *landwait += wait;
}
```

### 5. Processing a Departing Plane

```
/* Fly: process a plane that is actually taking off.
    Pre:  None.
    Post: Processes a plane p that is actually taking off. */
void Fly(Plane p, int curtime, int *ntakeoff, int *takeoffwait)
{
    int wait;
    wait = curtime - p.tm;
    printf("%3d : Plane %3d took off; in queue %d units.\n",
            curtime, p.id, wait);
    (*ntakeoff)++;
    *takeoffwait += wait;
}
```

### 6. Marking an Idle Time Unit

```
/* Idle: updates variables for idle runway.
    Pre:  None.
    Post: Updates variables for a time unit when the runway is idle. */
void Idle(int curtime, int *idletime)
{
    printf("%3d : Runway is idle.\n", curtime);
    (*idletime)++;
}
```

### 7. Finishing the Simulation

```
/* Conclude: write out statistics and conclude simulation.
    Pre:  None.
    Post: Writes out all the statistics and concludes the simulation. */
void Conclude(int nplanes, int nland, int ntakeoff,
              int nrefuse, int landwait, int takeoffwait,
              int idletime, int endtime,
              Queue *pt, Queue *pl)
{
    printf("Simulation has concluded after %d units.\n", endtime);
    printf("Total number of planes processed:   %3d\n", nplanes);
    printf("  Number of planes landed:          %3d\n", nland);
    printf("  Number of planes taken off:       %3d\n", ntakeoff);
    printf("  Number of planes refused use:     %3d\n", nrefuse);
    printf("  Number left ready to land:        %3d\n", QueueSize(pl));
    printf("  Number left ready to take off:    %3d\n", QueueSize(pt));
```

```
if (endtime > 0)
    printf("   Percentage of time runway idle:   %6.2f\n",
        ((double) idletime/endtime) * 100.0);
if (nland > 0)
    printf("   Average wait time to land:        %6.2f\n",
        (double) landwait/nland);
if (ntakeoff > 0)
    printf("   Average wait time to take off:    %6.2f\n",
        (double) takeoffwait/ntakeoff);
}
```

## 4.4.5 Pseudo-Random Numbers

A key step in our simulation is to decide, at each time unit, how many new planes become ready to land or take off. Although there are many ways in which these decisions can be made, one of the most interesting and useful is to make a random decision. When the program is run repeatedly with random decisions, the results will differ from run to run, and with sufficient experimentation, the simulation may display a range of behavior not unlike that of the actual system being studied.

The function RandomNumber in the outline of the airport simulation stands for a random number of planes arriving ready to land or ready to take off in a particular time unit.

*system random number generator*

We use the ANSI C library functions srand and rand to implement our random number generator.

The idea is to start with one number and apply a series of arithmetic operations that will produce another number with no obvious connection to the first. Hence the numbers we produce are not truly random at all, as each one depends in a definite way on its predecessor, and we should more properly speak of *pseudorandom* numbers. The number with which we begin a sequence of pseudorandom numbers is called the *seed* for the sequence.

*seed for pseudorandom numbers*

If we begin the simulation with the same value each time the program is run, then the whole sequence of pseudorandom numbers will be exactly the same, so we normally begin by setting the starting point for the pseudorandom integers to some random value, for example, the time of day:

```
/* Randomize: set starting point for pseudorandom integers. */
void Randomize(void)
{
    srand((unsigned int) (time(NULL) % 10000));
}
```

The ANSI C function srand takes one argument as the seed for a new sequence of pseudorandom numbers, and then the function rand is used to determine succeeding pseudorandom numbers in the sequence. The function prototypes for srand and rand (which follows) appear in stdlib.h. The function time returns the number of seconds elapsed since 00:00:00 GMT, January 1, 1970. The expression time(NULL) % 10000 produces a number between 0 and 9999—the number of seconds elapsed modulo 10000. This number provides a different starting point for srand each time it is run.

*uniform distribution*

We can then use the ANSI C function rand for producing each pseudorandom number from its predecessor. The function rand produces as its result an integer between 0 and INT_MAX. (Consult the file limits.h to determine the value of INT_MAX on your system.) Since all integers in this range are equally likely, the distribution of numbers is called a *uniform distribution*.

Several different kinds of random numbers are useful for different applications. For the airport simulation, we need one of the more sophisticated kinds, called *Poisson* random numbers.

To introduce the idea, let us note that saying that an average family has 2.6 children does not mean that each family has 2 children and 0.6 of a third. Instead, it means that, averaged over many families, the mean number of children is 2.6. Hence, for five families of sizes 4, 1, 0, 3, 5 the mean size is 2.6. Similarly, if the number of planes arriving to land in ten time units is 2, 0, 0, 1, 4, 1, 0, 0, 0, 1, then the mean number of planes arriving in one unit is 0.9.

*expected value*

Let us now start with a fixed number called the *expected value* $\nu$ of the random numbers. Then to say that a sequence of nonnegative integers satisfies a *Poisson distribution* with expected value $\nu$ means that, over long subsequences, the mean value of the integers in the sequence approaches $\nu$. We can now present a function that generates random integers according to a Poisson distribution with a given expected value, and this is just what we need for the airport simulation. The mathematical derivation of this function, however, requires statistics beyond the scope of this book.

*Poisson distribution*

*Poisson generator*

```
/* PoissonRandom: generate a pseudorandom integer according to the Poisson distri-
   bution.
   Pre:   None.
   Post:  Generates a random nonnegative integer according to a Poisson distribution
          with the expected value given as the parameter.
   Uses: exp, rand. */
int PoissonRandom(double expectedvalue)
{
    int n = 0;                              /* counter of iterations                */
    double limit;                           /* e^-v, where v is the expected value  */
    double x;                               /* pseudorandom number                  */
    limit = exp(-expectedvalue);
    x = rand()/(double) INT_MAX;
    while (x > limit) {
        n++;
        x *= rand()/(double) INT_MAX;
    }
    return n;
}
```

Because the rand function returns an integer between 0 and INT_MAX, we use

$$\text{rand()}/\text{(double)INT\_MAX}$$

to obtain a value between 0 and 1 that we use to calculate a pseudorandom integer according to a Poisson distribution.

## 4.4.6 SAMPLE RESULTS

We conclude this section with the output from a sample run of the airport simulation. You should note that there are some periods when the runway is idle and others when one or both of the queues are completely full, and in which some planes must be turned away. If you run this simulation again, you will obtain different results from those given here, but, if the expected values given to the program are the same, then there will be some correspondence between the numbers given in the summaries of the two runs.

This program simulates an airport with only one runway.
One plane can land or depart in each unit of time.
Up to 5 planes can be waiting to land or take off at any time.
How many units of time will the simulation run ? 30
Expected number of arrivals per unit time (real number) ? 0.47
Expected number of departures per unit time ? 0.47
    Plane 1 ready to land.
 1: Plane 1 landed; in queue 0 units.

*both queues are empty*
 2: Runway is idle.
    Plane 2 ready to land.
    Plane 3 ready to land.
 3: Plane 2 landed; in queue 0 units.
 4: Plane 3 landed; in queue 1 units.
    Plane 4 ready to land.
    Plane 5 ready to land.
    Plane 6 ready to take off.
    Plane 7 ready to take off.
 5: Plane 4 landed; in queue 0 units.
    Plane 8 ready to take off.
 6: Plane 5 landed; in queue 1 units.
    Plane 9 ready to take off.
    Plane 10 ready to take off.
 7: Plane 6 took off; in queue 2 units.
 8: Plane 7 took off; in queue 3 units.
 9: Plane 8 took off; in queue 3 units.
    Plane 11 ready to land.

*landing queue is*
*empty*
10: Plane 11 landed; in queue 0 units.
    Plane 12 ready to take off.
11: Plane 9 took off; in queue 4 units.
    Plane 13 ready to land.
    Plane 14 ready to land.
12: Plane 13 landed; in queue 0 units.
13: Plane 14 landed; in queue 1 units.
14: Plane 10 took off; in queue 7 units.
    Plane 15 ready to land.
    Plane 16 ready to take off.
    Plane 17 ready to take off.

15: Plane 15 landed; in queue 0 units.
    Plane 18 ready to land.
    Plane 19 ready to land.
    Plane 20 ready to take off.
    Plane 21 ready to take off.

16: Plane 18 landed; in queue 0 units.
    Plane 22 ready to land.

17: Plane 19 landed; in queue 1 units.
    Plane 23 ready to take off.
    Plane 23 told to try later.

*takeoff queue is full*

18: Plane 22 landed; in queue 1 units.
    Plane 24 ready to land.
    Plane 25 ready to land.
    Plane 26 ready to land.
    Plane 27 ready to take off.
    Plane 27 told to try later.

19: Plane 24 landed; in queue 0 units.
    Plane 28 ready to land.
    Plane 29 ready to land.
    Plane 30 ready to land.
    Plane 31 ready to land.
    Plane 31 directed to another airport.

*landing queue is full*

20: Plane 25 landed; in queue 1 units.
    Plane 32 ready to land.
    Plane 33 ready to take off.
    Plane 33 told to try later.

21: Plane 26 landed; in queue 2 units.

22: Plane 28 landed; in queue 2 units.

23: Plane 29 landed; in queue 3 units.
    Plane 34 ready to take off.
    Plane 34 told to try later.

24: Plane 30 landed; in queue 4 units.
    Plane 35 ready to take off.
    Plane 35 told to try later.
    Plane 36 ready to take off.
    Plane 36 told to try later.

25: Plane 32 landed; in queue 4 units.
    Plane 37 ready to take off.
    Plane 37 told to try later.

26: Plane 12 took off; in queue 15 units.

27: Plane 16 took off; in queue 12 units.

28: Plane 17 took off; in queue 13 units.

29: Plane 20 took off; in queue 13 units.
    Plane 38 ready to take off.

30: Plane 21 took off; in queue 14 units.

*summary*

Simulation has concluded after 30 units.
Total number of planes processed:   38
  Number of planes landed:          19
  Number of planes taken off:       10
  Number of planes refused use:      8
  Number left ready to land:         0
  Number left ready to take off:     1
  Percentage of time runway idle:    3.33
  Average wait time to land:         1.11
  Average wait time to take off:     8.60

## Programming Projects 4.4

**P1.** Combine all the functions for the airport simulation into a complete program. Experiment with several sample runs of the airport simulation, adjusting the values for the expected numbers of planes ready to land and take off. Find approximate values for these expected numbers that are as large as possible subject to the condition that it is very unlikely that a plane must be refused service. What happens to these values if the maximum size of the queues is increased or decreased?

**P2.** Modify the simulation to give the airport two runways, one always used for landings and one always used for takeoffs. Compare the total number of planes that can be served with the number for the one-runway airport. Does it more than double?

**P3.** Modify the simulation to give the airport two runways, one usually used for landings and one usually used for takeoffs. If one of the queues is empty, then both runways can be used for the other queue. Also, if the landing queue is full and another plane arrives to land, then takeoffs will be stopped and both runways used to clear the backlog of landing planes.

**P4.** Modify the simulation to have three runways, one always reserved for each of landing and takeoff and the third used for landings unless the landing queue is empty, in which case it can be used for takeoffs.

**P5.** Modify the original (one-runway) simulation so that when each plane arrives to land, it will (as part of its record) have a (randomly generated) fuel level, measured in units of time remaining. If the plane does not have enough fuel to wait in the queue, it is allowed to land immediately. Hence the planes in the landing queue may be kept waiting additional units, and so may run out of fuel themselves. Check this out as part of the landing function, and find about how busy the airport can become before planes start to crash from running out of fuel.

**P6.** Write a stub to take the place of the random-number function. The stub can be used both to debug the program and to allow the user to control exactly the number of planes arriving for each queue at each time unit.

# 4.5 Pointers and Linked Lists ━━━━━━━━━━━

## 4.5.1 Introduction and Survey

### 1. The Problem of Overflow

In the examples we have studied up to this point we have assumed that all items of data are kept within arrays, arrays that must be declared to have some size that is fixed when the program is written, and that can therefore not be changed while the program is running. When writing a program, we have had to decide on the maximum amount of memory that would be needed for these arrays and set this aside in the declarations. If we run the program on a small sample, then much of this space will never be used. If we decide to run the program on a large set of data, then we may exhaust the space set aside and encounter overflow, even when the computer memory itself is not fully used, simply because our original bounds on the array were too small.

*fixed bounds*

Even if we are careful to declare our arrays large enough to use up all the available memory, we can still encounter overflow, since one array may reach its limit while a great deal of unused space remains in others. Since different runs of the same program may cause different data structures to grow or shrink, it may be impossible to tell before the program actually executes which data structures will overflow.

*problem of overflow*

We now exhibit a way to keep data structures in memory without using arrays, whereby we can avoid these difficulties. These methods can be used for lists, stacks, queues, and other kinds of data structures that we shall study later.

### 2. Pointers

The idea we use is that of a pointer. A *pointer*, also called a *link* or a *reference*, is defined to be a variable that gives the location of some other variable, typically of a structure containing data that we wish to use. If we use pointers to locate all the structures in which we are interested, then we need not be concerned about where the structures themselves are actually stored, since by using a pointer, we can let the computer system itself locate the structure when required.

### 3. Diagram Conventions

Figure 4.5 shows pointers to several structures. Pointers are generally depicted as arrows and structures as rectangular boxes. In the diagrams, variables containing pointers are generally shown in shaded boxes. Hence in the diagram r is a pointer to the structure "Lynn" and v is a pointer to the structure "Jack." As you can see, the use of pointers is quite flexible: two pointers can refer to the same structure, as t and u do in Figure 4.5, or a pointer can refer to no structure at all. We denote this latter situation within diagrams by the electrical *ground symbol*, as shown for pointer s. Care must be exercised when using pointers, moreover, to be sure that, when they are moved, no structure is lost. In the diagram, the structure "Dave" is lost, with no pointer referring to it, and therefore there is no way to find it.

*pointers referring nowhere*

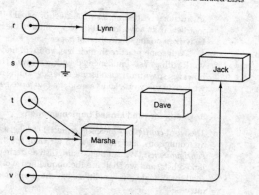

Figure 4.5. Pointers to structures

## 4. Linked Lists

*linked list*

The idea of a *linked list* is, for every structure in the list, to put a pointer into the structure giving the location of the next structure in the list. This idea is illustrated in Figure 4.6.

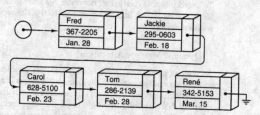

Figure 4.6. A linked list

As you can see from the illustration, a linked list is simple in concept. It uses the same idea as a children's treasure hunt, where each clue that is found tells where to find the next one. Or consider friends passing a popular cassette around. Fred has it, and has promised to give it to Jackie. Carol asks Jackie if she can borrow it, and then will next share it with Tom. And so it goes. A linked list may be considered analogous to following instructions where each instruction is given out only upon completion of the previous task. There is then no inherent limit on the number of tasks to be done, since each task may specify a new instruction, and there is no way to tell in advance how many instructions there are. The data-structure implementations studied up to now, on the other hand, are analogous to a list of instructions written on a single sheet of paper. It is then possible to see all the instructions in advance, but there is a limit to the number of instructions that can be written on the single sheet of paper.

With some practice in their use, you will find that linked lists are as easy to work with as lists implemented within arrays. The methods differ substantially, however, so we must spend some time developing new programming skills. Before we turn to this work, let us consider a few more general observations.

## 5. Contiguous and Linked Implementations

The word *contiguous* means *in contact, touching, adjoining*. The entries in an array are contiguous, and from now on we shall speak of a list kept in an array as a *contiguous list*. We can then distinguish as desired between contiguous lists and linked lists, and we shall use the unqualified word *list* only to include both. We shall speak analogously of linked or contiguous stacks and of linked or contiguous queues.

## 6. Pointers for Contiguous Lists

A pointer is simply a variable giving the location of some item, and for contiguous lists, stacks, and queues, we have in fact been using pointers informally throughout the book up to now.

The variable *top* is a pointer giving the location of the item on the top of a stack, and the variables *front* and *rear* give the locations of the front and rear of a queue. To avoid possible confusion, however, we shall generally reserve the word *pointer* for use with linked lists and continue to use the word *index* to refer to a location within an array.

## 7. Dynamic Memory Allocation

*time sharing*

As well as preventing unnecessary overflow problems caused by running out of room in arrays, the use of pointers has advantages in a multitasking or time-sharing environment. If we use arrays to reserve in advance the maximum amount of memory that our program might need, then this memory is assigned to us and will be unavailable for other tasks. If it is necessary to page our job out of memory, then there may be time lost as unused memory is copied to and from a disk. Instead of using arrays to hold all our items, we can begin very small, with space only for the program instructions and simple variables, and whenever we need space for an additional item, we can request the system for the needed memory. Similarly, when an item is no longer needed, its space can be returned to the system, which can then assign it to another user. In this way a program can start small and grow only as necessary, so that when it is small, it can run more efficiently, and when necessary it can grow to the limits of the computer system.

Even without multitasking this dynamic control of memory can prove useful. During one part of a task a large amount of memory may be needed for some purpose, which can later be released and then allocated again for another purpose, perhaps now containing data of a completely different type than before.

## 4.5.2 POINTERS AND DYNAMIC MEMORY IN C

C provides powerful facilities for processing pointers and standard functions for requesting additional memory and for releasing memory during program execution.

### 1. Static and Dynamic Variables

Variables that can be used during execution of a C program come in two varieties. *Static variables* are those that are declared and named, as usual, while writing the program. Space for them exists as long as the program in which they are declared is running. (There is a storage class for variables in C called static; the variables are known only in the function where they are declared and their space exists for the duration of the main program. We are using the term *static variable* here to denote any variable that is declared while writing the program.) *Dynamic variables* are created (and perhaps destroyed) during program execution. Since dynamic variables do not exist while the program is compiled, but only when it is run, they cannot be assigned names while it is being written.

The only way to access dynamic variables is by using pointers. Once it is created, however, a dynamic variable does contain data and must have a type like any other variable. Thus we can talk about creating a new dynamic variable of type $x$ and setting a pointer to point to it, or of moving a pointer from one dynamic variable of type $x$ to another, or of returning a dynamic variable of type $x$ to the system.

Static variables, on the other hand, cannot be created or destroyed during execution of the program in which they are declared, although pointer variables can be used to point to static variables. For example,

```
void f(void)
{
    char c;
    ...
}
```

The function f has a local variable c of type character. There will be space allocated for c when the function f executes. The function itself cannot destroy the space reserved for c or ask for more space for c. When f terminates, however, c is destroyed. The variable c is a static variable as opposed to a dynamic variable, for which the program controls the allocation and disposal of the space. If a dynamic variable is created in a function, then it can continue to exist even after the function terminates.

### 2. C Notation

C uses a star * to denote a pointer. If p is a pointer to a character, we declare it by

```
char *p;
```

If Node denotes the type of items in which we are interested, then we declare a pointer type that is bound to type Node with the declaration

```
typedef struct node {
    ...
} Node;
Node *q;
```

The type Node to which a pointer refers can be arbitrary, but in most applications it will be a structure. The words link and reference are also frequently used to designate pointer types.

### 3. Type Binding

C sets stringent rules for the use of pointers. Each pointer is **bound** to the type of variable to which it points, and the same pointer should not be used to point (at different times) to variables of different types. Variables of two different pointer types cannot be mixed with each other; C will allow assignments between two pointer variables of the same type, but it will produce a warning when you assign pointers of different types. If we have declarations

```
char *a, *b;
Node *x, *y;
```

then the assignments x = y;  and a = b;  are legal, but the assignment x = a;  is illegal.

### 4. NULL Pointers

Sometimes a pointer variable p has no dynamic variable to which it currently refers. This situation can be established by the assignment

```
p = NULL;
```

and it can subsequently be checked by a condition such as

```
if (p != NULL) ....
```

In diagrams we use the electrical ground symbol

for a NULL pointer.

NULL is a symbolic constant defined in the include file stdio.h, and, in fact, the value of NULL is the constant zero. This means that the constant NULL is generic in that it can be assigned to a variable of any pointer type. It also means that the statements

```
if (p != NULL) ...   and   if (p) ...
```

*equivalent forms*

do exactly the same thing. Both forms are commonly used in C programs. The first form shows more clearly that a pointer is being checked to see if it points to a dynamic variable. The second form, being more compact, is often easier to read when it appears inside a complicated expression. We shall use both forms interchangeably in the programs we write.

*undefined pointers*
*versus NULL pointers*

Note carefully the distinction between a pointer variable whose value is undefined and a pointer variable whose value is NULL. The assertion p == NULL means that p currently points to no dynamic variable. If the value of p is undefined, then p might point to any random location in memory. As with all variables, when the program begins execution, the values of pointer variables are undefined. Before we can use the value of a pointer variable p, therefore, we must either assign p = NULL or create a dynamic variable to which it points, as follows.

## 5. Creating and Destroying Dynamic Variables

The creation and destruction of dynamic variables is done with standard functions in C. If p has been declared as a pointer to type Node, then the statement

$$p = (Node *) \; malloc(sizeof(Node));$$

*malloc*

creates a new dynamic variable of type Node and assigns its location to the pointer p. The library function malloc allocates a block of memory and returns a pointer to that block of memory, or it returns NULL if there is not enough remaining memory to satisfy the request. The argument to malloc indicates, in bytes, the size of the

*sizeof*

block of memory that is requested. For our application, we determine this size by using the unary compile-time operator sizeof, which computes the size in bytes of any object or type. Hence,

$$sizeof(Node)$$

*type cast*

calculates the number of bytes occupied by a variable of Node. The placement of (Node *) before the call to malloc is a *type cast*: The value returned by malloc is a generic pointer; the type cast forces it to become Node.

If there is insufficient memory to create the new dynamic variable, malloc will fail and will return NULL. Your program should always check for a NULL pointer returned by malloc.

*free*

When a dynamic variable is no longer needed, the function call

$$free(p);$$

returns the space used by the dynamic variable to which p points to the system. After the function free(p) is called, the pointer variable p is undefined, and so cannot be used until it is assigned a new value. These actions are illustrated in Figure 4.7.

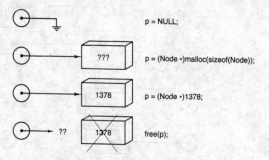

Figure 4.7. Allocating and freeing dynamic variables

Either a call p = malloc(...) or an assignment such as p = q or p = NULL is required before p can be used. After a call free(p), the value of p is undefined, so it is wise to set p = NULL immediately, to be sure that p is not used with an undefined value.

### 6. Following the Pointers

The star * that appears in the declaration of a C pointer can also be used in a statement that uses the pointer. For example, the declaration

char *p;

is read "p is a pointer to char" and when we use *p in an expression we read "what p points to." Again, the words *link* and *reference* are often used in this connection. The action of taking *p is sometimes called "dereferencing the pointer p."

*dereferencing*

### 7. Restrictions on Pointer Variables

The only use of variables of type Item * is to find the location of variables of type Item. Thus pointer variables can participate in assignment statements, can be checked for equality, can appear in calls to functions, and the programmer is allowed to do some limited arithmetic with pointers. Refer to Appendix C for more information on pointers.

*pointer operations*

*assignment*

In regard to assignment statements, it is important to remember the difference between p = q and *p = *q, both of which are legal (provided that p and q are bound to the same type), but which have quite different effects. The first statement makes p point to the same object to which q points, but does not change the value of either that object or of the other object that p was pointing to. The latter object will be lost unless there is some other pointer variable that still refers to it. The second statement, *p = *q, on the contrary, copies the value of the object *q into the object *p, so that we now have two objects with the same value, with p and q pointing to the two separate copies. Finally, the two assignment statements p = *q and *p = q have mixed types and are illegal (except in the unusual case that both p and q point to pointers of their same type!). Figure 4.8 illustrates these assignments.

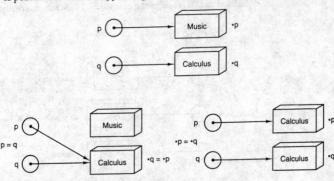

**Figure 4.8. Assignment of pointer variables**

## 4.5.3 THE BASICS OF LINKED LISTS

With these tools of pointers we can now begin to consider the implementation of linked lists into C.

### 1. Nodes and Type Declarations

Recall from Figure 4.6 that each entry of a linked list will be a structure containing not only the items of information but also a pointer to the next structure in the list. Translating this requirement into C declarations yields

```
typedef struct node {
    ListEntry entry;
    struct node *next;
} Node;
```

*use before declaration*   Note that we have a problem of circularity in this declaration. struct node *next; appears in the declaration of the structure node. This is called a *self-referential structure*. It means that the pointer next may point to a structure of the same type as the structure Node.

### 2. Beginning of the List

In our linked list we shall use the pointer next to move from any one node in the linked list to the next one, and thereby we can work our way through the list, once we have started. We must now, however, address a small problem that never arises with contiguous lists or other static variables and arrays: How do we find the beginning of the list?

Perhaps an analogy with reading a magazine article will help. If we are in the middle of reading an article, then upon reaching the bottom of a page we often find the instruction "Continued on page ...," and by following such instructions we can continue reading until we reach the end of the article. But how do we find the beginning? We look in the table of contents, which we expect to find in a fixed location near the beginning of the magazine.

For linked lists also we must refer to some fixed location to find the beginning; that is, we shall use a static variable to locate the first node of the list. One method *static head* of doing this is to make the first node in the list a static variable, even though all the remaining nodes are dynamically allocated. In this way the first node will have a unique name to which we can refer. Although we shall sometimes use this method, it has the disadvantage that the first node of the list is treated differently from all the others, a fact that can sometimes complicate the algorithms.

For linked stacks and queues and sometimes for other kinds of linked lists, we shall employ another method that avoids these problems. The *header* for a linked list is a pointer variable that locates the beginning of the list. The header will usually be a static variable, and by using its value we can arrive at the first (dynamic) node of the list. The header is also sometimes called the *base* or the *anchor* of the list. These terms are quite descriptive of providing a variable that ties down the beginning of the list, but since they are not so widely used, we shall generally employ the term *header*.

## 160 Chapter 4 • Queues and Linked Lists

*initialization*

When execution of the program starts we shall wish to initialize the linked list to be empty; with a header pointer, this is now easy. The header is a static pointer; so it exists when the program begins, and to set its value to indicate that its list is empty, we need only the assignment

### 3. The End of the List

Finding the end of a linked list is a much easier task than is finding its beginning. Since each node contains a pointer to the next node, the pointer field of the last node of the list has nowhere to point, so we give it the special value NULL. In this way we know that we are at the end of the list if and only if the node we are using has a NULL pointer to the next. Here we have one small advantage of linked lists over a contiguous implementation: There is no need to keep an explicit counter of the number of nodes in the list.

**Exercises 4.5**

These exercises are based on the following declarations, where the type Node is declared as follows.

typedef struct node {
        char c;
        struct node *next;
} Node;
Node *p, *q, *r;
Node x, y, z;
```

**E1.** For each of the following statements, either describe its effect, or state why it is illegal.

(a) p = (Node *) malloc(sizeof(Node));
(b) *q = (Node *) malloc(sizeof(Node));
(c) x = (Node *) malloc(sizeof(Node));
(d) p = r;
(e) q = y;
(f) r = NULL;
(g) z = *p;
(h) p = *x;
(i) free(y);
(j) free(*p);
(k) free(r);
(l) *q = NULL;
(m) *p = *x;
(n) z = NULL;
```

*swap*

**E2.** Write a C function to interchange pointers p and q, so that after the function is performed, p will point to the node to which q formerly pointed, and vice versa.

**E3.** Write a C function to interchange the values in the dynamic variables to which p and q point, so that after the function is performed *p will have the value formerly in *q and vice versa.

**E4.** Write a C function that makes p point to the same node to which q points, and frees the item to which p formerly pointed.

**E5.** Write a C function that creates a new variable with p pointing to it, and with contents the same as those of the node to which q points.

## 4.6 Linked Queues

In contiguous storage, queues were significantly harder to manipulate than were stacks, and even somewhat harder than simple lists, because it was necessary to treat straight-line storage as though it were arranged in a circle, and the extreme cases of full queues and empty queues caused difficulties. It is for queues that linked storage really comes into its own. Linked queues are just as easy to handle as are linked stacks. We need only keep two pointers, front and rear, that will point, respectively, to the beginning and the end of the queue. The operations of insertion and deletion are both illustrated in Figure 4.9.

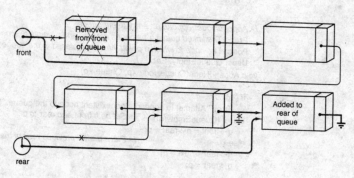

Figure 4.9. Operations on a linked queue

For all queues, we denote by queueentry the type designating the items in the queue. For linked queues, the structure of a node can then be declared as follows, in close analogy to what we have already done for stacks.

*type* queue

```
typedef char QueueEntry;
typedef struct queuenode {
    QueueEntry info;
    struct queuenode *next;
} QueueNode;
```

*type queue*

```
typedef struct queue {
    QueueNode *front;
    QueueNode *rear;
} Queue;
```

*initialize*

A queue should be initialized to be empty with the function:

```
/* CreateQueue: create the queue.
   Pre:  None.
   Post: The queue q has been initialized to be empty. */
void CreateQueue(Queue *q)
{
    q->front = q->rear = NULL;
}
```

Let us next turn to functions that process queue *nodes*. These will be considered private to the implementation, since the specifications for abstract queues specify only operations on entries, not nodes. First, to add a node p to the rear of a queue, we write:

```
/* AppendNode: append an entry to the queue.
   Pre:  The linked queue q has been created and p points to a node not already in q.
   Post: The node to which p points has been placed in the queue as its last entry.
   Uses: QueueEmpty, Error. */
void AppendNode(QueueNode *p, Queue *q)
{
    if (!p)
        Error("Attempt to append a nonexistent node to the queue.");
    else if (QueueEmpty(q))      /* Set both front and rear to p.                 */
        q->front = q->rear = p;
    else {                       /* Place p after previous rear of the queue.     */
        q->rear->next = p;
        q->rear = p;
    }
}
```

Note that this function includes error checking to prevent the insertion of a nonexistent node into the queue. The cases when the queue is empty or not must be treated separately, since the addition of a node to an empty queue requires setting both the front and the rear to the new node, whereas addition to a nonempty queue requires changing only the rear.

To remove a node from the front of a queue, we use the following function:

```
/* ServeNode: remove the first entry in the queue.
   Pre:   The linked queue q has been created and is not empty.
   Post:  The first node in the queue has been removed and parameter p points to this
          node.
   Uses: QueueEmpty, Error. */
void ServeNode(QueueNode **p, Queue *q)
{
    if (QueueEmpty(q))
        Error("Attempt to delete a node from an empty queue.");
    else {
        *p = q->front;                 /* Pull off the front entry of the queue.        */
        q->front = q->front->next;     /* Advance front of queue to the next node.      */
        if (QueueEmpty(q))             /* Is the queue now empty?                       */
            q->rear = NULL;
    }
}
```

The ∗∗ in front of the argument p indicates that the function expects 'a pointer to a pointer.' That is, the function receives a reference to a pointer; this is also commonly referred to as 'the address of a pointer.' (For more information on references see Appendix C.)

Again the possibility of an empty queue must be considered separately. It is an error to attempt deletion from an empty queue. It is, however, not an error for the queue to become empty after a deletion, but then the rear and front should both become NULL to indicate clearly that the queue is empty.

*simplicity*

If you compare these algorithms for linked queues with those needed for contiguous queues, you will see that the linked versions are both conceptually simpler and easier to program.

*implementations*

The functions we have developed process nodes; to enable us to change easily between contiguous and linked implementations of queues, we also need versions of functions Append and Serve that will process *entries* directly for linked queues. We leave writing these functions as exercises, along with the remaining functions for processing queues: CreateQueue, ClearQueue, QueueEmpty, QueueFull, QueueSize, QueueFront, and QueueFrontNode.

The functions Append and Serve that process *entries* of a linked queue are similar to the analogous functions for linked stacks. For Append, it is necessary first to use the malloc function to create a new node, then insert the new entry, and then use the function AppendNode to append the new node to the queue. Similarly, the function Serve requires use of both the functions free and ServeNode.

## Exercises 4.6

**E1.** By creating nodes and freeing nodes, write functions **(a)** Append and **(b)** Serve that will process entries for linked queues and that can be substituted directly for their contiguous counterparts.

**E2.** Write the following C functions for linked queues.

   **(a)** QueueEmpty.

   **(b)** ClearQueue.

   **(c)** QueueFront.

   **(d)** QueueFrontNode, which is to return a pointer to the *node* at the front of the queue, whereas QueueFront returns a copy of the front *entry*.

**E3.** For a linked queue, the function QueueSize requires a loop that moves through the entire queue to count the entries, since the number of entries in the queue is not kept as a separate member in the queue structure.

   **(a)** Write the C function QueueSize for a linked queue by using a loop that moves a pointer variable from node to node through the queue.

   **(b)** Consider modifying the declaration of a linked queue to add a count member to the structure. What changes will need to be made to all the functions for linked queues? Discuss the advantages and disadvantages of this modification compared to the original implementation of linked queues.

**E4.** A *circularly linked list*, illustrated in Figure 4.10, is a linked list in which the node at the tail of the list, instead of having a NULL pointer, points back to the node at the head of the list. We then need only one pointer tail to access both ends of the list, since we know that tail->next points back to the head of the list.

   **(a)** If we implement a queue as a circularly linked list, then we need only one pointer tail (or rear) to locate both the front and the rear. Write the C functions needed to process a queue stored in this way.

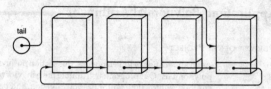

**Figure 4.10. A circularly linked list with tail pointer**

**(b)** What are the disadvantages of implementing this structure, as opposed to using the version requiring two pointers?

**E5.** With a deque stored as a circularly linked list with only one pointer to the tail of the list, three of the four functions to add a node to either end of the deque and to delete a node from either end become easy to implement, but the fourth does not.

**(a)** Which one of the four operations is the most difficult? Why?

**(b)** Write a C function to create an empty circularly linked deque.

**(c)** Write C functions for the three easy operations on a linked deque.

**(d)** Write a C function for the fourth operation.

**E6.** Write the functions needed to implement a deque in a doubly linked implementation.

**Programming
Projects 4.6**

**P1.** Assemble header files and functions for processing linked queues, suitable for use by an application program.

**P2.** Take the menu-driven demonstration program for a queue of characters (Section 4.3, Project P1) and substitute the linked queue functions for the contiguous queue functions. If you have designed the program and the functions carefully, then the program should work correctly with no further change.

**P3.** In the airport simulation developed in Section 4.4, replace the functions for processing contiguous queues with the functions for linked queues. If you have designed the functions carefully, the program should run in exactly the same way with no further change required.

# 4.7 Application: Polynomial Arithmetic

### 4.7.1 PURPOSE OF THE PROJECT

*calculator for polynomials*

As an application of linked queues, this section outlines a program for manipulating polynomials. Our program will imitate the behavior of a simple calculator that does addition, subtraction, multiplication, division, and perhaps some other operations, but one that performs these operations for polynomials.

*reverse Polish calculations*

There are many kinds of calculators available, and we could model our program after any of them. To provide a further illustration of the use of stacks, however, let us choose to model what is often called a *reverse Polish* calculator. In such a calculator, the operands (numbers usually, polynomials for us) are entered *before* the operation is specified. The operands are pushed onto a stack. When an operation is performed, it pops its operands from the stack and pushes its result back onto the stack. If ? denotes pushing an operand onto the stack, +, −, *, / represent arithmetic operations, and = means printing the top of the stack (but not popping it off), then ? ? + = means reading two operands, then calculating and printing their sum. The instruction ? ? + ? ? + * = requests four operands. If these are a, b, c, d, then the result printed is (a + b) * (c + d). Similarly, ? ? ? − = * ? + = pushes a, b, c onto the stack, replaces b, c by b − c and prints its value, calculates a * (b − c), pushes d on the stack, and finally calculates and prints (a * (b − c)) + d.

*no parentheses needed*

The advantage of a reverse Polish calculator is that any expression, no matter how complicated, can be specified without the use of parentheses.

This Polish notation is useful for compilers as well as for calculators, and its study forms the major topic of Chapter 12. For the present, however, a few minutes' practice with a reverse Polish calculator will make you quite comfortable with its use.

### 4.7.2 THE MAIN PROGRAM

#### 1. Outline

The task of the calculator program is quite simple in principle. It need only accept new commands and perform them as long as desired. In preliminary outline, the main program takes the form

*first outline*

```
/* Preliminary outline: program for manupulating polynomials */
int main(void)
{
   CreateStack(stack);
   while (there are more commands) {
      GetCommand(cmd);      /* command to execute           */
      DoCommand(cmd);
   }
   return 0;
}
```

### 2. Performing Commands

To turn this outline into C, we must specify what it means to obtain commands and how this will be done. Before doing so, let us make the decision to represent the commands by the characters ? , = , + , − , * , / . Given this decision, we can immediately write the function DoCommand in C, thereby specifying exactly what each command does:

```
/* DoCommand: do command cmd for polynomials.
   Pre:   The stack s has been created, and command is one of the operations allowed
          in the calculator.
   Post:  The specified operation command has been performed and the top entries of
          the stack s have been changed accordingly.
   Uses: Help, ReadPolynomial, WritePolymial, Add, Subtract, Multiply, Divide. */
void DoCommand(char command, Stack *s)
{
   switch(command) {
   case 'h' :                    /* Print help instructions for the user.        */
      Help();
      break;
   case '?' :                    /* Input a polynomial.                          */
      ReadPolynomial(s);
      break;
   case '=' :                    /* Print the polynomial on the top of the stack. */
      WritePolynomial(s);
      break;
   case '+' :                    /* Add top two polynomials and push answer.  */
      Add(s);
      break;
   case '-' :                    /* Subtract two polynomials and push answer. */
      Subtract(s);
      break;
   case '*' :                    /* Multiply two polynomials and push answer.  */
      Multiply(s);
      break;
   case '/' :                    /* Divide two polynomials and push answer.  */
      Divide(s);
      break;
   }
}
```

This function includes two additional commands: h prints a help screen for the user, and q quits the program.

### 3. Reading Commands: The Main Program

Now that we have decided that the commands are to be denoted as single characters, we could easily program function GetCommand to read one command at a time from the terminal. It is often convenient, however, to read a string of several commands at once, such as ? ? + ? ? + * = , and then perform them all before reading more. To allow for this, let us read a whole line of commands at once and set up a simple list to hold them. With this decision we can now write the main program in its final form, except for the additional declarations that we shall insert after choosing our data structures. We shall use a function ReadCommand to read the list of commands; this function will also be responsible for error checking.

```
#include "common.h"
#include "poly.h"


#define MAXCOMMAND 10

/* Implement calculator for polynomials.
   Pre:   None.
   Post:  Allows the user to do simple arithmetic with polynomials. */
```

*main program*
```
int main(void)
{
    int i, n;
    Stack stack;
    char command[MAXCOMMAND];
    Introduction( );
    Instructions( );
    CreateStack( &stack);

    do {
        n = ReadCommand(command, &stack);
        for (i = 0;  i < n;  i++)
            DoCommand(command[i], &stack);
    } while (n > 0);
    return 0;
}
```

### 4. Input Function

Before we turn to our principal task (deciding how to represent polynomials and writing functions to manipulate them), let us complete the preliminaries by writing the input function ReadCommand. The functions Introduction and Instructions will be left as exercises.

Function ReadCommand must check that the symbols typed in represent legitimate operations: It uses a set of characters validcommands (treated as a constant) for this task. If there is an error, then the command string must be re-entered from the start.

```
/* ReadCommand: read a command line and save it in command.
   Pre:   None.
   Post:  The parameter commandlist has been set to a list of legitimate commands
          ready to be performed by the calculator.
   Uses: Prompt. */

int ReadCommand(char commandlist[ ], Stack *s)

{
   int c, n;

   do {                         /* Read a valid command line.        */
      n = 0;                    /* number of characters read         */

      Prompt(s);

      while ((c = getchar()) != '\n') {

         c = tolower(c);
         if (strchr(" ,\t", c) != NULL)
            /* empty */;        /* Skip white-space characters.      */
         else if (c == 'q')
            return 0;           /* quit                              */
         else if (strchr("?+-*/=h", c) != NULL)
            commandlist[n++] = c;  /* valid command                  */
         else {
            printf("A command given is not valid; "
                   "please enter the line again.");
            fflush(stdin);
            break;
         }
      }
   } while (c != '\n');

   commandlist[n] = '\0';       /* Add end of string marker.         */
   return n;

}
```

The function Prompt displays a message and ignores extra newline characters.

*prompting user*

```
/* Prompt: prompt the user for command line.
   Pre:   None.
   Post:  Produces a prompt for the user and discards existing newline characters, if
          any.
   Uses: StackSize. */
void Prompt(Stack *s)
{
    int c;
    printf("\nThe stack size is %d\n", StackSize(s));
    printf("Enter in a command list of operations\n");
    while ((c = getchar()) == '\n')
        /* empty */ ;            /* Discard newlines, if any.                    */
    ungetc(c, stdin);           /* Back up to the last useful character.         */
}
```

### 5. Stubs and Testing

We have now written enough of our program that we should pause to compile it, debug it, and test it to make sure that what has been done so far is correct.

For the task of compiling the program, we must, of course, supply stubs for all the missing functions. At present, however, we have not even completed the type declarations: the most important one, that of a Polynomial, remains unspecified. We could make this type declaration almost arbitrarily and still be able to compile the program, but for testing, it is much better to make the temporary type declaration

```
typedef double Polynomial;
```

*temporary type declaration*

and test the program by running it as an ordinary reverse Polish calculator operating on real numbers. The following is then typical of the stubs that are needed:

```
Add(Stack *s)
{
    double x, y;
    Pop( &x, s);
    Pop( &y, s);
    Push(x + y, s);
}
```

Producing a skeleton program at this time also ensures that the stack and utility packages are properly integrated into the program.

### 4.7.3 DATA STRUCTURES AND THEIR IMPLEMENTATION

Let us now turn to our principal task by deciding how to represent polynomials and writing functions to manipulate them. If we carefully consider a polynomial such as

$$3x^5 - 2x^3 + x^2 + 4$$

*essence of a polynomial*

we see that the important information about the polynomial is contained in the coefficients and exponents of $x$; the variable $x$ itself is really just a place holder (a dummy variable). Hence, for purposes of calculation, we may think of a polynomial as made up of terms, each of which consists of a coefficient and an exponent. In a computer, we could similarly represent a polynomial as a *list* of pairs of coefficients and exponents. Each of these pairs constitutes a record, so a polynomial would be represented as a list of records. We would then build into our functions rules for performing arithmetic on two such lists. When we do this work, however, we find that we continually need to remove the first entry from the list, and we find that we need to insert new entries only at the end of the list. In other words, we find that the arithmetic operations treat the list as a queue, or, more precisely, as a *traversable queue*, since we frequently need to examine all the entries in the queue, but only deleting from the front and inserting at the rear.

*implementation of a polynomial*

Should we use a contiguous or a linked queue? If, in advance, we know a bound on the degree of the polynomials that can occur and if the polynomials that occur have nonzero coefficients in almost all their possible terms, then we should probably do better with contiguous queues. But if we do not know a bound on the degree, or if polynomials with only a few nonzero terms are likely to appear, then we shall find linked storage preferable. Let us in fact decide to represent a polynomial as a linked queue of *terms*, with each term a record consisting of a coefficient and an exponent. This representation is illustrated in Figure 4.11.

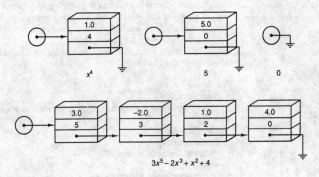

Figure 4.11. Polynomials as linked queues

*assumptions*

Each node contains one term of a polynomial, and we shall keep only nonzero terms in the queue. The polynomial that is always 0 (that is, it consists of only a 0 term) will be represented by an empty queue. We call this the *zero polynomial* or say that it is *identically 0*.

We can now match up all our decisions concerning data structures with our standard ways of declaring stacks, lists, and queues. We thereby obtain the following declarations for the main program.

```
typedef struct term {
    double coef;
    int exp;
} Term;
typedef struct term QueueEntry;
typedef struct queue Polynomial;
typedef Polynomial StackEntry;
```

We have not yet indicated the order of storing the terms of the polynomial. If we allow them to be stored in any order, then it might be difficult to recognize that

$$x^5 + x^2 - 3 \quad \text{and} \quad -3 + x^5 + x^2 \quad \text{and} \quad x^2 - 3 + x^5$$

*restriction*

all represent the same polynomial. Hence we adopt the usual convention that the terms of every polynomial are stored in the order of decreasing exponent within the linked queue, and we further assume that no two terms have the same exponent and that no term has a zero coefficient. (Recall that the polynomial that is identically 0 is represented as an empty queue.)

### 4.7.4 READING AND WRITING POLYNOMIALS

With polynomials implemented as queues, writing out a polynomial becomes simply a traversal of the queue, as follows.

```
/* WritePolynomial: write the polynomial at the top of the stack.
   Pre:   The stack s has been created and is not empty.
   Post:  The coefficients and exponents of the polynomial on the top of the stack s
          have been written out to the user.
   Uses: StackEmpty, Error, StackTop, TraverseQueue, QueueEmpty, WriteTerm. */
void WritePolynomial(Stack *s)
{
    Polynomial *p;
    if (StackEmpty(s))
        Error("Cannot write a polynomial since the stack is empty.");
    else {
        StackTop( &p, s);
        if (QueueEmpty( &p))
            printf("zero polynomial\n");
        else
            TraverseQueue(p, WriteTerm);
    }
}
```

We shall use a separate function WriteTerm to write out one term of the polynomial during the traversal.

```
/* WriteTerm: write a term of a polynomial.
   Pre:   A valid term currentterm exists.
   Post:  The term currentterm is printed. */
void WriteTerm(Term currentterm)
{
   if (currentterm.coef > 0.)
      printf(" +");
   printf("%5.2f x^%d", currentterm.coef, currentterm.exp);
}
```

As we read in a new polynomial, we shall be constructing a new queue, appending an entry to the queue for each term (coefficient-exponent pair) that we read from the input. This process of filling in a new term and appending it to the queue will reappear in almost every function for manipulating polynomials, at least in all those that change a polynomial. We therefore write this process as a separate utility that we can use whenever convenient in other functions to help construct a new polynomial.

```
/* AppendTerm: append a new term to the polynomial.
   Pre:   The polynomial p exists; coefficient and exponent are valid, with exponent less
          than the smallest exponent in p.
   Post:  A new term with the given coefficient and exponent has been added to the end
          of polynomial p.
   Uses:  AppendNode, MakeQueueNode. */
void AppendTerm(double coefficient, int exponent, Polynomial *p)
{
   Term newterm;

   newterm.coef = coefficient;
   newterm.exp = exponent;
   AppendNode(MakeQueueNode(newterm), p);

}
```

We can now use this function to make and insert new terms as we read coefficient-exponent pairs.

Like all functions that accept input directly from the user, our function for reading a new polynomial must carefully check its input to make sure that it meets the requirements of the problem. Making sure that the exponents in the polynomial appear in descending order is one of the larger tasks for our function. To do this, we continually compare the exponent of the current term with that of the previous term.

We shall use the special values of either a coefficient of 0 or an exponent of 0 to stop the reading process: Recall that a term with 0 coefficient is never stored in the polynomial, and, since the exponents are in descending order, a term with exponent of 0 must always be last. The resulting function follows.

```
/* ReadPolynomial: read a polynomial onto the stack.
  Pre:  The stack s has been created and is not full.
  Post: The user has supplied valid terms that have been assembled into the polyno-
        mial newpoly in order of decreasing exponents. The new polynomial is pushed
        onto the stack s.
  Uses: StackFull, Error, CreateQueue, AppendTerm, Push. */
void ReadPolynomial(Stack *s)
{
    double coefficient;
    int exponent, lastexponent;
    Polynomial newpoly;
    if (StackFull(s))
        Error("The stack is full: No more polynomials can be read at present.");
    else {
        CreateQueue( &newpoly);
        printf("Enter coefficients and exponents for the polynomial, "
               "one per line.\nExponents must be in decreasing order.\n"
               "Enter a coefficient of 0 or an exponent of 0 to terminate.\n");
        lastexponent = INT_MAX;
        while (1) {
            printf("coefficient? ");
            scanf("%lf", &coefficient);
            if (coefficient == 0.)
                break;
            printf("exponent? ");
            scanf("%d", &exponent);
            if (exponent >= lastexponent || exponent < 0)
                Error("Bad exponent.");
            else {
                AppendTerm(coefficient, exponent, &newpoly);
                if (exponent == 0)
                    break;
                lastexponent = exponent;
            }
        }
        Push(newpoly, s);
    }
}
```

## 4.7.5 ADDITION OF POLYNOMIALS

We now study one of the fundamental operations on polynomials, addition of two polynomials.

The requirement that the terms of a polynomial appear with descending exponents in the queue greatly simplifies their addition. To add two polynomials, we need only scan through them once each. If we find terms with the same exponent in the two polynomials, then we add the coefficients; otherwise, we copy the term of larger exponent into the sum and move on to the next term of that polynomial. When we reach the end of one of the polynomials, then any remaining part of the other is copied to the sum. We must also be careful not to include terms with zero coefficient in the sum.

```
/* Add: add two polynomials and push the answer onto stack.
   Pre:   The stack s has been created and contains at least two polynomials.
   Post:  The top two entries of the stack s have been popped off and added together.
          The sum is then pushed onto the stack s.
   Uses:  StackSize, Error, CreateQueue, Pop, QueueEmpty, QueueFront, ServeTerm,
          AppendTerm, MoveTerm, Push. */
void Add(Stack *s)
{
   Polynomial summand1, summand2, sum;
   Term firstterm, secondterm;
   double coefficient;
   if (StackSize(s) <= 1)
      Error("The stack does not contain enough "
         "polynomials for Add operation.");
   CreateQueue( &sum);
   Pop( &summand1, s);
   Pop( &summand2, s);
   while (!QueueEmpty( &summand1) && !QueueEmpty( &summand2)) {
      QueueFront( &firstterm, &summand1);
      QueueFront( &secondterm, &summand2);
      if (firstterm.exp == secondterm.exp) { /* Add terms with equal exponents.   */
         ServeTerm( &firstterm, &summand1);
         ServeTerm( &secondterm, &summand2);
         coefficient = firstterm.coef + secondterm.coef;
         if (coefficient != 0.)   /* Exclude terms with 0. coefficient.           */
            AppendTerm(coefficient, firstterm.exp, &sum);
      } else if (firstterm.exp > secondterm.exp)
         MoveTerm( &summand1, &sum);
      else
         MoveTerm( &summand2, &sum);
   }
   /* At this point one or both of the summands has been exhausted. At most one of
      the following loops will be executed. */
   while (!QueueEmpty( &summand1))
      MoveTerm( &summand1, &sum);
   while (!QueueEmpty( &summand2))
      MoveTerm( &summand2, &sum);
   Push(sum, s);
}
```

This function uses a short auxiliary function to move one term from one polynomial to another.

```
/* MoveTerm: move a term from one polynomial to another.
   Pre:    The polynomials incoming and outgoing exist.
   Post:   Removes a term from the incoming polynomial and appends in onto the out-
           going polynomial.
   Uses: ServeNode, AppendNode. */
void MoveTerm(Polynomial *incoming, Polynomial *outgoing)
{
   QueueNode *p;
   ServeNode( &p, incoming);
   AppendNode(p, outgoing);
}
```

## 4.7.6 COMPLETING THE PROJECT

### 1. The Missing Functions

At this point, the remaining functions for the calculator project are sufficiently similar to those already written that they can be left as exercises. Functions for the remaining arithmetical operations have the same general form as our function for addition. Some of these are easy: Subtraction is almost identical with addition. For multiplication, we can first write a function that multiplies a polynomial by a monomial, where *monomial* means a polynomial with only one term. This function requires only one traversal of the queue. Then we combine use of this function with the addition function to do a general multiplication. Division is more complicated.

### 2. Group Project

Production of a coherent set of functions for manipulating polynomials makes an interesting group project. Different members of the group can write functions or functions for different operations. Some of these are indicated as projects at the end of this section, but you may wish to include additional features as well. Any additional features should be planned carefully to be sure that they can be completed in a reasonable time, without disrupting other parts of the program.

*specifications*

After deciding on the division of work among its members, the most important decisions of the group relate to the exact ways in which the functions should communicate with each other, and especially with the calling program. If you wish to make any changes in the organization of the program, be certain that the precise details are spelled out clearly and completely for all members of the group.

*cooperation*

Next, you will find that it is too much to hope that all members of the group will complete their work at the same time, or that all parts of the project can be combined and debugged together. You will therefore need to use program stubs and drivers (see Section 1.4) to debug and test the various parts of the project. One member of the group might take special responsibility for this testing. In any case, you will find it very effective for different members to read, help debug, and test each other's subprograms.

*coordination*

Finally, there are the responsibilities of making sure that all members of the group complete their work on time, of keeping track of the progress of various aspects of the project, of making sure that no subprograms are integrated into the project before they are thoroughly debugged and tested, and then of combining all the work into the finished product.

---

**Exercises 4.7**

**E1.** A function in C can return a pointer as its result. Since a linked queue can be described by a single pointer to its head, we could define

> typedef struct queue *Polynomial;

Then we could write the arithmetic operations as, for example,

> Polynomial Subtract(Polynomial p, Polynomial q);

We could also write Pop(s) as a function that returns the top polynomial on the stack as its result. Then function DoCommand could then be shortened considerably by writing such statements as

> Push(Subtract(Pop(s), Pop(s)), s);

**(a)** Assuming that this statement works correctly, explain why it would still be bad programming style.

**(b)** It is possible that two different C compilers, both adhering strictly to ANSI standard C, would translate this statement in ways that would give different answers when the program runs. Explain how this could happen.

**E2.** Discuss the steps that would be needed to extend the polynomial calculator so that it would process polynomials in several variables.

**Programming Projects 4.7**

**P1.** Assemble the functions developed in this section and make the necessary changes in the code so as to produce a working skeleton for the calculator program, one that will read, write, and add polynomials. You will need to supply the functions Introduction and Instructions.

**P2.** Write the function Subtract and integrate it into the calculator.

**P3.** Write a function

> void MonomialMult(Term monomial, Polynomial *poly, Polynomial *product);

that multiplies poly by the one term monomial, returning the answer as product.

**P4.** Use the function of the preceding problem, together with the function Add, to write the function Multiply, and integrate the resulting function into the calculator.

**P5.** Write the function Divide and integrate it into the calculator.

**P6.** The function ReadCommand, as written, will accept any sequence of commands, but some sequences are illegal. If the stack begins empty, for example, then the sequence + ? ? is illegal, because it is impossible to add two polynomials before reading them in. Modify function ReadCommand as follows so that it will accept only legal sequences of commands. The function should set up a counter and initialize it to the number of polynomials on the stack. Whenever the command ? appears in the stream the counter is increased by one (since the read command ? will push an additional polynomial onto the stack), and whenever one of + , − , ∗ , / appears, it is decreased by one (since these commands will pop two polynomials and push one onto the stack). If the counter ever becomes zero or negative then the sequence is illegal.

**P7.** Many reverse Polish calculators not only use a stack but also provide memory locations where operands can be stored. Extend the project to provide for memory locations for polynomials, and provide additional commands to store the top of the stack into a memory location and to push the polynomial in a memory location onto the stack. There should be an array of 100 memory locations, and all 100 positions should be initialized to the zero polynomial when the program begins. The functions that access the memory should ask the user which location to use.

**P8.** Write a function that will discard the top polynomial on the stack, and include this capability as a new command.

**P9.** Write a function that will interchange the top two polynomials on the stack, and include this capability as a new command.

**P10.** Write a function that will add all the polynomials on the stack together, and include this capability as a new command.

**P11.** Write a function that will compute the derivative of a polynomial, and include this capability as a new command.

**P12.** Write a function that, given a polynomial and a real number, evaluates the polynomial at that number, and include this capability as a new command.

**P13.** Modify the function Divide so that the result of the function will be two new polynomials, the quotient and the remainder, where the remainder, if not 0, has degree strictly less than that of the divisor. First push the quotient onto the stack, then the remainder.

# 4.8 Abstract Data Types and Their Implementations

## 4.8.1 INTRODUCTION

Suppose that in deciphering a long and poorly documented program you found the following sets of instructions:

```
xxt->xlnk = w;      w->xlnk = NULL;      xxt = w;
```

and

```
if ((xxh == xxt + 1 && xxt >= 0) || (xxt == mxx && xxh == 0))
    tryagain();
else {
    xxt++;
    if (xxt > mxx)
        xxt = 0;
    xx[xxt] = wi;
}
```

In isolation it may not be clear what either of these sections of code is intended to do, and without further explanation, it would probably take some minutes to realize that in fact they have essentially the same function! Both segments are intended to append an item to the end of a queue, the first queue in a linked implementation and the second queue in contiguous storage.

*analogies*

Researchers working in different subjects frequently have ideas that are fundamentally similar but are developed for different purposes and expressed in different language. Often years will pass before anyone realizes the similarity of the work, but when the observation is made, insight from one subject can help with the other. In computer science, even so, the same basic idea often appears in quite different disguises that obscure the similarity. But if we can discover and emphasize the similarities, then we may be able to generalize the ideas and obtain easier ways to meet the requirements of many applications.

*similarity*

When we first introduced stacks and queues, we considered them only as they are implemented in contiguous storage, and yet upon introduction of linked stacks and queues, we had no difficulty in recognizing the same underlying logical structure. The obscurity of the code at the beginning of this section reflects the programmer's failure to recognize the general concept of a queue and to distinguish between this general concept and the particular implementation needed for each application.

*implementation*

The way in which an underlying structure is implemented can have substantial effects on program development, and on the capabilities and usefulness of the result. Sometimes these effects can be subtle. The underlying mathematical concept of a real number, for example, is usually (but not always) implemented by computer as a floating-point number with a certain degree of precision, and the inherent limitations in this implementation often produce difficulties with round-off error. Drawing a clear separation between the logical structure of our data and its implementation in computer memory will help us in designing programs. Our first step is to recognize the logical connections among the data and embody these connections in a logical data structure. Later we can consider our data structures and decide what is the best way to implement them for efficiency of programming and execution. By separating these decisions they both become easier, and we avoid pitfalls that attend premature commitment.

To help us clarify this distinction and achieve greater generality let us now reconsider some of the data structures we have studied from as general a perspective as we can.

## 4.8.2 GENERAL DEFINITIONS

### 1. Mathematical Concepts

Mathematics is the quintessence of generalization and therefore provides the language we need for our definitions. We start with the definition of a type:

**Definition**    A *type* is a set, and the elements of the set are called the *values* of the type.

We may therefore speak of the type *integer*, meaning the set of all integers, the type *real*, meaning the set of all real numbers, the type *character*, meaning the set of symbols that we wish to manipulate with our algorithms.

Notice that we can already draw a distinction between an abstract type and its implementation: The C type int, for example, is not the set of all integers; it consists only of the set of those integers directly represented in a particular computer, the largest of which is INT_MAX.

Similarly, the C type double generally means a certain set of floating-point numbers (separate mantissa and exponent) that is only a small subset of the set of all real numbers. The C type char also varies from computer to computer; sometimes it is the ASCII character set; sometimes it is the EBCDIC character set; sometimes it is some other set of symbols. Even so, all these types, both abstract types and implementations, are sets and hence fit the definition of a type.

### 2. Atomic and Structured Types

Types such as integer, real, and character are called *atomic* types because we think of their values as single entities only, not something we wish to subdivide. Computer languages like C, however, provide tools such as arrays, files, and pointers with which we can build new types, called *structured* types. A single value of a structured type (that is, a single element of its set) is an array or file or linked list. A value of a structured type has two ingredients: It is made up of *component* elements, and there is a *structure*, a set of rules for putting the components together.

*building types*

For our general point of view we shall use mathematical tools to provide the rules for building up structured types. Among these tools are sets, sequences, and functions. For the study of lists of various kinds the one that we need is the *finite sequence*, and for its definition we use mathematical induction. A definition by induction (like a proof by induction) has two parts: First is an initial case, and second is the definition of the general case in terms of preceding cases.

**Definition**  A *sequence of length* 0 is empty. A *sequence of length* $n \geq 1$ of elements from a set $T$ is an ordered pair $(S_{n-1}, t)$ where $S_{n-1}$ is a sequence of length $n - 1$ of elements from $T$, and $t$ is an element of $T$.

From this definition we can build up longer and longer sequences, starting with the empty sequence and adding on new elements from $T$, one at a time.

*sequential versus contiguous*

From now on we shall draw a careful distinction between the word *sequential*, meaning that the elements form a sequence, and the word *contiguous*, which we take to mean that the nodes have adjacent addresses in memory. Hence we shall be able to speak of a *sequential* list in either a *linked* or *contiguous* implementation.

### 3. Abstract Data Types

The definition of a finite sequence immediately makes it possible for us to attempt a definition of a list: a *list* of items of a type $T$ is simply a finite sequence of elements of the set $T$. Next we would like to define stacks and queues, but if you consider the definitions, you will realize that there will be nothing regarding the sequence of items to distinguish these structures from a list. The only difference among stacks, queues, and lists is in the *operations* by which changes or accesses can be made. Hence, before turning to these other structures, we should complete the definition of a simple list (as we have previously studied it) by specifying what operations can be done. Including a statement of these operations with the structural rules defining a finite sequence, we obtain

**Definition**  A *simple list* of elements of type $T$ is a finite sequence of elements of $T$ together with the operations

1. *Create* the list, leaving it empty.
2. Determine whether the list is *empty* or not.
3. Determine whether the list is *full* or not.
4. Find the *size* of the list.
5. *Add* a new entry at the end of the list, provided the list is not full.
6. *Traverse* the list, performing a given operation with each entry.
7. *Clear* the list to make it empty.

Stacks and queues can now be defined in a similar way.

**Definition**    A *stack* of elements of type $T$ is a finite sequence of elements of $T$ together with the operations

1. *Create* the stack, leaving it empty.
2. Determine whether the stack is *empty* or not.
3. Determine whether the stack is *full* or not.
4. Find the *size* of the stack.
5. *Push* a new entry onto the top of the stack, provided the stack is not full.
6. *Retrieve* the top entry in the stack, provided the stack is not empty.
7. *Pop* the entry off the top of the stack, provided the stack is not empty.
8. *Clear* the stack to make it empty.
9. *Traverse* the stack, performing a given operation with each entry.

**Definition**    A *queue* of elements of type $T$ is a finite sequence of elements of $T$ together with the operations

1. *Create* the queue, leaving it empty.
2. Determine whether the queue is *empty* or not.
3. Determine whether the queue is *full* or not.
4. Find the *size* of the queue.
5. *Append* a new entry onto the rear of the queue, provided the queue is not full.
6. *Retrieve* the front entry in the queue, provided the queue is not empty.
7. *Serve* (and remove) the entry from the front of the queue, provided the queue is not empty.
8. *Clear* the queue to make it empty.
9. *Traverse* the queue, performing a given operation with each entry.

In the strict sense, traversal is not allowed for stacks or queues, so, in this strict sense, we have defined ***traversable stacks*** and ***traversable queues***. Note that these definitions make no mention of the way in which the abstract data type (list, stack, or queue) is to be implemented. In the past several chapters we have studied different implementations of each of these types, and these new definitions fit any of these implementations equally well. These definitions produce what is called an

*abstract data type*    ***abstract data type***, often abbreviated as ***ADT***. The important principle is that the definition of any abstract data type involves two parts: First is a description of the way in which the components are related to each other, and second is a statement of the operations that can be performed on elements of the abstract data type.

### 4.8.3 REFINEMENT OF DATA SPECIFICATION

*top-down specification*

Now that we have obtained such general definitions of abstract data types, it is time to begin specifying more detail, since the objective of all this work is to find general principles that will help with designing programs, and we need more detail to accomplish this objective. There is, in fact, a close analogy between the process of top-down refinement of algorithms and the process of top-down specification of data structures that we have now begun. In algorithm design we begin with a general but precise statement of the problem and slowly specify more detail until we have developed a complete program. In data specification we begin with the selection of the mathematical concepts and abstract data types required for our problem and slowly specify more detail until finally we can describe our data structures in terms of a programming language.

*stages of refinement*

The number of stages required in this specification process depends on the application. The design of a large software system will require many more decisions than will the design of a single small program, and these decisions should be taken in several stages of refinement. Although different problems will require different numbers of stages of refinement, and the boundaries between these stages sometimes blur, we can pick out four levels of the refinement process.

*conceptual*

1. On the *abstract* level we decide how the data are related to each other and what operations are needed, but we decide nothing concerning how the data will actually be stored or how the operations will actually be done.

*algorithmic*

2. On the *data structures* level we specify enough detail so that we can analyze the behavior of the operations and make appropriate choices as dictated by our problem. This is the level, for example, at which we choose between contiguous lists and linked lists. Some operations are easier for contiguous lists and others for linked lists: finding the length of the list and retrieving the $k^{th}$ element are easier for contiguous lists; inserting and deleting are easier for linked lists. Some applications require many insertions or deletions at arbitrary positions in a list, so we prefer linked lists. For other problems contiguous lists prove better.

*programming*

3. On the *implementation* level we decide the details of how the data structures will be represented in computer memory.

4. On the *application* level we settle all details required for our particular application, such as names for variables or special requirements for the operations imposed by the application.

The first two levels are often called *conceptual* because at these levels we are more concerned with problem solving than with programming. The middle two levels can be called *algorithmic* because they concern precise methods for representing data and operating with it. The last two levels are specifically concerned with *programming*.

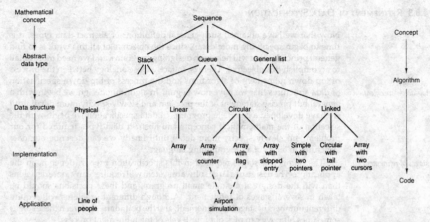

Figure 4.12. Refinement of a queue

Figure 4.12 illustrates these stages of refinement in the case of a queue. We begin with the mathematical concept of a sequence and then the queue considered as an abstract data type. At the next level, we choose from the various data structures shown in the diagram, ranging from the physical model (in which all items move forward as each one leaves the head of the queue) to the linear model (in which the queue is emptied all at once) to circular arrays and finally linked lists. Some of these data structures allow further variation in their implementation, as shown on the next level. At the final stage, the queue is coded for a specific application.

Let us conclude this section by restating its most important principles as programming precepts:

---

**Programming Precept**

*Let your data structure your program.*
*Refine your algorithms and data structures at the same time.*

---

---

**Programming Precept**

*Once your data are fully structured,*
*your algorithms should almost write themselves.*

---

**Exercises 4.8**   **E1.** Draw a diagram similar to that of Figure 4.12 showing levels of refinement for a stack.

**E2.** Give a formal definition of the term *deque*, using the definitions given for stack and queue as models.

**E3.** In mathematics the *Cartesian product* of sets $T_1, T_2, \ldots, T_n$ is defined as the set of all $n$-tuples $(t_1, t_2, \ldots, t_n)$ where $t_i$ is a member of $T_i$ for all $i, 1 \leq i \leq n$. Use the Cartesian product to give a precise definition of a *structure* that does not use a *union* to represent its contents.

## Pointers and Pitfalls

1. Before choosing implementations, be sure that all the data structures and their associated operations are fully specified on the abstract level.

2. In choosing between linked and contiguous implementations, consider the necessary operations on the data structure. Linked structures are more flexible in regard to insertions, deletions, and rearrangement; contiguous structures are sometimes faster.

3. Contiguous structures usually require less computer memory, computer time, and programming effort when the items in the structure are small and the algorithms are simple. When the structure holds large records, linked structures usually save space, time, and often programming effort.

## Review Questions

4.1
1. Define the term *queue*. What operations can be done on a queue?

2. How is a circular array implemented in a linear array?

3. List three different implementations of queues.

4.4
4. Define the term *simulation*.

4.5
5. Give two reasons why dynamic memory allocation is a valuable device.

6. Define the terms *linked* and *contiguous*.

7. What is a *pointer*?

8. Define the terms *static variable* and *dynamic variable*.

9. What is the difference between "p == NULL" and "p is undefined"?

10. Is the header for a linked list usually a static variable or a dynamic variable?

11. What is the basic step required to advance a pointer p one step through a linked list?

12. What condition is checked to determine if p has moved past the end of a list?

13. Why is it more difficult to move backward than forward in a linked list?

*4.6*
14. For linked queues, why are there separate operations Append and AppendNode for processing entries and nodes, respectively?

15. Why is it more important to have both the functions ClearQueue and Create-Queue for the linked implementation than for it is for the contiguous implementation?

16. Are the procedures for processing queues simpler for contiguous queues or for linked queues? Why?

17. What extreme case requires special treatment in writing the subprograms that process linked queues? Why?

*4.7*
18. Discuss some problems that occur in group programming projects that do not occur in individual programming projects. What advantages does a group project have over individual projects?

*4.8*
19. What are *atomic* and *structured* types?

20. What two parts must be in the definition of any abstract data type?

21. In an abstract data type, how much is specified about implementation?

22. Name (in order from abstract to concrete) four levels of refinement of data specification.

## References for Further Study

Queues are a standard topic covered by all data structures books. Most modern texts take the viewpoint of separating properties of data structures and their operations from the implementation of the data structures. Two examples of such books are:

JIM WELSH, JOHN ELDER, and DAVID BUSTARD, *Sequential Program Structures*, Prentice-Hall International, London, 1984, 385 pages.

DANIEL F. STUBBS and NEIL W. WEBRE, *Data Structures with Abstract Data Types and Pascal*, Brooks/Cole Publishing Company, Monterey, Calif., 1985, 459 pages.

For many topics concerning queues, the best source for additional information, historical notes, and mathematical analysis is KNUTH, volume 1 (reference in Chapter 3).

An elementary survey of computer simulations appears in *Byte* 10 (October 1985), pp. 149–251. A simulation of the National Airport in Washington, D.C., appears on pp. 186–190.

# 5

# General Lists

$T$HIS CHAPTER *turns from restricted
lists and related structures, like stacks
and queues, in which changes occur only
at the ends of the list, to more general
lists in which insertions, deletions, and
retrieval may occur at any point of the
list. After examining the specification and
implementation of such lists, we study
lists of characters, called strings, develop a
simple text editor as an application, and
finally consider the implementation of
linked lists within arrays.*

# 5.1 List Specifications

*operations,*
*information hiding,*
*and implementations*

When we first studied stacks, we practiced *information hiding* by separating our uses for stacks from the actual programming of these operations. In studying queues, we continued these methods and soon saw that many variations in *implementation* are possible. With general lists, we have much more flexibility and freedom in accessing and changing entries in any part of the list. The principles of information hiding are hence even more important for general lists than for restricted lists. Let us therefore begin by enumerating preconditions and postconditions for all the operations that we may wish to perform with lists.

*simple list operations*

In Section 2.2.1, we introduced several fundamental operations for a list, including CreateList, ClearList, ListEmpty, ListFull, and ListSize. The only operations that accessed entries of the list, however, were AddList, which added an entry at the end of a list, and TraverseList, which visited all the entries of the list. We now wish operations that will allow us to access *any* entry of the list. To develop these, let us take as our foundation all the declarations already made in Section 2.2.1 and supplement the list of operations as necessary.

*position in a list*

To find an entry, we shall simply use its *position* within the list, where the first entry in the list has position 0, the second position 1, and so on. Hence locating an entry of a list by its position is superficially like indexing an array, but there are important differences. First, if we insert an entry at a particular position, then the position numbers of all later entries increase by 1. If we delete an entry, then the positions of all following entries decrease by 1. Moreover, the position number

*implementation*
*independence*

for a list is defined without regard to the implementation. For a contiguous list, implemented in an array, the position will indeed be the index of the entry within the array. But we can also use the position to find an entry within a linked list, where no indices or arrays are used at all.

We can now give precise specifications for the remaining basic operations on a list. These are additional to the operations specified in Section 2.2.1.

---

void InsertList(Position p, ListEntry x, List *list);

*precondition:*   The list list has been created, list is not full, x is a valid list entry, and $0 \leq p \leq n$, where $n$ is the number of entries in list.

*postcondition:*  x has been inserted into position p in list; the entry formerly in position p (provided $p < n$) and all later entries have their position numbers increased by 1.

---

void DeleteList(Position p, ListEntry *x, List *list);

*precondition:*   The list list has been created, list is not empty, and $0 \leq p < n$, where $n$ is the number of entries in list.

*postcondition:*  The entry in position p of list has been returned as x and deleted from list; the entries in all later positions (provided $p < n - 1$) have their position numbers decreased by 1.

---

> void RetrieveList(Position p, ListEntry *x, List *list);
>
> *precondition:* The list list has been created, list is not empty, and $0 \le p < n$, where $n$ is the number of entries in list.
>
> *postcondition:* The entry in position p of list has been returned as x. list remains unchanged.

> void ReplaceList(Position p, ListEntry x, List *list);
>
> *precondition:* The list list has been created, list is not empty, x is a valid list entry, and $0 \le p < n$, where $n$ is the number of entries in list.
>
> *postcondition:* The entry in position p of list has been replaced by x. The other entries of list remain unchanged.

Other operations are possible for lists, but these will be left as exercises. Afterwards, we turn to implementation questions.

---

**Exercises 5.1**     Given the functions for operating with lists developed in this section and Section 2.2.1, write functions to do each of the following tasks. Be sure to specify the preconditions and postconditions for each function. You may use local variables of types List, ListEntry, and Position, but do not write any code that depends on the choice of implementation. Include code to detect an error if a precondition is violated.

**E1.** void InsertFirst(ListEntry x, List *list) inserts entry x into position 0 of list.

**E2.** void DeleteFirst(ListEntry *x, List *list) deletes the first entry of list, returning it as x.

**E3.** void InsertLast(ListEntry x, List *list) inserts x at the last entry of list.

**E4.** void DeleteLast(ListEntry x, List *list) deletes the last entry of list, returning it as x.

**E5.** void MedianList(ListEntry *x, List *list) returns x as the central entry if list has an odd number of entries, and as the left-central entry if list has an even number of entries.

**E6.** void InterchangeList(Position pos1, Position pos2, List *list) interchanges the entries at positions pos1 and pos2 of list.

**E7.** void ReverseTraverseList(List *list, void (*Visit)(ListEntry)) traverses list list in reverse order (from its last entry to its first).

**E8.** void CopyList(List *dest, List *source) copies all entries from source into dest; source remains unchanged. You may assume that dest already exists, but any entries already in dest are to be discarded.

**E9.** void JoinList(List *list1, List *list2) copies all entries from list1 onto the end of list2; list1 remains unchanged, as do all the entries previously in list2. list2 must already exist.

**E10.** void ReverseList(List *list) reverses the order of all entries in list.

**E11.** void SplitList(List *source, List *oddlist, List *evenlist) copies all entries from source so that those in odd-numbered positions make up oddlist and those in even-numbered positions make up evenlist. You may assume that oddlist and evenlist already exist, but any entries they may contain are to be discarded. The list source is to remain unchanged.

## 5.2 Implementation of Lists

At this point, we have specified how we wish lists to behave under all the operations we have discussed. It is now time to turn to the details of implementing lists in C. For the simple lists we have previously studied, as well as for stacks and queues, we have studied two kinds of implementations: contiguous implementations using an array and linked implementations using pointers. For general lists we have the same division, but we shall find several variations of further interest.

### 5.2.1 CONTIGUOUS IMPLEMENTATION

The contiguous implementation of general lists closely follows that developed in Section 2.3.1 for simple lists. The declaration of a list as a structure consisting of an array and a counter remains unchanged, and most of the functions (CreateList, ClearList, ListEmpty, ListFull, ListSize, TraverseList) remain identical.

Rather than adding a new entry only at the end of the list, as we did with simple lists, we now wish to insert a new entry at any position in the list. To do so, we must move entries within the array to make space to insert the new one. The resulting function is:

```
/* InsertList: insert a new entry in the list.
   Pre:   The list list has been created, list is not full, x is a valid list entry, 0 ≤ p ≤ n
          where n is the number of entries in list.
   Post:  x has been inserted into position p in list; the entry formerly in position p
          (provided p < n) and all later entries have their position numbers increased by
          1.
   Uses: Error, ListFull, ListSize. */
void InsertList(Position p, ListEntry x, List *list)
{
    int i;
    if (p < 0 || p > ListSize(list))
        Error("Attempt to insert in a position not in the list.");
    else if (ListFull(list))
        Error("Attempt to insert an entry into a full list.");
    else {
        for (i = ListSize(list) − 1; i >= p; i−−)   /* Move later entries.        */
            list->entry[i + 1] = list->entry[i];
        list->entry[p] = x;
        list->count++;
    }
}
```

How much work does this function do? If we insert an entry at the end of the list, then the function executes only a small, constant number of commands. If, on the other extreme, we insert an entry at the beginning of the list, then the function must move every entry in the list to make room, so, if the list is long, it will do much more work. In the average case, where we assume that all possible insertions are equally likely, the function will move about half the entries of the list. Thus we say that the amount of work the function does is approximately *proportional* to $n$, the length of the list.

Deletion, similarly, must move entries in the list to fill the hole left by the deleted entry. Hence deletion also requires time approximately proportional to $n$, the number of entries. Most of the remaining operations, on the other hand, do not use any loops and do their work in constant time. In summary,

> *In processing a contiguous list with $n$ entries:*
>
> InsertList *and* DeleteList *require time approximately proportional to* $n$.
>
> CreateList, ClearList, ListEmpty, ListFull, ListSize, ReplaceList, *and* Retrieve-List *operate in constant time.*

We have not included TraverseList in this discussion, since its time depends on the time used by its parameter Visit, something we do not know in general.

## 5.2.2 SIMPLY LINKED IMPLEMENTATION

### 1. Declarations

For the linked implementation of a general list, we can begin with declarations of pointers and nodes similar to those we used for linked stacks, queues, and simple lists:

```
typedef char ListEntry;
typedef struct listnode {
    ListEntry entry;
    struct listnode *next;
} ListNode;

typedef int Position;
typedef struct list {
    int count;
    ListNode *head;
} List;
```

The only additional declaration here is that of the type Position that we shall use to find a particular entry within the list.

Most of the operations for general lists in simply linked implementation are identical to the corresponding operations for the simply linked implementation of simple lists studied in Chapter 4, and these need not be repeated here.

## 2. Examples

To illustrate some other kinds of actions we need to perform with linked lists, let us consider for a moment the problem of editing text, and suppose that each node holds one word as well as the link to the next node. The sentence "Stacks are lists" appears as in (a) of Figure 5.1. If we *insert* the word "simple" before the word "lists" we obtain the list in (b). Next we decide to *replace* "lists" by "structures" and *insert* the three nodes "but important data" to obtain (c). Afterward, we decide to *delete* "simple but" and so arrive at list (d). Finally, we *traverse* the list to print its contents.

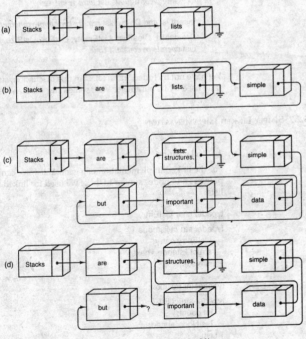

Figure 5.1. Actions on a linked list

### 3. Finding a List Position

Since we wish to be able to substitute our linked-list implementation directly for the equivalent contiguous-list implementation, we need a function that will take as its input a *position* (that is, an integer index into the list) and return a *pointer* to the corresponding node of the list. The easiest way, conceptually, to construct this function is to start at the beginning of the list and traverse it until we reach the desired node:

```
/* SetPosition: set current to point to a node at position p.
   Pre:   p is a valid position on list list; 0 ≤ p < list->count.
   Post:  The list pointer current points to the list node at position p.
   Uses: Error. */
void SetPosition(Position p, List *list, ListNode **current)
{
    int count;                        /* used to loop through positions        */
    ListNode *q;                      /* used to traverse list                 */
    if (p < 0 || p >= list->count)
        Error("Attempt to set a position not in the list.");
    else {                            /* Count from head of list to position p. */
        q = list->head;
        for (count = 1; count <= p; count++)
            q = q->next;
        *current = q;
    }
}
```

If all nodes are equally likely, then, on average, this function must move halfway through the list to find a given position. Hence, on average, its time requirement is approximately proportional to $n$, the size of the list.

### 4. Insertion

Next let us consider the problem of inserting a new entry into a linked list. If we have a new node that we wish to insert into the middle of a linked list, then, as shown in Figure 5.2, we must have a pointer to the node *preceding* the place where

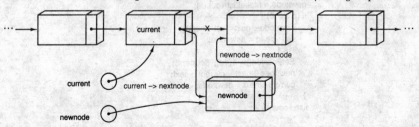

Figure 5.2. Insertion after a node

194	Chapter 5 • General Lists

the new node is to be inserted. If we let newnode point to the new node to be inserted and current point to the preceding node, then this action consists of the two statements

```
newnode->next = current->next;
current->next = newnode;
```

Note the order in which the two assignments of pointers are made. The next field of the new node newnode was previously undefined; hence we first assign it to its new value, current->next. This pointer then becomes free to receive its new value. If we attempted the assignment statements in the reverse order, then the value of current->next would be lost before it was used, and there would be no way to attach the new node newnode to the remainder of the list.

We can now build this code into a function for inserting a new entry into a linked list. Insertion at the beginning of the list must be treated as a special case, since the new entry then does not follow any other.

```
/* InsertList: insert a new entry in the list.
   Pre:  The list list has been created, list is not full, x is a valid list entry, 0 ≤ p ≤ n
         where n is the number of entries in list.
   Post: x has been inserted into position p in list; the entry formerly in position p
         (provided p < n) and all later entries have their position numbers increased
         by 1.
   Uses: Error, MakeListNode, SetPosition. */
void InsertList(Position p, ListEntry x, List *list)
{
    ListNode *newnode, *current;

    if (p < 0 || p > list->count)
        Error("Attempt to insert in a position not in the list.");
    else {
        newnode = MakeListNode(x);
        if (p == 0) {
            newnode->next = list->head;
            list->head = newnode;
        } else {
            SetPosition(p - 1, list, &current);
            newnode->next = current->next;
            current->next = newnode;
        }
        list->count++;
    }
}
```

InsertList requires an auxiliary function that obtains space for the new node being inserted:

```
/* MakeListNode: make a new ListNode.
   Pre:    The entry x is valid.
   Post:   The function creates a new ListNode, initializes it with x, and returns a pointer
           to the new node. */
ListNode *MakeListNode(ListEntry x)
{
    ListNode *p = malloc(sizeof(ListNode));   /* Obtain space from the system.     */
    if (p) {
        p->entry = x;
        p->next = NULL;                /* Set pointer field for safety's sake.     */
    } else
        Error("No space for additional node can be obtained.");
    return p;
}
```

### 5. Other Operations

The remaining operations for linked lists will all be left as exercises. Those that access a particular position in the list all need to use the function SetPosition, sometimes for the current position, and sometimes, as in InsertList, for the previous position. All these functions turn out to perform at most a constant number of steps other than those in SetPosition, except for ClearList (and TraverseList), which go through all entries of the list. We therefore have:

> *In processing a linked list with $n$ entries:*
>
> ClearList, InsertList, DeleteList, RetrieveList, *and* ReplaceList *require time approximately proportional to* $n$.
>
> CreateList, ListEmpty, ListFull, *and* ListSize *operate in constant time.*

Again, we have not included TraverseList in this discussion, since its time depends on the time used by its parameter Visit, something we do not know in general.

### 5.2.3 Variation: Keeping the Current Position

Many applications process the entries of a list in order, moving from one entry to the next. Many other applications refer to the same entry several times, doing Retrieve or Replace operations before moving to another entry. For all these applications, our current implementation of linked lists is very inefficient, since every operation that accesses an entry of the list begins by tracing through the list from its start until the desired position is reached. It would be much more efficient if, instead, we were able to *remember* the last-used position in the list and, if the next operation refers to the same or a later position, start tracing through the list from this last-used position.

Note, however, that remembering the last-used position will not speed up *every* application using lists. If, for example, some program accesses the entries of a linked list in reverse order, starting at its end, then every access will require tracing from the start of the list, since the links give only one-way directions. Remembering the last-used position gives no help in finding the one preceding it.

The enlarged declaration for a list now becomes:

```
typedef int Position;
typedef struct list {
    int count;
    ListNode *head;
    Position currentpos;
    ListNode *current;
} List;
```

We can then rewrite SetPosition to use and change these new fields of the record. Note that, since the current position is now part of the list record, there is no longer a need for SetPosition to return a pointer as an output parameter; instead, the calling function can refer to current directly within the list record.

```
/* SetPosition: set list->current to point to a node at position p.
   Pre:  p is a valid position on list list; 0 ≤ p < list->count.
   Post: The pointer list->current points to the list node at position p.
   Uses: Error. */
void SetPosition(Position p, List *list)
{
    if (p < 0 || p >= list->count)
        Error("Attempt to set a position not in the list.");
    else {
        if (p < list->currentpos) {
            list->currentpos = 0;
            list->current = list->head;
        }
        for (; list->currentpos != p; list->currentpos++)
            list->current = list->current->next;
    }
}
```

Note that, for repeated references to the same position, neither the body of the if statement nor the body of the for statement will be executed, and hence the function will take almost no time. If we move forward only one position, the body of the for statement will be executed only once, so again the function will be very fast. On the other hand, when it is necessary to move backwards through the list, then the function operates in almost the same way as the version of SetPosition used in the previous implementation.

With this revised version of SetPosition we can now revise the linked-list implementation to improve its efficiency. The changes needed to the various functions are minor, and they will all be left as exercises.

### 5.2.4 DOUBLY LINKED LISTS

Some applications of linked lists require that we frequently move both forward and backward through the list. In the last section we solved this problem by traversing the list from its beginning until the desired node was found, but this solution is generally unsatisfactory. Its programming is difficult, and the running time of the program will depend on the length of the list, which may be quite long.

There are several methods that can be used to overcome this problem of finding the node preceding the given one. In this section, we shall study the simplest and, in many ways, the most flexible and satisfying method.

#### 1. Declarations for a Doubly Linked List

*doubly linked list*

The idea, as shown in Figure 5.3, is to keep *two* links in each node, pointing in opposite directions. Hence, by following the appropriate link, we can move either direction through the linked list with equal ease. We call such a list a ***doubly linked list***.

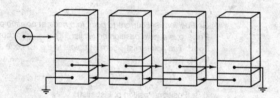

Figure 5.3. A doubly linked list

In a doubly linked list, the declaration of a node becomes

```
typedef char ListEntry;

typedef struct listnode {
    ListEntry entry;
    struct listnode *next;
    struct listnode *previous;
} ListNode;
```

and the declaration of the list becomes

```
typedef int Position;

typedef struct list {
    int count;
    ListNode *current;
    Position currentpos;
} List;
```

It is thus possible to move in either direction through the list while keeping only one pointer into the list.

Note that, in the declaration of a list, we keep only a pointer to the current node of the list. We do not even need to keep pointers to the head or the tail of the list, since they, like any other nodes, can be found by tracing back or forth from any given node.

### 2. Operations on Doubly Linked Lists

With a doubly linked list, traversals in either direction, finding a particular position, insertions, and deletions from arbitrary positions in the list can be accomplished without difficulty. Some of the functions that make changes in the list are longer than those for simply linked lists because it is necessary to update both forward and backward links when a node is inserted or deleted from the list.

First, to find a particular location within the list, we need only decide whether to move forward or backward from the initial position. Then we do a partial traversal of the list until we reach the desired position. The resulting function is:

/* SetPosition: set current *to point to a node at position* p.
   **Pre:**  p *is a valid position on list* list; $0 \le p <$ list->count.
   **Post:** *The pointer* list->current *points to the list node at position* p.
   **Uses:** Error. */

```
void SetPosition(Position p, List *list)
{
    if (p < 0 || p >= list->count)
        Error("Attempt to set a position not in the list.");
    else if (list->currentpos < p)
        for (; list->currentpos != p; list->currentpos + +)
            list->current = list->current->next;
    else if (list->currentpos > p)
        for (; list->currentpos != p; list->currentpos - -)
            list->current = list->current->previous;
}
```

Given this function, we can now write the insertion function, which is made somewhat longer by the need to adjust multiple links. Special care must be taken when the insertion is at one end of the list or into a previously empty list.

```
/* InsertList: insert a new entry in the list.
    Pre:  The list list has been created, list is not full, x is a valid list entry, 0 ≤ p ≤ n
          where n is the number of entries in list.
    Post: x has been inserted into position p in list; the entry formerly in position p
          (provided p < n) and all later entries have their position numbers increased
          by 1.
    Uses: Error, SetPosition. */
void InsertList(Position p, ListEntry x, List *list)
{
    ListNode *newnode, *following;

    if (p < 0 || p > list->count)
        Error("Attempt to insert in a position not in the list.");
    else {
        newnode = MakeListNode(x);
        if (p == 0) {              /* Insert at the beginning of the list.         */
            newnode->previous = NULL;
            if (list->count == 0)  /* The list was empty.                          */
                newnode->next = NULL;
            else {                 /* Insert at the start of the existing list.    */
                SetPosition(0, list);
                newnode->next = list->current;
                list->current->previous = newnode;
            }
        } else {                   /* Insert later in the list.                    */
            SetPosition(p - 1, list);
            following = list->current->next;
                           /* Insert between current and following. */
            newnode->next = following;
            newnode->previous = list->current;
            list->current->next = newnode;
            if (following)
                following->previous = newnode;
        }
        list->current = newnode;
        list->currentpos = p;
        list->count++;
    }
}
```

The cost of a doubly linked list, of course, is the extra space required in each node
for a second link. For most applications, however, the amount of space needed for
the information field entry in each node is much larger than the space needed for a
link, so the second link field in each node does not significantly increase the total
amount of storage space required for the list.

## 5.2.5 Comparison of Implementations

Now that we have seen several algorithms for manipulating linked lists and several variations in their structure and implementation, let us pause to assess some relative advantages of linked and of contiguous implementation of lists.

*advantages*

*overflow*

The foremost advantage of linked lists in dynamic storage is flexibility. Overflow is no problem until the computer memory is actually exhausted. Especially when the individual records are quite large, it may be difficult to determine the amount of contiguous static storage that might be needed for the required arrays, while keeping enough free for other needs. With dynamic allocation, there is no need to attempt to make such decisions in advance.

*changes*

Changes, especially insertions and deletions, can be made in the middle of a linked list more quickly than in the middle of a contiguous list. If the structures are large, then it is much quicker to change the values of a few pointers than to copy the structures themselves from one location to another.

*disadvantages*

*space use*

The first drawback of linked lists is that the links themselves take space—space that might otherwise be needed for additional data. In most systems, a pointer requires the same amount of storage (one word) as does an integer. Thus a list of integers will require double the space in linked storage that it would require in contiguous storage. On the other hand, in many practical applications, the nodes in the list are quite large, with data fields taking hundreds of words altogether. If each node contains 100 words of data, then using linked storage will increase the memory requirement by only one percent, an insignificant amount. In fact, if extra space is allocated to arrays holding contiguous lists to allow for additional insertions, then linked storage will probably require less space altogether. If each entry takes 100 words, then contiguous storage will save space only if all the arrays can be filled to more than 99 percent of capacity.

*random access*

The major drawback of linked lists is that they are not suited to random access. With contiguous storage, the program can refer to any position within a list as quickly as to any other position. With a linked list, it may be necessary to traverse a long path to reach the desired node. Access to a single node in linked storage may even take slightly more computer time, since it is necessary, first, to obtain the pointer and then go to the address. This last consideration, however, is usually of no importance. Similarly, you may find at first that writing functions to manipulate linked lists takes a bit more programming effort, but, with practice, this discrepancy will decrease.

*programming*

In summary, therefore, we can conclude:

*Contiguous storage is generally preferable*

> *when the records are individually very small;*
>
> *when the size of the list is known when the program is written;*
>
> *when few insertions or deletions need to be made except at the end of the list; and*
>
> *when random access is important.*

*Linked storage proves superior*

*when the records are large;*

*when the size of the list is not known in advance; and*

*when flexibility is needed in inserting, deleting, and rearranging the entries.*

Finally, to help choose one of the many possible variations in structure and implementation, the programmer should consider which of the operations will actually be performed on the list, and which of these are the most important. Is there *locality of reference?* That is, if one entry is accessed, is it likely that it will next be accessed again? Are the entries processed in order or not? If so, then it may be worthwhile to maintain the last-used position as part of the list structure. Is it necessary to move both directions through the list? If so, then doubly linked lists may prove advantageous.

---

**Exercises 5.2**

**E1.** Write C functions to implement the remaining operations for the contiguous implementation of a list, as follows:

(a) DeleteList

(b) ReplaceList

(c) RetrieveList

**E2.** Write C functions to implement the following operations for the (first) simply linked implementation of a list:

(a) ClearList            (c) ReplaceList

(b) DeleteList           (d) RetrieveList

**E3.** Write DeleteList for the (second) implementation of simply linked lists that remembers the last-used position.

**E4.** Indicate which of the following functions are the same for doubly linked lists (as implemented in this section) and for simply linked lists. For those that are different, write new versions for doubly linked lists. Be sure that each function conforms to the specifications given in Section 5.1.

(a) CreateList           (g) ReplaceList

(b) ClearList            (h) InsertList

(c) ListEmpty           (i) DeleteList

(d) ListFull             (j) TraverseList

(e) ListSize             (k) SetPosition

(f) RetrieveList

**Programming Projects 5.2**

**P1.** Prepare a collection of files containing the declarations for a contiguous list and all the functions for list processing.

**P2.** Write a menu-driven demonstration program for general lists, based on the one in Section 2.3.3, but with all the additional operations available for general lists. The list entries should be characters. Use the declarations and the functions for contiguous lists developed in Project P1.

**P3.** Create a collection of files containing declarations and functions for processing linked lists.

   (a) Use the simply linked lists as first implemented.

   (b) Use the simply linked lists that maintain a pointer to the last-used position.

   (c) Use doubly linked lists as implemented in this section.

**P4.** Start with the menu-driven demonstration program of Project P2, and, for the files supporting contiguous lists, substitute the collection of files with declarations and functions that support linked lists (from Project P3). If you have designed the declarations and the functions carefully, the program should operate correctly with no further change required.

**P5.** (a) Modify the implementation of doubly linked lists so that, along with the pointer to the last-used position, it will maintain pointers to both the first node and the last node of the list.

   (b) Use this implementation with the menu-driven demonstration program of Project P2 and thereby test that it is correct.

   (c) Discuss the advantages and disadvantages of this variation of doubly linked lists in comparison with the doubly linked lists of the text.

**P6.** (a) Write a program that will do addition, subtraction, multiplication, and division for arbitrarily large integers. Each integer should be represented as a list of its digits. Since the integers are allowed to be as large as you like, linked lists will be needed to prevent the possibility of overflow. For some operations, it is useful to move backwards through the list; hence, doubly linked lists are appropriate. Multiplication and division can be done simply as repeated addition and subtraction.

   (b) Rewrite multiply so that it is not based on repeated addition but on standard multiplication where the multiplicand1 is multiplied with each digit of multiplicand2 and then added.

   (c) Rewrite the divide operation so that it is not based on repeated subtraction but on long division. It may be necessary to write an additional function that determines if the dividend is absolutely larger than the divisor.

# 5.3 Strings

*definition*

In this section, we briefly discuss operations on a type of list called a *string*. Strings appear in most programs and a string is defined simply as an array of characters. Examples of strings are "This is a string" or "Name?", where the double quotes ("   ") are not part of the string. There is an *empty string*, denoted "". Strings, in C, are arrays of characters that end with the null byte '\0'. When we use strings surrounded by double quotes the compiler adds the null byte to the string; when we create the string by putting the characters into the array of characters, then it is our responsibility to add the null byte.

The definition

```
char *string = "This is a string.";
```

causes the compiler to allocate an array of 18 characters. The identifier string points to the start of this array and may be used like any other array variable, e.g. string[8] == 'a'.

The standard library includes capabilities for manipulating strings. Here are some of the operations available (declared in<string.h > ):

---

```
char *strcpy(char *to, char *from);
```

*precondition*:    The string from has been initialized.

*postcondition*:    The function copies string from to string to, including '\0'; it returns a pointer to the beginning of the string to.

---

```
char *strncpy(char *to, char *from, int n);
```

*precondition*:    The string from has been initialized.

*postcondition*:    The function copies at most n characters from string from to string to; it returns a pointer to the beginning of the string to. If from has less than n characters, the remaining positions are padded with '\0's.

---

```
char *strcat(char *to, char *from);
```

*precondition*:    The strings from and to have been initialized.

*postcondition*:    The function copies string from to the end of string to, including '\0'; it returns a pointer to the beginning of the string to.

---

```
char *strncat(char *to, char *from, int n);
```

*precondition*:    The strings from and to have been initialized.

*postcondition*:    The function copies at most n characters from string from to the end of string to, and terminates to with '\0'; it returns a pointer to the beginning of the string to.

---

```
int strcmp(char *s1, char *s2);
```

*precondition*:    The strings s1 and s2 have been initialized.

*postcondition*:    The function compares string s1 to string s2; it returns < 0 if s1 < s2, 0 if s1 == s2, or > 0 if s1 > s2.

```
int strncmp(char *s1, char *s2);
```
*precondition*: The strings s1 and s2 have been initialized.

*postcondition*: The function compares at most n characters of string s1 to string s2; it returns < 0 if s1 < s2, 0 if s1 == s2, or > 0 if s1 > s2.

```
char *strchr(char *s, char c);
```
*precondition*: The string s has been initialized.

*postcondition*: The function returns a pointer to the first occurrence of the character c in the string s, or it returns NULL if c is not present in s.

```
char *strrchr(char *s, char c);
```
*precondition*: The string s has been initialized.

*postcondition*: The function returns a pointer to the last occurrence of the character c in the string s, or it returns NULL if c is not present in s.

```
size_t strspn(char *s1, char *s2);
```
*precondition*: The strings s1 and s2 have been initialized.

*postcondition*: The function returns the length of the prefix of s1 that consists of characters that appear in s2. The type size_t is defined in the standard header file stdlib.h and it usually means unsigned int.

```
size_t strcspn(char *s1, char *s2);
```
*precondition*: The strings s1 and s2 have been initialized.

*postcondition*: The function returns the length of the prefix of s1 that consists of characters that do not appear in s2. The type size_t is defined in the standard header file stdlib.h and it usually means unsigned int.

---

char *strpbrk(char *s1, char *s2);

*precondition*: The strings s1 and s2 have been initialized.

*postcondition*: The function returns a pointer to the first occurrence in the string s1 of any character of the string s2, or it returns NULL if no character of s2 appears in s1.

---

char *strstr(char *s1, char *s2);

*precondition*: The strings s1 and s2 have been initialized.

*postcondition*: The function returns a pointer to the first occurrence of the string s2 in the string s1, or it returns NULL if the string s2 is not present in s1.

---

size_t strlen(char *s);

*precondition*: The string s has been initialized.

*postcondition*: The function returns the length of the string s. The length does not include the null byte '\0' at the end of the string s.

---

# 5.4 Application: A Text Editor

This section develops an application showing the use of both lists and the standard string functions we presented in the last section. Our project is the development of a miniature text-editing program. This program will allow only a few simple commands and is, therefore, quite primitive in comparison with a modern text editor or word processor. Even so, it illustrates some of the basic ideas involved in the construction of much larger and more sophisticated text editors.

## 5.4.1 SPECIFICATIONS

Our text editor will allow us to read a file into memory, where we shall say that it is stored in a *buffer*. We shall consider each line of text to be a *string*, and the buffer will be a *list* of these lines. We shall then devise editing commands that will do list operations on the lines in the buffer and will do string operations on the characters in a single line.

Since, at any moment, the user either may be typing characters to be inserted into a line or may be giving commands, a text editor should always be written to be as forgiving of invalid input as possible, recognizing illegal commands, and asking for confirmation before taking any drastic action like deleting the entire buffer.

Here is the list of commands to be included in the text editor. Each command is given by typing the letter shown in response to the prompt '?'. The command letter may be typed in either uppercase or lowercase.

*commands*

'R'  Read the text file, whose name was given in the command line, into the buffer. Any previous contents of the buffer are lost. At the conclusion, the current line will be the first line of the file.

'W'  Write the contents of the buffer to the text file whose name was given in the command line. Neither the current line nor the buffer is changed.

'I'  Insert a single new line typed in by the user at the current line number. The prompt 'I: ' requests the new line.

'D'  Delete the current line and move to the next line.

'F'  Find the first line, starting with the current line, that contains a target string that will be requested from the user.

'L'  Show the length in characters of the current line and the length in lines of the buffer.

'C'  Change the string requested from the user to a replacement text, also requested from the user, working within the current line only.

'Q'  Quit the editor; terminates immediately.

'H'  Print out help messages explaining all the commands. The program will also accept '?' as an alternative to 'H'.

'N'  Next line: advance one line through the buffer.

'P'  Previous line: back up one line in the buffer.

'B'  Beginning: go to the first line of the buffer.

'E'  End: go to the last line of the buffer.

'G'  Go to a user-specified line number in the buffer.

'S'  Substitute a line typed in by the user for the current line. The function should ask for the line number to be changed, print out the line for verification, and then request the new line.

'V'  View the entire contents of the buffer, printed out to the terminal.

**5.4.2 IMPLEMENTATION**

### 1. The Main Program

The tasks of the main program are to declare the variable required to hold the buffer that contains the current line number and a pointer to the current line, and then to coordinate execution of commands. We shall do this with a loop that first prints the contents of the current line to show the user where it is and what changes it has made, then requests a command, and then does the command. The resulting program follows.

```
/* Implement a simple editor.
   Pre:  None.
   Post: Reads in a file that contains lines (character strings), performs simple editing
         operations on the lines, and writes out the edited version.
   Uses: GetCommad, DoCommand. */

int main(int argc, char *argv[ ])
{
   char command;
   List buffer;

   CreateList( &buffer);
   OpenFiles(argc, argv, &buffer);

   do {
      GetCommand( &command, &buffer);
      DoCommand(command, &buffer);
   } while(command != 'q');

   return 0;
}
```

### 2. Receiving a Command

We now turn to the function that requests a command from the user. Since a text editor must be tolerant of invalid input, we must carefully check the commands typed in by the user and make sure that they are legal. The first step is to translate the uppercase letter into lowercase, as is done by the standard C library routine tolower, since the user cannot be expected to be consistent in typing uppercase or lowercase letters. The function GetCommand needs to obtain a response from the user, translate a letter to lowercase, and check that the response is valid.

```
/* GetCommand: get a new command.
   Pre:  None.
   Post: Returns a character command corresponding to the legal commands for the
         editor.
   Uses: ListSize, DisplayCurrentLine. */
void GetCommand(char *command, List *buffer)
{
   if(ListSize(buffer) == 0)
      printf("The buffer is empty.\n");
   else
      DisplayCurrentLine(buffer);
   printf("Please enter a command: ");
   do {
      while ((*command = getchar()) == ' ' || *command == '\t' ||
            *command == '\n')
         ;                          /* Skip white space characters.         */
      *command = tolower(*command);
      if (strchr("bcdefgh?ilnpqrsvw", *command) == NULL)
         printf("Press h for help or enter a valid command: ");
      else
         return;                    /* Received a valid command.            */
   } while (1);
}
```

## 3. Performing Commands

The function DoCommand that does the commands as specified consists essentially of one large switch statement that sends the work out to a different function for each command. Some of these functions (like NextLine and DeleteLine) are closely based on corresponding list-processing functions, but have additional processing to handle erroneous cases. Others we will need to write later; these operations may require more programming effort.

```
/* DoCommand: execute a command.
   Pre:  command is a valid command for the editor.
   Post: The command designated by command has been performed on the lines in
         the buffer or one line (depending on the command).
   Uses: All the functions that perform editor commands. */
void DoCommand(char command, List *buffer)
{
   switch(command) {
   case 'b':                        /* Go to beginning of buffer.           */
      GoToBeginning(buffer);
      break;
   case 'c':                        /* Change string to replacement text.   */
      ChangeString(buffer);
      break;
```

```
        case 'd' :              /* Delete the current line.                        */
          DeleteLine(buffer);
          break;
        case 'e' :              /* Go to the last line of the buffer.              */
          GoToEnd(buffer);
          break;
        case 'f' :              /* Find the first line containing target string.   */
          FindString(buffer);
          break;
        case 'g' :              /* Go to a user-specified line number.             */
          GoToLine(buffer);
          break;
        case '?' :
        case 'h' :              /* Display instructions explaining all commands.   */
          Help( );
          break;
        case 'i' :              /* Insert a new line at the current line number.   */
          InsertLine(buffer);
          break;
        case 'l' :              /* Show the length of current line and number of lines. */
          Length(buffer);
          break;
        case 'n' :              /* Move to next line of buffer.                    */
          NextLine(buffer);
          break;
        case 'p' :              /* Move to the previous line of buffer.            */
          PrecedingLine(buffer);
          break;
        case 'q' :              /* Terminate the editor immediately.               */
          break;
        case 'r' :              /* Read a text file into the buffer.               */
          ReadFile(buffer);
          break;
        case 's' :              /* Substitute a new line for the current line.     */
          SubstituteLine(buffer);
          break;
        case 'v' :              /* View the entire contents of the buffer.         */
          ViewBuffer(buffer);
          break;
        case 'w' :              /* Write the contents of the buffer into a text file. */
          WriteFile(buffer);
          break;
    }
}
```

To complete the project, we must, in turn, write each of the functions invoked by DoCommand.

### 4. Reading and Writing Files

Since this function destroys any previous contents of the buffer, it requests confirmation before proceeding unless, except in the case when the buffer is empty when it begins.

```
/* ReadFile: read the contents of the input file.
   Pre:    The buffer has been created.
   Post:   Reads the file contents of the input file into buffer, stopping at the end of file;
           any contents of the buffer before the read are discarded after approval from
           the user; leaves the current line at the first line of the buffer.
   Uses: ListEmpty, ClearList, CreateList, InsertList, UserSaysYes. */

void ReadFile(List *buffer)
{
   char line[MAXLINE];
   Boolean proceed = TRUE;

   if (!ListEmpty(buffer)) {
      printf("Buffer is not empty; the read will destroy it. "
             "OK to proceed? ");
      if ((proceed = UserSaysYes()) == TRUE)
         ClearList(buffer);
   }

   if (proceed) {
      CreateList(buffer);
      fseek(buffer->fpi, 0L, 0);   /* reset to the beginning of the file    */
      while (fgets(line, MAXLINE, buffer->fpi))
         InsertList(ListSize(buffer), line, buffer);
      buffer->currentpos = 0;
      buffer->current = buffer->head;
   }

}
```

*writing a file*    The function WriteFile is somewhat simpler than ReadFile, and it is left as an exercise.

### 5. Insertion of a Line

For insertion of a new line at the current line number, we must first check that the buffer is not full: Otherwise, there is no room for insertion. Then we read a string and use InsertList to insert the string into buffer.

```
/* InsertLine: insert a new line into the buffer.
   Pre:   The list buffer has been created.
   Post:  The line newline if valid is inserted into the list and currentpos is set to the
          newline.
   Uses: ListFull, ListSize, InsertList, Error. */


void InsertLine(List *buffer)
{

   int newline;
   char line[MAXLINE];

   if(ListFull(buffer))
      Error("Buffer is full; no insertion is possible.");

   else {
      printf("Where do you want to insert a new line? ");
      scanf("%d", &newline);
      if (newline < 0 || newline > ListSize(buffer)) {
         printf("That line number does not exist.");
      } else {
         printf("I: ");
         fflush(stdin);
         fgets(line, MAXLINE, stdin);
         InsertList(newline, line, buffer);
      }
   }


}
```

## 6. Searching for a String

Now we come to a more difficult task, that of searching for a line that contains a target string that the user will provide. We use the C library function strstr to check if the current line contains the target. If the target does not appear in the current line, then we search the entire buffer. If and when the target is found, then we highlight it by printing out the line where it was found, which now becomes the current line, together with a series of upward arrows ( ∧ ) showing where in the line the target appears.

```
/* FindString: find the line containing the string specified.
   Pre:  The list buffer has been created.
   Post: Obtains a target string from the user and moves through the buffer searching
         for the first line that contains the target string; prints the line where target is
         found, with the target highlighted. If the target is not found, no change is made,
         and the user is informed.
   Uses: ListEmpty. */
void FindString(List *buffer)
{
    int n;
    ListNode *p;
    char *s, *t, target[MAXLINE];
    if (ListEmpty(buffer))
        printf("Empty buffer; cannot search.\n");
    else {
        printf("String to search for? ");
        fflush(stdin);
        fgets(target, MAXLINE, stdin);
        target[strlen(target) - 1] = '\0';   /* Drop newline character.          */
        for (p = buffer->current, n = buffer->currentpos; p; p = p->next, n++)
            if ((s = strstr(p->entry, target)) != NULL)
                break;
        if (!p)
            printf("String was not found.\n");
        else {
            buffer->current = p;
            buffer->currentpos = n;
            printf("%2d: %s", n, p->entry);
            printf("    ");
            for (t = p->entry; t < s; t++)
                putchar(' ');
            for (; t < s + strlen(target); t++)
                putchar('^');
            putchar('\n');
        }
    }
}
```

## 7. Changing One String to Another

In accordance with the practice of several text editors, we shall allow the searches instituted by the Find command to be global, starting at the present position and continuing to the end of the buffer. We shall, however, treat the ChangeString command differently, so that it will make changes only in a line specified by the user. It is very easy for the user to make a mistake while typing a target or its replacement text. The FindString command changes nothing, so such a mistake is not too serious. If the ChangeString command were to work globally, a spelling error might cause changes in far different parts of the buffer from the previous location of the current line.

The function ChangeString obtains the target from the user, then locates it in the current string. If it is not found, the user is informed; otherwise, the user is requested to give the replacement text, after which a series of string operations remove the target from the current line and replace it with the replacement text.

```
/* ChangeString: change a string within buffer.
   Pre:   The list buffer has been created.
   Post:  If the line the user specifies is not in the buffer, then no change is made, and
          the user is informed. Otherwise, a target is obtained from the user and located
          in the line the user specified. If it is not found, the user is informed. Otherwise,
          a replacement string is obtained from the user and substituted for the target
          string.
   Uses: ListSize, SetPosition. */
void ChangeString(List *buffer)
{
    int n, len;
    char *s, rep[MAXLINE], text[MAXLINE], temp[MAXLINE];
    printf("Which line to change? ");
    scanf("%d", &n);                    /* Input the line number.                    */
    if (n < 0 || n >= ListSize(buffer))
        printf("No line to process.");
    else {
        SetPosition(n, buffer);
        printf("Text to replace? ");
        fflush(stdin);
        fgets(text, MAXLINE, stdin);    /* Input the target.                         */
        text[strlen(text) - 1] = '\0';  /* Drop newline character.                   */
        if ((s = strstr(buffer->current->entry, text)) == NULL)
            printf("String not found.");
        else {
            printf("Replacement text? ");
            fflush(stdin);
            fgets(rep, MAXLINE, stdin); /* Input the replacement.                    */
            rep[strlen(rep) - 1] = '\0';
            len = s - buffer->current->entry;
            strncpy(temp, buffer->current->entry, len);
            temp[len] = '\0';
            strcat(temp, rep);
            strcat(temp, buffer->current->entry + len + strlen(text));
            free(buffer->current->entry);
            buffer->current->entry = malloc(strlen(temp) + 1);
            strcpy(buffer->current->entry, temp);
        }
    }
}
```

**Programming Projects 5.4**

**P1.** Supply the following functions; test and exercise the text editor.

(a) WriteFile
(b) GoToBeginning
(c) GoToEnd
(d) GoToLine
(e) NextLine
(f) DeleteLine
(g) ViewBuffer
(h) Length
(i) LengthLine
(j) Help
(k) PrecedingLine
(l) SubstituteLine
(m) NextLine

**P2.** Add a feature to the text editor to put text into two columns, as follows. The user will select a range of line numbers, and the corresponding lines from the buffer will be placed into two queues, the first half of the lines in one, and the second half in the other. The lines will then be removed from the queues, one at a time from each, and combined with a predetermined number of blanks between them to form a line of the final result. (The white space between the columns is called the *gutter*.)

## 5.5 Linked Lists in Arrays

*old languages*

Several of the older but widely-used computer languages, such as FORTRAN, COBOL, and BASIC, do not provide facilities for dynamic storage allocation or pointers. Even when implemented in these languages, however, there are many problems where the methods of linked lists are preferable to those of contiguous lists, where, for example, the ease of changing a pointer rather than copying a large record proves advantageous. This section shows how to implement linked lists using only integer variables and arrays.

### 1. The Method

The idea is to begin with a large workspace array (or several arrays to hold different parts of a logical record, in the case when the programming language does not support records) and regard the array as our allocation of unused space. We then set up our own functions to keep track of which parts of the array are unused and to link entries of the array together in the desired order.

*dynamic memory*

The one feature of linked lists that we must invariably lose in this implementation method is the dynamic allocation of storage, since we must decide in advance how much space to allocate to each array. All the remaining advantages of linked lists, such as flexibility in rearranging large records or ease in making insertions or deletions anywhere in the list, will still apply, and linked lists still prove a valuable method.

The implementation of linked lists within arrays even proves valuable in languages like C that do provide pointers and dynamic memory allocation. The applications where arrays may prove preferable are those where

*advantages*

- the number of entries in a list is known in advance,

- the links are frequently rearranged, but relatively few insertions or deletions are made, and

- the same data are sometimes best treated as a linked list and other times as a contiguous list.

*multiple linkages*

An example of such an application is illustrated in Figure 5.4, which shows a small part of a student record system. Identification numbers are assigned to students first-come, first-served, so neither the names nor the marks in any particular course are in any special order. Given an identification number, a student's records may be found immediately by using the identification number as an index to look in the arrays. Sometimes, however, it is desired to print out the student records alphabetically by name, and this can be done by following the links stored in the array nextname. Similarly, student records can be ordered by marks in any course by following the links in the appropriate array.

To show how this implementation of linked lists works, let us traverse the linked list nextname shown in the first part of Figure 5.4. The list header (shown below the table) contains the value 8, which means that the entry in position 8, Arthur, E., is the first entry on the list. Position 8 of nextname then contains the value 0, which means that the name in position 0, Clark, F., comes next. In position 0, nextname contains 5, so Evans, B. comes next. Position 5 points to position 3 (Garcia, T.), which points to position 4 (Hall, W.), and position 4 points to position 1 (Smith, A.). In position 1, nextname contains a −1, which means that position 1 is the last entry on the linked list.

The array nextmath, similarly, describes a linked list giving the scores in the array math in descending order. The first entry is 5, which points to 3, and the following nodes in the order of the linked list are 1, 0, 4, and 8. The order in which the nodes appear in the linked list described by nextCS is 1, 3, 5, 8, 4, and 0.

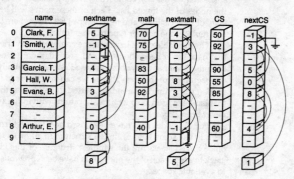

Figure 5.4. Linked lists in arrays

*shared lists and random access*

As the example in Figure 5.4 shows, implementation of linked lists in arrays can achieve the *flexibility* of linked lists for making changes, the ability to *share* the same information fields (such as the names in Figure 5.4) among several linked lists, and, by using indices to access entries directly, the advantage of *random access* otherwise available only for contiguous lists.

*indices*

In the implementation of linked lists in arrays, pointers become indices relative to the start of arrays, and the links of a list are stored in an array, each entry of which gives the index where, within the array, the next entry of the list is stored. To distinguish these indices from the pointers of a linked list in dynamic storage, we shall refer to links within arrays as *indices* and reserve the word *pointer* for links in dynamic storage.

For the sake of writing programs, we shall declare two arrays for each linked list, entry[ ] to hold the information in the nodes and nextnode[ ] to give the index of the next node. For most applications, entry is an array of records, or it is split into several arrays if the programming language does not provide for records. Both the arrays entry and nextnode will be indexed from 0 to MAXLIST − 1, where MAXLIST is a symbolic constant. Since we begin the indices with 0, we can make another

*nil indices*

arbitrary choice, and use the index value −1 to indicate the end of the list, just as the pointer value NULL is used in dynamic storage. This choice is also illustrated in Figure 5.4.

You should take a moment to trace through Figure 5.4, checking that the index values as shown correspond to the colored arrows shown from each entry to its successor.

## 2. Operations: Space Management

To obtain the flavor of implementing linked lists in arrays, let us rewrite some of the functions of this chapter with this implementation.

*stack of available space*

Our first task is to set up a list of available space and write functions to obtain a new node and to return a node to available space. For the sake of programming consistently with Section 5.2, we shall change our point of view slightly. All the space that we use will come from an array called workspace, whose entries will be the nodes of the linked list. Each of these nodes will be a record with two fields, entry of type ListEntry and next of type ListIndex, where ListIndex indexes the array and replaces the pointer type of other linked lists.

The available space in workspace comes in two varieties. First, there are nodes that have never been allocated, and, second, there are nodes that have previously been used but have now been released. We shall initially allocate space starting at the beginning of the array; hence we can keep track of how much space has been used at some time by an index lastused that indicates the position of the last node that has been used at some time. Locations with indices greater than lastused have never been allocated.

For the nodes that have been used and then returned to available space, we need to use some kind of linked structure to allow us to go from one to the next. Since linked stacks are the simplest structure of this kind, we shall use a linked stack to keep track of the nodes that have been previously used and then returned to available space.

This stack will be linked by means of indices in the array nextnode. Since the indices not only for the available space but for all the linked lists will coexist in the same array nextnode, this array is intrinsically global, and we shall treat it as a *global array with side effects* global variable. All functions that change indices in lists, therefore, will cause side effects by modifying the array nextnode.

To keep track of the stack of available space, we need an integer variable avail that will give the index of its top. If this stack is empty (which will be represented by avail = -1), then we will need to obtain a new node, that is, a position within the array that has not yet been used for any node. We do so by increasing the index variable lastused that will count the total number of positions within our array that have been used to hold list entries. When lastused reaches MAXLIST - 1 (the bound we have assumed for array size) and avail = -1, the workspace is full and no further space can be allocated. When the main program starts, both variables avail and lastused should be initialized to -1, avail to indicate that the stack of space previously used but now available is empty, and lastused to indicate that no space from the array has yet been assigned.

The available-space list is illustrated in Figure 5.5. This figure, by the way, also illustrates how two linked lists can coexist in the same array. The arrows shown on the left of the array nextnode describe a linked list that produces the names in the array info in alphabetical order. The arrows on the right side of array nextnode, with header variable avail, show the nodes in the stack of (previously used but now) available space. Notice that the indices that appear in the available-space list are precisely the indices in positions 10 or earlier that are not assigned to names in the array info. Finally, none of the entries in positions 11 or later has been assigned. This fact is indicated by the value lastused = 10. If we were to insert additional names into the list headed by firstname, we would first pop nodes from the stack with top avail, and only when the stack is empty would we increase lastused to insert a name in previously unused space.

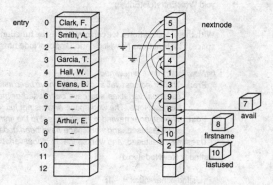

Figure 5.5. The array and stack of available space

The decisions we have made translate into the following declarations to be placed in the header file:

```
#define MAXLIST 10              /* Use a small value for testing.          */

typedef char ListEntry;
typedef int ListIndex;
typedef struct listnode {
    ListEntry entry;
    ListIndex next;
} ListNode;


typedef int Position;
typedef struct list {
    ListIndex head;
    int count;
} List;
extern ListIndex avail, lastused;
extern ListNode workspace[ ];

void CreateList(List *);
int CurrentPosition(Position, List *);
void DisposeNode(ListIndex, List *);
void Error(char *);
void InsertList(Position, ListEntry, List *);
ListIndex NewNode(void);
void SetPosition(Position, ListIndex *, List *);
void TraverseList(List *, void (*f)( ));
void WriteEntry(ListEntry);
```

With these declarations, we can now write the functions for keeping track of unused space. The functions NewNode and DisposeNode now take the form:

```
/* NewNode: make a new node.
    Pre:  The list indices avail and lastused have been initialized when they were defined
          as global variables and have been used or modified only by NewNode and
          DisposeNode. The workspace array is not full.
    Post: The list index newindex has been set to the first available place in workspace;
          avail, lastused, and workspace have been updated as necessary.
    Uses: avail, lastused, and workspace as global variables. */

ListIndex NewNode(void)
{
    ListIndex newindex = -1;
```

```
   if (avail != -1) {
      newindex = avail;
      avail = workspace[avail].next;
      workspace[newindex].next = 0;
   } else if (lastused < MAXLIST - 1) {
      newindex = ++lastused;
      workspace[newindex].next = 0;
   } else
      Error("Overflow: workspace for linked list is full.");
   return newindex;
}


/* DisposeNode: return a node to available space.
   Pre:   The list indices avail and lastused have been initialized when they were defined
          as global variables and have been used or modified only by NewNode and
          DisposeNode; oldindex is an occupied position in workspace.
   Post:  The list index oldindex has been pushed onto the linked stack of available
          space; avail, lastused, and workspace have been updated as necessary.
   Uses: avail, lastused, and workspace as global variables. */
void DisposeNode(ListIndex oldindex, List *list)
{
   ListIndex previous;
   if (oldindex == -1)
      Error("Disposing a nonexistent node in workspace array.");
   else {
      if (oldindex == list->head)
         list->head = workspace[oldindex].next;
      else {
         SetPosition(CurrentPosition(oldindex, list) - 1, &previous, list);
         workspace[previous].next = workspace[oldindex].next;
      }
      workspace[oldindex].next = avail;
      avail = oldindex;
   }
}
```

These two functions, of course, simply pop and push a stack. We could, if we wished, write separate functions for processing stacks and use those functions in place of programming the stack operations directly.

### 3. Other Operations

The translation of other functions so as to manipulate linked lists implemented within arrays proceeds in much the same way, and most of these will be left as exercises. To provide further models, however, let us write translations of the functions to traverse a list and to insert a new entry into a list.

```
/* TraverseList: traverse the list applying (*f)( ) to each element.
   Pre:  The list list exists.
   Post: The function (*f)( ) has been applied to each element of the list. */

void TraverseList(List *list, void (*f)( ))
{
   ListIndex current;

   for (current = list->head; current != -1; current = workspace[current].next)
      f(workspace[current].entry);
}



/* InsertList: insert a node into the list.
   Pre:  The linked list list has been created, list is not full, x is a valid list entry, and
         0 ≤ p ≤ n, where n is the number of entries in list.
   Post: x has been inserted into position p in list; the entry formerly in position p
         (provided p < n) and all later entries have their position numbers increased
         by 1.
   Uses: SetPosition, NewNode, Error. */

void InsertList(Position p, ListEntry x, List *list)
{
   ListIndex newindex, previous;

   if (p < 0 || p > list->count)
      Error("Inserting into a nonexistent position.");

   else {
      newindex = NewNode( );
      workspace[newindex].entry = x;
      if (p == 0) {
         workspace[newindex].next = list->head;
         list->head = newindex;
      } else {
         SetPosition(p-1, &previous, list);
         workspace[newindex].next = workspace[previous].next;
         workspace[previous].next = newindex;
      }
      list->count++;
   }
}
```

Compare these two functions with the equivalent ones for simply linked lists with
pointers and dynamic memory presented in Section 5.2. You will quickly see the
similarities and determine the changes that are required to translate functions from
one implementation to the other.

### 4. Linked-List Variations

Arrays with indices are not restricted to the implementation of simply linked lists. They are equally effective with doubly linked lists or with any other variation. For doubly linked lists, in fact, the ability to do arithmetic with indices allows an implementation (which uses negative as well as positive values for the indices) in which both forward and backward links can be included in a single index field. (See Exercise E5.)

**Exercises 5.5**

**E1.** Draw arrows showing how the list entries are linked together in each of the following nextnode tables. Some tables contain more than one list.

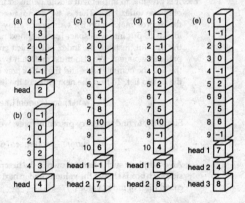

**E2.** Construct next tables showing how each of the following lists is linked into alphabetical order. Also, in each case, give the value of the variable head that starts the list.

| (a) | 0 | array | (c) | 0 | the | (d) | 0 | London |
|---|---|---|---|---|---|---|---|---|
| | 1 | stack | | 1 | of | | 1 | England |
| | 2 | queue | | 2 | and | | 2 | Rome |
| | 3 | list | | 3 | to | | 3 | Italy |
| | 4 | deque | | 4 | a | | 4 | Madrid |
| | 5 | scroll | | 5 | in | | 5 | Spain |
| | | | | 6 | that | | 6 | Oslo |
| (b) | 0 | push | | 7 | is | | 7 | Norway |
| | 1 | pop | | 8 | I | | 8 | Paris |
| | 2 | add | | 9 | it | | 9 | France |
| | 3 | delete | | 10 | for | | 10 | Warsaw |
| | 4 | insert | | 11 | as | | 11 | Poland |

**E3.** For the list of cities and countries in part (d) of the previous question, construct a next table that produces two linked lists, one containing all the cities in alphabetical order and the other containing all the countries in alphabetical order. Also give values to the two variables naming the lists.

**E4.** Write versions of each of the following functions for linked lists in arrays. Be sure that each function conforms to the specifications given in Section 5.1 and the declarations in this section.

(a) SetPosition      (e) ListFull       (i) DeleteList
(b) CreateList       (f) ListSize       (j) InsertList
(c) ClearList        (g) RetrieveList   (k) TraverseList
(d) ListEmpty        (h) ReplaceList

**E5.** It is possible to implement a doubly linked list in a workspace array by using only one index next. That is, we do not need to keep a separate field prev in the records making up the workspace array to find the backward links. The idea is to put into workspace[current].next not the index of the next entry on the list, but, instead, the index of the next entry *minus* the index of the entry preceding current. We also must maintain two pointers to successive nodes in the list, the current index and the index prev of the node just before current in the linked list. To find the next entry of the list, we calculate

    workspace[current].next + prev;

Similarly, to find the entry preceding prev, we calculate

    current − workspace[prev].next.

An example of such a list is shown in the first part of the following diagram. Inside each box is shown the value stored in next; on the right is the corresponding calculation of index values.

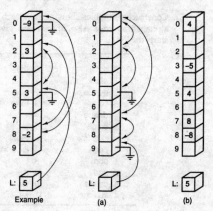

Example        (a)        (b)

The 3 in position 5 of the example is obtained as $3 = 2 - (-1)$, since position 2 is the next entry of the list, and nothing precedes position 5. In position 2 we have $8-5$, in position 8 we have $0-2$, and in position 0 we have $(-1)-8$, since position 0 comes last in the linked list.

**(a)** For the doubly linked list shown in the second part of the preceding diagram, show the values that will be stored in list.head and in the next fields of occupied nodes of the workspace.

**(b)** For the values of list.head and next shown in the third part of the preceding diagram, draw links showing the corresponding doubly linked list.

**(c)** With this implementation, write the function SetPosition.

**(d)** With this implementation, write the function InsertList.

**(e)** With this implementation, write the function DeleteList.

## 5.6 Generating Permutations

Our final sample project in this chapter illustrates the use both of general lists and of linked lists in arrays in a highly application-specific way. This project is to generate all the $n!$ permutations of $n$ objects as efficiently as possible. Recall that the permutations of $n$ different objects are all the ways to put them in different orders. For more information on permutations, see Appendix A.

The reason why there are $n!$ permutations of $n$ objects is that we can choose any of the $n$ objects to be first, then choose any of the $n - 1$ remaining objects second, and so on. These choices are independent, so the number of choices multiply. If we think of the number $n!$ as the product

$$n! = 1 \times 2 \times 3 \times \cdots \times n,$$

then the process of multiplication can be pictured as the tree in Figure 5.6. (Ignore the labels for the moment.) The root has two branches; each of its children has three branches; each node on the next level four branches, and so on.

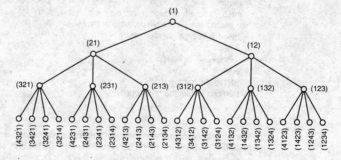

Figure 5.6. **Permutation generation by multiplication,** $n = 4$

### 1. The Idea

We can identify permutations with the nodes as given by the labels in Figure 5.6. At the top is 1 by itself. We can obtain the two permutations of $\{1, 2\}$ by writing 2 first on the left, then on the right of 1. Similarly, the six permutations of $\{1, 2, 3\}$ can be obtained by starting with one of the permutations $(2, 1)$ or $(1, 2)$ and inserting 3 into one of the three possible positions (left, center, or right). The task of generating permutations of $\{1, 2, \ldots, k\}$ can now be summarized as

> *Take a given permutation of $\{1, 2, \ldots, k - 1\}$ and put its entries into a list. Insert $k$, in turn, into each of the $k$ possible positions in this list, thereby obtaining $k$ distinct permutations of $\{1, 2, \ldots, k\}$.*

This algorithm illustrates the use of recursion to complete tasks that have been temporarily postponed. That is, we shall write a function that will first insert 1 into an empty list, and then use a recursive call to insert the remaining numbers from 2 to $n$ into the list. This first recursive call will insert 2 into the list containing only 1, and postpone further insertions to a recursive call. On the $n^{\text{th}}$ recursive call, finally, the integer $n$ will be inserted. In this way, having begun with a tree structure as motivation, we have now developed an algorithm for which the given tree becomes the recursion tree.

### 2. Refinement

Let us restate the algorithm in slightly more formal terms. We shall invoke our function as

Permute(1, $n$)

which will mean to insert all integers from 1 to $n$ to build all the $n!$ permutations. When it is time to insert the integer $k$, the remaining task is

*outline*

```
void Permute(k, n)
{
/* requires that 1 through k − 1 already be in the permutation list; then inserts the
   integers from k through n into the permutation list */
  for each of the k possible positions in the list {
    Insert k into the given position;
    if k == n
      ProcessPermutation
    else
      Permute(k + 1, n);
    Remove k from the given position;
  }
}
```

The function ProcessPermutation will make whatever disposition is desired of a complete permutation of $\{1, 2, \ldots, n\}$. We might wish only to print it out, or we might wish to send it as input to some other task.

### 3. The General Function

To translate this algorithm into C, we shall change some of the notation. We shall use

typedef int ListEntry;

and let perm denote the list containing the permutation being built. Instead of *k* we shall let newentry denote the integer being inserted, and write degree instead of *n* for the total number of objects being permuted. We then obtain the following function.

```
/* Permute: insert all entries in perm.
   Pre:  perm contains a permutation with entries 1 through newentry - 1.
   Post: All permutations with degree entries, built from the given permutation, have
         been constructed and processed.
   Uses: Permute recursively, ProcessPermutation. */

void Permute(int newentry, int degree, List *perm)
{
   int current = 0;

   for (current = 1;  current <= ListSize(perm) + 1;  current++) {
      InsertList(current, newentry, perm);
      if (newentry == degree)
         ProcessPermutation(perm);
      else
         Permute(newentry + 1, degree, perm);
      DeleteList(current, newentry, perm);
   }
}
```

Embedding this function into a working program is left as a project. For the required list functions, any of the implementations from Section 5.2 will be acceptable.

### 4. Data Structures: Optimization

The number *n*! increases very rapidly with *n*; the number of permutations goes up very quickly indeed with *n*. Hence this project is one of the few applications where optimization to increase the speed may be worth the effort, especially if we wish to use the program to study interesting questions concerning generating permutations.

Let us therefore now make some decisions regarding representation of the data with the view of increasing the program's speed as much as possible, even at the expense of readability. We use a list to hold the numbers being permuted. This list is available to the recursive invocations of the function as perm, and each recursive call updates the entries in this list. Since we must continually insert and delete entries into and from the list, linked storage will be more flexible than keeping the

*linked list in array*

entries in a contiguous list. But the total number of entries in the list never exceeds $n$, so we can (probably) improve efficiency by keeping the linked list within an array, rather than using dynamic memory allocation. Our links are thus integer indices relative to the start of the array. If we were, furthermore, to think of the array indices as starting with 0, then the index of each entry, as it is assigned, would happen to be the same as the value of the number being inserted, so there is no longer any need to keep this numerical value. Hence only the links need to be kept in the array.

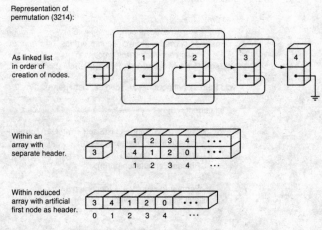

Representation of
permutation (3214):

As linked list
in order of
creation of nodes.

Within an
array with
separate header.

Within reduced
array with artificial
first node as header.

Figure 5.7. Permutation as a linked list in an array

This representation of a permutation as a linked list within an array is illustrated in Figure 5.7. The top diagram shows the permutation $(3, 2, 1, 4)$ as a linked list, and the second diagram shows it as a linked list inside an array with indices starting at 1, and with the convention that index 0 terminates the linked list. The third diagram omits the actual entries being permuted, since they are the same as the locations in the array, and thus it keeps only the links describing the linked list.

*artificial node*

Insertions and deletions are further simplified if we put an artificial first node at the beginning of the list (in position 0 of the array), so that insertions and deletions at the beginning of the (actual) list can be treated in the same way as those at other positions, always as insertions or deletions after a node. Hence we can obtain increased efficiency by using all these special conditions and writing the insertions and deletions into the function Permute, instead of using a generic list implementation.

### 5. Final Program

With these decisions we can write an optimized version of Permute.

```
/* Permute: insert all entries in perm.
   Pre:   perm contains a linked permutation with entries 1 through newentry − 1.
   Post:  All permutations with degree entries, built from the given permutation, have
          been constructed and processed.
   Uses:  Permute recursively, ProcessLinkedPermutation. */
void Permute(int newentry, int degree, int *perm)
{
   int current = 0;
   do {
      perm[newentry] = perm[current];
      perm[current] = newentry;
      if (newentry == degree)
         ProcessLinkedPermutation(perm);
      else
         Permute(newentry + 1, degree, perm);
      perm[current] = perm[newentry];
      current = perm[current];
   } while (current != 0);
}
```

The main program does little except to establish the declarations and initiate the process.

```
#define MAXDEGREE 20          /* large enough for all practical purposes        */
int main()
{
   int degree;
   int perm[MAXDEGREE + 1];
   printf("Number of elements to permute? ");
   scanf("%d", &degree);
   if (degree < 1 || degree > MAXDEGREE)
      printf("The number must be between 1 and %d\n", MAXDEGREE);
   else {
      perm[0] = 0;              /* Set the list to be initially empty.           */
      Permute(1, degree, perm); /* Install all entries from 1 to degree.         */
   }
   return 0;
}
```

Recall that the array perm describes a linked list of pointers and does not contain the objects being permuted. If, for example, it is desired to print the integers $1, \ldots, n$ being permuted, then the auxiliary function becomes

```
/* ProcessLinkedPermutation: print a permutation.
   Pre:   perm contains a permutation in linked form.
   Post:  The permutation has been printed at the terminal. */
void ProcessLinkedPermutation(int *perm)
{
    int current = 0;
    while (perm[current] != 0) {
        printf("%3d", perm[current]);
        current = perm[current];
    }
    putchar('\n');
}
```

With this, we have a complete program, and, in fact, one of the most efficient available programs for generating permutations at high speed.

---

**Programming Projects 5.6**

P1. Complete the permutation-generation program that uses one of the general list functions by writing its main program and a function ProcessPermutation that prints the permutation at the terminal. After testing your program, suppress printing the permutation and include the CPU timer functions provided with your compiler. Compare the performance of your program using each of the list implementations in Section 5.2. Also compare the performance with that of the optimized program written in the text.

P2. Modify the general version of Permute so that the position occupied by each number does not change by more than one to the left or to the right from any permutation to the next one generated. [This is a simplified form of one rule for *campanology* (ringing changes on church bells).]

---

## Pointers and Pitfalls

1. Don't confuse contiguous lists with arrays.

2. Choose your data structures as you design your algorithms, and avoid making premature decisions.

3. Always be careful about the extreme cases and handle them gracefully. Trace through your algorithm to determine what happens when a data structure is empty or full.

4. Don't optimize your code until it works perfectly, and then only optimize it if improvement in efficiency is definitely required. First try a simple implementation of your data structures. Change to a more sophisticated implementation only if the simple one proves too inefficient.

5. When working with general lists, first decide exactly what operations are needed, then choose the implementation that enables those operations to be done most easily.

6. In choosing between linked and contiguous implementations of lists, consider the necessary operations on the lists. Linked lists are more flexible in regard to insertions, deletions, and rearrangement; contiguous lists allow random access.

7. Contiguous lists usually require less computer memory, computer time, and programming effort when the items in the list are small and the algorithms are simple. When the list holds large records, linked lists usually save space, time, and often programming effort.

8. Dynamic memory and pointers allow a program to adapt automatically to a wide range of application sizes and provide flexibility in space allocation among different data structures. Static memory (arrays and indices) is sometimes more efficient for applications whose size can be completely specified in advance.

9. For advice on programming with linked lists in dynamic memory, see the guidelines in Chapter 4.

10. Avoid sophistication for sophistication's sake. If a simple method is adequate for your application, use it.

11. Don't reinvent the wheel. If a ready-made function is adequate for your application, use it.

# Review Questions

5.1

1. Which of the operations possible for general lists are also possible for queues? for stacks?

2. List three operations possible for general lists that are not allowed for either stacks or queues.

5.2

3. Is it easier to insert a new node before or after a specified node in a linked list? Why?

4. If the items in a list are integers (one word each), compare the amount of space required altogether if (a) the list is kept contiguously in an array 90 percent full, (b) the list is kept contiguously in an array 40 percent full, and (c) the list is kept as a linked list (where the pointers take one word each).

5. Repeat the comparisons of the previous exercise when the items in the list are records taking 200 words each.

6. What is an *alias* variable, and why is it dangerous?

7. What is the major disadvantage of linked lists in comparison with contiguous lists?

5.5

8. What are some reasons for implementing linked lists in arrays with indices instead of in dynamic memory with pointers?

## References for Further Study

The references given for stacks and queues continue to be appropriate for the current chapter. In particular, for many topics concerning list manipulation, the best source for additional information, historical notes, and mathematical analysis is KNUTH, volume 1. This book, however, does not take the principles of data abstraction into account.

For additional details regarding the implementation of pointer types in C, the authoritative reference is

BRIAN W. KERNIGHAN and DENNIS M. RITCHIE, *The C Programming Language*, second edition, Prentice Hall, Englewood Cliffs, N.J., 1988, 272 pages.

The algorithm that generates permutations by insertion into a linked list was published in the ACM *SIGCSE Bulletin* 14 (February 1982), 92–96. Useful surveys of many methods for generating permutations are

R. SEDGEWICK, "Permutation generation methods," *Computing Surveys* 9 (1977), 137–164; addenda, ibid., 314–317.

R. W. TOPOR, "Functional programs for generating permutations," *Computer Journal* 25 (1982), 257–263.

The applications of permutations to campanology (change ringing of bells) produce interesting problems amenable to computer study. An excellent source for further information is

F. J. BUDDEN, *The Fascination of Groups*, Cambridge University Press, Cambridge, England, 1972, pp. 451–479.

# 6

# Searching

THIS CHAPTER *introduces the problem of searching a list to find a particular entry. Our discussion centers on two well-known algorithms: sequential search and binary search. We shall develop several sophisticated mathematical tools, used both to demonstrate the correctness of algorithms and to calculate how much work they must do. These mathematical tools include loop invariants, comparison trees, and the big-O notation. Finally, we shall obtain lower bounds showing conditions under which any searching algorithm must do at least as much work as binary search.*

# 6.1 Searching: Introduction and Notation

Information retrieval is one of the most important applications of computers. We are given a name and are asked for an associated telephone listing. We are given an account number and are asked for the transactions occurring in that account. We are given an employee name or number and are asked for the personnel records of the employee.

### 1. Keys

*keys and records*

In these examples and a host of others, we are given one piece of information, which we shall call a **key**, and we are asked to find a record that contains other information associated with the key. We shall allow both the possibility that there is more than one record with the same key and that there is no record at all with a given key. See Figure 6.1.

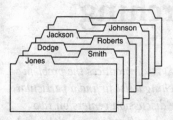

Figure 6.1. Records and their keys

### 2. Analysis

Searching for the keys that locate records is often the most time-consuming action in a program, and, therefore, the way the records are arranged and the choice of method used for searching can make a substantial difference in the program's performance. For this reason, we shall spend some time in this chapter studying how much work is done by each of the algorithms we develop. We shall find that counting the number of times that one key is compared with another gives us an excellent measure of the total amount of work that the algorithm will do and of the total amount of computer time it will require when it is run.

### 3. External and Internal Searching

The searching problem falls naturally into two cases. If there are many records, perhaps each one quite large, then it will be necessary to store the records in files on disk or tape, external to the computer memory. This case is called *external* searching. In the other case, the records to be searched are stored entirely within the computer memory. This case is called *internal* searching. In this book, we consider only internal searching. Although many of the methods we shall develop in this and later chapters are useful for external searching, a comprehensive study of methods for external searching lies beyond the scope of this book.

## 4. Implementation in C

To implement our programs in C, we establish some conventions. We shall be concerned only with contiguous lists in this chapter. Searching a linked structure is the major concern of Chapter 9, and we postpone consideration of linked structures until then.

*contiguous only*

Hence we shall always be searching in a contiguous list that we generally call list. What we have called records will be C structures, and they will be the entries in the list list. The C type that these records have we shall name as ListEntry, as we always have for lists. One of the fields of each list entry will be denoted key and have a type called KeyType. We thus assume that the program will have declarations of the form

```
typedef ... KeyType;
typedef struct listentry {
    ...
    KeyType key;
    ...
} ListEntry;
```

*examples*

Typical declarations for the key type are

```
typedef float KeyType;
typedef int KeyType;
typedef char * KeyType;
```

*target*

We begin with a *list* to be searched and use the standard declarations for the contiguous implementation of lists from Section 5.2.1. The key for which we are searching is always called the *target* of the search.

## 5. Parameters

*parameters*

Each searching function we write will have two input parameters. These parameters are the target and the list being searched. Its return value will be the location of the target. If the search was successful, then the function returns the position in the list where the target was found. If the search is unsuccessful, then the function returns −1.

We shall often need to compare two keys to determine which comes first or whether or not they are equal. If the keys are numbers, we can, of course, compare them by using such operations as '<' and '=='. If the keys are character strings, however, we shall need to use the standard C function strcmp instead. This function takes two strings as its arguments; it returns −1 if the first string precedes the second, 0 if they are equal, and +1 if the second string precedes the first.

We would like to code our algorithms in a way that will cover all the possibilities at once, so that we can change the code from processing numbers to processing strings as easily and quickly as we can. One method for doing this is to introduce new functions such as

> Boolean EQ(KeyType key1, KeyType key2);
> Boolean LT (KeyType key1, KeyType key2);

*function calls:*
*execution expense*

and using these in our routines whenever we need to compare keys. This method, however, induces a function call every time a pair of keys is compared. Since the time needed to compare keys is often the most critical part of our algorithms, the extra overhead associated with a function call is a high price to pay at execution time for every comparison of keys.

*special operators:*
*programming expense*

If, on the other hand, we code our algorithms either specifically for numerical keys or for character strings, then we lose generality. When we later wish to apply our algorithms to keys other than those for which they were coded, we must pay a high price in programming time to rewrite them for the new keys.

*macros*

The C language, fortunately, provides a feature that allows us to code our algorithms in as general a form as by using function calls and, at the same time, to achieve the same execution efficiency as using operators designed for a specific kind of keys. This feature is the provision of *macros*. When a function call appears in a program, the compiler writes in instructions that temporarily suspend the execution of the calling program and go to the function to begin executing its instructions. At its termination, the function executes instructions to return to the calling program and communicate the function result. Macros, on the other hand, are handled by a preprocessor, not the C compiler itself. When a macro is used, its instructions are copied into the program itself before it is compiled. Hence, at execution time, these instruction are done without the extra overhead of starting and stopping the execution of a function.

Macros are declared by using the #define direction to the preprocessor. Macros may use parameters just as functions can, but since macros are expanded before the compiler starts work, the formal parameters are not assigned types: When types are checked by the compiler, these formal parameters will already have been replaced by the actual arguments with which the macro was used.

For our applications, we shall need only simple macros. For numerical keys, the macros are

> #define EQ(a, b) ((a) == (b))
> #define LT (a, b) ((a) < (b))

If we wish to apply our algorithms to character strings, we simply replace these macro definitions with the following versions:

> #define EQ(a, b) (! strcmp((a), (b)))
> #define LT (a, b) (strcmp((a), (b)) < 0)

Note the extra parentheses around the parameters a and b in the macro text. These are required in case the actual parameters are expressions to make sure the operations in the macro expansion are performed in the correct order.

# 6.2 Sequential Search

### 1. Algorithm and Function

Beyond doubt, the simplest way to do a search is to begin at one end of the list and scan down it until the desired key is found or the other end is reached. This is our first method.

```
/* SequentialSearch: contiguous version.
   Pre:   The contiguous list list has been created.
   Post:  If an entry in list has key equal to target, then the function returns the location
          of the first such entry (success). Otherwise the function returns − 1 (failure). */
int SequentialSearch(List list, KeyType target)
{
    int location;
    for (location = 0;  location < list.count;  location++)
        if (EQ(list.entry[location].key, target))
            return location;
    return −1;
}
```

The for loop in this function keeps moving through the list as long as the target key target has not been found but terminates as soon as the target is found. If the search is successful, the function returns location of the target. If the search is unsuccessful, then the function returns −1.

### 2. Analysis

Let us now estimate the amount of work that sequential search will do, so that we can make comparisons with other methods later. Suppose that sequential search was run on a long list. The statements that appear outside the main loop, since they are done only once, take insignificant computer time compared to the work done inside the loop. For each pass through the loop, one key is compared with the target key, several other statements are executed, and several expressions are checked. But all these other statements and expressions are executed in lock step with the comparison of keys: They are all done once for each iteration of the loop.

Hence all the actions that we need to count relate directly to the comparison of keys. If someone else, using the same method, had written the functions, then differences in programming approach would likely make a difference in the running time. But all these cases still produce the same number of comparisons of keys. If the length of the list changes, then the work done by any implementation of the searching method will also change proportionately.

We shall study the way in which the number of comparisons of keys depends on the length of the list. Doing this study will give us the most useful information about the algorithm, information that can be applied equally well no matter what implementation or programming technique we decide to use when we actually write the program.

*importance of comparison count*

Hence if we wish to estimate how much computer time sequential search is likely to require, or if we wish to compare it with some other method, then knowing the number of comparisons of keys that it makes will give us the most useful information—information actually more useful than the total running time, which is too dependent on programming variations and on the particular machine being used.

No matter what algorithm for searching we develop, we can make a similar statement that we take as our fundamental premise in analyzing searching algorithms: The total work is reflected by the number of comparisons of keys that the algorithm makes.

> *To analyze the behavior of an algorithm that makes comparisons of keys, we shall use the count of these key comparisons as our measure of the work done.*

How many comparisons of keys does sequential search make when it is applied to a list of $n$ entries? Since sequential search compares the target to each key in the list in turn, the answer depends on if and where the target may be. If the function finds the target in the first position of the list, it does only one key comparison. If the target is second, the function does two key comparisons. If it is the last entry on the list, then the function does $n$ key comparisons. If the search is unsuccessful, then the target will have been compared to all entries in the list, for a total of $n$ comparisons of keys.

Our question, then, has several answers depending on if and where the target is found. If the search is unsuccessful, then the answer is $n$ key comparisons. The best performance for a successful search is 1 comparison, and the worst is $n$ comparisons.

We have obtained very detailed information about the performance of sequential search, information that is really too detailed for most uses, in that we generally will not know exactly where in a list a particular key may appear. Instead, it will generally be much more helpful if we can determine the *average* behavior of an algorithm. But what do we mean by average? One reasonable assumption, the one that we shall always make, is to take each possibility once and average the results.

*average behavior*

*provisos*

Note, however, that this assumption may be very far from the actual situation. Not all English words, for example, appear equally often in a typical essay. The telephone operator receives far more requests for the number of a large business than for that of an average family. The C compiler encounters the keywords if, for, and while far more often than the keywords enum, union, and goto.

There are a great many interesting, but exceedingly difficult, problems associated with analyzing algorithms where the input is chosen according to some statistical distribution. These problems, however, would take us too far afield to be considered here. We shall therefore limit our attention to the most important case, the one where all the possibilities are equally likely.

Under the assumption of equal likelihood we can find the average number of key comparisons done in a successful sequential search. We simply add the number needed for all the successful searches, and divide by $n$, the number of items in the list. The result is

$$\frac{1 + 2 + 3 + \cdots + n}{n}.$$

The first formula established in Appendix A is

$$1 + 2 + 3 + \cdots + n = \tfrac{1}{2}n(n + 1).$$

*average number of key comparisons*

Hence the average number of key comparisons done by sequential search in the successful case is

$$\frac{n(n + 1)}{2n} = \tfrac{1}{2}(n + 1).$$

### 3. Testing

An appropriate balance to the theoretical analysis of algorithms is empirical testing of the resulting functions. We set up sample data, run the functions, and compare the results with those of the analysis.

For searching routines, there are at least two numbers worth calculating, the average number of key comparisons done over many searches, and the amount of CPU time required. Let us now develop a function that can be used to test any searching routine.

To keep the testing general, we shall pass the search function as a parameter (pointer to a function). We use the function Time( ) as the CPU timer; the function uses a global variable compcounter as a comparison counter. The search function must increment compcounter every time it does a comparison of keys. Hence the versions of search functions used for testing will differ from the standard versions. The last parameter for TestSearch is the number searchcount of trials that will be made.

For test data let us use integers. Most of the searching methods later in this chapter require the data to be ordered, so we insert integers into our list in increasing order. We are interested in both successful and unsuccessful searches, so let us insert only odd integers into the list, and then look for odd integers for successful searches and even integers for unsuccessful searches. If the list has $n$ entries, then these will be $1, 3, 5, \ldots, 2n - 1$. For unsuccessful searches, we look for the integers $0, 2, 4, 6, \ldots, 2n$. In this way we test all possible failures, including keys less than the smallest key in the list, between each pair, and greater than the largest. To make the test more realistic, we use pseudo-random numbers to choose the target, by employing the function RandomInt:

```
/* RandomInt: generate a pseudorandom integer.
   Pre:   The seed contains an arbitrary value.
   Post:  Return a pseudorandom integer uniformly distributed over the range from low
          to high, inclusive.
   Uses: rand. */
int RandomInt(int low, int high)
{
   if (low > high)
      Error("RandomInt: low cannot be greater than high.");
   return (high - low + 1) * (rand( )/(double) INT_MAX) + low;
}
```

With these decisions, the resulting test function follows.

```
/* TestSearch: test a search routine.
   Pre:   The contiguous list list has been created.
   Post:  If an entry in list has key equal to target, then the function returns the location
          of one such entry (success). Otherwise the function returns − 1 (failure). */
void TestSearch(List list, int (*Search)(List list, KeyType target),
          int searchcount)
{
   float elapsedtime;          /* elapsed time between START and END     */
   int i, target;
   float average;              /* comparisons / searchcount              */
   extern long compcounter;
   compcounter = 0;            /* initialize the comparison counter      */
   (void) Time(START);
   if (list.count <= 0)
      average = 0.;
   else {                      /* Test with successful searches.         */
      for (i = 0; i < searchcount; i++) {
         target = 2 * RandomInt(1, list.count) − 1;  /* must be odd      */
         if (Search(list, target) == −1)
            printf("Error: %d not found\n", target);
      }
      average = (float) compcounter/searchcount;
   }
   elapsedtime = Time(END);
   printf("Successful search: %f comparisons\n", average);
   printf("Elapsed time to complete %d searches is %f seconds\n",
                searchcount, elapsedtime);
   compcounter = 0;            /* initialize the comparison counter      */
   (void) Time(START);
   if (list.count <= 0)
      average = 0.;
   else {                      /* Test with unsuccessful searches.       */
      for (i = 0; i < searchcount; i++) {
         target = 2 * RandomInt(0, list.count);  /* must be even         */
         if (Search(list, target) != −1)
            printf("Error: %d found improperly\n", target);
      }
      average = (float) compcounter/searchcount;
   }
   elapsedtime = Time(END);
   printf("Unsuccessful search: %f comparisons\n", average);
   printf("Elapsed time to complete %d searches is %f seconds\n",
                searchcount, elapsedtime);
}
```

The details of embedding this function into a working program are left as a project.

The Time function follows.

```
#include <time.h>

/* Time: calculate run time between two points.
   Pre:   START sets the starting time. END terminates the run time.
   Post:  At START return 0. At END return the time run since the function was called with
          START. */
float Time(int flag)
{
    static clock_t start;
    clock_t end;
    if (flag == START) {
        start = clock();
        return 0.0;
    } else {
        end = clock();
        return (end - start)/CLK_TCK;
    }
}
```

---

**Exercises 6.2**

**E1.** One good check for any algorithm is to see what it does in extreme cases. Determine what sequential search does when

    **(a)** there is only one item in the list.

    **(b)** the list is empty.

    **(c)** the list is full.

**E2.** Trace sequential search as it searches for each of the keys present in a list containing three items. Determine how many comparisons are made, and thereby check the formula for the average number of comparisons for a successful search.

**E3.** If we can assume that the keys in the list have been arranged in order (for example, numerical or alphabetical order), then we can terminate unsuccessful searches more quickly. If the smallest keys come first, then we can terminate the search as soon as a key greater than or equal to the target key has been found. If we assume that it is equally likely that a target key not in the list is in any one of the $n + 1$ intervals (before the first key, between a pair of successive keys, or after the last key), then what is the average number of comparisons for unsuccessful search in this version?

**E4.** At each iteration, sequential search checks two inequalities, one a comparison of keys to see if the target has been found, and the other a comparison of indices to see if the end of the list has been reached. A good way to speed up the algorithm by eliminating the second comparison is to make sure that eventually

*sentinel*

key target will be found, by increasing the size of the list, and inserting an extra item at the end with key target. Such an item placed in a list to ensure that a process terminates is called a *sentinel*. When the loop terminates, the search will have been successful if target was found before the last item in the list and unsuccessful if the final sentinel item was the one found.

Write a C function that embodies the idea of a sentinel in the contiguous version of sequential search using lists developed in Section 5.2.1.

**E5.** Find the number of comparisons of keys done by the function written in Exercise E4 for

(a) unsuccessful search.

(b) best successful search.

(c) worst successful search.

(d) average successful search.

**Programming Projects 6.2**

**P1.** Write a program to test sequential search and, later, other searching methods using lists developed in Section 5.2.1. You should make the appropriate declarations required to set up the list and put keys into it. The keys are the odd integers from 1 to $n$, where the user gives the value of $n$. Then successful searches can be tested by searching for odd integers, and unsuccessful searches can be tested by searching for even integers. Use the function TestSearch from the text to do the actual testing of the search routine. Modify the sequential search function so that it updates the counter compcounter each time it makes a key comparison. Write an appropriate Introduction function and a menu driver. For now, the only options are to fill the list with a user-given number of entries, to test SequentialSearch, and to quit. Later, other searching methods will be added as further options.

Find out how many comparisons are done for both unsuccessful and successful searches, and compare these results with the analyses in the text.

Run your program for representative values of $n$, such as $n = 10$, $n = 100$, $n = 1000$.

**P2.** Take the driver program written in Project P1 to test searching functions, and insert the version of sequential search that uses a sentinel (see Exercise E4). For various values of $n$, determine whether the version with or without a sentinel is faster. Find the cross-over point between the two versions, if there is one. That is, at what point is the extra time needed to insert a sentinel at the end of the list the same as the time needed for extra comparisons of indices in the version without a sentinel?

**P3.** (a) Write a version of sequential search for simply linked lists as developed in Section 5.2.2. (b) Write a version of the testing program from Project P1 for linked lists, and use it to test linked sequential search.

# 6.3 Coatrooms: A Project

This section introduces an abstract data type that serves as the basis for an interesting continuing project showing how several different data structures and algorithms can be used.

## 6.3.1 Introduction and Specification

*definition*

The idea of a coatroom is simple: A person carrying a bulky coat gives the coat to a coatroom attendant, receiving in exchange a small tag, much easier to carry. Eventually the person returns the tag to the attendant and claims the coat. In a computer system, similarly, there may be large records that need to be maintained but may not be used for some time. Rather than pass these large records from task to task or function to function, it would be better to put the large records into a coatroom, receive a tag in return, and pass only the tag from task to task. Whenever desired, a task can use the tag to claim the corresponding record.

*tag copies*

There are differences, of course, between a real coatroom and the computer system. It is trivial for a computer task to make a copy of a tag, but much more difficult for a person to duplicate a coatroom tag. Hence our programs must guard against one task attempting to use a duplicate tag to claim a coat that has already been claimed by another task and so is not in the coatroom.

*tags vs. keys*

Tags are very much like the keys used in searching a list. Both are used to find a record containing other information. There is, however, one important difference: The key is an intrinsic part of the record, put there by the client program; the tag is instead assigned by the computer system as it does coatroom processing.

Let us now specify more precisely the interface between a computer coatroom and the program that uses it, and with this interface list all the operations that can be done with a coatroom.

The client (calling) program needs to contain four declarations:

- The symbolic constant MAXCOATROOM gives the maximum number of coats that can be placed in a coatroom. This constant is used only for implementations of coatrooms in arrays. For implementations (with dynamic memory) with no inherent maximum size, this constant should not be used.

- The type Coat is a structure or other record that depends on the application. What is contained in a coat, how large it is, or how it is processed is not known and is of no concern to the coatroom operations.

- The declaration Coat * establishes one level of *indirection*. We will not actually pass coats between the coatroom and the application program, but instead *pointers* to coats, so the actual coatroom entries will be of type Coat *. If p is of type Coat *, then we can always obtain the coat itself by dereferencing p.

- The

    typedef int Tag;

attains uniformity by forcing all implementations of coatrooms to return integer tags. In this way, the program can read or write tag values if desired.

The remaining type and variable declarations, as well as declarations of all functions for processing coatrooms, should be placed in a separate *include* file. In this way, implementations can be changed with no change at all in the application program.

The first declaration to place in the coatroom *include* file is that of the type CoatRoom itself. In this chapter, CoatRoom will usually be a list; in later chapters we shall implement coatrooms with other data structures.

Next come the operations concerned with entire coatrooms.

---

void CreateCR(CoatRoom *cr);

*precondition*:    None.

*postcondition*:  The coatroom cr exists and is initialized to have 0 entries. All possible tag values are invalid for cr.

---

void ClearCR(CoatRoom *cr);

*precondition*:    cr has been created.

*postcondition*:  cr has been made empty; all pointers to coats that were in cr are lost. All possible tag values are invalid for cr. cr continues to exist, but it now has 0 entries.

---

Boolean IsEmptyCR(CoatRoom *cr);

*precondition*:    cr has been created.

*postcondition*:  The function returns TRUE or FALSE according as cr contains 0 or more pointers to coats. cr remains unchanged.

---

Boolean IsFullCR(CoatRoom *cr);

*precondition*:    cr has been created.

*postcondition*:  The function returns TRUE or FALSE according as cr contains MAX-COATROOM or fewer pointers to coats. If there is no inherent maximum number of pointers to coats in cr, then the function always returns the value FALSE. cr remains unchanged.

> int SizeCR(CoatRoom *cr);
>
> *precondition*:   cr has been created.
>
> *postcondition*:  The function returns the number of pointers to coats that cr currently contains. cr remains unchanged.

Next come the functions manipulating tags and pointers to coats:

> Tag CheckCR(CoatRoom *cr, Coat *p);
>
> *precondition*:   cr has been created and is not full; p points to a coat.
>
> *postcondition*:  The coat pointer p has been added to the coatroom cr, whose size increases by one entry; the function has made and returned a valid tag for cr.

> Coat *InspectCR(CoatRoom *cr, Tag t);
>
> *precondition*:   cr has been created, and t is a valid tag for cr.
>
> *postcondition*:  The function returns a pointer to the coat that was checked when t became a valid tag. cr and t remain unchanged. The coat remains checked and t remains valid.

> Coat *ClaimCR(CoatRoom *cr, Tag *t);
>
> *precondition*:   cr has been created and t is a valid tag for cr.
>
> *postcondition*:  The function returns a pointer to the coat that was checked when t became a valid tag. This pointer to a coat is deleted from cr, whose size decreases by one entry. Tag t becomes invalid.

> Boolean IsValidTagCR(CoatRoom *cr, Tag t);
>
> *precondition*:   cr has been created.
>
> *postcondition*:  The function returns TRUE or FALSE according as the tag t is currently valid or invalid for cr. cr and t remain unchanged.

Finally come two additional functions that are not strictly needed for most applications of coatrooms, but that are very useful for debugging and for demonstration programs.

---

void TraverseCR(CoatRoom *cr, void (*Visit)(Coat *p, Tag t));

*precondition*:    cr has been created.

*postcondition*: The function specified as parameter (*Visit)() has been performed once for every entry in cr, with the corresponding coat pointer p and tag t sent to the function Visit. The order in which the tags and coat pointers are processed is not specified.

---

void WriteMethodCR( );

*precondition*:    None.

*postcondition*: Writes part of one line giving a short description of the coatroom implementation.

---

WriteMethodCR is used to make an application program automatically identify the implementation of coatrooms that it is using.

Remember that the tags are produced by CheckCR in the coatroom implementation, not supplied by the application program. We have specified that the tags will be integers, but we have not said what integers to use. One possibility is for the implementation to produce small integers, say the position number within a list. This method, however, is dangerous in that a coat can be claimed and then its tag re-used for another coat. Then another task, using a duplicate of the tag, could inspect or claim a coat, expecting the first coat but getting the second instead.

*random tags*      A much better method for constructing tags is to use *random* integers. In this way, it becomes extremely unlikely that the same tag will ever be re-used. Random tags hence help the coatroom implementation guard against errors and increase the robustness of the program.

*choice of tags* is noted in the left margin beside the paragraph beginning "the implementation to produce small integers."

## 6.3.2 DEMONSTRATION AND TESTING PROGRAMS

### 1. Two Kinds of Demonstrations

*menu-driven demonstration*      The first kind of program that we can develop for using a coatroom is a menu-driven demonstration program. Such a program will be very similar to the menu-driven demonstrations for lists, stacks, and queues. About the only addition is that the coatroom demonstration must, when appropriate, ask the user to supply a tag number (integer) as well as the contents for the associated coat. A string of characters typed in by the user makes a good choice for a coat for this demonstration. The demonstration can be written so that either it passes on all input to the coatroom program, or it checks for erroneous input and thereby defends against user errors.

*timed-testing program*

The second kind of program is an attempt to perform more realistic tests on the performance of the coatroom under several conditions. This will include checking, inspecting, and claiming many coats in different orders and in different conditions. The program will use pseudorandom numbers to simulate possible applications more realistically.

Let us now develop an outline of such a project.

### 2. Declarations and Initialization

*size*

Ask the user to input the number of coats that will be checked. (This number would be very small for initial and debugging runs, but it will be in the thousands for the final tests.) Set MAXCOATROOM to 5,000.

*output*

Ask if the user wishes to have the transactions printed out as they happen. If the answer is yes, the program should print a line for each action it takes (such as checking a coat, inspecting a coat, and so on). This would normally be done during debugging runs with a small number of coats checked. For the large timed trials, the answer would be no, and the program would then print only summary lines showing the total number of coats checked, claimed, and so on, together with the CPU time required for each phase. A global Boolean variable is a good way to keep track of whether to print the transaction line or not. That is, you can declare a global Boolean variable, say doprint. Initialize it by setting doprint = UserSaysYes( ); . Use it in statements like

```
if (doprint) printf("Checked coat ");
```

Take

```
typedef int Coat;
```

*serial numbers*

For the contents of each coat take its serial number (that is, 0 for the first coat checked in, 1 for the second, and so on). If you claim (dispose of) a coat and then create another one, you just keep increasing the serial number—never re-use a serial number in the same run of the program.

Use the CPU timer function Time( ) from Section 6.2 to time each phase of the program.

### 3. Keeping Track of the Tags

*tag list*

Your program will need to keep a list of all the tags (remember that the tags are generated in the implementation, not in this main driver program) so that it can inspect and claim coats after they are checked in. The best and most elegant way to make this list is to use a list program from Chapter 5. After you have made a coat and checked it into the coatroom, you will need to put its tag, say currenttag, into the list. When you wish to inspect all the coats in the coatroom, you can use list traversal. To claim all the coats you can again use list traversal, with one more statement to dispose of the coat after you (perhaps) write out its serial number, and then clear the list since all the tags are now invalid.

### 4. Random Ordering

Most implementations of the coatroom will use random integers for the tags, but it also makes the program more realistic to mix up the order of the tags in their list several times during execution. A good way to do this follows. Suppose the coats are in positions 0 to $n - 1$ in the list. For each position $i$ from 0 to $n - 2$, generate a random integer in the range from $i$ to $n$, inclusive, and exchange the tags in positions $i$ and the random position. This will randomly mix up the order of the tags. Here is a function that accomplishes this task.

```
/* Mixup: rearrange a list using random numbers.
   Pre:   list is a list that has been created.
   Post:  The order of the entries in list has been permuted randomly.
   Uses: RandomInt, RetrieveList, ReplaceList, ListSize. */
void Mixup(List *list)
{
   ListEntry temp1, temp2;
   int curposition, newposition;
   for (curposition = 0; curposition < ListSize(*list) - 1; curposition++) {
      newposition = RandomInt(curposition, ListSize(*list) - 1);
      temp1 = RetrieveList(*list, curposition);
      temp2 = RetrieveList(*list, newposition);
      ReplaceList(list, temp2, curposition);
      ReplaceList(list, temp1, newposition);
   }
}
```

### 5. Overall Structure

Here are the phases of the main program. For each one of these, except the first and fifth, use the timer program to print the CPU time used in the phase.

1. Initialize the global variables, obtaining necessary information from the user.

2. Create the coatroom. (For most implementations, the time needed will be unmeasurably small; for others, it may not be.)

3. Check in the number of coats specified by the user.

4. Inspect all the coats once each, in the order of the tags in their list, which is the same as the order in which the coats were checked.

5. Use the function Mixup to rearrange all the tags in the list. Then again inspect all the coats in the coatroom once each. The time for Mixup should not be included in the CPU time for this or any phase.

6. Randomly permute the list of tags again. Then claim all the coats. After this phase, the coatroom will be empty, so then clear all the tags from their list.

7. This phase times a large number of transactions combining the three primary operations on a coatroom randomly. First, check in the number of coats previously specified by the user and keep their tags in the list. (Note that the coatroom was empty at the start of this phase.) Ask the user how many transactions are to be done. Inside a loop that will iterate once for each transaction, use random numbers, first, to select one of check, inspect, or claim with equal probability one third each. If the transaction turns out to be inspect or claim, select the tag to use randomly from those in the list. If you claim a coat, be sure to delete its tag from the list. If you start with a small number of coats, then your program may likely try to inspect or claim in an empty coatroom. Ignore such transactions, making sure they don't cause errors in your program.

An interesting test is to run the last phase with a small number of coats but a large number of transactions, to compare the behavior of small and large coatrooms.

---

**Programming Projects 6.3**

**P1.** Implement the coatroom program by using a list for the coatroom. The list entries will be records consisting of a tag and a pointer to a coat. The tags should be random integers (within an appropriate range, say up to 1000 * MAXCOATROOM). Use the standard list operations and a contiguous list with contiguous sequential search, so you can change the list implementation without changing the remainder of the coatroom program. Add newly checked coats to the end of the list. To inspect or claim a coat, use sequential search to find the tag in the list (the tags are the keys). The output message from WriteMethodCR should be something like "unordered list implementation."

**P2.** Write a simple menu-driven demonstration program for coatrooms that allows the user to choose operations and passes all requests through to the coatroom program. The coats should be strings of input from users.

**P3.** Write a more sophisticated menu-driven demonstration program for coatrooms that guards against user errors. If the user makes an illegal request, such as specifying an invalid tag, checking into a full coatroom, or inspecting or claiming from an empty coatroom, the program should issue a warning message and not pass the request to the coatroom package.

**P4.** Write the timed-testing program for coatrooms outlined in the text. Use the list-based coatroom package to verify that the program works correctly, but be sure that you will be able to substitute another package with no further change. Include the output from WriteMethodCR in the summary you print giving the number of transactions and times for the various phases.

# 6.4 Binary Search

Sequential search is easy to write and efficient for short lists, but a disaster for long ones. Imagine trying to find the name "Amanda Thompson" in a large telephone book by reading one name at a time starting at the front of the book! To find any entry in a long list, there are far more efficient methods, provided that the keys in the list are already sorted into order. One of the best is first to compare the target *method* key with one in the center of the list and then restrict our attention to only the first or second half of the list, depending on whether the target key comes before or after the central one. In this way, at each step, we reduce the length of the list to be searched by half. In only twenty steps, this method will locate any requested key in a list containing more than a million keys.

*restrictions* The method we are discussing is called *binary search*. This approach requires that the entries in the list be of a scalar or other type that can be regarded as having an order and that the list already be completely in order.

*random access* Since binary search requires jumping back and forth from one end of the list to the middle, it requires an implementation of the list in which this random access is rapid, as it is within an array, but not within a simply linked list. Hence we shall study binary search only for the array implementation.

What we are really doing here is introducing a new abstract data type, as follows.

**Definition** An *ordered list* is a list in which each entry contains a key, such that the keys are in order. That is, if entry $i$ comes before entry $j$ in the list, then the key of entry $i$ is less than or equal to the key of entry $j$.

The operations on an ordered list include all those for an ordinary list. For an ordered list, we have a few additional operations, such as the searching operations in this chapter and the ordered insertion of a new entry in the correct place determined by the order of the keys. We shall study this operation further in Chapter 7, but here is a simple, implementation-independent version of the function.

```
/* InsertOrder: insert an item into list maintaining correct order.
   Pre:   The contiguous list list has been created, is an ordered list, and is not full.
   Post:  The entry x has been inserted into list in a position such that the keys in all
          entries of list remain in correct order. */
void InsertOrder(List *list, ListEntry x)
{
    int current;
    ListEntry currententry;
    for (current = 0;  current < ListSize(*list); current++) {
        currententry = RetrieveList(*list, current);
        if (LE(x.key, currententry.key))
            break;
    }
    InsertList(list, x, current);
}
```

### 6.4.1 ALGORITHM DEVELOPMENT

*dangers*

Simple though the idea of binary search is, it is exceedingly easy to program it incorrectly. The method dates back at least to 1946, but the first version free of errors and unnecessary restrictions seems to have appeared only in 1962. One study (see the references at the end of the chapter) showed that about 90 percent of professional programmers fail to code binary search correctly, even after working on it for a full hour. Let us therefore take special care to make sure that we make no mistakes. To do this, we must state exactly what our variables designate; we must state precisely what conditions must be true before and after each iteration of the binary-search process; and we must make sure that this process will terminate properly.

Our binary search algorithm will use two indices, top and bottom, to enclose the part of the list in which we are looking for the target key. At each iteration, we shall reduce the size of this part of the list by about half. To help us keep track of the progress of the algorithm, let us write down a condition that we shall require to be true before every iteration. Such a statement is called an *invariant*.

> *The target key, provided it is present in the list, will be found between the indices* bottom *and* top, *inclusive.*

We establish the initial correctness of this statement by setting bottom to 0 and top to list.count − 1, where list.count is the number of entries in the list.

To do binary search, we first calculate the index middle halfway between bottom and top by calculating

$$\text{middle} = (\text{top} + \text{bottom})/2,$$

and then we compare the target key against the key at position middle, and change one of the indices top or bottom to reduce the list to either its bottom or top half.

*termination*

Next, we note that the binary-search process should terminate when top ≤ bottom, that is, when the remaining part of the list contains at most one item, providing that we have not terminated earlier by finding the target.

*termination*

Finally, we must make progress toward termination by ensuring that the number of items remaining to be searched, top − bottom +1, strictly decreases at each iteration of the process.

Several slightly different algorithms for binary search can be written.

### 6.4.2 THE FORGETFUL VERSION

Perhaps the simplest variation is to forget the possibility that the target key target might be found quickly and continue, whether target has been found or not, to subdivide the list until what remains has length 1.

This method is implemented as the following function, which, for simplicity, we write in recursive form, with the bounds on the sublist as additional parameters.

```
/* RecBinary1: recursive forgetful version of binary search.
   Pre:  The contiguous list list has been created, and bottom and top are indices of
         entries in the list.
   Post: If an entry in list between bottom and top, inclusive, has key equal to target,
         then the function returns the location of the first such entry (success). Other-
         wise, the function returns – 1 (failure). */
int RecBinary1(List list, KeyType target, int bottom, int top)
{
   int middle = –1;
   if (bottom < top) {             /* The list has size greater than 1.            */
      middle = (top + bottom)/2;
      if (GT(target, list.entry[middle].key))  /* Reduce to the top half of the list.  */
         middle = RecBinary1(list, target, middle + 1, top);
      else                         /* Reduce to the bottom half of the list.       */
         middle = RecBinary1(list, target, bottom, middle);
   } else if (bottom == top) {     /* The list has exactly 1 entry.                */
      if (EQ(target, list.entry[top].key))
         middle = top;
   }
   return middle;
}
```

The division of the list into sublists is described in the following diagram:

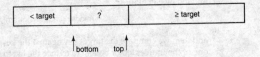

Note that this diagram shows only entries strictly less than target in the first part
of the list, whereas the last part contains entries greater than or equal to target. In
this way, when the middle part of the list is reduced to size 1 and hits the target,
it will be guaranteed to be the first occurrence of the target if it appears more than
once in the list.

If the list is empty, the function returns −1; otherwise it first calculates the
value of middle. As their average, middle is between bottom and top, and so middle
indexes a legitimate entry of the list.

*termination*    Note that the if statement that invokes the recursion is not symmetrical, since
the condition tested puts middle into the lower of the two intervals. On the other
hand, integer division of nonnegative integers always truncates downward. It
is only these two facts together that ensure that the recursion always terminates.
Let us determine what occurs toward the end of the search. The recursion will

continue only as long as top >bottom. But this condition implies that when middle is calculated we always have

$$bottom <= middle < top$$

since integer division truncates downward. Next, the if statement reduces the size of the interval from top − bottom either to top − (middle + 1) or to middle − bottom, both of which, by the inequality, are strictly less than top − bottom. Thus at each iteration the size of the interval strictly decreases, so the recursion will eventually terminate.

After the recursion terminates, we must finally check to see if the target key has been found, since all previous comparisons have tested only inequalities.

To adjust the parameters to our standard conventions, we use the following:

```
/* RecBinary1Search: front end for RecBinary1. */
int RecBinary1Search(List list, KeyType target)
{
    return RecBinary1(list, target, 0, list.count−1);
}
```

Since the recursion used in the preceding function is tail recursion, we can easily convert it into an iterative loop. At the same time, we can make the parameters consistent with other searching methods.

```
/* Binary1Search: forgetful version of binary search.
   Pre:   The contiguous list list has been created.
   Post:  If an entry in list has key equal to target, then the function returns the location
          of the first such entry (success). Otherwise the function returns − 1 (failure). */
int Binary1Search(List list, KeyType target)
{
    int bottom, middle, top;
    top = list.count − 1;          /* Initialize bounds to encompass entire list.       */
    bottom = 0;
    while (top > bottom) {          /* Check terminating condition.                      */
        middle = (top + bottom)/2;
        if (GT(target, list.entry[middle].key))
            bottom = middle + 1;    /* Reduce to the top half of the list.               */
        else
            top = middle;           /* Reduce to the bottom half of the list.            */
    }
    if (top == −1)
        return −1;                  /* Search for an empty list always fails.            */
    if (EQ(list.entry[top].key, target))
        return top;
    else
        return −1;
}
```

### 6.4.3 RECOGNIZING EQUALITY

Although Binary1Search is a simple form of binary search, it will often make unnecessary iterations because it fails to recognize that it has found the target before
continuing to iterate. Thus we may save computer time with a variation that checks
at each stage to see if it has found the target.

In recursive form this method becomes:

```
/* RecBinary2: recursive recognizing equality version of binary search.
   Pre:  The contiguous list list has been created, and bottom and top are indices of
         entries in the list.
   Post: If an entry in list between bottom and top, inclusive, has key equal to target,
         then the function returns the location of one such entry (success). Otherwise,
         the function returns - 1 (failure). */
int RecBinary2(List list, KeyType target, int bottom, int top)
{
   int middle = -1;
   if (bottom <= top) {
      middle = (top + bottom)/2;
      if (LT(target, list.entry[middle].key))  /* Reduce to the bottom half.       */
         middle = RecBinary2(list, target, bottom, middle - 1);
      else if (GT(target, list.entry[middle].key))  /* Reduce to the top half.     */
         middle = RecBinary2(list, target, middle + 1, top);
   }
   return middle;
}
```

As with RecBinary1Search we need a function RecBinary2Search to adjust the parameters to our standard conventions.

```
/* RecBinary2Search: front end for RecBinary2. */
int RecBinary2Search(List list, KeyType target)
{
   return RecBinary2(list, target, 0, list.count-1);
}
```

Again, this function can be translated into nonrecursive form with only the
standard parameters:

```
/* Binary2Search: recognizing equality version of binary search.
   Pre:  The contiguous list list has been created.
   Post: If an entry in list has key equal to target, then the function returns the location
         of one such entry (success). Otherwise the function returns - 1 (failure). */
```

```
int Binary2Search(List list, KeyType target)
{
    int bottom, middle, top;
    top = list.count - 1;          /* Initialize bounds to encompass entire list.      */
    bottom = 0;
    while (top >= bottom) {         /* Check terminating condition.                     */
        middle = (top + bottom)/2;
        if (EQ(target, list.entry[middle].key))
            return middle;
        else if (LT(target, list.entry[middle].key))
            top = middle - 1;      /* Reduce to the bottom half of the list.           */
        else
            bottom = middle + 1;   /* Reduce to the top half of the list.              */
    }
    return -1;
}
```

The operation of this version is described in the following diagram.

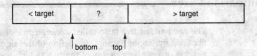

Notice that this diagram (in contrast to that for the first method) is symmetrical in that the first part contains only entries strictly less than target, and the last part contains only entries strictly greater than target. With this method, therefore, if target appears more than once in the list, then the algorithm may return any instance of the target.

*loop termination*

Proving that the loop in Binary2Search terminates is easier than the proof for Binary1Search. In Binary2Search, the form of the if statement within the loop guarantees that the length of the interval is reduced by more than half at each iteration.

*comparison of methods*

Which of these two versions of binary search will do fewer comparisons of keys? Clearly Binary2Search will, if we happen to find the target near the beginning of the search. But each iteration of Binary2Search requires two comparisons of keys, whereas Binary1Search requires only one. Is it possible that if many iterations are needed, then Binary1Search may do fewer comparisons? To answer this question we shall develop a new method in the next section.

---

**Exercises 6.4**

E1. Suppose that the list list contains the integers 1, 2, ..., 8 in this order. Trace through the steps of Binary1Search to determine what comparisons of keys are done in searching for each of the following targets: **(a)** 3, **(b)** 5, **(c)** 1, **(d)** 9, **(e)** 4.5.

E2. Repeat Exercise E1 using Binary2Search.

**E3.** [*Challenging*] Suppose that $L_1$ and $L_2$ are lists containing $n_1$ and $n_2$ integers, respectively, and both lists are already sorted into numerical order.

  **(a)** Use the idea of binary search to describe how to find the median of the $n_1 + n_2$ integers in the combined lists.

  **(b)** Write a function that implements your method.

**Programming Projects 6.4**

**P1.** Take the driver program of Project P1 of Section 6.2 (page 240), and incorporate Binary1Search and Binary2Search as new options. Compare their performance with each other and with sequential search.

**P2.** Incorporate the recursive versions of binary search (both variations) into the testing program of Project P1 of Section 6.2 (page 240). Compare the performance with the nonrecursive versions of binary search.

## 6.5 Comparison Trees

*definitions*

The *comparison tree* (also called *decision tree* or *search tree*) of an algorithm is obtained by tracing through the action of the algorithm, representing each comparison of keys by a *vertex* of the tree (which we draw as a circle). Inside the circle we put the index of the key against which we are comparing the target key. *Branches* (lines) drawn down from the circle represent the possible outcomes of the comparison and are labeled accordingly. When the algorithm terminates, we put either F (for failure) or the location where the target is found at the end of the appropriate branch, which we call a *leaf*, and draw as a square. Leaves are also sometimes called *end vertices* or *external vertices* of the tree. The remaining vertices are called the *internal vertices* of the tree.

The comparison tree for sequential search is especially simple; it is drawn in Figure 6.2.

*definitions*

The number of comparisons done by an algorithm in a particular search is the number of internal (circular) vertices traversed in going from the top of the tree (which is called its *root*) down the appropriate path to a leaf. The number of branches traversed to reach a vertex from the root is called the *level* of the vertex. Thus the root itself has level 0, the vertices immediately below it have level 1, and so on.

The number of vertices in the longest path that occurs is called the *height* of the tree. Hence a tree with only one vertex has height 1. In future chapters we shall sometimes allow trees to be empty, that is, to consist of no vertices at all, and we adopt the convention that an empty tree has height 0.

To complete the terminology we use for trees we shall now, as is traditional, mix our metaphors by thinking of family trees as well as botanical trees: We call the vertices immediately below a vertex $v$ the *children* of $v$ and the vertex immediately above $v$ the *parent* of $v$.

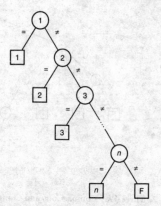

Figure 6.2. Comparison tree for sequential search

### 6.5.1 ANALYSIS FOR $n = 10$

#### 1. Shape of Trees

That sequential search on average does far more comparisons than binary search is obvious from comparing the shape of its tree with the shape of the trees for Binary1Search and Binary2Search, which for $n = 10$ are drawn in Figure 6.3 and Figure 6.4, respectively. Sequential search has a long, narrow tree, which means many comparisons, whereas the trees for binary search are much wider and shorter.

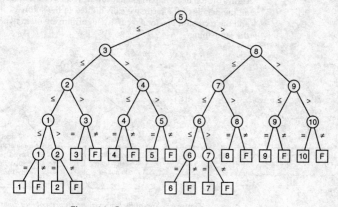

Figure 6.3. Comparison tree for Binary1Search, $n = 10$

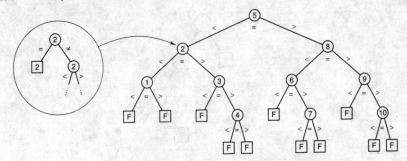

Figure 6.4. Comparison tree for Binary2Search, $n = 10$

## 2. Three-Way Comparisons and Compact Drawings

In the tree drawn for Binary2Search we have shown the algorithm structure more clearly (and reduced the space needed) by combining two comparisons to obtain one three-way comparison for each pass through the loop. Drawing the tree this way means that every vertex that is not a leaf terminates some successful search and the leaves correspond to unsuccessful searches. Thus the drawing in Figure 6.4 is more compact, but remember that two comparisons are really done for each of the vertices shown, except that only one comparison is done at the vertex at which the search succeeds in finding the target.

*two versions*

It is this compact way of drawing comparison trees that will become our standard method in future chapters.

It is also often convenient to show only part of a comparison tree. Figure 6.5 shows the top of a comparison tree for the recursive version of Binary2Search, with all the details of the recursive calls hidden in the subtrees. The comparison tree and the recursion tree for a recursive algorithm are often two ways of considering the same thing.

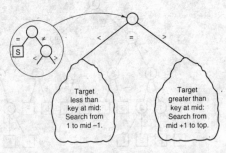

Figure 6.5. Top of the comparison tree, recursive Binary2Search

From the trees shown for Binary1Search and Binary2Search with $n = 10$, it is easy to read off how many comparisons will be done by each algorithm. In the worst case search, this number is simply one more than the height of the tree; in fact, for every search it is the number of interior vertices lying between the root and the vertex that terminates the search.

### 3. Binary1Search Comparison Count

*external path length*

In Binary1Search, every search terminates at a leaf; to obtain the average number of comparisons for both successful and unsuccessful searches, we need what is called the *external path length* of the tree: the sum of the number of branches traversed in going from the root once to every leaf in the tree. For the tree in Figure 6.3, the external path length is

$$(4 \times 5) + (6 \times 4) + (4 \times 5) + (6 \times 4) = 88.$$

Half the leaves correspond to successful searches, and half to unsuccessful searches. Hence the average number of comparisons needed for either a successful or unsuccessful search by Binary1Search is $\frac{44}{10} = 4.4$ when $n = 10$.

### 4. Binary2Search Comparison Count

*internal path length*

In the tree as it is drawn for Binary2Search, all the leaves correspond to unsuccessful searches; hence the external path length leads to the number of comparisons for an unsuccessful search. For successful searches, we need the *internal path length*, which is defined to be the sum, over all vertices that are not leaves, of the number of branches from the root to the vertex. For the tree in Figure 6.4, the internal path length is

$$0 + 1 + 2 + 2 + 3 + 1 + 2 + 3 + 2 + 3 = 19.$$

Recall that Binary2Search does two comparisons for each non-leaf except for the vertex that finds the target, and note that the number of these internal vertices traversed is one more than the number of branches (for each of the $n = 10$ internal vertices). We thereby obtain the average number of comparisons for a successful search to be

*average successful count*

$$2 \times \left( \frac{19}{10} + 1 \right) - 1 = 4.8.$$

The subtraction of 1 corresponds to the fact that one fewer comparison is made when the target is found.

For an unsuccessful search by Binary2Search, we need the external path length of the tree in Figure 6.4. This is

$$(5 \times 3) + (6 \times 4) = 39.$$

*average unsuccessful count*

We shall assume for unsuccessful searches that the $n + 1$ intervals (less than the first key, between a pair of successive keys, or greater than the largest) are all equally likely; for the diagram we therefore assume that all of the 11 failure leaves are equally likely. Thus the average number of comparisons for an unsuccessful search is

$$\frac{2 \times 39}{11} \approx 7.1.$$

### 5. Comparison of Algorithms

For $n = 10$, Binary1Search does slightly fewer comparisons both for successful and for unsuccessful searches. To be fair, however, we should note that the two comparisons done by Binary2Search at each internal vertex are closely related (the same keys are being compared), so that an optimizing compiler may not do as much work as two full comparisons. In that case, in fact, Binary2Search may be a slightly better choice than Binary1Search for successful searches when $n = 10$.

## 6.5.2 GENERALIZATION

What happens when $n$ is larger than 10? For longer lists, it may be impossible to draw the complete comparison tree, but from the examples with $n = 10$, we can make some observations that will always be true.

### 1. 2-trees

Let us define a *2-tree* as a tree in which every vertex except the leaves has exactly two children. Both versions of comparison trees that we have drawn fit this definition and are 2-trees. We can make several observations about 2-trees that will provide information about the behavior of binary search methods for all values of $n$.

*terminology*

Other terms for 2-tree are *strictly binary tree* and *extended binary tree*, but we shall not use these terms, because they are too easily confused with the term *binary tree*, which (when introduced in Chapter 9) has a somewhat different meaning.

*number of vertices in a 2-tree*

In a 2-tree, the number of vertices on any level can be no more than twice the number on the level above, since each vertex has either 0 or 2 children (depending on whether it is a leaf or not). Since there is one vertex on level 0 (the root), the number of vertices on level $t$ is at most $2^t$ for all $t \geq 0$. We thus have the facts:

**Lemma 6.1**    *The number of vertices on each level of a 2-tree is at most twice the number on the level immediately above.*

**Lemma 6.2**    *In a 2-tree, the number of vertices on level t is at most $2^t$ for $t \geq 0$.*

### 2. Analysis of Binary1Search

For Binary1Search both successful and unsuccessful searches terminate at leaves; there are thus $2n$ leaves. All these leaves, furthermore, must be on the same level or on two adjacent levels. (This observation can be proved by mathematical induction: It is true for a list of size 1, and when Binary1Search divides a larger list in half, the sizes of the two halves differ by at most 1, and the induction hypothesis shows that their leaves are on the same or adjacent levels.) The height (number of levels below root) of the tree is the maximum number of key comparisons that an algorithm does, and for Binary1Search is at most one more than the average number, since all leaves are on the same or adjacent levels. By Lemma 6.2, the height is also the smallest integer $t$ such that $2^t \geq 2n$. Take logarithms with base 2. (For a review of properties of logarithms, see Appendix A.) We obtain the result that the number of comparisons of keys done by Binary1Search in searching a list of $n$ items is approximately

*comparison count,*
Binary1Search

$$\lg n + 1.$$

As can be seen from the tree, the number of comparisons is essentially independent of whether the search is successful or not.

### 3. Notation

The notation for base 2 logarithms just used will be our standard notation. In analyzing algorithms we shall also sometimes need natural logarithms (taken with base $e = 2.71828\ldots$). We shall denote a natural logarithm by ln. We shall rarely need logarithms to any other base. We thus summarize,

*logarithms*

---

**Conventions**

*Unless stated otherwise, all logarithms will be taken with base* 2.
*The symbol* lg *denotes a logarithm with base* 2,
*and the symbol* ln *denotes a natural logarithm.*
*When the base for logarithms is not specified (or is not important),*
*then the symbol* log *will be used.*

---

*floor and ceiling*

After we take logarithms, we frequently need to move either up or down to the next integer. To specify this action, we define the *floor* of a real number $x$ to be the largest integer less than or equal to $x$, and the *ceiling* of $x$ to be the smallest integer greater than or equal to $x$. We denote the floor of $x$ by $\lfloor x \rfloor$ and the ceiling of $x$ by $\lceil x \rceil$.

### 4. Analysis of Binary2Search, Unsuccessful Search

To count the comparisons made by Binary2Search for a general value of $n$ for an unsuccessful search, we shall examine its comparison tree. For reasons similar to those given for Binary1Search, this tree is again full at the top, with all its leaves on at most two adjacent levels at the bottom. For Binary2Search, all the leaves correspond to unsuccessful searches, so there are exactly $n + 1$ leaves, corresponding to the $n + 1$ unsuccessful outcomes: less than the smallest key, between a pair of keys, and greater than the largest key. Since these leaves are all at the bottom of the tree, Lemma 6.2 implies that the number of leaves is approximately $2^h$, where $h$

*comparison count for*
Binary2Search,
*unsuccessful case*

is the height of the tree. Taking (base 2) logarithms, we obtain that $h \approx \lg(n + 1)$. This value is the approximate distance from the root to one of the leaves. Since two comparisons of keys are performed for each internal vertex, the number of comparisons done in an unsuccessful search is approximately $2\lg(n + 1)$.

### 5. The Path-Length Theorem

To calculate the average number of comparisons for a successful search, we first obtain an interesting and important relationship that holds for any 2-tree.

**Theorem 6.3**    *Denote the external path length of a 2-tree by $E$, the internal path length by $I$, and let $q$ be the number of vertices that are not leaves. Then*

$$E = I + 2q.$$

To prove the theorem we use the method of mathematical induction.

**Proof**    If the tree contains only its root, and no other vertices, then $E = I = q = 0$, and the first case of the theorem is trivially correct. Now take a larger tree, and let $\nu$ be some vertex that is not a leaf, but for which both the children of $\nu$ are leaves. Let $k$ be the number of branches on the path from the root to $\nu$. Now let us delete the two children of $\nu$ from the 2-tree. Since $\nu$ is not a leaf but its children are, the number of non-leaves goes down from $q$ to $q - 1$. The internal path length $I$ is reduced by the distance to $\nu$, that is, to $I - k$. The distance to each child of $\nu$ is $k + 1$, so the external path length is reduced from $E$ to $E - 2(k + 1)$, but $\nu$ is now a leaf, so its distance, $k$, must be added, giving a new external path length of

$$E - 2(k + 1) + k = E - k - 2.$$

Since the new tree has fewer vertices than the old one, by the induction hypothesis we know that

$$E - k - 2 = (I - k) + 2(q - 1).$$

Rearrangement of this equation gives the desired result.

### 6. Binary2Search, Successful Search

In the comparison tree of Binary2Search, the distance to the leaves is $\lg(n + 1)$, as we have seen. The number of leaves is $n + 1$, so the external path length is about

$$(n + 1)\lg(n + 1).$$

Theorem 6.3 then shows that the internal path length is about

$$(n + 1)\lg(n + 1) - 2n.$$

To obtain the average number of comparisons done in a successful search, we must first divide by $n$ (the number of non-leaves) and then add 1 and double, since two comparisons were done at each internal node. Finally, we subtract 1, since only one comparison is done at the node where the target is found. The result is approximately

$$\frac{2(n + 1)}{n} \lg(n + 1) - 3$$

comparisons of keys.

### 6.5.3 COMPARISON OF METHODS

*simplified counts*

Note the similarities and differences in the formulae for the two versions of binary search. Recall, first, that we have already made some approximations in our calculations, and hence our formulae are only approximate. For large values of $n$ the difference between $\lg n$ and $\lg(n + 1)$ is insignificant, and $(n + 1)/n$ is very nearly 1. Hence we can simplify our results as follows:

|  | *Successful search* | *Unsuccessful search* |
| --- | --- | --- |
| Binary1Search | $\lg n + 1$ | $\lg n + 1$ |
| Binary2Search | $2\lg n - 3$ | $2\lg n$ |

*assessment*

In all four cases the times are proportional to $\lg n$, except for small constant terms, and the coefficients of $\lg n$ are, in all cases, the number of comparisons inside the loop. The fact that the loop in Binary2Search can terminate early contributes disappointingly little to improving its speed for a successful search; it does not reduce the coefficient of $\lg n$ at all, but only reduces the constant term from $+1$ to $-3$.

A moment's examination of the comparison trees will show why. More than half of the vertices occur at the bottom level, and hence their loops cannot terminate early. More than half the remaining ones could terminate only one iteration early. Thus, for large $n$, the number of vertices relatively high in the tree, say, in the top half of the levels, is negligible in comparison with the number at the bottom level. It is only for this negligible proportion of the vertices that Binary2Search can achieve better results than Binary1Search, but it is at the cost of nearly doubling the number of comparisons for all searches, both successful and unsuccessful.

With the smaller coefficient of $\lg n$, Binary1Search will do fewer comparisons when $n$ is sufficiently large, but with the smaller constant term, Binary2Search may do fewer comparisons when $n$ is small. But for such a small value of $n$, the overhead in setting up binary search and the extra programming effort probably make it a more expensive method to use than sequential search. Thus we arrive at the conclusion, quite contrary to what we would intuitively conclude, that Binary2Search is probably not worth the effort, since for large problems Binary1Search is better, and for small problems, SequentialSearch is better. To be fair, however, with some computers and optimizing compilers, the two comparisons needed in Binary2Search will not take double the time of the one in Binary1Search, so in such a situation Binary2Search might prove the better choice.

*conclusions*

Our object in doing analysis of algorithms is to help us decide which may be better under appropriate circumstances. Disregarding the foregoing provisos, we have now been able to make such a decision, and have available to us information that might otherwise not be obvious.

The number of comparisons of keys done in the average successful case by SequentialSearch, Binary1Search, and Binary2Search are graphed in Figure 6.6. The
numbers shown in the graphs are from test runs of the functions; they are not approximations. The first graph in Figure 6.6 compares the three functions for small
values of $n$, the number of items in the list. In the second graph we compare the

*logarithmic graphs*    numbers over a much larger range by employing a ***log-log graph*** in which each
unit along an axis represents doubling the corresponding coordinate. In the third
graph we wish to compare the two versions of binary search; a ***semilog graph*** is appropriate here, so that the vertical axis maintains linear units while the horizontal
axis is logarithmic.

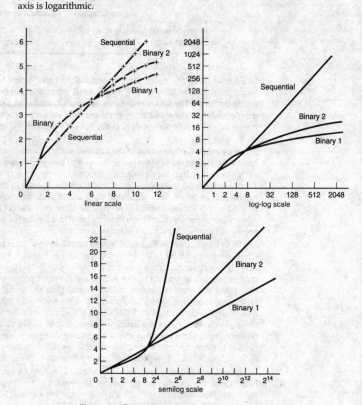

Figure 6.6. Comparison of average successful searches

### 6.5.4 A GENERAL RELATIONSHIP

*hypotheses*

Before leaving this section, let us use Theorem 6.3 to obtain a relationship between the average number of key comparisons for successful and for unsuccessful searches, a relationship that holds for any searching method for which the comparison tree can be drawn as we did for Binary2Search. That is, we shall assume that the leaves of the comparison tree correspond to unsuccessful searches, that the internal vertices correspond to successful searches, and that two comparisons of keys are made for each internal vertex, except that only one is made at the vertex where the target is found. If $I$ and $E$ are the internal and external path lengths of the tree, respectively, and $n$ is the number of items in the list, so that $n$ is also the number of internal vertices in the tree, then, as in the analysis of Binary2Search, we know that the average number of comparisons in a successful search is

$$S = 2\left(\frac{I}{n} + 1\right) - 1 = \frac{2I}{n} + 1$$

and the average number for an unsuccessful search is $U = 2E/(n+1)$. By Theorem 6.3, $E = I + 2n$. Combining these expressions, we can therefore conclude that

**Theorem 6.4**    *Under the specified conditions, the average numbers of key comparisons done in successful and unsuccessful searches are related by*

$$S = \left(1 + \frac{1}{n}\right)U - 3.$$

In other words, the average number of comparisons for a successful search is almost exactly the same as that for an unsuccessful search. Knowing that an item is in the list is very little help in finding it, if you are searching by means of comparisons of keys.

---

**Exercises 6.5**

E1. Draw the comparison trees for (i) Binary1Search and (ii) Binary2Search when **(a)** $n = 5$, **(b)** $n = 7$, **(c)** $n = 8$, **(d)** $n = 13$. Calculate the external and internal path lengths for each of these trees, and verify that the conclusion of Theorem 6.3 holds.

E2. Sequential search has less overhead than binary search, and so may run faster for small $n$. Find the break-even point where the same number of comparisons of keys is made between SequentialSearch and Binary1Search. Compute in terms of the formulæ for the number of comparisons done in the average successful search.

**E3.** Suppose that you have a list of 10,000 names in alphabetical order in an array and you must frequently look for various names. It turns out that 20 percent of the names account for 80 percent of the retrievals. Instead of doing a binary search over all 10,000 names every time, consider the possibility of splitting the list into two, a high-frequency list of 2000 names, and a low-frequency list of the remaining 8000 names. To look up a name, you will first use binary search on the high-frequency list, and 80 percent of the time you will not need to go on to the second stage, where you use binary search on the low-frequency list. Is this scheme worth the effort? Justify your answer by finding the number of comparisons done for the average successful search, both in the new scheme and in a binary search of a single list of 10,000 names.

**E4.** If you modified binary search so that it divided the list not essentially in half at each pass, but instead into two pieces of sizes about one-third and two-thirds of the remaining list, then what would be the approximate effect on its average count of comparisons?

**Programming Projects 6.5**

**P1.** (a) Write a "ternary" search function analogous to Binary2Search that examines the key one-third of the way through the list, and if the target key is greater, then examines the key two-thirds of the way through, and thus in any case at each pass reduces the length of the list by a factor of three. (b) Include your function as an additional option in the testing program of Project P1 of Section 6.2 (page 240), and compare its performance with other methods.

**P2.** (a) Write a program that will do a "hybrid" search, using Binary1Search for large lists and switching to sequential search when the search is reduced to a sufficiently small sublist. (Because of different overhead, the best switch-over point is not necessarily the same as your answer to Exercise E2.) (b) Include your function as an additional option in the testing program of Project P1 of Section 6.2 (page 240), and compare its performance to other methods.

**P3.** (a) Produce an implementation of a coatroom (see Section 6.3, Project P1) based on an ordered list, where the list is ordered according to the size of the tag. Use ordered insertion to check in a new coat, and use binary search to inspect or claim a coat. (b) Test your functions with the menu-driven demonstration program. (c) Substitute your functions into the timed-testing program and compare its performance with other implementations.

## 6.6 Lower Bounds

We know that for an ordered contiguous list, binary search is much faster than sequential search. It is only natural to ask if we can find another method that is much faster than binary search.

### 1. Polishing Programs

One approach is to attempt to polish and refine our programs to make them run faster. By being clever we may be able to reduce the work done in each iteration by a bit and thereby speed up the algorithm. One method, called *Fibonacci search*, even manages to replace the division inside the loop of binary search by certain subtractions (with no auxiliary table needed), which on some computers will speed up the function.

*basic algorithms and small variations*

Fine tuning of a program may be able to cut its running time in half, or perhaps reduce it even more, but limits will soon be reached if the underlying algorithm remains the same. The reason why binary search is so much faster than sequential search is not that there are fewer steps within its loop (there are actually more) or that the code is optimized, but that the loop is iterated fewer times, about $\lg n$ times instead of $n$ times, and as the number $n$ increases, the value of $\lg n$ grows much more slowly than does the value of $n$.

In the context of comparing underlying methods, the differences between Binary1Search and Binary2Search become insignificant. For large lists Binary2Search may require nearly double the time of Binary1Search, but the difference between $2\lg n$ and $\lg n$ is negligible compared to the difference between $n$ and $2\lg n$.

### 2. Arbitrary Searching Algorithms

Let us now ask whether it is possible for any search algorithm to exist that will, in the worst and the average cases, be able to find its target using significantly fewer comparisons of keys than binary search. We shall see that the answer is *no*, providing that we stay within the class of algorithms that rely only on comparisons of keys to determine where to look within an ordered list.

*general algorithms and comparison trees*

Let us start with an arbitrary algorithm that searches an ordered list by making comparisons of keys, and imagine drawing its comparison tree in the same way as we drew the tree for Binary1Search. That is, each internal node of the tree will correspond to some comparison of keys and each leaf to one of the possible outcomes. (If the algorithm is formulated as three-way comparisons like those of Binary2Search, then we expand each internal vertex into two, as shown for one vertex in Figure 6.4.) The possible outcomes to which the leaves correspond include not only the successful discovery of the target but also the different kinds of failure that the algorithm may distinguish. Binary search of a list of length $n$ produces $k = 2n + 1$ outcomes, consisting of $n$ successful outcomes and $n + 1$ different kinds of failure (less than the smallest key, between each pair of keys, or larger than the largest key). On the other hand, our sequential search function produced only $k = n + 1$ possible outcomes since it distinguished only one kind of failure.

*height and external path length*

As with all search algorithms that compare keys, the height of our tree will equal the number of comparisons that the algorithm does in its worst case, and (since all outcomes correspond to leaves) the external path length of the tree divided by the number of possible outcomes will equal the average number of comparisons done by the algorithm. We therefore wish to obtain lower bounds on the height and the external path length in terms of $k$, the number of leaves.

### 3. Observations on 2-trees

Here is the result on 2-trees that we shall need:

**Lemma 6.5**    *Let $T$ be a 2-tree with $k$ leaves. Then the height $h$ of $T$ satisfies $h \geq \lceil \lg k \rceil$ and the external path length $E(T)$ satisfies $E(T) \geq k \lg k$. The minimum values for $h$ and $E(T)$ occur when all the leaves of $T$ are on the same level or on two adjacent levels.*

**Proof**    We begin the proof by establishing the assertion in the last sentence. Suppose that some leaves of $T$ are on level $r$ and some are on level $s$, where $r > s + 1$. Now take two leaves on level $r$ that are both children of the same vertex $v$, detach them from $v$, and attach them as children of some (former) leaf on level $s$. Then we have changed $T$ into a new 2-tree $T'$ that still has $k$ leaves, the height of $T'$ is certainly no more than that of $T$, and the external path length of $T'$ satisfies

$$E(T') = E(T) - 2r + (r-1) - s + 2(s+1) = E(T) - r + s + 1 < E(T)$$

since $r > s + 1$. The terms in this expression are obtained as follows. Since two leaves at level $r$ are removed, $E(T)$ is reduced by $2r$. Since vertex $v$ has become a leaf, $E(T)$ is increased by $r - 1$. Since the vertex on level $s$ is no longer a leaf, $E(T)$ is reduced by $s$. Since the two leaves formerly on level $r$ are now on level $s + 1$, the term $2(s+1)$ is added to $E(T)$. This process is illustrated in Figure 6.7.

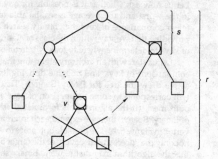

Figure 6.7. Moving leaves higher in a 2-tree

We can continue in this way to move leaves higher up the tree, reducing the external path length and possibly the height each time, until finally all the leaves are on the same or adjacent levels. The height and the external path length will then be minimal amongst all 2-trees with $k$ leaves.

*proof of $h \geq \lceil \lg k \rceil$*    To prove the remaining assertions in Lemma 6.5, let us from now on assume that $T$ has minimum height and path length amongst the 2-trees with $k$ leaves, so all leaves of $T$ occur on levels $h$ and (possibly) $h - 1$, where $h$ is the height of $T$. By Lemma 6.2, the number of vertices on level $h$ (which are necessarily leaves) is at most $2^h$. If all the leaves are on level $h$, then $k \leq 2^h$. If some of the leaves are on level $h - 1$, then each of these (since it has no children) reduces the number of possible vertices on level $h$ by 2, so the bound $k \leq 2^h$ continues to hold. We take logarithms to obtain $h \geq \lg k$ and, since the height is always an integer, we move up to the ceiling $h \geq \lceil \lg k \rceil$.

*proof of $E(T) \geq k \lg k$*    For the bound on the external path length, let $x$ denote the number of leaves of $T$ on level $h - 1$, so that $k - x$ leaves are on level $h$. These vertices are children of exactly $\frac{1}{2}(k - x)$ vertices on level $h - 1$, which, with the $x$ leaves, comprise all vertices on level $h - 1$. Hence, by Lemma 6.2,

$$\tfrac{1}{2}(k - x) + x \leq 2^{h-1},$$

which becomes $x \leq 2^h - k$. We now have

$$E(T) = (h - 1)x + h(k - x)$$
$$= kh - x$$
$$\geq kh - (2^h - k)$$
$$= k(h + 1) - 2^h.$$

From the bound on the height, we already know that $2^{h-1} < k \leq 2^h$. If we set $h = \lg k + \epsilon$, then $\epsilon$ satisfies $0 \leq \epsilon < 1$, and substituting $\epsilon$ into the bound for $E(T)$ we obtain

$$E(T) \geq k(\lg k + 1 + \epsilon - 2^\epsilon).$$

It turns out that, for $0 \leq \epsilon < 1$, the quantity $1 + \epsilon - 2^\epsilon$ is between 0 and 0.0861. Thus the minimum path length is quite close to $k \lg k$ and, in any case, is at least $k \lg k$, as was to be shown. With this, the proof of Lemma 6.5 is complete.

### 4. Lower Bounds for Searching

Finally, we return to the study of our arbitrary searching algorithm. Its comparison tree may not have all leaves on two adjacent levels, but, even if not, the bounds in Lemma 6.5 will still hold. Hence we may translate these bounds into the language of comparisons, as follows.

**Theorem 6.6**    *Suppose that an algorithm uses comparisons of keys to search for a target in a list. If there are $k$ possible outcomes, then the algorithm must make at least $\lceil \lg k \rceil$ comparisons of keys in its worst case and at least $\lg k$ in its average case.*

Observe that there is very little difference between the worst-case bound and the average-case bound. By Theorem 6.4, moreover, for many algorithms it does not much matter whether the search is successful or not, in determining the bounds in the above theorems. When we apply Theorem 6.6 to algorithms such as binary search for which, on an ordered list of length $n$, there are $n$ successful and $n + 1$ unsuccessful outcomes, we obtain a worst-case bound of

$$\lceil \lg(2n + 1) \rceil \geq \lceil \lg(2n) \rceil = \lceil \lg n \rceil + 1$$

and an average-case bound of $\lg n + 1$ comparisons of keys. When we compare these numbers with those obtained in the analysis of Binary1Search, we obtain

**Corollary 6.7**    Binary1Search *is optimal in the class of all algorithms that search an ordered list by making comparisons of keys. In both the average and worst cases,* Binary1Search *achieves the optimal bound.*

### 5. Other Ways to Search

The bounds in Theorem 6.6 do not imply that no algorithm can run faster than binary search, only those that rely only on comparisons of keys. As a simple example, suppose that the keys are the integers from 1 to $n$ themselves. If we know that the target key $x$ is an integer in this range, then we would never perform a search algorithm to locate its item; we would simply store the items in an array indexed from 1 to $n$ and immediately look in index $x$ to find the desired item.

*interpolation search*

This idea can be extended to obtain another method called *interpolation search*. We assume that the keys are either numerical or are information, such as words, that can be readily encoded as numbers. The method also assumes that the keys in the list are uniformly distributed, that is, that the probability of a key being in a particular range equals its probability of being in any other range of the same length. To find the target key target, interpolation search then estimates, according to the magnitude of the number target relative to the first and last entries of the list, about where target would be in the list and looks there. It then reduces the size of the list according as target is less than or greater than the key examined. It can be shown that on average, with uniformly distributed keys, interpolation search will take about $\lg \lg n$ comparisons of keys, which, for large $n$, is somewhat fewer than binary search requires. If, for example, $n = 1,000,000$ then Binary1Search will require about $\lg 10^6 + 1 \approx 21$ comparisons, while interpolation search may need only about $\lg \lg 10^6 \approx 4.32$ comparisons.

Finally, we should repeat that, even for search by comparisons, our assumption that requests for all keys are equally likely may be far from correct. If one or two keys are much more likely than the others, then even sequential search, if it looks for those keys first, may be faster than any other method. The importance of search, or more generally, information retrieval, is so fundamental that much of data structures is devoted to its methods, and in later chapters we shall return to these problems again and again.

---

**Exercise 6.6**

**E1.** Suppose that, like Binary2Search, a search algorithm makes three-way comparisons. Let each internal node of its comparison tree correspond to a successful search and each leaf to an unsuccessful search.

    **(a)** Use Lemma 6.5 to obtain a theorem like Theorem 6.6 giving lower bounds for worst and average case behavior for an unsuccessful search by such an algorithm.

    **(b)** Use Theorem 6.4 to obtain a similar result for successful searches.

    **(c)** Compare the bounds you obtain with the analysis of Binary2Search.

**Programming Project 6.6**

**P1.** **(a)** Write a program to do interpolation search and verify its correctness (especially termination). See the references at the end of the chapter for suggestions and program analysis. **(b)** Include your function as another option in the testing program of Project P1 of Section 6.2 (page 240) and compare its performance with the other methods.

## 6.7 Asymptotics

### 6.7.1 INTRODUCTION

The time has come to distill important generalizations from our analyses of searching algorithms. As we have progressed, we have been able to see more clearly which aspects of algorithm analysis are of great importance and which parts can safely be neglected. If a section of a program is performed only once outside any loops, for example, then the amount of time it uses is negligible compared to the amount of time used inside loops. We have found that, although binary search is more difficult to program and to analyze than sequential search, and even though it runs more slowly when applied to a very short list, for a longer list it will run far faster than sequential search.

*designing algorithms*
*for small problems*

The design of efficient methods to work on small problems is an important subject to study, since a large program may need to do the same or similar small tasks many times during its execution. As we have discovered, for small problems, the large overhead of a sophisticated method may make it inferior to a simpler method. For a list of three or four entries, sequential search is certainly superior to binary search. To improve efficiency in the algorithm for a small problem, the programmer must necessarily devote attention to details specific to the computer system and programming language, and there are few general observations that will help with this task.

*choice of method for*
*large problems*

The design of efficient algorithms for large problems is an entirely different matter. In studying binary search, we have seen that the overhead becomes relatively unimportant; it is the basic idea that will make all the difference between success and a problem too large to be attacked.

*asymptotics*

The word *asymptotics* that titles this section means the study of functions of a parameter $n$, as $n$ becomes larger and larger without bound. In comparing searching algorithms, we have seen that a count of the number of comparisons of keys accurately reflects the total running time for large problems, since it has generally been true that all the other operations (such as incrementing and comparing indices) have gone in lock step with comparison of keys.

*basic actions*

In fact, the frequency of such basic actions is much more important than is a total count of all operations including the housekeeping. The total including housekeeping is too dependent on the choice of programming language and on the programmer's particular style, so dependent that it tends to obscure the general methods. Variations in housekeeping details or programming technique can easily triple the running time of a program, but such a change probably will not make the difference between whether the computation is feasible or not. A change in fundamental method, on the other hand, can make a vital difference. If the number of basic actions is proportional to the size $n$ of the input, then doubling $n$ will about double the running time, no matter how the housekeeping is done. If the number of basic actions is proportional to $\lg n$, then doubling $n$ will hardly change the running time. If the number of basic actions is proportional to $n^2$, then the running time will quadruple, and the computation may still be feasible, but may be uncomfortably

*goal*

long. If the number of basic operations is proportional to $2^n$, then doubling $n$ will square this number. A computation that took 1 second might involve a million ($10^6$) basic operations, and doubling the input might require $10^{12}$ basic operations, increasing the running time from 1 second to $11\frac{1}{2}$ days.

Our desire in formulating general principles that will apply to the analysis of many classes of algorithms, then, is to have a notation that will accurately reflect the way in which the computation time will increase with the size, but that will ignore superfluous details with little effect on the total. We wish to concentrate on one or two basic operations within the algorithm, without too much concern for all the housekeeping operations that will accompany them. If an algorithm does $f(n)$ basic operations when the size of its input is $n$, then its total running time will be at most $cf(n)$, where $c$ is a constant that depends on the algorithm, on the way in which it is programmed, and on the computer used, but $c$ does not depend on the size $n$ of the input (at least when $n$ is past a few initial cases).

## 6.7.2 THE BIG-O NOTATION

The ideas we have been discussing are embodied in the following notation:

**Definition**     If $f(n)$ and $g(n)$ are functions defined for positive integers, then to write

$$f(n) \text{ is } O(g(n))$$

[read $f(n)$ is *big O* of $g(n)$] means that there exists a constant $c$ such that $|f(n)| \le c|g(n)|$ for all sufficiently large positive integers $n$.

Under these conditions we also say that "$f(n)$ has *order* at most $g(n)$" or "$f(n)$ grows no more rapidly than $g(n)$."

### 1. Examples

As a first example, consider the function $f(n) = 100n$. Then $f(n)$ is $O(n)$, since $f(n) \le cn$ for the constant $c = 100$. Any larger constant $c > 100$ will also work just as well.

Next consider the function $f(n) = 4n + 200$. Since $f(n) \le 4n$ is not true for large values of $n$, we cannot show that $f(n)$ is $O(n)$ by taking $c = 4$. But we can choose any larger value for $c$. If we choose $c = 5$, for example, then we will find that $f(n) \le 5n$ whenever $n \ge 200$, and therefore $f(n)$ is again $O(n)$.

For the next example, take $f(n) = n^2$. Suppose we were to try to show that $f(n)$ is $O(n)$. Doing so would mean that we could find a *constant* such that $n^2 \le cn$ for all sufficiently large $n$. When we take $n$ to be a large positive integer and divide both sides of the inequality by $n$, we obtain $n \le c$ for *all* large integers and a *constant* $c$. This statement is obviously nonsense: We can choose the integer $n$ to be larger than $c$. Hence we must conclude that $n^2$ is not $O(n)$.

The final example of polynomials in $n$ that we shall choose is $f(n) = 3n^2 - 100n$. For small values of $n$, $f(n)$ is less than $n$, but for reasons similar to the last example, for any constant $c$, $f(n)$ will be greater than $cn$ when $n$ is sufficiently large. Hence $f(n)$ is not $O(n)$. On the other hand, when $c = 3$ we have $f(n) \le 3n^2$, so it is true that $f(n)$ is $O(n^2)$. Even if we were to change $f(n)$ to $3n^2 + 100n$, we would still have that $f(n)$ is $O(n^2)$. In this case, we would not be able to use $c = 3$, but any larger value for $c$ would work.

## 2. General Observations

These examples of polynomials generalize to the first and most important rule about the big-O notation. To obtain the order of a polynomial function, we simply need to extract the term with the highest degree, disregarding all constants and all terms with a lower degree. More formally, we have:

> If $f(n)$ is a polynomial in $n$ with degree $r$, then $f(n)$ is $O(n^r)$, but $f(n)$ is not $O(n^s)$ for any power $s$ less than $r$.

Logarithms form a second class of functions that appear frequently in studying algorithms. We have already used logarithms in the analysis of binary search, and we have seen that the logarithm of $n$ grows much more slowly than $n$ itself. In fact, the general observation is true:

> Any logarithm of $n$ grows more slowly (as $n$ increases) than any positive power of $n$. Hence $\log n$ is $O(n^k)$ for any $k > 0$, but $n^k$ is never $O(\log n)$ for any power $k > 0$.

## 3. Common Orders

When we apply the big-O notation, $f(n)$ will normally be the operation count or running time for some algorithm, and we wish to choose the form of $g(n)$ to be as simple as possible. We thus write $O(1)$ to mean computing time that is bounded by a constant (not dependent on $n$); $O(n)$ means that the time is directly proportional to $n$, and is called *linear time*. We call $O(n^2)$ *quadratic time*, $O(n^3)$ *cubic*, $O(2^n)$ *exponential*. These five orders, together with *logarithmic time* $O(\log n)$ and $O(n \log n)$, are the ones most commonly used in analyzing algorithms.

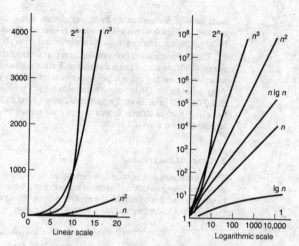

Figure 6.8. Growth rates of common functions

Figure 6.8 shows how these seven functions (with constant 1) grow with $n$, and the relative sizes of some of these numbers are shown in Figure 6.9. The number in the lower right corner of the table in Figure 6.9 is beyond comprehension: If every electron in the universe ($10^{50}$ of them) were a supercomputer doing a hundred million ($10^8$) operations per second since the creation of the universe (perhaps 30 billion years, or about $10^{18}$ seconds), then a computation requiring $2^{1000}$ operations would have done only about $10^{76}$ operations, so it would have to go $10^{225}$ *times* as long! A computation requiring $2^n$ operations is feasible only for *very* small values of $n$.

| $n$ | 1 | $\lg n$ | $n$ | $n \lg n$ | $n^2$ | $n^3$ | $2^n$ |
|---|---|---|---|---|---|---|---|
| 1 | 1 | 0.00 | 1 | 0 | 1 | 1 | 2 |
| 10 | 1 | 3.32 | 10 | 33 | 100 | 1000 | 1024 |
| 100 | 1 | 6.64 | 100 | 66 | 10,000 | 1,000,000 | $1.268 \times 10^{30}$ |
| 1000 | 1 | 9.97 | 1000 | 997 | 1,000,000 | $10^9$ | $1.072 \times 10^{301}$ |

Figure 6.9. Relative sizes of functions

Notice especially how much slower $\lg n$ grows than $n$; this is essentially the reason why binary search is superior to sequential search for large lists. Notice how the functions 1 and $\lg n$ become farther and farther below all the others for large $n$.

### 4. Algorithm Analyses

We can now express the conclusions of our algorithm analyses very simply:

- On a list of length $n$, sequential search has running time $O(n)$.

- On an ordered list of length $n$, binary search has running time $O(\log n)$.

- Retrieval from a contiguous list of length $n$ has running time $O(1)$.

- Retrieval from a linked list of length $n$ has running time $O(n)$.

## 6.7.3 IMPRECISION OF THE BIG-O NOTATION

Note that the constant $c$ in the definition of the big-O notation depends on which functions $f(n)$ and $g(n)$ are under discussion. Thus we can write that $17n^3 - 5$ is $O(n^3)$ (here $c = 17$ will do, as will any larger $c$), and also $35n^3 + 100$ is $O(n^3)$ (here $c \geq 35$).

### 1. Poor Uses

Note also that it is equally correct to write that $35n^3$ is $O(n^7)$ as that $35n^3$ is $O(n^3)$. It is correct but uninformative to write that both binary and sequential search have running time that is $O(n^5)$. If $h(n)$ is any function that grows faster than $g(n)$, then a function that is $O(g(n))$ must also be $O(h(n))$. Hence the big-O notation can be used imprecisely, but we shall always refrain from doing so, instead using the smallest possible of the seven functions shown in Figure 6.8.

A common but incorrect way to use the big-O notation is to write a sentence such as "Binary search operates in $O(\log n)$ time whereas sequential search takes $O(n)$ time." This statement, while correct, does *not* imply that binary search is faster than sequential search. Indeed, it is correct to note that binary search also takes $O(n)$ time.

### 2. Keeping the Dominant Term

We would often like to have a more precise measure of the amount of work done by an algorithm, and we can obtain one by using the big-O notation within an expression, as follows. We define

$$f(n) = g(n) + O(h(n))$$

*search comparisons*

to mean that $f(n) - g(n)$ is $O(h(n))$. Instead of thinking of $O(h(n))$ as the class of all functions growing no faster than $ch(n)$ for some constant $c$, we think of $O(h(n))$ as a single but arbitrary such function. We then use this function to represent all the terms of our calculation in which we are not interested, generally all the terms except the one that grows the most quickly.

The results of some of our algorithm analyses can now be summarized as follows:

- For a successful search in a list of length $n$, sequential search has running time $\frac{1}{2}n + O(1)$.

- For a successful search in an ordered list of length $n$, binary search has running time $2\lg n + O(1)$.

- Retrieval from a contiguous list of length $n$ has running time $O(1)$.

- Retrieval from a simply linked list of length $n$ has average running time $\frac{1}{2}n + O(1)$.

In using the big-O notation in expressions, it is necessary always to remember that $O(h(n))$ does not stand for a well-defined function, but for an arbitrary function *danger* from a large class. Hence ordinary algebra cannot be done with $O(h(n))$. For example, we might have two expressions

$$n^2 + 4n - 5 = n^2 + O(n) \text{ and } n^2 - 9n + 7 = n^2 + O(n)$$

but $O(n)$ represents different functions in the two expressions, so we cannot equate the right sides or conclude that the left sides are equal.

### 6.7.4 Ordering of Common Functions

Although the seven functions graphed in Figure 6.8 are the only ones we shall usually need for algorithm analysis, a few simple rules will enable you to determine the order of many other kinds of functions.

1. *The powers of $n$ are ordered according to the exponent: $n^a$ is $O(n^b)$ if and only if $a \leq b$.*

2. *The order of $\log n$ is independent of the base taken for the logarithms; that is, $\log_a n$ is $O(\log_b n)$ for all $a, b > 1$.*

3. *A logarithm grows more slowly than any positive power of $n$: $\log n$ is $O(n^a)$ for any $a > 0$, but $n^a$ is never $O(\log n)$ for $a > 0$.*

4. *Any power $n^a$ is $O(b^n)$ for all $a$ and all $b > 1$, but $b^n$ is never $O(n^a)$ for any $b > 1$ or for any $a$.*

5. *If $a < b$, then $a^n$ is $O(b^n)$, but $b^n$ is not $O(a^n)$.*

6. *If $f(n)$ is $O(g(n))$ and $h(n)$ is an arbitrary function, then $f(n)h(n)$ is $O(g(n)h(n))$.*

7. *The above rules may be applied recursively (a chain rule) by substituting any function of $n$ for $n$. For example, $\log \log n$ is $O((\log n)^{1/2})$. To verify this fact, replace $n$ by $\log n$ in the statement "$\log n$ is $O(n^{1/2})$."*

**Exercises 6.7**

**E1.** For each of the following pairs of functions, find the smallest integer value of $n > 1$ for which the first becomes larger than the second.

    **(a)** $n^2$ and $15n + 5$           **(c)** $0.1n$ and $10 \lg n$

    **(b)** $2^n$ and $8n^4$             **(d)** $0.1n^2$ and $100n \lg n$

**E2.** Arrange the following functions into increasing order; that is, $f(n)$ should come before $g(n)$ in your list if and only if $f(n)$ is $O(g(n))$.

| 1000000 | $(\lg n)^3$ | $2^n$ |
|---|---|---|
| $n \lg n$ | $n^3 - 100n^2$ | $n + \lg n$ |
| $\lg \lg n$ | $n^{0.1}$ | $n^2$ |

**E3.** Let $x$ and $y$ be real numbers with $0 < x < y$. Prove that $n^x$ is $O(n^y)$, but $n^y$ is not $O(n^x)$.

**E4.** Show that logarithmic time does not depend on the base $a$ chosen for the logarithms. That is, prove that $\log_a n$ is $O(\log_b n)$ for any real numbers $a > 1$ and $b > 1$.

**Programming Project 6.7**

**P1.** Write a program to test on your computer how long it takes to do $n \lg n$, $n^2$, $n^5$, $2^n$, and $n!$ additions for $n = 5, 10, 15, 20$.

# Pointers and Pitfalls

1. In designing algorithms be very careful of the extreme cases, such as empty lists, lists with only one item, or full lists (in the contiguous case).

2. Be sure that all your variables are properly initialized.

3. Double check the termination conditions for your loops, and make sure that progress toward termination always occurs.

4. In case of difficulty, formulate statements that will be correct both before and after each iteration of a loop, and verify that they hold.

5. Avoid sophistication for sophistication's sake. If a simple method is adequate for your application, use it.

6. Don't reinvent the wheel. If a ready-made routine is adequate for your application, use it.

7. Sequential search is slow but robust. Use it for short lists or if there is any doubt that the keys in the list are properly ordered.

8. Be extremely careful if you must reprogram binary search. Verify that your algorithm is correct and test it on all the extreme cases.

9. Drawing trees is an excellent way both to trace the action of an algorithm and to analyze its behavior.

10. Rely on the big-O analysis of algorithms for large applications but not for small applications.

# Review Questions

6.4

1. Name three conditions under which sequential search of a list is preferable to binary search.

6.5

2. In searching a list of $n$ items, how many comparisons of keys are done, on average, by (a) SequentialSearch, (b) Binary1Search, and (c) Binary2Search?

3. Why was binary search implemented only for contiguous lists, not for linked lists?

4. Draw the comparison tree for Binary1Search for searching a list of length (a) 1, (b) 2, and (c) 3.

5. Draw the comparison tree for Binary2Search for searching a list of length (a) 1, (b) 2, and (c) 3.

6. If the height of a 2-tree is 3, what are (a) the largest and (b) the smallest number of vertices that can be in the tree?

7. Define the terms *internal* and *external path length* of a 2-tree. State the path length theorem.

6.6

8. What is the smallest number of comparisons that any method relying on comparisons of keys must make, on average, in searching a list of $n$ items?

9. If Binary2Search does 20 comparisons for the average successful search, then about how many will it do for the average unsuccessful search, assuming that the possibilities of the target less than the smallest key, between any pair of keys, or larger than the largest key are all equally likely?

6.7

10. What is the purpose of the big-O notation?

# References for Further Study

The primary reference for this chapter is KNUTH, Volume 3. (See the end of Chapter 3 for bibliographic details.) Sequential search occupies pp. 389–405; binary search is covered in pp. 406–414; then comes Fibonacci search, and a section on history. KNUTH studies every method we have touched, and many others besides. He does algorithm analysis in considerably more detail than we have, writing his algorithms in a pseudo-assembly language and counting operations in detail there.

The coatroom project is taken from the following reference, which includes several interesting extensions and further applications.

JOSEPH BERGIN, "Coatroom: An ADT which is useful in implementation of object oriented programming (with positive pedagogical side effects)," *ACM SIGCSE Bulletin* 22 (1990), 45–46, 62.

Proving the correctness of the binary search algorithm is the topic of

JON BENTLEY, "Programming pearls: Writing correct programs" (regular column), *Communications of the ACM* 26 (1983), 1040–1045.

In this column BENTLEY shows how to formulate a binary search algorithm from its requirements, points out that about 90 percent of professional programmers whom he has taught were unable to write the program correctly in one hour, and gives a formal verification of correctness.

The following paper studies 26 published versions of binary search, pointing out correct and erroneous reasoning and drawing conclusions applicable to other algorithms:

R. LESUISSE, "Some lessons drawn from the history of the binary search algorithm," *The Computer Journal* 26 (1983), 154–163.

Theorem 6.4 (successful and unsuccessful searches take almost the same time on average) is due to

T. N. HIBBARD, *Journal of the ACM* 9 (1962), 16–17.

Interpolation search is presented in

C. C. GOTLIEB and L. R. GOTLIEB, *Data Types and Structures*, Prentice-Hall, Englewood Cliffs, N. J., 1978, pp. 133–135.

# 7

# Sorting

**T**HIS CHAPTER *studies several important methods for sorting lists, both contiguous and linked. At the same time, we shall develop further tools that help with the analysis of algorithms.*

# 7.1 Introduction and Notation

We live in a world obsessed with keeping information, and to find it, we must keep it in some sensible order. Librarians make sure that no one misplaces a book; income tax authorities trace down every dollar we earn; credit bureaus keep track of almost every detail of our actions. We once saw a cartoon in which a keen filing clerk, anxious to impress the boss, said frenetically, "Let me make sure these files are in alphabetical order before we throw them out." If we are to be the masters of this explosion instead of its victims, we had best learn how to keep track of it all!

*practical importance*

Several years ago, it was estimated, more than half the time on many commercial computers was spent in sorting. This is perhaps no longer true, since sophisticated methods have been devised for organizing data, methods that do not require that it be kept in any special order. Eventually, nonetheless, the information does go out to people, and then it must often be sorted in some way.

Because sorting is so important, a great many algorithms have been devised for doing it. In fact, so many good ideas appear in sorting methods that an entire course could easily be built around this one theme. Amongst the differences in environment that require different methods, the most important is the distinction between *external* and *internal*, that is, whether there are so many records to be sorted that they must be kept in external files on disks, tapes, or the like, or whether they can all be kept internally in high-speed memory. In this chapter, we consider only internal sorting.

*external and internal sorting*

It is not our intention to present anything close to a comprehensive treatment of internal sorting methods. For such a treatment, see Volume 3 of the monumental work of D. E. KNUTH (reference given at end of Chapter 3). KNUTH expounds about twenty-five sorting methods and claims that they are "only a fraction of the algorithms that have been devised so far." We shall study only a few methods in detail, chosen, first, because they are good—each one can be the best choice under some circumstances; second, because they illustrate much of the variety appearing in the full range of methods; and third, because they are relatively easy to write and understand, without too many details to complicate their presentation. A considerable number of variations of these methods then appear as exercises.

*reference*

Throughout this chapter we use the same notation as in previous chapters, so that list will be a *list* of entries to be sorted into order by a *key* field within each list entry. To compare keys we shall use macros, as described in Chapter 6, so that our routines can easily be transformed from sorting one kind of keys to another. The macros that we shall need are taken from EQ (equal), LT (less than), GT (greater than), LE (less than or equal), and GE (greater than or equal). The declarations for a list and the names assigned to various types and operations will be the same as in previous chapters.

*notation*

In one case we must sometimes exercise special care: Two or more of the entries in a list may have the same key. In this case of duplicate keys, sorting might produce different orders of the entries with duplicate keys. If the order of entries with duplicate keys makes a difference to an application, then we must be especially careful in constructing sorting algorithms.

*basic operations*

In studying searching algorithms, it soon became clear that the total amount of work done was closely related to the number of comparisons of keys. The same observation is true for sorting algorithms, but sorting algorithms must also either change pointers or move entries around within the list, and therefore time spent this way is also important, especially in the case of large entries kept in a contiguous list. Our analyses will therefore concentrate on these two basic actions.

*analysis*

As before, both the worst-case performance and the average performance of a sorting algorithm are of interest. To find the average, we shall consider what would happen if the algorithm were run on all possible orderings of the list (with $n$ entries, there are $n!$ such orderings altogether) and take the average of the results.

## 7.2 Insertion Sort

### 7.2.1 ORDERED LISTS

When first introducing binary search in Section 6.4, we mentioned that an *ordered list* is really a new abstract data type, which we defined as a list in which each entry contains a key, and such that the keys are in order; that is, if entry $i$ comes before entry $j$ in the list, then the key of entry $i$ is less than or equal to the key of entry $j$. To compare keys, we shall use the same macros, such as LT, LE, and EQ described in Chapter 6, so that our functions can easily be transformed from sorting one kind of keys to another.

For ordered lists, we shall often use three new operations that have no counterparts for other lists, since they use keys rather than positions to locate the entry. One operation *retrieves* an entry with a specified key from the ordered list. The second operation *inserts* a new entry into an ordered list by using the key in the new entry to determine where in the list to insert it. The third operation *sorts* a list which may not be ordered but which has keys in its entries, so that the resulting list is ordered.

Retrieval by key from an ordered list is exactly the same as searching. We have already studied this problem in Chapter 6. Ordered insertion will serve as the basis for our first sorting method.

First, let us consider a contiguous list. In this case, it is necessary to move entries in the list to make room for the insertion. To find the place where the insertion is to be made, we must search. One method for performing ordered insertion into a contiguous list is first to do a binary search to find the correct location, then move the entries as required and insert the new entry. This method is left as an exercise. Since so much time is needed to move entries no matter how the search is done, it turns out in many cases to be just as fast to use sequential search as binary search. By doing sequential search from the *end* of the list, the search and the movement of entries can be combined in a single loop, thereby reducing the overhead required in the function.

An example of ordered insertion appears in Figure 7.1. We begin with the ordered list shown in part (a) of the figure and wish to insert the new entry hen. In contrast to the implementation-independent version of InsertOrder from Section 6.4, we shall start comparing keys at the *end* of the list, rather than at its beginning. Hence we first compare the new key hen with the last key ram shown in the colored box in part (a). Since hen comes before ram, we move ram one position down, leaving the empty position shown in part (b). We next compare hen with the key pig shown in the colored box in part (b). Again, hen belongs earlier, so we move pig down and compare hen with the key dog shown in the colored box in part (c). Since hen comes after dog, we have found the proper location and can complete the insertion as shown in part (d).

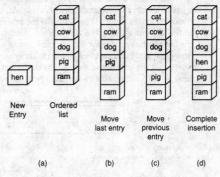

Figure 7.1. Ordered insertion

## 7.2.2 SORTING BY INSERTION

Our first sorting method for a list is based on the idea of insertion into an ordered list. To sort an unordered list, we think of removing its entries one at a time and then inserting each of them into an initially empty new list, always keeping the entries in the new list in the proper order according to their keys.

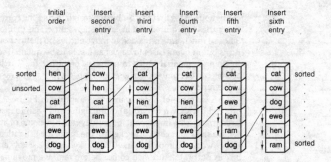

Figure 7.2. Example of insertion sort

*example*

    This method is illustrated in Figure 7.2, which shows the steps needed to sort a list of six words. At each stage, the words that have not yet been inserted into the sorted list are shown in colored boxes, and the sorted part of the list is shown in white boxes. In the initial diagram, the first word hen is shown as sorted, since a list of length 1 is automatically ordered. All the remaining words are shown as unsorted at this stage. At each step of the process, the first unsorted word (shown in the uppermost gray box) is inserted into its proper place in the sorted part of the list. To make room for the insertion, some of the sorted words must be moved down the list. Each move of a word is shown as a colored arrow in Figure 7.2. By starting at the end of the sorted part of the list, we can move entries at the same time as we do comparisons to find where the new entry fits.

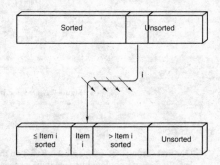

Figure 7.3. The main step of contiguous insertion sort

    The main step required to insert an entry denoted i into the sorted part of the list is shown in Figure 7.3. In the function that follows, we instead denote this item as fu. Let us now write the function.

```
/* InsertionSort: sort contiguous list by the insertion sort method.
   Pre:  The contiguous list list has been created. Each entry of list contains a key.
   Post: The entries of list have been rearranged so that the keys in all the entries are
         sorted into nondecreasing order. */
void InsertionSort(List *list)
{
    Position fu;              /* position of first unsorted entry       */
    Position place;           /* searches sorted part of list           */
    ListEntry current;        /* holds entry temporarily removed from list */
    for (fu = 1; fu < list->count; fu++)
        if (LT(list->entry[fu].key, list->entry[fu - 1].key)) {
            current = list->entry[fu];
            for (place = fu - 1; place >= 0; place--) {
                list->entry[place + 1] = list->entry[place];
                if (place == 0 || LE(list->entry[place - 1].key, current.key))
                    break;
            }
            list->entry[place] = current;
        }
}
```

*contiguous insertion sort*

The action of the program is nearly self-explanatory. Since a list with only one entry is automatically sorted, the loop on fu (first unsorted entry) starts with the second entry. If it is in the correct place, nothing needs to be done. Otherwise, the new entry is pulled out of the list into the variable current, and the second for loop pushes entries one position down the list until the correct position is found, and finally current is inserted there before proceeding to the next unsorted entry. The case when current belongs in the first position of the list must be treated specially, since in this case there is no entry with a smaller key that would terminate the search. We treat this special case by testing the value of place (is it equal to zero?) before we invoke LE; when place is equal to zero the logical AND fails, we do not invoke LE, and we break out of the loop.

## 7.2.3 LINKED VERSION

*algorithm*

For a linked version of insertion sort, since there is no movement of data, there is no need to start searching at the *end* of the sorted sublist. Instead, we shall traverse the original list, taking one entry at a time and inserting it in the proper place in the sorted list. The pointer variable ls (last sorted entry) will give the end of the sorted part of the list, and ls->next will give the first entry that has not yet been inserted into the sorted sublist. We shall let fu (first unsorted entry) also point to this entry, and use a pointer current to search the sorted part of the list to find where to insert fu. If fu belongs before the current head of the list, then we insert it there. Otherwise, we move current down the list until current->entry.key >= fu->entry.key and then insert fu before current. To enable insertion before current we keep a second pointer trailing in lock step one position closer to the head than current.

A *sentinel* is an extra entry added to one end of a list to ensure that a loop will terminate without having to include a separate check. Since we have

ls->next = fu,

the node fu is already in place to serve as a sentinel for the search, and the loop moving current is simplified.

Finally, let us note that a list with 0 or 1 entry is already sorted, so that we can check these cases separately and thereby avoid trivialities elsewhere. The details appear in the following function.

```
/* InsertionSort: sort linked list by the insertion sort method.
   Pre:  The linked list list has been created. Each entry of list contains a key.
   Post: The entries of list have been rearranged so that the keys in all the entries are
         sorted into nondecreasing order. */
void InsertionSort(List *list)
{
    ListNode *fu;            /* the first unsorted node to be inserted       */
    ListNode *ls;            /* the last sorted node (tail of sorted sublist) */
    ListNode *current, *trailing;
    if (list->head) {
        ls = list->head;            /* An empty list is already sorted.       */
        while (ls->next) {
            fu = ls->next;          /* Remember first unsorted node.          */
            if (LT(fu->entry.key, list->head->entry.key)) {
                ls->next = fu->next;
                fu->next = list->head;
                list->head = fu;    /* Insert first unsorted at the head of sorted list. */
            } else {                /* Search the sorted sublist.             */
                trailing = list->head;
                for (current = trailing->next; GT(fu->entry.key, current->entry.key);
                     current = current->next)
                    trailing = current;
                /* First unsorted node now belongs between trailing and current. */
                if (fu == current)
                    ls = fu;
                else {
                    ls->next = fu->next;
                    fu->next = current;
                    trailing->next = fu;
                }
            }
        }
    }
}
```

*linked insertion sort*

Even though the mechanics of the linked version are quite different from those of the contiguous version, you should be able to see that the basic method is the same. The only real difference is that the contiguous version searches the sorted sublist in reverse order, while the linked version searches it in increasing order of position within the list.

## 7.2.4 ANALYSIS

Since the basic ideas are the same, let us analyze only the performance of the contiguous version of the program. We also restrict our attention to the case when the list list is initially in random order (meaning that all possible orderings of the keys are equally likely). When we deal with entry $i$, how far back must we go to insert it? There are $i$ possible positions: not moving it at all, moving it one position, up to moving it $i - 1$ positions to the front of the list. Given randomness, these are equally likely. The probability that it need not be moved is thus $1/i$, in which case only one comparison of keys is done, with no moving of entries.

*inserting one entry*

The remaining case, in which entry $i$ must be moved, occurs with probability $(i - 1)/i$. Let us begin by counting the average number of iterations of the second for loop. Since all of the $i - 1$ possible positions are equally likely, the average number of iterations is

$$\frac{1 + 2 + \cdots + (i - 1)}{i - 1} = \frac{(i - 1)i}{2(i - 1)} = \frac{i}{2}.$$

One key comparison and one assignment are done for each of these iterations, with one more key comparison done outside the loop, along with two assignments of entries. Hence, in this second case, entry $i$ requires, on average, $\frac{1}{2}i + 1$ comparisons and $\frac{1}{2}i + 2$ assignments.

When we combine the two cases with their respective probabilities, we have

$$\frac{1}{i} \times 1 + \frac{i - 1}{i} \times \left(\frac{i}{2} + 1\right) = \frac{i + 1}{2}$$

comparisons and

$$\frac{1}{i} \times 0 + \frac{i - 1}{i} \times \left(\frac{i}{2} + 2\right) = \frac{i + 3}{2} - \frac{2}{i}$$

assignments.

*inserting all entries*

We wish to add these numbers from $i = 2$ to $i = n$, but to avoid complications in the arithmetic, we first use the big-O notation (see Section 6.7.2) to approximate each of these expressions by suppressing the terms bounded by a constant. We thereby obtain $\frac{1}{2}i + O(1)$ for both the number of comparisons and the number of assignments of entries. In making this approximation, we are really concentrating on the actions within the main loop and suppressing any concern about operations done outside the loop or variations in the algorithm that change the amount of work only by some bounded amount.

To add $\frac{1}{2}i + O(1)$ from $i = 2$ to $i = n$, we apply Theorem A.1 on page 580 (the sum of the integers from 1 to $n$), obtaining

$$\sum_{i=2}^{n} \left(\tfrac{1}{2}i + O(1)\right) = \frac{1}{2}\sum_{i=2}^{n} i + O(n) = \tfrac{1}{4}n^2 + O(n)$$

for both the number of comparisons of keys and the number of assignments of entries.

So far we have nothing with which to compare this number, but we can note that as $n$ becomes larger, the contributions from the term involving $n^2$ become much larger than the remaining terms collected as $O(n)$. Hence as the size of the list grows, the time needed by insertion sort grows like the square of this size.

*best and worst cases*      The worst-case analysis of insertion sort will be left as an exercise. We can observe quickly that the best case for insertion sort occurs when the list is already in order, when insertion sort will do nothing except $n - 1$ comparisons of keys. We can now show that there is no sorting method that can possibly do better in its best case.

**Theorem 7.1.**     *Verifying that a list of n entries is in the correct order requires at least $n - 1$ comparisons of keys.*

**Proof**     Consider an arbitrary program that checks whether a list of $n$ entries is in order or not (and perhaps sorts it if it is not). The program will first do some comparison of keys, and this comparison will involve some two entries from the list. Sometime later, at least one of these two entries must be compared with a third, or else there would be no way to decide where these two should be in the list relative to the third. Thus this second comparison involves only one new entry not previously in a comparison. Continuing in this way, we see that there must be another comparison involving some one of the first three entries and one new entry. Note that we are not necessarily selecting the comparisons in the order in which the algorithm does them. Thus, except for the first comparison, each one that we select involves only one new entry not previously compared. All $n$ of the entries must enter some comparison, for there is no way to decide whether an entry is in the right place unless it is compared to at least one other entry. Thus to involve all $n$ entries *end of proof*     requires at least $n - 1$ comparisons, and the proof is complete.

With this theorem we find one of the advantages of insertion sort: It verifies that a list is correctly sorted as quickly as can be done. Furthermore, insertion sort remains an excellent method whenever a list is nearly in the correct order and few entries are many positions away from their correct locations.

---

**Exercises 7.2**     **E1.** By hand, trace through the steps insertion sort will use on each of the following lists. In each case, count the number of comparisons that will be made and the number of times an entry will be moved.

**(a)** The following three words to be sorted alphabetically:

triangle     square     pentagon

**(b)** The three words in part (a) to be sorted according to the number of sides of the corresponding polygon, in increasing order

**(c)** The three words in part (a) to be sorted according to the number of sides of the corresponding polygon, in decreasing order

**(d)** The following seven numbers to be sorted into increasing order:

26   33   35   29   19   12   22

(e) The same seven numbers in a different initial order, again to be sorted into increasing order:

$$12 \quad 19 \quad 33 \quad 26 \quad 29 \quad 35 \quad 22$$

(f) The following list of 14 names to be sorted into alphabetical order:

Tim Dot Eva Roy Tom Kim Guy Amy Jon Ann Jim Kay Ron Jan

**E2.** What initial order for a list of keys will produce the worst case for insertion sort in the contiguous version? In the linked version?

**E3.** How many key comparisons and entry assignments does contiguous insertion sort make in its worst case?

**E4.** Modify the linked version of insertion sort so that a list that is already sorted, or nearly so, will be processed rapidly.

**Programming Projects 7.2**

**P1.** Write a program that can be used to test and evaluate the performance of insertion sort and, later, other methods. The following outline should be used.

(a) Create several files of integers to be used to test sorting methods. Make files of several sizes, for example, sizes 20, 200, and 2000. Make files that are in order, in reverse order, in random order, and partially in order. By keeping all this test data in files (rather than generating it with random numbers each time the testing program is run), the same data can be used to test different sorting methods, and hence it will be easier to compare their performance.

(b) Write a menu-driven program for testing various sorting methods. One option is to read a file of integers into a list. Other options will be to run one of various sorting methods on the list, to print the unsorted or the sorted list, and to quit. After the list is sorted and (perhaps) printed, it should be discarded so that testing a later sorting method will start with the same input data. This can be done either by copying the unsorted list to a second list and sorting that one, or by arranging the program so that it reads the data file again before each time it starts sorting.

(c) Use the code in the program to calculate and print (1) the CPU time, (2) the number of comparisons of keys, and (3) the number of assignments of list entries during sorting a list. Counting comparisons and assignments requires setting up global variables and inserting code into each sorting function to increment one of these global variables each time a key comparison or entry assignment is made.

(d) Use the contiguous list functions as developed in Section 5.2.1, use the contiguous version of insertion sort, and assemble statistics on the performance of contiguous insertion sort for later comparison with other methods.

(e) Use the linked list functions as developed in Section 5.2.2, use the linked version of insertion sort, assemble its performance statistics, and compare them with contiguous insertion sort. Why is the count of entry assignments of little interest for this version?

**P2.** Rewrite the contiguous version of InsertionSort so that it uses binary search to locate where to insert the next entry. Compare the time needed to sort a list with that of the original function InsertionSort. Is it reasonable to use binary search in the linked version of InsertionSort? Why or why not?

*scan sort*

**P3.** There is an even easier sorting method, which, instead of using two pointers to move through the list, uses only one. We can call it *scan sort*, and it proceeds by starting at one end and moving forward, comparing adjacent pairs of keys, until it finds a pair out of order. It then swaps this pair of entries, and starts moving the other way, continuing to swap pairs until it finds a pair in the correct order. At this point it knows that it has moved the one entry as far back as necessary, so that the first part of the list is sorted, but, unlike insertion sort, it has forgotten how far forward has been sorted, so it simply reverses direction and sorts forward again, looking for a pair out of order. When it reaches the far end of the list, then it is finished.

**(a)** Write a C program to implement scan sort for contiguous lists. Your program should use only one position variable (other than list->count), one variable of type ListEntry to be used in making swaps, and no other local variables.

**(b)** Compare the timings for your program with those of InsertionSort.

*bubble sort*

**P4.** A well-known algorithm called *bubble sort* proceeds by scanning the list from left to right, swapping entries whenever a pair of adjacent keys is found to be out of order. In this first pass, the largest key in the list will have "bubbled" to the end, but the earlier keys may still be out of order. Thus the pass scanning for pairs out of order is put in a loop that first makes the scanning pass go all the way to list->count, and at each iteration stops it one position sooner. **(a)** Write a C function for bubble sort. **(b)** Find the performance of bubble sort on various kinds of lists, and compare the results with those for insertion sort.

## 7.3 Selection Sort

Insertion sort has one major disadvantage. Even after most entries have been sorted properly into the first part of the list, the insertion of a later entry may require that many of them be moved. All the moves made by insertion sort are moves of only one position at a time. Thus to move an entry 20 positions up the list requires 20 separate moves. If the entries are small, perhaps a key alone, or if the entries are in linked storage, then the many moves may not require excessive time. But if the entries are very large, such as personnel files or student transcripts—records containing hundreds of components, and these records must be kept in contiguous storage, then it would be far more efficient if an entry being moved could immediately be placed in its final position. Our next sorting method accomplishes this goal.

### 7.3.1 THE ALGORITHM

An example of this sorting method appears in Figure 7.4, which shows the steps needed to sort a list of six words alphabetically. At the first stage, we scan the list to find the word that comes last in alphabetical order. This word, ram, is shown in a colored box. We then exchange this word with the word in the last position, as shown in the second part of Figure 7.4. Now we repeat the process on the shorter list obtained by omitting the last entry. Again the word that comes last is shown in a colored box; it is exchanged with the last entry still under consideration; and so we continue. The words that are not yet sorted into order are shown in gray boxes at each stage, except for the one that comes last, which is shown in a colored box. When the unsorted list is reduced to length 1, the process terminates.

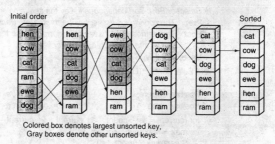

Colored box denotes largest unsorted key,
Gray boxes denote other unsorted keys.

**Figure 7.4. Example of selection sort**

This method translates into an algorithm called *selection sort*. The general step in selection sort is illustrated in Figure 7.5. The entries with large keys will be sorted in order and placed at the end of the list. The entries with smaller keys are not yet sorted. We then look through the unsorted entries to find the one with the largest key and swap it with the last unsorted entry. In this way, at each pass through the main loop, one more entry is placed in its final position.

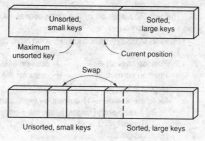

**Figure 7.5. The general step in selection sort**

## 7.3.2 CONTIGUOUS IMPLEMENTATION

Since selection sort minimizes data movement by putting one entry in its final position at every pass, the algorithm is primarily useful for contiguous lists with large entries for which movement of entries is expensive. If the entries are small, or if the list is linked, so that only pointers need be changed to sort the list, then insertion sort is usually faster than selection sort. We therefore give only a contiguous version of selection sort. The algorithm uses a function called MaxKey, which finds the maximum key on the part of the list list given as the parameters. The function Swap simply swaps the two entries with the given indices. For convenience in the discussion to follow, we write these two as separate functions.

```
/* SelectionSort: sort contiguous list by the selection sort method.
    Pre:   The contiguous list list has been created. Each entry of list contains a key.
    Post:  The entries of list have been rearranged so that the keys in all the entries are
           sorted into nondecreasing order.
    Uses: MaxKey, Swap. */
void SelectionSort(List *list)
{
    Position current;              /* position of place being correctly filled   */
    Position max;                  /* position of largest remaining key          */
    for (current = list->count - 1; current > 0; current--) {
        max = MaxKey(0, current, list);
        Swap(max, current, list);
    }
}
```

*contiguous selection sort*

Note that when all entries in a list but one are in the correct place, then the remaining one must be also. Thus the for loop stops at 1.

```
/* MaxKey: find the position of the largest key in the sublist.
    Pre:   The contiguous list list has been created. low and high are valid positions in
           list.
    Post:  The position of the entry between low and high with the largest key is re-
           turned. */
Position MaxKey(Position low, Position high, List *list)
{
    Position largest;             /* position of largest key so far            */
    Position current;             /* index for the contiguous list             */
    largest = low;
    for (current = low + 1; current <= high; current++)
        if (LT(list->entry[largest].key, list->entry[current].key))
            largest = current;
    return largest;
}
```

```
/* Swap: swap two entries in the contiguous list.
Pre:    The contiguous list list has been created. low and high are valid positions in
        list.
Post:   The entry at position low is swapped with the entry at position high. */
void Swap(Position low, Position high, List *list)
{
    ListEntry temp = list->entry[low];
    list->entry[low] = list->entry[high];
    list->entry[high] = temp;
}
```

### 7.3.3 ANALYSIS

*À propos* of algorithm analysis, the most remarkable fact about this algorithm is that both of the loops that appear are for loops, which means that we can calculate in advance exactly how many times they will iterate. In the number of comparisons it

*ordering unimportant*

makes, selection sort pays no attention to the original ordering of the list. Hence for a list that is nearly correct to begin with, selection sort is likely to be much slower than insertion sort. On the other hand, selection sort does have the advantage of predictability: its worst-case time will differ little from its best.

*advantage of selection sort*

The primary advantage of selection sort regards data movement. If an entry is in its correct final position, then it will never be moved. Every time any pair of entries is swapped, then at least one of them moves into its final position, and therefore at most $n - 1$ swaps are done altogether in sorting a list of $n$ entries. This is the very best that we can expect from any method that relies entirely on swaps to move its entries.

We can analyze the performance of function SelectionSort in the same way that it is programmed. The main function does nothing except some bookkeeping and calling the subprograms. Function Swap is called $n - 1$ times, and each call does 3 assignments of entries, for a total count of $3(n - 1)$. The function MaxKey is called $n - 1$ times, with the length of the sublist ranging from $n$ down to 2. If $t$ is the number of entries on the part of the list for which it is called, then MaxKey does

*comparison count for selection sort*

exactly $t - 1$ comparisons of keys to determine the maximum. Hence, altogether, there are $(n - 1) + (n - 2) + \cdots + 1 = \frac{1}{2}n(n - 1)$ comparisons of keys, which we approximate to $\frac{1}{2}n^2 + O(n)$.

### 7.3.4 COMPARISONS

Let us pause for a moment to compare the counts for selection sort with those for insertion sort. The results are

|  | Selection | Insertion (average) |
|---|---|---|
| Assignments of entries | $3.0n + O(1)$ | $0.25n^2 + O(n)$ |
| Comparisons of keys | $0.5n^2 + O(n)$ | $0.25n^2 + O(n)$ |

The relative advantages of the two methods appear in these numbers. When $n$ becomes large, $0.25n^2$ becomes much larger than $3n$, and if moving entries is a slow process, then insertion sort will take far longer than will selection sort. But the amount of time taken for comparisons is, on average, only about half as much for insertion sort as for selection sort. If the list entries are small, so that moving them is not slow, then insertion sort will be faster than selection sort.

---

**Exercises 7.3**

**E1.** By hand, trace through the steps selection sort will use on each of the following lists. In each case, count the number of comparisons that will be made and the number of times an entry will be moved.

(a) The following three words to be sorted alphabetically:

triangle    square    pentagon

(b) The three words in part (a) to be sorted according to the number of sides of the corresponding polygon, in increasing order

(c) The three words in part (a) to be sorted according to the number of sides of the corresponding polygon, in decreasing order

(d) The following seven numbers to be sorted into increasing order:

26  33  35  29  19  12  22

(e) The same seven numbers in a different initial order, again to be sorted into increasing order:

12  19  33  26  29  35  22

(f) The following list of 14 names to be sorted into alphabetical order:

Tim Dot Eva Roy Tom Kim Guy Amy Jon Ann Jim Kay Ron Jan

*count sort*

**E2.** There is a simple algorithm called *count sort* that will construct a new, sorted list from list in a new array, provided we are guaranteed that all the keys in list are different from each other. Count sort goes through list once, and for each key list->entry[i].key scans list to count how many keys are less than list->entry[i].key. If $c$ is this count, then the proper position in the sorted list for this key is $c + 1$. Determine how many comparisons of keys will be done by count sort. Is it a better algorithm than selection sort?

**Programming Projects 7.3**

**P1.** Run the test program written in Project P1 of Section 7.2 (page 287), to compare selection sort with insertion sort (contiguous version). Use the same files of test data used with insertion sort.

**P2.** Write and test a linked version of selection sort. Explain why selection sort is not especially good for linked lists.

# 7.4 Shell Sort

As we have seen, in some ways insertion sort and selection sort behave in opposite ways. Selection sort moves the entries very efficiently but does many redundant comparisons. In its best case, insertion sort does the minimum number of comparisons, but is inefficient in moving entries only one place at a time. Our goal now is to derive another method avoiding as much as possible the problems with both of these. Let us start with insertion sort and ask how we can reduce the number of times it moves an entry.

*diminishing increments*

The reason why insertion sort can move entries only one position is that it compares only adjacent keys. If we were to modify it so that it first compares keys far apart, then it could sort the entries far apart. Afterward, the entries closer together would be sorted, and finally the increment between keys being compared would be reduced to 1, to ensure that the list is completely in order. This is the idea implemented in 1959 by D. L. SHELL in the sorting method bearing his name. This method is also sometimes called *diminishing-increment sort*. Before describing the algorithm formally, let us work through a simple example of sorting names.

*example*

Figure 7.6 shows what will happen when we first sort all names that are at distance 5 from each other (so there will be only two or three names on each such list), then re-sort the names using increment 3, and finally perform an ordinary insertion sort (increment 1).

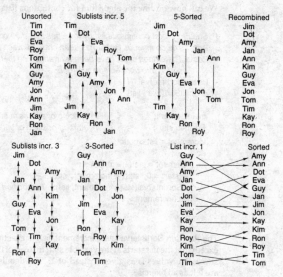

Figure 7.6. Example of Shell sort

You can see that, even though we make three passes through all the names, the early passes move the names close to their final positions, so that at the final pass (which does an ordinary insertion sort), all the entries are very close to their final positions so the sort goes rapidly.

*choice of increments*

There is no magic about the choice of 5, 3, and 1 as increments. Many other choices might work as well or better. It would, however, probably be wasteful to choose powers of 2, such as 8, 4, 2, and 1, since then the same keys compared on one pass would be compared again at the next, whereas by choosing numbers that are not multiples of each other, there is a better chance of obtaining new information from more of the comparisons. Although several studies have been made of Shell sort, no one has been able to prove that one choice of the increments is greatly superior to all others. Various suggestions have been made. If the increments are chosen close together, as we have done, then it will be necessary to make more passes, but each one will likely be quicker. If the increments decrease rapidly, then fewer but longer passes will occur. The only essential feature is that the final increment be 1, so that at the conclusion of the process, the list will be checked to be completely in order. For simplicity in the following algorithm, we start with increment = list->count and at each pass reduce the increment by

$$\text{increment} = \text{increment}/3 + 1;$$

We can now outline the algorithm for contiguous lists.

```
/* ShellSort: sort contiguous list by the Shell sort method.
   Pre:  The contiguous list list has been created. Each entry of list contains a key.
   Post: The entries of list have been rearranged so that the keys in all the entries are
         sorted into nondecreasing order.
   Uses: SortInterval. */
void ShellSort(List *list)
```

*Shell sort*

```
{
    int increment;            /* spacing of entries in sublist        */
    Position start;           /* starting position of sublist         */
    increment = list->count;
    do {
        increment = increment/3 + 1;
        for (start = 0;  start < increment;  start++)
            SortInterval(start, increment, list);  /* modified insert sort   */
    } while (increment > 1);
}
```

The function SortInterval(start, increment, list) is exactly the function InsertionSort, except that the list starts at the variable start instead of 0 and the increment between successive values is as given instead of 1. The details of modifying InsertionSort are left as an exercise.

Since the final pass through Shell sort has increment 1, Shell sort really is insertion sort optimized by the preprocessing stage of first sorting sublists using larger increments. Hence the proof that Shell sort works correctly is exactly the same as the proof that insertion sort works correctly. And, although we have good reason to think that the preprocessing stage will speed up the sorting considerably by eliminating many moves of entries by only one position, we have not actually proved that Shell sort will ever be faster than insertion sort.

*analysis*

The analysis of Shell sort turns out to be exceedingly difficult, and to date, good estimates on the number of comparisons and moves have been obtained only under special conditions. It would be very interesting to know how these numbers depend on the choice of increments, so that the best choice might be made. But even without a complete mathematical analysis, running a few large examples on a computer will convince you that Shell sort is quite good. Very large empirical studies have been made of Shell sort, and it appears that the number of moves, when $n$ is large, is in the range of $n^{1.25}$ to $1.6n^{1.25}$. This constitutes a substantial improvement over insertion sort.

---

**Exercises 7.4**

**E1.** By hand, sort the list of 14 names in the "unsorted" column of Figure 7.6 using Shell sort with increments of **(a)** 8, 4, 2, 1 and **(b)** 7, 3, 1. Count the number of comparisons and moves that are made in each case.

**E2.** Explain why Shell sort is ill suited for use with linked lists.

**Programming Projects 7.4**

**P1.** Rewrite InsertionSort to serve as the SortInterval function used in ShellSort.

**P2.** Test ShellSort with the program of Project P1 of Section 7.2 (page 287), using the same data files as for insertion sort, and compare the results.

---

## 7.5 Lower Bounds

Now that we have seen a method that performs much better than our first attempts, it is appropriate to ask,

> *How fast is it possible to sort?*

To answer, we shall limit our attention (as we did when answering the same question for searching) to sorting methods that rely entirely on comparisons between pairs of keys to do the sorting.

*comparison tree*

Let us take an arbitrary sorting algorithm of this class and consider how it sorts a list of $n$ entries. Imagine drawing its comparison tree. Sample comparison trees for insertion sort and selection sort applied to three numbers $a$, $b$, $c$ are shown in Figure 7.7. As each comparison of keys is made, it corresponds to an interior vertex (drawn as a circle). The leaves (square nodes) show the order that the numbers have after sorting.

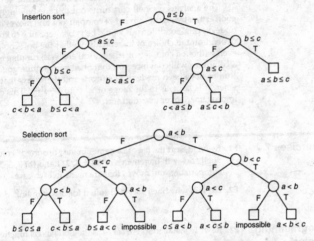

Figure 7.7. Comparison trees, insertion and selection sort, $n = 3$

Note that the diagrams show clearly that, on average, selection sort makes more comparisons of keys than insertion sort. In fact, selection sort makes redundant comparisons, repeating comparisons that have already been made.

*comparison trees:*
*height and path length*

The comparison tree of an arbitrary sorting algorithm displays several features of the algorithm. Its height is the largest number of comparisons that will be made, and hence gives the worst-case behavior of the algorithm. The external path length, after division by the number of leaves, gives the average number of comparisons that the algorithm will do. The comparison tree displays all the possible sequences of comparisons that can be made as all the different paths from the root to the leaves. Since these comparisons control how the entries are rearranged during sorting, any two different orderings of the list must result in some different decisions, hence different paths through the tree, which must then end in different leaves. The number of ways that the list containing $n$ entries could originally have been ordered is $n!$ (see Section A.3.1), and thus the number of leaves in the tree must be at least $n!$. Lemma 6.5 now implies that the height of the tree is at least $\lceil \lg n! \rceil$ and its external path length is at least $n! \lg n!$. (Recall that $\lceil k \rceil$ means the smallest integer not less than $k$.) Translating these results into the number of comparisons, we obtain

**Theorem 7.2**   *Any algorithm that sorts a list of n entries by use of key comparisons must, in its worst case, perform at least $\lceil \lg n! \rceil$ comparisons of keys, and, in the average case, it must perform at least $\lg n!$ comparisons of keys.*

Stirling's formula (Theorem A.5 on page 590) gives an approximation to the factorial of an integer, which, after taking the base 2 logarithm, is

$$\lg n! \approx (n + \tfrac{1}{2})\lg n - (\lg e)n + \lg\sqrt{2\pi} + \frac{\lg e}{12n}.$$

*approximating* $\lg n!$   The constants in this expression have the approximate values

$$\lg e \approx 1.442695041 \quad \text{and} \quad \lg\sqrt{2\pi} \approx 1.325748069.$$

Stirling's approximation to $\lg n!$ is very close indeed, much closer than we shall ever need for analyzing algorithms. For almost all purposes, the following rough approximation will prove quite satisfactory:

$$\lg n! \approx (n + \tfrac{1}{2})(\lg n - 1\tfrac{1}{2})+2$$

and often we use only the approximation $\lg n! = n \lg n + O(n)$.

*other methods*   Before ending this section we should note that there are sometimes methods for sorting that do not use comparisons and can be faster. For example, if you know in advance that you have 100 entries and that their keys are exactly the integers between 1 and 100 in some order, with no duplicates, then the best way to sort them is not to do any comparisons, but simply, if a particular entry has key $i$, then place it in location $i$. With this method we are (at least temporarily) regarding the entries to be sorted as being in a table rather than a list, and then we can use the key as an index to find the proper place in the table for each entry. Project P1 suggests an extension of this idea to an algorithm.

---

**Exercises 7.5**   **E1.** Draw the comparison trees for **(a)** insertion sort and **(b)** selection sort applied to four objects.

**E2.** **(a)** Find a sorting method for four keys that is optimal in the sense of doing the smallest possible number of key comparisons in its worst case. **(b)** Find how many comparisons your algorithm does in the average case (applied to four keys). Modify your algorithm to make it come as close as possible to achieving the lower bound of $\lg 4! \approx 4.585$ key comparisons. Why is it impossible to achieve this lower bound?

**E3.** Suppose that you have a shuffled deck of 52 cards, 13 cards in each of 4 suits, and you wish to sort the deck so that the 4 suits are in order and the 13 cards within each suit are also in order. Which of the following methods is fastest?

   **(a)** Go through the deck and remove all the clubs; then sort them separately. Proceed to do the same for the diamonds, the hearts, and the spades.

   **(b)** Deal the cards into 13 piles according to the rank of the card. Stack these 13 piles back together and deal into 4 piles according to suit. Stack these back together.

   **(c)** Make only one pass through the cards, by placing each card in its proper position relative to the previously sorted cards.

**Programming Projects 7.5**

The sorting projects for this section are specialized methods requiring keys of a particular type, pseudorandom numbers between 0 and 1. Hence they are not intended to work with the testing program devised for other methods, nor to use the same data as the other methods studied in this chapter.

*interpolation sort*

**P1.** Construct a list of $n$ pseudorandom numbers between 0 and 1. Suitable values for $n$ are 10 (for debugging) and 500 (for comparing the results with other methods). Write a program to sort these numbers into an array via the following **interpolation sort**. First, clear the array (to all 0). For each number from the old list, multiply it by $n$, take the integer part, and look in that position of the table. If that position is 0, put the number there. If not, move left or right (according to the relative size of the current number and the one in its place) to find the place to insert the new number, moving the entries in the table over if necessary to make room (as in the fashion of insertion sort). Show that your algorithm will really sort the numbers correctly. Compare its running time with that of the other sorting methods applied to randomly ordered lists of the same size.

*linked distribution sort*

**P2.** [suggested by B. LEE] Write a program to perform a linked distribution sort, as follows. Take the keys to be pseudorandom numbers between 0 and 1, as in the previous project. Set up an array of linked lists, and distribute the keys into the linked lists according to their magnitude. The linked lists can either be kept sorted as the numbers are inserted or sorted during a second pass, during which the lists are all connected together into one sorted list. Experiment to determine the optimum number of lists to use. (It seems that it works well to have enough lists so that the average length of each list is about 3.)

# 7.6 Divide-and-Conquer Sorting

## 7.6.1 THE MAIN IDEAS

*shorter is easier*

Making a fresh start is often a good idea, and we shall do so by forgetting (temporarily) almost everything that we know about sorting. Let us try to apply only one important principle that has shown up in the methods we have previously studied and that we already know from common experience: It is much easier to sort short lists than long ones. If the number of entries to be sorted doubles, then the work more than doubles (with insertion or selection sort it quadruples, roughly). Hence if we can find a way to divide the list into two roughly equal-sized lists and sort them separately, then we will save work. If, for example, you were working in a library and were given a thousand index cards to put in alphabetical order, then a good way would be to distribute them into piles according to the first letter and sort the piles separately.

*divide-and-conquer*

Here again we have an application of the idea of dividing a problem into smaller but similar subproblems, that is, of *divide-and-conquer*.

First, we note that comparisons by computer are usually two-way branches, so we shall divide the entries to sort into two lists at each stage of the process.

What method, you may ask, should we use to sort the reduced lists? Since we have (temporarily) forgotten all the other methods we know, let us simply use the same method, divide-and-conquer, again, repeatedly subdividing the list. But we won't keep going forever: Sorting a list with only one entry doesn't take any work, even if we know no formal sorting methods.

In summary, let us informally outline divide-and-conquer sorting:

```
Sort(list)
{
    if the list has length greater than 1 then
    {
        Partition the list into lowlist, highlist;
        Sort(lowlist);
        Sort(highlist);
        Combine(lowlist, highlist);
    }
}
```

We still must decide how we are going to partition the list into two sublists and, after they are sorted, how we are going to combine the sublists into a single list. There are two methods, each of which works very well in different circumstances.

*mergesort*

■ *Mergesort*: In the first method, we simply chop the list into two sublists of sizes as nearly equal as possible and then sort them separately. Afterward, we carefully merge the two sorted sublists into a single sorted list. Hence this method is called **mergesort**.

*quicksort*

*pivot*

■ *Quicksort*: The second method does more work in the first step of partitioning the list into two sublists, and the final step of combining the sublists then becomes trivial. This method was invented and christened **quicksort** by C. A. R. HOARE. To partition the list, we first choose some key from the list for which, we hope, about half the keys will come before and half after. We shall use the name *pivot* for this selected key. We next partition the entries so that all those with keys less than the pivot come in one sublist, and all those with greater keys come in another. Finally, then, we sort the two reduced lists separately, put the sublists together, and the whole list will be in order.

## 7.6.2 An Example

Before we refine our methods into detailed functions, let us work through a specific example. We take the following seven numbers to sort:

26  33  35  29  19  12  22.

## 1. Mergesort Example

The first step of mergesort is to chop the list into two. When (as in this example) the list has odd length, let us establish the convention of making the left sublist one entry larger than the right sublist. Thus we divide the list into

$$26 \quad 33 \quad 35 \quad 29 \qquad \text{and} \qquad 19 \quad 12 \quad 22$$

*first half*

and first consider the left sublist. It is again chopped in half as

$$26 \quad 33 \qquad \text{and} \qquad 35 \quad 29.$$

For each of these sublists, we again apply the same method, chopping each of them into sublists of one number each. Sublists of length one, of course, require no sorting. Finally, then, we can start to merge the sublists to obtain a sorted list. The sublists 26 and 33 merge to give the sorted list 26 33, and the sublists 35 and 29 merge to give 29 35. At the next step, we merge these two sorted sublists of length two to obtain a sorted sublist of length four,

$$26 \quad 29 \quad 33 \quad 35.$$

*second half*

Now that the left half of the original list is sorted, we do the same steps on the right half. First, we chop it into the sublists

$$19 \quad 12 \qquad \text{and} \qquad 22.$$

The first of these is divided into two sublists of length one, which are merged to give 12 19. The second sublist, 22, has length one, so it needs no sorting. It is now merged with 12 19 to give the sorted list

$$12 \quad 19 \quad 22.$$

Finally, the sorted sublists of lengths four and three are merged to produce

$$12 \quad 19 \quad 22 \quad 26 \quad 29 \quad 33 \quad 35.$$

The way that all these sublists and recursive calls are put together is shown by the recursion tree for mergesort drawn in Figure 7.8. The order in which the recursive calls occur is shown by the colored path. The numbers in each sublist passed to a recursive call are shown in black, and the numbers in their order after the merge is done are shown in color. The calls for which no further recursion is required (sublists of length 1) are the leaves of the tree and are drawn as squares.

## 2. Quicksort Example

Let us again work through the same example, this time applying quicksort, and keeping careful account of the execution of steps from our outline of the method.

*choice of pivot*

To use quicksort, we must first decide, in order to partition the list into two pieces, what key to choose as the pivot. We are free to choose any number we wish, but, for consistency, we shall adopt a definite rule. Perhaps the simplest rule is to choose the first number on a list as the pivot, and we shall do so in this example. For practical applications, however, other choices are usually better.

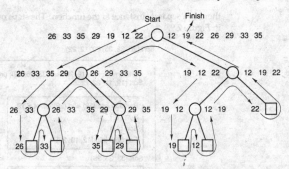

**Figure 7.8. Recursion tree, mergesort of 7 numbers**

*partition*

Our first pivot, then, is 26, and the list partitions into sublists

$$19 \quad 12 \quad 22 \quad \text{and} \quad 33 \quad 35 \quad 29$$

consisting, respectively, of the numbers less than and greater than the pivot. We have left the order of the entries in the sublists unchanged from that in the original list, but this decision also is arbitrary. Some versions of quicksort put the pivot into one of the sublists, but we choose to place the pivot into neither sublist.

We now arrive at the next line of the outline, which tells us to sort the first sublist. We thus start the algorithm over again from the top, but this time applied to the shorter list

$$19 \quad 12 \quad 22.$$

*lower half*

The pivot of this list is 19, which partitions its list into two sublists of one number each, 12 in the first and 22 in the second. With only one entry each, these sublists do not need sorting, so we arrive at the last line of the outline, whereupon we combine the two sublists with the pivot between them to obtain the sorted list

$$12 \quad 19 \quad 22.$$

Now the call to the sort function is finished for this sublist, so it returns whence it was called. It was called from within the sort function for the full list of seven numbers, so we now go on to the next line of that function.

*inner and outer function calls*

We have now used the function twice, with the second instance occurring within the first instance. Note carefully that the two instances of the function are working on different lists and are as different from each other as is executing the same code twice within a loop. It may help to think of the two instances as having different colors, so that the instructions in the second (inner) call could be written out in full in place of the call, but in a different color, thereby clearly distinguishing them as a separate instance of the function. The steps of this process are illustrated in Figure 7.9.

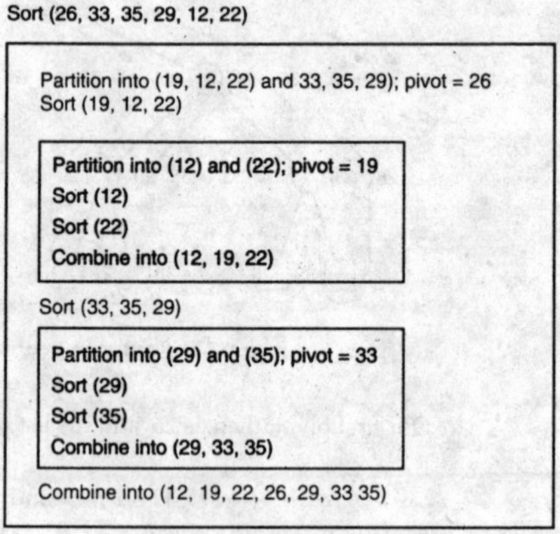

Sort (26, 33, 35, 29, 12, 22)

Partition into (19, 12, 22) and 33, 35, 29); pivot = 26
Sort (19, 12, 22)

Partition into (12) and (22); pivot = 19
Sort (12)
Sort (22)
Combine into (12, 19, 22)

Sort (33, 35, 29)

Partition into (29) and (35); pivot = 33
Sort (29)
Sort (35)
Combine into (29, 33, 35)

Combine into (12, 19, 22, 26, 29, 33 35)

Figure 7.9. Execution trace of quicksort

Returning to our example, we find the next line of the first instance of the function to be another call to sort another list, this time the three numbers

33   35   29.

*upper half* As in the previous (inner) call, the pivot 33 immediately partitions the list, giving sublists of length one that are then combined to produce the sorted list

29   33   35.

Finally, this call to sort returns, and we reach the last line of the (outer) instance that sorts the full list. At this point, the two sorted sublists of length three are combined with the original pivot of 26 to obtain the sorted list

12   19   22   26   29   33   35.

*recombine* After this step, the process is complete.

The easy way to keep track of all the calls in our quicksort example is to draw its recursion tree, as shown in Figure 7.10. The two calls to Sort at each level are shown as the children of the vertex. The sublists of size 1 or 0, which need no sorting, are drawn as the leaves. In the other vertices (to avoid cluttering the diagram), we include only the pivot that is used for the call. It is, however, not hard to read all the numbers in each sublist (but not necessarily in their original order). The numbers in the sublist at each recursive call are the number at the corresponding vertex and those at all descendents of the vertex.

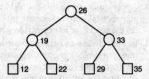

Figure 7.10. Recursion tree, quicksort of 7 numbers

*example*

If you are still uneasy about the workings of recursion, then you will find it helpful to pause and work through sorting the list of 14 names introduced in previous sections, using both mergesort and quicksort. As a check, Figure 7.11 provides the tree of calls for quicksort in the same abbreviated form used for the previous example. This tree is given for two versions, one where the pivot is the first key in each sublist, and one where the central key (center left for even-sized lists) is the pivot.

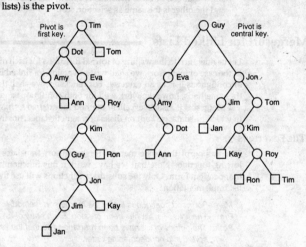

Figure 7.11. Recursion trees, quicksort of 14 names

**Exercises 7.6**

**E1.** Apply quicksort to the list of seven numbers considered in this section, where the pivot in each sublist is chosen to be **(a)** the last number in the sublist and **(b)** the center (or left-center) number in the sublist. In each case, draw the tree of recursive calls.

**E2.** Apply mergesort to the list of 14 names considered for previous sorting methods:

Tim Dot Eva Roy Tom Kim Guy Amy Jon Ann Jim Kay Ron Jan

**E3.** Apply quicksort to this list of 14 names, and thereby sort them by hand into alphabetical order. Take the pivot to be **(a)** the first key in each sublist and **(b)** the center (or left-center) key in each sublist. See Figure 7.11.

**E4.** In both divide-and-conquer methods, we have attempted to divide the list into two sublists of approximately equal size, but the basic outline of sorting by divide-and-conquer remains valid without equal-sized halves. Consider dividing the list so that one sublist has size 1. This leads to two methods, depending on whether the work is done in splitting one element from the list or in combining the sublists.

**(a)** Split the list by finding the entry with the largest key and making it the sublist of size 1. After sorting the remaining entries, the sublists are combined easily by placing the entry with largest key last.

**(b)** Split off the last entry from the list. After sorting the remaining entries, merge this entry into the list.

Show that one of these methods is exactly the same method as insertion sort and the other is the same as selection sort.

# 7.7 Mergesort for Linked Lists

Let us now turn to the writing of formal functions for each of our sorting methods. In the case of mergesort, we shall write a version for linked lists and leave the case of contiguous lists as an exercise. For quicksort, we shall do the reverse. Both of these methods, however, work well for both contiguous and linked lists.

Mergesort is also an excellent method for *external sorting*, that is, for problems in which the data are kept on disks or magnetic tapes, not in high-speed memory.

## 7.7.1 THE FUNCTIONS

Our outline of the basic method for mergesort translates directly into the following function. Note that we have written this function in an implementation-independent form. Only the subsidiary functions will use the specifics of a linked-list implementation.

```
/* MergeSort: sort contiguous list by the merge sort method.
   Pre:   The linked list list has been created. Each entry of list contains a key.
   Post:  The entries of list have been rearranged so that the keys in all the entries are
          sorted into nondecreasing order.
   Uses: Divide, Merge. */
void MergeSort(List *list)
{
    List secondhalf;              /* holds the second half of the list after division    */
    if (ListSize(list) > 1) {     /* Is there a need to sort?                            */
        Divide(list, &secondhalf);  /* Divide the list in half.                          */
        MergeSort(list);            /* Sort the first half.                              */
        MergeSort( &secondhalf);    /* Sort the second half.                             */
        Merge(list, &secondhalf, list);  /* Merge the two sorted sublists.               */
    }
}
```

*merge sort*

The first subsidiary function called by MergeSort, Divide(list, secondhalf), takes the list list, divides it in half, and returns with the first half in list and the second half in secondhalf.

*/\* Divide: divide the list into two parts.*
  *  **Pre:**   *The linked list* list *has been created.*
  *  **Post:**  *List* list *has been reduced to its first half, and the second half of the entries*
                *from* list *are in the linked list* secondhalf. *If* list *has an odd number of entries,*
                *then its first half will be one entry larger than its second. \*/*

*chop a linked list in half*

```
void Divide(List *list, List *secondhalf)
{
    ListNode *current, *midpoint;
    if ((midpoint = list->head) == NULL)
        secondhalf->head = NULL;
    else {
        for (current = midpoint->next; current; ) {
            current = current->next;
            if (current) {
                midpoint = midpoint->next;
                current = current->next;
            }
        }
        secondhalf->head = midpoint->next;
        midpoint->next = NULL;
    }
}
```

The second function, Merge(first, second, out), merges the lists first and second, returning the merged list as its third parameter out. The action of function Merge is illustrated in Figure 7.12.

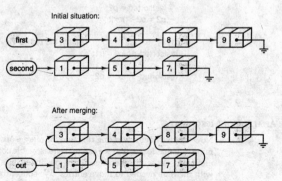

Figure 7.12. Merging two sorted linked lists

/* *Merge: merge two lists producing a third list.*
   **Pre:**   first *and* second *are ordered linked lists and have been created.*
   **Post:**  out *is an ordered linked list containing all entries that were in* first *and sec-*
        *ond. The original lists* first *and* second *have been destroyed.* */
void Merge(List *first, List *second, List *out)

*merge two sorted*
*linked lists*

```
{
    ListNode *p1, *p2;          /* pointers to traverse first and second lists    */
    ListNode *lastsorted;       /* always points to last node of sorted list      */
    if (!first->head)
        *out = *second;
    else if (!second->head)
        *out = *first;
    else {
        p1 = first->head;       /* First find the head of the merged list.         */
        p2 = second->head;
        if (LE(p1->entry.key, p2->entry.key)) {
            *out = *first;
            p1 = p1->next;
        } else {
            *out = *second;
            p2 = p2->next;
        }
        lastsorted = out->head;  /* lastsorted gives last entry of merged list.     */
        while (p1 && p2)
            if (LE(p1->entry.key, p2->entry.key)) {
                lastsorted->next = p1;
                lastsorted = p1;
                p1 = p1->next;
            } else {
                lastsorted->next = p2;
                lastsorted = p2;
                p2 = p2->next;
            }
        if (p1)                  /* Attach the remaining list.                      */
            lastsorted->next = p1;
        else
            lastsorted->next = p2;
    }
}
```

## 7.7.2 ANALYSIS OF MERGESORT

Now that we have a working function for mergesort, it is time to pause and determine its behavior, so that we can make reasonable comparisons with other sorting
methods. As with other algorithms on linked lists, we need not be concerned
with the time needed to move entries. We concentrate instead on the number of
comparisons of keys that the function will do.

*merge function*

### 1. Counting Comparisons

Comparison of keys is done at only one place in the complete mergesort function. This place is within the main loop of the merge function. After each comparison, one of the two nodes is sent to the output list. Hence the number of comparisons certainly cannot exceed the number of entries being merged. To find the total lengths of these lists, let us again consider the recursion tree of the algorithm, which for simplicity we show in Figure 7.13 for the case when $n = 2^m$ is a power of 2.

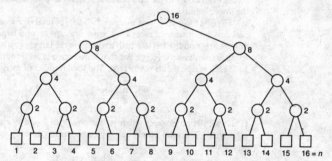

Figure 7.13. Lengths of sublist merges

It is clear from the tree of Figure 7.13 that the total lengths of the lists on each level is precisely $n$, the total number of entries. In other words, every entry is treated in precisely one merge on each level. Hence the total number of comparisons done on each level cannot exceed $n$. The number of levels, excluding the leaves (for which no merges are done), is $\lg n$ rounded up to the next smallest integer, the ceiling $\lceil \lg n \rceil$. The number of comparisons of keys done by mergesort on a list of $n$ entries, therefore, is no more than $\lceil \lg n \rceil$.

### 2. Contrast with Insertion Sort

Recall (Section 7.2.4) that insertion sort does more than $\frac{1}{4}n^2$ comparisons of keys, on average, in sorting $n$ entries. As soon as $n$ becomes greater than 16, $\lg n$ becomes less than $\frac{1}{4}n$. When $n$ is of practical size for sorting a list, $\lg n$ is far less than $\frac{1}{4}n$, and therefore the number of comparisons done by mergesort is far less than the number done by insertion sort. When $n = 1024$, for example, then $\lg n = 10$, so that the bound on comparisons for mergesort is 10,240, whereas the average number that insertion sort will do is more than 250,000. A problem requiring a half-hour of computer time using insertion sort will probably require hardly a minute using mergesort.

$n \lg n$

The appearance of the expression $n \lg n$ in the preceding calculation is by no means accidental, but relates closely to the lower bounds established in Section 7.5, where it was proved that any sorting method that uses comparisons of keys must do at least

$$\lg n! \approx n \lg n - 1.44n + O(\log n)$$

comparisons of keys. When $n$ is large, the first term of this expression becomes more important than what remains. We have now found, in mergesort, an algorithm that comes within reach of this lower bound.

### 3. Improving the Count

By being somewhat more careful we can, in fact, obtain a more accurate count of comparisons made by mergesort, one that will show that its actual performance comes even closer to the best possible number of comparisons of keys allowed by the lower bound.

First, let us observe that merging two lists of total size $k$ never requires $k$ comparisons, but instead at most $k - 1$, since after the second largest key has been put out, there is nothing left to which to compare the largest key, so it goes out without another comparison. Hence we should reduce our total count of comparisons by 1 for each merge that is performed. The total number of merges is essentially

$$\frac{n}{2} + \frac{n}{4} + \frac{n}{8} + \cdots + 1 = n - 1.$$

(This calculation is exact when $n$ is a power of 2 and is a good approximation otherwise.) The total number of key comparisons done by mergesort is therefore less than

$$n \lg n - n + 1.$$

Second, we should note that it is possible for one of the two lists being merged to be finished before the other, and then all entries in the second list will go out with no further comparisons, so that the number of comparisons may well be less than we have calculated. Every element of one list, for example, might precede every element of the second list, so that all elements of the second list would come out using no comparisons. The exercises outline a proof that the total count can be reduced, on average, to

*improved count*

$$n \lg n - 1.1583n + 1,$$

and the correct coefficient of $n$ is likely close to $-1.25$. We thus see that, not only is the leading term as small as the lower bound permits, but the second term is also quite close. By refining the merge function even more, the method can be brought within a few percent of the theoretically optimal number of comparisons (see the references).

### 4. Conclusions

*advantages of linked mergesort*

From these remarks, it may appear that mergesort is the ultimate sorting method, and, indeed, for linked lists in random order, it is difficult to surpass. We must remember, however, that considerations other than comparing keys are important. The program we have written spends significant time finding the center of the list, so that it can break it in half. The exercises discuss one method for saving some of this time. The linked version of mergesort uses space efficiently. It needs no large auxiliary arrays or other lists, and since the depth of recursion is only $\lg n$, the amount of space needed to keep track of the recursive calls is very small.

### 5. Contiguous Mergesort

*three-way trade-off for merging*

For contiguous lists, unfortunately, mergesort is not such an unqualified success. The difficulty is in merging two contiguous lists without substantial expense in one of (1) space, (2) computer time, or (3) programming effort. The first and most straightforward way to merge two contiguous lists is to use an auxiliary array large enough to hold the combined list and copy the entries into the array as the lists are merged. This method requires extra space proportional to $n$. For a second method, we could put the sublists to be merged next to each other, forget the amount of order they already have, and use a method like insertion sort to put the combined list into order. This approach uses almost no extra space, but uses computer time proportional to $n^2$, compared to time proportional to $n$ for a good merging algorithm. Finally (see the references), algorithms have been invented that will merge two contiguous lists in time proportional to $n$ while using only a small, fixed amount of extra space. These algorithms, however, are quite complicated.

---

**Exercises 7.7**

**E1.** An article in a professional journal stated, "This recursive process [mergesort] takes time $O(n \log n)$, and so runs 64 times faster than the previous method [insertion sort] when sorting 256 numbers." Criticize this statement.

**E2.** The count of key comparisons in merging is usually too high, since it does not account for the fact that one list may be finished before the other. It might happen, for example, that all entries in the first list come before any in the second list, so that the number of comparisons is just the length of the first list. For this exercise, assume that all numbers in the two lists are different and that all possible arrangements of the numbers are equally likely.

(a) Show that the average number of comparisons performed by our algorithm to merge two ordered lists of length 2 is $\frac{8}{3}$. [*Hint*: Start with the ordered list 1, 2, 3, 4. Write down the six ways of putting these numbers into two ordered lists of length 2, and show that four of these ways will use 3 comparisons, and two will use 2 comparisons.]

(b) Show that the average number of comparisons done to merge two ordered lists of length 3 is 4.5.

(c) Show that the average number of comparisons done to merge two ordered lists of length 4 is 6.4.

(d) Use the foregoing results to obtain the improved total count of key comparisons for mergesort.

(e) Show that, as $m$ tends to infinity, the average number of comparisons done to merge two ordered lists of length $m$ approaches $2m - 2$.

**E3.** [*Very challenging*] The straightforward method for merging two contiguous lists, by building the merged list in a separate array, uses extra space proportional to the number of entries in the two lists, but can be written to run efficiently, with time proportional to the number of entries. Try to devise a merging method for contiguous lists that will require as little extra space as possible, but that will still run in time (linearly) proportional to the number of entries in the lists. [There is a solution using only a small, constant amount of extra space. See the references.]

*fixed-space linear-time merging*

**Programming Projects 7.7**

**P1.** Implement mergesort for linked lists on your computer. Use the same conventions and the same test data used for implementing and testing the linked version of insertion sort. Compare the performance of mergesort and insertion sort for short and long lists, as well as for lists nearly in correct order and in random order.

**P2.** Our mergesort program for linked lists spends significant time locating the center of each sublist, so that it can be broken in half. Implement the following modification that will save most of this time. First set up a record to describe a linked list that will contain not only **(a)** a pointer to the head of the list, but also **(b)** a pointer to the center of the list and **(c)** the length of the list. At the beginning, the original list must be traversed once to determine this information. With this information, it becomes easy to break the list in half and obtain the lengths of the sublists. The center of a sublist can be found by traversing only half the sublist. Rewrite the mergesort function to pass the records describing linked lists as calling parameters, and use them to simplify the subdivision of the lists.

**P3.** Our mergesort function pays little attention to whether or not the original list was partially in the correct order. In *natural mergesort* the list is broken into sublists at the end of an increasing sequence of keys, instead of arbitrarily at its halfway point. This exercise requests the implementation of two versions of natural mergesort.

*natural mergesort*

In the first version, the original list is traversed only once, and only two sublists are used. As long as the order of the keys is correct, the nodes are placed in the first sublist. When a key is found out of order, the first sublist is ended and the second started. When another key is found out of order, the second sublist is ended, and the second sublist merged into the first. Then the second sublist is repeatedly built again and merged into the first. When the end of the original list is reached, the sort is finished. This first version is simple to program, but as it proceeds, the first sublist is likely to become much longer than the second, and the performance of the function will degenerate toward that of insertion sort.

*one sorted list*

The second version ensures that the lengths of sublists being merged are closer to being equal and, therefore, that the advantages of divide-and-conquer are fully used. This method keeps a (small) auxiliary array containing (a) the lengths and (b) pointers to the heads of the ordered sublists that are not yet merged. The entries in this array should be kept in order according to the length of sublist. As each (naturally ordered) sublist is split from the original list, it is put into the auxiliary array. If there is another list in the array whose length is between half and twice that of the new list, then the two are merged, and the process repeated. When the original list is exhausted, any remaining sublists in the array are merged (smaller lengths first) and the sort is finished.

*several sorted lists*

There is nothing sacred about the ratio of 2 in the criterion for merging sublists. Its choice merely ensures that the number of entries in the auxiliary array cannot exceed $\lg n$ (prove it!). A smaller ratio (required to be greater than 1) will make the auxiliary table larger, and a larger ratio will lessen the advantages of divide-and-conquer. Experiment with test data to find a good ratio to use.

**P4.** Devise a version of mergesort for contiguous lists. The difficulty is to produce a function to merge two sorted lists in contiguous storage. It is necessary to use some additional space other than that needed by the two lists. The easiest solution is to use two arrays, each large enough to hold all the entries in the two original lists. The two sorted sublists occupy different parts of the same array. As they are merged, the new list is built in the second array. After the merge is complete, the new list can, if desired, be copied back into the first array. Otherwise, the roles of the two arrays can be reversed for the next stage.

# 7.8 Quicksort for Contiguous Lists

We now turn to the method of quicksort, in which the list is first partitioned into lower and upper sublists for which all keys are, respectively, less than some pivot key or greater than the pivot key. Quicksort can be developed for linked lists with little difficulty, and this will be pursued as one of the projects for this section. The most important applications of quicksort, however, are to contiguous lists, where it can prove to be very fast, and where it has the advantage over contiguous mergesort of not requiring a choice between using substantial extra space for an auxiliary array or investing great programming effort in implementing a complicated and difficult merge algorithm.

## 7.8.1 THE MAIN FUNCTION

Our task in developing contiguous quicksort consists essentially in writing an algorithm for partitioning entries in a list by use of a pivot key, swapping the entries within the list so that all those with keys before the pivot come first, then the entry with the pivot key, and then the entries with larger keys. We shall let pivotpos provide the position of the pivot in the partitioned list.

Since the partitioned sublists are kept in the same array, in the proper relative positions, the final step of combining sorted sublists is completely vacuous and thus is omitted from the function.

To apply the sorting function recursively to sublists, the bounds low and high of the sublists need to be parameters for the function. Our other sorting functions, however, had the list list as the only parameter, so for consistency of notation we do the recursion in a function RecQuickSort that is invoked by the following function:

```
/* QuickSort: sort contiguous list by the quicksort method.
   Pre:  The contiguous list list has been created. Each entry of list contains a key.
   Post: The entries of list have been rearranged so that the keys in all the entries are
         sorted into nondecreasing order.
   Uses: RecQuickSort. */
void QuickSort(List *list)
{
   RecQuickSort(list, 0, list->count − 1);
}
```

*main function*
QuickSort

The actual quicksort function for contiguous lists is then

```
/* RecQuickSort: use recursive method to sort list.
   Pre:  The contiguous list list has been created. Each entry of list contains a key. low
         and high are valid positions on the list list.
   Post: The entries of list have been rearranged so that the keys in all the entries are
         sorted into nondecreasing order.
   Uses: RecQuickSort, Partition. */
void RecQuickSort(List *list, Position low, Position high)
{
    Position pivotpos;            /* position of the pivot after partitioning      */
    if (low < high) {
        pivotpos = Partition(list, low, high);
        RecQuickSort(list, low, pivotpos - 1);
        RecQuickSort(list, pivotpos + 1, high);
    }
}
```

*recursive*
*RecQuickSort*

### 7.8.2 PARTITIONING THE LIST

Now we must construct the function Partition. There are several methods that we might use (one of which is suggested as an exercise), methods that sometimes are faster than the algorithm we develop but that are intricate and difficult to get correct. The algorithm we develop is much simpler and easier to understand, and it is certainly not slow; in fact, it does the smallest possible number of key comparisons of any partitioning algorithm.

#### 1. Algorithm Development

Given a pivot value $p$, we must rearrange the entries of the list and compute pivotpos so that the pivot is at pivotpos, all entries to its left have keys less than $p$, and all entries to its right have larger keys. To allow for the possibility that more than one entry has key equal to $p$, we insist that the entries to the left of pivotpos have keys strictly less than $p$, and the entries to its right have keys greater than or equal to $p$, as shown in the following diagram:

*goal (postcondition)*

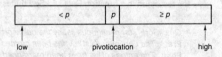

To reorder the entries this way, we must compare each key to the pivot. We shall use a for loop (running on a variable i) to do this. We shall use a second variable pivotpos such that all entries at or before location pivotpos have keys less than $p$. Suppose that the pivot $p$ starts in the first position, and let us leave it there temporarily. Then in the middle of the loop the list has the following property:

*loop invariant*

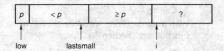

When the function inspects entry i, there are two cases. If the entry is greater than or equal to $p$, then i can be increased and the list still has the required property. If the entry is less than $p$, then we restore the property by increasing pivotpos and *restore the invariant* swapping that entry (the first of those at least $p$) with entry i, as shown in the following diagrams:

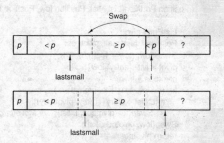

When the loop terminates, we have the situation:

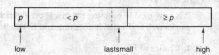

*final position*     and we then need only swap the pivot from position low to position pivotpos to obtain the desired final arrangement.

## 2. Choice of Pivot

We are not bound to the choice of the first entry in the list as the pivot; we can choose any entry we wish and swap it with the first entry before beginning the loop that partitions the list. In fact, the first entry is often a poor choice for pivot, since if the list is already sorted, then the first key will have no others less than it, and so one of the sublists will be empty. Hence, let us instead choose a pivot near *pivot from center* the center of the list, in the hope that our choice will partition the keys so that about half come on each side of the pivot.

### 3. Coding

With these decisions, we obtain the following function, in which we use the swap function from Section 7.3.2 (page 291).

```
/* Partition: partition a list.
    Pre:   The contiguous list list has been created; low and high are valid positions on
           the list list.
    Post:  The center (or left center) entry of list has been chosen as a pivot and moved
           to index pivotpos. All entries of list between indices low and high, inclusive,
           have been rearranged so that those with keys less than the pivot come before
           pivotpos and the remaining entries come after pivotpos.
    Uses: Swap. */
Position Partition(List *list, Position low, Position high)
{
    ListEntry pivot;
    Position i, lastsmall, pivotpos;
    Swap(low, (low + high)/2, list);
    pivot = list->entry[low];
    pivotpos = low;
    for (i = low + 1; i <= high; i++)
        if (LT(list->entry[i].key, pivot.key))
            Swap(++pivotpos, i, list);    /* Move large entry to right and small to left.   */
    Swap(low, pivotpos, list);
    return pivotpos;
}
```

## 7.8.3 ANALYSIS OF QUICKSORT

It is now time to examine the quicksort algorithm carefully, to determine when it works well and when it does not, and how much computation it performs.

### 1. Choice of Pivot

Our choice of a key at the center of the list to be the pivot is arbitrary. This choice may succeed in dividing the list nicely in half, or we may be unlucky and find that one sublist is much larger than the other. Some other methods for choosing the pivot are considered in the exercises. An extreme case for our method occurs for the following list, where every one of the pivots selected turns out to be the largest key in its sublist:

*worst case*

$$2 \quad 4 \quad 6 \quad 7 \quad 3 \quad 1 \quad 5$$

Check it out, using the Partition function in the text. When quicksort is applied to this list, its label will appear to be quite a misnomer, since at the first recursion the nonempty sublist will have length 6, at the second 5, and so on.

If we were to choose the pivot as the first key or the last key in each sublist, then the extreme case would occur when the keys are in their natural order or in their reverse order. These orders are more likely to happen than some random order, and therefore choosing the first or last key as pivot is likely to cause problems.

## 2. Count of Comparisons and Swaps

Let us determine the number of comparisons and swaps that contiguous quicksort makes. Let $C(n)$ be the number of comparisons of keys made by quicksort when applied to a list of length $n$, and let $S(n)$ be the number of swaps of entries. We have $C(1) = C(0) = 0$. The partition function compares the pivot with every other key in the list exactly once, and thus Partition accounts for exactly $n - 1$ key comparisons. If one of the two sublists it creates has length $r$, then the other sublist will have length exactly $n - r - 1$. The number of comparisons done in the two recursive calls will then be $C(r)$ and $C(n - r - 1)$. Thus we have

*total number of comparisons*

$$C(n) = n - 1 + C(r) + C(n - r - 1).$$

To solve this equation we need to know $r$. In fact, our notation is somewhat deceptive, since the values of $C(\ )$ depend not only on the length of the list but also on the exact ordering of the entries in it. Thus we shall obtain different answers in different cases, depending on the ordering.

## 3. Comparison Count, Worst Case

First, consider the worst case for comparisons. We have already seen that this occurs when the pivot fails to split the list at all, so that one sublist has $n - 1$ entries and the other is empty. In this case, since $C(0) = 0$, we obtain $C(n) = n - 1 + C(n - 1)$. An expression of this form is called a ***recurrence relation*** because it expresses its answer in terms of earlier cases of the same result. We wish to solve the recurrence, which means to find an equation for $C(n)$ that does not involve $C(\ )$ on the other side. Various (sometimes difficult) methods are needed to solve recurrence relations, but in this case we can do it easily by starting at the bottom instead of the top:

*recurrence relation*

$$
\begin{aligned}
C(1) &= 0. & & \\
C(2) &= 1 + C(1) & &= 1. \\
C(3) &= 2 + C(2) & &= 2 + 1. \\
C(4) &= 3 + C(3) & &= 3 + 2 + 1. \\
&\ \ \vdots & &\ \ \vdots \\
C(n) &= n - 1 + C(n - 1) & &= (n - 1) + (n - 2) + \cdots + 2 + 1 \\
& & &= \tfrac{1}{2}(n - 1)n = \tfrac{1}{2}n^2 - \tfrac{1}{2}n.
\end{aligned}
$$

In this calculation we have applied Theorem A.1 on page 580 to obtain the sum of the integers from 1 to $n - 1$.

*selection sort*

Recall that selection sort makes about $\tfrac{1}{2}n^2 - \tfrac{1}{2}n$ key comparisons, and making too many comparisons was the weak point of selection sort (as compared with insertion sort). Hence in its worst case, quicksort is as bad as the worst case of selection sort.

## 4. Swap Count, Worst Case

Next let us determine how many times quicksort will swap entries, again in its worst case. The partition function does one swap inside its loop for each key less than the pivot and two swaps outside its loop. In its worst case, the pivot is the largest key in the list, so the partition function will then make $n + 1$ swaps. With $S(n)$ the total number of swaps on a list of length $n$, we then have the recurrence

$$S(n) = n + 1 + S(n - 1)$$

in the worst case. The partition function is called only when $n \geq 2$, and $S(2) = 3$ in the worst case. Hence, as in counting comparisons, we can solve the recurrence by working downward, and we obtain

*answer*

$$S(n) = (n + 1) + n + \cdots + 3 = \tfrac{1}{2}(n + 1)(n + 2) - 3 = 0.5n^2 + 1.5n - 1$$

swaps in the worst case.

### 5. Comparison with Insertion Sort and Selection Sort

In its worst case, contiguous insertion sort must make about twice as many comparisons and assignments of entries as it does in its average case, giving a total of $0.5n^2 + O(n)$ for each operation. Each swap in quicksort requires three assignments of entries, so quicksort in its worst case does $1.5n^2 + O(n)$ assignments, or, for large $n$, about three times as many as insertion sort. But moving entries was the weak point of insertion sort in comparison to selection sort. Hence, in its worst case, quicksort (so-called) is worse than the poor aspect of insertion sort, and, in regard to key comparisons, it is also as bad as the poor aspect of selection sort. Indeed, in the worst-case analysis, quicksort is a disaster, and its name is nothing less than false advertising.

*poor worst-case behavior*

There must be some other reason that quicksort was not long ago consigned to the scrap heap of programs that never worked. The reason is the *average* behavior of quicksort when applied to lists in random order, which turns out to be one of the best of any sorting methods (using key comparisons and applied to contiguous lists) yet known!

*excellent average-case behavior*

## 7.8.4 AVERAGE-CASE ANALYSIS OF QUICKSORT

To do the average-case analysis, we shall assume that all possible orderings of the list are equally likely, and for simplicity, we take the keys to be just the integers from 1 to $n$.

### 1. Counting Swaps

When we select the pivot in the function Partition, it is equally likely to be any one of the keys. Denote by $p$ whatever key is selected as pivot. Then after the partition, key $p$ is guaranteed to be in position $p$, since the keys $1, \ldots, p - 1$ are all to its left and $p + 1, \ldots, n$ are to its right.

The number of swaps that will have been made in one call to Partition is $p + 1$, consisting of one swap in the loop for each of the $p - 1$ keys less than $p$ and two swaps outside the loop. Let us denote by $S(n)$ the average number of swaps done by quicksort on a list of length $n$ and by $S(n, p)$ the average number of swaps on a list of length $n$ where the pivot for the first partition is $p$. We have now shown that, for $n \geq 2$,

$$S(n, p) = (p + 1) + S(p - 1) + S(n - p).$$

We must now take the average of these expressions, since $p$ is random, by adding them from $p = 1$ to $p = n$ and dividing by $n$. The calculation uses the formula for the sum of the integers (Theorem A.1), and the result is

$$S(n) = \frac{n}{2} + \frac{3}{2} + \frac{2}{n}\Big(S(0) + S(1) + \cdots + S(n-1)\Big).$$

## 2. Solving the Recurrence Relation

The first step toward solving this recurrence relation is to note that, if we were sorting a list of length $n-1$, we would obtain the same expression with $n$ replaced by $n-1$, provided that $n \geq 2$:

$$S(n-1) = \frac{n-1}{2} + \frac{3}{2} + \frac{2}{n-1}\Big(S(0) + S(1) + \cdots + S(n-2)\Big).$$

Multiplying the first expression by $n$, the second by $n-1$, and subtracting, we obtain

$$nS(n) - (n-1)S(n-1) = n + 1 + 2S(n-1),$$

or

$$\frac{S(n)}{n+1} = \frac{S(n-1)}{n} + \frac{1}{n}.$$

We can solve this recurrence relation as we did a previous one by starting at the bottom. The result is

$$\frac{S(n)}{n+1} = \frac{S(2)}{3} + \frac{1}{3} + \cdots + \frac{1}{n}.$$

The sum of the reciprocals of integers is studied in Section A.2.8, where it is shown that

$$1 + \frac{1}{2} + \cdots + \frac{1}{n} = \ln n + O(1).$$

The difference between this sum and the one we want is bounded by a constant, so we obtain

$$S(n)/(n+1) = \ln n + O(1),$$

or, finally,

$$S(n) = n \ln n + O(n).$$

To compare this result with those for other sorting methods, we note that

$$\ln n = (\ln 2)(\lg n)$$

and $\ln 2 \approx 0.69$, so that

$$S(n) \approx 0.69(n \lg n) + O(n).$$

### 3. Counting Comparisons

Since a call to the partition function for a list of length $n$ makes exactly $n - 1$ comparisons, the recurrence relation for the number of comparisons made in the average case will differ from that for swaps in only one way: Instead of $p + 1$ swaps in the partition function, there are $n - 1$ comparisons. Hence the first recurrence for the number $C(n, p)$ of comparisons for a list of length $n$ with pivot $p$ is

$$C(n, p) = n - 1 + C(p - 1) + C(n - p).$$

When we average these expressions for $p = 1$ to $p = n$, we obtain

$$C(n) = n + \frac{2}{n}\big(C(0) + C(1) + \cdots + C(n - 1)\big).$$

Since this recurrence for the number $C(n)$ of key comparisons differs from that for $S(n)$ only by the factor of $\frac{1}{2}$ in the latter, the same steps used to solve for $S(n)$ will yield

$$C(n) \approx 2n \ln n + O(n) \approx 1.39n \lg n + O(n).$$

## 7.8.5 COMPARISON WITH MERGESORT

*key comparisons*

The calculation just completed shows that, on average, quicksort does about 39 percent more comparisons of keys than required by the lower bound and, therefore, also about 39 percent more than does mergesort. The reason, of course, is that mergesort is carefully designed to divide the list into halves of essentially equal size, whereas the sizes of the sublists for quicksort cannot be predicted in advance. Hence it is possible that quicksort's performance can be seriously degraded, but such an occurrence is unlikely in practice, so that averaging the times of poor performance with those of good performance yields the result just obtained.

*data movement*

Concerning data movement, we did not derive detailed information for merge-sort since we were primarily interested in the linked version. If, however, we consider the version of contiguous mergesort that builds the merged sublists in a second array, and reverses the use of arrays at each pass, then it is clear that, at each level of the recursion tree, all $n$ entries will be copied from one array to the other. The number of levels in the recursion tree is $\lg n$, and it therefore follows that the number of assignments of entries in contiguous mergesort is $n \lg n$. For quicksort, on the other hand, we obtained a count of about $0.69n \lg n$ swaps, on average. A good (machine language) implementation should accomplish a swap of entries in two assignments. Therefore, again, quicksort does about 39 percent more assignments of entries than does mergesort. The exercises, however, outline

*optimization*

another partition function that does, on average, only about one-third as many swaps as the version we developed. With this refinement, therefore, contiguous quicksort may perform fewer than half as many assignments of data entries as contiguous mergesort.

**Exercises 7.8**

**E1.** How will the quicksort routine (as presented in the text) function if all the keys in the list are equal?

**E2.** [Due to KNUTH] Describe an algorithm that will arrange a contiguous list whose keys are real numbers so that all the entries with negative keys will come first, followed by those with nonnegative keys. The final list need not be completely sorted. Make your algorithm do as few movements of entries and as few comparisons as possible. Do not use an auxiliary array.

**E3.** [Due to HOARE] Suppose that, instead of sorting, we wish only to find the $m^{th}$ smallest key in a given list of size $n$. Show how quicksort can be adapted to this problem, doing much less work than a complete sort.

**E4.** Given a list of integers, develop a function, similar to the partition function, that will rearrange the integers so that either all the integers in even-numbered positions will be even or all the integers in odd-numbered positions will be odd. (Your function will provide a proof that one or the other of these goals can always be attained, although it may not be possible to establish both at once.)

**E5.** A different method for choosing the pivot in quicksort is to take the median of the first, last, and central keys of the list. Describe the modifications needed to the QuickSort to implement this choice. How much extra computation will be done? For $n = 7$, find an ordering of the keys

$$1, 2, \ldots, 7$$

that will force the algorithm into its worst case. How much better is this worst case than that of the original algorithm?

**E6.** A different approach to the selection of pivot is to take the mean (average) of all the keys in the list as the pivot. The resulting algorithm is called *meansort*.

*meansort*

**(a)** Write a function to implement meansort. The partition function must be modified, since the mean of the keys is not necessarily one of the keys in the list. On the first pass, the pivot can be chosen any way you wish. As the keys are then partitioned, running sums and counts are kept for the two sublists, and thereby the means (which will be the new pivots) of the sublists can be calculated without making any extra passes through the list.

**(b)** In meansort, the relative *sizes* of the keys determine how nearly equal the sublists will be after partitioning; the initial *order* of the keys is of no importance, except for counting the number of swaps that will take place. How bad can the worst case for meansort be in terms of the relative sizes of the two sublists? Find a set of $n$ integers that will produce the worst case for meansort.

**E7.** [Requires elementary probability theory] A good way to choose the pivot is to use a random-number generator to choose the position for the next pivot at each call to RecQuickSort. Using the fact that these choices are independent, find the probability that quicksort will happen upon its worst case.

    **(a)** Do the problem for $n = 7$.

    **(b)** Do the problem for general $n$.

**E8.** At the cost of a few more comparisons of keys, the partition function can be rewritten so that the number of swaps is reduced by a factor of about 3, from $\frac{1}{2}n$ to $\frac{1}{6}n$ on average. The idea is to use two indices moving from the ends of the lists toward the center and to perform a swap only when a large key is found by the low position and a small key by the high position. This exercise outlines the development of such a function.

*optimize Partition*

    **(a)** Establish two indices i and j, and maintain the invariant property that all keys before position i are less than or equal to the pivot and all keys after position j are greater than the pivot. For simplicity, swap the pivot into the first position, and start the partition with the second element. Write a loop that will increase the position i as long as the invariant holds and another loop that will decrease j as long as the invariant holds. Your loops must also ensure that the indices do not go out of range, perhaps by checking that i ≤ j. When a pair of entries, each on the wrong side, is found, then they should be swapped and the loops repeated. What is the termination condition of this outer loop? At the end, the pivot can be swapped into its proper place.

    **(b)** Using the invariant property, verify that your function works properly.

    **(c)** Show that each swap performed within the loop puts two entries into their final positions. From this, show that the function does at most $1/2n + O(1)$ swaps in its worst case for a list of length $n$.

    **(d)** If, after partitioning, the pivot belongs in position $p$, then the number of swaps that the function does is approximately the number of entries originally in one of the $p$ positions at or before the pivot, but whose keys are greater than or equal to the pivot. If the keys are randomly distributed, then the probability that a particular key is greater than or equal to the pivot is $\frac{1}{n}(n - p - 1)$. Show that the average number of such keys, and hence the average number of swaps, is approximately $\frac{p}{n}(n - p)$. By taking the average of these numbers from $p = 1$ to $p = n$, show that the number of swaps is approximately $\frac{n}{6} + O(1)$.

    **(e)** The need to check to make sure that the indices i and j in the partition stay in bounds can be eliminated by using the pivot key as a sentinel to stop the loops. Implement this method in your function. Be sure to verify that your function works correctly in all cases.

(f) [Due to WIRTH] Consider the following simple and "obvious" way to write the loops using the pivot as a sentinel:

```
do {
    do i = i + 1 while (LT(list->entry[i].key, pivot.key));
    do j = j - 1 while (GT(list->entry[j].key, pivot.key));
    Swap(i, j, list);
} while (i < j);
```

Find a list of keys for which this version fails.

**Programming Projects 7.8**

**P1.** Implement quicksort (for contiguous lists) on your computer, and test it with the program from Project P1 of Section 7.2 (page 287). Compare its performance with that of all the other sorting methods you have studied.

**P2.** Write a version of quicksort for linked lists, integrate it into the linked version of the testing program from Project P1 of Section 7.2 (page 287), and compare its performance with that of other sorting methods for linked lists.

*linked quicksort*

Use the first entry of a sublist as the pivot for partitioning. The partition function for linked lists is somewhat simpler than for contiguous lists, since minimization of data movement is not a concern. To partition a sublist, you need only traverse it, deleting each entry as you go, and then add the entry to one of two lists depending on the size of its key relative to the pivot.

Since Partition now produces two new lists, you will, however, require a short additional function to recombine the sorted sublists into a single linked list.

**P3.** Because it may involve more overhead, quicksort may be inferior to simpler methods for short lists. Through experiment, find a value where, on average for lists in random order, quicksort becomes more efficient than insertion sort. Write a hybrid sorting function that starts with quicksort and, when the sublists are sufficiently short, switches to insertion sort. Determine if it is better to do the switch-over within the recursive function or to terminate the recursive calls when the sublists are sufficiently short to change methods and then at the very end of the process run through insertion sort once on the whole list.

# 7.9 Heaps and Heapsort

Quicksort has the disadvantage that, even though its usual performance is excellent, some kinds of input can make it misbehave badly. In this section we study another sorting method that overcomes this problem. This algorithm, called *heapsort*, sorts a contiguous list of length $n$ with $O(n \log n)$ comparisons and movements of entries, even in its worst case. Hence it achieves worst-case bounds better than those of quicksort, and for contiguous lists is better than mergesort, since it needs only a small and constant amount of space apart from the list being sorted.

*corporate hierarchy*    Heapsort is based on a tree structure that reflects the pecking order in a corporate hierarchy. Imagine the organizational structure of corporate management as a tree, with the president at the top. When the president retires, the vice-presidents compete for the top job; one then wins promotion and creates a vacancy. The junior executives are thus always competing for promotion whenever a vacancy arises. Now (quite unrealistically) imagine that the corporation always does its "downsizing" by pensioning off its most expensive employee, the president. Hence a vacancy continually appears at the top, employees are competing for promotion, and as each employee reaches the "top of the heap" that position again becomes vacant. With this, we have the essential idea of our sorting method.

## 7.9.1 Two-Way Trees as Lists

Let us begin with a complete 2-tree such as the one shown in Figure 7.14, and number the vertices, beginning with the root, from left to right on each level.

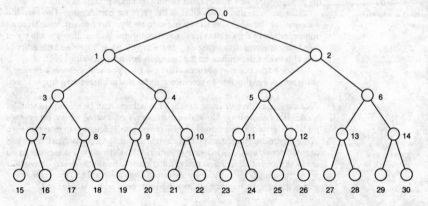

Figure 7.14. Complete 2-tree with 31 vertices

We can now put the 2-tree into a list by storing each node in the position shown by its label. We conclude that

*The left and right children of the node with position $k$ are in positions $2k + 1$ and $2k + 2$ of the list, respectively. If these positions are beyond the end of the list, then these children do not exist.*

With this idea, we can define what we mean by a heap.

**Definition**     A *heap* is a list in which each entry contains a key, and, for all positions $k$ in the list, the key at position $k$ is at least as large as the keys in positions $2k + 1$ and $2k + 2$, provided these positions exist in the list.

In this way, a heap is analogous to a corporate hierarchy in which each employee (except those at the bottom of the heap) supervises exactly two others.

In explaining the use of heaps, we shall draw trees like Figure 7.15 to show the hierarchical relationships, but algorithms operating on heaps always treat them as a particular kind of list.

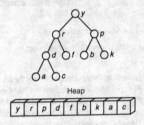

Figure 7.15. A heap as a tree and as a list

**NOTE**

Note that a heap is definitely *not* an ordered list. The first entry, in fact, must have the largest key in the heap, whereas the first key is smallest in an ordered list. In a heap, there is no necessary ordering between the keys in locations $k$ and $k + 1$ if $k > 0$.

**Remark**     Many C manuals and textbooks refer to the area used for dynamic memory as the "heap"; this use of the word "heap" has nothing to do with the present definition.

## 7.9.2 HEAPSORT

### 1. Method

*two-phase function*     Heapsort proceeds in two phases. First, we must arrange the entries in the list so that they satisfy the requirements for a heap (analogous to organizing a corporate hierarchy). Second, we repeatedly remove the top of the heap and promote another entry to take its place.

For this second phase, we recall that the root of the tree (which is the first entry of the list as well as the top of the heap) has the largest key. This key belongs at the end of the list. We therefore move the first entry to the last position, replacing an entry current. We then decrease a counter lu (last unsorted) that keeps track of the size of the unsorted part of the list, thereby excluding the largest entry from further sorting. The entry current that has been removed from the last position, however, may not belong on the top of the heap, and therefore we must insert current into the proper position to restore the heap property before continuing to loop in the same way.

From this description, you can see that heapsort requires random access to all parts of the list. We must therefore decide:

> *Heapsort is suitable only for contiguous lists.*

### 2. The Main Function

Let us now crystallize heapsort by writing it in C, using our standard conventions.

```
/* HeapSort: sort contiguous list by the heap sort method.
   Pre:   The contiguous list list has been created. Each entry of list contains a key.
   Post:  The entries of list have been rearranged so that the kevs in all the entries are
          sorted into nondecreasing order.
   Uses: BuildHeap, InsertHeap. */
void HeapSort(List *list)
{
   Position lu;                /* Entries beyond lu have been sorted.          */
   ListEntry current;          /* holds entry temporarily removed from list    */
   BuildHeap(list);            /* First phase: turn list into a heap.          */
   for (lu = list->count - 1; lu >= 1; lu--) {
      current = list->entry[lu];   /* Extract last element from list.          */
      list->entry[lu] = list->entry[0];  /* Move top of heap to end of list.   */
      InsertHeap(current, 0, lu - 1, list);
   }
}
```

### 3. An Example

Before we begin work on the two functions BuildHeap and InsertHeap, let us see what happens in the first few stages of sorting the heap shown in Figure 7.15. These stages are shown in Figure 7.16. In the first step, the largest key, *y*, is moved from the first to the last entry of the list. The first diagram shows the resulting tree, with *y* removed from further consideration, and the entry that was formerly last, *c*, put aside as the temporary variable current. To find how to rearrange the heap and insert *c*, we look at the two children of the root. Each of these is guaranteed to have a larger key than any other entry in its subtree, and hence the largest of these two entries and *c* belongs in the root. We therefore promote *r* to the top of the heap, and repeat the process on the subtree whose root has just been removed. Hence the larger of $d$ and $f$ is now inserted where $r$ was formerly. At the next step, we would compare current = $c$ with the two children of $f$, but these do not exist, so the promotion of entries through the tree ceases, and current = $c$ is inserted in the empty position formerly occupied by $f$.

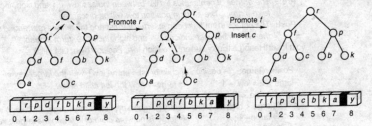

Figure 7.16. First stage of HeapSort

At this point, we are ready to repeat the algorithm, again moving the top of the heap to the end of the list and restoring the heap property. The sequence of actions that occurs in the complete sort of the list is shown in Figure 7.17.

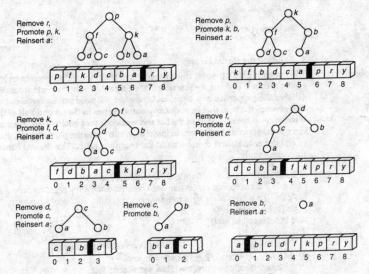

Figure 7.17. Trace of HeapSort

### 4. The Function InsertHeap

It is only a short step from this example to a formal function for inserting the entry current into the heap.

```
/* InsertHeap: insert an entry into the heap.
    Pre:  The entries of contiguous list list between indices low + 1 and high, inclusive,
          form a heap. The entry in position low will be discarded.
    Post: The entry current has been inserted into list and the entries rearranged so that
          the entries between indices low and high, inclusive, form a heap. */
void InsertHeap(ListEntry current, Position low, Position high, List *list)
{
    Position large;  /* position of child of list->entry[low] with the larger key */
    large = 2 * low + 1;            /* large is now the left child of low.               */
    while (large <= high) {
        if (large < high && LT(list->entry[large].key, list->entry[large + 1].key))
            large++;                /* large is now the child of low with the largest key. */
        if (GE(current.key, list->entry[large].key))
            break;
        else {                      /* Promote entry[large] and move down the tree.       */
            list->entry[low] = list->entry[large];
            low = large;
            large = 2 * low + 1;
        }
    }
    list->entry[low] = current;
}
```

### 5. Building the Initial Heap

*initialization*

The remaining task that we must specify is to build the initial heap from a list in arbitrary order. To do so, we first note that a 2-tree with only one node automatically satisfies the properties of a heap, and therefore we need not worry about any of the leaves of the tree, that is, about any of the entries in the second half of the list. If we begin at the midpoint of the list and work our way back toward the start, we can use the function InsertHeap to insert each entry into the partial heap consisting of all later entries, and thereby build the complete heap. The desired function is therefore simply:

```
/* BuildHeap: build a heap from a random contiguous list.
    Pre:  The contiguous list list has been created. Each entry of list contains a key.
    Post: The entries of list have been rearranged so that list becomes a heap.
    Uses: InsertHeap. */
void BuildHeap(List *list)
{
    Position low;                   /* Entries beyond low form a heap.                    */
    for (low = list->count/2 - 1; low >= 0; low--)
        InsertHeap(list->entry[low], low, list->count, list);
}
```

### 7.9.3 ANALYSIS OF HEAPSORT

From the example we have worked out, it is not at all clear that heapsort is efficient, and, in fact, heapsort is not a good choice for short lists. It seems quite strange that we can sort by moving large keys slowly toward the beginning of the list before finally putting them away at the end. When $n$ becomes large, however, such small quirks become unimportant, and heapsort proves its worth as one of very few sorting algorithms for contiguous lists that is guaranteed to finish in time $O(n \log n)$ with minimal space requirements.

*worst-case insertion*

First, let us determine how much work InsertHeap does in its worst case. At each pass through the loop, the position low is at least doubled; hence the number of passes cannot exceed lg(high/low); this is also the height of the subtree rooted at list->entry[low]. Each pass through the loop does two comparisons of keys (usually) and one assignment of entries. Therefore, the number of comparisons done in InsertHeap is at most $2\lg(\text{high/low})$ and the number of assignments $\lg(\text{high/low})$.

Let $m = \lfloor \frac{1}{2}n \rfloor$ (that is, the greatest integer that does not exceed $\frac{1}{2}n$). In Build-Heap we make $m$ calls to InsertHeap, for values of $k = $ low ranging from $m - 1$ down to 0. Hence the total number of comparisons is about

*first phase*

$$2 \sum_{k=0}^{m-1} \lg\left(\frac{n}{k}\right) = 2(m \lg n - \lg m!) \approx 5m \approx 2.5n,$$

since, by Stirling's approximation (Theorem A.5 on page 590) and $\lg m = \lg n - 1$, we have

$$\lg m! \approx m \lg m - 1.5m \approx m \lg n - 2.5m.$$

*second phase*

Similarly, in the sorting and insertion phase, we have about

$$2 \sum_{k=2}^{n} \lg k = 2 \lg n! \approx 2n \lg n - 3n$$

comparisons. This term dominates that of the initial phase, and hence we conclude that the number of comparisons is $2n \lg n + O(n)$.

*total worst-case counts*

One assignment of entries is done in InsertHeap for each two comparisons (approximately). Therefore the total number of assignments is $n \lg n + O(n)$.

In summary, we can state:

*In its worst case for sorting a list of length $n$, heapsort performs $2n \lg n + O(n)$ comparisons of keys and $n \lg n + O(n)$ assignments of entries.*

*comparison with quicksort*

From Section 7.8.4 we can see that the corresponding numbers for quicksort in the average case are $1.39n \lg n + O(n)$ comparisons and $0.69n \lg n + O(n)$ swaps, which can be reduced to $0.23n \lg n + O(n)$ swaps. Hence the worst case for heapsort is somewhat poorer than is the average case for quicksort. Quicksort's worst case, however, is $O(n^2)$, which is far worse than the worst case of heapsort for large $n$. An average-case analysis of heapsort appears to be very complicated, but empirical studies show that (as for selection sort) there is relatively little difference between the average and worst cases, and heapsort usually takes about twice as long as quicksort.

Heapsort, therefore, should be regarded as something of an insurance policy: On average, heapsort costs about half again as much as quicksort, but heapsort avoids the slight possibility of a catastrophic degradation of performance.

### 7.9.4 PRIORITY QUEUES

To conclude this section, we briefly mention another application of heaps.

**Definition**    A *priority queue* consists of entries, each of which contains a key called the *priority* of the entry. A priority queue has only two operations other than the usual creation, clearing, size, full, and empty operations:

> Insert an entry.
>
> Remove the entry having the largest (or smallest) key.

If entries have equal keys, then any entry with the largest key may be removed first.

*applications*    In a time-sharing computer system, for example, a large number of tasks may be waiting for the CPU. Some of these tasks have higher priority than others. Hence the set of tasks waiting for the CPU forms a priority queue. Other applications of priority queues include simulations of time-dependent events (like the airport simulation in Section 4.4) and solution of sparse systems of linear equations by row reduction.

*implementations*    We could represent a priority queue as a sorted contiguous list, in which case removal of an entry is immediate, but insertion would take time proportional to $n$, the number of entries in the queue. Or we could represent it as an unsorted list, in which case insertion is rapid but removal is slow.

Now consider the properties of a heap. The entry with largest key is on the top and can be removed immediately. It will, however, take time $O(\log n)$ to restore the heap property for the remaining keys. If, however, another entry is to be inserted immediately, then some of this time may be combined with the $O(\log n)$ time needed to insert the new entry. Thus the representation of a priority queue as a heap proves advantageous for large $n$, since it is represented efficiently in contiguous storage and is guaranteed to require only logarithmic time for both insertions and deletions.

---

**Exercises 7.9**    **E1.** Show the list corresponding to each of the following trees under the representation that the children of the entry in position $k$ are in positions $2k + 1$ and $2k + 2$. Which of these are heaps? For those that are not, state the position in the list at which the heap property is violated.

**E2.** By hand, trace the action of HeapSort on each of the following lists. Draw the initial tree to which the list corresponds, show how it is converted into a heap, and show the resulting heap as each entry is removed from the top and the new entry inserted.

(a) The following three words to be sorted alphabetically:

triangle    square    pentagon

(b) The three words in part (a) to be sorted according to the number of sides of the corresponding polygon, in increasing order.

(c) The three words in part (a) to be sorted according to the number of sides of the corresponding polygon, in decreasing order.

(d) The following seven numbers to be sorted into increasing order:

26  33  35  29  19  12  22

(e) The same seven numbers in a different initial order, again to be sorted into increasing order:

12  19  33  26  29  35  22

(f) The following list of 14 names to be sorted into alphabetical order:

Tim Dot Eva Roy Tom Kim Guy Amy Jon Ann Jim Kay Ron Jan

**E3.** (a) Design a function that will insert a new entry into a heap, obtaining a new heap. (The function InsertHeap in the text requires that the root be unoccupied, whereas, for this exercise, the root will already contain the entry with largest key, which must remain in the heap. Your function will increase the count of entries in the list.)

(b) Analyze the time and space requirements of your function.

**E4.** (a) Design a function that will delete the entry with the largest key (the root) from the top of the heap and restore the heap properties of the resulting, smaller list.

(b) Analyze the time and space requirements of your function.

**E5.** (a) Design a function that will delete the entry with index $i$ from a heap and restore the heap properties of the resulting, smaller list.

(b) Analyze the time and space requirements of your function.

**E6.** Consider a heap of $n$ keys, with $x_k$ being the key in position $k$ (in the contiguous representation) for $0 \le k \le n - 1$. Prove that the height of the subtree rooted at $x_k$ is the greatest integer not exceeding $\lg(n/k)$, for all $k$ satisfying $0 \le k \le n-1$. [*Hint*: Use "backward" induction on $k$, starting with the leaves and working back toward the root, which is $x_0$.]

**E7.** Define the notion of a *ternary heap*, analogous to an ordinary heap except that each node of the tree except the leaves has three children. Devise a sorting method based on ternary heaps, and analyze the properties of the sorting method.

**Programming Project 7.9**

**P1.** Implement heapsort (for contiguous lists) on your computer, integrate it into the test program of Project P1 of Section 7.2 (page 287), and compare its performance with all the previous sorting algorithms.

# 7.10 Review: Comparison of Methods

In this chapter we have studied and carefully analyzed quite a variety of sorting methods. Perhaps the best way to summarize this work is to emphasize in turn each of the three important efficiency criteria:

- Use of storage space;
- Use of computer time; and
- Programming effort.

## 1. Use of space

In regard to space, most of the algorithms we have discussed use little space other than that occupied by the original list, which is rearranged in its original place to be in order. The exceptions are quicksort and mergesort, where the recursion does require a small amount of extra storage to keep track of the sublists that have not yet been sorted. But in a well-written function, the amount of extra space used for recursion is $O(\log n)$ and will be trivial in comparison with that needed for other purposes.

Finally, we should recall that a major drawback of mergesort for contiguous lists is that the straightforward version requires extra space equal to that occupied by the original list.

In many applications the list to be sorted is much too large to be kept in high-speed memory, and when this is the case, other methods become necessary. A frequent approach is to divide the list into sublists that can be sorted internally within high-speed memory and then merge the sorted sublists externally. Hence much work has been invested in developing merging algorithms, primarily when it is necessary to merge many sublists at once. We shall not discuss this topic further.

*external sorting and merging*

## 2. Computer Time

The second efficiency criterion is use of computer time, which we have already carefully analyzed for each of the methods we have developed. In summary, the simple methods insertion sort and selection sort have time that increases like $n^2$ as the length $n$ of the list increases; Shell sort is much faster; and the remaining methods are usually the fastest, with time that is $O(n \log n)$. Quicksort, however, has a worst-case time that increases like $n^2$. Heapsort is something of an insurance policy. It usually is more costly than quicksort, but avoids the slight possibility of a serious degradation in performance.

## 3. Programming Effort

The third efficiency criterion is often the most important of all: this criterion is the efficient and fruitful use of the programmer's time.

If a list is small, the sophisticated sorting techniques designed to minimize computer time requirements are usually worse or only marginally better in achieving their goal than are the simpler methods. If a program is to be run only once or twice and there is enough machine time, then it would be foolish for a programmer to spend days or weeks investigating many sophisticated algorithms that might, in the end, only save a few seconds of computer time.

When programming in languages such as most dialects of FORTRAN, COBOL, or BASIC that do not support recursion, implementation of mergesort and quicksort becomes considerably more complicated, although it can be done by using stacks to hold the values of variables, as we observed in Chapter 3. See Appendix B.

Shell sort comes not far behind mergesort and quicksort in performance, does not require recursion, and is easy to program. One should therefore never sell Shell sort short.

The saving of programming time is an excellent reason for choosing a simple algorithm, even if it is inefficient, but two words of caution should always be remembered. First, saving programming time is never an excuse for writing an incorrect program, one that may usually work but can sometimes misbehave. Murphy's law will then inevitably come true. Second, simple programs, designed to be run only a few times and then discarded, often instead find their way into applications not imagined when they were first written. Lack of care in the early stages will then prove exceedingly costly later.

For many applications, insertion sort can prove to be the best choice. It is easy to write and maintain, and it runs efficiently for short lists. Even for long lists, if they are nearly in the correct order, insertion sort will be very efficient. If the list is completely in order, then insertion sort verifies this condition as quickly as can be done.

### 4. Statistical Analysis

The final choice of algorithm will depend not only on the length of list, the size of records, and their representation in storage, but very strongly on the way in which the records can be expected to be ordered before sorting. The analysis of algorithms from the standpoint of probability and statistics is of great importance. For most algorithms, we have been able to obtain results on the mean (average) performance, but the experience of quicksort shows that the amount by which this performance changes from one possible ordering to another is also an important factor to consider.

*mean*

*standard deviation*

The **standard deviation** is a statistical measure of this variability. Quicksort has an excellent mean performance, and the standard deviation is small, which signifies that the performance is likely to differ little from the mean. For algorithms such as selection sort, heapsort, and mergesort, the best-case and worst-case performances differ little, which means that the standard deviation is almost 0. Other algorithms, such as insertion sort, for example, will have a much larger standard deviation in their performance. The particular distribution of the orderings of the incoming lists is therefore an important consideration in choosing a sorting method. To enable intelligent decisions, the professional computer scientist needs to be knowledgeable about important aspects of mathematical statistics as they apply to algorithm analysis.

### 5. Empirical Testing

Finally, in all these decisions, we must be careful to temper the theoretical analysis of algorithms with empirical testing. Different computers and compilers will produce different results. It is most instructive, therefore, to see by experiment how the different algorithms behave in different circumstances.

**Exercises 7.10**   **E1.** Classify the sorting methods we have studied into one of the following categories: (a) the method does not require access to the entries at one end of the list until the entries at the other end have been sorted; (b) the method does not require access to the entries that have already been sorted; (c) the method requires access to all entries in the list throughout the process.

**E2.** Some of the sorting methods we have studied are not suited for use with linked lists. Which ones, and why not?

**E3.** Rank the sorting methods we have studied (both for linked and contiguous lists) according to the amount of extra storage space that they require for indices or pointers, for recursion, and for copies of the entries being sorted.

**E4.** Which of the methods we studied would be a good choice in each of the following applications? Why? If the representation of the list in contiguous or linked storage makes a difference in your choice, state how.

  **(a)** You wish to write a general-purpose sorting program that will be used by many people in a variety of applications.

  **(b)** You wish to sort 1000 numbers once. After you finish, you will not keep the program.

  **(c)** You wish to sort 50 numbers once. After you finish, you will not keep the program.

  **(d)** You need to sort 5 entries in the middle of a long program. Your sort will be called hundreds of times by the long program.

  **(e)** You have a list of 1000 keys to sort in high-speed memory, and key comparisons can be made quickly, but each time a key is moved, a corresponding 500 block file on disk must also be moved, and doing so is a slow process.

  **(f)** There is a twelve foot long shelf full of computer science books all catalogued by number. A few of these have been put back in the wrong places by readers, but rarely are the books more than one foot from where they belong.

  **(g)** You have a stack of 500 library index cards in random order to sort alphabetically.

  **(h)** You are told that a list of 5000 words is already in order, but you wish to check it to make sure, and sort any words found out of order.

**E5.** Discuss the advantages and disadvantages of designing a general sorting function as a hybrid between quicksort and Shell sort. What criteria would you use to switch from one to the other? Which would be the better choice for what kinds of lists?

**E6.** Summarize the results of the test runs of the sorting methods of this chapter for your computer. Also include any variations of the methods that you have written as exercises. Make charts comparing the following:

  **(a)** the number of key comparisons.

  **(b)** the number of assignments of entries.

  **(c)** the total running time.

  **(d)** the working storage requirements of the program.

  **(e)** the length of the program.

  **(f)** the amount of programming time required to write and debug the program.

**E7.** Write a one-page guide to help a user of your computer system select one of our sorting algorithms according to the desired application.

*stable sorting methods*

**E8.** A sorting function is called *stable* if, whenever two entries have equal keys, then these two entries will be in the same order on completion of the sorting function that they were in before sorting. Stability is important if a list has already been sorted by one key and is now being sorted by another key, and it is desired to keep as much of the original ordering as the new ordering allows. Determine which of the sorting methods of this chapter are stable and which are not. For those that are not, produce a list (as short as possible) containing some entries with equal keys whose orders are not preserved. In addition, see if you can discover simple modifications to the algorithm that will make it stable.

## Pointers and Pitfalls

1. Many computer systems have a general-purpose sorting utility. If you can access this utility and it proves adequate for your application, then use it rather than writing a sorting program from scratch.

2. In choosing a sorting method, take into account the ways in which the keys will usually be arranged before sorting, the size of the application, the amount of time available for programming, the need to save computer time and space, the way in which the data structures are implemented, the cost of moving data, and the cost of comparing keys.

3. Divide-and-conquer is one of the most widely applicable and most powerful methods for designing algorithms. When faced with a programming problem, see if its solution can be obtained by first solving the problem for two (or more) problems of the same general form but of a smaller size. If so, you may be able to formulate an algorithm that uses the divide-and-conquer method and program it using recursion.

4. Mergesort, quicksort, and heapsort are powerful sorting methods, more difficult to program than the simpler methods, but much more efficient when applied to large lists. Consider the application carefully to determine whether the extra effort needed to implement one of these sophisticated algorithms will be justified.

5. Priority queues are important for many applications, and heaps provide an excellent implementation of priority queues.

6. Heapsort is like an insurance policy: It is usually slower than quicksort, but it guarantees that sorting will be completed in $O(n \log n)$ comparisons of keys, something that quicksort cannot always do.

# Review Questions

7.2

1. How many comparisons of keys are required to verify that a list of $n$ entries is in order?

2. Explain in twenty words or less how insertion sort works.

7.3

3. Explain in twenty words or less how selection sort works.

4. On average, about how many more comparisons does selection sort do than insertion sort on a list of 20 entries?

5. What is the advantage of selection sort over all the other methods we studied?

7.4

6. What disadvantage of insertion sort does Shell sort overcome?

7.5

7. What is the lower bound on the number of key comparisons that any sorting method must make to put $n$ keys into order, if the method uses key comparisons to make its decisions? Give both the average- and worst-case bounds.

8. What is the lower bound if the requirement of using comparisons to make decisions is dropped?

7.6

9. Define the term *divide-and-conquer*.

10. Explain in twenty words or less how mergesort works.

11. Explain in twenty words or less how quicksort works.

7.7

12. Explain why mergesort is better for linked lists than for contiguous lists.

7.8

13. In quicksort, why did we choose the pivot from the center of the list rather than from one of the ends?

14. On average, about how many more comparisons of keys does quicksort make than the optimum? About how many comparisons does it make in the worst case?

7.9

15. What is a heap?

16. How does heapsort work?

17. Compare the worst-case performance of heapsort with the worst-case performance of quicksort, and compare it also with the average-case performance of quicksort.

7.10

18. When are simple sorting algorithms better than sophisticated ones?

# References for Further Study

The primary reference for this chapter is the comprehensive series by D. E. KNUTH (bibliographic details on page 124). Internal sorting occupies Volume 3, pp. 73–180. KNUTH does algorithm analysis in considerably more detail than we have. He writes all algorithms in a pseudo-assembly language and does detailed operation counts there. He studies all the methods we have, several more, and many variations.

The original references to Shell sort and quicksort are, respectively,

D. L. SHELL, "A high-speed sorting procedure," *Communications of the ACM* 2 (1959), 30–32.

C. A. R. HOARE, "Quicksort," *Computer Journal* 5 (1962), 10–15.

The unified derivation of mergesort and quicksort, that can also be used to produce insertion sort and selection sort, is based on the work

JOHN DARLINGTON, "A synthesis of several sorting algorithms," *Acta Informatica* 11 (1978), 1–30.

Mergesort can be refined to bring its performance very close to the optimal lower bound. One example of such an improved algorithm, whose performance is within 6 percent of the best possible, is

R. MICHAEL TANNER, "Minimean merging and sorting: An algorithm," *SIAM J. Computing* 7 (1978), 18–38.

A relatively simple contiguous merge algorithm that operates in linear time with a small, constant amount of additional space appears in

BING-CHAO HUANG and MICHAEL A. LANGSTON, "Practical In-Place Merging," *Communications of the ACM* 31 (1988), 348–352.

The algorithm for partitioning the list in quicksort was discovered by NICO LOMUTO and was published in

JON L. BENTLEY, "Programming pearls: How to sort," *Communications of the ACM* 27 (1984), 287–291.

The "Programming pearls" column contains many elegant algorithms and helpful suggestions for programming that have been collected into the following two books:

JON L. BENTLEY, *Programming Pearls*, Addison–Wesley, Reading, Mass., 1986, 195 pages.

JON L. BENTLEY, *More Programming Pearls: Confessions of a Coder*, Addison–Wesley, Reading, Mass., 1988, 224 pages.

An extensive analysis of the quicksort algorithm is given in

ROBERT SEDGEWICK, "The analysis of quicksort programs," *Acta Informatica* 7 (1976–77), 327–355.

The exercise on meansort (taking the mean of the keys as pivot) comes from

DALIA MOTZKIN, "MEANSORT," *Communications of the ACM* 26 (1983), 250–251; 27 (1984), 719–722.

Heapsort was discovered and so named by

J. W. J. WILLIAMS, *Communications of the ACM* 7 (1964), 347–348.

A simple but complete development of algorithms for heaps and priority queues appears in

JON L. BENTLEY, "Programming pearls: Thanks, heaps," *Communications of the ACM* 28 (1985), 245–250.

There is, of course, a vast literature in probability and statistics with potential applications to computers. A classic treatment of elementary probability and statistics is

W. FELLER, *An Introduction to Probability Theory and Its Applications*, Vol. 1, second edition, Wiley–Interscience, New York, N.Y., 1957.

# 8

# Tables and Information Retrieval

THIS CHAPTER *continues the study of information retrieval begun in Chapter 6 but concentrates on tables instead of lists. We begin with ordinary rectangular arrays, then other kinds of arrays, and then we generalize to the study of hash tables. One of our major purposes again is to analyze and compare various algorithms, to see which are preferable under different conditions. Applications in the chapter include a sorting method based on tables and a version of the Life game using a hash table.*

# 8.1 Introduction: Breaking the lg n Barrier

In Chapter 6 we showed that, by use of key comparisons alone, it is impossible to complete a search of $n$ items in fewer than $\lg n$ comparisons, on average. But this result speaks only of searching by key comparisons. Perhaps some method other than key comparisons may allow us to locate a given item even more quickly.

In fact, we commonly do so. If we have 500 different records, with an index between 1 and 500 assigned to each, then we would never think of using sequential or binary search to locate a record. We would simply store the records in an array of size 500, and use the index $n$ to locate the record of item $n$ by ordinary table lookup.

*table lookup*

Both table lookup and searching share the same essential purpose, that of *information retrieval*. We begin with a key (which may be complicated or simply an index) and wish to find the location of the entry (if any) with that key. In other words, both table lookup and our searching algorithms provide *functions* from the set of keys to locations in a list or array. The functions are in fact one-to-one from the set of keys that actually occur to the set of locations that actually occur, since we assume that each entry has only one key, and there is only one entry with a given key.

*functions for information retrieval*

In this chapter we study ways to implement and access tables in contiguous storage, beginning with ordinary rectangular arrays, and then considering tables with restricted location of nonzero entries, such as triangular tables. We turn afterward to more general problems, with the purpose of introducing and motivating the use first of access tables and then hash tables for information retrieval.

*tables*

We shall see that, depending on the shape of the table, several steps may be needed to retrieve an entry, but, even so, the time required remains $O(1)$—that is, it is bounded by a constant that does not depend on the size of the table—and thus table lookup can be more efficient than any searching method.

*conventions*

Before beginning our discussion we should establish some conventions. In C, all arrays are indexed starting from 0 and are referenced using individually bracketed index expressions like `somearray[i*2][j + 1][k]`. We will, however, sometimes talk about arrays with arbitrary upper and lower bounds, which are not directly available in C. So, for general discussions of arrays, we will use parenthesized index expressions like $(i_0, i_1, \ldots, i_n)$. When referring to a specific C implementation we will use proper C syntax, namely $[i_0][i_1]\ldots[i_n]$.

# 8.2 Rectangular Arrays

Because of the importance of rectangular arrays, almost all high-level languages provide convenient and efficient means to store and access them, so that generally the programmer need not worry about the implementation details. Nonetheless, computer storage is fundamentally arranged in a contiguous sequence (that is, in a straight line with each entry next to another), so for every access to a rectangular array, the machine must do some work to convert the location within a rectangle to a position along a line. Let us take a slightly closer look at this process.

## 1. Row-Major and Column-Major Ordering

Perhaps the most natural way to read a rectangular array is to read the entries of the first row from left to right, then the entries of the second row, and so on until the last row has been read. This is also the order in which most compilers store a rectangular array, and is called *row-major ordering*. For example, if the rows of an array are numbered from 1 to 2 and the columns are numbered from 1 to 3, then the order of indices with which the entries are stored in row-major ordering is

$$(1, 1) \qquad (1, 2) \qquad (1, 3) \qquad (2, 1) \qquad (2, 2) \qquad (2, 3).$$

*FORTRAN*

Standard FORTRAN instead uses *column-major ordering*, in which the entries of the first column come first, and so on. This example in column-major ordering is

$$(1, 1) \qquad (2, 1) \qquad (1, 2) \qquad (2, 2) \qquad (1, 3) \qquad (2, 3).$$

Figure 8.1 further illustrates row- and column-major orderings for an array with three rows and four columns.

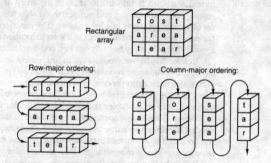

Figure 8.1. Sequential representation of a rectangular array

## 2. Indexing Rectangular Arrays

In the general problem, the compiler must be able to start with an index $(i, j)$ and calculate where the corresponding entry of the array will be stored. We shall derive a formula for this calculation. For simplicity we shall use only row-major ordering and suppose that the rows are numbered from 0 to $m - 1$ and the columns from 0 to $n - 1$. The general case is treated as an exercise. Altogether, the array will have $mn$ entries, as must its sequential implementation. We number the entries in the array from 0 to $mn - 1$. To obtain the formula calculating the position where $(i, j)$ goes, we first consider some special cases. Clearly $(0, 0)$ goes to position 0, and, in fact, the entire first row is easy: $(0, j)$ goes to position $j$. The first entry of the second row, $(1, 0)$, comes after $(0, n - 1)$, and thus goes into position $n$. Continuing, we see that $(1, j)$ goes to position $n + j$. Entries of the next row will have two full rows, that is, $2n$ entries, preceding them. Hence entry $(2, j)$ goes to position $2n + j$. In general, the entries of row $i$ are preceded by $ni$ earlier entries,

*index function,*
*rectangular array*

so the desired formula is

$$\text{Entry } (i, j) \text{ goes to position } ni + j.$$

A formula of this kind, which gives the sequential location of an array entry, is called an *index function*.

### 3. Variation: An Access Table

The index function for rectangular arrays is certainly not difficult to calculate, and the compilers of most high-level languages will simply write into the machine-language program the necessary steps for its calculation every time a reference is made to a rectangular array. On small machines, however, multiplication can be quite slow, so a slightly different method can be used to eliminate the multiplications.

*access table,*
*rectangular array*
This method is to keep an auxiliary array, a part of the multiplication table for $n$. The array will contain the values

$$0, \quad n, \quad 2n, \quad 3n, \quad \ldots, \quad (m-1)n.$$

Note that this array is much smaller (usually) than the rectangular array, so that it can be kept permanently in memory without losing too much space. Its entries then need be calculated only once (and note that they can be calculated using only addition). For all later references to the rectangular array, the compiler can find the position for $(i, j)$ by taking the entry in position $i$ of the auxiliary table, adding $j$, and going to the resulting position.

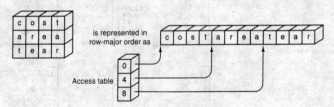

Figure 8.2. Access table for a rectangular array

This auxiliary table provides our first example of an *access table* (see Figure 8.2). In general, an access table is an auxiliary array used to find data stored elsewhere. An access table is also sometimes called an *access vector*.

---

**Exercises 8.2**

**E1.** What is the index function for a two-dimensional rectangular array with bounds

$$(0 .. m - 1, 0 .. n - 1)$$

under column-major ordering?

**E2.** Give the index function, with row-major ordering, for a two dimensional array with arbitrary bounds

$$(r .. s, t .. u).$$

**E3.** Find the index function, with the generalization of row-major ordering, for an array with $d$ dimensions and arbitrary bounds for each dimension.

## 8.3 Tables of Various Shapes ━━━━━━━━━━━━━━━━━━━━━

*matrix*

Information that is usually stored in a rectangular array may not require every position in the rectangle for its representation. If we define a *matrix* to be an array of numbers, then often some of the positions within the matrix will be required to be 0. Several such examples are shown in Figure 8.3. Even when the entries in a table are not numbers, the positions actually used may not be all of those in a rectangle, and there may be better implementations than using a rectangular array and leaving some positions vacant. In this section, we examine ways to implement tables of various shapes, ways that will not require setting aside unused space in a rectangular array.

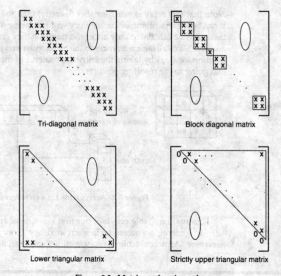

Tri-diagonal matrix

Block diagonal matrix

Lower triangular matrix

Strictly upper triangular matrix

**Figure 8.3. Matrices of various shapes**

### 8.3.1 TRIANGULAR TABLES

Let us consider the representation of a lower triangular table as shown in Figure 8.3. Such a table can be defined formally as a table in which all indices $(i, j)$ are required to satisfy $i \geq j$. We can implement a triangular table in a contiguous array by sliding each row out after the one above it, as shown in Figure 8.4.

To construct the index function that describes this mapping, we again make the slight simplification of assuming that the rows and the columns are numbered starting with 0. To find the position where $(i, j)$ goes, we now need to find where

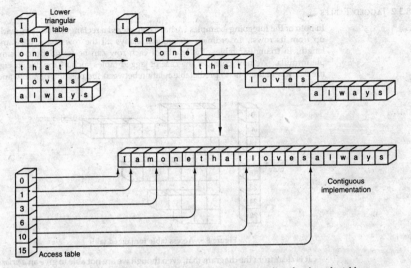

**Figure 8.4. Contiguous implementation of a triangular table**

row $i$ starts, and then to locate column $j$ we need only add $j$ to the starting point of row $i$. If the entries of the contiguous array are also numbered starting with 0, then the index of the starting point will be the same as the number of entries that precede row $i$. Clearly there are 0 entries before row 0, and only the one entry of row 0 precedes row 1. For row 2 there are $1 + 2 = 3$ preceding entries, and in general we see that preceding row $i$ there are exactly

$$1 + 2 + \cdots + i = \tfrac{1}{2}i(i + 1)$$

*index function, rectangular table*

entries. Hence the desired function is that entry $(i, j)$ of the triangular table corresponds to entry

$$\tfrac{1}{2}i(i + 1) + j$$

of the contiguous array.

*access table, triangular table*

As we did for rectangular arrays, we can again avoid all multiplications and divisions by setting up an access table whose entries correspond to the row indices of the triangular table. Position $i$ of the access table will permanently contain the value $\tfrac{1}{2}i(i + 1)$. The access table will be calculated only once at the start of the program, and then used repeatedly at each reference to the triangular table. Note that even the initial calculation of this access table requires no multiplication or division, but only addition to calculate its entries in the order

$$0, \quad 1, \quad 1 + 2, \quad (1 + 2) + 3, \quad \cdots .$$

### 8.3.2 JAGGED TABLES

In both of the foregoing examples we have considered a rectangular table as made up from its rows. In ordinary rectangular arrays all the rows have the same length; in triangular tables, the length of each row can be found from a simple formula. We now consider the case of jagged tables such as the one in Figure 8.5, where there is no predictable relation between the position of a row and its length.

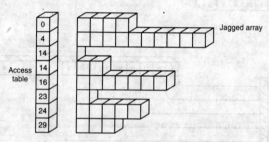

Figure 8.5. Access table for jagged table

It is clear from the diagram that, even though we are not able to give an *a priori* function to map the jagged table into contiguous storage, the use of an access table remains as easy as in the previous examples, and elements of the jagged table can be referenced just as quickly. To set up the access table, we must construct the jagged table in its natural order, beginning with its first row. Entry 0 of the access table is, as before, the start of the contiguous array. After each row of the jagged table has been constructed, the index of the first unused position of the contiguous storage should then be entered as the next entry in the access table and used to start constructing the next row of the jagged table.

### 8.3.3 INVERTED TABLES

Next let us consider an example illustrating multiple access tables, by which we can refer to a single table of records by several different keys at once.

Consider the problem faced by the telephone company in accessing the records of its customers. To publish the telephone book, the records must be sorted alphabetically by the name of the subscriber, but to process long-distance charges, the accounts must be sorted by telephone number. To do routine maintenance, the company also needs to have its subscribers sorted by address, so that a repairman *multiple records* may be able to work on several lines with one trip. Conceivably, the telephone company could keep three (or more) sets of its records, one sorted by name, one by number, and one by address. Doing this would, however, not only be very wasteful of storage space, but it would introduce endless headaches if one set of records were updated but another was not. Erroneous and unpredictable information might be given to the user.

*multiple access tables*

By using access tables we can avoid the multiple sets of records, and we can still find the records by any of the three keys almost as quickly as if the records were fully sorted by that key. For the names we set up one access table. The first entry in this table is the position where the records of the subscriber whose name is first in alphabetical order are stored, the second entry gives the location of the second (in alphabetical order) subscriber's records, and so on. A second access table gives the location of the subscribers' records sorted by telephone number from the smallest to largest in numerical order. Yet a third access table gives the locations of the records sorted lexicographically by address.

*unordered records for ordered access tables*

Notice that in this method all the fields that are treated as keys are processed in the same way. There is no particular reason why the records themselves need to be sorted according to one key rather than another, or, in fact, why they need to be sorted at all. The records themselves can be kept in an arbitrary order—say, the order in which they were first entered into the system. It also makes no difference whether the records are in an array, with entries in the access tables being indices of the array, or whether the records are in dynamic storage, with the access tables holding pointers to individual records. In any case, it is the access tables that are used for information retrieval, and, as ordinary contiguous arrays, they may be used for table lookup, or binary search, or any other purpose for which a contiguous implementation is appropriate.

An example of this scheme for a small number of accounts is shown in Figure 8.6.

| Index | Name | Address | Phone |
|---|---|---|---|
| 1 | Hill, Thomas M. | High Towers #317 | 2829478 |
| 2 | Baker, John S. | 17 King Street | 2884285 |
| 3 | Roberts, L. B. | 53 Ash Street | 4372296 |
| 4 | King, Barbara | High Towers #802 | 2863386 |
| 5 | Hill, Thomas M. | 39 King Street | 2495723 |
| 6 | Byers, Carolyn | 118 Maple Street | 4394231 |
| 7 | Moody, C. L. | High Towers #210 | 2822214 |

| Access Tables | | |
|---|---|---|
| Name | Address | Phone |
| 2 | 3 | 5 |
| 6 | 7 | 7 |
| 1 | 1 | 1 |
| 5 | 4 | 4 |
| 4 | 2 | 2 |
| 7 | 5 | 3 |
| 3 | 6 | 6 |

Figure 8.6. Multikey access tables: an inverted table

**Exercises 8.3**

**E1.** The *main diagonal* of a square matrix consists of the entries for which the row and column indices are equal. A *diagonal matrix* is a square matrix in which all entries not on the main diagonal are 0. Describe a way to store a diagonal matrix without using space for entries that are necessarily 0, and give the corresponding index function.

**E2.** A *tri-diagonal matrix* is a square matrix in which all entries are 0 except possibly those on the main diagonal and on the diagonals immediately above and below it. That is, $T$ is a tri-diagonal matrix means that $T[i][j] = 0$ unless $|i - j| \leq 1$.

(a) Devise a space-efficient storage scheme for tri-diagonal matrices, and give the corresponding index function.

(b) The *transpose* of a matrix is the matrix obtained by interchanging its rows with the corresponding columns. That is, matrix $B$ is the transpose of matrix $A$ means that $B[j][i] = A[i][j]$ for all indices $i$ and $j$ corresponding to positions in the matrix. Design an algorithm that transposes a tri-diagonal matrix using the storage scheme devised in the previous part of the exercise.

**E3.** An *upper triangular matrix* is a square array in which all entries below the main diagonal are 0. Describe the modifications necessary to use the access table method to store an upper triangular matrix.

**E4.** Consider a table of the triangular shape shown in Figure 8.7, where the columns are indexed from $-n$ to $n$ and the rows from 0 to $n$.

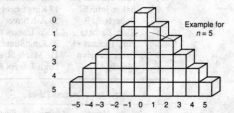

Figure 8.7. A table symmetrically triangular around 0

(a) Devise an index function that maps a table of this shape into a sequential array.

(b) Write a function that will generate an access table for finding the first entry of each row of a table of this shape within the contiguous array.

(c) Write a function that will reflect the table from left to right. The entries in column 0 (the central column) remain unchanged, those in columns $-1$ and 1 are swapped, and so on.

**Programming Projects 8.3**

Implement the method described in the text that uses an access table to store a lower triangular table, as applied in the following projects.

**P1.** Write a function that will read the entries of a lower triangular table from the terminal.

**P2.** Write a function that will print a lower triangular table at the terminal.

**P3.** Suppose that a lower triangular table is a table of distances between cities, as often appears on a road map. Write a function that will check the triangle rule: The distance from city $A$ to city $C$ is never more than the distance from $A$ to city $B$, plus the distance from $B$ to $C$.

**P4.** Embed the functions of the previous projects into a complete program for demonstrating lower triangular tables.

## 8.4 Tables: A New Abstract Data Type

At the beginning of this chapter we studied several *index functions* used to locate entries in tables, and then we turned to *access tables*, which were arrays used for the same purpose as index functions. The analogy between functions and table lookup is indeed very close: With a function, we start with an argument and calculate a corresponding value; with a table, we start with an index and look up a corresponding value. Let us now use this analogy to produce a formal definition of the term *table*, a definition that will, in turn, motivate new ideas that come to fruition in the following section.

### 1. Functions

In mathematics a *function* is defined in terms of two sets and a correspondence from elements of the first set to elements of the second. If $f$ is a function from a set $A$ to a set $B$, then $f$ assigns to each element of $A$ a unique element of $B$. The set $A$ is called the *domain* of $f$, and the set $B$ is called the *codomain* of $f$. The subset of $B$ containing just those elements that occur as values of $f$ is called the *range* of $f$. This definition is illustrated in Figure 8.8.

*domain, codomain, and range*

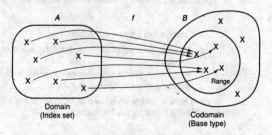

**Figure 8.8. The domain, codomain, and range of a function**

*index set, value type*

Table access begins with an index and uses the table to look up a corresponding value. Hence for a table we call the domain the *index set*, and we call the codomain the *base type* or *value type*. (Recall that in Section 4.8 a *type* was defined as a set of values.) If, for example, we have the array declaration

float somearray[n];

then the index set is the set of integers between 0 and $n-1$, and the base type is the set of all real numbers. As a second example, consider a triangular table with m rows whose entries have type Item. The base type is then simply type Item and the index type is the set of ordered pairs of integers

$$\{(i,j) \mid 0 \leq j \leq i \leq m-1\}.$$

## 2. An Abstract Data Type

We are now well on the way toward defining *table* as a new abstract data type, but recall from Section 4.8 that to complete the definition, we must also specify the operations that can be performed. Before doing so, let us summarize what we know.

**Definition**

A *table* with index set $I$ and base type $T$ is a function from $I$ into $T$ together with the following operations.

1. *Table access*: Evaluate the function at any index in $I$.
2. *Table assignment*: Modify the function by changing its value at a specified index in $I$ to the new value specified in the assignment.

These two operations are all that are provided by C and some other languages, but that is no reason why we cannot allow the possibility of further operations. If we compare the definition of a list, we find that we allowed insertion and deletion as well as access and assignment. We can do the same with tables.

3. *Creation*: Set up a new function.
4. *Clearing*: Remove all elements from the index set $I$, so there is no remaining domain.
5. *Insertion*: Adjoin a new element $x$ to the index set $I$ and define a corresponding value of the function at $x$.
6. *Deletion*: Delete an element $x$ from the index set $I$ and restrict the function to the resulting smaller domain.

Even though these last operations are not available directly in C, they remain very useful for many applications, and we shall study them further in the next section. In some other languages, such as APL and SNOBOL, tables that change size while the program is running are an important feature. In any case, we should always be careful to program *into* a language and never allow our thinking to be limited by the restrictions of a particular language.

### 3. Implementation

*index functions and access tables*

The definition just given is that of an abstract data type and in itself says nothing about implementation, nor does it speak of the index functions or access tables studied earlier. Index functions and access tables are, in fact, implementation methods for more general tables. An index function or access table starts with a general index set of some specified form and produces as its result an index in some subscript range, such as a subrange of the integers. This range can then be used directly as subscripts for arrays provided by the programming language. In this way, the implementation of a table is divided into two smaller problems: finding an access table or index function and programming an array. You should note that both of these are special cases of tables, and hence we have an example of solving a problem by dividing it into two smaller problems of the same nature. This process is illustrated in Figure 8.9.

*divide and conquer*

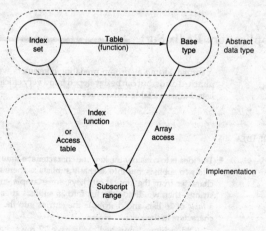

**Figure 8.9. Implementation of a table**

### 4. Comparisons

Let us compare the abstract data types *list* and *table*. The underlying mathematical construction for a list is the sequence, and for a table, it is the set and the function.

*lists and tables*

Sequences have an implicit order—a first element, a second, and so on—but sets and functions have no such order. (If the index set has some natural order, then sometimes this order is reflected in the table, but this is not a necessary aspect of using tables.) Hence information retrieval from a list naturally involves a search like the ones studied in the previous chapter, but information retrieval from a table

*retrieval*

requires different methods, access methods that go directly to the desired entry. The time required for searching a list generally depends on the number $n$ of entries in the list and is at least $\lg n$, but the time for accessing a table does not usually depend on the number of entries in the table; that is, it is usually $O(1)$. For this reason, in many applications, table access is significantly faster than list searching.

*traversal*

On the other hand, traversal is a natural operation for a list but not for a table. It is generally easy to move through a list performing some operation with every entry in the list. In general, it may not be nearly so easy to perform an operation on every entry in a table, particularly if some special order for the entries is specified in advance.

*tables and arrays*

Finally, we should clarify the distinction between the terms *table* and *array*. In general, we shall use *table* as we have defined it in this section and restrict the term *array* to mean the programming feature available in C and most high-level languages and used for implementing both tables and contiguous lists.

# 8.5 Application: Radix Sort

A formal sorting algorithm predating computers was first devised for use with punched cards, but can be developed into a very efficient sorting method for linked lists that uses a table and queues.

## 8.5.1 THE IDEA

The idea is to consider the key one character at a time and to divide the entries, not into two sublists, but into as many sublists as there are possibilities for the given character from the key. If our keys, for example, are words or other alphabetic strings, then we divide the list into 26 sublists at each stage. That is, we set up a *table* of 26 lists and distribute the entries into the lists according to one of the characters in the key.

Old-fashioned punched cards have 12 rows; hence mechanical card sorters were designed to work on only one column at a time and divide the cards into 12 piles.

A person sorting words by this method might first distribute the words into 26 lists according to the initial letter, then divide each of these sublists into further *method*

sublists according to the second letter, and so on. The following idea eliminates this multiplicity of sublists: Partition the items into the table of sublists first by the *least* significant position, not the most significant. After this first partition, the sublists from the table are put back together as a single list, in the order given by the character in the least significant position. The list is then partitioned into the table according to the second least significant position and recombined as one list. When, after repetition of these steps, the list has been partitioned by the most significant place and recombined, it will be completely sorted.

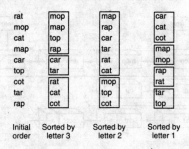

Figure 8.10. Trace of a radix sort

This process is illustrated by sorting the list of nine three-letter words in Figure 8.10. The words are in the initial order shown in the left column. They are first divided into three lists according to their third letter, as shown in the second column, where the colored boxes indicate the resulting sublists. The order of the words in each sublist remains the same as it was before the partition. Next, the sublists are put back together as shown in the second column of the diagram, and they are now distributed into two sublists according to the second letter. The result is shown in the colored boxes of the third column. Finally, these sublists are recombined and distributed into four sublists according to the first letter. When these sublists are recombined, the whole list is sorted.

### 8.5.2 IMPLEMENTATION

We shall implement this method in C for linked lists, where the keys are strings of characters of fixed length. After each time the items have been partitioned into sublists in a table, the sublists must be recombined into a single list so that the items can be redistributed according to the next most significant position in the key. We shall treat the sublists as queues, since entries are always inserted at the end of a sublist and, when recombining the sublists, removed from the beginning.

For clarity of presentation, we use the general list and queue functions for this processing. Doing so, however, entails unnecessary data movement, since all that is necessary is to implement the queues in linked storage. To recombine these linked queues into one list, we need only connect the rear of each queue to the front of the next queue. This process is illustrated in Figure 8.11 for the same list of nine words used previously. At each stage, the links shown in black are those within one of the queues, and the links shown in color are those added to recombine the queues into a single list. Programming this optimization of radix sort is left as a project.

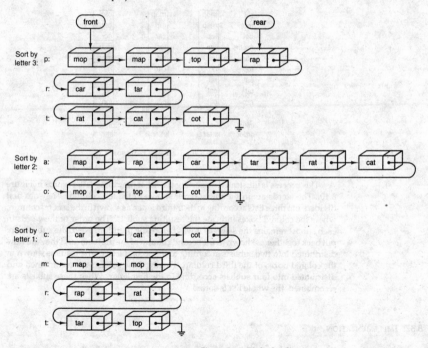

**Figure 8.11. Linked radix sort**

We shall set up an array of 28 linked queues. Position 0 corresponds to a blank character, positions 1 through 26 to the letters (with upper- and lowercase regarded as the same), and position 27 corresponds to any other character that appears in the key. Within a loop running from the least to most significant positions of the key, we shall traverse the linked list and add each item to the end of the appropriate queue. After the list has been thus partitioned, we recombine the queues into one list. At the end of the major loop on positions in the key, the list will be completely sorted.

With regard to declarations and notation, finally, let us use the standard declarations and operations for a list (from Chapter 5) and for a queue (from Chapter 4). We assume the declaration

typedef char QueueEntry[KEYSIZE];

where the symbolic constant KEYSIZE is defined appropriately.

## 1. The Main Function

The sorting function then takes the following form:

```
/* RadixSort: sort a list using radix sort method.
   Pre:    The linked list list has been created. The entries in list all contain keys that are
           arrays of letters of size KEYSIZE.
   Post:   The entries of list have been sorted so all their keys are in alphabetical order.
   Uses: Functions for queues (chapter 5) and lists (chapter 6). */
void RadixSort(List *list)
{
   int i, j;
   Node *x;
   Queue queues[MAXQUEUEARRAY];
   for (i = 0; i < MAXQUEUEARRAY; i++)
      CreateQueue( &queues[i]);
   for (j = KEYSIZE - 2; j >= 0; j--) {
      while( !ListEmpty(list)) {
         DeleteList(0, &x, list);
         AppendNode(x, &queues[QueuePosition(x->entry[j])]);
      }
      Rethread(list, queues);
   }
}
```

This function uses two subsidiary subprograms: QueuePosition determines into which queue a particular key should go, and Rethread recombines the queues as a single list.

## 2. Selecting a Position

The function QueuePosition checks whether the character is in the alphabet and assigns it to the appropriate position and assigns all non-alphabetical characters other than blanks to position 27. Blanks are assigned to position 0. It is also adjusted to make no distinction between upper- and lowercase. As with most functions manipulating characters, QueuePosition is system dependent; it will work with the ASCII encoding, but may require modification for other systems.

```
/* QueuePosition: determine the queue position (0 through 27) for a character.
   Pre:   None.
   Post:  If c is a letter of the alphabet (either upper or lower case) then the function
          returns the position of c within the alphabet (from 1 for 'a' or 'A' to 26 for 'z' or
          'Z'). Otherwise, if c is a blank then 0 is returned, else the function returns 27.
   Uses:  System requirement that the letters have adjacent codes (true for ASCII, not
          true for EBCDIC) */
int QueuePosition(char c)
{
   if (c == ' ')
      return 0;
   else if (isalpha(c))
      return tolower(c) - 'a' + 1;
   else
      return 27;
}
```

### 3. Connecting the Queues

The function Rethread connects the 28 queues together as a single list. A project requests rewriting this function in an implementation-dependent way that will operate much more quickly than the current version.

```
/* Rethread: rethread a list from an array of queues.
   Pre:   All 28 linked queues in array queues have been created; the list has been
          created and is empty.
   Post:  All the queues are combined to form one list list; all the queues are empty. */
void Rethread(List *list, Queue queues[ ])
{
   int i;
   Node *x;
   for (i = 0; i < MAXQUEUEARRAY; i++)
      while(!QueueEmpty( &queues[i])) {
         ServeNode( &x, &queues[i]);
         InsertList(ListSize(list), x, list);
      }
}
```

### 8.5.3 ANALYSIS

Note that the time used by radix sort is proportional to $nk$, where $n$ is the number of items being sorted and $k$ is the number of characters in a key. The time for all our other sorting methods depends on $n$ but not directly on the length of a key. The best time was that of mergesort, which was $n \lg n + O(n)$. The relative performance of the methods will therefore relate in some ways to the relative sizes of $nk$ and

$n \lg n$. If the keys are long but there are relatively few of them, then $k$ is large and $n$ relatively small, and other methods (such as mergesort) will outperform radix sort; but if $k$ is small and there are a large number of keys, then radix sort will be faster than any other method we have studied.

---

**Exercises 8.5**

E1. Trace the action of radix sort on the list of 14 names used to trace other sorting methods:

Tim Dot Eva Roy Tom Kim Guy Amy Jon Ann Jim Kay Ron Jan

E2. Trace the action of radix sort on the following list of seven numbers considered as two-digit integers:

26   33   35   29   19   12   22

E3. Trace the action of radix sort on the preceding list of seven numbers considered as six-digit binary integers.

**Programming Projects 8.5**

P1. Design, program, and test a version of radix sort that is implementation independent, with alphabetic keys.

P2. The radix-sort program presented in the book is very inefficient, since its implementation-independent features force a large amount of data movement. Design a project that is implementation dependent and saves all the data movement. In Rethread you need only link the rear of one queue to the front of the next. Compare the performance of this version with that of other sorting methods for linked lists.

# 8.6 Hashing

## 8.6.1 SPARSE TABLES

### 1. Index Functions

We can continue to exploit table lookup even in situations where the key is no longer an index that can be used directly as in array indexing. What we can do is to set up a one-to-one correspondence between the keys by which we wish to retrieve information and indices that we can use to access an array. The index function that we produce will be somewhat more complicated than those of previous sections, since it may need to convert the key from, say, alphabetic information to an integer, but in principle it can still be done.

The only difficulty arises when the number of possible keys exceeds the amount of space available for our table. If, for example, our keys are alphabetical words of eight letters, then there are $26^8 \approx 2 \times 10^{11}$ possible keys, a number likely greater than the number of positions that will be available in high-speed memory. In practice, however, only a small fraction of these keys will actually occur. That is, the table is *sparse*. Conceptually, we can regard it as indexed by a very large set, but with relatively few positions actually occupied. In C, for example, we might think in terms of conceptual declarations such as

typedef sparse table of Entry type SparseTable[MAXENTRY];

Even though it may not be possible to implement a declaration such as this directly, it is often helpful in problem solving to begin with such a picture, and only slowly tie down the details of how it is put into practice.

## 2. Hash Tables

*index function not one to one*

The idea of a *hash table* (such as the one shown in Figure 8.12) is to allow many of the different possible keys that might occur to be mapped to the same location in an array under the action of the index function. Then there will be a possibility that two records will want to be in the same place, but if the number of records that actually occur is small relative to the size of the array, then this possibility will cause little loss of time. Even when most entries in the array are occupied, hash methods can be an effective means of information retrieval.

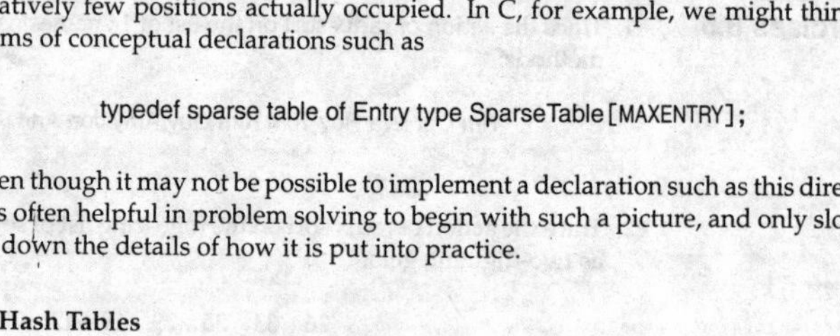

Figure 8.12. A hash table

*hash function*

We begin with a *hash function* that takes a key and maps it to some index in the array. This function will generally map several different keys to the same index. If the desired record is in the location given by the index, then our problem is solved; otherwise we must use some method to resolve the *collision* that may have occurred between two records wanting to go to the same location. There are thus two questions we must answer to use hashing. First, we must find good hash functions, and, second, we must determine how to resolve collisions.

*collision*

Before approaching these questions, let us pause to outline informally the steps needed to implement hashing.

### 3. Algorithm Outlines

First, an array must be declared that will hold the hash table. With ordinary arrays the keys used to locate entries are usually the indices, so there is no need to keep them within the array itself, but for a hash table, several possible keys will

*keys in table*    correspond to the same index, so one field within each record in the array must be reserved for the key itself.

*initialization*    Next, all locations in the array must be initialized to show that they are empty. How this is done depends on the application; often it is accomplished by setting the key fields to some value that is guaranteed never to occur as an actual key. With alphanumeric keys, for example, a key consisting of all blanks might represent an empty position.

*insertion*    To insert a record into the hash table, the hash function for the key is first calculated. If the corresponding location is empty, then the record can be inserted, else if the keys are equal, then insertion of the new record would not be allowed, and in the remaining case (a record with a different key is in the location), it becomes necessary to resolve the collision.

*retrieval*    To retrieve the record with a given key is entirely similar. First, the hash function for the key is computed. If the desired record is in the corresponding location, then the retrieval has succeeded; otherwise, while the location is nonempty and not all locations have been examined, follow the same steps used for collision resolution. If an empty position is found, or all locations have been considered, then no record with the given key is in the table, and the search is unsuccessful.

## 8.6.2 Choosing a Hash Function

The two principal criteria in selecting a hash function are that it should be easy and quick to compute and that it should achieve an even distribution of the keys that actually occur across the range of indices. If we know in advance exactly what keys will occur, then it is possible to construct hash functions that will be very efficient, but generally we do not know in advance what keys will occur. Therefore, the usual

*method*    way is for the hash function to take the key, chop it up, mix the pieces together in various ways, and thereby obtain an index that (like the pseudorandom numbers generated by computer) will be uniformly distributed over the range of indices.

Note, however, that there is nothing random about a hash function. If the function is evaluated more than once on the same key, then it gives the same result every time, so the key can be retrieved without fail.

It is from this process that the word *hash* comes, since the process converts the key into something that bears little resemblance to the original. At the same time, it is hoped that any patterns or regularities that may occur in the keys will be destroyed, so that the results will be uniformly distributed.

Even though the term *hash* is very descriptive, in some books the more technical terms **scatter-storage** or **key-transformation** are used in its place.

We shall consider three methods that can be put together in various ways to build a hash function.

## 1. Truncation

Ignore part of the key, and use the remaining part directly as the index (considering non-numeric fields as their numerical codes). If the keys, for example, are eight-digit integers and the hash table has 1000 locations, then the first, second, and fifth digits from the right might make the hash function, so that 62538194 maps to 394. Truncation is a very fast method, but it often fails to distribute the keys evenly through the table.

## 2. Folding

Partition the key into several parts and combine the parts in a convenient way (often using addition or multiplication) to obtain the index. For example, an eight-digit integer can be divided into groups of three, three, and two digits, the groups added together, and truncated if necessary to be in the proper range of indices. Hence 62538194 maps to $625 + 381 + 94 = 1100$, which is truncated to 100. Since all information in the key can affect the value of the function, folding often achieves a better spread of indices than does truncation by itself.

## 3. Modular Arithmetic

Convert the key to an integer (using the above devices as desired), divide by the size of the index range, and take the remainder as the result. This amounts to using the C modulus operator %. The spread achieved by taking a remainder depends very much on the modulus (in this case, the size of the hash array). If the modulus is a power of a small integer like 2 or 10, then many keys tend to map to the same index, while other indices remain unused. The best choice for modulus is often, *prime modulus* but not always, a prime number, which usually has the effect of spreading the keys quite uniformly. (We shall see later that a prime modulus also improves an important method for collision resolution.) Hence, rather than choosing a hash table size of 1000, it is often better to choose either 997 or 1009; $2^{10} = 1024$ would usually be a poor choice. Taking the remainder is usually the best way to conclude calculating the hash function, since it can achieve a good spread at the same time that it ensures that the result is in the proper range.

## 4. C Example

As a simple example, let us write a hash function in C for transforming a key consisting of alphanumeric characters into an integer in the range

$$0 .. \text{HASHSIZE} - 1.$$

That is, we shall begin with the type

```
typedef char *Key;
```

We can then write a simple hash function as follows:

```
/* Hash: determine the hash value of key s.
   Pre:  s is a valid key type.
   Post: s has been hashed, returning a value between 0 and HASHSIZE – 1 */
int Hash(Key s)
{
    unsigned h = 0;
    while (*s)
        h += *s++;
    return h % HASHSIZE;
}
```

We have simply added the integer codes corresponding to each of the characters in the string. There is no reason to believe that this method will be better (or worse), however, than any number of others. We could, for example, subtract some of the codes, multiply them in pairs, or ignore every other character. Sometimes an application will suggest that one hash function is better than another; sometimes it requires experimentation to settle on a good one.

### 8.6.3 COLLISION RESOLUTION WITH OPEN ADDRESSING

#### 1. Linear Probing

The simplest method to resolve a collision is to start with the hash address (the location where the collision occurred) and do a sequential search through the table for the desired key or an empty location. Hence this method searches in a straight line, and it is therefore called *linear probing*. The table should be considered circular, so that when the last location is reached, the search proceeds to the first location of the table.

#### 2. Clustering

The major drawback of linear probing is that, as the table becomes about half full, there is a tendency toward *clustering*; that is, records start to appear in long strings of adjacent positions with gaps between the strings. Thus the sequential searches needed to find an empty position become longer and longer. Consider the example

*example of clustering*

in Figure 8.13, where the occupied positions are shown in color. Suppose that there

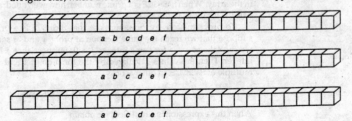

**Figure 8.13. Clustering in a hash table**

are $n$ locations in the array and that the hash function chooses any of them with equal probability $1/n$. Begin with a fairly uniform spread, as shown in the top diagram. If a new insertion hashes to location *b*, then it will go there, but if it hashes to location *a* (which is full), then it will also go into *b*. Thus the probability that *b* will be filled has doubled to $2/n$. At the next stage, an attempted insertion into any of locations *a, b, c,* or *d* will end up in *d*, so the probability of filling *d* is $4/n$. After this, *e* has probability $5/n$ of being filled, and so as additional insertions are made the most likely effect is to make the string of full positions beginning at location *a* longer and longer. Hence the performance of the hash table starts to degenerate toward that of sequential search.

*instability*     The problem of clustering is essentially one of instability; if a few keys happen randomly to be near each other, then it becomes more and more likely that other keys will join them, and the distribution will become progressively more unbalanced.

### 3. Increment Functions

If we are to avoid the problem of clustering, then we must use some more sophisticated way to select the sequence of locations to check when a collision occurs. There are many ways to do so. One, called *rehashing*, uses a second hash function *rehashing* to obtain the second position to consider. If this position is filled, then some other method is needed to get the third position, and so on. But if we have a fairly good spread from the first hash function, then little is to be gained by an independent second hash function. We will do just as well to find a more sophisticated way of determining the distance to move from the first hash position and apply this method, whatever the first hash location is. Hence we wish to design an increment function that can depend on the key or on the number of probes already made and that will avoid clustering.

### 4. Quadratic Probing

If there is a collision at hash address $h$, this method probes the table at locations $h + 1, h + 4, h + 9, \ldots$, that is, at locations $h + i^2$ (% HASHSIZE) for $i = 1, 2, \ldots$. That is, the increment function is $i^2$.

Quadratic probing substantially reduces clustering, but it is not obvious that it will probe all locations in the table, and in fact it does not. For some values of HASHSIZE, for example powers of 2, the function will probe relatively few positions in the array. When HASHSIZE is a prime number, however, quadratic probing reaches half the locations in the array.

*proof*     To prove this observation, suppose that HASHSIZE is a prime number. Also suppose that we reach the same location at probe $i$ and at some later probe that we can take as $i + j$ for some integer $j > 0$. Suppose that $j$ is the smallest such integer. Then the values calculated by the function at $i$ and at $i + j$ differ by a multiple of HASHSIZE. In other words,

$$h + i^2 \equiv h + (i + j)^2 \ (\% \ \text{HASHSIZE}).$$

When this expression is simplified, we obtain

$$j^2 + 2ij = j(j + 2i) \equiv 0 \ (\% \ \text{HASHSIZE}).$$

This last expression means that HASHSIZE divides (with no remainder) the product $j(j + 2i)$. The only way that a prime number can divide a product is to divide one of its factors. Hence HASHSIZE either divides $j$ or it divides $j + 2i$. If the first case occurred, then we would have made HASHSIZE probes before duplicating probe $i$. (Recall that $j$ is the smallest positive integer such that probe $i + j$ duplicates probe $i$.) The second case, however, will occur sooner, when $j =$ HASHSIZE $- 2i$, or, if this expression is negative, at this expression increased by HASHSIZE. Hence the total number of distinct positions that will be probed is exactly

$$\text{(HASHSIZE} + 1)/2.$$

It is customary to regard the table as full when this number of positions has been probed, and the results are quite satisfactory.

*alculation*

Note that quadratic probing can be accomplished without doing multiplications: After the first probe at position $x$, the increment is set to 1. At each successive probe, the increment is increased by 2 after it has been added to the previous location. Since

$$1 + 3 + 5 + \cdots + (2i - 1) = i^2$$

for all $i \geq 1$ (you can prove this fact by mathematical induction), probe $i$ will look in position $x + 1 + 3 + \cdots + (2i - 1) = x + i^2$, as desired.

### 5. Key-Dependent Increments

Rather than having the increment depend on the number of probes already made, we can let it be some simple function of the key itself. For example, we could truncate the key to a single character and use its code as the increment. In C, we might write

increment = *key;

A good approach, when the remainder after division is taken as the hash function, is to let the increment depend on the quotient of the same division. An optimizing compiler should specify the division only once, so the calculation will be fast, and the results generally satisfactory.

In this method, the increment, once determined, remains constant. If HASHSIZE is a prime, it follows that the probes will step through all the entries of the array before any repetitions. Hence overflow will not be indicated until the array is completely full.

### 6. Random Probing

A final method is to use a pseudorandom number generator to obtain the increment. The generator used should be one that always generates the same sequence provided it starts with the same seed. (See Chapter 4.) The seed, then, can be specified as some function of the key. This method is excellent in avoiding clustering, but is likely to be slower than the others.

### 7. C Algorithms

To conclude the discussion of open addressing, we continue to study the C example already introduced, which used alphanumeric keys of the type

typedef char *Key;

We set up the hash table with the declarations

```
/* declarations for a hash table with open addressing */
#define HASHSIZE 997
typedef char *Key;
typedef struct item {
    Key key;
} Entry;
typedef Entry HashTable[HASHSIZE];
```

*initialization*

The hash table must be created by setting the key field of each item to NULL. This is the task of the function CreateTable, whose specifications are:

> void CreateTable(HashTable H);
>
> *precondition*:  None.
>
> *postcondition*:  The hash table H has been created and initialized to be empty.

There should also be a function ClearTable that returns a table that already has been created to an empty state. Its specifications follow, but its code (for the case of hash tables using open addressing) will be identical to that of CreateTable.

> void ClearTable(HashTable H);
>
> *precondition*:  The hash table H has been created.
>
> *postcondition*:  The hash table H has been cleared and is empty.

Although we have started to specify hash-table operations, we shall not continue to develop a complete and general set of functions. Since the choice of a good hash function depends strongly on the kind of keys used, hash-table operations are usually too dependent on the particular application to be assembled into a set of functions.

To show how the code for further routines will be written, we shall continue to follow the example of the hash function already written in Section 8.6.2, page 357, and we shall use quadratic probing for collision resolution. We have shown that the maximum number of probes that can be made this way is (HASHSIZE + 1)/2, and we keep a counter pc to check this upper bound.

With these conventions, let us write a function to insert a new entry newentry into the hash table H.

```
/* Insert: insert an item using open addressing and linear probing.
   Pre:  The hash table H has been created and is not full. H has no current entry with
         key equal to that of newitem.
   Post: The item newitem has been inserted into H.
   Uses: Hash. */
void Insert(HashTable H, Entry newitem)
{
    int pc = 0;            /* probe count to be sure that table is not full   */
    int probe;             /* position currently probed in H                  */
    int increment = 1;     /* increment used for quadratic probing            */
    probe = Hash(newitem.key);

    while (H[probe].key != NULL &&  /* Is the location empty?                  */
      strcmp(newitem.key, H[probe].key) && /* Duplicate key present?          */
      pc <= HASHSIZE/2) {           /* Has overflow occurred?                  */
        pc++;
        probe = (probe + increment) % HASHSIZE;
        increment += 2;             /* Prepare increment for next iteration.   */
    }
    if (H[probe].key == NULL)
        H[probe] = newitem;         /* Insert the new entry.                   */
    else if (strcmp(newitem.key, H[probe].key) == 0)
        Error("The same key cannot appear twice in the hash table.");
    else
        Error("Hash table is full; insertion cannot be made.");
}
```

A function to retrieve the record (if any) with a given key will have a similar
form and is left as an exercise. The retrieval function should return the full entry
associated with a target key. Its specifications are:

---

int RetrieveTable(HashTable H, Key target);

*precondition*:  The hash table H has been created.

*postcondition*:  If an entry in H has key equal to target, then the function returns
the index for the entry. Otherwise, the function returns $-1$.

---

### 8. Deletions

Up to now, we have said nothing about deleting entries from a hash table. At
first glance, it may appear to be an easy task, requiring only marking the deleted
location with the special key indicating that it is empty. This method will not work.
The reason is that an empty location is used as the signal to stop the search for a
target key. Suppose that, before the deletion, there had been a collision or two and
that some entry whose hash address is the now-deleted position is actually stored
elsewhere in the table. If we now try to retrieve that entry, then the now-empty

*special key*

position will stop the search, and it is impossible to find the entry, even though it is still in the table.

One method to remedy this difficulty is to invent another special key, to be placed in any deleted position. This special key would indicate that this position is free to receive an insertion when desired but that it should not be used to terminate the search for some other entry in the table. Using this second special key will, however, make the algorithms somewhat more complicated and a bit slower. With the methods we have so far studied for hash tables, deletions are indeed awkward and should be avoided as much as possible.

### 8.6.4 COLLISION RESOLUTION BY CHAINING

*linked storage*

Up to now we have implicitly assumed that we are using only contiguous storage while working with hash tables. Contiguous storage for the hash table itself is, in fact, the natural choice, since we wish to be able to refer quickly to random positions in the table, and linked storage is not suited to random access. There is, however, no reason why linked storage should not be used for the records themselves. We can take the hash table itself as an array of pointers to the records, that is, as an array of linked lists. An example appears in Figure 8.14.

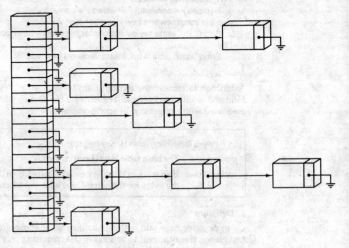

Figure 8.14. A chained hash table

*chaining*

It is traditional to refer to the linked lists from the hash table as *chains* and call this method collision resolution by *chaining*.

## 1. Advantages of Chaining

There are several advantages to this point of view. The first, and the most important when the records themselves are quite large, is that considerable space *space saving* may be saved. Since the hash table is a contiguous array, enough space must be set aside at compilation time to avoid overflow. If the records themselves are in the hash table, then if there are many empty positions (as is desirable to help avoid the cost of collisions), these will consume considerable space that might be needed elsewhere. If, on the other hand, the hash table contains only pointers to the records, pointers that require only one word each, then the size of the hash table may be reduced by a large factor (essentially by a factor equal to the size of the records), and will become small relative to the space available for the records, or for other uses.

*collision resolution*
The second major advantage of keeping only pointers in the hash table is that it allows simple and efficient collision handling. We need only add a link field to each record, and organize all the records with a single hash address as a linked list. With a good hash function, few keys will give the same hash address, so the linked lists will be short and can be searched quickly. Clustering is no problem at all, because keys with distinct hash addresses always go to distinct lists.

*overflow*
A third advantage is that it is no longer necessary that the size of the hash table exceed the number of records. If there are more records than entries in the table, it means only that some of the linked lists are now sure to contain more than one record. Even if there are several times more records than the size of the table, the average length of the linked lists will remain small and sequential search on the appropriate list will remain efficient.

*deletion*
Finally, deletion becomes a quick and easy task in a chained hash table. Deletion proceeds in exactly the same way as deletion from a simple linked list.

## 2. Disadvantage of Chaining

These advantages of chained hash tables are indeed powerful. Lest you believe that chaining is always superior to open addressing, however, let us point out one *use of space* important disadvantage: All the links require space. If the records are large, then this space is negligible in comparison with that needed for the records themselves; but if the records are small, then it is not.

*small records*
Suppose, for example, that the links take one word each and that the entries themselves take only one word (which is the key alone). Such applications are quite common, where we use the hash table only to answer some yes–no question about the key. Suppose that we use chaining and make the hash table itself quite small, with the same number $n$ of entries as the number of entries. Then we shall use $3n$ words of storage altogether: $n$ for the hash table, $n$ for the keys, and $n$ for the links to find the next node (if any) on each chain. Since the hash table will be nearly full, there will be many collisions, and some of the chains will have several entries. Hence searching will be a bit slow. Suppose, on the other hand, that we use open addressing. The same $3n$ words of storage put entirely into the hash table will mean that it will be only one third full, and therefore there will be relatively few collisions and the search for any given entry will be faster.

### 3. C Algorithms

A chained hash table in C takes the simple declaration

$$\text{typedef List HashTable[HASHSIZE];}$$

where List refers to the linked implementation of lists studied in Chapter 5.

*initialization*  The code needed to create the hash table is

```
for(i = 0; i < HASHSIZE; i++)
    CreateList(H[i]);
```

To clear a chained hash table that has previously been created is a different task, in contrast to open addressing, where it was the same as creating the table. To clear the table, we must clear the linked list in each of the table positions. This task can be done by using the linked-list function ClearList.

We can even use the list processing functions to access the hash table. The hash function itself is no different from that used with open addressing; for data retrieval, we can simply use a linked version of SequentialSearch. The essence of RetrieveTable is

$$\text{SequentialSearch(H[Hash(target)], target);}$$

The details of converting this into a full function are left as an exercise.

Similarly, the essence of insertion is the one line

$$\text{InsertList(0, newentry, H[newentry.key]);}$$

Here we have chosen to insert the new entry as the first node of its list, since that is the easiest. As you can see, both insertion and retrieval are simpler than the versions for open addressing, since collision resolution is not a problem and we can make use of the previous work done for linked lists.

*deletion*  Deletion from a chained hash table is also much simpler than it is from a table with open addressing. To delete the entry with a given key, we need only use sequential search to find the entry where it is located within its chain in the hash table, and then we delete this entry from its linked list. The specifications for this function are:

---

Entry *DeleteTable(HashTable H, Key target);

*precondition*:   The chained hash table H has been created and contains an entry with key equal to target.

*postcondition*:  The entry with key equal to target has been deleted from H and its pointer has been returned.

---

Writing the corresponding function is left as an exercise.

**Exercises 8.6**

**E1.** Prove by mathematical induction that $1+3+5+\cdots+(2i-1)=i^2$ for all integers $i > 0$.

**E2.** Write a function to insert an entry into a hash table with open addressing using linear probing.

**E3.** Write a function to retrieve an entry from a hash table with open addressing using **(a)** linear probing; **(b)** quadratic probing.

**E4.** In a student project for which the keys were integers, one student thought that he could mix the keys well by using a trigonometric function, which had to be converted to an integer index, so he defined his hash function as

$$abs(sin(n));$$

What was wrong with this choice? He then decided to replace the function sin(n) by exp(n). Criticize this choice.

**E5.** Devise a simple, easy-to-calculate hash function for mapping three-letter words to integers between $0$ and $n-1$, inclusive. Find the values of your function on the words

PAL  LAP  PAM  MAP  PAT  PET  SET  SAT  TAT  BAT

for $n = 11, 13, 17, 19$. Try for as few collisions as possible.

**E6.** Suppose that a hash table contains HASHSIZE = 13 entries indexed from 0 through 12 and that the following keys are to be mapped into the table:

10  100  32  45  58  126  3  29  200  400  0

**(a)** Determine the hash addresses and find how many collisions occur when these keys are reduced % HASHSIZE.

**(b)** Determine the hash addresses and find how many collisions occur when these keys are first folded by adding their digits together (in ordinary decimal representation) and then reducing % HASHSIZE.

*perfect hash functions*

**(c)** Find a hash function that will produce no collisions for these keys. (A hash function that has no collisions for a fixed set of keys is called *perfect*.)

**(d)** Repeat the previous parts of this exercise for HASHSIZE = 11. (A hash function that produces no collision for a fixed set of keys that completely fill the hash table is called *minimal perfect*.)

**E7.** Another method for resolving collisions with open addressing is to keep a separate array called the *overflow table*, into which are put all entries that collide with an occupied location. They can either be inserted with another hash function or simply inserted in order, with sequential search used for retrieval. Discuss the advantages and disadvantages of this method.

**E8.** Write the following functions for processing a chained hash table, using the list-processing operations of Section 5.1 to implement the operations.

    **(a)** CreateTable

    **(b)** ClearTable

    **(c)** InsertTable

    **(d)** RetrieveTable

    **(e)** DeleteTable

**E9.** Write the following functions for processing a chained hash table. Do not use the list-processing functions; instead, write instructions directly into the hash-table for processing the pointers describing the linked chains.

    **(a)** CreateTable

    **(b)** ClearTable

    **(c)** InsertTable

    **(d)** RetrieveTable

    **(e)** DeleteTable

**E10.** Write a deletion algorithm for a hash table with open addressing using linear probing, using a second special key to indicate a deleted entry (see Part 8 of Section 8.6.3 on page 361). Change the retrieval and insertion algorithms accordingly.

**E11.** With linear probing, it is possible to delete an entry without using a second special key, as follows. Mark the deleted entry empty. Search until another empty position is found. If the search finds a key whose hash address is at or before the first empty position, then move it back there, make its previous position empty, and continue from the new empty position. Write an algorithm to implement this method. Do the retrieval and insertion algorithms need modification?

**Programming Projects 8.6**

*coatroom*

**P1.** Use a chained hash table to implement the coatroom operations of Section 6.3. You will need to program one additional operation (not a standard hash-table operation): traversal of a chained hash table. Your hash function should take advantage of the fact that the keys (that is, tags) are already random integers. In deciding on the size of your hash table, note that a large table will cause the create, clear, and traverse operations to be slow, whereas a small table will entail collisions and therefore slow down insertion, retrieval, and deletion. Test your program with the coatroom demonstration program, and then run the timed-test program with the hash-table package, comparing the results with those for sequential and binary search.

**P2.** Consider the following 32 C reserved words.

| | | | | |
|---|---|---|---|---|
| auto | break | case | char | const |
| continue | default | do | double | else |
| enum | extern | float | for | goto |
| if | int | long | register | return |
| short | signed | sizeof | static | struct |
| switch | typedef | union | unsigned | void |
| volatile | while | | | |

(a) Devise an integer-valued function that will produce different values when applied to all 32 reserved words. [You may find it helpful to write a short program that reads the words from a file, applies the function you devise, and determines what collisions occur.]

(b) Find the smallest integer HASHSIZE such that, when the values of your function are reduced % HASHSIZE, all 32 values remain distinct.

(c) Modify your function as necessary until you can achieve HASHSIZE = 32 in the preceding part. (You will then have discovered a *minimal perfect* hash function for the 32 C reserved words.)

**P3.** Write a program that will read a molecular formula such as $H_2SO_4$ and will write out the molecular weight of the compound that it represents. Your program should be able to handle bracketed radicals such as in $Al_2(SO_4)_3$. [*Hint*: Use recursion to find the molecular weight of a bracketed radical. *Simplifications:* You may find it helpful to enclose the whole formula in parentheses(...). You will need to set up a hash table of atomic weights of elements, indexed by their abbreviations. For simplicity, the table may be restricted to the more common elements. Some elements have one-letter abbreviations, and some two. For uniformity you may add blanks to the one-letter abbreviations.]

*molecular weight*

# 8.7 Analysis of Hashing

### 1. The Birthday Surprise

The likelihood of collisions in hashing relates to the well-known mathematical diversion: How many randomly chosen people need to be in a room before it becomes likely that two people will have the same birthday (month and day)? Since (apart from leap years) there are 365 possible birthdays, most people guess that the answer will be in the hundreds, but in fact, the answer is only 24 people.

We can determine the probabilities for this question by answering its opposite: With $m$ randomly chosen people in a room, what is the probability that no two have the same birthday? Start with any person, and check that person's birthday off on a calendar. The probability that a second person has a different birthday is 364/365. Check it off. The probability that a third person has a different birthday is now 363/365. Continuing this way, we see that if the first $m - 1$ people have different birthdays, then the probability that person $m$ has a different birthday is

$(365 - m + 1)/365$. Since the birthdays of different people are independent, the probabilities multiply, and we obtain that the probability that $m$ people all have different birthdays is

*probability*

$$\frac{364}{365} \times \frac{363}{365} \times \frac{362}{365} \times \cdots \times \frac{365 - m + 1}{365}.$$

This expression becomes less than 0.5 whenever $m \geq 24$.

In regard to hashing, the birthday surprise tells us that with any problem of

*collisions likely*

reasonable size, we are almost certain to have some collisions. Our approach, therefore, should not be only to try to minimize the number of collisions, but also to handle those that occur as expeditiously as possible.

## 2. Counting Probes

As with other methods of information retrieval, we would like to know how many comparisons of keys occur on average during both successful and unsuccessful attempts to locate a given target key. We shall use the word *probe* for looking at one entry and comparing its key with the target.

The number of probes we need clearly depends on how full the table is. Therefore (as for searching methods), we let $n$ be the number of entries in the table, and we let $t$ (which is the same as HASHSIZE) be the number of positions in the

*load factor*

array. The *load factor* of the table is $\lambda = n/t$. Thus $\lambda = 0$ signifies an empty table; $\lambda = 0.5$ a table that is half full. For open addressing, $\lambda$ can never exceed 1, but for chaining there is no limit on the size of $\lambda$. We consider chaining and open addressing separately.

## 3. Analysis of Chaining

With a chained hash table we go directly to one of the linked lists before doing any probes. Suppose that the chain that will contain the target (if it is present) has $k$ entries.

*unsuccessful retrieval*

If the search is unsuccessful, then the target will be compared with all $k$ of the corresponding keys. Since the entries are distributed uniformly over all $t$ lists (equal probability of appearing on any list), the expected number of entries on the one being searched is $\lambda = n/t$. Hence the average number of probes for an unsuccessful search is $\lambda$.

*successful retrieval*

Now suppose that the search is successful. From the analysis of sequential search, we know that the average number of comparisons is $\frac{1}{2}(k + 1)$, where $k$ is the length of the chain containing the target. But the expected length of this chain is no longer $\lambda$, since we know in advance that it must contain at least one node (the target). The $n - 1$ nodes other than the target are distributed uniformly over all $t$ chains; hence the expected number on the chain with the target is $1 + (n-1)/t$. Except for tables of trivially small size, we may approximate $(n-1)/t$ by $n/t = \lambda$. Hence the average number of probes for a successful search is very nearly

$$\frac{1}{2}(k + 1) \approx \frac{1}{2}(1 + \lambda + 1) = 1 + \frac{1}{2}\lambda.$$

In summary:

*Retrieval from a chained hash table with load factor $\lambda$ requires approximately $1 + \frac{1}{2}\lambda$ probes in the successful case and $\lambda$ probes in the unsuccessful case.*

### 4. Analysis of Open Addressing

For our analysis of the number of probes done in open addressing, let us first ignore the problem of clustering by assuming that not only are the first probes random, but after a collision, the next probe will be random over all remaining positions of *random probes* the table. In fact, let us assume that the table is so large that all the probes can be regarded as independent events.

Let us first study an unsuccessful search. The probability that the first probe hits an occupied cell is $\lambda$, the load factor. The probability that a probe hits an empty cell is $1 - \lambda$. The probability that the unsuccessful search terminates in exactly two probes is therefore $\lambda(1 - \lambda)$, and, similarly, the probability that exactly $k$ probes are made in an unsuccessful search is $\lambda^{k-1}(1 - \lambda)$. The expected number $U(\lambda)$ of probes in an unsuccessful search is therefore

$$U(\lambda) = \sum_{k=1}^{\infty} k\lambda^{k-1}(1 - \lambda).$$

*unsuccessful retrieval* This sum is evaluated in Section A.1; we obtain thereby

$$U(\lambda) = \frac{1}{(1 - \lambda)^2}(1 - \lambda) = \frac{1}{1 - \lambda}.$$

To count the probes needed for a successful search, we note that the number needed will be exactly one more than the number of probes in the unsuccessful search made before inserting the entry. Now let us consider the table as beginning empty, with each entry inserted one at a time. As these entries are inserted, the load factor grows slowly from 0 to its final value, $\lambda$. It is reasonable for us to approximate this step-by-step growth by continuous growth and replace a sum with an integral. We conclude that the average number of probes in a successful search is approximately

*successful retrieval*
$$S(\lambda) = \frac{1}{\lambda} \int_0^{\lambda} U(\mu)\,d\mu = \frac{1}{\lambda} \ln \frac{1}{1 - \lambda}.$$

In summary:

> *Retrieval from a hash table with open addressing, random probing, and load factor $\lambda$ requires approximately*
>
> $$\frac{1}{\lambda} \ln \frac{1}{1 - \lambda}$$
>
> *probes in the successful case and $1/(1 - \lambda)$ probes in the unsuccessful case.*

*linear probing* Similar calculations may be done for open addressing with linear probing, where it is no longer reasonable to assume that successive probes are independent. The details, however, are rather more complicated, so we present only the results. For the complete derivation, consult the references at the end of the chapter.

*Retrieval from a hash table with open addressing, linear probing, and load factor* $\lambda$ *requires approximately*

$$\frac{1}{2}\left(1 + \frac{1}{1-\lambda}\right)$$

*probes in the successful case and*

$$\frac{1}{2}\left(1 + \frac{1}{(1-\lambda)^2}\right)$$

*probes in the unsuccessful case.*

## 5. Theoretical Comparisons

Figure 8.15 gives the values of the above expressions for different values of the load factor.

| Load factor | 0.10 | 0.50 | 0.80 | 0.90 | 0.99 | 2.00 |
|---|---|---|---|---|---|---|
| *Successful search, expected number of probes:* | | | | | | |
| Chaining | 1.05 | 1.25 | 1.40 | 1.45 | 1.50 | 2.00 |
| Open, Random probes | 1.05 | 1.4 | 2.0 | 2.6 | 4.6 | — |
| Open, Linear probes | 1.06 | 1.5 | 3.0 | 5.5 | 50.5 | — |
| *Unsuccessful search, expected number of probes:* | | | | | | |
| Chaining | 0.10 | 0.50 | 0.80 | 0.90 | 0.99 | 2.00 |
| Open, Random probes | 1.1 | 2.0 | 5.0 | 10.0 | 100. | — |
| Open, Linear probes | 1.12 | 2.5 | 13. | 50. | 5000. | — |

Figure 8.15. Theoretical comparison of hashing methods

We can draw several conclusions from this table. First, it is clear that chaining consistently requires fewer probes than does open addressing. On the other hand, traversal of the linked lists is usually slower than array access, which can reduce the advantage, especially if key comparisons can be done quickly. Chaining comes into its own when the records are large, and comparison of keys takes significant time. Chaining is also especially advantageous when unsuccessful searches are common, since with chaining, an empty list or very short list may be found, so that often no key comparisons at all need be done to show that a search is unsuccessful.

For successful searches in a table with open addressing, the simpler method of linear probing is not significantly slower than more sophisticated methods of collision resolution, at least until the table is almost completely full. For unsuccessful searches, however, clustering quickly causes linear probing to degenerate into a long sequential search. We might conclude, therefore, that if searches are quite likely to be successful, and the load factor is moderate, then linear probing is quite satisfactory, but in other circumstances another method (such as quadratic probing) should be used.

## 6. Empirical Comparisons

It is important to remember that the computations giving Figure 8.15 are only approximate, and also that in practice nothing is completely random, so that we can always expect some differences between the theoretical results and actual computations. For sake of comparison, therefore, Figure 8.16 gives the results of one empirical study, using 900 keys that are pseudorandom numbers between 0 and 1.

| Load factor | 0.1 | 0.5 | 0.8 | 0.9 | 0.99 | 2.0 |
|---|---|---|---|---|---|---|
| *Successful search, average number of probes:* | | | | | | |
| Chaining | 1.04 | 1.2 | 1.4 | 1.4 | 1.5 | 2.0 |
| Open, Quadratic probes | 1.04 | 1.5 | 2.1 | 2.7 | 5.2 | — |
| Open, Linear probes | 1.05 | 1.6 | 3.4 | 6.2 | 21.3 | — |
| *Unsuccessful search, average number of probes:* | | | | | | |
| Chaining | 0.10 | 0.50 | 0.80 | 0.90 | 0.99 | 2.00 |
| Open, Quadratic probes | 1.13 | 2.2 | 5.2 | 11.9 | 126. | — |
| Open, Linear probes | 1.13 | 2.7 | 15.4 | 59.8 | 430. | — |

Figure 8.16. Empirical comparison of hashing methods

*conclusions*

In comparison with other methods of information retrieval, the important thing to note about all these numbers is that they depend only on the load factor, not on the absolute number of entries in the table. Retrieval from a hash table with 20,000 entries in 40,000 possible positions is no slower, on average, than is retrieval from a table with 20 entries in 40 possible positions. With sequential search, a list 1000 times the size will take 1000 times as long to search. With binary search, this ratio is reduced to 10 (more precisely, to lg 1000), but still the time needed increases with the size, which it does not with hashing.

Finally, we should emphasize the importance of devising a good hash function, one that executes quickly and maximizes the spread of keys. If the hash function is poor, the performance of hashing can degenerate to that of sequential search.

**Exercises 8.7**    **E1.** Suppose that each entry in a hash table occupies $s$ words of storage (exclusive of the pointer field needed if chaining is used), and suppose that there are $n$ entries in the hash table, which has a total of $t$ possible positions ($t$ is the same as HASHSIZE).

**(a)** If the load factor is $\lambda$ and open addressing is used, determine how many words of storage will be required for the hash table.

**(b)** If chaining is used, then each node will require $s + 1$ words, including the pointer field. How many words will be used altogether for the $n$ nodes?

**(c)** If the load factor is $\lambda$ and chaining is used, how many words will be used for the hash table itself? (Recall that with chaining the hash table itself contains only pointers requiring one word each.)

**(d)** Add your answers to the two previous parts to find the total storage requirement for load factor $\lambda$ and chaining.

**(e)** If $s$ is small, then open addressing requires less total memory for a given $\lambda$, but for large $s$, chaining requires less space altogether. Find the break-even value for $s$, at which both methods use the same total storage. Your answer will depend on the load factor $\lambda$.

**E2.** One reason why the answer to the birthday problem is surprising is that it differs from the answers to apparently related questions. For the following, suppose that there are $n$ people in the room, and disregard leap years.

**(a)** What is the probability that someone in the room will have a birthday on a random date drawn from a hat?

**(b)** What is the probability that at least two people in the room will have that same random birthday?

**(c)** If we choose one person and find that person's birthday, what is the probability that someone else in the room will share the birthday?

**E3.** In a chained hash table, suppose that it makes sense to speak of an order for the keys, and suppose that the nodes in each chain are kept in order by key. Then a search can be terminated as soon as it passes the place where the key should be, if present. How many fewer probes will be done, on average, in an unsuccessful search? In a successful search? How many probes are needed, on average, to insert a new node in the right place? Compare your answers with the corresponding numbers derived in the text for the case of unordered chains.

*ordered hash table*

E4. In our discussion of chaining, the hash table itself contained only pointers, list headers for each of the chains. One variant method is to place the first actual entry of each chain in the hash table itself. (An empty position is indicated by an impossible key, as with open addressing.) With a given load factor, calculate the effect on space of this method, as a function of the number of words (except links) in each entry. (A link takes one word.)

**Programming Project 8.7**

P1. Produce a table like Figure 8.16 for your computer, by writing and running test programs to implement the various kinds of hash tables and load factors.

## 8.8 Conclusions: Comparison of Methods

In this chapter and Chapter 6, we have explored four quite different methods of information retrieval: sequential search, binary search, table lookup, and hashing. If we are to ask which of these is best, we must first select the criteria by which to answer, and these criteria will include both the requirements imposed by the application and other considerations that affect our choice of data structures, since

*choice of data structures*

the first two methods are applicable only to lists and the second two to tables. In many applications, however, we are free to choose either lists or tables for our data structures.

*table lookup*

In regard both to speed and convenience, ordinary lookup in contiguous tables is certainly superior, but there are many applications to which it is inapplicable, such as when a list is preferred or the set of keys is sparse. It is also inappropriate whenever insertions or deletions are frequent, since such actions in contiguous storage may require moving large amounts of information.

Which of the other three methods is best depends on other criteria, such as the form of the data.

*other methods*

Sequential search is certainly the most flexible of our methods. The data may be stored in any order, with either contiguous or linked representation. Binary search is much more demanding. The keys must be in order, and the data must be in random-access representation (contiguous storage). Hashing requires even more, a peculiar ordering of the keys well suited to retrieval from the hash table, but generally useless for any other purpose. If the data are to be available immediately for human inspection, then some kind of order is essential, and a hash table is inappropriate.

*near miss*

Finally, there is the question of the unsuccessful search. Sequential search and hashing, by themselves, say nothing except that the search was unsuccessful. Binary search can determine which data have keys closest to the target, and perhaps thereby can provide useful information.

## 8.9  Application: The Life Game Revisited

At the end of Chapter 2 we noted that the bounds we used for the arrays in CONWAY's game of Life were highly restrictive and artificial. The Life cells are supposed to be on an unbounded grid. In other words, we would really like to have the C declaration

typedef Cell Grid[int] [int];

*unbounded array*
*sparse table*

which is, of course, illegal. Since only a limited number of these cells will actually be occupied at any one time, we should really regard the grid for the Life game as a sparse table, and therefore a hash table proves an attractive way to represent the grid.

### 8.9.1  CHOICE OF ALGORITHM

Before we specify our data structures more precisely, let us consider the basic algorithm that we might use. We already have two versions of the Life simulation, and we should not introduce a third unless we know that it will prove a significant improvement. The first version scanned the entire grid at each generation, an action that is not suitable for a sparse array (where it would be impossibly slow). The second version, on the other hand, was designed essentially to treat the grid as a sparse array. It never explicitly scans through cells that are dead, but uses four lists to locate all cells that need attention. Rather than writing a complete new program from scratch, let us therefore see how far we can go to use the overall structure of the second program Life2 in conjunction with a hash table to represent the sparse array.

*modify* Life2

### 8.9.2  SPECIFICATION OF DATA STRUCTURES

*use of space*

We have already decided to represent our sparse array of cells as a hash table, but we have not yet decided between open addressing and chaining. For each cell we must keep the status of the cell (alive or dead), the number of living neighbors, and (since the key itself must be explicitly kept when using a hash table) the row and column of the cell. With these four entries in each record, there are few space considerations to advise our decision. With chaining, the size of each record will increase 25 percent to accommodate the necessary pointer, but the hash table itself will be smaller and can take a higher load factor than with open addressing. With open addressing, the records will be smaller, but more room must be left vacant in the hash table to avoid long searches and possible overflow.

*flexibility*

After space considerations, the second question we should ask concerns flexibility. Do we need to make deletions, and, if so, when? We could keep track of all cells until the memory is full, and then delete those that are not needed. But this would require rehashing the full array, which would be slow. With chaining, we can easily dispose of cells as soon as they are not needed, and thereby reduce the number of cells in the hash table as much as possible.

*access*

Finally, we should review the requirements for accessing the cells. As we work with a given cell, we need to locate its eight neighbors, and we can use the hash table to do so. Some of these neighbors may be inserted into the four lists maylive, maydie, newlive, and newdie. When we later retrieve a cell from one of these lists, we could again use the hash table to find it, but doing so would be repeating work. If we use chaining, then we can add a cell to a list either by inserting the cell itself or a pointer to it, rather than by inserting its coordinates as before. In this way we can locate the cell directly with no need for any search. At the same time, linked lists can help to avoid problems with unnecessary overflow.

*specification*

For reasons both of flexibility and time saving, therefore, let us decide to use dynamic memory allocation, a chained hash table, and linked lists.

*list implementation*

The most obvious way to implement the four lists is by connecting the cells into one of the lists by means of a pointer field. This would need to be a second pointer field in the structure for a cell, since the first pointer field is used for chains from the hash table. A subtle problem arises, however. We have no guarantee that the same cell may not simultaneously be on two of the lists, and with only one available pointer field, the entries of the two lists will become mixed up. The obvious way to cure this problem is to keep a total of five pointer fields for each cell, one for the hash-table chain and four for possible use in the four lists. This solution wastes space, since many of the cells will not be on any of the four lists, and very few (if any) will be on more than one.

*indirect linked list*

A much better way is to put pointers to cells into the four lists, not the cells themselves. The result for one of the lists is illustrated in Figure 8.17. Each node of the list thus contains two pointers: one to a cell and one to the next node of the list.

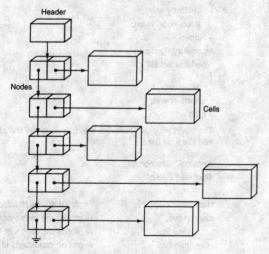

Figure 8.17. An indirect linked list

### 8.9.3 THE MAIN PROGRAM

With these decisions made, we can now tie down the representation and notation for our data structures by writing the main program. Since we are following the method of Life2, the action part is almost identical with that of Life2. The necessary declarations appear in life3.h:

```
#define HASHSIZE 997
#define FACTOR 101

typedef enum state { DEAD, ALIVE } State;
typedef struct cell
{
    State status;
    int neighborcount;
    int row,
        col;
    struct cell *next;
} Cell;
typedef Cell *HashTable[HASHSIZE];
typedef Cell *ListEntry;

typedef struct node
{
    ListEntry entry;
    struct node *next;
} Node;
typedef int Position;
typedef struct list
{
    int count;
    Node *head;
} List;
```

The main program contains the definitions of the global variables for hash table and the four lists.

```
#include "common.h"
#include "life3.h"

HashTable map;            /* global: the hash table map                       */
List newlive,             /* global: the cells that have just been vivified   */
     newdie,              /* global: the cells that have just died            */
     maylive,             /* global: candidates to vivify in the next generation */
     maydie;              /* global: candidates to kill in the next generation   */
```

*Life3, main program*

```
/* Life3 - Third version of Life
    Pre:    The user supplies an initial configuration of living cells.
    Post:   The program prints a sequence of maps showing the changes in the configu-
            ration of living cells according to the rules for the game of Life.
    Uses:   Introduction, Initialized, WriteMap, and simple list functions. */
void main(void)
{
```

*initialization*

```
    Introduction( );
    Initialize(map, &newlive, &newdie, &maylive, &maydie);
    WriteMap( );
    printf("Proceed with the demonstration");
```

*main loop*

```
    while (UserSaysYes( )) {
        TraverseList( &maylive, Vivify);
        ClearList( &maylive);
        TraverseList( &maydie, Kill);
        ClearList( &maydie);
        WriteMap( );
        TraverseList( &newlive, AddNeighbors);
        ClearList( &newlive);
        TraverseList( &newdie, SubtractNeighbors);
        ClearList( &newdie);
        printf("Do you want to continue viewing new generations");
    }
}
```

## 8.9.4 FUNCTIONS

Let us now write several of the functions, so as to show how processing of the cells and of the lists transpires. The remaining functions will be left as exercises.

### 1. Function Vivify

The task of Vivify is, within a traversal of the list maylive, to determine whether each cell on it satisfies the conditions to become alive, vivify it if so and add it to the list newlive.

```
/* Vivify: vivify a cell if it should become alive.
    Pre:    The cell pointed by cell is a candidate to become alive.
    Post:   Checks that cell in the hash table map pointed by cell meets all requirements
            to become alive. If not, no change is made. If so, then the pointer to the cell
            is added to the list newlive. The cell status is set to ALIVE.
    Uses:   Function AddList, the list newlive as global variables (side effects). */
```

*make cells alive*

```
void Vivify(ListEntry cell)
{
    if (cell->status == DEAD && cell->neighborcount == 3) {
        cell->status = ALIVE;
        AddList(cell, &newlive);
    }
}
```

If you compare this function with the corresponding one for Life2, you will note that the only changes are the dereferencing of current (since the lists are now indirect) and the removal of references to the hedge, which does not exist in Life3, since the grid has no boundaries.

### 2. Function AddNeighbors

The task of this function is to increase the neighbor count by 1 for each neighbor of a cell from the list newlive and to add cells to lists maylive and maydie when appropriate.

Finding the neighbors of a given cell will require using the hash table; we shall postpone this task by referring to

Cell *GetCell(int row, int col);

*hash table retrieval*

which will return a pointer to the cell being sought, creating the cell if it was not previously in the hash table.

```
/* AddNeighbors: add the neighbors for cell.
    Pre:  cell is a pointer to a cell that has just become alive.
    Post: The neighbors of the cell pointed to by cell have had their neighbor count
          increased. If the increased neighbor count makes the cell a candidate to be
          vivified [resp. killed] then the pointer to the cell has been added to the list
          maylive [resp. maydie].
    Uses: AddList, GetCell, changes lists maylive and maydie as global variables (side
          effects). */
```

*update neighbor counts*

```
void AddNeighbors(ListEntry cell)
{
    int nbrrow,                      /* loop index for row of neighbor loops     */
        nbrcol;                      /* column loop index                        */
    Cell *neighbor;                  /* pointer to a structure form of a neighbor */
```

*bounds for loop*

```
    for (nbrrow = cell->row - 1; nbrrow <= cell->row + 1; nbrrow++)
        for (nbrcol = cell->col - 1; nbrcol <= cell->col + 1; nbrcol++)
```

*find a neighbor*

```
            if (nbrrow != cell->row || nbrcol != cell->col) {  /* Skip cell itself.  */
                neighbor = GetCell(nbrrow, nbrcol);
```

*put cells into lists.*

```
                switch (++neighbor->neighborcount) {
                case 0: Error("Impossible case in AddNeighbors.");
                    break;
                case 3:
                    if (neighbor->status == DEAD)
                        AddList(neighbor, &maylive);
                    break;
                case 4:
                    if (neighbor->status == ALIVE)
                        AddList(neighbor, &maydie);
                    break;
                }                       /* switch statement   */
            }
}
```

Again, the differences between this function and that of Life2 are minimal, consisting mainly of the need to use GetCell rather than accessing an array directly.

### 3. Processing the Hash Table

We now turn to the first basic difference from Life2, the function GetCell that explicitly references the hash table. The task of the function

Cell *GetCell(int row, int col);

*task*

is first to look in the hash table for the cell with the given coordinates. If the search is successful, then the function returns a pointer to the cell; otherwise, it must create a new cell, assign it the given coordinates, initialize its other fields to the default values, and put it in the hash table as well as return a pointer to it.

This outline translates into the following function.

```
/* GetCell: get a cell from the hash table.
   Pre:   The hash table map has been initialized.
   Post:  The function returns a pointer to the cell(row, col) from the hash table map if it
          is present; otherwise the cell is created, initialized, and put into the hash table
          map, and a pointer to it is returned. */
Cell *GetCell(int row, int col)
{
   Cell *p;
   int location = Hash(row, col);
   for (p = map[location]; p; p = p->next)
     if (p->row ==  row && p->col == col)
        break;
   if (!p) {
      p = (Cell *)malloc(sizeof(Cell));
      p->row = row;
      p->col = col;
      p->status = DEAD;
      p->neighborcount = 0;
      p->next = map[location];
      map[location] = p;
   }
   return p;
}
```

### 4. The Hash Function

Our hash function will differ slightly from those earlier in the chapter, in that its argument already comes in two parts (row and column), so that some kind of folding can be done easily. Before deciding how, let us for a moment consider the special case of a small array, where the function is one-to-one and is exactly the index function. When there are exactly maxrow entries in each row, the index i, j maps to

i + maxrow * j

to place the rectangular array into contiguous storage, one row after the next.

It should prove effective to use a similar mapping for our hash function, where we replace maxrow by some convenient number (like a prime) that will maximize the spread and reduce collisions. Hence we obtain

```
/* Hash: calculate hash value.
   Pre:  None.
   Post: Calculated a value between 0 and HASHSIZE − 1, inclusive. */
int Hash(int row, int col)
{
    return abs(row + FACTOR * col) % HASHSIZE;
}
```

### 5. Other Subprograms

The remaining subprograms all bear considerable resemblance either to one of the preceding functions or to the corresponding function in Life2, and these subprograms can therefore safely be left as projects.

---

**Programming Projects 8.9**

**P1.** Write the function Kill.

**P2.** Write the function SubtractNeighbors. When a cell is dead and has a neighbor count of 0, it is supposed to be deleted from the hash table. However, there may easily be more than one pointer to this cell, since maylive and maydie may contain redundant entries. Hence deletion must be delayed until processing maylive and maydie is complete, since otherwise they might refer to cells that have been disposed. For this project, write SubtractNeighbors so that it leaves such cells in the table.

**P3.** Modify the program so that dead cells with a neighbor count of 0 will be deleted from the hash table. To do so, set up a linked stack of available space. Modify SubtractNeighbors so that it deletes dead cells with a neighbor count of 0 from the hash table and pushes such cells onto the stack. Modify GetCell so that, before creating a new cell, it pops a cell from the stack if it is nonempty.

---

## Pointers and Pitfalls

1. Use top-down design for your data structures, just as you do for your algorithms. First determine the logical structure of the data, then slowly specify more detail, and delay implementation decisions as long as possible.

2. Before considering detailed structures, decide what operations on the data will be required, and use this information to decide whether the data belong in a *list* or a *table*. Traversal of the data structure or access to all the data in a prespecified order generally implies choosing a list. Access to any entry in time $O(1)$ generally implies choosing a table.

3. For the design and programming of lists, see Chapter 5.

4. Use the logical structure of the data to decide what kind of table to use: an ordinary array, a table of some special shape, a system of inverted tables, or a hash table. Choose the simplest structure that allows the required operations and that meets the space requirements of the problem. Don't write complicated functions to save space that will then remain unused.

5. Let the structure of the data help you decide whether an index function or an access table is better for accessing a table of data. Use the features built into your programming language whenever possible.

6. In using a hash table, let the nature of the data and the required operations help you decide between chaining and open addressing. Chaining is generally preferable if deletions are required, if the records are relatively large, or if overflow might be a problem. Open addressing is usually preferable when the individual records are small and there is no danger of overflowing the hash table.

7. Hash functions must usually be custom-designed for the kind of keys used for accessing the hash table. In designing a hash function, keep the computations as simple and as few as possible while maintaining a relatively even spread of the keys over the hash table. There is no obligation to use every part of the key in the calculation. For important applications, experiment by computer with several variations of your hash function, and look for rapid calculation and even distribution of the keys.

8. Recall from the analysis of hashing that some collisions will almost inevitably occur, so don't worry about the existence of collisions if the keys are spread nearly uniformly through the table.

9. For open addressing, clustering is unlikely to be a problem until the hash table is more than half full. If the table can be made several times larger than the space required for the records, then linear probing should be adequate; otherwise more sophisticated collision resolution may be required. On the other hand, if the table is many times larger than needed, then initialization of all the unused space may require an inordinate length of time.

# Review Questions

8.1

1. In terms of the big-O notation, compare the difference in time required for table lookup and for list searching.

8.2

2. What are *row-major* and *column-major* ordering?

8.3

3. Why do *jagged tables* require access tables instead of index functions?

4. For what purpose are *inverted tables* used?

5. What is the difference in purpose, if any, between an *index function* and an *access table*?

8.4

6. What operations are available for an abstract table?

7. What operations are usually easier for a list than for a table?

**8.** In 20 words or less, describe how *radix sort* works.

**9.** In radix sort, why are the keys usually partitioned first by the least significant position, not the most significant?

**10.** What is the difference in purpose, if any, between an *index function* and a

*hash function*?

**11.** What objectives should be sought in the design of a hash function?

**12.** Name three techniques often built into hash functions.

**13.** What is *clustering* in a hash table?

**14.** Describe two methods for minimizing clustering.

**15.** Name four advantages of a chained hash table over open addressing.

**16.** Name one advantage of open addressing over chaining.

**17.** If a hash function assigns 30 keys to random positions in a hash table of size 300, about how likely is it that there will be no collisions?

# References for Further Study

The primary reference for this chapter is KNUTH, Volume 3. (See page 124 for bibliographic details.) Hashing is the subject of Volume 3, pp. 506–549. KNUTH studies every method we have touched, and many others besides. He does algorithm analysis in considerably more detail than we have, writing his algorithms in a pseudoassembly language, and counting operations in detail there.

An alternative treatment that includes careful analysis of algorithms for searching, hashing, as well as other topics, is

LYDIA I. KRONSJO, *Algorithms: Their Complexity and Efficiency*, John Wiley, New York, 1979.

The following book (pp. 156–185) considers arrays of various kinds, index functions, and access tables in considerable detail:

C. C. GOTLIEB and L. R. GOTLIEB, *Data Types and Structures*, Prentice-Hall, Englewood Cliffs, N.J., 1978.

An interesting study of hash functions and the choice of constants used is:

B. J. MCKENZIE, R. HARRIES, and T. C. BELL, "Selecting a hashing algorithm," *Software Practice and Experience* 20 (1990), 209–224.

Extensions of the birthday surprise are considered in

M. S. KLAMKIN and D. J. NEWMAN, *Journal of Combinatorial Theory* 3 (1967), 279–282.

# 9

# Binary Trees

LINKED LISTS *have great advantages of flexibility over the contiguous representation of data structures, but they have one weak feature: They are sequential lists; that is, they are arranged so that it is necessary to move through them only one position at a time. In this chapter we overcome these disadvantages by studying trees as data structures, using the methods of pointers and linked lists for their implementation. Data structures organized as trees will prove valuable for a range of applications, especially for problems of information retrieval.*

## 9.1 Introduction to Binary Trees

For some time, we have been drawing trees to illustrate the behavior of algorithms. We have drawn comparison trees showing the comparisons of keys in searching and sorting algorithms; we have drawn trees of subprogram calls; and we have drawn recursion trees. If, for example, we consider applying binary search to the following list of names, then the order in which comparisons will be made is shown in the comparison tree of Figure 9.1.

Amy Ann Dot Eva Guy Jan Jim Jon Kay Kim Ron Roy Tim Tom

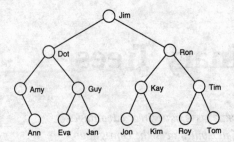

Figure 9.1. Comparison tree for binary search

### 9.1.1 DEFINITIONS

In binary search, when we make a comparison with a key, we then move either left or right depending on the outcome of the comparison. It is thus important to keep the relation of *left* and *right* in the structure we build. It is also possible that the part of the tree on one side or both below a given node is empty. In the example of Figure 9.1, the name Amy has an empty left subtree. For all the leaves, both subtrees are empty.

We can now give the formal definition of a new data structure.

*Definition*  A **binary tree** is either empty, or it consists of a node called the **root** together with two binary trees called the **left subtree** and the **right subtree** of the root.

*abstract data type*  Note that this definition is that of a mathematical structure. To specify binary trees as an abstract data type, we must state what operations can be performed on binary trees. Rather than doing so at once, we shall develop the operations as the chapter progresses.

Note also that this definition makes no reference to the way in which binary trees will be implemented in memory. As we shall presently see, a linked representation is natural and easy to use, but other methods are possible as well. Note, finally, that this definition makes no reference to keys or the way in which they are ordered. Binary trees are used for many purposes other than searching; hence we have kept the definition general.

Before we consider general properties of binary trees further, let us return to the general definition and see how its recursive nature works out in the construction of small binary trees.

*small binary trees*

*recursion base*

The first case, the base case that involves no recursion, is that of an empty binary tree. For other kinds of trees, we might never think of allowing an empty one, but for binary trees it is convenient, not only in the definition, but in algorithms, to allow for an empty tree. The empty tree will usually be the base case for recursive algorithms and will determine when the algorithm stops.

The only way to construct a binary tree with one node is to make that node its root and to make both the left and right subtrees empty. Thus a single node with no branches is the one and only binary tree with one node.

With two nodes in the tree, one of them will be the root and the other will be in a subtree. Thus either the left or right subtree must be empty, and the other will contain exactly one node. Hence there are two different binary trees with two nodes.

*left and right*

At this point, you should note that the concept of a binary tree differs from some of the examples of trees that we have previously seen, in that left and right are important for binary trees. The two binary trees with two nodes can be drawn as

and

which are different from each other. We shall never draw any part of a binary tree to look like

since there is no way to tell if the lower node is the left or the right child of its parent.

*comparison trees*

We should, furthermore, note that binary trees are not the same class as the 2-trees we studied in the analysis of algorithms in Chapter 6 and Chapter 7. Each node in a 2-tree has either 0 or 2 children, never 1, as can happen with a binary tree. Left and right are not fundamentally important for studying the properties of comparison trees, but they are crucial in working with binary trees.

*binary trees with three nodes*

For the case of a binary tree with three nodes, one of these will be the root, and the others will be partitioned between the left and right subtrees in one of the ways

$$2+0 \qquad 1+1 \qquad 0+2.$$

Since there are two binary trees with two nodes and only one empty tree, the first case gives two binary trees. The third case, similarly, gives two more binary trees. In the second case the left and right subtrees both have one node, and there is only one binary tree with one node, so there is one binary tree in the second case. Altogether, then, there are five binary trees with three nodes.

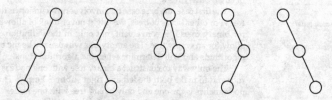

Figure 9.2. The binary trees with three nodes

These binary trees with three nodes are all shown in Figure 9.2. The steps that we went through to construct these binary trees are typical of those needed for larger cases. We begin at the root and think of the remaining nodes as partitioned between the left and right subtrees. The left and right subtrees are then smaller cases for which we know the results from earlier work.

Before proceeding, you should pause to construct all fourteen binary trees with four nodes. This exercise will further help you establish the ideas behind the definition of binary trees.

### 9.1.2 Traversal of Binary Trees

One of the most important operations on a binary tree is *traversal*, moving through all the nodes of the binary tree, visiting each one in turn. As for traversal of other data structures, the action we shall take when we *visit* each node will depend on the application.

For lists, the nodes came in a natural order from first to last, and traversal followed the same order. For trees, however, there are many different orders in which we could traverse all the nodes. When we write an algorithm to traverse a binary tree, we shall almost always wish to proceed so that the same rules are applied at each node, and we thereby adhere to a general pattern.

At a given node, then, there are three tasks we shall wish to do in some order: We shall visit the node itself; we shall traverse its left subtree; and we shall traverse its right subtree. The key distinction in traversal orders is to decide if we are to visit the node itself before traversing either subtree, between the subtrees, or after traversing both subtrees.

If we name the tasks of visiting a node $V$, traversing the left subtree $L$, and traversing the right subtree $R$, then there are six ways to arrange them:

$$VLR \qquad LVR \qquad LRV \qquad VRL \qquad RVL \qquad RLV.$$

## 1. Standard Traversal Orders

By standard convention, these six are reduced to three by permitting only the ways in which the left subtree is traversed before the right. The three mirror images are clearly similar. The three ways with left before right are given special names that we shall use from now on:

| V L R | L V R | L R V |
|:-:|:-:|:-:|
| *Preorder* | *Inorder* | *Postorder* |

*preorder, inorder, and postorder*

These three names are chosen according to the step at which the given node is visited. With **preorder traversal**, the node is visited before the subtrees; with **inorder traversal**, it is visited between them; and with **postorder traversal**, the root is visited after both of the subtrees.

Inorder traversal is also sometimes called **symmetric order**, and postorder traversal was once called **endorder**. We shall not use these terms.

## 2. Simple Examples

As a first example, consider the following binary tree:

*preorder*

Under preorder traversal, the root, labeled 1, is visited first. Then the traversal moves to the left subtree. The left subtree contains only the node labeled 2, and it is visited second. Then preorder traversal moves to the right subtree of the root, finally visiting the node labeled 3. Thus preorder traversal visits the nodes in the order 1, 2, 3.

*inorder*

Before the root is visited under inorder traversal, we must traverse its left subtree. Hence the node labeled 2 is visited first. This is the only node in the left subtree of the root, so the traversal moves to the root, labeled 1, next, and finally to the right subtree. Thus inorder traversal visits the nodes in the order 2, 1, 3.

*postorder*

With postorder traversal, we must traverse both the left and right subtrees before visiting the root. We first go to the left subtree, which contains only the node labeled 2, and it is visited first. Next, we traverse the right subtree, visiting the node 3, and, finally, we visit the root, labeled 1. Thus postorder traversal visits the nodes in the order 2, 3, 1.

As a second, slightly more complicated example, let us consider the following binary tree:

*preorder*

First, let us determine the preorder traversal. The root, labeled 1, is visited first. Next, we traverse the left subtree. But this subtree is empty, so its traversal does nothing. Finally, we must traverse the right subtree of the root. This subtree contains the vertices labeled 2, 3, 4, and 5. We must therefore traverse this subtree, again using the preorder method. Hence we next visit the root of this subtree, labeled 2, and then traverse the left subtree of 2. At a later step, we shall traverse the right subtree of 2, which is empty, so nothing will be done. But first we traverse the left subtree, which has root 3. Preorder traversal of the subtree with root 3 visits the nodes in the order 3, 4, 5. Finally, we do the empty right subtree of 2. Thus the complete preorder traversal of the tree visits the nodes in the order 1, 2, 3, 4, 5.

*inorder*

For inorder traversal, we must begin with the left subtree of the root, which is empty. Hence the root, labeled 1, is the first node visited, and then we traverse its right subtree, which is rooted at node 2. Before we visit node 2, we must traverse its left subtree, which has root 3. The inorder traversal of this subtree visits the nodes in the order 4, 3, 5. Finally, we visit node 2 and traverse its right subtree, which does nothing since it is empty. Thus the complete inorder traversal of the tree visits the nodes in the order 1, 4, 3, 5, 2.

*postorder*

For postorder traversal, we must traverse both the left and right subtrees of each node before visiting the node itself. Hence we first would traverse the empty left subtree of the root 1, then the right subtree. The root of a binary tree is always the last node visited by a postorder traversal. Before visiting the node 2, we traverse its left and right (empty) subtrees. The postorder traversal of the subtree rooted at 3 gives the order 4, 5, 3. Thus the complete postorder traversal of the tree visits the nodes in the order 4, 5, 3, 2, 1.

### 3. Expression Trees

The choice of the names *preorder*, *inorder*, and *postorder* for the three most important traversal methods is not accidental, but relates closely to a motivating example of considerable interest, that of expression trees.

*expression tree*

An *expression tree* is built up from the simple operands and operators of an (arithmetical or logical) expression by placing the simple operands as the leaves of a binary tree and the operators as the interior nodes. For each binary operator, the left subtree contains all the simple operands and operators in the left operand of the given operator, and the right subtree contains everything in the right operand.

*operators*

For a unary operator, one of the two subtrees will be empty. We traditionally write some unary operators to the left of their operands, such as '−' (unary negation) or the standard functions like log( ) and cos( ). Other unary operators are written on the right, such as the factorial function ( )! or the function that takes the square of a number, ( )$^2$. Sometimes either side is permissible, such as the derivative operator, which can be written as $d/dx$ on the left, or as ( )' on the right, or the incrementing operator ++ in the C language (where the actions on the left and right are different). If the operator is written on the left, then in the expression tree we take its left subtree as empty, so that the operands appear on the right side of the operator in the tree, just as they do in the expression. If the operator appears

**NOTE**

on the right, then its right subtree will be empty, and the operands will be in the left subtree of the operator.

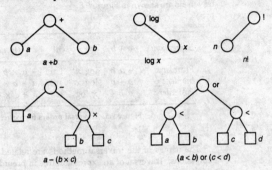

**Figure 9.3. Expression trees**

The expression trees of a few simple expressions are shown in Figure 9.3, together with the slightly more complicated example of the quadratic formula in Figure 9.4, where we denote exponentiation by ↑.

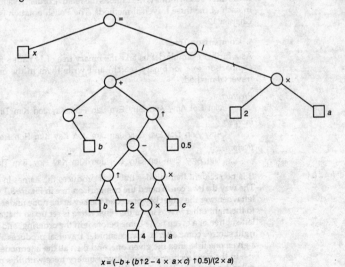

$$x = (-b + (b \uparrow 2 - 4 \times a \times c) \uparrow 0.5)/(2 \times a)$$

**Figure 9.4. Expression tree of the quadratic formula**

You should take a few moments to traverse each of these expression trees in preorder, inorder, and postorder. To help you check your work, the results of such traversals are shown in Figure 9.5.

| Expression: | $a + b$ | $\log x$ | $n!$ | $a - (b \times c)$ | $(a < b)$ or $(c < d)$ |
|---|---|---|---|---|---|
| Preorder : | $+ \, a \, b$ | $\log \, x$ | $! \, n$ | $- \, a \times b \, c$ | or $< \, a \, b \, < \, c \, d$ |
| Inorder : | $a + b$ | $\log \, x$ | $n \, !$ | $a - b \times c$ | $a < b$ or $c < d$ |
| Postorder : | $a \, b \, +$ | $x \, \log$ | $n \, !$ | $a \, b \, c \times -$ | $a \, b \, < \, c \, d \, <$ or |

Figure 9.5. Traversal orders for expression trees

*Polish form*

The names of the traversal methods are related to the **Polish forms** of the expressions: Traversal of an expression tree in preorder yields the **prefix form**, in which every operator is written before its operand(s); inorder traversal gives the **infix form** (the customary way to write the expression); and postorder traversal gives the **postfix form**, in which all operators appear after their operand(s). A moment's consideration will convince you of the reason: The left and right subtrees of each node are its operands, and the relative position of an operator to its operands in the three Polish forms is the same as the relative order of visiting the components in each of the three traversal methods. The Polish notation is the major topic of Chapter 12.

### 4. Comparison Trees

As a further example, let us take the binary tree of 14 names from Figure 9.1 (the comparison tree for binary search) and write them in the order given by each traversal method:

*Preorder*:

    Jim Dot Amy Ann Guy Eva Jan Ron Kay Jon Kim Tim Roy Tom

*Inorder*:

    Amy Ann Dot Eva Guy Jan Jim Jon Kay Kim Ron Roy Tim Tom

*Postorder*:

    Ann Amy Eva Jan Guy Dot Jon Kim Kay Roy Tom Tim Ron Jim

*ordered keys*

It is no accident that inorder traversal produces the names in alphabetical order. The way that we constructed the comparison tree in Figure 9.1 was to move to the left whenever the target key preceded the key in the node under consideration, and to the right otherwise. Hence the binary tree is set up so that all the nodes in the left subtree of a given node come before it in the ordering, and all the nodes in its right subtree come after it. Hence inorder traversal produces all the nodes before a given one first, then the given one, and then all the later nodes.

In the next section, we shall study binary trees with this property. They are called *binary search trees*, since they are very useful and efficient for problems requiring searching.

### 9.1.3 LINKED IMPLEMENTATION OF BINARY TREES

A binary tree has a natural implementation in linked storage. As usual for linked structures, we shall wish all the nodes to be acquired as dynamic storage, so we shall need a separate pointer variable to enable us to find the tree. Our usual name for this pointer variable will be *root*, since it will point to the root of the tree. With this pointer variable, it is easy to recognize an empty binary tree as precisely the condition

*root*

root = NULL,

and to create a new, empty binary tree we need only assign its root pointer to NULL.

#### 1. Declarations

Each node of a binary tree (as the root of some subtree) has both a left and a right subtree, which we can reach with pointers by declaring

```
typedef struct treenode TreeNode;
typedef struct treenode {
    TreeEntry entry;
    TreeNode *left;
    TreeNode *right;
} TreeNode;
```

The type TreeEntry depends on the application. These declarations turn the comparison tree for the 14 names from the first tree diagram of this section, Figure 9.1, into the linked binary tree of Figure 9.6. As you can see, the only difference

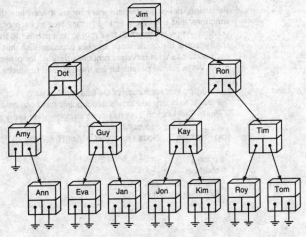

Figure 9.6. A linked binary tree

between the comparison tree and the linked binary tree is that we have explicitly shown the NULL links in the latter, whereas it is customary in drawing trees to omit all empty subtrees and the branches going to them.

## 2. First Operations

```
/* CreateTree: create a tree.
   Pre:  None.
   Post: An empty binary search tree has been created to which root points. */
void CreateTree(TreeNode **root)
{
   *root = NULL;
}
```

```
/* TreeEmpty: TRUE if the tree is emtpy.
   Pre:  The tree to which root points has been created.
   Post: The function returns the value TRUE or FALSE according as the tree is empty or
         not. */
Boolean TreeEmtpy(TreeNode *root)
{
   return root == NULL;
}
```

## 3. Traversal

Recursion makes it especially easy for us to translate the definitions into formal functions that traverse a linked binary tree in each of the three ways we have studied. As usual, we shall take root to be a pointer to the root of the tree, and we shall assume the existence of another function Visit that does the desired task for each node. As with traversal functions defined for other data structures, we shall make Visit a formal parameter for the traversal functions.

*visit root first*

```
/* Preorder: visit each node of the tree in preorder.
   Pre:  The binary tree to which root points has been created.
   Post: The function Visit has been performed on every entry in the binary tree in
         preorder sequence. */
void Preorder(TreeNode *root, void (*Visit)(TreeEntry x))
{
  if (root) {
   Visit(root->entry);
   Preorder(root->left, Visit);
   Preorder(root->right, Visit);
  }
}
```

*visit root in middle*

```
/* Inorder: visit each node of the tree in inorder.
   Pre:   The binary tree to which root points has been created.
   Post:  The function Visit has been performed on every entry in the binary tree in
          inorder sequence. */
void Inorder(TreeNode *root, void (*Visit)(TreeEntry x))
{
  if (root) {
    Inorder(root->left, Visit);
    Visit(root->entry);
    Inorder(root->right, Visit);
  }
}
```

*visit root last*

```
/* Postorder: visit each node of the tree in postorder.
   Pre:   The binary tree to which root points has been created.
   Post:  The function Visit has been performed on every entry in the binary tree in
          postorder sequence. */
void Postorder(TreeNode *root, void (*Visit)(TreeEntry x))
{
  if (root) {
    Postorder(root->left, Visit);
    Postorder(root->right, Visit);
    Visit(root->entry);
  }
}
```

---

**Exercises 9.1**

**E1.** Construct the 14 binary trees with four nodes.

**E2.** Determine the order in which the vertices of the following binary trees will be visited under (1) preorder, (2) inorder, and (3) postorder traversal.

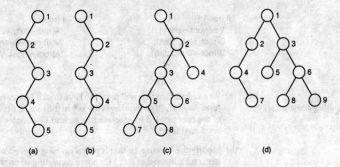

(a)   (b)   (c)   (d)

**E3.** Draw expression trees for each of the following expressions, and show the order of visiting the vertices in (1) preorder, (2) inorder, and (3) postorder:

**(a)** $\log n!$
**(b)** $(a - b) - c$
**(c)** $a - (b - c)$
**(d)** $(a < b)$ and $(b < c)$ and $(c < d)$

TreeSize

**E4.** Write a function int TreeSize(Tree *root) that will count all the nodes of a linked binary tree.

**E5.** Write a function that will count the leaves (i.e., the nodes with both subtrees empty) of a linked binary tree.

**E6.** Write a function int TreeHeight(Tree *root) that will find the height of a linked binary tree, where an empty tree is considered to have height 0 and a tree with only one node has height 1.

ClearTree

**E7.** Write a function void ClearTree(Tree *root) that will traverse a binary tree (in whatever order you find works best) and dispose of all its nodes.

CopyTree

**E8.** Write a function void CopyTree(Tree *root, Tree **newroot) that will make a copy of a linked binary tree. The function should obtain the necessary new nodes from the system and copy the entry field from the nodes of the old tree to the new one.

double-order traversal

**E9.** Write a function to perform a *double-order traversal* of a binary tree, meaning that at each node of the tree, the function first visits the node, then traverses its left subtree (in double order), then visits the node again, then traverses its right subtree (in double order).

**E10.** For each of the binary trees in Exercise E2, determine the order in which the nodes will be visited in the mixed order given by invoking function A:

```
void A(TreeNode *root,                    void B(TreeNode *root,
     void (*Visit)(TreeEntry x))                void (*Visit)(TreeEntry x))
{                                         {
  if (root) {                               if (root) {
    Visit(root->entry);                       A(root->left, Visit);
    B(root->left, Visit);                     Visit(root->entry);
    B(root->right, Visit);                    A(root->right, Visit)
  }                                         }
}                                         }
```

printing a binary tree

**E11. (a)** Write a function that will print the keys from a binary tree in the *bracketed form* (key : LT, RT) where key is the key in the root, LT denotes the left subtree of the root printed in bracketed form, and RT denotes the right subtree in bracketed form.

**(b)** Modify the function so that it prints nothing instead of (: , ) for an empty tree, and x instead of (x: , ) for a tree consisting of only one node with the key x.

**E12.** Write a function that will interchange all left and right subtrees in a linked binary tree. See the example in Figure 9.7.

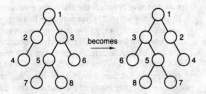

Figure 9.7. Reversal of a binary tree

*level-by-level traversal*

**E13.** Write a function that will traverse a binary tree level by level. That is, the root is visited first, then the immediate children of the root, then the grandchildren of the root, and so on. [*Hint*: Use a queue to keep track of the children of a node until it is time to visit them.]

*width*

**E14.** Write a function that will return the width of a linked binary tree, that is, the maximum number of nodes on the same level.

*doubly linked list*

**E15.** Write a function that converts a binary tree into a doubly linked list, in which the nodes have the order of inorder traversal of the tree. At the conclusion of the function, the pointer root should point to the leftmost node of the doubly linked list, and the links right and left should be used to move through the list, and be NULL at the two ends of the list.

*traversal sequences*

For the following exercises, it is assumed that the keys stored in the nodes of the binary trees are all distinct, but it is not assumed that the trees are binary search trees. That is, there is no necessary connection between the ordering of the keys and their location in the trees. If a tree is traversed in a particular order, and each key printed when its node is visited, the resulting sequence is called the sequence corresponding to that traversal.

**E16.** Suppose that you are given two sequences that supposedly correspond to the preorder and inorder traversals of a binary tree. Prove that it is possible to reconstruct the binary tree uniquely.

**E17.** Either prove or disprove (by finding a counterexample) the analogous result for inorder and postorder traversal.

**E18.** Either prove or disprove the analogous result for preorder and postorder traversal.

**E19.** Find a pair of (short) sequences of the same keys that could not possibly correspond to the preorder and inorder traversals of the same binary tree.

## 9.2 Binary Search Trees

*the dilemma*

Consider the problem of searching a linked list for some target key. There is no way to move through the list other than one node at a time, and hence searching through the list must always reduce to a sequential search. As you know, sequential search is usually very slow in comparison with binary search. Hence, assuming we can keep the keys in order, searching becomes much faster if we use a contiguous list and binary search. Suppose we also frequently need to make changes in the list, inserting new entries or deleting old entries. Then it is much slower to use a contiguous list than a linked list, because insertion or deletion in a contiguous list requires moving many of the entries every time, whereas a linked list requires only adjusting a few pointers.

The pivotal problem for this section is:

*Can we find an implementation for ordered lists in which we can search quickly (as with binary search on a contiguous list) and in which we can make insertions and deletions quickly (as with a linked list)?*

Binary trees provide an excellent solution to this problem. By making the entries of an ordered list into the nodes of a binary tree, we shall find that we can search for a target key in $O(\log n)$ steps, just as with binary search, and we shall obtain algorithms for inserting and deleting entries also in time $O(\log n)$.

*comparison trees*

When we studied binary search, we drew comparison trees showing the progress of binary search by moving either left (if the target key is smaller than the one in the current node of the tree) or right (if the target key is larger). An example of such a comparison tree appears in Figure 9.1 and again in Figure 9.6, where it is shown as a linked binary tree. From these diagrams, it may already be clear that the way in which we can keep the advantages of linked storage and obtain the speed of binary search is to store the nodes as a binary tree with the structure of the comparison tree itself, with links used to describe the relations of the tree.

The essential feature of the comparison tree is that, when we move to the left subtree, we move to smaller keys, and, when we move to the right subtree, we move to larger keys. This special condition on keys in the nodes of a binary tree is the essential part of the following important definition:

*Definition*

A **binary search tree** is a binary tree that is either empty or in which every node contains a key and satisfies the conditions:

1. The key in the left child of a node (if it exists) is less than the key in its parent node.

2. The key in the right child of a node (if it exists) is greater than the key in its parent node.

3. The left and right subtrees of the root are again binary search trees.

The first two properties describe the ordering relative to the key in the root node, and the third property extends them to all nodes in the tree; hence we can continue to use the recursive structure of the binary tree. After we examine the root of the tree, we shall move to either its left or right subtree, and this subtree is again a binary search tree. Thus we can use the same method again on this smaller tree.

*distinct keys*

We have written this definition in a way that ensures that no two entries in a binary search tree can have equal keys, since the keys in the left subtree are strictly smaller than the key in the root, and those in the right subtree are strictly greater. It is possible to change the definition to allow entries with equal keys, but doing so makes the algorithms somewhat more complicated. Therefore, we always assume:

> *No two entries in a binary search tree may have equal keys.*

The tree shown in Figure 9.1 and Figure 9.6 is automatically a binary search tree, since the decision to move left or right at each node is based on the same comparisons of keys used in the definition of a search tree.

## 9.2.1 ORDERED LISTS AND IMPLEMENTATIONS

When the time comes to start formulating functions to manipulate binary search trees, there are at least three different points of view that we might take:

*three views*

- We can regard binary search trees as a new abstract data type with its own definition and its own operations;

- Since binary search trees are special kinds of binary trees, we may consider their operations as special kinds of binary tree operations;

- Since the entries in binary search trees contain keys, and since they are applied for information retrieval in the same way as ordered lists, we may study binary search trees as a new implementation of the abstract data type *ordered list*.

In practice, programmers sometimes take each of these points of view, and so shall we. We shall find later in this section that the keys in a binary search tree can be regarded as already sorted into order, and it is therefore appropriate to think of using a binary search tree for the same applications as an ordered list. Our main tool for this is traversal, which we borrow from general binary trees. For many applications, however, it is easiest to regard binary search trees as a different abstract data type, and this we shall usually do.

*use of pointers*

Since the linked implementation is by far the most natural way to program operations on binary search trees, we shall often change the specifications and parameters to use pointers to nodes rather than to use entries directly as we have with lists and tables.

We have already introduced a typedef and functions that allow us to manipulate the nodes of a binary tree, and we can continue to use these same definitions for binary search trees. The items of information in any binary tree are declared to have a type called TreeEntry, the links are of a type Tree *, and each node contains a left and right link in addition to an entry.

Recall that, for ordered lists, we used ListEntry as the name for the entries in the list, each of which contained a key field. If we wish to make our declarations compatible with those given for ordered lists in previous chapters, we need only declare

**typedef ListEntry TreeEntry;**

and the entries in our binary search tree become compatible with those in an ordered list.

*keys*

Recall that each entry in an ordered list contains a key of a type called KeyType. This condition is equally required for the entries of type TreeEntry in a binary search tree. We leave KeyType unspecified, assuming that it is some type, such as a number or a string, for which any two keys can be compared to determine which should be first.

Since binary search trees are a special kind of binary tree, we can apply the operations already defined for general binary trees to binary search trees without difficulty. These operations include CreateTree, ClearTree, TreeEmpty, TreeSize, and the traversal functions Preorder, Inorder, and Postorder.

## 9.2.2 TREESEARCH

The first important new operation for binary search trees is the one from which their name comes: a function to search through a linked binary search tree for an entry with a particular target key.

### 1. Method

To search for the target, we first compare it with the key at the root of the tree. If it is the same, then we are finished. If it is not the same, we go to the left subtree or right subtree as appropriate and repeat the search in that subtree.

Let us, for example, search for the name Kim in the binary search tree of Figure 9.1 and Figure 9.6. We first compare Kim with the key in the root, Jim. Since Kim comes after Jim in alphabetical order, we move to the right and next compare Kim with Ron. Since Kim comes before Ron, we move left and compare Kim with Kay. Now Kim comes later, so we move to the right and find the desired node.

What event will be the termination condition for the search? Clearly if we find the key, the function finishes successfully. If not, then we continue searching until we hit an empty subtree. By using a pointer to move through the tree, we can return the value of the pointer to send the results of the search back to the calling program. Thus we have:

*specifications*

---

Tree *TreeSearch(Tree *root, KeyType target);

*precondition:*   The binary search tree to which root points has been created.

*postcondition:*   If an entry in the binary search tree has key equal to target, then the return value points to such a node; otherwise, the function returns NULL.

---

### 2. Recursive Version

Perhaps the simplest way to write the function for searching is to use recursion:

*recursive search*

```
/* TreeSearch: search for target starting at node root.
   Pre:   The tree to which root points has been created.
   Post:  The function returns a pointer to a tree node that matches target or NULL if the
          target is not in the tree. */
TreeNode *TreeSearch(TreeNode *root, KeyType target)
{
    if (root)
        if (LT(target, root->entry.key))
            root = TreeSearch(root->left, target);
        else if (GT(target, root->entry.key))
            root = TreeSearch(root->right, target);
    return root;
}
```

### 3. Recursion Removal

*tail recursion*

Recursion occurs in this function only as *tail recursion*, that is, as the last statement executed in the function. By using a loop, it is always possible to change tail recursion into iteration. In this function, we write a loop in place of the cascaded if statements, and we use the variable position to move through the tree. The body of the function then consists essentially of the statement

```
while (position && NE(target, position->entry.key))
    if (LT(target, position->entry.key))
        position = position->left;
    else
        position = position->right;
```

### 4. Behavior of the Algorithm

Recall that TreeSearch is based closely on binary search. If we apply binary search to an ordered list and draw its comparison tree, then we see that binary search does exactly the same comparisons as TreeSearch will do if it is applied to this same tree. We already know from Section 6.5 that binary search performs $O(\log n)$ comparisons for a list of length $n$. This performance is excellent in comparison to other methods, since $\log n$ grows very slowly as $n$ increases.

*example*

Suppose, as an example, that we apply binary search to the list of seven letters *a, b, c, d, e, f,* and *g.* The resulting tree is shown in part (a) of Figure 9.8. If TreeSearch is applied to this tree, it will do the same number of comparisons as binary search.

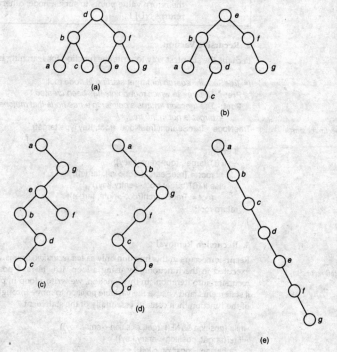

(a)

(b)

(c)

(d)

(e)

**Figure 9.8. Several binary search trees with the same keys**

It is quite possible, however, that the same letters may be built into a binary search tree of a quite different shape, such as any of those shown in the remaining parts of Figure 9.8.

*optimal tree*

The tree shown as part (a) of Figure 9.8 is the best possible for searching. It is as "bushy" as possible: It has the largest possible number of vertices for its height. The number of vertices between the root and the target, inclusive, is the number of comparisons that must be done to find the target. The bushier the tree, therefore, the smaller the number of comparisons that will usually need to be done.

*typical tree*

It is not always possible to predict in advance what shape of binary search tree we will have, and the tree shown in part (b) of Figure 9.8 is more typical of what happens than is the tree in part (a). In the tree of part (b), a search for the target *c* requires four comparisons, but only three in that of part (a). The tree in part (b), however, remains fairly bushy and its performance is only a little poorer than that of part (a).

*poor tree*

In part (c) of Figure 9.8, however, the tree has degenerated quite badly, so that a search for target *c* requires six comparisons. In parts (d) and (e), the tree reduces to a single chain. When applied to chains like these, TreeSearch can do nothing

*chains*

except go through the list entry by entry. In other words, TreeSearch, when applied to such a chain, degenerates to sequential search. In its worst case on a tree with *n* nodes, therefore, TreeSearch may require as many as *n* comparisons to find its target.

In practice, if the keys are built into a binary search tree in random order, then it is extremely unlikely that a binary search tree degenerates as badly as the trees shown in parts (d) and (e) of Figure 9.8. Instead, trees like those of parts (a) and (b) are much more likely. Hence TreeSearch almost always performs nearly as well as binary search. In Section 9.2.4, in fact, we shall see that, for random binary search trees, the performance of TreeSearch is only about 39 percent slower than the optimum of $\lg n$ comparisons, and it is therefore far superior to the *n* comparisons needed by sequential search.

## 9.2.3 Insertion into a Binary Search Tree

### 1. The Problem

The next important operation for us to consider is the insertion of a new node into a binary search tree in such a way that the keys remain properly ordered; that is, so that the resulting tree satisfies the definition of a binary search tree. The formal specifications for this operation are:

*specifications*

| |
|---|
| Tree *InsertTree(Tree *root, Tree *newnode); |
| *precondition*: The binary search tree to which root points has been created. The parameter newnode points to a node that has been created and contains a key in its entry. |
| *postcondition*: *newnode has been inserted into the tree in such a way that the properties of a binary search tree are preserved. |

### 2. Examples

Before we turn to writing this function, let us study some simple examples. Figure 9.9 shows what happens when we insert the keys *e, b, d, f, a, g, c* into an initially empty tree in the order given.

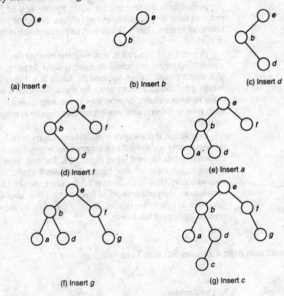

(a) Insert *e*

(b) Insert *b*

(c) Insert *d*

(d) Insert *f*

(e) Insert *a*

(f) Insert *g*

(g) Insert *c*

Figure 9.9. Insertions into a binary search tree

When the first entry, *e*, is inserted, it becomes the root, as shown in part (a). Since *b* comes before *e*, its insertion goes into the left subtree of *e*, as shown in part (b). Next we insert *d*, first comparing it to *e* and going left, then comparing it to *b* and going right. The next insertion, *f*, goes to the right of the root, as shown in part (d) of Figure 9.9. Since *a* is the earliest key inserted so far, it moves left from *e* and then from *b*. The key *g*, similarly, comes last in alphabetical order, so its insertion moves as far right as possible, as shown in part (f). The insertion of *c*, finally, compares first with *e*, goes left, then right from *b* and left from *d*. Hence we obtain the binary search tree shown in the last part of Figure 9.9.

It is quite possible that a different order of insertion can produce the same binary search tree. The final tree in Figure 9.9, for example, can be obtained by inserting the keys in either of the orders

*different orders, same tree*

*e, f, g, b, a, d, c*     or     *e, b, d, c, a, f, g,*

as well as several other orders.

*natural order*

One case is of special importance. Suppose that the keys are inserted into an initially empty tree in their natural order $a, b, \ldots, g$. Then $a$ will go into the root, $b$ will become its right child, $c$ will move to the right of $a$ and $b$, and so on. The insertions will produce a chain for the binary search tree, as shown in the final part of Figure 9.8. Such a chain, as we have already seen, is very inefficient for searching. Hence we conclude:

> *If the keys to be inserted into an empty binary search tree are in their natural order,* *then function* InsertTree *will produce a tree that degenerates into an inefficient chain.* InsertTree *should never be used with keys that are already sorted into order.*

The same conclusion holds if the keys are in reverse order or if they are nearly but not quite sorted into order.

### 3. Method

It is only a small step from the example we have worked to the general method for inserting a new node into a binary search tree.

The first case, inserting a node into an empty tree, is easy. We need only make root point to the new node. If the tree is not empty, then we must compare the key with the one in the root. If it is less, then the new node must be inserted into the left subtree; if it is more, then it must be inserted into the right subtree. If the keys are equal, then we shall adopt the convention of inserting the duplicate key into the right subtree.

Note that we have described insertion by using recursion. After we compare the new key with the one in the root, we use exactly the same insertion method either on the left or right subtree that we previously used at the root.

### 4. Recursive Function

From this outline, we can now write our function, using the declarations from the beginning of this section.

```
/* InsertTree: insert a new node in the tree.
   Pre:  The binary search tree to which root points has been created. The parameter
         newnode points to a node that has been created and contains a key in its entry.
   Post: The node newnode has been inserted into the tree in such a way that the
         properties of a binary search tree are preserved. */
```

*recursive insertion*

```c
TreeNode *InsertTree(TreeNode *root, TreeNode *newnode)
{
    if (!root) {
        root = newnode;
        root->left = root->right = NULL;
    } else if (LT(newnode->entry.key, root->entry.key))
        root->left = InsertTree(root->left, newnode);
    else
        root->right = InsertTree(root->right, newnode);
    return root;
}
```

Note how this function handles duplicate keys: It inserts a new key that duplicates a previous key on the right side of the old entry. By doing this, when we later traverse the tree (doing left subtrees before right subtrees), the entries with duplicate keys will be visited in the same order in which they were inserted. Since comparisons of keys are made in the same order as they are in TreeSearch, the searching function will always find the first entry that was inserted with a given key.

The use of recursion in the function InsertTree is not essential, since it is tail recursion. We leave translation of InsertTree into nonrecursive form as an exercise.

In regard to performance, InsertTree makes the same comparisons of keys that TreeSearch would make in looking for the key being inserted. InsertTree also changes a few pointers, but does not move entries or do any other operations that take a large amount of space or time. Therefore the performance of InsertTree will be very much the same as that of TreeSearch:

InsertTree *can usually insert a new node into a random binary search tree with* $n$ *nodes in* $O(\log n)$ *steps. It is possible, but extremely unlikely, that a random tree may degenerate so that insertions require as many as* $n$ *steps. If the keys are inserted in sorted order into an empty tree, however, this degenerate case will occur.*

A more precise analysis is given in Theorem 9.3 on page 421.

### 9.2.4 TREESORT

Recall from our discussion of traversing binary trees that, when we traverse a binary search tree in inorder, the keys will come out in sorted order. The reason is that all the keys to the left of a given key precede it (or are equal), and all those that come to its right follow it (or are equal). By recursion, the same facts are applied again and again until the subtrees have only one key. Hence inorder traversal always gives the sorted order for the keys.

#### 1. The Method

*treesort*

This observation is the basis for an interesting sorting method, called *treesort*. We simply take the entries to be sorted, use InsertTree to build them into a binary search tree, and use inorder traversal to put them out in order.

#### 2. Comparison with Quicksort

Let us briefly study what comparisons of keys are done by treesort. The first node goes into the root of the binary search tree, with no key comparisons. As each succeeding node comes in, its key is first compared to the key in the root and then it goes either into the left subtree or the right subtree. Notice the similarity with quicksort, where at the first stage every key is compared with the first pivot key, and then put into the left or the right sublist. In treesort, however, as each node comes in it goes into its final position in the linked structure. The second node becomes the root of either the left or right subtree (depending on the comparison of its key with the root key). From then on, all keys going into the same subtree are compared to this second one. Similarly in quicksort all keys in one sublist are compared to the second pivot, the one for that sublist. Continuing in this way, we can make the following observation.

**Theorem 9.1**    *Treesort makes exactly the same comparisons of keys as does quicksort when the pivot for each sublist is chosen to be the first key in the sublist.*

*advantages*

As we know, quicksort is usually an excellent method. Among the methods we studied, only mergesort, on average, makes fewer key comparisons. Hence, on average, we can expect treesort also to be an excellent sorting method in terms of key comparisons. In fact, from Section 7.8.4 we can conclude:

**Corollary 9.2**    *In the average case, on a randomly ordered list of length $n$, treesort performs*

$$2n \ln n + O(n) \approx 1.39n \lg n + O(n)$$

*comparisons of keys.*

Treesort has one advantage over quicksort. Quicksort needs to have access to all the items to be sorted throughout the sorting process. With treesort, the nodes need not all be available at the start of the process, but are built into the tree one by one as they become available. Hence treesort is preferable for applications where the nodes are received one at a time. The major advantage of treesort is that its search tree remains available for later insertions and deletions, and that the tree can subsequently be searched in logarithmic time, whereas all our previous sorting methods either required contiguous lists, for which insertions and deletions are difficult, or produced linked lists for which only sequential search is available.

*drawbacks*

The major drawback of treesort is already implicit in Theorem 9.1. Quicksort has a very poor performance in its worst case, and, although a careful choice of pivots makes this case extremely unlikely, the choice of pivot to be the first key in each sublist makes the worst case appear whenever the keys are already sorted. If the keys are presented to treesort already sorted, then treesort too will be a disaster—the search tree it builds will reduce to a chain. Treesort should never be used if the keys are already sorted, or are nearly so.

There are few other reservations about treesort that are not equally applicable to all linked structures. For small problems with small items, contiguous storage is usually the better choice, but for large problems and bulky records, linked storage comes into its own.

## 9.2.5 DELETION FROM A BINARY SEARCH TREE

In the discussion of treesort, we mentioned the ability to make changes in the binary search tree as an advantage. We have already obtained an algorithm that inserts a new node into the binary search tree, and it can be used to update the tree as easily as to build it from scratch. But we have not yet considered how to delete a node from the tree. If the node to be deleted is a leaf, then the process is easy: We need only replace the link to the deleted node by NULL. The process remains easy if the deleted node has only one subtree: We adjust the link from the parent of the deleted node to point to its subtree.

When the node to be deleted has both left and right subtrees nonempty, however, the problem is more complicated. To which of the subtrees should the parent of the deleted node now point? What is to be done with the other subtree? This problem is illustrated in Figure 9.10, together with one possible solution. (An exercise outlines another, sometimes better solution.) What we do is to attach the right subtree in place of the deleted node, and then hang the left subtree onto an appropriate node of the right subtree.

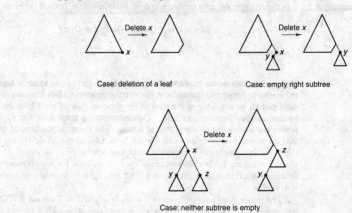

Figure 9.10. Deletion of a node from a binary search tree

To which node of the right subtree should the former left subtree be attached? Since every key in the left subtree precedes every key of the right subtree, it must be as far to the left as possible, and this point can be found by taking left branches until an empty left subtree is found.

*requirements*    We can now devise a function to implement this plan. As a calling parameter, it will use a pointer to the node to be deleted. Since the object is to update the binary search tree, we must assume that the corresponding actual parameter is the address of one of the links of the tree, and not just a copy, or else the tree structure itself will not be changed as it should. In other words, if the node at the left of x is to be deleted, the call should be

DeleteNodeTree( &x->left);

and, if the root is to be deleted, the call should be

DeleteNodeTree( &root);

On the other hand, the following call will not work properly:

y = x->left;

DeleteNodeTree( &y);

```
/* DeleteNodeTree: delete a new node from the tree.
   Pre:  The parameter p is the address of an actual link (not a copy) in a binary search
         tree, and p is not NULL.
   Post: The node p has been deleted from the binary search tree and the resulting
         smaller tree has the properties required of a binary search tree. */
void DeleteNodeTree(TreeNode **p)
{
    TreeNode *r = *p, *q;       /* used to find place for left subtree            */
    if (r == NULL)
        Error("Attempt to delete a nonexistent node from binary search tree");
    else if (r->right == NULL) {
        *p = r->left;           /* Reattach left subtree.                         */
        free(r);                /* Release node space.                            */
    } else if (r->left == NULL) {
        *p = r->right;          /* Reattach right subtree.                        */
        free(r);
    } else {                    /* Neither subtree is empty.                      */
        for (q = r->right; q->left; q = q->left)
            ;                   /* leftmost node of right subtree                 */
        q->left = r->left;      /* Reattach left subtree.                         */
        *p = r->right;          /* Reattach right subtree.                        */
        free(r);
    }
}
```

*deletion*

You should trace through this function to check that all pointers are updated properly, especially in the case when neither subtree is empty. Note the steps needed to make the loop stop at a node with an empty left subtree, but not to end at the empty subtree itself.

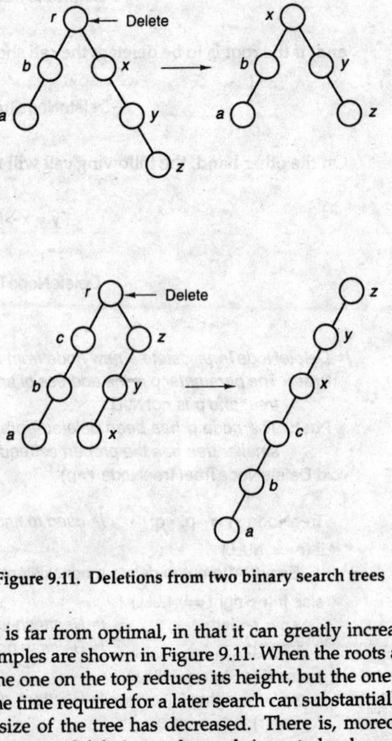

Figure 9.11. Deletions from two binary search trees

This function is far from optimal, in that it can greatly increase the height of the tree. Two examples are shown in Figure 9.11. When the roots are deleted from these two trees, the one on the top reduces its height, but the one below increases its height. Thus the time required for a later search can substantially increase, even though the total size of the tree has decreased. There is, moreover, often some tendency for insertions and deletions to be made in sorted order, which will further elongate the binary search tree. Hence, to optimize the use of binary search trees, we need methods to make the left and right subtrees more nearly balanced. We shall consider such methods later in this chapter.

*balancing*

For many applications, we are not given a pointer to a node that needs to be deleted; instead we are given a *key* for which the corresponding node must be deleted. To accomplish this, we combine a search through the tree with the preceding deletion function. The result follows.

*/* DeleteKeyTree: delete a new node from the tree.*
  **Pre:**   *root is the root of a binary search tree with a node containing key equal to target.*
  **Post:**  *The node with key equal to target has been deleted and returned. The resulting tree has the properties required of a binary search tree.*
  **Uses:** DeleteKeyTree *recursively,* DeleteNodeTree. */*

```
void DeleteKeyTree(TreeNode **root, TreeNode **keyposition, KeyType target)
{
    if (*root == NULL)
        Error("Attempt to delete a key not present in the binary search tree");
    else if (EQ(target, (*root)->entry.key)) {
        *keyposition = *root;
        DeleteNodeTree(root);
    } else if (LT(target, (*root)->entry.key))
        DeleteKeyTree(root, keyposition, target);
    else
        DeleteKeyTree(root, keyposition, target);
}
```

---

**Exercises 9.2**

The first several exercises are based on the following binary search tree. Answer each part of each exercise independently, using the original tree as the basis for each part.

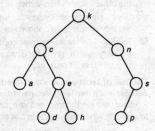

**E1.** Show the keys with which each of the following targets will be compared in a search of the preceding binary search tree.

| | | |
|---|---|---|
| **(a)** *c* | **(d)** *a* | **(g)** *f* |
| **(b)** *s* | **(e)** *d* | **(h)** *b* |
| **(c)** *k* | **(f)** *m* | **(i)** *t* |

**E2.** Insert each of the following keys into the preceding binary search tree. Show the comparisons of keys that will be made in each case. Do each part independently, inserting the key into the original tree.

| | | | | | |
|---|---|---|---|---|---|
| **(a)** *m* | | **(c)** *b* | | **(e)** *c* | |
| **(b)** *f* | | **(d)** *t* | | **(f)** *s* | |

**E3.** Delete each of the following keys from the preceding binary search tree, using the algorithm developed in this section. Do each part independently, deleting the key from the original tree.

| | | | | | |
|---|---|---|---|---|---|
| **(a)** *a* | | **(c)** *n* | | **(e)** *e* | |
| **(b)** *p* | | **(d)** *s* | | **(f)** *k* | |

**E4.** Draw the binary search trees that InsertTree will construct for the list of 14 names presented in each of the following orders and inserted into a previously empty binary search tree.

(a) Jan Guy Jon Ann Jim Eva Amy Tim Ron Kim Tom Roy Kay Dot

(b) Amy Tom Tim Ann Roy Dot Eva Ron Kim Kay Guy Jon Jan Jim

(c) Jan Jon Tim Ron Guy Ann Jim Tom Amy Eva Roy Kim Dot Kay

(d) Jon Roy Tom Eva Tim Kim Ann Ron Jan Amy Dot Guy Jim Kay

**E5.** All parts of this exercise refer to the binary search trees shown in Figure 9.8 and concern the different orders in which the keys $a, b, \ldots, g$ can be inserted into an initially empty binary search tree.

(a) Give four different orders for inserting the keys, each of which will yield the binary search tree shown in part (a).

(b) Give four different orders for inserting the keys, each of which will yield the binary search tree shown in part (b).

(c) Give four different orders for inserting the keys, each of which will yield the binary search tree shown in part (c).

(d) Explain why there is only one order for inserting the keys that will produce a binary search tree that reduces to a given chain, such as the one shown in part (d) or in part (e).

**E6.** The use of recursion in InsertTree is not essential, since it is tail recursion. Rewrite InsertTree in nonrecursive form. [You will need a local pointer variable to move through the tree, and you may find it useful to keep a Boolean variable to indicate when the insertion can actually take place.]

*deletion*

**E7.** Write a function that will delete a node from a linked binary tree, using the following method in the case when the node to be deleted has both subtrees nonempty. First, find the immediate predecessor of the node under inorder traversal by moving to its left child and then as far right as possible. (The immediate successor would work just as well.) The immediate predecessor is guaranteed to have at most one child (why?), so it can be deleted from its current position without difficulty. It can then be placed into the tree in the position formerly occupied by the node that was supposed to be deleted, and the properties of a binary search tree will still be satisfied (why?).

**Programming Projects 9.2**

**P1.** Prepare the files containing the declarations for a binary search tree and the functions developed in this section. The files should be suitable for use in any application program.

**P2.** Produce a menu-driven demonstration program to illustrate the use of binary search trees. The entries may consist of keys alone, and the keys should be single characters. The minimum capabilities that the user should be able to demonstrate include creating (initializing) the tree, insertion and deletion of an entry with a given key, searching for a target key, and traversal of the tree in the three standard orders. The project may be enhanced by the inclusion of additional capabilities written as exercises in this and the previous section. These include determining the size of the tree, printing out all the entries arranged to show the shape of the tree, and traversal of the tree in various ways.

Keep the functions in your project as modular as possible, so that you can later replace the files for a binary search tree by functionally equivalent files for another kind of tree.

**P3.** Write a function for treesort that can be added to Project P1 of Section 7.2 (page 287). Determine whether it is necessary for the list structure to be contiguous or linked. Compare the results with those for the other sorting methods in Chapter 7.

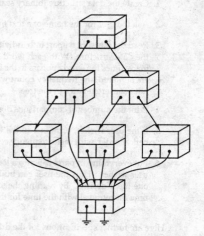

Figure 9.12. Binary search tree with sentinel

**P4.** Write a function for searching, using a binary search tree with sentinel as follows: Introduce a new sentinel node, and keep a pointer (of type TreeNode) called sentinel to it. See Figure 9.12. Replace all the NULL links within the binary search tree with links to the sentinel. Then, for each search, store the target key into the sentinel node before starting the search. Delete the test for an unsuccessful search from TreeSearch, since it cannot now occur. Instead, a search that now finds the sentinel sentinel is actually an unsuccessful search. Run this function on the test data of the preceding project to compare the performance of this version with the original TreeSearch.

*coatroom*

**P5.** Use a binary search tree to implement the coatroom operations of Section 6.3. Test your program with the coatroom demonstration program, and then run the timed-test program with the binary search tree package, comparing the results with those for the other implementations.

**P6.** Different authors tend to use different vocabularies and to use common words with differing frequencies. Given an essay or other text, it is interesting to find what distinct words are used and how many times each is used. The purpose of this project is to compare several different kinds of binary search trees useful for this information retrieval problem. The current, first part of the project is to produce a driver program and the information-retrieval package using ordinary binary search trees. Here is an outline of the main driver program:

1. Create the data structure (binary search tree).

2. Ask the user for the name of a text file and open it to read.

3. Read the file, split it apart into individual words, and insert the words into the data structure. With each word will be kept a frequency count (how many times the word appears in the input), and when duplicate words are encountered, the frequency count will be increased. The same word will not be inserted twice in the tree.

4. Print the number of comparisons done and the CPU time used in part 3.

5. If the user wishes, print out all the words in the data structure, in alphabetical order, with their frequency counts.

6. Put everything in parts 2–5 into a loop that will run as many times as the user wishes. Thus the user can build the data structure with more than one file if desired. By reading the same file twice, the user can compare time for retrieval with the time for the original insertion.

Here are further specifications for the driver program:

■ The input to the driver will be a file of type text. The program will be executed with several different files; the name of the file to be used should be requested from the user while the program is running.

■ A word is defined as a sequence of letters, together with apostrophes (') and hyphens (-), provided that the apostrophe or hyphen is both immediately preceded and followed by a letter. Uppercase and lowercase letters should be regarded as the same (by translating all letters into either uppercase or lowercase, as you prefer). A word is to be truncated to its first 20 characters (that is, only 20 characters are to be stored in the data structure) but words longer than 20 characters may appear in the text. Non-alphabetic characters (such as digits, blanks, punctuation marks, control characters) may appear in the text file. The appearance of any of these terminates a word, and the next word begins only when a letter appears.

■ Be sure to write your driver so that it will not be changed at all when you change implementation of data structures later.

Here are specifications for the functions to be implemented first with binary search trees, that is, by declaring typedef TreeNode *Structure; and using appropriate binary search tree operations.

---

void Create(Structure *s);

*precondition:*  None.

*postcondition:* s is created and is empty.

---

Structure Update(Structure s, char *w, int *ncomp);

*precondition:*  s has been created; w points to a word.

*postcondition:* If w was not already present in s, then w has been inserted into s and its frequency count is 1. If w was already present in s, then its frequency count has been increased by 1. ncomp is the number of comparisons of words done.

---

void Print(Structure s);

*precondition:*  s has been created.

*postcondition:* All words in s are printed at the terminal in alphabetical order together with their frequency counts.

---

void WriteMethod();

*precondition:*  None.

*postcondition:* The function has written a short string identifying the abstract data type used for Structure.

## 9.3 Building a Binary Search Tree

Suppose that we have a list of nodes that is already in order, or perhaps a file of records, with keys already sorted alphabetically. If we wish to use these nodes to look up information, add additional nodes, or make other changes, then we would like to take the list or file of nodes and make it into a binary search tree.

We could, of course, start out with an empty binary tree and simply use the tree insertion algorithm to insert each node into it. But the nodes were given already in order, so the resulting search tree will become one long chain, and using it will be too slow—with the speed of sequential search rather than binary search. We wish instead, therefore, to take the nodes and build them into a tree that will be as bushy as possible, so as to reduce both the time to build the tree and all subsequent search time. When the number of nodes, $n$, is 31, for example, we wish to build the tree of Figure 9.13.

*goal*

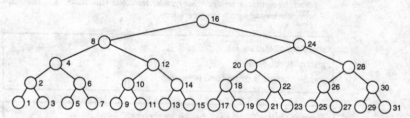

Figure 9.13. Complete binary tree with 31 nodes

In Figure 9.13 the nodes are numbered in their natural order, that is, in inorder sequence, which is the order in which they will be received and built into the tree. If you examine the diagram for a moment, you may notice an important property of the labels. The labels of the leaves are all odd numbers; that is, they are not divisible by 2. The labels of the nodes one level above the leaves are 2, 6, 10, 14, 18, 22, 26, and 30. These numbers are all double an odd number; that is, they are all even, but are not divisible by 4. On the next level up, the labels are 4, 12, 20, and 28, numbers that are divisible by 4, but not by 8. Finally, the nodes just below the root are labeled 8 and 24, and the root itself is 16. The key observation is

> *If the nodes of a complete binary tree are labeled in inorder sequence, then each node is exactly as many levels above the leaves as the highest power of 2 that divides its label.*

Let us now put one more constraint on our problem: Let us suppose that we do not know in advance how many nodes will be built into the tree. If the nodes are coming from a file or a linked list, then this assumption is quite reasonable, since we may not have any convenient way to count the nodes before receiving them.

This assumption also has the advantage that it will stop us from worrying about the fact that, when the number of nodes is not exactly one less than a power of 2, the resulting tree will not be complete and cannot be as symmetrical as the one in Figure 9.13. Instead, we shall design our algorithm as though it were completely symmetrical, and after receiving all nodes we shall determine how to tidy up the tree.

### 9.3.1 GETTING STARTED

There is no doubt what to do with node number 1 when it arrives. It will be a leaf, and therefore its left and right pointers should both be set to NULL. Node number 2 goes above node 1, as shown in Figure 9.14. Since node 2 links to node 1, we obviously must keep some way to remember where node 1 is. Node 3 is again a leaf, but it is in the right subtree of node 2, so we must remember a pointer to node 2.

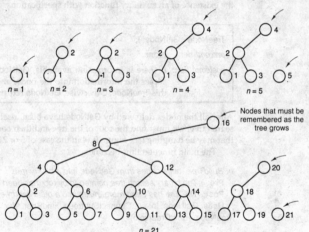

Figure 9.14. Building the first nodes into a tree

Does this mean that we must keep a list of pointers to all nodes previously processed, to determine how to link in the next one? The answer is no, since when node 3 is received, all connections for node 1 are complete. Node 2 must be remembered until node 4 is received, to establish the left link from node 4, but then a pointer to node 2 is no longer needed. Similarly, node 4 must be remembered until node 8 has been processed. In Figure 9.14, colored arrows point to each node that must be remembered as the tree grows.

It should now be clear that to establish future links, we need only remember pointers to one node on each level, the last node processed on that level. We keep these pointers in an array called lastnode that will be quite small. For example, a tree with 20 levels can accommodate $2^{20} - 1 > 1,000,000$ nodes.

As each new node arrives, it is clearly the last one received in the order, so we can set its right pointer to NULL (at least temporarily). The left pointer of the new node is NULL if it is a leaf. Otherwise it is the entry in lastnode one level lower than the new node. So that we can treat the leaves in the same way as other nodes, we consider the leaves to be on level 0, index the array lastnode from −1 to the maximum height allowed, and ensure that lastnode[0] == NULL.

### 9.3.2 DECLARATIONS AND THE MAIN FUNCTION

We can now write down declarations of the variables needed for our task, and, while we are at it, we can outline the main function. The first step will be to receive all the nodes and insert them into the tree. To obtain each new node, we assume the existence of an auxiliary function with specifications:

---

TreeNode *GetNode( );

*precondition:*  None.

*postcondition:*  If there is information available, GetNode creates a TreeNode, copies the information into the node, and returns a pointer to this TreeNode. Otherwise, GetNode returns NULL.

---

After all the nodes delivered by GetNode have been inserted into the new binary search tree, we must find the root of the tree and then connect any right subtrees that may be dangling (see Figure 9.14 in the case of 5 or 21 nodes).

The main function thus becomes

```
/* BuildTree: build nodes from GetNode into a binary tree.
   Pre:  The binary search tree pointed to by root has been created.
   Post: The tree has been reorganized into a balanced tree.
   Uses: GetNode, Insert, ConnectSubtrees, FindRoot. */
```
*main function*
```
TreeNode *BuildTree(void)
{
   TreeNode *newnode;
   int count = 0;                  /* number of nodes so far              */
   int level;                      /* number of steps above leaves        */
   TreeNode *lastnode[MAXHEIGHT];  /* pointers to last node on each level */
   for (level = 0; level < MAXHEIGHT; level++)
      lastnode[level] = NULL;
   while ((newnode = GetNode()) != NULL)
      Insert(newnode, ++count, lastnode);
   newnode = FindRoot(lastnode);
   ConnectSubtrees(lastnode);
   return newnode;                 /* Return root of the tree.            */
}
```

### 9.3.3 INSERTING A NODE

The discussion in the previous section shows how to set up the left links of each node correctly, but for some of the nodes the right link should not permanently have the value NULL. When a new node arrives, it cannot yet have a proper right subtree, since it is the latest node (under the ordering) so far received. The node, however, may be the right child of some previous node. On the other hand, it may instead be a left child, in which case its parent node has not yet arrived. We can tell which case occurs by looking in the array lastnode. If level denotes the level of the new node, then its parent has level level + 1. We look at lastnode[level + 1]. If its right link is still NULL, then its right child must be the new node; if not, then its right child has already arrived, and the new node must be the left child of some future node.

We can now formally describe how to insert a new node into the tree.

*insertion*

```
/* Insert: insert newnode as the rightmost node of a partial tree.
   Pre:   newnode is a valid pointer of an entry to be inserted into the binary search
          tree.
   Post:  newnode has been inserted as rightmost node of a partial binary search tree.
   Uses: Power2. */
void Insert(TreeNode *newnode, int count, TreeNode *lastnode[ ])
{
    int level = Power2(count) + 1;
    newnode->right = NULL;
    newnode->left = lastnode[level-1];
    lastnode[level] = newnode;
    if (lastnode[level + 1] && !lastnode[level + 1]->right)
        lastnode[level + 1]->right = newnode;
}
```

This function uses another function to find the level of node that newnode points to:

```
#define ODD(x) ((x)/2*2 != (x))
/* Power2: find the highest power of 2 that divides count.
   Pre:   x is a valid integer.
   Post:  The function finds the highest power of 2 that divides x; requires x != 0. */
int Power2(int x)
{
    int level;
    for (level = 0;  !ODD(x);  level++)
        x /= 2;
    return level;
}
```

### 9.3.4 Finishing the Task

Finding the root of the tree is easy: the root is the highest node in the tree; hence its pointer is the highest entry not equal to NULL in the array lastnode. We therefore have

*finding the root*

```
/* FindRoot: find root of tree (highest entry in lastnode).
    Pre:  The array lastnode contains pointers to the occupied levels of the binary search
          tree.
    Post: Return a pointer to the root of the newly created binary search tree. */

TreeNode *FindRoot(TreeNode *lastnode[ ])
{
    int level;
    for (level = MAXHEIGHT - 1; level > 0 && ! lastnode [level]; level - -)
        ;

    if (level <= 0)
        return NULL;
    else
        return lastnode [level];
}
```

Finally, we must determine how to tie in any subtrees that may not yet be connected properly after all the nodes have been received. The difficulty is that some nodes in the upper part of the tree may still have their right links set to NULL, even though further nodes have come in that belong in their right subtrees.

Any node for which the right child is still NULL will be one of the nodes in lastnode. Its right child should be set to the highest node in lastnode that is not already in its left subtree. We thus arrive at the following algorithm.

*tying subtrees together*

```
/* ConnectSubtrees: connect free subtrees from lastnode [ ].
    Pre:  The nearly completed binary search tree has been initialized. The array last-
          node has been initialized and contains the information needed to complete the
          binary search tree.
    Post: The binary search tree has been completed. */

void ConnectSubtrees(TreeNode *lastnode[ ])
{
    TreeNode *p;
    int level, templevel;
    for (level = MAXHEIGHT - 1; level > 2 && ! lastnode [level]; level - -)
        ;                              /* Find the highest node: root.              */
```

```
    while (level > 2) {              /* Levels 1 and 2 are already OK.              */
      if (lastnode [level] ->right)
        level--;                     /* Search for highest dangling node.          */
      else {                         /* Right subtree is undefined.                */
        p = lastnode [level] ->left;
        templevel = level - 1;
        do {                         /* Find highest entry not in left subtree.    */
          p = p->right;
        } while (p && p ==  lastnode [--templevel]);
        lastnode [level] ->right = lastnode [templevel];
        level = templevel;
      }
    }
  }
}
```

## 9.3.5 EVALUATION

The algorithm of this section produces a binary search tree that is not always completely balanced. If 32 nodes come in, for example, then node 32 will become the root of the tree, and all 31 remaining nodes will be in its left subtree. Thus the leaves are five steps removed from the root. If the root were chosen optimally, then most of the leaves would be four steps from it, and only one would be five steps. Hence one comparison more than necessary will usually be done.

One extra comparison in a binary search is not really a very high price, and it is easy to see that a tree produced by our method is never more than one level away from optimality. There are sophisticated methods for building a binary search tree that is as balanced as possible, but much remains to recommend a simpler method, one that does not need to know in advance how many nodes are in the tree.

The exercises outline ways in which our algorithm can be used to take an arbitrary binary search tree and rearrange the nodes to bring it into better balance, so as to improve search times. Again, there are more sophisticated methods (which, however, will likely be slower) for rebalancing a tree. In Section 9.4 we shall study AVL trees, in which we perform insertions and deletions in such a way as always to maintain the tree in a state of near balance. For many practical purposes, however, the simpler algorithm described in this section should prove sufficient.

## 9.3.6 RANDOM SEARCH TREES AND OPTIMALITY

To conclude this section, let us ask whether it is worthwhile, on average, to keep a binary search tree balanced or to rebalance it. If we assume that the keys have arrived in random order, then, on average, how many more comparisons are needed in a search of the resulting tree than would be needed in a completely balanced tree?

*extended binary tree*

In answering the question, we first convert the binary search tree into a 2-tree, as follows. Think of all the vertices of the binary tree as drawn as circles, and add on new, square vertices replacing all the empty subtrees (NULL links). This process is shown in Figure 9.15. All the vertices of the original binary tree become internal vertices of the 2-tree, and the new vertices are all external (leaves). A successful search terminates at an interior vertex of the 2-tree, and an unsuccessful search at a leaf. Hence the internal path length leads us to the number of comparisons for a successful search, and the external path length leads us to the number for an unsuccessful search. Since two comparisons are done at each internal node, the number of comparisons done in searching once for each key in the tree is, in fact, twice the internal path length.

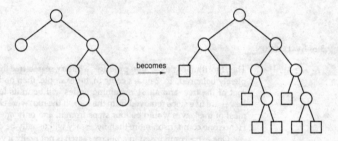

Figure 9.15. Extension of a binary tree into a 2-tree

We shall assume that the $n!$ possible orderings of keys are equally likely in building the tree. When there are $n$ nodes in the tree, we denote by $S(n)$ the number of comparisons done in the average successful search and by $U(n)$ the number in the average unsuccessful search.

*counting comparisons*

The number of comparisons needed to find any key in the tree is exactly one more than the number of comparisons that were needed to insert it in the first place, and inserting it required the same comparisons as the unsuccessful search showing that it was not yet in the tree. We therefore have the relationship

$$S(n) = 1 + \frac{U(0) + U(1) + \cdots + U(n-1)}{n}.$$

The relation between internal and external path length, as presented in Theorem 6.4, states that

$$S(n) = \left(1 + \frac{1}{n}\right) U(n) - 3.$$

*recurrence relation*

The last two equations together give

$$(n + 1)U(n) = 4n + U(0) + U(1) + \cdots + U(n - 1).$$

We solve this recurrence by writing the equation for $n - 1$ instead of $n$:

$$nU(n - 1) = 4(n - 1) + U(0) + U(1) + \cdots + U(n - 2),$$

and subtracting, to obtain

$$U(n) = U(n - 1) + \frac{4}{n + 1}.$$

The sum

$$H_n = 1 + \frac{1}{2} + \frac{1}{3} + \cdots + \frac{1}{n}$$

*harmonic number*

is called the $n^{th}$ **harmonic number**, and it is shown in Theorem A.4 on page 588 that this number is approximately the natural logarithm $\ln n$. Since $U(0) = 0$, we can now evaluate $U(n)$ by starting at the bottom and adding:

$$U(n) = 4\left[\frac{1}{2} + \frac{1}{3} + \cdots + \frac{1}{n + 1}\right] = 4H_{n+1} - 4 \approx 4\ln n.$$

By Theorem 6.4, the number of comparisons for a successful search is also approximately $4\ln n$. Since searching any binary search tree requires two comparisons per node and the optimal height is $\lg n$, the optimal number of comparisons is $2\lg n$. But (see Section A.2)

$$\ln n = (\ln 2)(\lg n).$$

Converting natural logarithms to base 2 logarithms, we finally obtain

**Theorem 9.3**     *The average number of nodes visited in a search of the average binary search tree with $n$ nodes is approximately $2\ln n = (2\ln 2)(\lg n) \approx 1.39\lg n$, and the number of key comparisons is approximately $4\ln n = (4\ln 2)(\lg n) \approx 2.67\lg n$.*

**Corollary 9.4**     *The average binary search tree requires approximately $2\ln 2 \approx 1.39$ times as many comparisons as a completely balanced tree.*

*cost of not balancing*    In other words, the average cost of not balancing a binary search tree is approximately 39 percent more comparisons. In applications where optimality is important, this cost must be weighed against the extra cost of balancing the tree, or of maintaining it in balance. Note especially that these latter tasks involve not only the cost of computer time, but the cost of the extra programming effort that will be required.

---

**Exercises 9.3**

E1. Draw the sequence of partial binary search trees (like Figure 9.14) that the method in this section will construct for $n = 6$, $n = 7$, and $n = 8$.

E2. Write GetNode for the case when type Structure is an ordered list. The function will thus delete the first entry of the list, put it into a tree node, and return a pointer to that node.

E3. Write GetNode for the case when the input structure is a binary search tree, so the type Structure is the same as TreeNode * and s points to the root of the tree. The function will need to find and delete the leftmost node of the binary search tree and return a pointer to it (newnode). [This version, with BuildTree, gives a function to rebalance a binary search tree.]

E4. Write a version of GetNode that will read a key from a text file, one key per line, create a tree node containing the key, and return a pointer to the node. When the end of the file is reached, the value NULL is returned. [This version, with BuildTree, gives a function that reads a binary search tree from an ordered file.]

E5. There are 3! = 6 possible orderings of three keys, but only 5 distinct binary trees with three nodes. Therefore these binary trees are not equally likely to occur as search trees. Find which one of the five binary search trees corresponds to each of the six possible orders. Thereby find the probability for building each of the binary search trees from randomly ordered input.

E6. There are 4! = 24 possible orderings of four keys, but only 14 distinct binary trees with four nodes. Therefore these binary trees are not equally likely to occur as search trees. Find which one of the 14 binary search trees corresponds to each of the 24 possible orders. Thereby find the probability for building each of the binary search trees from randomly ordered input.

---

## 9.4 Height Balance: AVL Trees

The algorithm of Section 9.3 can be used to build a nearly balanced binary search tree, or to restore balance when it is feasible to restructure the tree completely. In many applications, however, insertions and deletions occur continually, with no predictable order. In some of these applications, it is important to optimize search times by keeping the tree very nearly balanced at all times. The method in this section for achieving this goal was described in 1962 by two Russian mathematicians, G. M. ADEL'SON-VEL'SKII and E. M. LANDIS, and the resulting binary search trees are called *AVL trees* in their honor.

*nearly optimal height*　　　AVL trees achieve the goal that searches, insertions, and deletions in a tree with $n$ nodes can all be achieved in time that is $O(\log n)$, even in the worst case. The height of an AVL tree with $n$ nodes, as we shall establish, can never exceed $1.44 \lg n$, and thus even in the worst case, the behavior of an AVL tree could not be much below that of a random binary search tree. In almost all cases, however, the actual length of a search is very nearly $\lg n$, and thus the behavior of AVL trees closely approximates that of the ideal, completely balanced binary search tree.

## 9.4.1 DEFINITION

In a completely balanced tree, the left and right subtrees of any node would have the same height. Although we cannot always achieve this goal, by building a search tree carefully we can always ensure that the heights of every left and right subtree never differ by more than 1. We accordingly make the following definition:

**Definition**　　An *AVL tree* is a binary search tree in which the heights of the left and right subtrees of the root differ by at most 1 and in which the left and right subtrees are again AVL trees.

　　With each node of an AVL tree is associated a *balance factor* that is *left higher*, *equal height*, or *right higher* according, respectively, as the left subtree has height greater than, equal to, or less than that of the right subtree.

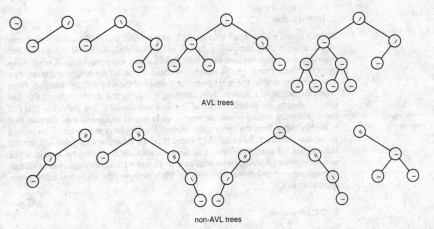

AVL trees

non-AVL trees

Figure 9.16. Examples of AVL trees and other binary trees

In drawing diagrams, we shall show a left-high node by ' / ', a node whose balance factor is equal by ' – ', and a right-high node by ' \ '. Figure 9.16 shows several small AVL trees, as well as some binary trees that fail to satisfy the definition.

Note that the definition does not require that all leaves be on the same or adjacent levels. Figure 9.17 shows several AVL trees that are quite skewed, with right subtrees having greater height than left subtrees.

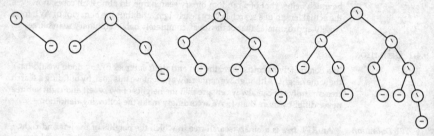

**Figure 9.17. AVL trees skewed to the right**

## 9.4.2 INSERTION OF A NODE

### 1. Introduction

We can insert a new node into an AVL tree by first using the usual binary tree insertion algorithm, comparing the key of the new node with that in the root, and inserting the new node into the left or right subtree as appropriate. It often turns out that the new node can be inserted without changing the height of the subtree, in which case neither the height nor the balance of the root will be changed. Even when the height of a subtree does increase, it may be the shorter subtree that has grown, so only the balance factor of the root will change. The only case that can *problem* cause difficulty occurs when the new node is added to a subtree of the root that is strictly taller than the other subtree, and the height is increased. This would cause one subtree to have height 2 more than the other, whereas the AVL condition is that the height difference is never more than 1. Before we consider this situation more carefully, let us illustrate in Figure 9.18 the growth of an AVL tree through several insertions, and then we shall tie down the ideas by outlining our algorithm in C.

### 2. C Conventions

The basic structure of our algorithm will be the same as the ordinary recursive binary tree insertion algorithm of Section 9.2.3 (page 403), but with certain additions to accommodate the structure of AVL trees. First, each structure corresponding to

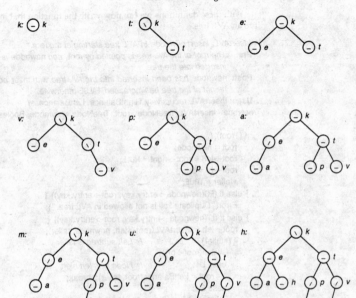

Figure 9.18. Simple insertions of nodes into an AVL tree

a node will have an additional field (along with its information field and left and right pointers), defined as

BalanceFactor bf;

where we employ the enumerated data type

typedef enum BalanceFactor { LH, EH, RH } BalanceFactor;

which symbols denote *left higher, equal height,* and *right higher,* respectively.

Second, we must keep track of whether an insertion has increased the height or not, so that the balance factors can be changed appropriately. This we do by including an additional calling parameter taller of type Boolean. The task of restoring balance when required will be done in the subsidiary functions LeftBalance and RightBalance.

With these definitions we can now write the function that inserts a new node into an AVL tree.

```
/* InsertAVL: insert newnode in AVL tree starting at the root.
   Pre:  The root of the AVL tree is pointed by root, and newnode is a new node to be
         inserted into the tree.
   Post: newnode has been inserted into the AVL tree with taller equal to TRUE if the
         height of the tree has increased, FALSE otherwise.
   Uses: InsertAVL recursively, RightBalance, LeftBalance. */
TreeNode *InsertAVL(TreeNode *root, TreeNode *newnode, Boolean *taller)
{
   if (!root) {
      root = newnode;
      root->left = root->right = NULL;
      root->bf = EH;
      *taller = TRUE;
   } else if (EQ(newnode->entry.key, root->entry.key)) {
      Error("Duplicate key is not allowed in AVL tree.");
   } else if (LT(newnode->entry.key, root->entry.key)) {
      root->left = InsertAVL(root->left, newnode, taller);
      if (*taller)                    /* Left subtree is taller.                   */
         switch(root->bf) {
         case LH:                     /* Node was left high.                        */
            root = LeftBalance(root, taller); break;
         case EH:
            root->bf = LH; break;   /* Node is now left high.                     */
         case RH:
            root->bf = EH;    /* Node now has balanced height.              */
            *taller = FALSE; break;
         }
   } else {
      root->right = InsertAVL(root->right, newnode, taller);
      if (*taller)                    /* Right subtree is taller.                  */
         switch(root->bf) {
         case LH:
            root->bf = EH;    /* Node now has balanced height.              */
            *taller = FALSE; break;
         case EH:
            root->bf = RH; break;  /* Node is right high.                        */
         case RH:                     /* Node was right high.                      */
            root = RightBalance(root, taller); break;
         }
   }
   return root;
}
```

### 3. Rotations

Let us now consider the case when a new node has been inserted into the taller subtree of the root and its height has increased, so that now one subtree has height 2 more than the other, and the tree no longer satisfies the AVL requirements. We must now rebuild part of the tree to restore its balance. To be definite, let us assume that we have inserted the new node into the right subtree, its height has increased, and the original tree was right higher. That is, we wish to consider the case covered by the function RightBalance. Let $r$ be the root of the tree and $x$ the root of its right subtree.

There are three cases to consider, depending on the balance factor of $x$.

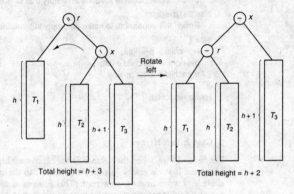

Figure 9.19. First case: Restoring balance by a left rotation

### 4. Case 1: Right Higher

*left rotation*

The first case, when $x$ is right higher, is illustrated in Figure 9.19. The action needed in this case is called a **left rotation**; we have rotated the node $x$ upward to the root, dropping $r$ down into the left subtree of $x$; the subtree $T_2$ of nodes with keys between those of $r$ and $x$ now becomes the right subtree of $r$ rather than the left subtree of $x$. A left rotation is succinctly described in the following C function. Note especially that, when done in the appropriate order, the steps constitute a rotation of the values in three pointer variables. Note also that, after the rotation, the height of the rotated tree has decreased by 1; it had previously increased because of the insertion; hence the height finishes where it began.

/* RotateLeft: rotate a binary tree to the left.
   **Pre:**   p is the root of the nonempty AVL subtree being rotated, and its right child is
           nonempty.
   **Post:**  The right child of p becomes the new p. The old p becomes the left child of
           the new p. */

```
TreeNode *RotateLeft(TreeNode *p)
{
    TreeNode *rightchild = p;

    if (!p)
        Error("It is impossible to rotate an empty tree in RotateLeft.");
    else if (!p->right)
        Error("It is impossible to make an empty subtree the root in RotateLeft.");
    else {
        rightchild = p->right;
        p->right = rightchild->left;
        rightchild->left = p;
    }
    return rightchild;
}
```

### 5. Case 2: Left Higher

*double rotation*

The second case, when the balance factor of $x$ is left higher, is slightly more complicated. It is necessary to move two levels, to the node $w$ that roots the left subtree of $x$, to find the new root. This process is shown in Figure 9.20 and is called a **double rotation**, because the transformation can be obtained in two steps by first rotating the subtree with root $x$ to the right (so that $w$ becomes its root), and then rotating the tree with root $r$ to the left (moving $w$ up to become the new root).

In this second case, the new balance factors for $r$ and $x$ depend on the previous balance factor for $w$. The diagram shows the subtrees of $w$ as having equal heights, but it is possible that $w$ may be either left or right higher. The resulting balance factors are

| old w | new r | new x |
| --- | --- | --- |
| – | – | – |
| / | – | \ |
| \ | / | – |

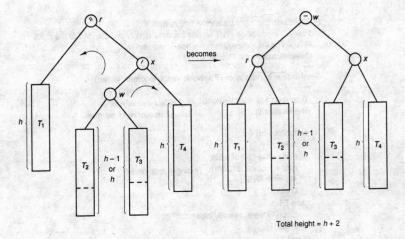

becomes

One of $T_2$ or $T_3$ has height $h$.
Total height = $h + 3$

Total height = $h + 2$

Figure 9.20. Second case: Restoring balance by a double rotation

## 6. Case 3: Equal Height

It would appear, finally, that we must consider a third case, when the two subtrees of $x$ have equal heights, but this case, in fact, can never happen. To see why, let us recall that we have just inserted a new node into the subtree rooted at $x$, and this subtree now has height 2 more than the left subtree of the root. The new node went either into the left or right subtree of $x$. Hence its insertion increased the height of only one subtree of $x$. If these subtrees had equal heights after the insertion, then the height of the full subtree rooted at $x$ was not changed by the insertion, contrary to what we already know.

## 7. C Function for Balancing

It is now straightforward to incorporate these transformations into a C function. The forms of functions RotateRight and LeftBalance are clearly similar to those of RotateLeft and RightBalance, respectively, and are left as exercises.

```
/* RightBalance: right balance a binary tree.
   Pre:  A node of an AVL tree has become doubly unbalanced to the right.
   Post: The AVL properties have been restored.
   Uses: RotateRight, RotateLeft. */

TreeNode *RightBalance(TreeNode *root, Boolean *taller)
{
    TreeNode *rs = root->right;    /* right subtree of root              */
    TreeNode *ls;                  /* left subtree of right subtree      */

    switch(rs->bf) {
    case RH :
        root->bf = rs->bf = EH;
        root = RotateLeft(root);   /* single rotation left               */
        *taller = FALSE;
        break;
    case EH :
        Error("Tree is already balanced");
        break;
    case LH :                      /* double rotation left               */
        ls = rs->left;
        switch(ls->bf) {
        case RH :
            root->bf = LH;
            rs->bf = EH;
            break;
        case EH :
            root->bf = rs->bf = EH;
            break;
        case LH :
            root->bf = EH;
            rs->bf = RH;
            break;
        }
        ls->bf = EH;
        root->right = RotateRight(rs);
        root = RotateLeft(root);
        *taller = FALSE;
    }
    return root;
}
```

Examples of insertions requiring single and double rotations are shown in Figure 9.21.

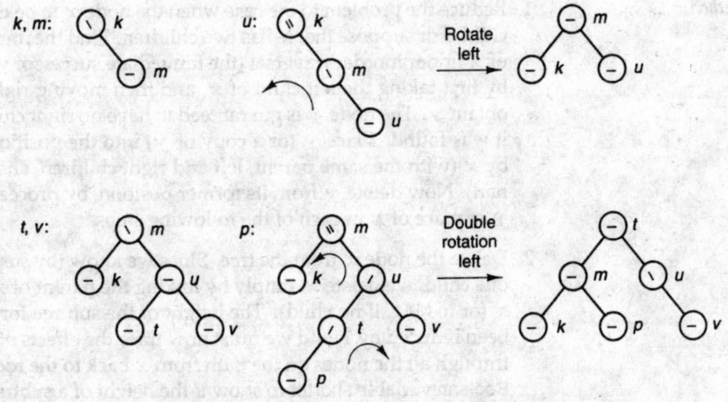

**Figure 9.21. AVL insertions requiring rotations**

### 8. Behavior of the Algorithm

The number of times that function InsertAVL calls itself recursively to insert a new node can be as large as the height of the tree. At first glance it may appear that each one of these calls might induce either a single or double rotation of the appropriate subtree, but, in fact, at most only one (single or double) rotation will ever be done. *counting rotations* To see this, let us recall that rotations are done only in the functions RightBalance and LeftBalance and that these functions are called only when the height of a subtree has increased. When these functions return, however, the rotations have removed the increase in height, so, for the remaining (outer) recursive calls, the height has not increased, and no further rotations or changes of balance factors are done.

Most of the insertions into an AVL tree will induce no rotations. Even when rotations are needed, they will usually occur near the leaf that has just been inserted. Even though the algorithm to insert into an AVL tree is complicated, it is reasonable to expect that its running time will differ little from insertion into an ordinary search tree of the same height. Later we shall see that we can expect the height of AVL trees to be much less than that of random search trees, and therefore both insertion and retrieval will be significantly more efficient in AVL trees than in random binary search trees.

## 9.4.3 DELETION OF A NODE

Deletion of a node $x$ from an AVL tree requires the same basic ideas, including single and double rotations, that are used for insertion. We shall give only the steps of an informal outline of the method, leaving the writing of complete algorithms as a programming project.

*method*

1. Reduce the problem to the case when the node $x$ to be deleted has at most one child. For suppose that $x$ has two children. Find the immediate predecessor $y$ of $x$ under inorder traversal (the immediate successor would be just as good), by first taking the left child of $x$, and then moving right as far as possible to obtain $y$. The node $y$ is guaranteed to have no right child, because of the way it was found. Place $y$ (or a copy of $y$) into the position in the tree occupied by $x$ (with the same parent, left and right children, and balance factor that $x$ had). Now delete $y$ from its former position, by proceeding as follows, using $y$ in place of $x$ in each of the following steps.

2. Delete the node $x$ from the tree. Since we know (by step 1) that $x$ has at most one child, we delete $x$ simply by linking the parent of $x$ to the single child of $x$ (or to NULL, if no child). The height of the subtree formerly rooted at $x$ has been reduced by 1, and we must now trace the effects of this change on height through all the nodes on the path from $x$ back to the root of the tree. We use a Boolean variable shorter to show if the height of a subtree has been shortened. The action to be taken at each node depends on the value of shorter, on the balance factor of the node, and sometimes on the balance factor of a child of the node.

3. The Boolean variable shorter is initially TRUE. The following steps are to be done for each node $p$ on the path from the parent of $x$ to the root of the tree, provided shorter remains TRUE. When shorter becomes FALSE, then no further changes are needed, and the algorithm terminates.

4. *Case 1:* The current node $p$ has balance factor equal. The balance factor of $p$ is changed accordingly as its left or right subtree has been shortened, and shorter becomes FALSE.

5. *Case 2:* The balance factor of $p$ is not equal, and the taller subtree was shortened. Change the balance factor of $p$ to equal, and leave shorter as TRUE.

6. *Case 3:* The balance factor of $p$ is not equal, and the shorter subtree was shortened. The height requirement for an AVL tree is now violated at $p$, so we apply a rotation, as follows, to restore balance. Let $q$ be the root of the taller subtree of $p$ (the one not shortened). We have three cases according to the balance factor of $q$.

7. *Case 3a:* The balance factor of $q$ is equal. A single rotation (with changes to the balance factors of $p$ and $q$) restores balance, and shorter becomes FALSE.

8. *Case 3b:* The balance factor of $q$ is the same as that of $p$. Apply a single rotation, set the balance factors of $p$ and $q$ to equal, and leave shorter as TRUE.

9. *Case 3c:* The balance factors of $p$ and $q$ are opposite. Apply a double rotation (first around $q$, then around $p$), set the balance factor of the new root to equal and the other balance factors as appropriate, and leave shorter as TRUE.

In cases 3a, b, c, the direction of the rotations depends on whether a left or right subtree was shortened. Some of the possibilities are illustrated in Figure 9.22, and an example of deletion of a node appears in Figure 9.23.

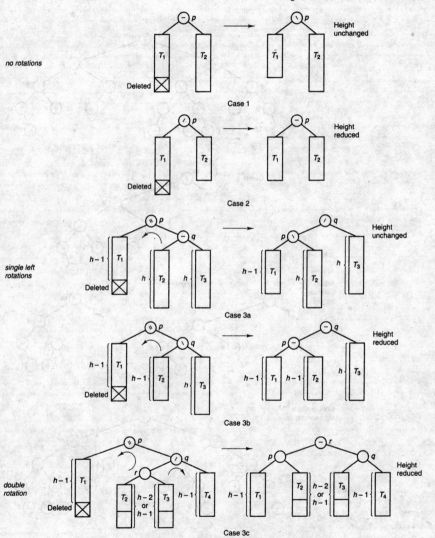

Figure 9.22. Sample cases, deletion from an AVL tree

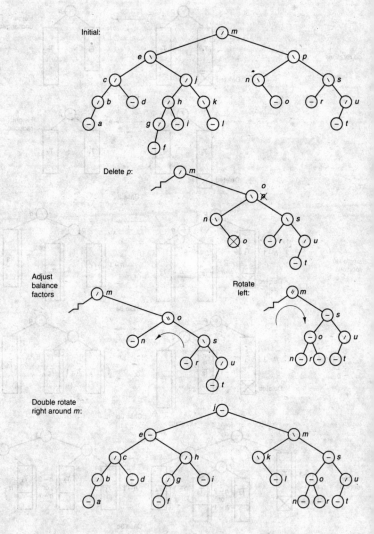

**Figure 9.23. Example of deletion from an AVL tree**

### 9.4.4 THE HEIGHT OF AN AVL TREE

It turns out to be very difficult to find the height of the average AVL tree, and thereby to determine how many steps are done, on average, by the algorithms of this section. It is much easier, however, to find what happens in the worst case, and these results show that the worst-case behavior of AVL trees is essentially no worse than the behavior of random trees. Empirical evidence suggests that the average behavior of AVL trees is much better than that of random trees, almost as good as that which could be obtained from a perfectly balanced tree.

*worst-case analysis*

To determine the maximum height that an AVL tree with $n$ nodes can have, we can instead ask what is the minimum number of nodes that an AVL tree of height $h$ can have. If $F_h$ is such a tree, and the left and right subtrees of its root are $F_l$ and $F_r$, then one of $F_l$ and $F_r$ must have height $h - 1$, say $F_l$, and the other has height either $h - 1$ or $h - 2$. Since $F_h$ has the minimum number of nodes among AVL trees of height $h$, it follows that $F_l$ must have the minimum number of nodes among AVL trees of height $h - 1$ (that is, $F_l$ is of the form $F_{h-1}$), and $F_r$ must have height $h - 2$ with minimum number of nodes (so that $F_r$ is of the form $F_{h-2}$).

*Fibonacci trees*

The trees built by the above rule, which are therefore as sparse as possible for AVL trees, are called **Fibonacci trees**. The first few are shown in Figure 9.24.

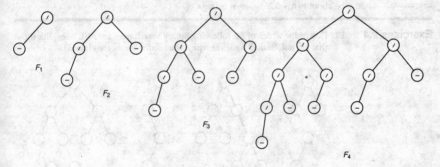

**Figure 9.24. Fibonacci trees**

*counting nodes of a Fibonacci tree*

If we write $|T|$ for the number of nodes in a tree $T$, we then have (counting the root as well as the subtrees) the recurrence relation

$$|F_h| = |F_{h-1}| + |F_{h-2}| + 1,$$

where $|F_0| = 1$ and $|F_1| = 2$. By adding 1 to both sides, we see that the numbers $|F_h| + 1$ satisfy the definition of the Fibonacci numbers (see Section A.4), with the subscripts changed by 3. By the evaluation of Fibonacci numbers in Section A.4, we therefore see that

$$|F_h| + 1 \approx \frac{1}{\sqrt{5}} \left[ \frac{1 + \sqrt{5}}{2} \right]^{h+2}$$

*height of a Fibonacci tree*

Next, we solve this relation for $h$ by taking the logarithms of both sides, and discarding all except the largest terms. The approximate result is that

$$h \approx 1.44 \lg |F_h|.$$

*worst-case bound*

This means that the sparsest possible AVL tree with $n$ nodes has height approximately $1.44 \lg n$. A perfectly balanced binary tree with $n$ nodes has height about $\lg n$, and a degenerate tree has height as large as $n$. Hence the algorithms for manipulating AVL trees are guaranteed to take no more than about 44 percent more time than the optimum. In practice, AVL trees do much better than this. It can be shown that, even for Fibonacci trees, which are the worst case for AVL trees, the average search time is only 4 percent more than the optimum. Most AVL trees are not nearly as sparse as Fibonacci trees, and therefore it is reasonable to expect that average search times for average AVL trees are very close indeed to the optimum.

*average-case observation*

Empirical studies, in fact, show that the average number of comparisons seems to be about $\lg n + 0.25$ when $n$ is large.

**Exercises 9.4**     E1. Determine which of the following binary search trees are AVL trees. For those that are not, find all nodes at which the requirements are violated.

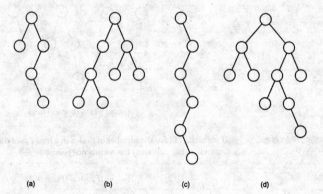

(a)          (b)          (c)          (d)

**E2.** In each of the following, insert the keys, in the order shown, to build them into an AVL tree.

(a) A, Z, B, Y, C, X.

(b) A, B, C, D, E, F.

(c) M, T, E, A, Z, G, P.

(d) A, Z, B, Y, C, X, D, W, E, V, F.

(e) A, B, C, D, E, F, G, H, I, J, K, L.

(f) A, V, L, T, R, E, I, S, O, K.

**E3.** Delete each of the keys inserted in Exercise E2 from the AVL tree, in LIFO order (last key inserted is first deleted).

**E4.** Delete each of the keys inserted in Exercise E2 from the AVL tree, in FIFO order (first key inserted is first deleted).

**E5.** Start with the following AVL tree and delete each of the following keys. Do each deletion independently, starting with the original tree each time.

(a) *k*

(b) *c*

(c) *j*

(d) *a*

(e) *g*

(f) *m*

(g) *h*

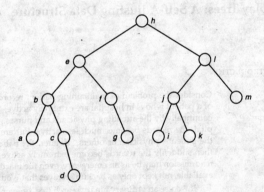

**E6.** Write a function that returns the height of an AVL tree by tracing only one path from the root to a leaf, not by investigating all the nodes in the tree.

**E7.** Write a function that returns a pointer to the leftmost leaf closest to the root of a nonempty AVL tree.

**E8.** Prove that the number of (single or double) rotations done in deleting a key from an AVL tree cannot exceed half the height of the tree.

**Programming Projects 9.4**

**P1.** Write a C function to delete a node from an AVL tree, following the steps outlined in the text.

**P2.** Substitute the functions for AVL insertion and deletion into the menu-driven demonstration program for binary search trees from Section 9.2, Project P2 (page 411), thereby obtaining a demonstration program for AVL trees.

*coatroom*

**P3.** Use an AVL tree to implement the coatroom operations of Section 6.3. Test your package with the coatroom demonstration program, and then run the timed-test program with the AVL tree package, comparing the results with those for the other implementations.

**P4.** Substitute the function for AVL insertion into the information-retrieval project of Project P6 of Section 9.2 (page 412). Compare the performance of AVL trees with ordinary binary search trees for various combinations of input text files.

# 9.5 Splay Trees: A Self-Adjusting Data Structure ▬▬▬▬

## 9.5.1 INTRODUCTION

*hospital records*

Consider the problem of maintaining patient records in a hospital. The records of a patient who is in hospital are extremely active, being consulted and updated continually by the attending physicians and nurses. When the patient leaves hospital, the records become much less active, but are still needed occasionally by the patient's physician or others. If, later, the patient is readmitted to hospital, then suddenly the records become extremely active again. Since, moreover, this readmission may be as an emergency, even the inactive records should be quickly available, not kept only as backup archives that would be slow to access.

*access time*

If we use an ordinary binary search tree, or even an AVL tree, for the hospital records, then the records of a newly admitted patient will go into a leaf position, far from the root, and therefore will be slow to access. Instead, we wish to keep records that are newly inserted or frequently accessed very close to the root, while records that are inactive may be placed far off, near or in the leaves. But we cannot shut down the hospital's record system even for an hour to rebuild the tree into the desired shape. Instead, we need to make the tree into a *self-adjusting* data structure that *automatically* changes its shape to bring records closer to the root as they are more frequently accessed, allowing inactive records to drift slowly out toward the leaves.

*self-adjusting trees*

*Splay trees* are binary search trees that achieve our goals by being self-adjusting in a quite remarkable way: Every time we access a node of the tree, whether for insertion or retrieval, we perform radical surgery on the tree, lifting the newly-accessed node all the way up, so that it becomes the root of the modified tree. Other nodes are pushed out of the way as necessary to make room for this new root. Nodes that are frequently accessed will frequently be lifted up to become the root, and they will never drift too far from the top position. Inactive nodes, on the other hand, will slowly be pushed farther and farther from the root.

*amortized analysis*

It is possible that splay trees can become highly unbalanced, so that a single access to a node of the tree can be quite expensive. Later in this section, however, we shall prove that, over a long sequence of accesses, splay trees are not at all expensive, and are guaranteed to require not many more operations even than AVL trees. The analytical tool used is called *amortized algorithm analysis*, since, like insurance calculations, the few expensive cases are averaged in with many less expensive cases to obtain excellent performance over a long sequence of operations.

We perform the radical surgery on splay trees by using rotations of a similar form to those used for AVL trees, but now with many rotations done for every insertion or retrieval in the tree. In fact, rotations are done all along the path from the root to the most recently accessed node. Let us now discuss precisely how this work proceeds.

## 9.5.2 SPLAYING STEPS

When a single rotation is performed in a binary search tree, such as shown in Figure 9.19 (page 427), some nodes move higher in the tree and some lower. In a left rotation, the parent node moves down and its right child moves up one level. A double rotation, as shown in Figure 9.20 (page 429), is made up of two single rotations, and one node moves up two levels, while others move down or remain on the same level. By beginning with the just-accessed node and working up the path to the root, we could do single rotations at each step, thereby lifting the accessed node all the way to the root. This method would achieve the goal of making the accessed node into the root, but, it turns out, the performance of the tree amortized over many accesses may not be good.

*zig and zag*

Instead, the key idea of splaying is to move the accessed node *two* levels up the tree at each step. First some simple terminology: Consider the path going from the root *down* to the accessed node. Each time we move left going down this path, we say that we *zig*, and each time we move right we say that we *zag*. A move of two steps left (going down) is then called *zig-zig*, two steps right *zag-zag*, left then right *zig-zag*, and right then left *zag-zig*. These four cases are the only possibilities in moving two steps down the path. If the length of the path is odd, however, there will be one more step needed at its end, either a *zig* (left) move, or a *zag* (right) move.

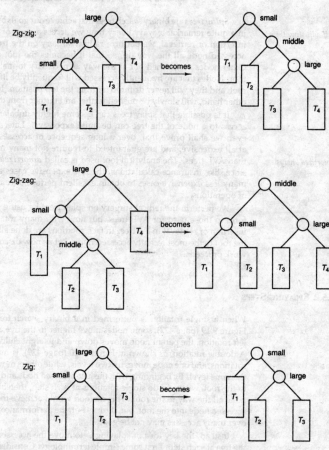

**Figure 9.25. Splay rotations**

The rotations done in splaying for each of zig-zig, zig-zag, and zig moves are shown in Figure 9.25. The zig-zag case is identical to that of an AVL double rotation, and the zig case is identical to a single rotation. The zig-zig case, however, is *not* the same as would be obtained by lifting the node twice with single rotations, as shown in Figure 9.26.

Let us fix these ideas in mind by working through an example, as shown in Figure 9.27.

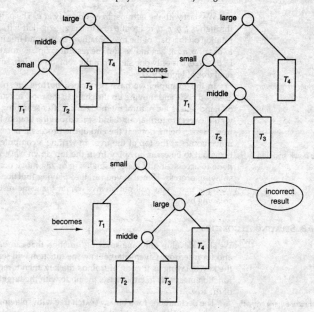

Figure 9.26. Zig-zig incorrectly replaced by single rotations

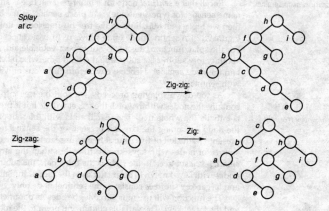

Figure 9.27. Example of splaying

We start with the leftmost tree and splay at *c*. The path from the root to *c* goes through *h, f, b, e, d, c*. From *e* to *d* to *c* is zig-zig (left-left), so we perform a zig-zig rotation on this part of the tree, obtaining the second tree in Figure 9.27. From *f* to *b* to *c* is now a zig-zag move, and the resulting zig-zag rotation yields the third tree. In this tree, *c* is only one step from the root, on the left, so a zig rotation yields the final tree of Figure 9.27.

*bottom-up splaying*

In this example, we have performed ***bottom-up*** splaying, beginning at the accessed node and moving up the chain to the root. In working through examples by hand, this is the natural method, since, after searching from the top down, one would expect to turn around and splay from the bottom back up to the top of the tree. Hence, being done at the end of the process if necessary, a single zig or zag move occurs at the top of the tree. In writing a computer algorithm, however, it

*top-down splaying*

turns out to be easier to splay from the top down *while* we are searching for the node to access. In this case, a single zig or zag move occurs at the bottom of the splaying process. Hence, if you run the splaying function we shall develop on the example trees, you will not always obtain the same results as doing bottom-up splaying by hand.

### 9.5.3 SPLAYING ALGORITHM

We shall develop only one splaying function that can be used both for retrieval and for insertion. Given a target key, the function will search through the tree for the key, splaying as it goes. If it finds the key, then it retrieves it; if not, then the function inserts it. In either case, the node with the target key ends up as the root of the tree.

*ordinary binary search trees*

The declarations for a binary search tree with splaying are identical to those of an ordinary binary tree. A splay tree does *not* keep track of heights and does *not* use any balance factors like an AVL tree.

*sentinel node* sentinel

Recall that a ***sentinel*** node for a binary search tree is an extra node, which we name sentinel (of type TreeNode). We place sentinel at the bottom of the tree, and then we replace all NULL links in the tree by TreeNode ∗ links to sentinel. (Review Figure 9.12.) A sentinel node often allows us to avoid checking for empty subtrees. For the splay function, this turns out to be a valuable aid. We never need worry about empty subtrees; a subtree that would otherwise be empty will always contain the node sentinel. Hence we write our functions only for binary search trees with sentinel.

*three-way tree split*

As top-down splaying proceeds, we split the tree into three parts. One part contains the nodes within which the target will lie if it is present. This ***central*** part is initially the whole tree. The search ends with the root of the central tree being the node containing the target if present, or the sentinel node if the target is not present. To the left of this central tree of unsearched nodes is the second part, the subtree of nodes with keys known to be less than the target, which we call the ***smaller-key*** subtree. To the right is the third part, the subtree called ***larger-key*** of nodes with keys known to be greater than the target. Initially, both the smaller-key and larger-key subtrees consist of the sentinel node only.

*variables*

The function will use four variables besides its parameters (the root of the tree and the target key). The variable current will point to the root of the central subtree of nodes not yet searched. The nodes are split off in such a way that *every* key in the smaller-key subtree is less than *every* key in the central subtree; hence to split off more nodes from the central subtree we need a pointer lastsmall to the largest (that is, the rightmost) node in the smaller-key subtree. Similarly, we need a pointer firstlarge to the smallest (leftmost) node of the larger-key subtree.

As the search progresses, we compare the target to the key in the root *current of the central subtree. Suppose the target is greater. Then the search will move to the right, but we need to take *current and its left subtree and adjoin them to the smaller-key tree. This is accomplished by the following function.

```
/* LinkLeft: link to the left side.
   Pre:   target > current->entry.key.
   Post:  Moves current and its left subtree into the tree of keys known to be less than
          target; therefore reassigns lastsmall to old current and moves current to its
          right child. */
TreeNode *LinkLeft(TreeNode *current, TreeNode **lastsmall)
{
   (*lastsmall)->right = current;
   *lastsmall = current;
   return current->right;
}
```

Since this function changes the right child of current, we need the fourth variable, child, that will tell us with which node to continue the search for the target.

A similar function LinkRight attaches *current and its right subtree to the larger-key subtree, in which case we move the search and the pointer current to its left child.

*splaying steps*    Now we come to the actual splaying steps, which are accomplished with surprising ease. A zig move takes current to its left child, and moves the old *current and its right subtree into the larger-key (right) subtree; this is precisely the action of LinkRight. For a zig-zig move, we must first do a right rotation, so that the left child of *current becomes the new *current, and then both nodes are linked into the larger-key subtree. In other words, we must do

$$\text{RotateRight( );  LinkRight( );}$$

where the function RotateRight is an ordinary right rotation:

```
/* RotateRight: rotate a binary tree to the right.
   Pre:   current points to a node of a binary search tree with sentinel.
   Post:  Rotates rightward the edge joining current and its left child. */
TreeNode *RotateRight(TreeNode *current)
{
   TreeNode *leftchild = current->left;
   current->left = leftchild->right;
   leftchild->right = current;
   return leftchild;
}
```

For a zig-zag move we must move *current and its right subtree into the larger-key subtree, and we must move its left child and the left subtree of that child into the smaller-key subtree. This is accomplished by

LinkRight( );  LinkLeft( );

The three symmetrical cases zag, zag-zag, and zag-zig are similar.

*termination*     When the search finishes, the root of the central subtree is the target node or the sentinel node. If the target is found, it becomes the root of the whole tree, but, before that, its left and right subtrees are now known to belong in the smaller-key and larger-key subtrees, respectively, so they must be moved there. If the sentinel is found, a new root is created.

*reassembly of the tree*     Finally, the left and right subtrees of the new root should now be the smaller-key and larger-key subtrees. How do we find the roots of these subtrees, since we have kept pointers only to their rightmost and leftmost nodes, respectively? We must remember what happened at the beginning of the search. Initially, both these subtrees consisted of *sentinel alone. When a node (and subtree) are attached to the smaller-key subtree, they are attached on its right, by changing lastsmall->right. Since lastsmall is initially sentinel, we can now, at the end of the search, find the first node inserted into the smaller-key subtree, and thus its root, simply as sentinel->right. Similarly, sentinel->left points to the root of the larger-key subtree.

With all this preliminary work, we can finally write the function for retrieving and inserting a node with splaying in a binary search tree.

```
/* TreeSplay: find or insert target in a splay tree.
   Pre:  The splay tree to which root points has been created.
   Post: The tree has been splayed around the key target. If a node with key target
         was in the tree, it has now become the root. If not, then a new node has been
         created as the root, with key target.
   Uses: LinkLeft, LinkRight, RotateLeft, RotateRight, MakeNode, SetNode. */

TreeNode *TreeSplay(TreeNode *root, KeyType target)
{
    TreeNode *current;        /* the current position in the tree                   */
    TreeNode *child;          /* one of the children of current                     */
    TreeNode *lastsmall;      /* largest key known to be less than the target       */
    TreeNode *firstlarge;     /* smallest key known to be greater than the target   */
    extern TreeNode *sentinel;

    sentinel->entry.key = target;   /* Establish sentinel for searching.            */
    lastsmall = firstlarge = sentinel;
```

```
for (current = root; NE(current->entry.key, target); )
    if (LT(current->entry.key, target)) {
        child = current->right;
        if (EQ(target, child->entry.key)) {
            current = LinkLeft(current, &lastsmall);
        } else if (GT(target, child->entry.key)) {
            current = RotateLeft(current);
            current = LinkLeft(current, &lastsmall);
        } else {
            current = LinkLeft(current, &lastsmall);
            current = LinkRight(current, &firstlarge);
        }
    } else {
        child = current->left;
        if (EQ(target, child->entry.key)) {
            current = LinkRight(current, &firstlarge);
        } else if (LT(target, child->entry.key)) {
            current = RotateRight(current);
            current = LinkRight(current, &firstlarge);
        } else {
            current = LinkRight(current, &firstlarge);
            current = LinkLeft(current, &lastsmall);
        }
    }

if (current == sentinel) {
    printf("Target has been inserted as root of the tree.");
    root = current = MakeNode(target, sentinel);
} else {
    printf("Target was found; it is now the root of the tree.");
}
lastsmall->right = current->left;     /* Move remaining central nodes.   */
firstlarge->left = current->right;
current->right = sentinel->left;      /* root of larger-key subtree       */
current->left = sentinel->right;      /* root of smaller-key subtree      */
root = current;                       /* Define the new root.             */
SetNode(sentinel, 0, sentinel);       /* Re-establish standard use of sentinel. */

return root;
}
```

All things considered, this is really quite a subtle and sophisticated algorithm in its pointer manipulations and economical use of resources.

## 9.5.4 AMORTIZED ALGORITHM ANALYSIS: INTRODUCTION

We now wish to determine the behavior of splaying over long sequences of operations, but before doing so, let us introduce the amortized analysis of algorithms with simpler examples.

### 1. Introduction

*definition*

In the past, we have considered two kinds of algorithm analysis, *worst-case* analysis and *average-case* analysis. In both of these, we have taken a single event or single situation and attempted to determine how much work an algorithm does to process it. Amortized analysis differs from both these kinds of analysis in that it considers a long *sequence* of events rather than a single event in isolation. Amortized analysis then gives a *worst-case* estimate of the cost of a long sequence of events.

It is quite possible that one event in a sequence affects the cost of later events. One task may be difficult and expensive to perform, but it may leave a data structure in a state where the tasks which follow become much easier. Consider, for example, a stack where any number of entries may be pushed on at once, and any number may be popped off at once. If there are $n$ entries in the stack, then the worst-case cost of a multiple pop operation is obviously $n$, since all the entries might be popped off at once. If, however, almost all the entries are popped off (in one expensive pop operation), then a subsequent pop operation cannot be expensive, since few entries remain. Let us allow a pop of 0 entries at a cost of 0. Then, if we start with $n$ entries in the stack and do a series of $n$ multiple pops, the amortized worst-case cost of each pop is only 1, even though the worst-case cost is $n$, the reason being that the $n$ multiple pops together can only remove the $n$ entries from the stack, so their total cost cannot exceed $n$.

*multiple pops*

*amortization*

In the world of finance, *amortization* means to spread a large expense over a period of time, such as using a mortgage to spread the cost of a house (with interest) over many monthly payments. Accountants amortize a large capital expenditure over the income-producing activities for which it is used. Insurance actuaries amortize high-risk cases over the general population.

### 2. Average versus Amortized Analysis

Amortized analysis is not the same as average-case analysis, since the former considers a sequence of *related* situations and the latter all possible *independent* situations. For sorting methods, we did average-case analysis over all possible cases. It makes no sense to speak of sorting the same list twice in a row, and therefore amortized analysis does not usually apply to sorting.

*sorting*

We can, however, contrive an example where it does. Consider a list which is first sorted, then, after some use of the list, has a new entry inserted into a random position of the list. After further use, the list is then sorted again. Later, another entry is inserted at random, and so on. What sorting method should we use? If we rely on average-case analysis, we might choose quicksort. If we prefer worst-case analysis, then we might choose mergesort or heapsort with guaranteed performance of $O(n \log n)$. Amortized analysis, however, will lead us to insertion sort: Once the list is sorted and a new entry inserted at random, insertion sort will move it to its proper place with $O(n)$ performance. Since the list is nearly sorted, quicksort (with the best average-case performance) may provide the worst actual performance, since some choices of pivot may force it to nearly its worst case.

### 3. Tree Traversal

As another example, consider the inorder traversal of a binary tree, where we measure the cost of visiting one vertex as the number of branches traversed to reach that vertex from the last one visited. The best-case cost is 1, when we go from a vertex to one of its children or to its parent. The worst-case cost, for a tree with $n$ vertices, is $n - 1$, as shown by the tree that is one long chain to the left, where it takes $n - 1$ branches to reach the first (leftmost) vertex. In this chain, however, all the remaining vertices are reached in only 1 step each, as the traversal moves from each vertex to its parent. In a completely balanced binary tree of size $n$, some vertices require as many as $\lg n$ steps, others only 1.

If, however, we amortize the cost over a traversal of the entire binary tree, then the cost of going from each vertex to the next is less than 2. To see this, note first that every binary tree with $n$ vertices has precisely $n - 1$ branches, since every vertex except the root has just one branch coming down into it. A complete traversal of the tree goes over every branch twice, once going down and once up. (Here we have included going up the path to the root after the last, rightmost vertex has been visited.) Hence the total number of steps in a full traversal is $2(n - 1)$, and the amortized number of steps from one vertex to the next is $2(n - 1)/n < 2$.

### 4. Credit Balance: Making costs level

Suppose you are working with your household budget. If you are employed, then (you hope) your income is usually fairly stable from month to month. Your expenses, however, may not be. Some months large amounts are due for insurance, or tuition, or a major purchase. Other months have no extraordinary expenses. To keep your bank account solvent, you then need to save enough during the months with low expenses so that you can pay all the large bills as they come due. At the beginning of the month with large bills, you have a large bank balance. After paying the bills, your bank balance is much smaller, but you are just as well off, because you now owe less money.

*credit function*

We wish to apply this idea to algorithm analysis. To do so, we invent a function, which we call a ***credit balance***, that behaves like the bank balance of a well-budgeted family. The credit function will be chosen in such a way that it will be large when the next operation is expensive, and smaller when the next operation can be done quickly. We then think of the credit function as helping to bear some of the cost of expensive operations, and, for inexpensive operations, we set aside more than the actual cost, using the excess to build up the credit function for future use.

To make this idea more precise, suppose that we have a sequence of $m$ operations on a data structure, and let $t_i$ be the *actual* cost of operation $i$ for $1 \le i \le m$. Let the values of our credit function be $c_0, c_1, \ldots, c_m$, where $c_0$ is the credit balance before the first operation and $c_i$ is the credit balance after operation $i$, for $1 \le i \le m$. Then we make the fundamental definition:

**Definition**   The *amortized cost* $a_i$ of each operation is defined to be

$$a_i = t_i + c_i - c_{i-1}$$

for $i = 1, 2, \ldots, m$, where $t_i$ and $c_i$ are as just defined.

This equation says that the amortized cost is the actual cost plus the amount that our credit balance has changed while doing the operation.

Remember that our credit balance is just an accounting tool: We are free to invent any function we wish, but some are much better than others. Our goal is to help with budgeting; therefore, our goal is:

*goal*

*Choose the credit-balance function $c_i$ so as to make the amortized costs $a_i$ as nearly equal as possible, no matter how the actual costs $t_i$ may vary.*

We now wish to use the amortized cost to help us calculate the total actual cost of the sequence of $m$ operations. The fundamental definition rearranges as $t_i = a_i + c_{i-1} - c_i$, and the total actual cost is then

$$\sum_{i=1}^{m} t_i = \sum_{i=1}^{m} (a_i + c_{i-1} - c_i) = \left( \sum_{i=1}^{m} a_i \right) + c_0 - c_m.$$

Except for the first and last values, all the credit balances cancel each other out and therefore do not enter the final calculation. For future reference, we restate this fact as a lemma:

**Lemma 9.5**   *The total actual cost and total amortized cost of a sequence of $m$ operations on a data structure are related by*

$$\sum_{i=1}^{m} t_i = \left( \sum_{i=1}^{m} a_i \right) + c_0 - c_m.$$

Our goal is to choose the credit-balance function in such a way that the $a_i$ are nearly equal; it will then be easy to calculate the right-hand side of this equation, and therefore the total actual cost of the sequence of $m$ operations as well.

*telescoping sum*

A sum like this one, where the terms have alternate plus and minus signs, so that they cancel when added, is called a *telescoping sum*, since it may remind you of a toy (or portable) telescope made up of several short tubes that slide inside each other but may be extended to make up one long telescope tube.

**5. Incrementing Binary Integers**

Let us tie down these ideas by studying one more simple example. Then it will be time to apply these ideas to prove a fundamental and surprising theorem about splay trees.

The example we consider is an algorithm that continually increments a binary (base 2) integer by 1. We start at the right side; while the current bit is 1, we change it to 0 and move left, stopping when we reach the far left or hit a 0 bit, which we change to 1 and stop. The cost of performing this algorithm is the number of bits (binary digits) that are changed. The results of applying this algorithm 16 times to a four digit integer are shown in the first three columns of Figure 9.28.

| step $i$ | integer | $t_i$ | $c_i$ | $a_i$ |
|----------|---------|-------|-------|-------|
|          | 0 0 0 0 |       | 0     |       |
| 1        | 0 0 0 1 | 1     | 1     | 2     |
| 2        | 0 0 1 0 | 2     | 1     | 2     |
| 3        | 0 0 1 1 | 1     | 2     | 2     |
| 4        | 0 1 0 0 | 3     | 1     | 2     |
| 5        | 0 1 0 1 | 1     | 2     | 2     |
| 6        | 0 1 1 0 | 2     | 2     | 2     |
| 7        | 0 1 1 1 | 1     | 3     | 2     |
| 8        | 1 0 0 0 | 4     | 1     | 2     |
| 9        | 1 0 0 1 | 1     | 2     | 2     |
| 10       | 1 0 1 0 | 2     | 2     | 2     |
| 11       | 1 0 1 1 | 1     | 3     | 2     |
| 12       | 1 1 0 0 | 3     | 2     | 2     |
| 13       | 1 1 0 1 | 1     | 3     | 2     |
| 14       | 1 1 1 0 | 2     | 3     | 2     |
| 15       | 1 1 1 1 | 1     | 4     | 2     |
| 16       | 0 0 0 0 | 4     | 0     | 0     |

Figure 9.28. Cost and amortized cost of incrementing binary integers

For the credit balance in this example, we take the total number of 1's in the binary integer. Clearly, the number of digits that must be changed is exactly one more than the number of 1's in the rightmost part of the integer, so it is reasonable that the more 1's there are, the more digits must be changed. With this choice, we can calculate the amortized cost of each step, using the fundamental formula. The result is shown in the last column of Figure 9.28, and turns out to be 2 for every step except the last, which is 0. Hence we conclude that we can increment a four digit binary integer with an amortized cost of two digit changes, even though the actual cost varies from one to four.

### 9.5.5 AMORTIZED ANALYSIS OF SPLAYING

After all this preliminary introduction, we can now use the techniques of amortized algorithm analysis to determine how much work our splay-tree algorithm does over a long sequence of retrievals and insertions. As a measure of the actual complexity we shall take the depth within the tree that the desired node has before splaying. All the actions of the algorithm—key comparisons and rotations—go in lock step with this depth. The number of iterations of the main loop that the function makes, for example, is about half this depth.

First, let us introduce some simple notation. We let $T$ be a binary search tree on which we are performing a splay insertion or retrieval. We let $T_i$ denote the tree $T$ as it has been transformed after step $i$ of the splaying process, with $T_0 = T$. If $x$ is any node in $T_i$, then we denote by $T_i(x)$ the subtree of $T_i$ with root $x$, and we denote by $|T_i(x)|$ the number of nodes in this subtree.

We assume that we are splaying at a node $x$, and we consider a bottom-up splay, so $x$ begins somewhere in the tree $T$, but, after $m$ splaying steps, ends up as the root of $T$.

*rank*

For each step $i$ of the splaying process and each vertex $x$ in $T$, we define the *rank* at step $i$ of $x$ to be

$$r_i(x) = \lg |T_i(x)|.$$

This rank function behaves something like an idealized height: It depends on the size of the subtree with root $x$, not on its height, but it indicates what the height of the subtree would be if it were completely balanced.

If $x$ is a leaf, then $|T_i(x)| = 1$, so $r_i(x) = 0$. Nodes close to the fringe of the tree have small ranks; the root has the largest rank in the tree.

The amount of work that the algorithm must do to insert or retrieve in a subtree is clearly related to the height of the subtree, and so, we hope, to the rank of the subtree's root. We would like to define the credit balance in such a way that large and tall trees would have a large credit balance and short or small trees a smaller balance, since the amount of work in splaying increases with the height of the tree. We shall use the rank function to achieve this. In fact, we shall portion out the credit balance of the tree among all its vertices by always requiring the following to hold:

---

**The Credit Invariant**

*The Credit Invariant*

*For every node $x$ of $T$ and after every step $i$ of splaying, node $x$ has credit equal to its rank $r_i(x)$.*

---

The total credit balance for the tree is then defined simply as the sum of the individual credits for all the nodes in the tree,

$$c_i = \sum_{x \in T_i} r_i(x).$$

If the tree is empty or contains only one node, then its credit balance is 0. As the tree grows, its credit balance increases, and this balance should reflect the work needed to build the tree. The investment of credit in the tree is done in two ways:

- We invest the actual work done in the operation. We have already decided to count this as one unit for each level that the target node rises during the splaying process. Hence each splaying step counts as two units, except for a zig or a zag step, which count as one unit.

- Since the shape of the tree changes during splaying, we must either add or remove credit invested in the tree so as to maintain the Credit Invariant at all times. (As we discussed in the last section, this is essentially an accounting device to even out the costs of different steps.)

This investment is summarized by the equation defining the amortized complexity $a_i$ of step $i$,

$$a_i = t_i + c_i - c_{i-1},$$

where $t_i$ is the actual work and $c_i - c_{i-1}$ gives the change in the credit balance.

Our principal goal now is, by using the definitions given and the way splaying works, to determine bounds on $a_i$ that, in turn, will allow us to find the cost of the whole splaying process, amortized over a sequence of retrievals and insertions.

First, we need a preliminary mathematical observation.

**Lemma 9.6**     If $\alpha$, $\beta$, and $\gamma$ are positive real numbers with $\alpha + \beta \leq \gamma$, then

$$\lg \alpha + \lg \beta \leq 2 \lg \gamma - 2.$$

**Proof**     We have $\left(\sqrt{\alpha} - \sqrt{\beta}\right)^2 \geq 0$, since the square of any real number is nonnegative. This expands and simplifies to

$$\sqrt{\alpha\beta} \leq \frac{\alpha + \beta}{2}.$$

(This inequality is called the *arithmetic–geometric mean inequality*.) Since $\alpha + \beta \leq \gamma$, we obtain $\sqrt{\alpha\beta} \leq \gamma/2$. Squaring both sides and taking (base 2) logarithms gives the result in the lemma.

We next analyze the various kinds of splaying steps separately.

**Lemma 9.7**     If the $i^{\text{th}}$ splaying step is a zig-zig or zag-zag step at node $x$, then its amortized complexity $a_i$ satisfies

$$a_i < 3(r_i(x) - r_{i-1}(x)).$$

**Proof**     This case is illustrated as follows:

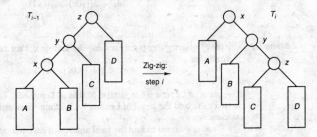

The actual complexity $t_i$ of a zig-zig or a zag-zag step is 2 units, and only the sizes of the subtrees rooted at $x$, $y$, and $z$ change in this step. Therefore, all terms in the summation defining $c_i$ cancel against those for $c_{i-1}$ except those indicated in the following equation:

$$a_i = t_i + c_i - c_{i-1}$$
$$= 2 + r_i(x) + r_i(y) + r_i(z) - r_{i-1}(x) - r_{i-1}(y) - r_{i-1}(z)$$
$$= 2 + r_i(y) + r_i(z) - r_{i-1}(x) - r_{i-1}(y)$$

We obtain the last line by taking the logarithm of $|T_i(x)| = |T_{i-1}(z)|$, which is the observation that the subtree rooted at $z$ before the splaying step has the same size as that rooted at $x$ after the step.

Lemma 9.6 can now be applied to cancel the 2 in this equation (the actual complexity). Let $\alpha = |T_{i-1}(x)|$, $\beta = |T_i(z)|$, and $y = |T_i(x)|$. From the diagram for this case, we see that $T_{i-1}(x)$ contains components $x$, $A$, and $B$; $T_i(z)$ contains components $z$, $C$, and $D$; and $T_i(x)$ contains all these components (and $y$ besides). Hence $\alpha + \beta < y$, so Lemma 9.6 implies $r_{i-1}(x) + r_i(z) \le 2r_i(x) - 2$, or $2r_i(x) - r_{i-1}(x) - r_i(z) - 2 \ge 0$. Adding this nonnegative quantity to the right side of the last equation for $a_i$, we obtain

$$a_i \le 2r_i(x) - 2r_{i-1}(x) + r_i(y) - r_{i-1}(y).$$

Before step $i$, $y$ is the parent of $x$, so $|T_{i-1}(y)| > |T_{i-1}(x)|$. After step $i$, $x$ is the parent of $y$, so $|T_i(x)| > |T_i(y)|$. Taking logarithms, we have $r_{i-1}(y) > r_{i-1}(x)$ and $r_i(x) > r_i(y)$. Hence we finally obtain

$$a_i < 3r_i(x) - 3r_{i-1}(x),$$

which is the assertion in Lemma 9.7 that we wished to prove.

**Lemma 9.8**   If the $i^{th}$ splaying step is a zig-zag or zag-zig step at node $x$, then its amortized complexity $a_i$ satisfies
$$a_i < 2(r_i(x) - r_{i-1}(x)).$$

**Lemma 9.9**   If the $i^{th}$ splaying step is a zig or a zag step at node $x$, then its amortized complexity $a_i$ satisfies
$$a_i < 1 + (r_i(x) - r_{i-1}(x)).$$

The proof of Lemma 9.8 is similar to that of Lemma 9.7 (even though the result is stronger), and the proof of Lemma 9.9 is straightforward; both of these are left as exercises.

Finally, we need to find the total amortized cost of a retrieval or insertion. To do so, we must add the costs of all the splay steps done during the retrieval or insertion. If there are $m$ such steps, then at most one, (the last) can be a zig or zag step to which Lemma 9.9 applies, and the others all satisfy the bounds in Lemmas

9.7 and 9.8, of which the coefficient of 3 in Lemma 9.7 provides the weaker bound. Hence we obtain that the total amortized cost is

$$\sum_{i=1}^{m} a_i = \sum_{i=1}^{m-1} a_i + a_m$$

$$\leq \sum_{i=1}^{m-1} \left(3r_i(x) - 3r_{i-1}(x)\right) + \left(1 + 3r_m(x) - 3r_{m-1}(x)\right)$$

$$= 1 + 3r_m(x) - 3r_0(x)$$

$$\leq 1 + 3r_m(x)$$

$$= 1 + 3\lg n.$$

In this derivation, we have used the fact that the sum telescopes, so that only the first rank $r_0(x)$ and the final rank $r_m(x)$ remain. Since $r_0(x) \geq 0$, its omission only increases the right side, and since at the end of the splaying process $x$ is the root of the tree, we have $r_m(x) = \lg n$, where $n$ is the number of nodes in the tree.

With this, we have now completed the proof of the principal result of this section:

**Theorem 9.10**   *The amortized cost of an insertion or retrieval with splaying in a binary search tree with n nodes does not exceed*

$$1 + 3\lg n$$

*upward moves of the target node in the tree.*

Finally, we can relate this amortized cost to the actual cost of each of a long sequence of splay insertions or retrievals. To do so, we apply Lemma 9.5, noting that the summations now are over a sequence of retrievals or insertions, not over the steps of a single retrieval or insertion. We see that the total actual cost of a sequence of $m$ splay accesses differs from the total amortized cost only by $c_0 - c_m$, where $c_0$ and $c_m$ are the credit balances of the initial and final trees, respectively. If the tree never has more than $n$ nodes, then these balances are somewhere between 0 and $\lg n$, so we need not add more than $\lg n$ to the cost in Theorem 9.10 to obtain:

**Corollary 9.11**   *The total complexity of a sequence of m insertions or retrievals with splaying in a binary search tree which never has more than n nodes does not exceed*

$$m(1 + 3\lg n) + \lg n$$

*upward moves of a target node in the tree.*

In this result, each splaying step counts as two upward moves, except for zig or zag steps, which count as one move each.

The fact that insertions and retrievals in a splay tree, over a long sequence, are *guaranteed* to take only $O(\log n)$ time is quite remarkable, given that, at any time, it is quite possible for a splay tree to degenerate into a highly unbalanced shape.

**Exercises 9.5**     **E1.** Consider the following binary search tree:

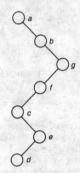

Splay this tree at each of the following keys in turn:

d  b  g  f  a  d  b  d

Each part builds on the previous; that is, use the final tree of each solution as the starting tree for the next part.     [*Check*: The tree should be completely balanced after the last part, as well as after one previous part.]

**E2.** Define a *rank* function $r(x)$ for the nodes of any binary tree as follows:

If $x$ is the root, then $r(x) = 0$.

If $x$ is the left child of a node $y$, then $r(x) = r(y) - 1$.

If $x$ is the right child of a node $y$, then $r(x) = r(y) + 1$.

We define the *credit balance* of a tree during a traversal to be the rank of the node being visited. For each of the following binary trees, determine the ranks at each node and prepare a table like Figure 9.28 (page 449) showing the actual cost, credit balance, and amortized cost (in edges traversed) of each step of an inorder traversal.

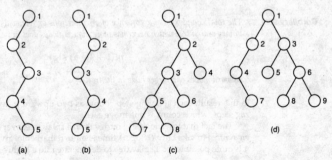

E3. Generalize the amortized analysis given in the text for incrementing four digit binary integers to $n$ digit binary integers.

E4. Prove Lemma 9.8. The method is similar to the proof of Lemma 9.7.

E5. Prove Lemma 9.9. This proof does not require Lemma 9.6 or any intricate calculations.

**Programming Projects 9.5**

P1. Substitute the function for splay retrieval and insertion into the menu-driven demonstration program for binary search trees in Section 9.2, Project P2 (page 411) (using a version with a sentinel sentinel), thereby obtaining a demonstration program for splay trees.

*coatroom*

P2. Use a splay tree to implement the coatroom operations of Section 6.3. Test your program with the coatroom demonstration program, and then run the timed-test program with the splay-tree program, comparing the results with those for the other implementations. Why are you likely to find this performance disappointing?

*information retrieval*

P3. Substitute the function for splay retrieval and insertion into the information-retrieval program of Project P6 of Section 9.2 (page 412). Compare the performance of splay trees with ordinary binary search trees for various combinations of input text files.

# Pointers and Pitfalls

1. Consider binary search trees as an alternative to ordered lists (indeed, as a way of implementing the abstract data type *list*). At the cost of an extra pointer field in each node, binary search trees allow random access (with $O(\log n)$ key comparisons) to all nodes while maintaining the flexibility of linked lists for insertions, deletions, and rearrangement.

2. Consider binary search trees as an alternative to tables (indeed, as a way of implementing the abstract data type *table*). At the cost of access time that is $O(\log n)$ instead of $O(1)$, binary search trees allow traversal of the data structure in the order specified by the keys while maintaining the advantage of random access provided by tables.

3. In choosing your data structures, always carefully consider what operations will be required. Binary trees are especially appropriate when random access, traversal in a predetermined order, and flexibility in making insertions and deletions are all required.

4. While choosing data structures and algorithms, remain alert to the possibility of highly unbalanced binary search trees. If the incoming data are likely to be in random order, then an ordinary binary search tree should prove entirely adequate. If the data may come in a sorted or nearly sorted order, then the algorithms should take appropriate action. If there is only a slight possibility of serious imbalance, it might be ignored. If, in a large project, there is greater

likelihood of serious imbalance, then there may still be appropriate places in the software where the trees can be checked for balance and rebuilt if necessary. For applications in which it is essential to maintain logarithmic access time at all times, AVL trees provide nearly perfect balance at a slight cost in computer time and space, but with considerable programming cost. If it is necessary for the tree to adapt dynamically to changes in the frequency of the data, then a splay tree may be the best choice.

5. Binary trees are defined recursively; algorithms for manipulating binary trees are usually best written recursively. In programming with binary trees, be aware of the problems generally associated with recursive algorithms. Be sure that your algorithm terminates under any condition and that it correctly treats the trivial case of an empty tree.

6. Although binary trees are usually implemented as linked structures, remain aware of the possibility of other implementations. In programming with linked binary trees, keep in mind the pitfalls attendant on all programming with linked lists.

# Review Questions

9.1

1. Define the term *binary tree*.

2. What is the difference between a binary tree and an ordinary tree in which each vertex has at most two branches?

3. Give the order of visiting the vertices of each of the following binary trees under (a) preorder, (b) inorder, and (c) postorder traversal.

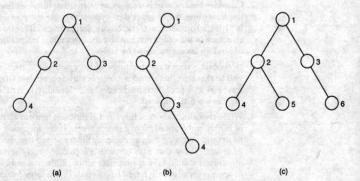

(a)  (b)  (c)

**4.** Draw the expression trees for each of the following expressions, and show the result of traversing the tree in **(a)** preorder, **(b)** inorder, and **(c)** postorder.

(a) $a - b$.

(b) $n/m!$.

(c) $\log m!$.

(d) $(\log x) + (\log y)$.

(e) $x \times y \le x + y$.

(f) $a > b$ or $b \ge a$.

9.2

**5.** Define the term *binary search tree*.

**6.** If a binary search tree with $n$ nodes is well balanced, what is the approximate number of comparisons of keys needed to find a target? What is the number if the tree degenerates to a chain?

**7.** In twenty words or less, explain how treesort works.

**8.** What is the relationship between treesort and quicksort?

**9.** What causes deletion from a search tree to be more difficult than insertion into a search tree?

9.3

**10.** When is the algorithm for building a binary search tree developed in Section 9.3 useful, and why is it preferable to simply using the function for inserting an item into a search tree for each item in the input?

**11.** How much slower, on average, is searching a random binary search tree than is searching a completely balanced binary search tree?

9.4

**12.** What is the purpose for AVL trees?

**13.** What condition defines an AVL tree among all binary search trees?

**14.** Draw a picture explaining how balance is restored when an insertion into an AVL tree puts a node out of balance.

**15.** How does the worst-case performance of an AVL tree compare with the worst-case performance of a random binary search tree? How does it compare with its average-case performance? How does the average-case performance of an AVL tree compare with that of a random binary search tree?

9.5

**16.** In twenty words or less, describe what *splaying* does.

**17.** What is the purpose for splaying?

**18.** What is *amortized* algorithm analysis?

**19.** What is a *credit-balance function*, and how is it used?

**20.** In the big-O notation, what is the cost of splaying amortized over a sequence of retrievals and insertions? Why is this surprising?

## References for Further Study ━━━━━━━━━━━━━━━━━━━━━━━━━━

The most comprehensive source of information on binary trees is the series of books by KNUTH. The properties of binary trees, other classes of trees, traversal, path length, and history, altogether occupy pages 305–405 of Volume 1. Volume 3, pages 422–480, discusses binary search trees, AVL trees, and related topics. The proof of Theorem 9.2 is from Volume 3, page 427.

An alternative study of binary trees, with Pascal programs presented in detail, is

N. WIRTH, *Algorithms + Data Structures = Programs*, Prentice-Hall, Englewood Cliffs, N. J., 1976.

This book also contains (pages 189–264) an exposition, with Pascal algorithms, of binary trees, balancing methods, and generalizations, including (pages 215–226) algorithms for insertion and deletion in AVL trees.

A mathematical analysis of the behavior of AVL trees appears in

E. M. REINGOLD, J. NIEVERGELT, N. DEO, *Combinatorial Algorithms: Theory and Practice*, Prentice Hall, Englewood Cliffs, N. J., 1977.

The original reference for AVL trees is

G. M. ADEL'SON-VEL'SKII and E. M. LANDIS, *Dokl. Akad. Nauk SSSR* 146 (1962), 263–266; English translation: *Soviet Math. (Dokl.)* 3 (1962), 1259–1263.

Several algorithms for constructing a balanced binary search tree are discussed in

HSI CHANG and S. S. IYENGAR, "Efficient algorithms to globally balance a binary search tree," *Communications of the ACM* 27 (1984), 695–702.

The notions of splay trees and amortized algorithm analysis, together with the derivation of the algorithm we present, are due to:

D. D. SLEATOR and R. E. TARJAN, "Self-adjusting binary search trees," *Journal of the ACM* 32 (1985), 652–686.

Good sources for more advanced presentations of topics related to this chapter are:

HARRY R. LEWIS and LARRY DENENBERG, *Data Structures & Their Algorithms*, Harper Collins, 1991, 509 pages.

DERICK WOOD, *Data Structures, Algorithms, and Performance*, Addison-Wesley, 1993, 594 pages.

Another interesting method of adjusting the shape of a binary search tree, called *weighted path length* trees and based on the frequencies with which the nodes are accessed, appears in the following paper, easy to read and with a survey of related results:

G. ARGO, "Weighting without waiting: the weighted path length tree," *Computer Journal*, 34 (1991), 444–449.

# 10

# Multiway
# Trees

THIS CHAPTER continues the study
of trees as data structures, now
concentrating on trees with possibly more
than two branches at each node. We begin
with establishing a simple connection with
binary trees. Second, we study a class
of trees called tries, which share some
properties with table lookup. Next we
investigate B-trees, which prove invaluable
for problems of external information
retrieval. Each of these sections is
independent of the others. In the following
section, we apply the idea of B-trees to
obtain another class of binary search trees,
called red-black trees. Finally, the chapter
illustrates the use of trees to describe the
execution of an algorithm by studying
lookahead trees used in game playing.

## 10.1  Orchards, Trees, and Binary Trees ━━━━━━━━━━━━━━━

Binary trees, as we have seen, are a powerful and elegant form of data structures. Even so, the restriction to no more than two children at each node is severe, and there are many possible applications for trees as data structures where the number of children of a node can be arbitrary. This section elucidates a pleasant and helpful surprise: Binary trees provide a convenient way to represent what first appears to be a far broader class of trees.

### 10.1.1  On the Classification of Species

Since we have already sighted several kinds of trees in the applications we have studied, we should, before exploring further, put our gear in order by settling the definitions. In mathematics, the term *tree* has a quite broad meaning: It is any set of points (called vertices) and any set of pairs of distinct vertices (called edges or branches) such that (1) there is a sequence of edges (a path) from any vertex to any other, and (2) there are no circuits, that is, no paths starting from a vertex and returning to the same vertex.

*free tree*
*rooted tree*

In computer applications we usually do not need to study trees in such generality, and when we do, for emphasis we call them *free trees*. Our trees are almost always tied down by having one particular vertex singled out as the *root*, and for emphasis we call such a tree a *rooted tree*.

A rooted tree can be drawn in our usual way by picking it up by its root and shaking it so that all the branches and vertices hang downward, with the leaves at the bottom. Even so, rooted trees still do not have all the structure that we usually use. In a rooted tree there is still no way to tell left from right, or, when one vertex has several children, to tell which is first, second, and so on. If for no other reason, the restraint of sequential execution of instructions (not to mention sequential organization of storage) usually imposes an order on the children of each vertex. Hence we define an ***ordered tree*** to be a rooted tree in which the children
*ordered tree*
of each vertex are assigned an order.

Note that ordered trees for which no vertex has more than two children are still not the same class as binary trees. If a vertex in a binary tree has only one child, then it could be either on the left side or on the right side, and the two resulting binary trees are different, but both would be the same as ordered trees.

*2-tree*

As a final remark related to the definitions, let us note that the 2-trees that we studied as part of algorithm analysis are rooted trees (but not necessarily ordered trees) with the property that every vertex has either 0 or 2 children. Thus 2-trees do not coincide with any of the other classes we have introduced.

Figure 10.1 shows what happens for the various kinds of trees with a small number of vertices. Note that each class of trees after the first can be obtained by taking the trees from the previous class and distinguishing those that differ under the new criterion. Compare the list of five ordered trees with four vertices with the list of fourteen binary trees with four vertices constructed in Exercise E1 of Section 9.1 (page 393). You will find that, again, the binary trees can be obtained from the appropriate ordered trees by distinguishing a left branch from a right branch.

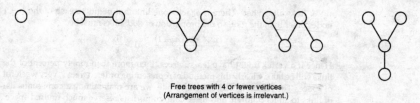

Free trees with 4 or fewer vertices
(Arrangement of vertices is irrelevant.)

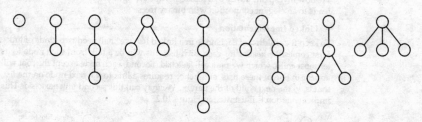

Rooted trees with 4 or fewer vertices
(Root is at the top of tree.)

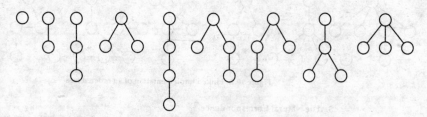

Ordered trees with 4 or fewer vertices

**Figure 10.1. Various kinds of trees**

### 10.1.2 Ordered Trees

#### 1. Computer Implementation

If we wish to use an ordered tree as a data structure, the obvious way to implement it in computer memory would be to extend the standard way to implement a binary tree, keeping as many fields in each node as there may be subtrees, in place of the two links needed for binary trees. Thus in a tree where some nodes have as many as ten subtrees, we would keep ten link fields in each node. But this will result in a great many of the link fields being NULL. In fact, we can easily determine exactly *multiple links* how many. If the tree has $n$ nodes and each node has $k$ link fields, then there are

$n \times k$ links altogether. There is exactly one link that points to each of the $n - 1$ nodes other than the root, so the proportion of NULL links must be

$$\frac{(n \times k) - (n - 1)}{n \times k} > 1 - \frac{1}{k}.$$

Hence if a vertex might have ten subtrees, then more than ninety percent of the links will be NULL. Clearly this method of representing ordered trees is very wasteful of space. The reason is that, for each node, we are maintaining a contiguous list of links to all its children, and these contiguous lists reserve much unused space. We now investigate a way that replaces these contiguous lists with linked lists and leads to an elegant connection with binary trees.

## 2. Linked Implementation

To keep the children of each node in a linked list, we shall need two kinds of links. First comes the header for each such list; this will be a link from each node to its leftmost child, which we may call firstchild. Second, each node except the root will appear in one of these lists, and hence requires a link to the next node on the list, that is, to the next child of the parent. We may call this second link nextchild. This implementation is illustrated in Figure 10.2.

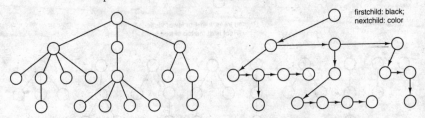

Figure 10.2. Linked implementation of an ordered tree

## 3. The Natural Correspondence

For each node of the ordered tree we have defined two links (that will be NULL if not otherwise defined), firstchild and nextchild. By using these two links we now have the structure of a binary tree; that is, the linked implementation of an ordered tree is a linked binary tree. If we wish, we can even form a better picture of a binary tree by taking the linked representation of the ordered tree and rotating it a few degrees clockwise, so that downward (firstchild) links point leftward and the horizontal (nextchild) links point downward and to the right.

## 4. Inverse Correspondence

Suppose that we reverse the steps of the foregoing process, beginning with a binary tree and trying to recover an ordered tree. The first observation that we must make is that not every binary tree is obtained from a rooted tree by the above process: Since the nextchild link of the root is always NULL, the root of the corresponding binary tree will always have an empty right subtree. To study the inverse correspondence more carefully, we must consider another class of data structures.

### 10.1.3 FORESTS AND ORCHARDS

*forest*

*orchard*

*recursive definitions*

In our work so far with binary trees we have profited from using recursion, and for other classes of trees we shall continue to do so. Employing recursion means reducing a problem to a smaller one. Hence we should see what happens if we take a rooted tree or an ordered tree and strip off the root. What is then left is (if not empty) a set of rooted trees or an ordered set of ordered trees, respectively.

The standard term for an arbitrary set of trees is *forest*, but when we use this term, we generally assume that the trees are rooted. The phrase *ordered forest* is sometimes used for an ordered set of ordered trees, but we shall adopt the equally descriptive (and more colorful) term *orchard* for this class.

Note that not only can we obtain a forest or an orchard by removing the root from a rooted tree or an ordered tree, respectively, but we can build a rooted or an ordered tree by starting with a forest or an orchard, attaching a new vertex at the top, and adding branches from the new vertex (which will be the root) to the roots of all trees in the forest or the orchard.

We shall use this observation to give a new, recursive definition of ordered trees and orchards, one that yields a formal proof of the connection with binary trees. First, let us consider how to start. Recall that it is possible for a binary tree to be empty; that is, it may have no vertices. It is also possible for a forest or an orchard to be empty; that is, it may contain no trees. It is, however, not possible for a rooted or an ordered tree to be empty, since it is guaranteed to contain a root, at least. If we wish to start building trees and forests, we can note that the tree with only one vertex is obtained by attaching a new root to an empty forest. Once we have this tree, we can make a forest consisting of as many one-vertex trees as we wish and attach a new root to build all rooted trees of height 1. In this way we can continue to construct all the rooted trees in turn in accordance with the following mutually recursive definitions.

**Definition**

A *rooted tree* consists of a single vertex $v$, called the *root* of the tree, together with a forest $F$, whose trees are called the *subtrees* of the root.

A *forest* $F$ is a (possibly empty) set of rooted trees.

A similar construction works for ordered trees and orchards.

**Definition**

An *ordered tree* $T$ consists of a single vertex $v$, called the *root* of the tree, together with an orchard $O$, whose trees are called the *subtrees* of the root $v$. We may denote the ordered tree with the ordered pair

$$T = \{v, O\}.$$

An *orchard* $O$ is either the empty set $\varnothing$, or consists of an ordered tree $T$, called the *first tree* of the orchard, together with another orchard $O'$ (which contains the remaining trees of the orchard). We may denote the orchard with the ordered pair

$$O = (T, O').$$

Notice how the ordering of trees is implicit in the definition of orchard. A nonempty orchard contains a first tree, and the remaining trees form another orchard, which again has a first tree that is the second tree of the original orchard. Continuing to examine the remaining orchard yields the third tree, and so on, until the remaining orchard is the empty one.

### 10.1.4 THE FORMAL CORRESPONDENCE

We can now obtain the principal result of this section.

**Theorem 10.1**    *Let S be any finite set of vertices. There is a one-to-one correspondence f from the set of orchards whose set of vertices is S to the set of binary trees whose set of vertices is S.*

**Proof**    Let us use the notation introduced in the definitions to prove the theorem. First, we need a similar notation for binary trees: A binary tree $B$ is either the empty set $\varnothing$ or consists of a root vertex $\nu$ with two binary trees $B_1$ and $B_2$. We may thus denote a binary tree with the ordered triple

$$B = [\nu, B_1, B_2].$$

We shall prove the theorem by mathematical induction on the number of vertices in $S$. The first case to consider is the empty orchard $\varnothing$, which will correspond to the empty binary tree:

$$f(\varnothing) = \varnothing.$$

If the orchard $O$ is not empty, then it is denoted by the ordered pair

$$O = (T, O_2)$$

where $T$ is an ordered tree and $O_2$ another orchard. The ordered tree $T$ is denoted as the pair

$$T = \{\nu, O_1\}$$

where $\nu$ is a vertex and $O_1$ is another orchard. We substitute this expression for $T$ in the first expression, obtaining

$$O = (\{\nu, O_1\}, O_2).$$

By the induction hypothesis, $f$ provides a one-to-one correspondence from orchards with fewer vertices than in $S$ to binary trees, and $O_1$ and $O_2$ are smaller than $O$, so the binary trees $f(O_1)$ and $f(O_2)$ are determined by the induction hypothesis. We define the correspondence $f$ from the orchard to a binary tree by

$$f(\{v, O_1\}, O_2) = [v, f(O_1), f(O_2)].$$

It is now obvious that the function $f$ is a one-to-one correspondence between orchards and binary trees with the same vertices. For any way to fill in the symbols $v$, $O_1$, and $O_2$ on the left side, there is exactly one way to fill in the same symbols on the right, and vice versa.

### 10.1.5 ROTATIONS

We can also use this notational form of the correspondence to help us form the picture of the transformation from orchard to binary tree. In the binary tree $[v, f(O_1), f(O_2)]$ the left link from $v$ goes to the root of the binary tree $f(O_1)$, which in fact was the first child of $v$ in the ordered tree $\{v, O_1\}$. The right link from $v$ goes to the vertex that was formerly the root of the next ordered tree to the right. That is, "left link" in the binary tree corresponds to "first child" in an ordered tree, and "right link" corresponds to "next sibling." In geometrical terms, the transformation reduces to the rules:

1. Draw the orchard so that the first child of each vertex is immediately below the vertex, rather than centering the children below the vertex.

2. Draw a vertical link from each vertex to its first child, and draw a horizontal link from each vertex to its next sibling.

3. Remove the remaining original links.

4. Rotate the diagram 45 degrees clockwise, so that the vertical links appear as left links and the horizontal links as right links.

This process is illustrated in Figure 10.3.

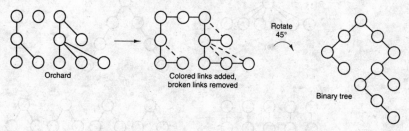

Orchard

Colored links added,
broken links removed

Rotate
45°

Binary tree

Figure 10.3.  Conversion from orchard to binary tree

### 10.1.6 SUMMARY

We have seen three ways to describe the correspondence between orchards and binary trees:

- firstchild and nextchild links,
- rotations of diagrams,
- formal notational equivalence.

Most people find the second way, rotation of diagrams, the easiest to remember and to picture. It is the first way, setting up links to give the correspondence, that is usually needed in actually writing computer programs. The third way, the formal correspondence, finally, is the one that proves most useful in constructing proofs of various properties of binary trees and orchards.

**Exercises 10.1**   **E1.** Convert each of the following orchards into a binary tree.

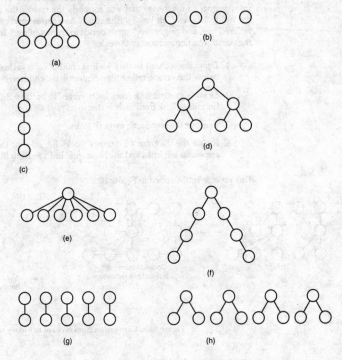

(a)   (b)   (c)   (d)   (e)   (f)   (g)   (h)

**E2.** Convert each of the following binary trees into an orchard.

(a)

(b)

(c)

(d)

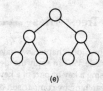

(e)

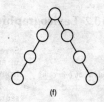

(f)

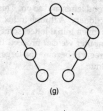

(g)

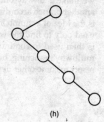

(h)

**E3.** Draw all the

    **(a)** free trees,

    **(b)** rooted trees, and

    **(c)** ordered trees

    with five vertices.

**E4.** We can define the *preorder traversal* of an orchard as follows: If the orchard is empty, do nothing. Otherwise, first visit the root of the first tree, then traverse the orchard of subtrees of the first tree in preorder, and then traverse the orchard of remaining trees in preorder. Prove that preorder traversal of an orchard and preorder traversal of the corresponding binary tree will visit the vertices in the same order.

E5. We can define the *inorder traversal* of an orchard as follows: If the orchard is empty, do nothing. Otherwise, first traverse the orchard of subtrees of the first tree's root in inorder, then visit the root of the first tree, and then traverse the orchard of remaining subtrees in inorder. Prove that inorder traversal of an orchard and inorder traversal of the corresponding binary tree will visit the vertices in the same order.

E6. Describe a way of traversing an orchard that will visit the vertices in the same order as postorder traversal of the corresponding binary tree. Prove that your traversal method visits the vertices in the correct order.

# 10.2 Lexicographic Search Trees: Tries ▬▬▬▬▬

Several times in previous chapters we have contrasted searching a list with looking up an entry in a table. We can apply the idea of table lookup to information retrieval from a tree by using a key or part of a key to make a *multiway branch*.

*multiway branching*

Instead of searching by comparison of entire keys, we can consider a key as a sequence of characters (letters or digits, for example), and use these characters to determine a multiway branch at each step. If our keys are alphabetic names, then we make a 26-way branch according to the first letter of the name, followed by another branch according to the second letter, and so on. This multiway branching is the idea of a thumb index in a dictionary. A thumb index, however, is generally used only to find the words with a given initial letter; some other search method is then used to continue. In a computer we can proceed two or three levels by multiway branching, but then the tree will become too large, and we shall need to resort to some other device to continue.

## 10.2.1 TRIES

One method is to prune from the tree all the branches that do not lead to any key. In English, for example, there are no words that begin with the letters 'bb', 'bc', 'bf', 'bg', ..., but there are words beginning with 'ba', 'bd', or 'be'. Hence all the branches and nodes for nonexistent words can be removed from the tree. The resulting tree is called a *trie*. (This term originated as letters extracted from the word *retrieval*, but it is usually pronounced like the word "try.")

A trie of order $m$ can be defined formally as being either empty or consisting of an ordered sequence of exactly $m$ tries of order $m$.

## 10.2.2 SEARCHING FOR A KEY

A trie describing the words (as listed in the *Oxford English Dictionary*) made up only from the letters *a*, *b*, and *c* is shown in Figure 10.4. Along with the branches to the next level of the trie, each node contains a pointer to a structure of information about the key, if any, that has been found when the node is reached. The search for a particular key begins at the root. The first letter of the key is used as an index to determine which branch to take. An empty branch means that the key being sought is not in the tree. Otherwise, we use the second letter of the key to determine the branch at the next level, and so continue. When we reach the end of the word, the information pointer directs us to the desired information. A NULL information pointer shows that the string is not a word in the trie. Note, therefore, that the word *a* is a prefix of the word *aba*, which is a prefix of the word *abaca*. On the other hand, the string *abac* is not an English word, and therefore has a NULL information pointer.

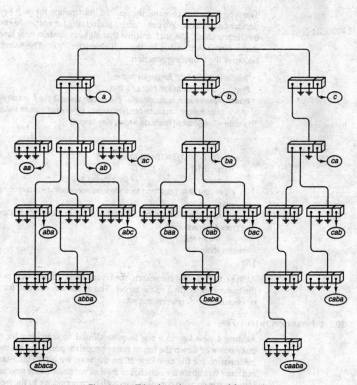

Figure 10.4. Trie of words constructed from *a*, *b*, *c*

## 10.2.3 C ALGORITHM

The search process described above translates easily into a function. First we need some declarations which we put in the file trie.h.

```
#define MAXLENGTH 10        /* maximum length of a key                    */
#define LETTERS 26          /* number of letters in the alphabet          */
typedef char Key[MAXLENGTH];  /* contains only 'a' through 'z'            */
typedef struct trienode Trienode;

struct trienode {
    Trienode *branch[LETTERS];
    Entry *ref;
};
```

The type Entry that contains the desired information for each key is assumed to be declared elsewhere. We use indirect addressing for entries to keep the space taken by the trie small. We shall assume that all keys contain only lowercase letters and that a key is terminated by the null character '\0'. The searching method then becomes the following function.

```
/* TrieSearch: Search for target in trie.
   Pre:   root points to the root of a trie.
   Post:  If the search is successful, the return value is the trie entry which points to the
          information structure holding target; otherwise, return value is NULL. */
```

*trie retrieval*

```
Trienode *TrieSearch(Trienode *root, Key target)
{
    int i;
    for (i = 0; i < MAXLENGTH && root; i++)
        if (target[i] == '\0')
            break;              /* terminates search                      */
            /* root is left pointing to node with information for target. */
        else
            root = root->branch[target[i] - 'a'];  /* Move down appropriate branch. */
    if (root && !root->ref)
        return NULL;
    return root;
}
```

At the conclusion of the search, the return value (if not NULL) points to the node in the trie corresponding to the target. The actual information for the entry can then be obtained by dereferencing ref.

## 10.2.4 INSERTION INTO A TRIE

Adding a new key to a trie is quite similar to searching for the key: We must trace our way down the trie to the appropriate point and set the ref pointer to the information for the new key. If, on the way, we hit a NULL branch in the trie, we must not terminate the search, but instead we must create new nodes and put them into the trie so as to complete the path corresponding to the new key. We thereby obtain the following function.

```
/* InsertTrie: insert a new key into a trie.
   Pre:  root is the root of a trie, newkey is a key not already in the trie, and newentry
         points to its associated information.
   Post: This new entry has been inserted into the trie. */
```

*trie insertion*

```
Trienode *InsertTrie(Trienode *root, Key newkey, Entry *newentry)
{
   int i;
   Trienode *saveroot;

   if (!root)                          /* Create a new trie with all empty subtries.      */
      root = CreateNode();

   saveroot = root;

   for (i = 0;  i < MAXLENGTH;  i++)
      if (newkey[i] == '\0')  /* Terminate the search.                                    */
         break;
      else {
         if (!root->branch[newkey[i] - 'a'])
            /* Make a new node on the route for newkey. */
            root->branch[newkey[i] - 'a'] = CreateNode();
         /* Move down the appropriate branch. */
         root = root->branch[newkey[i] - 'a'];
      }

   /* At this point, we have tested for all characters of newkey. */
   if (root->ref != NULL)
      Warning("Tried to insert a duplicate key.");
   else
      root->ref = newentry;
   return saveroot;
}
```

Function CreateNode, used to allocate new nodes, is as follows.

```
/* CreateNode: create a new node.
   Pre:  None.
   Post: The return value is a Trienode that has been allocated and initialized. */

Trienode *CreateNode(void)
{
   int ch;
   Trienode *new = (Trienode *)malloc(sizeof(Trienode));

   for (ch = 0;  ch < LETTERS;  ch++)
      new->branch[ch] = NULL;
   new->ref = NULL;
   return new;
}
```

### 10.2.5 DELETION FROM A TRIE

The same general plan used for searching and insertion also works for deletion from a trie. We trace down the path corresponding to the key being deleted, and when we reach the appropriate node, we set the corresponding ref field to NULL. If now, however, this node has all its fields NULL (all branches and the ref field), then we should dispose of this node. To do so, we can set up a stack of pointers to the nodes on the path from the root to the last node reached. Alternatively, we can use recursion in the deletion algorithm and avoid the need for an explicit stack. In either case, we shall leave the programming as an exercise.

### 10.2.6 ASSESSMENT OF TRIES

The number of steps required to search a trie (or insert into it) is proportional to the number of characters making up a key, not to a logarithm of the number of keys as in other tree-based searches. If this number of characters is small relative to the (base 2) logarithm of the number of keys, then a trie may prove superior to a binary tree. If, for example, the keys consist of all possible sequences of five letters, then the trie can locate any of $n = 26^5 = 11,881,376$ keys in 5 iterations, whereas the best

*comparison with binary search*

that binary search can do is $\lg n \approx 23.5$ key comparisons.

In many applications, however, the number of characters in a key is larger, and the set of keys that actually occur is sparse in the set of all possible keys. In these applications, the number of iterations required to search a trie may very well exceed the number of key comparisons needed for a binary search.

The best solution, finally, may be to combine the methods. A trie can be used for the first few characters of the key, and then another method can be employed for the remainder of the key. If we return to the example of the thumb index in a dictionary, we see that, in fact, we use a multiway tree to locate the first letter of the word, but we then use some other search method to locate the desired word among those with the same first letter.

---

**Exercises 10.2**    **E1.** Draw the tries constructed from each of the following sets of keys.

  **(a)** All three-digit integers containing only 1, 2, 3 (in decimal representation).

  **(b)** All three-letter sequences built from a, b, c, d where the first letter is a.

  **(c)** All four-digit binary integers (built from 0 and 1).

  **(d)** The words

  a   ear   re   rare   area   are   ere   era   rarer   rear   err

  built from the letters *a, e, r.*

(e) The words

> gig  i  inn  gin  in  inning  gigging  ginning

built from the letters *g, i, n.*

(f) The words

> pal  lap  a  papa  al  papal  all  ball  lab

built from the letters *a, b, l, p.*

**E2.** Write a function that will traverse a trie and print out all its words in alphabetical order.

**E3.** Write a function that will traverse a trie and print out all its words, with the order determined first by the length of the word, with shorter words first, and, second, by alphabetical order for words of the same length.

**E4.** Write a function that will delete a word from a trie.

**Programming Project 10.2**

**P1.** Construct a menu-driven demonstration program for tries. The keys should be words constructed from the 26 lowercase letters, up to 8 characters long. The only information that should be kept in the Entry structure (with the key) is a serial number indicating when the word was inserted.

# 10.3 External Searching: B-Trees

In our work throughout this book we have assumed that all our data structures are kept in high-speed memory; that is, we have considered only *internal* information retrieval. For many applications, this assumption is reasonable, but for many other important applications, it is not. Let us now turn briefly to the problem of *external* information retrieval, where we wish to locate and retrieve records stored in a disk file.

## 10.3.1 ACCESS TIME

The time required to access and retrieve a word from high-speed memory is a few microseconds at most. The time required to locate a particular record on a disk is measured in milliseconds, and for floppy disks can exceed a second. Hence the time required for a single access is thousands of times greater for external retrieval than for internal retrieval. On the other hand, when a record is located on a disk, the normal practice is not to read only one word, but to read in a large *page* or *block* of information at once. Typical sizes for blocks range from 256 to 1024 characters or words.

Our goal in external searching must be to minimize the number of disk accesses, since each access takes so long compared to internal computation. With each access, however, we obtain a block that may have room for several records. Using these records we may be able to make a multiway decision concerning which block to access next. Hence multiway trees are especially appropriate for external searching.

## 10.3.2 MULTIWAY SEARCH TREES

Binary search trees generalize directly to multiway search trees in which, for some integer $m$ called the *order* of the tree, each node has at most $m$ children. If $k \le m$ is the number of children, then the node contains exactly $k - 1$ keys, which partition all the keys in the subtrees into $k$ subsets. If some of these subsets are empty, then the corresponding children in the tree are empty. Figure 10.5 shows a 5-way search tree in which some of the children of some nodes are empty.

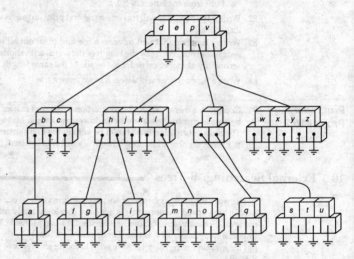

Figure 10.5. A 5-way search tree

## 10.3.3 BALANCED MULTIWAY TREES

Our goal is to devise a multiway search tree that will minimize file accesses; hence we wish to make the height of the tree as small as possible. We can accomplish this by insisting, first, that no empty subtrees appear above the leaves (so that the division of keys into subsets is as efficient as possible); second, that all leaves be on the same level (so that searches will all be guaranteed to terminate with about the same number of accesses); and, third, that every node (except the leaves) have at least some minimal number of children. We shall require that each node (except the leaves) have at least half as many children as the maximum possible. These conditions lead to the following formal definition.

**Definition**   A *B-tree of order* $m$ is an $m$-way tree in which

1. All leaves are on the same level.
2. All internal nodes except the root have at most $m$ nonempty children, and at least $\lceil m/2 \rceil$ nonempty children.
3. The number of keys in each internal node is one less than the number of its nonempty children, and these keys partition the keys in the children in the fashion of a search tree.
4. The root has at most $m$ children, but may have as few as 2 if it is not a leaf, or none if the tree consists of the root alone.

The tree in Figure 10.5 is not a B-tree, since some nodes have empty children, and the leaves are not all on the same level. Figure 10.6 shows a B-tree of order 5 whose keys are the 26 letters of the alphabet.

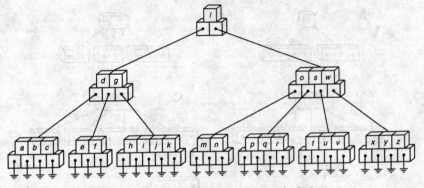

Figure 10.6. A B-tree of order 5

## 10.3.4 INSERTION INTO A B-TREE

*method*

The condition that all leaves be on the same level forces a characteristic behavior of B-trees: In contrast to binary search trees, B-trees are not allowed to grow at their leaves; instead, they are forced to grow at the root. The general method of insertion is as follows. First, a search is made to see if the new key is in the tree. This search (if the key is truly new) will terminate in failure at a leaf. The new key is then added to the leaf node. If the node was not previously full, then the insertion is finished.

When a key is added to a full node, then the node splits into two nodes on the same level, except that the median key is not put into either of the two new nodes, but is instead sent up the tree to be inserted into the parent node. When a search is later made through the tree, therefore, a comparison with the median key will serve to direct the search into the proper subtree. When a key is added to a full root, then the root splits in two and the median key sent upward becomes a new root.

This process is greatly elucidated by studying an example such as the growth of the B-tree of order 5 shown in Figure 10.7. We shall insert the keys

*a g f b k d h m j e s i r x c l n t u p*

into an initially empty tree, in the order given.

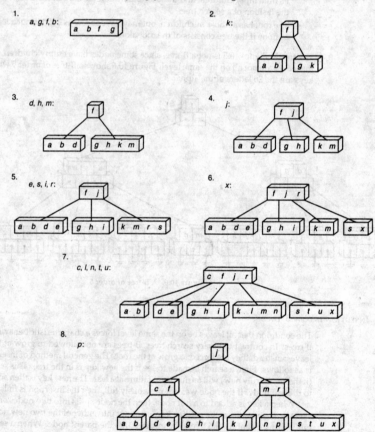

**Figure 10.7. Growth of a B-tree**

The first four keys will be inserted into one node, as shown in the first diagram of Figure 10.7. They are sorted into the proper order as they are inserted. There is no room, however, for the fifth key, *k*, so its insertion causes the node to split into two, and the median key, *f*, moves up to enter a new node, which is a new root. Since the split nodes are now only half full, the next three keys can be inserted without difficulty. Note, however, that these simple insertions can require rearrangement of the keys within a node. The next insertion, *j*, again splits a node, and this time it is *j* itself that is the median key, and therefore moves up to join *f* in the root.

*node splitting*

*upward propagation*

The next several insertions proceed similarly. The final insertion, that of *p*, is more interesting. This insertion first splits the node originally containing *k l m n*, sending the median key *m* upward into the node containing *c f j r*, which is, however, already full. Hence this node in turn splits, and a new root containing *j* is created.

*improving balance*

Two comments regarding the growth of B-trees are in order. First, when a node splits, it produces two nodes that are now only half full. Later insertions, therefore, can more likely be made without the need to split nodes again. Hence one splitting prepares the way for several simple insertions. Second, it is always a median key that is sent upward, not necessarily the key being inserted. Hence repeated insertions tend to improve the balance of the tree, no matter in what order the keys happen to arrive.

## 10.3.5 C Algorithms: Searching and Insertion

To develop C algorithms for searching and insertion in a B-tree, let us begin with the declarations needed to set up a B-tree. For simplicity we shall construct our B-tree entirely in high-speed memory, using C pointers to describe its structure. In most applications, these pointers would be replaced by the addresses of various blocks or pages on a disk, and taking a pointer reference would become making a disk access.

### 1. Declarations

We assume that Key and Treeentry are defined already. Each entry contains a key, along with other information. Within one node there will be a list of entries and a list of pointers to the children of the node. Since these lists are short, we shall, for simplicity, use contiguous arrays and a separate variable count for their representation.

```
#define MAX 4              /* maximum number of keys in node:   MAX = m − 1 */
#define MIN 2              /* minimum number of keys in node:   MIN = ⌈m/2⌉ − 1 */
typedef struct treenode Treenode;

struct treenode {
    int count;                 /* Except for the root, the lower limit is MIN      */
    Treeentry entry [MAX + 1];
    Treenode *branch [MAX + 1];
};
```

The way in which the indices are arranged implies that in some of our algorithms we shall need to investigate branch[0] separately, and then consider each key in association with the branch on its right.

## 2. Searching

As a simple first example we write a function to search through a B-tree for a target key. The input parameters for the function are the target key and a pointer to the root of the B-tree. The function value is a pointer to the node where the target was found in the tree, or NULL if it was not found. The last parameter is the position of the target within that node.

The general method of searching by working our way down through the tree is similar to a search through a binary search tree. In a multiway tree, however, we must examine each node more extensively to find which branch to take at the next step. This examination is done by the auxiliary function SearchNode that returns a Boolean value indicating if the search was successful and targetpos, which is the position of the target if found, and otherwise is the number of the branch on which to continue the search.

```
/* SearchTree: traverse B-tree looking for target.
   Pre:  The B-tree pointed to by root has been created.
   Post: If the key target is present in the B-tree, then the return value points to the
         node containing target in position targetpos. Otherwise, the return value is
         NULL and targetpos is undefined.
   Uses: SearchTree recursively, SearchNode. */
```

*B-tree retrieval*

```
Treenode *SearchTree(Key target, Treenode *root, int *targetpos)
{
    if (!root)
        return NULL;

    else if (SearchNode(target, root, targetpos))
        return root;

    else
        return SearchTree(target, root->branch[*targetpos], targetpos);
}
```

This function has been written recursively to exhibit the similarity of its structure to that of the insertion function to be developed shortly. The recursion is tail recursion, however, and can easily be replaced by iteration if desired.

## 3. Searching a Node

This function determines if the target is in the current node, and, if not, finds which of the count + 1 branches will contain the target key. For convenience, the possibility of taking branch 0 is considered separately, and then a sequential search is made through the remaining possibilities, starting at the end so that the key in index 1 can serve as a sentinel to stop the search.

```
/* SearchNode: searches keys in node for target.
   Pre:   target is a key and current points to a node of a B-tree
   Post:  Searches keys in node for target; returns location pos of target, or branch on
          which to continue search. */
```

*sequential search*

```
Boolean SearchNode(Key target, Treenode *current, int *pos)
{
    if (LT(target, current->entry[1].key)) {  /* Take the leftmost branch.         */
        *pos = 0;
        return FALSE;

    } else {                        /* Start a sequential search through the keys.  */
        for (*pos = current->count;
            LT(target, current->entry[*pos].key) && *pos > 1;  (*pos)--)
            ;
        return EQ(target, current->entry[*pos].key);
    }
}
```

For B-trees of large order, this function should be modified to use binary search instead of sequential search. In some applications, a significant amount of information is stored with each key of the B-tree, so that the order of the B-tree will be relatively small, and sequential search within a node is appropriate. In many applications, only keys are kept in the nodes, so the order is much larger, and binary search should be used to locate the position of a key within a node.

Yet another possibility is to use a linked binary search tree instead of a sequential array of entries for each node; this possibility will be investigated at length later in this chapter.

### 4. Insertion: The Main Function

Insertion into a B-tree can be most naturally formulated as a recursive function, since, after insertion in a subtree has been completed, a (median) key may remain that must be reinserted higher in the tree. Recursion allows us to keep track of the position within the tree and work our way back up the tree without need for an explicit auxiliary stack.

*parameters*

We shall assume that the key being inserted is not already in the tree. The insertion function then needs only two parameters: newentry, the key being inserted, and root, the root of the B-tree. For the recursion, however, we need three additional output parameters. The first of these is a Boolean value which indicates whether the root of the subtree has split into two, also producing a (median) key to be reinserted higher in the tree. When this happens, we shall adopt the convention that the old root node contains the left half of the entries and a new node contains the right half of the entries. When a split occurs, the second output parameter medentry is the median key, and the last parameter medright is a pointer to the new node, the right half of the former root of the subtree.

To keep all these parameters straight, we shall do the recursion in a function called PushDown. This situation is illustrated in Figure 10.8.

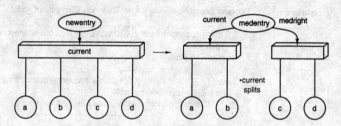

Figure 10.8. Action of PushDown function

The recursion is started by the main function InsertTree. If the outermost call to function PushDown should return TRUE, then there is a key to be placed in a new root, and the height of the entire tree will increase. The main function appears as follows.

```
/* InsertTree: inserts entry into the B-tree.
   Pre:   The B-tree to which root points has been created, and no entry in the B-tree
          has key equal to newentry.key.
   Post:  newentry has been inserted into the B-tree; the root is returned.
   Uses: PushDown. */
Treenode *InsertTree(Treeentry newentry, Treenode *root)
{
    Treeentry medentry;        /* node to be reinserted as new root            */
    Treenode *medright;        /* subtree on right of medentry                 */
    Treenode *newroot;         /* used when the height of the tree increases   */
    if (PushDown(newentry, root, &medentry, &medright)) {
                               /* Tree grows in height.                        */
        newroot = (Treenode *)malloc(sizeof(Treenode)); /* Make a new root.    */
        newroot->count = 1;
        newroot->entry[1] = medentry;
        newroot->branch[0] = root;
        newroot->branch[1] = medright;
        return newroot;
    }
    return root;
}
```

*B-tree insertion: main function*

### 5. Recursive Insertion into a Subtree

Next we turn to the recursive function PushDown, which uses a parameter current to point to the root of the subtree being searched. In a B-tree, a new key is first inserted into a leaf. We shall thus use the condition current == NULL to terminate the recursion; that is, we shall continue to move down the tree searching for newentry until we hit an empty subtree. Since the B-tree does not grow by adding new leaves, we do not then immediately insert newentry, but instead return TRUE and send the key (now called medentry) back up for insertion.

When a recursive call returns TRUE, then we attempt to insert the key medentry in the current node. If there is room, then we are finished. Otherwise, the current node *current splits into *current and *medright and a (possibly different) median key medentry is sent up the tree. The function uses three auxiliary functions: SearchNode (same as for searching); PushIn puts the key medentry into node *current provided that there is room; and Split chops a full node *current into two.

```
/* PushDown: recursively move down tree searching for newentry.
   Pre:   newentry belongs in the subtree to which current points.
   Post:  newentry has been inserted into the subtree to which current points; if TRUE
          is returned, then the height of the subtree has grown, and medentry needs to
          be reinserted higher in the tree, with subtree medright on its right.
   Uses: PushDown recursively, SearchNode, Split, PushIn. */
Boolean PushDown(Treeentry newentry, Treenode *current, Treeentry *medentry,
                 Treenode **medright)
{
    int pos;                        /* branch on which to continue the search      */
    if (current == NULL) {          /* cannot insert into empty tree; terminates   */
        *medentry = newentry;
        *medright = NULL;
        return TRUE;
    } else {                        /* Search the current node.                    */
        if (SearchNode(newentry.key, current, &pos))
            Warning("Inserting duplicate key into B-tree");
        if (PushDown(newentry, current->branch[pos], medentry, medright))
            if (current->count < MAX) {  /* Reinsert median key.                   */
                PushIn(*medentry, *medright, current, pos);
                return FALSE;
            } else {
                Split(*medentry, *medright, current, pos, medentry, medright);
                return TRUE;
            }
        return FALSE;
    }
}
```

*found the leaf where key goes*

*insert into node*

*split node*

### 6. Insert a Key into a Node

The next function inserts the key medentry and its right-hand pointer medright into the node *current.

This function requires that there is room in the node *current to accommodate one additional key.

```
/* PushIn: inserts a key into a node
  Pre:   medentry belongs at index pos in node *current, which has room for it.
  Post:  Inserts key medentry and pointer medright into *current at index pos. */

void PushIn(Treeentry medentry, Treenode *medright, Treenode *current, int pos)
{
                                    /* index to move keys to make room for medentry */
    int i;

    for (i = current->count; i > pos; i--) {
                                    /* Shift all the keys and branches to the right. */
        current->entry[i + 1] = current->entry[i];
        current->branch[i + 1] = current->branch[i];
    }

    current->entry[pos + 1] = medentry;
    current->branch[pos + 1] = medright;
    current->count++;

}
```

### 7. Splitting a Full Node

The next function inserts the key medentry with subtree pointer medright into the full node *current, splits the right half off as new node *newright, and sends the median key newmedian upward for reinsertion later.

It is, of course, not possible to insert key medentry directly into the full node: we must instead first determine whether medentry will go into the left or right half, divide the node (at position median) accordingly, and then insert medentry into the appropriate half.

While this work proceeds, we shall leave the median key newmedian in the left half.

```
/* Split: splits a full node.
  Pre:   medentry belongs at index pos of node *current which is full.
  Post:  Splits node *current with entry medentry and pointer medright at index pos
         into nodes *current and *newright with median entry newmedian.
  Uses: PushIn. */
```

```
void Split(Treeentry medentry, Treenode *medright, Treenode *current, int pos,
        Treeentry *newmedian, Treenode **newright)
{
    int i;                          /* used for copying from *current to new node   */
    int median;                     /* median position in the combined, overfull node */
    if (pos <= MIN)                 /* Determine if new key goes to left or right half. */
        median = MIN;
    else
        median = MIN + 1;
    /* Get a new node and put it on the right. */
    *newright = (Treenode *)malloc(sizeof(Treenode));
    for (i = median + 1; i <= MAX; i++) {  /* Move half the keys.   */
        (*newright)->entry[i – median] = current->entry[i];
        (*newright)->branch[i – median] = current->branch[i];
    }
    (*newright)->count = MAX – median;
    current->count = median;
    if (pos <= MIN)                 /* Push in the new key.   */
        PushIn(medentry, medright, current, pos);
    else
        PushIn(medentry, medright, *newright, pos – median);
    *newmedian = current->entry[current->count];
    (*newright)->branch[0] = current->branch[current->count];
    current->count – –;
}
```

*find splitting point*

*move keys to right node*

*insert new key*

## 10.3.6 DELETION FROM A B-TREE

### 1. Method

During insertion, the new entry always goes first into a leaf. For deletion we shall also wish to remove an entry from a leaf. If the entry that is to be deleted is not in a leaf, then its immediate predecessor (or successor) under the natural order of keys is guaranteed to be in a leaf (prove it!). Hence we can promote the immediate predecessor (or successor) into the position occupied by the deleted entry, and delete the entry from the leaf.

If the leaf contains more than the minimum number of entries, then one can be deleted with no further action. If the leaf contains the minimum number, then we first look at the two leaves (or, in the case of a node on the outside, one leaf) that are immediately adjacent to each other and are children of the same node. If one of these has more than the minimum number of entries, then one of them can be moved into the parent node, and the entry from the parent moved into the leaf where the deletion is occurring. If, finally, the adjacent leaf has only the minimum number of entries, then the two leaves and the median entry from the parent can all be combined as one new leaf, which will contain no more than the maximum number of entries allowed. If this step leaves the parent node with too few entries, then the process propagates upward. In the limiting case, the last entry is removed from the root, and then the height of the tree decreases.

### 2. Example

The process of deletion in our previous B-tree of order 5 is shown in Figure 10.9. The first deletion, *h*, is from a leaf with more than the minimum number of entries, and hence causes no problem. The second deletion, *r*, is not from a leaf, and therefore the immediate successor of *r*, which is *s*, is promoted into the position of *r*, and then *s* is deleted from its leaf. The third deletion, *p*, leaves its node with too few entries. The key *s* from the parent node is therefore brought down and replaced by the key *t*.

Deletion of *d* has more extensive consequences. This deletion leaves the node with too few entries, and neither of its sibling nodes can spare an entry. The node is therefore combined with one of the siblings and with the median entry from the parent node, as shown by the dashed line in the first diagram and the combined node *a b c e* in the second diagram. This process, however, leaves the parent node with only the one key *f*. The top three nodes of the tree must therefore be combined, yielding the tree shown in the final diagram of Figure 10.9.

### 3. C Functions

We can write a deletion algorithm with overall structure similar to that used for insertion. Again we shall use recursion, with a separate main function to start the recursion. Rather than attempting to pull an entry down from a parent node during an inner recursive call, we shall allow the recursive function to return even though there are too few entries in its root node. The outer call will then detect this occurrence and move entries as required.

The main function is:

*B-tree deletion*

```
/* DeleteTree: deletes target from the B-tree.
   Pre:   target is the key of some entry in the B-tree to which root points.
   Post:  This entry has been deleted from the B-tree.
   Uses:  RecDeleteTree. */
Treenode *DeleteTree(Key target, Treenode *root)
{
    Treenode *oldroot;          /* used to dispose of an empty root        */
    RecDeleteTree(target, root);

    if (root->count == 0) {     /* Root is empty.                          */
        oldroot = root;
        root = root->branch[0];
        free(oldroot);
    }
    return root;
}
```

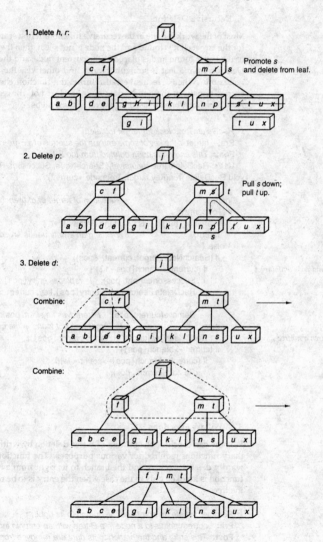

Figure 10.9. Deletion from a B-tree

### 4. Recursive Deletion

Most of the work is done in the recursive function. It first searches the current node for the target. If it is found and the node is not a leaf, then the immediate successor of the key is found and is placed in the current node, and the successor is deleted. Deletion from a leaf is straightforward, and otherwise the process continues by recursion. When a recursive call returns, the function checks to see if enough entries remain in the appropriate node, and, if not, moves entries as required. Auxiliary functions are used in several of these steps.

```
/* RecDeleteTree: look for target to delete.
   Pre:  target is the key of some entry in the subtree of a B-tree to which current points.
   Post: This entry has been deleted from the B-tree.
   Uses: RecDeleteTree recursively, SearchNode, Successor, Remove, Restore. */
void RecDeleteTree(Key target, Treenode *current)
{
   int pos;                    /* location of target or of branch on which to search */
   if (!current) {
      Warning("Target was not in the B-tree.");
      return;                  /* Hitting an empty tree is an error.                 */
   } else {
      if (SearchNode(target, current, &pos))
         if (current->branch[pos - 1]) {
            Successor(current, pos);  /* replaces entry[pos] by its successor       */
            RecDeleteTree(current->entry[pos].key, current->branch[pos]);
         } else
            Remove(current, pos);   /* removes key from pos of *current             */
      else                        /* Target was not found in the current node.       */
         RecDeleteTree(target, current->branch[pos]);
      if (current->branch[pos])
         if (current->branch[pos]->count < MIN)
            Restore(current, pos);
   }
}
```

*found node with target* and *search a subtree* are margin notes.

### 5. Auxiliary Functions

We now can conclude the process of B-tree deletion by writing several of the auxiliary functions required for various purposes. The function Remove straightforwardly deletes an entry and the branch to its right from a node of a B-tree. This function is invoked only in the case when the entry is to be removed from a leaf of the tree.

```
/* Remove: delete an entry and the branch to its right.
   Pre:  current points to a node in a B-tree with an entry in index pos.
   Post: This entry and the branch to its right are removed from *current. */
```

*remove key from a leaf*

```
void Remove(Treenode *current, int pos)
{
    int i;                        /* index for moving entries        */
    for (i = pos + 1; i <= current->count; i++) {
        current->entry[i-1] = current->entry[i];
        current->branch[i-1] = current->branch[i];
    }
    current->count--;
}
```

The function Successor is invoked when an entry must be deleted from a node that is not a leaf. In this case, the immediate successor (in order of keys) is found by first taking the branch to the right of the entry and then taking leftmost branches until a leaf is reached. The leftmost entry in this leaf then replaces the entry to be deleted.

```
/* Successor: replaces an entry by its immediate successor.
    Pre:   current points to a node in a B-tree with an entry in index pos.
    Post:  This entry is replaced by its immediate successor under order of keys. */
```

*copy successor of key*

```
void Successor(Treenode *current, int pos)
{
    Treenode *leaf;               /* used to move down the tree to a leaf    */
    /* Move as far leftward as possible. */
    for (leaf = current->branch[pos]; leaf->branch[0]; leaf = leaf->branch[0])
        ;
    current->entry[pos] = leaf->entry[1];
}
```

Finally, we must show how to restore current->branch[pos] to the minimum number of entries if a recursive call has reduced its count below the minimum. The function we write is somewhat biased to the left; that is, it looks first to the sibling on the left to take an entry, and uses the right sibling only when there are no entries to spare in the left one. The steps that are needed are illustrated in Figure 10.10.

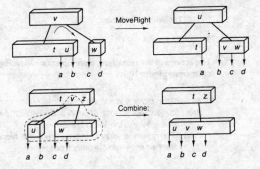

Figure 10.10. Restoration of the minimum number of entries.

```
/* Restore: restore the minimum number of entries.
   Pre:   current points to a node in a B-tree with an entry in index pos; the branch to
          the right of pos has one too few entries.
   Post:  An entry taken from elsewhere is to restore the minimum number of entries by
          entering it at current->branch[pos].
   Uses: MoveLeft, MoveRight, Combine. */

void Restore(Treenode *current, int pos)

{
   if (pos == 0)                    /* case: leftmost key                    */

      if (current->branch[1]->count > MIN)
         MoveLeft(current, 1);

      else
         Combine(current, 1);


   else if (pos == current->count)  /* case: rightmost key                   */

      if (current->branch[pos-1]->count > MIN)
         MoveRight(current, pos);

      else
         Combine(current, pos);


                                    /* remaining cases */
   else if (current->branch[pos-1]->count > MIN)
      MoveRight(current, pos);

   else if (current->branch[pos + 1]->count > MIN)
      MoveLeft(current, pos + 1);

   else
      Combine(current, pos);
}
```

The actions of the remaining three functions MoveRight, MoveLeft, and Combine are clear from Figure 10.10.

```
/* MoveRight: move a key to the right.
   Pre:   current points to a node in a B-tree with entries in the branches pos and
          pos - 1, with too few in branch pos.
   Post:  The rightmost entry from branch pos - 1 has moved into *current, which has
          sent an entry into the branch pos. */
```

*move a key to the right*

```
void MoveRight(Treenode *current, int pos)
{
    int c;
    Treenode *t;
    t = current->branch[pos];
    for (c = t->count; c > 0; c--) {
    /* Shift all keys in the right node one position. */
        t->entry[c + 1] = t->entry[c];
        t->branch[c + 1] = t->branch[c];
    }
    t->branch[1] = t->branch[0];    /* Move key from parent to right node.        */
    t->count++;
    t->entry[1] = current->entry[pos];
    t = current->branch[pos-1];    /* Move last key of left node into parent.     */
    current->entry[pos] = t->entry[t->count];
    current->branch[pos] ->branch[0] = t->branch[t->count];
    t->count--;
}
```

```
/* MoveLeft: move a key to the left.
```
    **Pre:**  current *points to a node in a B-tree with entries in the branches* pos *and*
        pos − 1, *with too few in branch* pos − 1.
    **Post:** *The leftmost entry from branch* pos *has moved into* *current, *which has sent*
        *an entry into the branch* pos − 1. */

*move a key to the left*

```
void MoveLeft(Treenode *current, int pos)
{
    int c;
    Treenode *t;
    t = current->branch[pos-1];    /* Move key from parent into left node.        */
    t->count++;
    t->entry[t->count] = current->entry[pos];
    t->branch[t->count] = current->branch[pos] ->branch[0];
    t = current->branch[pos];    /* Move key from right node into parent.         */
    current->entry[pos] = t->entry[1];
    t->branch[0] = t->branch[1];
    t->count--;
    for (c = 1; c <= t->count; c++) {
    /* Shift all keys in right node one position leftward. */
        t->entry[c] = t->entry[c + 1];
        t->branch[c] = t->branch[c + 1];
    }
}
```

*/* Combine: combine adjacent nodes.*

**Pre:** current *points to a node in a B-tree with entries in the branches* pos *and* pos − 1, *with too few to move entries.*

**Post:** *The nodes at branches* pos − 1 *and* pos *have been combined into one node, which also includes the entry formerly in* ∗current *at index* pos. */*

*combine adjacent nodes*

```
void Combine(Treenode *current, int pos)
{
    int c;
    Treenode *right;
    Treenode *left;
    right = current->branch[pos];
    left = current->branch[pos-1];    /* Work with the left node.          */
    left->count++;                    /* Insert the key from the parent.   */
    left->entry[left->count] = current->entry[pos];
    left->branch[left->count] = right->branch[0];
    for (c = 1; c <= right->count; c++) {  /* Insert all keys from right node.  */
        left->count++;
        left->entry[left->count] = right->entry[c];
        left->branch[left->count] = right->branch[c];
    }
    for (c = pos; c < current->count; c++) {  /* Delete key from parent node.  */
        current->entry[c] = current->entry[c + 1];
        current->branch[c] = current->branch[c + 1];
    }
    current->count--;
    free(right);                      /* Dispose of the empty right node.  */
}
```

**Exercises 10.3**

**E1.** Insert the six remaining letters of the alphabet in the order

$$z, v, o, q, w, y$$

into the final B-tree of Figure 10.7 (page 476).

**E2.** Insert the entries below, in the order stated, into an initially empty B-tree of order **(a)** 3, **(b)** 4, **(c)** 7.

$$a\ g\ f\ b\ k\ d\ h\ m\ j\ e\ s\ i\ r\ x\ c\ l\ n\ t\ u\ p$$

**E3.** What is the smallest number of entries that, when inserted in an appropriate order, will force a B-tree of order 5 to have height 2 (that is, 3 levels)?

**E4.** Draw all the B-trees of order 5 (between 2 and 4 keys per node) that can be constructed from the keys 1, 2, 3, 4, 5, 6, 7, and 8.

**E5.** If a key in a B-tree is not in a leaf, prove that both its immediate predecessor and immediate successor (under the natural order) are in leaves.

**E6.** Suppose that disk hardware allows us to choose the size of a disk record any way we wish, but that the time it takes to read a record from the disk is $a + bd$, where $a$ and $b$ are constants and $d$ is the order of the B-tree. (One node in the B-tree is stored as one record on the disk.) Let $n$ be the number of entries in the B-tree. Assume for simplicity that all the nodes in the B-tree are full (each node contains $d - 1$ entries).

  **(a)** Explain why the time needed to do a typical B-tree operation (searching or insertion, for example) is approximately $(a + bd)\log_d n$.

  **(b)** Show that the time needed is minimized when the value of $d$ satisfies $d(\ln d - 1) = a/b$. (Note that the answer does not depend on the number $n$ of entries in the B-tree.) [*Hint:* For fixed $a$, $b$, and $n$, the time is a function of $d$: $f(d) = (a + bd)\log_d n$. Note that $\log_d n = (\ln n)/(\ln d)$. To find the minimum, calculate the derivative $f'(d)$ and set it to 0.]

  **(c)** Suppose $a$ is 20 milliseconds and $b$ is 0.1 millisecond. (The records are very short.) Use a calculator to find the value of $d$ (approximately) that minimizes the time.

  **(d)** Suppose $a$ is 20 milliseconds and $b$ is 10 milliseconds. (The records are longer.) Use a calculator to find the value of $d$ (approximately) that minimizes the time.

**E7.** Write a function that will traverse a linked B-tree, visiting all its entries in order of keys (smaller keys first).

**E8.** Define *preorder* traversal of a B-tree recursively to mean visiting all the entries in the root node first, then traversing all the subtrees, from left to right, in preorder. Write a function that will traverse a B-tree in preorder.

**E9.** Define *postorder* traversal of a B-tree recursively to mean first traversing all the subtrees of the root, from left to right, in postorder, then visiting all the entries in the root. Write a function that will traverse a B-tree in postorder.

**E10.** Remove the tail recursion from the function Search.

**E11.** Rewrite the function SearchNode to use binary search.

**E12.** A *B\*-tree* is a B-tree in which every node, except possibly the root, is at least two-thirds full, rather than half full. Insertion into a B\*-tree moves entries between sibling nodes (as done during deletion) as needed, thereby delaying splitting a node until two sibling nodes are completely full. These two nodes can then be split into three, each of which will be at least two-thirds full.

  **(a)** Specify the changes needed to the insertion algorithm so that it will maintain the properties of a B\*-tree.

  **(b)** Specify the changes needed to the deletion algorithm so that it will maintain the properties of a B\*-tree.

  **(c)** Discuss the relative advantages and disadvantages of B\*-trees compared to ordinary B-trees.

**Programming
Projects 10.3**

**P1.** Combine all the functions of this section into a menu-driven demonstration program for B-trees. If you have designed the demonstration program for binary search trees from Section 9.2, Project P2 (page 411) with sufficient care, you should be able to make a direct replacement of one package of operations by another.

*coatroom*

**P2.** Use a B-tree of order 5 to implement the coatroom operations of Section 6.3. Test your package with the coatroom demonstration program, and then run the timed-test program with the B-tree package, comparing the results with those for the other implementations.

**P3.** Substitute the functions for B-tree retrieval and insertion into the information-retrieval project of Project P6 of Section 9.2 (page 412). Compare the performance of B-trees with binary search trees for various combinations of input text files and various orders of B-trees.

# 10.4 Red-Black Trees

## 10.4.1 INTRODUCTION

*B-tree nodes*

In the last section, we used a contiguous list to store the entries within a single node of a B-tree. Doing so was appropriate because the number of entries in one node is usually relatively small, and because we were emulating methods that might be used in external files on a disk, where dynamic memory may not be available.

*binary tree
representation*

In general, however, we may use any ordered structure we wish for storing the entries in each B-tree node. Small binary search trees turn out to be an excellent choice. We need only be careful to distinguish between the links within a single B-tree node and the links from one B-tree node to another. Let us therefore draw the links within one node as curly colored lines and the links between B-tree nodes as straight black lines. Figure 10.11 shows a B-tree of order 4 constructed this way.

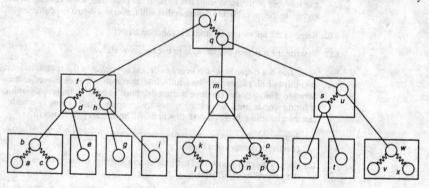

**Figure 10.11. A B-tree of order 4 as a binary search tree**

### 10.4.2 DEFINITION AND ANALYSIS

This construction is especially useful for a B-tree of order 4 (like Figure 10.11), where each node of the tree contains one, two, or three entries. A node with one key is the same in the B-tree and the binary search tree; a node with three entries transforms as:

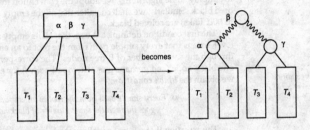

A node with two entries has two possible representations:

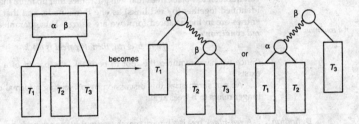

If we wished, we could always use only one of these two, but there is no reason to do so, and we shall find that our algorithms naturally produce both possible forms, so let us allow either form to represent a B-tree node with two entries.

*first definition*
Hence we obtain the fundamental definition of this section: A **red-black tree** is a binary search tree, with links colored red or black, obtained from a B-tree of order 4 in the way just described. (It is standard to refer to *red*, even if the color used in drawing is not red.) After we have converted a B-tree into a red-black tree, we can use it like any other binary search tree. In particular, searching and traversal of a red-black tree are exactly the same as for an ordinary binary search tree; we simply ignore the color of the links. Insertion and deletion, however, require more care to maintain the underlying B-tree structure. Let us therefore translate the requirements for a B-tree into corresponding requirements for red-black trees.

*colored nodes*

First, however, let us adopt some more notation: We shall consider each *node* of a red-black tree as colored with the same color as the link immediately *above* it; hence we shall often speak of red nodes and black nodes instead of red links and black links. In this way, we need keep only one extra bit for each node to indicate its color.

*root color*

Since the root has no link above it, it does not obtain a color in this way. In order to simplify some algorithms, we adopt the convention that the root is always colored black. Similarly, we shall consider that all the empty subtrees (corresponding to NULL links) are colored black.

The first condition defining a B-tree, that all its empty subtrees are on the same level, means that every simple path from the root to an empty subtree (NULL) goes through the same number of B-tree nodes. The corresponding red-black tree has one black node (and perhaps one or two red nodes) for each B-tree node. Hence we obtain the **black condition**:

*black condition*

> *Every simple path from the root to an empty subtree goes through the same number of black nodes.*

The assertion that a B-tree satisfies search-tree properties is automatically satisfied for a red-black tree, and, for order 4, the remaining parts of the definition amount to saying that each node contains one, two, or three entries. We need a condition on red-black trees that will guarantee that no more than three nodes are identified together (by red links) as one B-tree node, and that nodes with three entries are in the balanced form we are using. This guarantee comes from the **red condition**:

*red condition*

> *If a node is red, then its parent is black.*

(Since we have required the root to be black, the parent of a red node always exists.)

We can summarize this discussion by presenting a formal definition that no longer refers to B-trees at all:

**Definition**

A **red-black tree** is a binary search tree in which each node has either the color *red* or *black*, and which satisfies:

1. Every simple path from the root to an empty subtree (a NULL link) goes through the same number of black nodes.

2. If a node is red, then its parent exists and is black.

From this definition it follows that no path from the root to an empty subtree can be more than twice as long as another, since, by the red condition, no more than half the nodes on such a path can be red, and, by the black condition, there are the same number of black nodes on each such path. Hence we obtain:

**Theorem 10.2**     *The height of a red-black tree containing $n$ nodes is no more than $2 \lg n$.*

*search performance*

Hence the time for searching a red-black tree with $n$ nodes is $O(\log n)$ in every case. We shall find that the time for insertion is also $O(\log n)$, but first we need to devise the associated algorithm.

### 10.4.3 INSERTION

*overall outline*

Let us begin with the standard recursive algorithm for insertion into a binary search tree. That is, we compare the new key with the key at the root (if the tree is nonempty) and then recursively insert the new entry into the left or right subtree of the root. This process terminates when we hit an empty subtree, whereupon we create a new node and attach it to the tree in place of the empty subtree.

*new node*

Should this new node be red or black? Were we to make it black, we would increase the number of black nodes on one path (and only one path), thereby violating the black condition. Hence the new node must be red. (Recall also that insertion of a new entry into a B-tree first goes into an existing node, a process that corresponds to attaching a new red node to a red-black tree.) If the parent of the new red node is black, then the insertion is finished, but if the parent is red, then we have introduced a violation of the red condition into the tree. The major work of the insertion algorithm is to remove such a violation, and we shall find several different cases that we shall need to process separately.

*postpone work*

*status variable*

Our algorithm is considerably simplified, however, if we do not consider these cases immediately, but instead postpone the work as long as we can. Hence, when we make a node red, we do not immediately try to repair the tree, but instead simply return from the recursive call with a status indicator set to indicate that the node just processed is red.

*parent node: red violation*

After this return, we are again processing the parent node. If it is black, then the conditions for a red-black tree are satisfied and the process terminates. If it is red, then again we do not immediately attempt to repair the tree, but instead we set the status variable to indicate that we have two red nodes together, and then simply return from the recursive call. It turns out, in this case, to be helpful to use the status variable also to indicate if the two red nodes are related as left child or right child.

After returning from the second recursive call we are processing the grandparent node. Here is where our convention that the root will always be black is helpful: Since the parent node is red, it cannot be the root, and hence the grandparent exists. This grandparent, moreover, is guaranteed to be black, since its child (the parent node) is red, and the only violation of the red condition is farther down the tree.

*grandparent node: restoration*

Finally, at the recursive level of the grandparent node, we can transform the tree to restore the red-black conditions. We shall examine only the cases where the parent is the left child of the grandparent; those where it is the right child are symmetric. We need to distinguish two cases according to the color of the other (the right) child of the grandparent, that is, the "aunt" or "uncle" of the original node.

*black aunt*

First suppose this aunt node is black. This case also covers the possibility that the aunt node does not exist. (Recall that an empty subtree is considered black.) Then the red-black properties are restored by a single or double rotation to the right, as shown in the first two parts of Figure 10.12. You will need to verify that, in both these diagrams, the rotation (and associated color changes) removes the violation of the red condition and preserves the black condition by not changing the number of black nodes on any path down the tree.

*red aunt*

Now suppose the aunt node is red, as shown in the last two parts of Figure 10.12. Here the transformation is simpler: No rotation occurs, but the colors are changed. The parent and aunt nodes become black, and the grandparent node becomes red. Again, you should verify that the number of black nodes on any path down the tree remains the same. Since the grandparent node has become red, however, it is quite possible that the red condition is still violated: The great-grandparent node may be red. Hence the process may not terminate. We need to set the status indicator to show that we have a newly red node, and then we can continue to work out of the recursion. Any violation of the red condition, however, moves two levels up the tree, and, since the root is black, the process will eventually terminate. It is also possible that this process will change the root from black to red; hence, in the outermost call, we need to make sure that the root is changed back to black if necessary.

### 10.4.4 C INSERTION

Let us now take this method of insertion and translate it into C. We assume that Key and Treeentry are defined already so our declarations become:

```
typedef struct treenode Treenode;

struct treenode {
    Treeentry entry;
    Boolean red;
    Treenode *left, *right;
};

typedef enum outcome { OK, REDNODE, RIGHTRED, LEFTRED } Outcome;
/* These outcomes from a call to the recursive insertion function describe the following
   results of the call:
```

OK:       *The color of the current root (of the subtree) has not changed; the tree now satisfies the conditions for a red-black tree.*

REDNODE:  *The current root has changed from black to red; modification may or may not be needed to restore the red-black properties.*

RIGHTRED: *The current root and its right child are now both red; a color flip or rotation is needed.*

LEFTRED:  *The current root and its left child are now both red; a color flip or rotation is needed.*

```
                                    */
```

As usual, we shall do almost all the work within a recursive function, so the main insertion function only does some setup and error checking. Since we want only one status-indicator variable that will continually change as the insertion proceeds, we declare status in the main function. The only other tasks of the main insertion

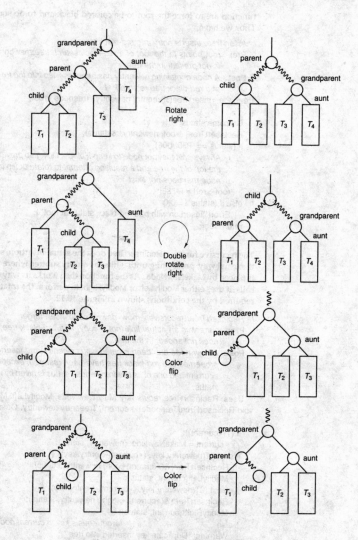

Figure 10.12. Restoring red-black conditions

function are to force the root to be colored black and to do some error checking. Thus we have:

```
/* InsertTree: inserts entry into red-black tree.
   Pre:  root points to the root of a red-black search tree; newentry is an entry which
         is not present in the tree.
   Post: A node containing newentry has been inserted into the tree and the properties
         of a red-black tree restored. */
Treenode *InsertTree(Treeentry newentry, Treenode *root)
{
   Outcome status;
   RecInsertTree( &root, newentry, &status);
   if (status == REDNODE)
      /* Always split the root node to keep it black. Doing so prevents two red nodes at
         the top of the tree and a resulting attempt to rotate or flip colors using a parent
         node that does not exist. */
      root->red = FALSE;
   else if (status != OK)
      Error("Insertion with bad red-black status at root");
   return root;
}
```

The recursive function RecInsertTree does the actual insertion, searching the tree in the usual way, proceeding until it hits the empty subtree where the actual insertion is placed by MakeNewNode. As the function then works its way out of the recursive calls, it uses either ModifyLeft or ModifyRight to perform the rotations and color flips required by the conditions shown in Figure 10.12.

```
/* RecInsertTree: recursively move down tree to insert target.
   Pre:  current is an actual link (not a copy) in a red-black tree; target is a key that
         does not appear in the tree.
   Post: A new node has been created with newentry and inserted into the tree; the
         properties of a red-black tree have been restored, except possibly at the root
         *current and one of its children, whose status is given by the output parameter
         status.
   Uses: RecInsertTree recursively, MakeNewNode, ModifyLeft, ModifyRight. */
void RecInsertTree(Treenode **current, Treeentry newentry, Outcome *status)
{
   if (!(*current))
      *current = MakeNewNode(newentry, status);
   else if (LT(newentry.key, (*current)->entry.key)) {
      RecInsertTree( &(*current)->left, newentry, status);
      ModifyLeft(current, status);
   } else if (GT(newentry.key, (*current)->entry.key)) {
      RecInsertTree( &(*current)->right, newentry, status);
      ModifyRight(current, status);
   } else                        /* target equals key in current node.          */
      Warning("Duplicate key inserted into tree");
}
```

The function ModifyLeft updates the status variable and recognizes the situations shown in Figure 10.12 that require rotations or color flips. It is in this function that our decision to postpone the restoration of the red-black properties pays off. When ModifyLeft is invoked, we know that the insertion was made in the left subtree of the current node; we know its color; and, by using the status variable, we know the condition of the subtree into which the insertion went. By using all this information, we can now determine exactly what actions, if any, are needed to restore the red-black properties.

```
/* ModifyLeft: update node after left insertion.
    Pre:    An insertion has been made in the left subtree of *current which has returned
            the value of status for this subtree.
    Post:   Any color change or rotation needed for the tree rooted at current has been
            made, and status has been updated.
    Uses: RotateRight, FlipColor, DRotateRight. */

void ModifyLeft(Treenode **current, Outcome *status)
{
    /* The value of status describes the left subtree of current. */
    switch (*status) {
    case OK:                        /* No action needed, as tree is already OK.        */
        break;
    case REDNODE:
        if ((*current)->red)
            *status = LEFTRED;      /* Both current and left child are red.             */
        else
            *status = OK;           /* current is black and left is red, so now OK.     */
        break;
    case LEFTRED:
        if (!(*current)->right)     /* An empty subtree behaves like black.             */
            RotateRight(current, status);
        else if ((*current)->right->red)  /* Both children are red.                     */
            FlipColor(current, status);
        else                        /* Right child is black; left is red.               */
            RotateRight(current, status);
        break;
    case RIGHTRED:
        if (!(*current)->right)     /* An empty subtree behaves like black.             */
            DRotateRight(current, status);
        else if ((*current)->right->red)  /* Both children are red.                     */
            FlipColor(current, status);
        else                        /* Right child is black; left is red.               */
            DRotateRight(current, status);
        break;
    }
}
```

ModifyRight is similar, treating the mirror images of the situations shown in Figure 10.12. The actions of the rotation and color-flip functions are shown in Figure 10.12, and these may all safely be left as exercises. The rotation functions may be based on those for AVL trees, but for red-black trees it becomes important to set the colors and the status indicator correctly.

The only remaining function is MakeNewNode, which is also straightforward.

```
/* MakeNewNode: create and initialize a new node.
   Pre:  target is a key to be put in a new node.
   Post: A new red node has been created containing key target and status becomes
         REDNODE. */
Treenode *MakeNewNode(Treeentry newentry, Outcome *status)
{
    Treenode *new = (Treenode *)malloc(sizeof(Treenode));
    new->entry = newentry;
    new->red = TRUE;
    new->left = new->right = NULL;
    *status = REDNODE;
    return new;
}
```

---

**Exercises 10.4**

**E1.** Insert the keys *c, o, r, n, f, l, a, k, e, s* into an initially empty red-black tree.

**E2.** Insert the keys *a, b, c, d, e, f, g, h, i, j, k* into an initially empty red-black tree.

**E3.** Find a binary search tree whose nodes cannot be colored so as to make it a red-black tree.

**E4.** Find a red-black tree that is not an AVL tree.

**E5.** Prove that any AVL tree can have its nodes colored so as to make it a red-black tree. [You may find it easier to prove the following stronger statement: An AVL tree of height $h$ can have its nodes colored as a red-black tree with exactly $\lceil h/2 \rceil$ black nodes on each path to an empty subtree, and, if $h$ is odd, then both children of the root are black.]

**Programming Projects 10.4**

**P1.** Complete red-black insertion by writing the missing functions: ModifyRight, FlipColor, RotateLeft, RotateRight, DRotateLeft, and DRotateRight. Be sure that, at the end of each function, the colors of affected nodes have been set properly, and the variable status correctly indicates the current condition. By including extensive error testing for illegal situations, you can simplify the process of correcting your work.

**P2.** Substitute the function for red-black insertion into the menu-driven demonstration program for binary search trees from Section 9.2, Project P2 (page 411), thereby obtaining a demonstration program for red-black trees. You may leave deletion not implemented.

**P3.** Substitute the function for red-black insertion into the information-retrieval project of Project P6 of Section 9.2 (page 412). Compare the performance of red-black trees with other search trees for various combinations of input text files.

## 10.5 Tree-Structured Programs: Look-Ahead in Games

In games of mental skill the person who can anticipate what will happen several moves in advance has an advantage over a competitor who looks only for immediate gain. In this section we develop a computer algorithm to play games by looking at moves several steps in advance. This algorithm can be described in terms of a tree; afterward we show how recursion can be used to program this structure.

### 10.5.1 GAME TREES

We can picture the sequences of possible moves by means of a *game tree*, in which the root denotes the initial situation and the branches from the root denote the legal moves that the first player could make. At the next level down, the branches correspond to the legal moves by the second player in each situation, and so on, with branches from vertices at even levels denoting moves by the first player, and from vertices at odd levels denoting moves by the second player.

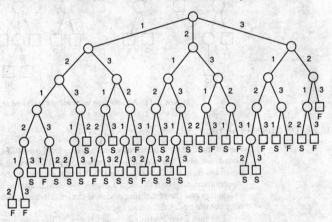

Figure 10.13. Tree for the game of Eight

*Eight*

The complete game tree for the trivial game of *Eight* is shown in Figure 10.13. In this game the first player chooses one of the numbers 1, 2, or 3. At each later turn the appropriate player chooses one of 1, 2, or 3, but the number previously chosen is not allowed. A running sum of the numbers chosen is kept, and if a player brings this sum to exactly eight, then the player wins. If the player takes the sum over eight, then the other player wins. No draws are possible. In the diagram, F denotes a win by the first player, and S a win by the second player. Even a trivial game like Eight produces a good-sized tree. Games of real interest like Chess or Go have trees so huge that there is no hope of investigating all the branches, and a program that runs in reasonable time can examine only a few levels below the current vertex in the tree. People playing such games are also unable to see every possibility to the end of the game, but they can make intelligent choices, because, with experience, a person comes to recognize that some situations in a game are much better than others, even if they do not guarantee a win.

*evaluation function*    For any interesting game that we propose to play by computer, therefore, we shall need some kind of *evaluation function* that will examine the current situation and return a number assessing its benefits. To be definite, we shall assume that large numbers reflect favorable situations for the first player, and therefore small (or more negative) numbers show an advantage for the second player.

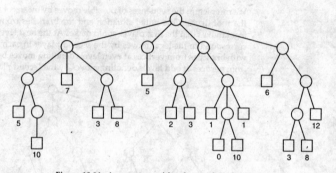

Figure 10.14. A game tree with values assigned at the leaves

## 10.5.2 THE MINIMAX METHOD

Part of the tree for a fictitious game appears in Figure 10.14. Since we are looking ahead, we need the evaluation function only at the leaves of the tree (that is, the positions from which we shall not look further ahead in the game), and, from this information, we wish to select a move. We shall draw the leaves of the game tree as squares and the remaining nodes as circles. Hence Figure 10.14 provides values only for the nodes drawn as squares.

The move we eventually select is one of the branches coming directly from the root, at the top level of the tree. We take the evaluation function from the perspective of this player, which means that this player selects the maximum value possible. At the next level down, the other player will select the smallest value possible, and so on.

*tracing the tree*    By working up from the bottom of the tree, we can assign values to all the vertices. Let us trace this process part of the way through Figure 10.14, starting at the lower left side of the tree. The first unlabeled node is the circle above the square labeled 10. Since there is no choice for the move made at this node, it must also have the value 10. Its parent node has two children now labeled 5 and 10. This parent node is on the third level of the tree. That is, it represents a move by the first player, who wishes to maximize the value. Hence, this player will choose the move with value 10, and so the value for the parent node is also 10.

Next let us move up one level in the tree to the node with three children. We now know that the leftmost child has value 10, and the second child has value 7. The value for the rightmost child will be the maximum of the values of its two children, 3 and 8. Hence its value is 8. The node with three children is on the second level; that is, it represents a move by the player who wishes to minimize the value. Thus this player will choose the center move of the three possibilities, and the value at this node is therefore 7.

And thus the process continues. You should take a moment to complete the evaluation of all the nodes in Figure 10.14. The result is shown in Figure 10.15. The value of the current situation turns out to be 7, and the current (first) player will choose the leftmost branch as the best move.

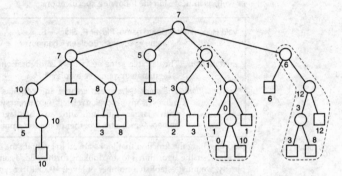

**Figure 10.15.** Minimax evaluation of a game tree

The dotted lines shown in color will be explained later, in one of the projects. It turns out, by keeping track of the minimum and maximum found so far, that it is not necessary to evaluate every node in a game tree, and, in Figure 10.15, the nodes enclosed in the dotted lines need not be evaluated. Since in evaluating a game tree

*minimax*

we alternately take minima and maxima, this process is called a *minimax* method.

## 10.5.3 ALGORITHM DEVELOPMENT

Next let us see how the minimax method can be embodied in a formal algorithm for looking ahead in a game-playing program. We wish to write a general-purpose algorithm that can be used with any two-player game; we shall therefore leave various types and data structures unspecified, since their choice will depend on the particular game being played.

First, we shall need to use a function that we call Recommend to return the moves to be investigated at the next level of look-ahead. We have our choice of sev-

*recommended moves*

eral data structures to hold these moves. The order in which they are investigated in later stages of look-ahead is unimportant, so they could be kept as a set, or a list, or a stack. For simplicity of programming, let us use a stack. The entries in the stack are moves; that is, we have typedef Move Stackentry. The declaration of type Move depends on the game.

Function Recommend will also return a value recvalue that depends on the current situation in the game (but not yet on which of the recommended moves is eventually made). The value will normally be a number. Whether it is an integer or a real number depends on the game.

As its input, Recommend uses both the current configuration of the game and a specification of which player is about to move. For the player, we use the enumerated type declaration typedef enum player { FIRST, SECOND } Player; and always take the first player as the one who wishes to maximize the value, whereas the second player wishes to minimize the value. Recommend performs other operations as well, as indicated in the following specifications.

---

void Recommend(Board game, Player P, Stack * S,
               Value * recvalue, Boolean * gameover);

*precondition:*  The variable game describes a configuration of the game which is legitimate for a move by player P.

*postcondition:*  The stack S has been created and contains the recommended moves (if any); recvalue reflects the current situation of the game, with a larger value indicating an advantage to the first player; gameover indicates whether or not the game is finished.

---

*termination*

Before writing the function that looks ahead to evaluate the game tree, we should decide when the algorithm is to stop looking further. For a game of reasonable complexity, we must establish a number of levels MAXDEPTH beyond which the search will not go. The other condition for termination is when gameover becomes TRUE. The basic task of looking ahead in the tree can now be described simply with the following recursive algorithm.

*outline*

```
void LookAhead()
{
    Use Recommend to obtain a stack S of possible moves;
    if (the recursion terminates (depth == 0 or gameover))
        Return one move and associated value;
    else {
        for each recommended move from S
            Tentatively make the move and recursively LookAhead for the
                best move for the other player;
        Select the best value for P among the values returned in the loop;
        Return the corresponding move and value as the result;
    }
}
```

### 10.5.4 REFINEMENT

To specify the details of this algorithm, we must, finally, employ two more functions that depend on the game. The functions MakeMove(Board game, Player P, Move m) and UndoMove(Board game, Player P, Move m) make and undo tentative moves as indicated. In the formal function, we also rearrange some of the steps from the outline.

```
/* LookAhead: finds the next move
   Pre:  The game is in a legitimate position for player P; it is the turn of player P, and
         at least one move is possible.
   Post: After looking ahead depth levels through the game tree the function returns
         the recommended move recmove, which has a calculated value of recvalue.
   Uses: Stack functions; functions Recommend, MakeMove, UndoMove, LookAhead
         (recursively), and a constant INFINITY (larger than the value of any move). */
void LookAhead(Board game, int depth, Player P, Move *recmove, Value *recvalue)
{
   Player opponent;            /* opponent of P                                 */
   Move oppmove;               /* recommended move for opponent                 */
   Value oppvalue;             /* value returned for opponent's move            */
   Stack S;                    /* stack of recommended moves for P              */
   Move tentmove;              /* tentative move being tried in tree            */
   Boolean gameover;

   Recommend(game, P, &S, recvalue, &gameover);
   if (gameover || depth == 0)
      if (!StackEmpty(&S))
         Pop(recmove, &S);    /* Return any one move as the answer.            */
            /* The value recvalue has been set by Recommend. */
   else {
      /* Investigate all recommended moves. */

      if (P == FIRST) {        /* Prepare to maximize recvalue.                 */
         opponent = SECOND;
         *recvalue = -INFINITY; /* Set to a value less than any that occurs.   */
      } else {                 /* Prepare to minimize recvalue.                 */
         opponent = FIRST;
         *recvalue = INFINITY; /* Set to a value greater than any that occurs. */
      }
      while (!StackEmpty(&S)) {
         Pop(&tentmove, &S);
         MakeMove(game, P, tentmove);
         LookAhead(game, depth - 1, opponent, &oppmove, &oppvalue);
         UndoMove(game, P, tentmove);
         if ((P == FIRST && oppvalue > *recvalue) ||
             (P == SECOND && oppvalue < *recvalue)) {
            *recvalue = oppvalue;
            *recmove = tentmove;
         }
      }
   }
}
```

**Exercises 10.5**     **E1.** Assign values of +1 for a win by the first player and $-1$ for a win by the second player in the game of Eight, and evaluate its game tree by the minimax method, as shown in Figure 10.13.

**E2.** A variation of the game of *Nim* begins with a pile of sticks, from which a player can remove 1, 2, or 3 sticks at each turn. The player must remove at least 1 (but no more than remain on the pile). The player who takes the last stick loses. Draw the complete game tree that begins with **(a)** 5 and **(b)** 6 sticks. Assign appropriate values for the leaves of the tree, and evaluate the other nodes by the minimax method.

**E3.** Draw the top three levels (showing the first two moves) of the game tree for the game of tic-tac-toe (Noughts and Crosses), and calculate the number of vertices that will appear on the fourth level. You may reduce the size of the tree by taking advantage of symmetries: At the first move, for example, show only three possibilities (the center square, a corner, or a side square) rather than all nine. Further symmetries near the root will reduce the size of the game tree.

**Programming**     **P1.** Write a main routine and the other functions needed to play Eight against a
**Projects 10.5**           human opponent. The function Recommend can return all legal moves at each turn.

**P2.** Write a look-ahead program for playing tic-tac-toe. In the simplest version, function Recommend returns all empty positions as recommended moves. Approximately how many possibilities will then be investigated in a complete search of the game tree? Implement this simple method. Second, modify the function Recommend so that it searches for two marks in a row with the third empty, and thereby recommends moves more intelligently. Compare the running times of the two versions.

**P3.** If you have worked your way through the tree in Figure 10.14 in enough detail, you may have noticed that it is not necessary to obtain the values for all the vertices while doing the minimax process, for there are some parts of the tree in which the best move certainly cannot appear. Let us suppose that we work our way through the tree starting at the lower left, and filling in the value for a parent vertex as soon as we have the values for all its children. After we have done all the vertices in the two main branches on the left, we find values of 7 and 5, and therefore the maximum value will be at least 7. When we go to the next vertex on level 1 and its left child, we find that the value of this child is 3. At this stage, we are taking minima, so the value to be assigned to the parent on level 1 cannot possibly be more than 3 (it is actually 1). Since 3 is less than 7, the first player will take the leftmost branch instead, and we can exclude the other branch. The vertices that, in this way, need never be evaluated, are shown within dotted lines in color in Figure 10.15.

*alpha-beta pruning*

The process of eliminating vertices in this way is called *alpha-beta pruning*. The Greek letters $\alpha$ (alpha) and $\beta$ (beta) are generally used to denote the cutoff points found.

Modify the function LookAhead so that it uses alpha-beta pruning to reduce the number of branches investigated. Compare the performance of the two versions in playing several games.

## Pointers and Pitfalls

1. Trees are flexible and powerful structures both for modeling problems and for organizing data. In using trees in problem solving and in algorithm design, first decide on the kind of tree needed (ordered, rooted, free, or binary) before considering implementation details.

2. Most trees can be described easily by using recursion; their associated algorithms are often best formulated recursively.

3. For problems of information retrieval, consider the size, number, and location of the records along with the type and structure of the entries while choosing the data structures to be used. For small records or small numbers of entries, high-speed internal memory will be used, and binary search trees will likely prove adequate. For information retrieval from disk files, methods employing multiway branching, such as tries, B-trees, and hash tables, will usually be superior. Tries are particularly well suited to applications where the keys are structured as a sequence of symbols and where the set of keys is relatively dense in the set of all possible keys. For other applications, methods that treat the key as a single unit will often prove superior. B-trees, together with various generalizations and extensions, can be usefully applied to many problems concerned with external information retrieval.

## Review Questions

10.1

1. Define the terms (a) *free tree*, (b) *rooted tree*, and (c) *ordered tree*.

2. Draw all the different (a) free trees, (b) rooted trees, and (c) ordered trees with three vertices.

3. Name three ways describing the correspondence between orchards and binary trees, and indicate the primary purpose for each of these ways.

10.2

4. What is a trie?

5. How may a trie with six levels and a five-way branch in each node differ from the rooted tree with six levels and five children for every node except the leaves? Will the trie or the tree likely have fewer nodes, and why?

6. Discuss the relative advantages in speed of retrieval of a trie and a binary search tree.

*10.3*

7. How does a multiway search tree differ from a trie?

8. What is a B-tree?

9. What happens when an attempt is made to insert a new entry into a full node of a B-tree?

10. Does a B-tree grow at its leaves or at its root? Why?

11. In deleting an entry from a B-tree, when is it necessary to combine nodes?

12. For what purposes are B-trees especially appropriate?

*10.4*

13. What is the relationship between red-black trees and B-trees?

14. State the black and the red conditions.

15. How is the height of a red-black tree related to its size?

*10.5*

16. Explain the *minimax* method for finding the value of a game.

17. Determine the value of the following game tree by the *minimax* method.

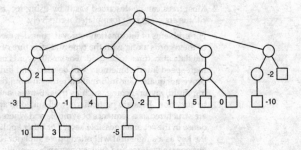

## References for Further Study

One of the most thorough available studies of trees is in the series of books by KNUTH. The correspondence from ordered trees to binary trees appears in Volume 1, pp. 332–347. Volume 3, pp. 471–505, discusses multiway trees, B-trees, and tries.
Tries were first studied in

EDWARD FREDKIN, "Trie memory," *Communications of the ACM* 3 (1960), 490–499.

The original reference for B-trees is

R. BAYER and E. McCREIGHT, "Organization and maintenance of large ordered indexes," *Acta Informatica* 1 (1972), 173–189.

An interesting survey of applications and variations of B-trees is

D. COMER, "The ubiquitous B-tree," *Computing Surveys* 11 (1979), 121–137.

The following book contains (pp. 242–264) an exposition of B-trees with Pascal algorithms for insertion and deletion.

N. WIRTH, *Algorithms + Data Structures = Programs*, Prentice-Hall, Englewood Cliffs, N. J., 1976, p. 170.

For an alternative treatment of red-black trees, including a deletion algorithm, see:

THOMAS H. CORMEN, CHARLES E. LEISERSON, and RONALD L. RIVEST, *Introduction to Algorithms*, M.I.T. Press, Cambridge, Mass., and McGraw Hill, New York, 1990, 1028 pages.

This book gives comprehensive coverage of many different kinds of algorithms. A more extensive mathematical analysis of red-black trees appears in

DERICK WOOD, *Data Structures, Algorithms, and Performance*, Addison-Wesley, 1993, 594 pages.

The following book (pp. 290–302) contains more extensive discussion and analysis of game trees and look-ahead programs.

E. HOROWITZ and S. SAHNI, *Fundamentals of Computer Algorithms*, Computer Science Press, 1978, 626 pages.

# 11

# Graphs

THIS CHAPTER *introduces important mathematical structures called graphs that have applications in subjects as diverse as sociology, chemistry, geography, and electrical engineering. We shall study methods to represent graphs in the data structures available to us and shall construct several important algorithms for processing graphs. Finally, we look at the possibility of using graphs themselves as data structures.*

# 11.1 Mathematical Background

### 11.1.1 DEFINITIONS AND EXAMPLES

*graphs and directed graphs*

A *graph* $G$ consists of a set $V$, whose members are called the *vertices* of $G$, together with a set $E$ of pairs of distinct vertices from $V$. These pairs are called the *edges* of $G$. If $e = (v, w)$ is an edge with vertices $v$ and $w$, then $v$ and $w$ are said to *lie on* $e$, and $e$ is said to be *incident* with $v$ and $w$. If the pairs are unordered, then $G$ is called an *undirected graph*; if the pairs are ordered, then $G$ is called a *directed graph*. The term *directed graph* is often shortened to *digraph*, and the unqualified term *graph* usually means *undirected graph*.

*drawings*

The natural way to picture a graph is to represent vertices as points or circles and edges as line segments or arcs connecting the vertices. If the graph is directed, then the line segments or arcs have arrowheads indicating the direction. Figure 11.1 shows several examples of graphs.

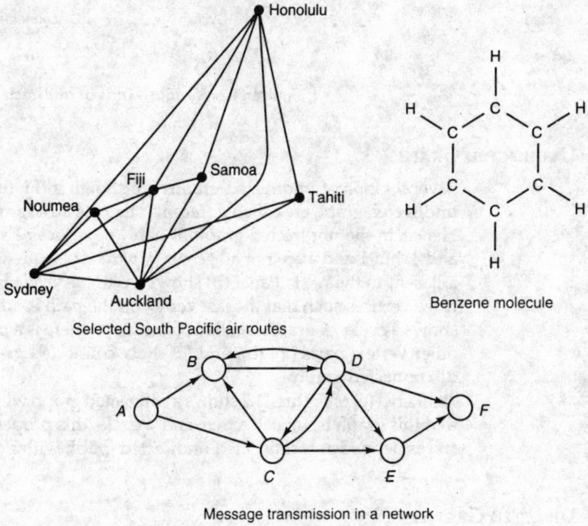

Selected South Pacific air routes

Benzene molecule

Message transmission in a network

Figure 11.1. Examples of graphs

The places in the first part of Figure 11.1 are the vertices of the graph, and the air routes connecting them are the edges. In the second part, the hydrogen and carbon atoms (denoted H and C) are the vertices, and the chemical bonds are the edges. The third part of Figure 11.1 shows a directed graph, where the nodes of the network ($A, B, \ldots, F$) are the vertices and the edges from one to another have the directions shown by the arrows.

*applications*

Graphs find their importance as models for many kinds of processes or structures. Cities and the highways connecting them form a graph, as do the components on a circuit board with the connections among them. An organic chemical compound can be considered a graph with the atoms as the vertices and the bonds between them as edges. The people living in a city can be regarded as the vertices of a graph with the relationship *is acquainted with* describing the edges. People working in a corporation form a directed graph with the relation "supervises" describing the edges. The same people could also be considered as an undirected graph, with different edges describing the relationship "works with."

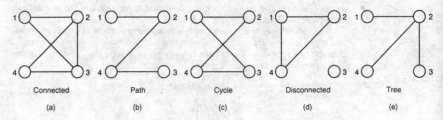

Figure 11.2. Various kinds of undirected graphs

### 11.1.2 UNDIRECTED GRAPHS

*paths, cycles, connected*

Several kinds of undirected graphs are shown in Figure 11.2. Two vertices in an undirected graph are called **adjacent** if there is an edge from the first to the second. Hence, in the undirected graph of part (a), vertices 1 and 2 are adjacent, as are 3 and 4, but 1 and 4 are not adjacent. A **path** is a sequence of distinct vertices, each adjacent to the next. Panel (b) shows a path. A **cycle** is a path containing at least three vertices such that the last vertex on the path is adjacent to the first. Panel (c) shows a cycle. A graph is called **connected** if there is a path from any vertex to any other vertex; parts (a), (b), and (c) show connected graphs, and part (d) shows a disconnected graph.

*free tree*

Panel (e) of Figure 11.2 shows a connected graph with no cycles. You will notice that this graph is, in fact, a tree, and we take this property as the definition: A **free tree** is defined as a connected undirected graph with no cycles.

### 11.1.3 DIRECTED GRAPHS

*directed paths and cycles*

For directed graphs, we can make similar definitions. We require all edges in a path or a cycle to have the same direction, so that following a path or a cycle means always moving in the direction indicated by the arrows. Such a path (cycle) is called a **directed** path (cycle). A directed graph is called **strongly connected** if there is a directed path from any vertex to any vertex. If we suppress the direction of the edges and the resulting undirected graph is connected, we call the directed graph **weakly connected**. Figure 11.3 illustrates directed cycles, strongly connected directed graphs, and weakly connected directed graphs.

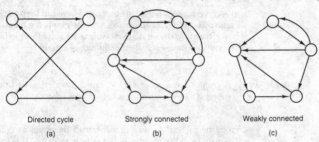

|                   |                      |                    |
| :---------------: | :------------------: | :----------------: |
| Directed cycle    | Strongly connected   | Weakly connected   |
| (a)               | (b)                  | (c)                |

Figure 11.3. Examples of directed graphs.

*multiple edges*

*self-loops*

The directed graphs in parts (b) and (c) of Figure 11.3 show pairs of vertices with directed edges going both ways between them. Since directed edges are ordered pairs and the ordered pairs $(v, w)$ and $(w, v)$ are distinct if $v \neq w$, such pairs of edges are permissible in directed graphs. Since the corresponding unordered pairs are not distinct, however, in an undirected graph there can be at most one edge connecting a pair of vertices. Similarly, since the vertices on an edge are required to be distinct, there can be no edge from a vertex to itself. We should remark, however, that (although we shall not do so) sometimes these requirements are relaxed to allow multiple edges connecting a pair of vertices and self-loops connecting a vertex to itself.

# 11.2 Computer Representation

If we are to write programs for solving problems concerning graphs, then we must first find ways to represent the mathematical structure of a graph as some kind of data structure. There are several methods in common use, which differ fundamentally in the choice of abstract data type used to represent graphs, and there are several variations depending on the implementation of the abstract data type. In other words, we begin with one mathematical system (a *graph*), then we study how it can be described in terms of abstract data types (*sets*, *tables*, and *lists* can all be used, as it turns out), and finally we choose implementations for the abstract data type that we select.

## 1. The Set Representation

Graphs are defined in terms of sets, and it is natural to look first to sets to determine their representation as data. First, we have a set of vertices, and, second, we have the edges as a set of pairs of vertices. Rather than attempting to represent this set of pairs directly, we divide it into pieces by considering the set of edges attached to each vertex separately. In other words, we can keep track of all the edges in the graph by keeping, for all vertices $v$ in the graph, the set $E_v$ of edges containing $v$, or, equivalently, the set $A_v$ of all vertices adjacent to $v$. In fact, we can use this idea to produce a new, equivalent definition of a graph:

**Definition**    A *graph* $G$ consists of a set $V$, called the *vertices* of $G$, and, for all $v \in V$, a subset $A_v$ of $V$, called the set of vertices *adjacent* to $v$.

From the subsets $A_v$ we can reconstruct the edges as ordered pairs by the rule: The pair $(v, w)$ is an edge if and only if $w \in A_v$. It is easier, however, to work with sets of vertices than with pairs. This new definition, moreover, works for both directed and undirected graphs. The graph is *undirected* provided that it satisfies the following symmetry property: $w \in A_v$ implies $v \in A_w$ for all $v, w \in V$. This property can be restated in less formal terms: It means that an undirected edge between $v$ and $w$ can be regarded as made up of two directed edges, one from $v$ to $w$ and the other from $w$ to $v$.

## 2. Implementation of Sets

There are two general ways for us to implement sets of vertices in data structures and algorithms. One way is to represent the set as a *list* of its elements; this method we shall study presently. The other implementation, often called a *bit string*, keeps a Boolean value (hence a single bit) for each possible member of the set to indicate whether or not it is in the set. Some languages, such as Pascal, provide these sets as part of the language. Other programming languages, such as C, however, do not provide sets as part of the language. We can overcome this difficulty, however, and at the same time obtain a better representation of graphs.

*sets as bit strings*

## 3. Adjacency Tables

One way to implement a graph in C is with a two-dimensional array of Boolean values. For simplicity, we shall consider that these vertices are indexed with the integers from 0 to $n-1$, where n denotes the number of vertices. Since we shall wish n to be variable, we shall also introduce a constant MAXVERTEX bounding the number of vertices, with which we can fully specify the first representation of a graph:

*first implementation: adjacency table*

```
typedef Boolean AdjacencyTable [MAXVERTEX] [MAXVERTEX];

typedef struct graph {
   int n;                         /* number of vertices in the graph        */
   AdjacencyTable A;
} Graph;
```

*meaning*

The adjacency table A has a natural interpretation: A[v][w] is TRUE if and only if vertex v is adjacent to vertex w. If the graph is directed, we interpret A[v][w] as indicating whether or not the edge from v to w is in the graph. If the graph is undirected, then the adjacency table is symmetric, that is, A[v][w] == A[w][v] for all v and w. The representation of a graph by adjacency sets and by an adjacency table is illustrated in Figure 11.4.

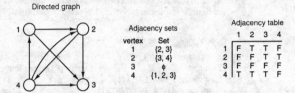

Figure 11.4. Adjacency set and an adjacency table

### 4. Adjacency Lists

Another way to represent a set is as a *list* of its elements. For representing a graph, we shall then have both a list of vertices and, for each vertex, a list of adjacent vertices. We shall consider implementation of graphs by using both contiguous lists and simply linked lists. For more advanced applications, however, it is often useful to employ more sophisticated implementations of lists as binary or multiway search trees or as heaps.

Note that, by identifying vertices with their indices in the previous representations, we have *ipso facto* implemented the vertex set as a contiguous list, but now we should make a deliberate choice concerning the use of contiguous or linked lists.

### 5. Linked Implementation

Greatest flexibility is obtained by using linked lists for both the vertices and the adjacency lists. This implementation is illustrated in part (a) of Figure 11.5 and results in a declaration such as the following:

*second implementation: linked lists*

```
typedef struct vertex Vertex;
typedef struct edge Edge;
struct vertex {
    Edge *firstedge;        /* start of the adjacency list        */
    Vertex *nextvertex;     /* next vertex on the linked list     */
};
struct edge {
    Vertex *endpoint;       /* vertex to which the edge points    */
    Edge *nextedge;         /* next edge on the adjacency list     */
};
typedef Vertex *Graph;      /* header for the list of vertices     */
```

### 6. Contiguous Implementation

Although this linked implementation is very flexible, it is sometimes awkward to navigate through the linked lists, and many algorithms require random access to vertices. Therefore the following contiguous implementation is often better. For a contiguous adjacency list, we must keep a counter, and for this we use standard notation from graph theory: The *valence* of a vertex is defined as the number of edges on which it lies, and hence it is also the number of vertices adjacent to it. This contiguous implementation is illustrated in part (b) of Figure 11.5.

*third implementation: contiguous lists*

```
typedef int AdjacencyList[MAXVERTEX];

typedef struct graph {
    int n;                    /* number of vertices in the graph        */
    int valence[MAXVERTEX];
    AdjacencyList A[MAXVERTEX];
} Graph;
```

### 7. Mixed Implementation

The final implementation uses a contiguous list for the vertices and linked storage for the adjacency lists. This mixed implementation is illustrated in part (c) of Figure 11.5.

*fourth implementation: mixed lists*

```
typedef struct edge {
    Vertex endpoint;
    struct edge *nextedge;
} Edge;
typedef struct graph {
    int n;                    /* number of vertices in the graph        */
    Edge *firstedge[MAXVERTEX];
} Graph;
```

### 8. Information Fields

Many applications of graphs require not only the adjacency information specified in the various representations but also further information specific to each vertex or each edge. In the linked representations, this information can be included as additional fields within appropriate records, and, in the contiguous representations, it can be included by making array entries into records.

*networks, weights*

An especially important case is that of a *network*, which is defined as a graph in which a numerical *weight* is attached to each edge. For many algorithms on networks, the best representation is an adjacency table, where the entries are the weights rather than Boolean values. We shall return to this topic later in the chapter.

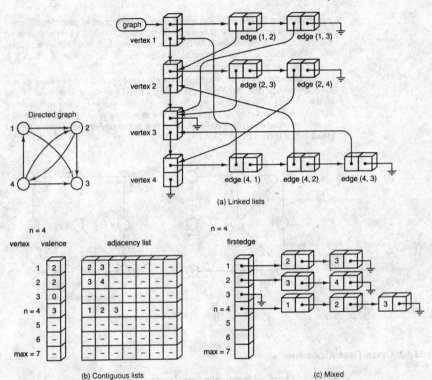

Figure 11.5. Implementations of a graph with lists

## 11.3 Graph Traversal

### 11.3.1 METHODS

In many problems, we wish to investigate all the vertices in a graph in some systematic order, just as with binary trees, where we developed several systematic traversal methods. In tree traversal, we had a root vertex with which we generally started; in graphs, we often do not have any one vertex singled out as special, and therefore the traversal may start at an arbitrary vertex. Although there are many possible orders for visiting the vertices of the graph, two methods are of particular importance..

*depth-first*

      ***Depth-first traversal*** of a graph is roughly analogous to preorder traversal of an ordered tree. Suppose that the traversal has just visited a vertex $v$, and let $w_1, w_2, \ldots, w_k$ be the vertices adjacent to $v$. Then we shall next visit $w_1$ and keep $w_2, \ldots, w_k$ waiting. After visiting $w_1$, we traverse all the vertices to which it is adjacent before returning to traverse $w_2, \ldots, w_k$.

*breadth-first*

      ***Breadth-first traversal*** of a graph is roughly analogous to level-by-level traversal of an ordered tree. If the traversal has just visited a vertex $v$, then it next visits *all* the vertices adjacent to $v$, putting the vertices adjacent to these in a waiting list to be traversed after all vertices adjacent to $v$ have been visited. Figure 11.6 shows the order of visiting the vertices of one graph under both depth-first and breadth-first traversals.

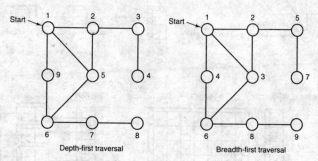

Figure 11.6. Graph traversal

## 11.3.2 DEPTH-FIRST ALGORITHM

      Depth-first traversal is naturally formulated as a recursive algorithm. Its action, when it reaches a vertex $v$, is

```
Visit(v);
for all vertices w adjacent to v do
    Traverse(w, Visit);
```

*complications*

      In graph traversal, however, two difficulties arise that cannot appear for tree traversal. First, the graph may contain cycles, so our traversal algorithm may reach the same vertex a second time. To prevent infinite recursion, we therefore introduce a Boolean-valued array visited, set visited[v] to TRUE immediately before visiting v, and check the value of visited[w] before processing w. Second, the graph may not be connected, so the traversal algorithm may fail to reach all vertices from a single starting point. Hence we enclose the action in a loop that runs through all vertices.

With these refinements, we obtain the following outline of depth-first traversal. Further details depend on the choice of implementation of graphs, and we postpone them to application programs.

*main function*

```
/* DepthFirst: depth-first traversal of a graph.
   Pre:  The graph G has been created.
   Post: The function Visit has been performed at each vertex of G in depth-first order.
   Uses: Function Traverse produces the recursive depth-first order. */
void DepthFirst(Graph G, void (*Visit)(Vertex))
{
    Boolean visited[MAXVERTEX];
    Vertex v;
    for (all v in G)
        visited[v] = FALSE;
    for (all v in G)
        if (!visited[v])
            Traverse(v, Visit);
}
```

The recursion is performed in the following function, to be declared along with the previous one.

*recursive traversal*

```
/* Traverse: recursive traversal of a graph
   Pre:  v is a vertex of the graph G.
   Post: The depth-first traversal, using function Visit, has been completed for v and
         for all vertices adjacent to v.
   Uses: Traverse recursively. */
void Traverse(Vertex v, void (*Visit)(Vertex))
{
    Vertex w;
    visited[v] = TRUE;
    Visit(v);
    for (all w adjacent to v)
        if (!visited[w])
            Traverse(w, Visit);
}
```

### 11.3.3 Breadth-First Algorithm

*stacks and queues*

Since using recursion and programming with stacks are essentially equivalent, we could formulate depth-first traversal with a stack, pushing all unvisited vertices adjacent to the one being visited onto the stack and popping the stack to find the next vertex to visit. The algorithm for breadth-first traversal is quite similar to the resulting algorithm for depth-first traversal, except that a queue is needed instead of a stack. Its outline follows.

```
                        /* BreadthFirst: breadth-first traversal of a graph.
                        Pre:   The graph G has been created.
                        Post:  The function Visit has been performed at each vertex of G, where the vertices
                               are chosen in breadth-first order.
                        Uses:  Queue functions. */
breadth-first traversal  void BreadthFirst(Graph G, void (*Visit)(Vertex))
                        {
                            Queue Q;                    /* QueueEntry defined to be Vertex.              */
                            Boolean visited[MAXVERTEX];
                            Vertex v, w;
                            for (all v in G)
                                visited[v] = FALSE;
                            CreateQueue(Q);
                            for (all v in G)
                                if (!visited[v]) {
                                    Append(v, Q);
                                    do {
                                        Serve(v, Q);
                                        if (!visited[v]) {
                                            visited[v] = TRUE;
                                            Visit(v);
                                        }
                                        for (all w adjacent to v)
                                            if (!visited[w])
                                                Append(w, Q);
                                    } while (!QueueEmpty(Q));
                                }
                        }
```

# 11.4 Topological Sorting

### 11.4.1 THE PROBLEM

*topological order*

If $G$ is a directed graph with no directed cycles, then a **topological order** for $G$ is a sequential listing of all the vertices in $G$ such that, for all vertices $v, w \in G$, if there is an edge from $v$ to $w$, then $v$ precedes $w$ in the sequential listing. Throughout this section, we shall consider only directed graphs that have no directed cycles. The term **acyclic** is often used to mean that a graph has no cycles.

*applications*

Such graphs arise in many problems. As a first application of topological order, consider the courses available at a university as the vertices of a directed graph, where there is an edge from one course to another if the first is a prerequisite for the second. A topological order is then a listing of all the courses such that all prerequisites for a course appear before it does. A second example is a glossary of technical terms that is ordered so that no term is used in a definition before it is itself defined. Similarly, the author of a textbook uses a topological order for the topics in the book. Two different topological orders of a directed graph are shown in Figure 11.7.

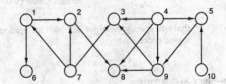

Directed graph with no directed cycles

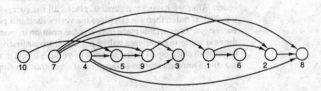

Depth-first ordering

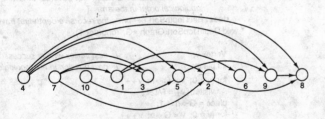

Breadth-first ordering

Figure 11.7. Topological orderings of a directed graph

As an example of algorithms for graph traversal, we shall develop functions that produce a topological ordering of the vertices of a directed graph that has no cycles. We shall develop two functions: first, for depth-first traversal, and, then, for breadth-first traversal. Both functions will operate on a graph G given in the mixed *graph representation*    implementation (with a contiguous list of vertices and linked adjacency lists), and both functions will produce an array of type

**Vertex toporder[MAXVERTEX];**

that will specify the order in which the vertices should be listed to obtain a topological order.

## 11.4.2 DEPTH-FIRST ALGORITHM

*method*    In a topological order, each vertex must appear before all the vertices that are its successors in the directed graph. For a depth-first topological ordering, we therefore start by finding a vertex that has no successors and place it last in the order. After we have, by recursion, placed all the successors of a vertex into the topological order, then we can place the vertex itself in a position before any of its successors. The variable place indicates the position in the topological order where the next vertex to be ordered will be placed. Since we first order the last vertices, we begin with place equal to the number of vertices in the graph. The main function is a direct implementation of the general algorithm developed in the last section.

```
/* DepthTopSort: generate depth-first topological ordering
   Pre:  G is a directed graph with no cycles implemented with a contiguous list of
         vertices and linked adjacency lists.
   Post: The function makes a depth-first traversal of G and generates the resulting
         topological order in the array T.
   Uses: RecDepthSort performs the recursive depth-first traversal. */
void DepthTopSort(Graph *G, Toporder T)
{
   Vertex v;              /* next vertex whose successors are to be ordered    */
   int place;             /* next position in the topological order to be filled    */
   for (v = 0; v < G->n; v++)
      visited[v] = FALSE;
   place = G->n - 1;
   for (v = 0; v < G->n; v++)
      if (!visited[v])
         RecDepthSort(G, v, &place, T);
}
```

The function RecDepthSort that performs the recursion, based on the outline for the general function Traverse, first places all the successors of v into their positions in the topological order and then places v into the order.

/* RecDepthSort: perform recursion for DepthTopSort.

   **Pre:** v *is a vertex of the graph G and place is the next location in the topological*
   *order* T *to be determined (starting from the end of the final ordered list).*

   **Post:** *The procedure puts all the successors of v and finally v itself into the topolog-*
   *ical order* T *in depth-first order.*

   **Uses:** *Global array* visited *and RecDepthSort recursively.* */

*recursive traversal*   void RecDepthSort(Graph *G, int v, int *place, Toporder T)
```
{
    Vertex curvertex;          /* vertex adjacent to v                              */
    Edge *curedge;             /* traverses list of vertices adjacent to v          */
    visited[v] = TRUE;
    curedge = G->firstedge[v];  /* Find the first vertex succeeding v.              */
    while (curedge) {
        curvertex = curedge->endpoint;  /* curvertex is adjacent to v.             */
        if (!visited[curvertex])
            RecDepthSort(G, curvertex, place, T);
                                /* Order the successors of curvertex.                */
        curedge = curedge->nextedge;
                                /* Go on to the next immediate successor of v.       */
    }
    T[*place] = v;             /* Put v itself into the topological order.          */
    (*place)--;
}
```

Since this algorithm visits each node of the graph exactly once and follows each
edge once, doing no searching, its running time is $O(n+e)$, where $n$ is the number
*performance*    of vertices and $e$ is the number of edges in the graph.

## 11.4.3 BREADTH-FIRST ALGORITHM

*method*    In a breadth-first topological ordering of a directed graph with no cycles, we start
by finding the vertices that should be first in the topological order and then apply
the fact that every vertex must come before its successors in the topological order.
The vertices that come first are those that are not successors of any other vertex.
To find these, we set up an array predecessorcount whose entry at index v is the
number of immediate predecessors of vertex v. The vertices that are not successors
are those with no predecessors. We therefore initialize the breadth-first traversal
by placing these vertices into the queue of vertices to be visited. As each vertex is
visited, it is removed from the queue, assigned the next available position in the
topological order (starting at the beginning of the order), and then removed from
further consideration by reducing the predecessor count for each of its immediate
successors by one. When one of these counts reaches zero, all predecessors of the
corresponding vertex have been visited, and the vertex itself is then ready to be
processed, so it is added to the queue. We therefore obtain the following function.

```
/* BreadthTopSort: generate breadth-first topological ordering
   Pre:  G is a directed graph with no cycles implemented with a contiguous list of
         vertices and linked adjacency lists.
   Post: The function makes a breadth-first traversal of G and generates the resulting
         topological order in T.
   Uses: Functions for processing queues. */
void BreadthTopSort(Graph *G, Toporder T)
{
    int predecessorcount[MAXVERTEX];
                                 /* number of immediate predecessors of each vertex */
    Queue Q;                     /* vertices ready to be placed into the order      */
    Vertex v;                    /* vertex currently being visited                  */
    Vertex succ;                 /* one of the immediate successors of v            */
    Edge *curedge;               /* traverses the adjacency list of v               */
    int place;                   /* next position in topological order              */
    /* Initialize all the predecessor counts to 0. */
    for (v = 0; v < G->n; v++)
        predecessorcount[v] = 0;
    /* Increase the predecessor count for each vertex that is a successor. */
    for (v = 0; v < G->n; v++)
        for (curedge = G->firstedge[v]; curedge; curedge = curedge->nextedge)
            predecessorcount[curedge->endpoint]++;
    CreateQueue(&Q);
    /* Place all vertices with no predecessors into the queue. */
    for (v = 0; v < G->n; v++)
        if (predecessorcount[v] == 0)
            Append(v, &Q);
    /* Start the breadth-first traversal. */
    place = -1;
    while (!QueueEmpty(Q)) {
        /* Visit v by placing it into the topological order. */
        Serve(&v, &Q);
        place++;
        T[place] = v;
        /* Traverse the list of immediate successors of v. */
        for (curedge = G->firstedge[v]; curedge; curedge = curedge->nextedge) {
            /* Reduce the predecessor count for each immediate successor. */
            succ = curedge->endpoint;
            predecessorcount[succ]--;
            if (predecessorcount[succ] == 0)
                /* succ has no further predecessors, so it is ready to process. */
                Append(succ, &Q);
        }
    }
}
```

*breadth-first
topological order*

This algorithm requires some of the functions for processing queues. The entries in the queue are to be vertices, and the queue can be implemented in any of the ways described in Chapter 4.

*performance*     As with depth-first traversal, the time required by the breadth-first function is $O(n + e)$, where $n$ is the number of vertices and $e$ is the number of edges in the directed graph.

## 11.5 A Greedy Algorithm: Shortest Paths

### 1. The Problem

As a final application of graphs, one requiring somewhat more sophisticated reasoning, we consider the following problem. We are given a directed graph $G$ in which every edge has a nonnegative *weight* attached, and our problem is to find a path from one vertex $v$ to another $w$ such that the sum of the weights on the

*shortest path*    path is as small as possible. We call such a path a ***shortest path***, even though the weights may represent costs, time, or some quantity other than distance.

We can think of $G$ as a map of airline routes, for example, with each vertex representing a city and the weight on each edge the cost of flying from one city to the second. Our problem is then to find a routing from city $v$ to city $w$ such that the total cost is a minimum. Consider the directed graph shown in Figure 11.8. The shortest path from vertex 0 to vertex 1 goes via vertex 2 and has a total cost of 4, compared to the cost of 5 for the edge directly from 0 to 1 and the cost of 8 for the path via vertex 4.

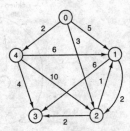

Figure 11.8. A directed graph with weights

*source*     It turns out that it is just as easy to solve the more general problem of starting at one vertex, called the ***source***, and finding the shortest path to every other vertex, instead of to just one destination vertex. For simplicity, we take the source to be vertex 0, and our problem then consists of finding the shortest path from vertex 0 to every vertex in the graph. We require that the weights are all nonnegative.

## 2. Method

The algorithm operates by keeping a set $S$ of those vertices whose shortest distance from 0 is known. Initially, 0 is the only vertex in $S$. At each step, we add to $S$ a remaining vertex for which the shortest path from 0 has been determined. The problem is to determine which vertex to add to $S$ at each step. Let us think of the vertices already in $S$ as having been labeled with some color, and think of the edges making up the shortest paths from the source 0 to these vertices as also colored.

*distance table*

We shall maintain a table $D$ that gives, for each vertex $v$, the distance from 0 to $v$ along a path all of whose edges are colored, except possibly the last one. That is, if $v$ is in $S$, then $D[v]$ gives the shortest distance to $v$ and all edges along the corresponding path are colored. If $v$ is not in $S$, then $D[v]$ gives the length of the path from 0 to some vertex $w$ in $S$ plus the weight of the edge from $w$ to $v$, and all the edges of this path except the last one are colored. The table $D$ is initialized by setting $D[v]$ to the weight of the edge from 0 to $v$ if it exists and to $\infty$ if not.

*greedy algorithm*

To determine what vertex to add to $S$ at each step, we apply the *greedy* criterion of choosing the vertex $v$ with the smallest distance recorded in the table $D$, such that $v$ is not already in $S$.

*verification*

We must prove that, for this vertex $v$, the distance recorded in $D$ really is the length of the shortest path from 1 to $v$. For suppose that there were a shorter path from 0 to $v$, such as shown in Figure 11.9. This path first leaves $S$ to go to some vertex $x$, then goes on to $v$ (possibly even reentering $S$ along the way). But if this path is shorter than the colored path to $v$, then its initial segment from 0 to $x$ is also shorter, so that the greedy criterion would have chosen $x$ rather than $v$ as the

*end of proof*

next vertex to add to $S$, since we would have had $D[x] < D[v]$.

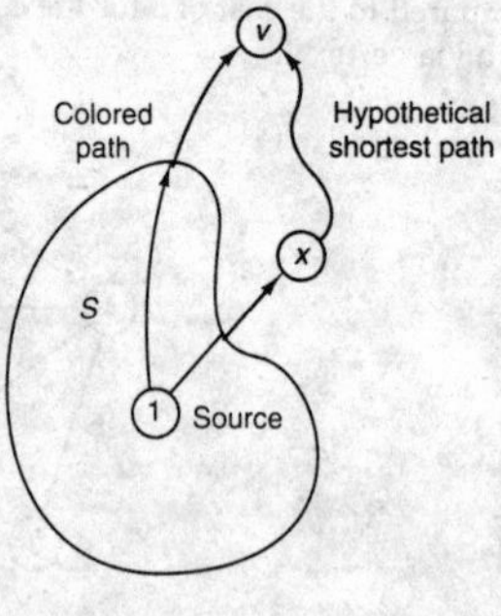

Figure 11.9. Finding a shortest path

When we add $v$ to $S$, we think of $v$ as now colored and also color the shortest path from 0 to $v$ (every edge of which except the last was actually already colored). Next, we must update the entries of $D$ by checking, for each vertex $w$ not in $S$, whether a path through $v$ and then directly to $w$ is shorter than the previously

*maintain the invariant*

recorded distance to $w$. That is, we replace $D[w]$ by $D[v]$ plus the weight of the edge from $v$ to $w$ if the latter quantity is smaller.

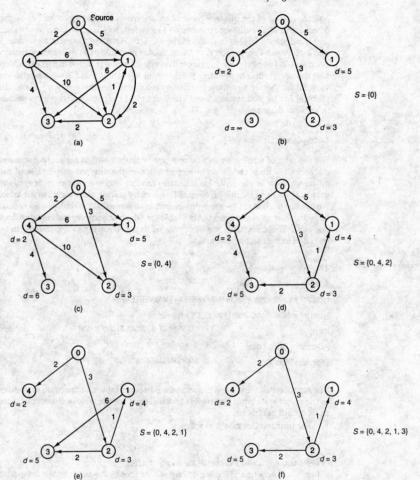

Figure 11.10. Example of shortest paths

### 3. Example

Before writing a formal function incorporating this method, let us work through the example shown in Figure 11.10. For the directed graph shown in part (a), the initial situation is shown in part (b): The set $S$ (colored vertices) consists of 0 alone, and the entries of the distance table $D$ are shown as numbers in color beside the other vertices. The distance to vertex 4 is shortest, so 4 is added to $S$ in part (c), and the distance $D[4]$ is updated to the value 6. Since the distances to vertices 1 and 2 via vertex 4 are greater than those already recorded in $T$, their entries remain unchanged. The next closest vertex to 0 is vertex 2, and it is added in part (d), which also shows the effect of updating the distances to vertices 1 and 3, whose paths via vertex 2 are shorter than those previously recorded. The final two steps, shown in parts (e) and (f), add vertices 1 and 3 to $S$ and yield the paths and distances shown in the final diagram.

## 4. Implementation

For the sake of writing a function to embody this algorithm for finding shortest distances, we must choose an implementation of the directed graph. Use of the adjacency-table implementation facilitates random access to all the vertices of the graph, as we need for this problem. Moreover, by storing the weights in the table, we can use the table to give weights as well as adjacencies. We shall place a special large value ∞ in any position of the table for which the corresponding edge does not exist. These decisions are incorporated in the following C declarations to be included in the calling program.

*graph representation*

```
#include <limits.h>
#define INFINITY INT_MAX        /* value for ∞                           */
typedef int AdjacencyTable[MAXVERTEX][MAXVERTEX];
typedef int DistanceTable[MAXVERTEX];
int n;                          /* number of vertices in the graph       */
AdjacencyTable cost;            /* describes the graph                   */
DistanceTable D;                /* shortest distances from vertex 0      */
```

The function that we write will accept the adjacency table and the count of vertices in the graph as its input parameters and will produce the table of closest distances as its output parameter.

The function Distance is as follows:

```
/* Distance: calculates the cost of the shortest path.
   Pre:  A directed graph is given which has n vertices by the weights given in the table
         cost.
   Post: The function finds the shortest path from vertex 0 to each vertex of the graph
         and returns the path that it finds in the array D. */
```

*shortest-distance function*

```
void Distance(int n, AdjacencyTable cost, DistanceTable D)
{
    Boolean final[MAXVERTEX];    /* Has the distance from 0 to v been found?   */
                                 /* final[v] is true iff v is in the set S.    */
    int i;                       /* repetition count for the main loop         */
                 /* One distance is finalized on each pass through the loop. */
    int w;                       /* a vertex not yet added to the set S        */
    int v;                       /* vertex with minimum tentative distance in D[] */
    int min;                     /* distance of v, equals D[v]                 */
    final[0] = TRUE;             /* Initialize with vertex 0 alone in the set S. */
    D[0] = 0;
    for (v = 1; v < n; v++) {
        final[v] = FALSE;
        D[v] = cost[0][v];
    }
    /* Start the main loop; add one vertex v to S on each pass. */
    for (i = 1; i < n; i++) {
        min = INFINITY;                /* Find the closest vertex v to vertex 0. */
        for (w = 1; w < n; w++)
            if (!final[w])
                if (D[w] < min) {
                    v = w;
                    min = D[w];
                }
        final[v] = TRUE;               /* Add v to the set S.                    */
        for (w = 1; w < n; w++)        /* Update the remaining distances in D.   */
            if (!final[w])
                if (min + cost[v][w] < D[w])
                    D[w] = min + cost[v][w];
    }
}
```

*performance*

To estimate the running time of this function, we note that the main loop is executed $n - 1$ times, and within the main loop are two other loops, each executed $n - 1$ times, so these loops contribute a multiple of $(n - 1)^2$ operations. Statements done outside the loops contribute only $O(n)$, so the running time of the algorithm is $O(n^2)$.

## 11.6 Graphs as Data Structures

In this chapter, we have studied a few applications of graphs, but we have hardly begun to scratch the surface of the broad and deep subject of graph algorithms. In many of these algorithms, graphs appear, as they have in this chapter, as mathematical structures capturing the essential description of a problem rather than as computational tools for its solution.

*mathematical structures and data structures*

Note that in this chapter we have spoken of graphs as mathematical structures, and not as data structures, for we have used graphs to formulate mathematical problems, and, to write algorithms, we have then implemented the graphs within data structures such as tables and lists. Graphs, however, can certainly be regarded as data structures themselves, data structures that embody relationships among the data more complicated than those describing a list or a tree.

*flexibility and power*

Because of their generality and flexibility, graphs are powerful data structures that prove valuable in more advanced applications such as the design of database management systems. Such powerful tools are meant to be used, of course, whenever necessary, but they must always be used with care so that their power is not turned to confusion. Perhaps the best safeguard in the use of powerful tools is to insist on regularity, that is, to use the powerful tools only in carefully defined and well-understood ways. Because of the generality of graphs, it is not always easy to impose this discipline on their use.

*irregularity*

In this world, nonetheless, irregularities will always creep in, no matter how hard we try to avoid them. It is the bane of the systems analyst and programmer to accommodate these irregularities while trying to maintain the integrity of the underlying system design. Irregularity even occurs in the very systems that we use as models for the data structures we devise, models such as the family trees whose terminology we have always used. An excellent illustration of what can happen is the following classic story, quoted by N. WIRTH[1] from a Zurich newspaper of July 1922.

> I married a widow who had a grown-up daughter. My father, who visited us quite often, fell in love with my step-daughter and married her. Hence, my father became my son-in-law, and my step-daughter became my mother. Some months later, my wife gave birth to a son, who became the brother-in-law of my father as well as my uncle. The wife of my father, that is my step-daughter, also had a son. Thereby, I got a brother and at the same time a grandson. My wife is my grandmother, since she is my mother's mother. Hence, I am my wife's husband and at the same time her step-grandson; in other words, I am my own grandfather.

---

**Exercises 11.6**  **E1.** **(a)** Find all the cycles in each of the following graphs. **(b)** Which of these graphs are connected? **(c)** Which of these graphs are free trees?

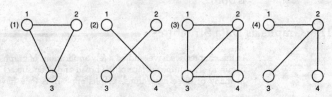

---

[1] *Algorithms + Data Structures = Programs*, Prentice Hall, Englewood Cliffs, N. J., 1976, page 170.

**E2.** For each of the graphs shown in Exercise E1, give the implementation of the graph as **(a)** an adjacency table, **(b)** a linked vertex list with linked adjacency lists, **(c)** a contiguous vertex list of contiguous adjacency lists.

**E3.** A graph is *regular* if every vertex has the same valence (that is, if it is adjacent to the same number of other vertices). For a regular graph, a good implementation is to keep the vertices in a linked list and the adjacency lists contiguous. The length of all the adjacency lists is called the *degree* of the graph. Write C declarations for this implementation of regular graphs.

**E4.** The topological sorting functions as presented in the text are deficient in error checking. Modify the **(a)** depth-first and **(b)** breadth-first functions so that they will detect any (directed) cycles in the graph and indicate what vertices cannot be placed in any topological order because they lie on a cycle.

**Programming Projects 11.6**

**P1.** Write C functions called ReadGraph that will read from the terminal the number of vertices in an undirected graph and lists of adjacent vertices. Be sure to include error checking. The graph is to be implemented as

**(a)** an adjacency table;
**(b)** a linked vertex list with linked adjacency lists;
**(c)** a contiguous vertex list of linked adjacency lists.

**P2.** Write C functions called WriteGraph that will write pertinent information specifying a graph to the terminal. The graph is to be implemented as

**(a)** an adjacency table;
**(b)** a linked vertex list with linked adjacency lists;
**(c)** a contiguous vertex list of linked adjacency lists.

**P3.** Use the functions ReadGraph and WriteGraph to implement and test the topological sorting functions developed in this section for

**(a)** depth-first order and
**(b)** breadth-first order.

**P4.** Implement and test the function for determining shortest distances in directed graphs with weights.

# Pointers and Pitfalls

1. Graphs provide an excellent way to describe the essential features of many applications, thereby facilitating specification of the underlying problems and formulation of algorithms for their solution. Graphs sometimes appear as data structures but more often as mathematical abstractions useful for problem solving.

2. Graphs may be implemented in many ways by the use of different kinds of data structures. Postpone implementation decisions until the applications of graphs in the problem-solving and algorithm-development phases are well understood.

3. Many applications require graph traversal. Let the application determine the traversal method: depth first, breadth first, or some other order. Depth-first traversal is naturally recursive (or can use a stack). Breadth-first traversal normally uses a queue.

4. Greedy algorithms represent only a sample of the many paradigms useful in developing graph algorithms. For further methods and examples, consult the references.

# Review Questions

11.1
1. In the sense of this chapter, what is a *graph*? What are *edges* and *vertices*?

2. What is the difference between an *undirected* and a *directed* graph?

3. Define the terms *adjacent*, *path*, *cycle*, and *connected*.

4. What does it mean for a directed graph to be strongly connected? Weakly connected?

11.2
5. Describe three ways to implement graphs in computer memory.

11.3
6. Explain the difference between *depth-first* and *breadth-first* traversal of a graph.

7. What data structures are needed to keep track of the waiting vertices during **(a)** depth-first and **(b)** breadth-first traversal?

11.4
8. For what kind of graphs is *topological sorting* defined?

9. What is a *topological order* for such a graph?

11.5
10. Why is the algorithm for finding shortest distances called *greedy*?

# References for Further Study

The study of graphs and algorithms for their processing is a large subject and one that involves both mathematics and computing science. Three books, each of which contains many interesting algorithms, are

R. E. TARJAN, *Data Structures and Network Algorithms*, Society for Industrial and Applied Mathematics, Philadelphia, 1983, 131 pages.

SHIMON EVEN, *Graph Algorithms*, Computer Science Press, Rockville, Md., 1979, 249 pages.

E. M. REINGOLD, J. NIEVERGELT, N. DEO, *Combinatorial Algorithms: Theory and Practice*, Prentice-Hall, Englewood Cliffs, N. J., 1977, 433 pages.

The original reference for the greedy algorithm determining the shortest paths in a graph is

E. W. DIJKSTRA, "A note on two problems in connexion with graphs," *Numerische Mathematik* 1 (1959), 269–271.

# 12

# Case Study: The Polish Notation

*T*HIS CHAPTER *studies the Polish notation for arithmetic or logical expressions, first in terms of problem solving, and then as applied to a program that interactively accepts an expression, compiles it, and evaluates it. This chapter illustrates uses of recursion, stacks, tables, and trees, as well as their interplay in problem solving and algorithm design.*

## 12.1 The Problem

One of the most important accomplishments of the early designers of computer languages was allowing a programmer to write arithmetic expressions in something close to their usual mathematical form. It was a real triumph to design a compiler that understood expressions such as

$$(x + y) * exp(x - z) - 4.0$$
$$a * b + c/d - c * (x + y)$$
$$(p \text{ \&\& } q) \text{ || } (x <= 7.0)$$

*etymology:* FORTRAN    and produced machine-language output. In fact, the name FORTRAN stands for

FORmula TRANSlator

in recognition of this very accomplishment. It often takes only one simple idea that, when fully understood, will provide the key to an elegant solution of a difficult problem, in this case the translation of expressions into sequences of machine-language instructions.

The triumph of the method to be developed in this chapter is that, in contrast to the first approach a person might take, it is not necessary to make repeated scans through the expression to decipher it, and, after a preliminary translation, neither parentheses nor priorities of operators need be taken into account, so that evaluation of the expression can be achieved with great efficiency.

### 12.1.1 THE QUADRATIC FORMULA

Before we discuss this idea, let us briefly imagine the problems an early compiler designer might have faced when confronted with a fairly complicated expression. Even the quadratic formula produces problems:

$$x = (-b + (b \uparrow 2 - (4 \times a) \times c) \uparrow \tfrac{1}{2})/(2 \times a)$$

*notation*    Here, and throughout this chapter, we denote exponentiation by '↑'. When we take square roots, we limit our attention to only the positive root.

Which operations must be done before others? What are the effects of parentheses? When can they be omitted? As you answer these questions for this example, you will probably look back and forth through the expression several times.

In considering how to translate such expressions, the compiler designers soon settled on the conventions that are familiar now: Operations are ordinarily done left to right, subject to the priorities assigned to operators, with exponentiation highest, then multiplication and division, then addition and subtraction. This order can be altered by parentheses. For the quadratic formula the order of operations is

$$x = (-b + (b \uparrow 2 - (4 \times a) \times c) \uparrow \tfrac{1}{2}) / (2 \times a)$$

| | ↑ | ↑ ↑ | | ↑ ↑ | | ↑ | | ↑ | | ↑ | | ↑ | | ↑ | ↑ |
|---|---|---|---|---|---|---|---|---|---|---|---|---|---|---|---|

↑  ↑ ↑   ↑ ↑    ↑     ↑     ↑     ↑  ↑

10  1 7   2 5    3     4     6     9  8

Note that assignment = really is an operator that takes the value of its right operand and assigns it to the left operand. The priority of = will be the lowest of any operator, since it cannot be done until the expression is fully evaluated.

### 1. Unary Operators and Priorities

With one exception, all the operators in the quadratic equation are *binary*, that is, they have two operands. The one exception is the leading minus sign in $-b$. This is a *unary* operator, and unary operators provide a slight complication in determining priorities. Normally we interpret $-2^2$ as $-4$, which means that negation is done after exponentiation, but we interpret $2^{-2}$ as $\frac{1}{4}$ and not as $-4$, so that here negation is done first. It is reasonable to assign unary operators the same priority as exponentiation and, in order to preserve the usual algebraic conventions, to evaluate operators of this priority from right to left. Doing this, moreover, also gives the ordinary interpretation of 2 ↑ 3 ↑ 2 as

$$2^{(3^2)} = 512 \quad \text{and not as} \quad (2^3)^2 = 64.$$

There are unary operators other than negation. These include such operations as taking the factorial of $x$ (denoted $x!$), the derivative of a function $f$ (denoted $f'$), as well as all functions of a single variable, such as the trigonometric, exponential, and logarithmic functions. the Boolean operator not, which negates a Boolean variable.

Several binary operators produce Boolean results: the operators && and || as well as the comparison operators == , ! =, <, ≤, >, and ≥. These comparisons are normally done after the arithmetic operators, but before && , || , and assignment.

*priority list*    We thus obtain the following list of priorities to reflect our usual customs in evaluating operators:

| Operators | Priority |
|---|---|
| ↑,    all unary operators | 6 |
| *   /   % | 5 |
| +    − (binary) | 4 |
| ==   != | 3 |
| <   <=   >   >= | 2 |
| &&   || | 1 |
| = | 0 |

Note that the priorities shown in this table are not the same as those used in C, where && has higher priority that || . As long as we are designing our own system, however, we are free to set our own conventions in any way we wish. By using the priorities shown in the table, we interpret expressions in a way that most people find more natural than the way that C uses.

## 12.2 The Idea

### 12.2.1 EXPRESSION TREES

Drawing a picture is often an excellent way to gain insight into a problem. For our current problem, the appropriate picture is the *expression tree*, as first introduced in Section 9.1.2. Recall that an expression tree is a binary tree in which the leaves are the simple operands and the interior vertices are the operators. If an operator is binary, then it has two nonempty subtrees that are its left and right operands (either simple operands or subexpressions). If an operator is unary, then only one of its subtrees is nonempty, the one on the left or right according as the operator is written on the right or left of its operand. You should review Figure 9.3 for several simple expression trees, as well as Figure 9.4 for the expression tree of the quadratic formula.

Let us determine how to evaluate an expression tree such as, for example, the one shown in part (a) of Figure 12.1. It is clear that we must begin with one of the leaves, since it is only the simple operands for which we know the values when starting. To be consistent, let us start with the leftmost leaf, whose value is 2.9. Since, in our example, the operator immediately above this leaf is unary negation, we can apply it immediately and replace both the operator and its operand by the result, −2.9. This step results in the diamond-shaped node in part (b) of the diagram.

The parent of the diamond-shaped node in part (b) is a binary operator, and its second operand has not yet been evaluated. We cannot, therefore, apply this operator yet, but must instead consider the next two leaves, as shown by the colored path. After moving past these two leaves, the path moves to their parent operator, which can now be evaluated, and the result placed in the second diamond-shaped node, as shown in part (c).

At this stage, both operands of the addition are available, so we can perform it, obtaining the simplified tree in part (d). And so we continue, until the tree has been reduced to a single node, which is the final result. In summary, we have processed the nodes of the tree in the order

$$2.9 \quad - \quad 2.7 \quad 3.0 \quad / \quad + \quad 5.5 \quad 2.5 \quad - \quad ! \quad \times$$

*postorder traversal*    The general observation is that we should process the subtree rooted at any given operator in the order:

*Evaluate the left subtree; evaluate the right subtree; perform the operator.*

(If the operator is unary, then one of these steps is vacuous.) This order is precisely a postorder traversal of the expression tree. We have already observed in Section 9.1.2 that the postorder traversal of an expression tree yields the postfix form of the expression, in which each operator is written after its operands, instead of between them.

This simple idea is the key to efficient calculation of expressions by computer.

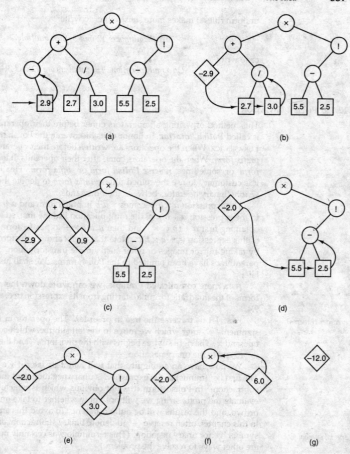

Figure 12.1. Evaluation of an expression tree

As a matter of fact, our customary way of writing arithmetic or logical expressions with the operator between its operands is slightly illogical. The instruction

*Take the number* 12 *and multiply by* ....

is incomplete until the second factor is given. In the meantime it is necessary to remember both a number and an operation. From the viewpoint of establishing uniform rules it makes more sense either to write

*Take the numbers 12 and 3; then multiply.*

or to write

*Do a multiplication. The numbers are 12 and 3.*

### 12.2.2 POLISH NOTATION

This method of writing all operators either before their operands, or after them, is called *Polish notation*, in honor of its discoverer, the Polish mathematician JAN ŁUKASIEWICZ. When the operators are written before their operands, it is called the *prefix form*. When the operators come after their operands, it is called the *postfix form*, or, sometimes, *reverse Polish form* or *suffix form*. Finally, in this context, it is customary to use the coined phrase *infix form* to denote the usual custom of writing binary operators between their operands.

The expression $a \times b$ becomes $\times a\ b$ in prefix form and $a\ b \times$ in postfix form. In the expression $a + b \times c$, the multiplication is done first, so we convert it first, obtaining first $a + (b\ c \times)$ and then $a\ b\ c \times +$ in postfix form. The prefix form of this expression is $+ a \times b\ c$. Note that prefix and postfix forms are not related by taking mirror images or other such simple transformation. Note also that all parentheses have been omitted in the Polish forms. We shall justify this omission later.

As a more complicated example, we can write down the prefix and postfix forms of the quadratic formula, starting from its expression tree, as shown in Figure 9.4.

*preorder traversal*    First, let us traverse the tree in preorder. The operator in the root is the assignment '=', after which we move to the left subtree, which consists only of the operand $x$. The right subtree begins with the division '/', and then moves leftward to '+' and to the unary negation '−'.

We now have an ambiguity that will haunt us later if we do not correct it. The first '−' (minus) in the expression is unary negation, and the second is binary subtraction. In Polish form it is not obvious which is which. When we go to evaluate the prefix string we will not know whether to take one operand for '−' or two, and the results will be quite different. To avoid this ambiguity we shall, in this chapter, often reserve '−' to denote binary subtraction, and use the special symbol '@' for unary negation. (This terminology is certainly not standard. There are other ways to resolve the problem.)

*special symbol @*

The preorder traversal of Figure 9.4 up to this point has yielded

$$=\quad x\quad /\quad +\quad @\quad b$$

and the next step is to traverse the right subtree of the operator '+'. The result is the sequence

$$\uparrow\quad -\quad \uparrow\quad b\quad 2\quad \times\quad \times\quad 4\quad a\quad c\quad \tfrac{1}{2}$$

Finally, we traverse the right subtree of the division '/', obtaining

$$\times \quad 2 \quad a.$$

Hence the complete prefix form for the quadratic formula is

$$= \quad x \quad / \quad + \quad @ \quad b \quad \uparrow \quad - \quad \uparrow \quad b \quad 2 \quad \times \quad \times \quad 4 \quad a \quad c \quad \tfrac{1}{2} \quad \times \quad 2 \quad a.$$

You should verify yourself that the postfix form is

$$x \quad b \quad @ \quad b \quad 2 \quad \uparrow \quad 4 \quad a \quad \times \quad c \quad \times \quad - \quad \tfrac{1}{2} \quad \uparrow \quad + \quad 2 \quad a \quad \times \quad / \quad = .$$

### 12.2.3 C Method

Before concluding this section, we should remark that most C compilers do not use Polish forms in translating expressions into machine language (although other languages do). Some C compilers, instead, use the method of recursive descent. In this method, each priority of operator requires a separate function for its compilation.

*parsing*    Translation of an expression by recursive descent is called ***top-down parsing***, whereas this chapter's method of translating an expression by looking at each of its components in turn is an example of ***bottom-up parsing***.

---

**Exercises 12.2**    (a) Draw the expression tree for each of the following expressions. Using the tree, convert the expression into (b) prefix and (c) postfix form. Use the table of priorities developed in this section, not those in C.

**E1.** $a + b < c$

**E2.** $a < b + c$

**E3.** $a - b < c - d \ || \ e < f$

**E4.** $n! \ / \ (k! \times (n - k)!)$ (Formula for binomial coefficients)

**E5.** $s = (n/2) \times (2 \times a + (n - 1) \times d)$ (This is the sum of the first $n$ terms of an arithmetic progression.)

**E6.** $g = a \times (1 - r^n)/(1 - r)$ (Sum of first $n$ terms of a geometric progression.)

**E7.** $a = 1 \ || \ b \times c \ == \ 2 \ || \ (a > 1 \ \&\& \ b < 3)$

## 12.3 Evaluation of Polish Expressions

We first introduced the postfix form as a natural order of traversing an expression tree in order to evaluate the corresponding expression. Later in this section we shall formulate an algorithm for evaluating an expression directly from the postfix form, but first (since it is even simpler) we consider the prefix form.

### 12.3.1 EVALUATION OF AN EXPRESSION IN PREFIX FORM

Preorder traversal of a binary tree works from the top down. The root is visited first, and the remainder of the traversal is then divided into two parts. The natural way to organize the process is as a recursive, divide-and-conquer algorithm. The same situation holds for an expression in prefix form. The first symbol (if there is more than one) is an operator (the one that will actually be done last), and the remainder of the expression comprises the operand(s) of this operator (one for a unary operator, two for a binary operator). Our function for evaluating the prefix form should hence begin with this first symbol. If it is a unary operator, then the function should invoke itself recursively to determine the value of the operand. If the first symbol is a binary operator, then it should make two recursive calls for its two operands. The recursion terminates in the remaining case: When the first symbol is a simple operand, it is its own prefix form and the function should only return its value.

The following outline thus summarizes the evaluation of an expression in prefix form:

*outline*

```
/* Evaluate: evaluate an expression in prefix form. */
Value Evaluate(expression)
{
    Value x, y;

    Let token be the first symbol in the expression,
    and remove token from the expression

    if (token is a unary operator) {
        x = Evaluate(expression);
        return result of applying operator token to x;

    } else if (token is a binary operator) {
        x = Evaluate(expression);
        y = Evaluate(expression);
        return result of applying operator token to x and y;

    } else {
        return token;
    }
}
```

### 12.3.2 C CONVENTIONS

To tie down the details in this outline, let us establish some conventions and rewrite the algorithm in C. The operators and operands in our expression may well have names that are more than one character long; hence we do not scan the expression one character at a time. Instead we define a ***token*** to be a single operator or operand from the expression. To emphasize that the function scans through the expression only once, we shall employ an auxiliary function

```
void GetToken(Token token, Expression expr);
```

that will move through the expression and return one token at a time in token. We need to know whether the token is an operand, a unary operator, or a binary operator, so we assume the existence of a function Kind( ) that will return one of the three constants from an enumerated type,

```
OPERAND,   UNARYOP,   BINARYOP.
```

For simplicity we shall assume that all the operands and the results of evaluating the operators are of the same type, which for now we leave unspecified and call Value. In many applications, this type would be one of integer or double.

Finally, we must assume the existence of three auxiliary functions that return a result of type Value. The first two,

```
Value DoUnary(Token token, Value x);
```

```
Value DoBinary(Token token, Value x, Value y);
```

actually perform the given operation on their operand(s). They need to recognize the symbols used for the operation token and the operands x and y, and invoke the necessary machine-language instructions. Similarly,

```
Value GetValue(Token token);
```

returns the actual value of a simple operand token, and might need, for example, to convert a constant from decimal to binary form, or look up the value of a variable. The actual form of these functions will depend very much on the application. We cannot settle all these questions here, but want only to concentrate on designing one important part of a compiler or expression evaluator.

## 12.3.3 C FUNCTION FOR PREFIX EVALUATION

With these preliminaries we can now specify more details in our outline, translating it into a C function to evaluate prefix expressions.

```
/* EvaluatePrefix: evaluate an expression in prefix form.
   Pre:   expr is an expression in prefix form.
   Post:  The expression has been evaluated (and perhaps consumed in the process)
          giving the value returned. */
Value EvaluatePrefix(Expression expr)
{
    Token token;
    Value x, y;
    GetToken(token, expr);
    switch(Kind(token)) {
    case OPERAND :
        return GetValue(token);
    case UNARYOP :
        x = EvaluatePrefix(expr);
        return DoUnary(token, x);
    case BINARYOP :
        x = EvaluatePrefix(expr);
        y = EvaluatePrefix(expr);
        return DoBinary(token, x, y);
    }
}
```

## 12.3.4 EVALUATION OF POSTFIX EXPRESSIONS

It is almost inevitable that the prefix form so naturally calls for a recursive function for its evaluation, since the prefix form is really a "top-down" formulation of the algebraic expression: The outer, overall actions are specified first, then later in the expression the component parts are spelled out. On the other hand, in the postfix form the operands appear first, and the whole expression is slowly built up from its simple operands and the inner operators in a "bottom-up" fashion. Therefore iterative programs using stacks appear more natural for the postfix form. (It is of course possible to write either recursive or nonrecursive programs for either form. We are here discussing only the motivation, or what first appears more natural.)

To evaluate an expression in postfix form, it is necessary to remember the operands until their operator is eventually found some time later. The natural way *stacks* to remember them is to put them on a stack. Then when the first operator to be done is encountered, it will find its operands on the top of the stack. If it puts its result back on the stack, then its result will be in the right place to be an operand for a later operator. When the evaluation is complete, the final result will be the only value on the stack. In this way, we obtain a function to evaluate a postfix expression.

At this time we should note a significant difference between postfix and prefix expressions. There was no need, in the prefix function, to check explicitly that the end of the expression had been reached, since the entire expression automatically constituted the operand(s) for the first operator. Reading a postfix expression from left to right, however, we can encounter sub-expressions that are, by themselves, legitimate postfix expressions. For example, if we stop reading

$$b \quad 2 \quad \uparrow \quad 4 \quad a \quad \times \quad c \quad \times \quad -$$

after the '↑', we find that it is a legal postfix expression. To remedy this problem we shall suppose that the expression ends with a newline character, and the function Kind recognizes the newline and returns the special value ENDEXPR.

The remaining defined types, as well as the other auxiliary functions are the same as for the prefix evaluation.

```
/* EvaluatePostfix: evaluate expression in postfix form.
    Pre:   expr is an expression in prefix form.
    Post:  The expression has been evaluated (and perhaps consumed in the process)
           giving the value returned. */
Value EvaluatePostfix(Expression expr)
{
    KindType type;
    Token token;
    Value x, y;
    Stack stack;
    CreateStack( &stack);
    do {
        GetToken(token, expr);
        switch (type = Kind(token)) {
        case OPERAND :
            Push(GetValue(token), &stack);
            break;
        case UNARYOP :
            Pop( &x, &stack);
            Push(DoUnary(token, x), &stack);
            break;
        case BINARYOP :
            Pop( &y, &stack);
            Pop( &x, &stack);
            Push(DoBinary(token, x, y), &stack);
            break;
        case ENDEXPR :
            Pop( &x, &stack);
            if (! StackEmpty( &stack))
                Error("Incorrect expression");
            break;
        }
    } while (type != ENDEXPR);
    return x;
}
```

## 12.3.5 Proof of the Program: Counting Stack Entries

So far we have given only an informal motivation for the preceding program, and it may not be clear that it will produce the correct result in every case. Fortunately it is not difficult to give a formal justification of the program and, at the same time, to discover a useful criterion as to whether an expression is properly written in postfix form or not.

The method we shall use is to keep track of the number of entries in the stack. When each operand is obtained, it is immediately pushed onto the stack. A unary operator first pops, then pushes the stack, and thus makes no change in the number of entries. A binary operator pops the stack twice and pushes it once, giving a net decrease of one entry in the stack. More formally, we have

*running-sum condition*

> *For a sequence E of operands, unary operators, and binary operators, form a running sum by starting at the left end of E and counting +1 for each operand, 0 for each unary operator, and −1 for each binary operator. E satisfies the **running-sum condition** provided that this running sum never falls below 1, and is exactly 1 at the right-hand end of E.*

The sequence of running sums for the postfix form of an expression is illustrated in Figure 12.2. We shall prove the next two theorems at the same time.

$a = 2$
$b = -7$
$c = 3$

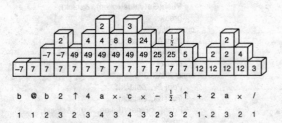

Figure 12.2. Stack frames and running sums, quadratic formula

**Theorem 12.1**    *If E is a properly formed expression in postfix form, then E must satisfy the running sum condition.*

**Theorem 12.2**
*A properly formed expression in postfix form will be correctly evaluated by Evalu-atePostfix.*

**Proof**
We shall prove the theorems together by using mathematical induction on the length of the expression $E$ being evaluated.

*induction proof*
The starting point for the induction is the case that $E$ is a single operand alone, with length 1. This operand contributes +1, and the running-sum condition is satisfied. The function, when applied to a simple operand alone, gets its value, pushes it on the stack (which was previously empty) and at the end pops it as the final value of the function, thereby evaluating it correctly.

For the induction hypothesis we now assume that $E$ is a properly formed postfix expression of length more than 1, that the program correctly evaluates all postfix expressions of length less than that of $E$, and that all such shorter expressions satisfy the running-sum condition. Since the length of $E$ is more than 1, $E$ is constructed at its last step either as $F$ $op$, where $op$ is a unary operator and $F$ a postfix expression, or as $F$ $G$ $op$, where $op$ is a binary operator and $F$ and $G$ are postfix expressions.

In either case the lengths of $F$ and $G$ are less than that of $E$, so by induction hypothesis both of them satisfy the running-sum condition, and the function would evaluate either of them separately and would obtain the correct result.

*unary operator*
First, take the case when $op$ is a unary operator. Since $F$ satisfies the running-sum condition, the sum at its end is exactly +1. As a unary operator, $op$ contributes 0 to the sum, so the full expression $E$ satisfies the running-sum condition. When the function reaches the end of $F$, similarly, it will, by induction hypothesis, have evaluated $F$ correctly and left its value as the unique stack entry. The unary operator $op$ is then finally applied to this value, which is popped as the final result.

*binary operator*
Finally take the case when $op$ is binary, so $E$ has the form $F$ $G$ $op$ when $F$ and $G$ are postfix expressions. When the function reaches the last token of $F$, then the value of $F$ will be the unique entry on the stack. Similarly, the running sum will be 1. At the next token the program starts to evaluate $G$. By the induction hypothesis the evaluation of $G$ will also be correct and its running sum alone never falls below 1, and ends at exactly 1. Since the running sum at the end of $F$ is 1, the combined running sum never falls below 2, and ends at exactly 2 at the end of $G$. Thus the evaluation of $G$ will proceed and never disturb the single entry on the bottom of the stack, which is the result of $F$. When the evaluation reaches the final binary operator $op$, the running sum is correctly reduced from 2 to 1, and the operator finds precisely its two operands on the stack, where after evaluation it leaves its unique result. This completes the proof of Theorems 12.1 and 12.2.

This error checking by keeping a running count of the number of entries on the stack provides a handy way to verify that a sequence of tokens is in fact a properly formed postfix expression, and is especially useful because its converse is also true:

**Theorem 12.3**    *If E is any sequence of operands and operators that satisfies the running-sum condition, then E is a properly formed expression in postfix form.*

**Proof**    We shall again use mathematical induction to prove Theorem 12.3. The starting point is an expression containing only one token. Since the running sum (same as final sum) for a sequence of length 1 will be 1, this one token must be a simple operand. One simple operand alone is indeed a syntactically correct expression.

*induction proof*    Now for the inductive step, suppose that the theorem has been verified for all expressions strictly shorter than $E$, and $E$ has length greater than 1. If the last token of $E$ were an operand, then it would contribute +1 to the sum, and since the final *case: operand*    sum is 1, the running sum would have been 0 one step before the end, contrary to the assumption that the running-sum condition is satisfied. Thus the final token of $E$ must be an operator.

*case: unary operator*    If the operator is unary, then it can be omitted and the remaining sequence still satisfies the condition on running sums. Therefore by induction hypothesis, it is a syntactically correct expression, and all of $E$ then also is.

*case: binary operator*    Finally suppose that the last token is a binary operator *op*. To show that $E$ is syntactically correct, we must find where in the sequence the first operand of *op* ends and the second one starts, by using the running sum. Since the operator *op* contributes −1 to the sum, it was 2 one step before the end. This 2 means that there were two items on the stack, the first and second operands of *op*. As we step backward through the sequence $E$, eventually we will reach a place where there is only one entry on the stack (running sum 1), and this one entry will be the first operand of *op*. Thus the place to break the sequence is at the last position before the end where the running sum is exactly 1. Such a position must exist, since at the far left end of $E$ (if not before) we will find a running sum of 1. When we break $E$ at its last 1, then it takes the form $F$ $G$ *op*. The subsequence $F$ satisfies the condition on running sums, and ends with a sum of 1, so by induction hypothesis it is a correctly formed postfix expression. Since the running sums during $G$ of $F$ $G$ *op* never again fall to 1, and end at 2 just before *op*, we may subtract 1 from each of them and conclude that the running sums for $G$ alone satisfy the condition. Thus by induction hypothesis $G$ is also a correctly formed postfix expression. Thus both $F$ and $G$ are correct expressions, and can be combined by the binary operator *op* into a correct expression $E$. Thus the proof of the theorem is complete.

We can take the proof one more step, to show that the last position where a sum of 1 occurs is the *only* place where the sequence $E$ can be split into syntactically correct subsequences $F$ and $G$. For suppose it was split elsewhere. If at the end of $F$ the running sum is not 1, then $F$ is not a syntactically correct expression. If the running sum is 1 at the end of $F$, but reaches 1 again during the $G$ part of $F$ $G$ *op*, then the sums for $G$ alone would reach 0 at that point, so $G$ is not correct. We have now shown that there is only one way to recover the two operands of a binary operator. Clearly there is only one way to recover the single operand for a unary operator. Hence we can recover the infix form of an expression from its postfix form, together with the order in which the operations are done, which we can denote by bracketing the result of every operation in the infix form with another pair of parentheses.

We have therefore proved:

**Theorem 12.4**     *An expression in postfix form that satisfies the running-sum condition corresponds to exactly one fully bracketed expression in infix form. Hence no parentheses are needed to achieve the unique representation of an expression in postfix form.*

Similar theorems hold for the prefix form; their proofs are left as exercises. The preceding theorems provide both a theoretical justification of the use of Polish notation and a convenient way to check an expression for correct syntax.

## 12.3.6 RECURSIVE EVALUATION OF POSTFIX EXPRESSIONS

Most people find that the recursive function for evaluating prefix expressions is easier to understand than the stack-based, nonrecursive function for evaluating postfix expressions. In this (optional) section we show how the stack can be eliminated in favor of recursion for postfix evaluation.

First, however, let us see why the natural approach leads to a recursive function for prefix evaluation but not for postfix. We can describe both prefix and postfix expressions by the syntax diagrams of Figure 12.3. In both cases there are three possibilities: The expression consists of only a single operand, or the outermost operator is unary, or it is binary.

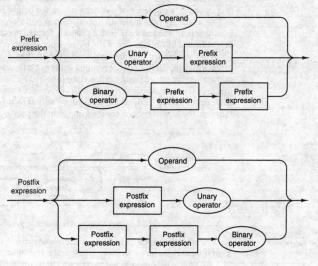

Figure 12.3. Syntax diagrams of Polish expressions

*prefix evaluation*

In tracing through the diagram for prefix form, the first token we encounter in the expression determines which of the three branches we take, and there are then no further choices to make (except within recursive calls, which need not be considered just now). Hence the structure of the recursive function for prefix evaluation closely resembles the syntax diagram.

*postfix evaluation*

With the postfix diagram, however, there is no way to tell from the first token (which will always be an operand) which of the three branches to take. It is only when the last token is encountered that the branch is determined. This fact does, however, lead to one easy recursive solution: Read the expression from right to left, reverse all the arrows on the syntax diagram, and use the same function as for prefix evaluation!

If we wish, however, to read the expression in the usual way from left to right, then we must work harder. Let us consider separately each of the three kinds of tokens in a postfix form. We have already observed that the first token in the expression must be an operand; this follows directly from the fact that the running sum after the first token is (at least) 1. Since unary operators do not change the running sum, unary operators can be inserted anywhere after the initial operand. It is the third case, binary operators, whose study leads to the solution.

*running sum*

Consider the sequence of running sums, and the place(s) in the sequence where the sum drops from 2 to 1. Since binary operators contribute −1 to the sum, such places must exist if the postfix expression contains any binary operators, and correspond to the places in the expression where the two operands of the binary operator constitute the whole expression to the left. Such situations are illustrated in the stack frames of Figure 12.2. The entry on the bottom of the stack is the first operand; a sequence of positions where the height is at least 2, starting and ending at exactly two, make up the calculation of the second operand, and, taken in isolation, this sequence is itself a properly formed postfix expression. A drop in height from 2 to 1 marks one of the binary operators in which we are interested.

After the binary operator, more unary operators may appear, and then the process may repeat itself (if the running sums again increase) with more sequences that are self-contained postfix expressions followed by binary and unary operators. In summary, we have shown that postfix expressions are described by the syntax diagram of Figure 12.4, which translates easily into the recursive function that follows. The C conventions are the same as in the previous functions.

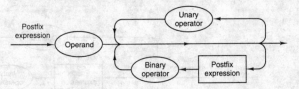

Figure 12.4. Alternative syntax diagram, postfix expression

*left recursion*

The situation appearing in the postfix diagram of Figure 12.3 is called **left recursion**, and the steps we have taken in the transition to the diagram in Figure 12.4 are typical of those needed to remove left recursion.

First is a function that initiates the recursion.

```
/* EvaluatePostfix: evaluate expression in postfix form.
   Pre:  expr is an expression in prefix form.
   Post: The expression has been evaluated (and perhaps consumed in the process)
         giving the value returned. */
Value EvaluatePostfix(Expression expr)
{
   Value result;
   Token token;
   GetToken(token, expr);
   if (Kind(token) == OPERAND)
      result = RecEvaluate(token, expr);
   else
      Error("Postfix expression does not start with operand");
   if (Kind(token) == ENDEXPR)
      return result;
   else
      Error("Missing end expression");
}
```

The actual recursion uses the first token separately from the remainder of the expression.

```
/* RecEvaluate: recursively evaluate expression in postfix form.
   Pre:  The token token exists and it is guaranteed to be an operand when RecEval-
         uated is invoked. expr is the remaining expression.
   Post: At conclusion, token is the first token beyond the expression evaluated and will
         be a binary operator, unless the end of the expression has been reached. */
Value RecEvaluate(Token token, Expression expr)
{
   KindType type;
   Value x;
   Value result;
   result = GetValue(token);
   for (GetToken(token, expr); (type = Kind(token)) == OPERAND ||
                          type == UNARYOP; GetToken(token, expr)) {
      if (type == UNARYOP)
         result = DoUnary(token, result);
      else {
         x = RecEvaluate(token, expr);
         if (Kind(token) == BINARYOP)
            result = DoBinary(token, result, x);
         else
            Error("Expecting binary operator");
      }
   }
   return result;
}
```

**Exercises 12.3**    **E1.** Trace the action on each of the following expressions by the function EvaluatePostfix in **(a)** nonrecursive and **(b)** recursive versions. For the recursive function, draw the tree of recursive calls, indicating at each node which tokens are being processed. For the nonrecursive function, draw a sequence of stack frames showing which tokens are processed at each stage.

(a) $a \quad b \quad + \quad c \quad \times$

(b) $a \quad b \quad c \quad + \quad \times$

(c) $a \quad ! \quad b \quad ! \quad / \quad c \quad d \quad - \quad a \quad ! \quad - \quad \times$

(d) $a \quad b \quad < \quad c \quad d \quad \times \quad < \quad e \quad ||$

**E2.** Trace the action of EvaluatePrefix on each of the following expressions by drawing a tree of recursive calls showing which tokens are processed at each stage.

(a) $/ \quad + \quad x \quad y \quad ! \quad n$

(b) $/ \quad + \quad ! \quad x \quad y \quad n$

(c) $\&\& \quad < \quad x \quad y \quad || \quad == \quad + \quad x \quad y \quad z \quad > \quad x \quad 0$

**E3.** Which of the following are syntactically correct postfix expressions? Show the error in each incorrect expression. Translate each correct expression into infix form, using parentheses as necessary to avoid ambiguities.

(a) $a \quad b \quad c \quad + \quad \times \quad a \quad / \quad c \quad b \quad + \quad d \quad / \quad -$

(b) $a \quad b \quad + \quad c \quad a \quad \times \quad b \quad c \quad / \quad d \quad -$

(c) $a \quad b \quad + \quad c \quad a \quad \times \quad - \quad c \quad \times \quad + \quad b \quad c \quad -$

(d) $a \quad @ \quad b \quad \times$

(e) $a \quad \times \quad b \quad @$

(f) $a \quad b \quad \times \quad @$

(g) $a \quad b \quad @ \quad \times$

**E4.** Translate each of the following expressions from prefix form into postfix form.

(a) $/ \quad + \quad x \quad y \quad ! \quad n$

(b) $/ \quad + \quad ! \quad x \quad y \quad n$

(c) $\&\& \quad < \quad x \quad y \quad || \quad == \quad + \quad x \quad y \quad z \quad > \quad x \quad 0$

**E5.** Translate each of the following expressions from postfix form into prefix form.

(a) $a \quad b \quad + \quad c \quad \times$

(b) $a \quad b \quad c \quad + \quad \times$

(c) $a \quad ! \quad b \quad ! \quad / \quad c \quad d \quad - \quad a \quad ! \quad - \quad \times$

(d) $a \quad b \quad < \quad c \quad d \quad \times \quad < \quad e \quad \|$

**E6.** Formulate and prove theorems analogous to Theorems

(a) 12.1,

(b) 12.3, and

(c) 12.4 for the prefix form of expressions.

# 12.4 Translation from Infix Form to Polish Form

Few programmers habitually write algebraic or logical expressions in Polish form, even though doing so might be more consistent and logical than the customary infix form. To make convenient use of the algorithms we have developed for evaluating Polish expressions, we must therefore develop an efficient method to translate arbitrary expressions from infix form into Polish notation.

As a first simplification, we shall consider only an algorithm for translating infix expressions into postfix form. Secondly, we shall not consider unary operators that are placed to the right of their operands. Such operators would cause no conceptual difficulty in the development of the algorithm, but they make the resulting function appear a little more complicated.

One method that we might consider for developing our algorithm would be, first, to build the expression tree from the infix form, and then to traverse the tree to obtain the postfix form. It turns out, however, that building the tree from the infix form is actually more complicated than constructing the postfix form directly.

Since, in postfix form, all operators come after their operands, the task of translation from infix to postfix form amounts to moving operators so that they come after their operands instead of before or between them. In other words:

*Delay each operator until its right-hand operand has been translated. Pass each simple operand through to the output without delay.*

This action is illustrated in Figure 12.5.

Infix form:

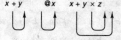

Postfix form:

$$x\, y + \quad x\, @ \quad x\, y\, z \times +$$

Infix form:

Postfix form:

$$x\, b\, @\, b\, 2\!\uparrow\, 4\, a \times c \times - \tfrac{1}{2}\!\uparrow\, + 2\, a \times / =$$

**Figure 12.5.  Delaying operators in postfix form**

The major problem we must resolve is to find what token will terminate the right-hand operand of a given operator and thereby mark the place at which that operator should be placed. To do this, we must take both parentheses and priorities of operators into account.

The first problem is easy. If a left parenthesis is in the operand, then everything up to and including the matching right parenthesis must also be in the operand. For the second problem, that of taking account of the priorities of operators, we shall consider binary operators separately from operators of priority 6, namely, unary operators and exponentiation. The reason for this is that operators of priority 6 are evaluated from right to left, whereas binary operators of lower priority are evaluated from left to right.

*finding the end of the right operand*

Let $op_1$ be a binary operator of a priority evaluated from left to right, and let $op_2$ be the first nonbracketed operator to the right of $op_1$. If the priority of $op_2$ is less than or equal to that of $op_1$, then $op_2$ will not be part of the right operand of $op_1$, and its appearance will terminate the right operand of $op_1$. If the priority of $op_2$ is greater than that of $op_1$, then $op_2$ is part of the right operand of $op_1$, and we can continue through the expression until we find an operator of priority less than or equal to that of $op_1$; this operator will then terminate the right operand of $op_1$.

*right-to-left evaluation*

Next, suppose that $op_1$ has priority 6 (it is unary or exponentiation), and recall that operators of this priority are to be evaluated from right to left. If the first operand $op_2$ to the right of $op_1$ has equal priority, it therefore will be part of the right operand of $op_1$, and the right operand is terminated only by an operator of strictly smaller priority.

There are two more ways in which the right-hand operand of a given operator can terminate: The expression can end, or the given operator may itself be within a bracketed subexpression, in which case its right operand will end when an unmatched right parenthesis ')' is encountered. In summary, we have the rules:

> If $op$ is an operator in an infix expression, then its right-hand operand contains all tokens on its right until one of the following is encountered:
>
> 1. *the end of the expression;*
> 2. *an unmatched right parenthesis '* ) *';*
> 3. *an operator of priority less than or equal to that of* $op$, *and not within a bracketed sub-expression, if* $op$ *has priority less than 6; or*
> 4. *an operator of priority strictly less than that of* $op$, *and not within a bracketed subexpression, if* $op$ *has priority 6.*

*stack of operators*

From these rules, we can see that the appropriate way to remember the operators being delayed is to keep them on a stack. If operator $op_2$ comes on the right of operator $op_1$ but has higher priority, then $op_2$ will be output before $op_1$ is. Thus the operators are output in the order last in, first out.

The key to writing an algorithm for the translation is to make a slight change in our point of view by asking, as each token appears in the input, which of the operators previously delayed (that is, on the stack) now have their right operands terminated because of the new token, so that it is time to move them into the output. The preceding conditions then become:

1. *At the end of the expression, all operators are output.*
2. *A right parenthesis causes all operators found since the corresponding left parenthesis to be output.*
3. *An operator of priority not 6 causes all other operators of greater or equal priority to be output.*
4. *An operator of priority 6 causes all other operators of strictly greater priority to be output, if such operators exist.*

To implement the second rule, we shall put each left parenthesis on the stack when it is encountered. Then, when the matching right parenthesis appears and the operators have been popped from the stack, the pair can both be discarded.

We can now incorporate these rules into a function. To do so, we shall use the same auxiliary types and functions as in the last section, except that now the function Kind(...) can return two additional values:

LEFTPAREN          RIGHTPAREN

that denote, respectively, left and right parentheses. The stack will now contain tokens (operators) rather than values. In addition to GetToken(...) that obtains the next token from the input (infix expression), we use an auxiliary function

void PutToken(Token token, Expression expr);

that puts the given token into the postfix expression. Thus these two functions might read and write with files or might only refer to lists already set up, depending on the desired application. Finally, we shall use a function Priority(op) that will return the priority of an operator op.

With these conventions we can write the function that translates the expression from the infix to postfix form.

```
/* InfixtoPostfix: translate from infix to postfix form.
   Pre:  The input is a valid expression in infix form.
   Post: The ouput is the input expression converted into a postfix expression. */

void InfixtoPostfix(Expression expr, Expression postfix)
{
    Stack stack;
    StackEntry topentry;
    Token token, tmp;
    KindType type;

    CreateStack( &stack);
    do {
        GetToken(token, expr);
        switch (type = Kind(token)) {

        case OPERAND :
            PutToken(token, postfix);
            break;
```

```
    case LEFTPAREN :
        Push(token, &stack);
        break;

    case RIGHTPAREN :
        for (Pop(token, &stack); Kind(token) != LEFTPAREN; Pop(token, &stack))
            PutToken(token, postfix);
        break;

    case UNARYOP :              /* Treat both kinds together.                    */

    case BINARYOP :
        do {
            if (StackEmpty( &stack))
                break;
            else {
                StackTop( &topentry, &stack);
                if (Kind(topentry) == LEFTPAREN)
                    break;
                else if (Priority(topentry) < Priority(token))
                        break;
                    else if (Priority(topentry) == Priority(token)
                            && Priority(token) == MAXPRIORITY)
                        break;
                else {
                    Pop(tmp, &stack);
                    PutToken(tmp, postfix);
                }
            }
        } while (1);
        Push(token, &stack);
        break;

    case ENDEXPR :
        while(! StackEmpty( &stack)) {
            Pop(token, &stack);
            PutToken(token, postfix);
        }
        break;

    }
} while (type != ENDEXPR);
}
```

Figure 12.6 shows the steps performed to translate the quadratic formula

$$x = (@b + (b^2 - 4 \times a \times c)^{\frac{1}{2}})/(2 \times a)$$

into postfix form, as an illustration of this algorithm. (Recall that we are using '@' to denote unary negation.)

| Input Token | Contents of Stack (rightmost token is on top) | | | | | | Output Token(s) |
|---|---|---|---|---|---|---|---|
| $x$ | | | | | | | $x$ |
| = | = | | | | | | |
| ( | = | ( | | | | | |
| @ | = | ( | @ | | | | |
| $b$ | = | ( | @ | | | | $b$ |
| + | = | ( | + | | | | @ |
| ( | = | ( | + | ( | | | |
| $b$ | = | ( | + | ( | | | $b$ |
| ↑ | = | ( | + | ( | ↑ | | |
| 2 | = | ( | + | ( | ↑ | | 2 |
| − | = | ( | + | ( | − | | ↑ |
| 4 | = | ( | + | ( | − | | 4 |
| × | = | ( | + | ( | − | × | |
| $a$ | = | ( | + | ( | − | × | $a$ |
| × | = | ( | + | ( | − | × | × |
| $c$ | = | ( | + | ( | − | × | $c$ |
| ) | = | ( | + | | | | × − |
| ↑ | = | ( | + | ↑ | | | |
| $\frac{1}{2}$ | = | ( | + | ↑ | | | $\frac{1}{2}$ |
| ) | = | | | | | | ↑ + |
| / | = | / | | | | | |
| ( | = | / | ( | | | | |
| 2 | = | / | ( | | | | 2 |
| × | = | / | ( | × | | | |
| $a$ | = | / | ( | × | | | $a$ |
| ) | = | / | | | | | × |
| ENDEXPR | | | | | | | / = |

Figure 12.6. Translation of the quadratic formula into postfix form

This completes the discussion of translation into postfix form. There will clearly be similarities in describing the translation into prefix form, but some difficulties arise because of the seemingly irrelevant fact that, in European languages, we read from left to right. If we were to translate an expression into prefix form working from left to right, then not only would the operators need to be rearranged but operands would need to be delayed until after their operators were output. But the relative order of operands is not changed in the translation, so the appropriate data structure to keep the operands would not be a stack (it would in fact be a queue). Since stacks would not do the job, neither would recursive programs with no explicit auxiliary storage, since these two kinds of programs can do equivalent tasks. Thus a left-to-right translation into prefix form would need a different approach. The trick is to translate into prefix form by working from right to left through the expression, using methods quite similar to the left-to-right postfix translation that we have developed. The details are left as an exercise.

---

**Exercises 12.4**

**E1.** Devise an algorithm to translate an expression from prefix form into postfix form. Use the C conventions of this chapter.

**E2.** Write a C algorithm to translate an expression from postfix form into prefix form. Use the C conventions of this chapter.

**E3.** A *fully bracketed* expression is one of the following forms:

   **i.** a simple operand;

   **ii.** $(op\ E)$ where $op$ is a unary operator and $E$ is a fully bracketed expression;

   **iii.** $(E\ op\ F)$ where $op$ is a binary operator and $E$ and $F$ are fully bracketed expressions.

Hence, in a fully bracketed expression, the results of every operation are enclosed in parentheses. Examples of fully bracketed expressions are $((a+b)-c)$, $(-a)$, $(a+b)$, $(a+(b+c))$. Write C algorithms that will translate expressions from (a) prefix and (b) postfix form into fully bracketed form.

**E4.** Rewrite InfixtoPostfix as a recursive function that uses no stack or other array.

**Programming Project 12.4**

**P1.** Construct a menu-driven demonstration program for Polish expressions. The input to the program should be an expression in any of infix, prefix, or postfix form. The program should then, at the user's request, translate the expression into any of fully bracketed infix, prefix, or postfix, and print the result. The operands should be single letters or digits only. The operators allowed are:

| | | | | | | | | | | | |
|---|---|---|---|---|---|---|---|---|---|---|---|
| *binary:* | + | − | * | / | ↑ | : | < | > | & | \| | = |
| *left unary:* | # | @ | $ | | | | | | | | |
| *right unary:* | ! | ' | " | % | | | | | | | |

In addition, the program should allow parentheses '(' and ')' in infix expressions only. The meanings of some of the special symbols used in this project are:

| | | | |
|---|---|---|---|
| & | Boolean &&, 'and' | \| | Boolean \|\|, 'or' |
| : | Assign (as in =) | ! | Factorial (on right) |
| ' | Derivative (on right) | " | Second derivative (on right) |
| % | Percent (on right) | @ | Unary negation |
| # | Boolean not | $ | Ignored by program |

# 12.5 An Interactive Expression Evaluator

There are many applications for a program that can evaluate a function that is typed in interactively while the program is running. One such application is a program that will draw the graph of a mathematical function. Suppose that you are writing such a program to be used to help first-year calculus students graph functions. Most of these students will not know how to write or compile programs, so you wish to include in your program some way that the user can put in an expression for a function such as

$$x \times \log(x) - x^{1.25}$$

while the program is running, which the program can then graph for appropriate values of x.

*goal*

The goal of this section is to describe such a program, and especially to complete the writing of two subprograms to help with this problem. The first subprogram will take as input an expression involving constants, variable(s), arithmetic operators, and standard functions, with bracketing allowed, as typed in from the terminal. It will then translate the expression into postfix form and keep it in a list of tokens. The second subprogram will evaluate this postfix expression for values of the variable(s) given as its calling parameter(s) and return the answer, which can then be graphed.

*purpose*

We undertake this project for several reasons. It shows how to take the ideas already developed for working with Polish notation and build these ideas into a complete, concrete, and functioning program. In this way, the project illustrates a problem-solving approach to program design, in which we begin with solutions to the key questions and complete the structure with auxiliary functions as needed.

*robustness*

Finally, since this project is intended for use by people with little computer experience, it provides opportunity to test *robustness*, that is, the ability of the program to withstand unexpected or incorrect input without catastrophic failure.

## 12.5.1 Overall Structure

To allow the user flexibility in changing the graphing, let us make the program menu driven, so that the action of the main program has the following familiar form:

```
Dictionary lexicon;
/* Read infix expression, change it to postfix, and graph it. */
void main(void)
{
    Expression infix, postfix;
    PlotParameter plotdata;
    char cmd;
    int hashtable[MAXTOKEN];
    Introduction();
    Initialize( &infix, &postfix, hashtable, &plotdata);
    while ((cmd = GetCommand()) != 'q')
        DoCommand(cmd, &infix, &postfix, hashtable, &plotdata);
}
```

The division of work among various functions is done by DoCommand:

```
/* DoCommand: do one command.
   Pre:   cmd contains a valid command.
   Post:  Performed the given command cmd on the expression infix or postfix. */
void DoCommand(char cmd, Expression *infix, Expression *postfix,
               int hashtable[ ], PlotParameter *plotdata)
{
   if (EndExpression(postfix) && strchr("rhq", cmd) == NULL)
      ErrorInform(WARNING, "Please read an expression before doing "
                           "any other operation.");
   else
      switch(cmd) {
      case 'g':
         DrawGraph(postfix, plotdata);
         break;
      case 'h':
         Help();
         break;
      case 'l':
         ReadNewGraphLimits(plotdata);
         break;
      case 'n':
         ReadNewParameters(plotdata);
         break;
      case 'p':
         WriteParameters(plotdata);
         break;
      case 'q':
         break;
      case 'r':
         while (!ReadExpression(infix, hashtable, plotdata));
         InfixtoPostfix(infix, postfix);
         break;
      case 'w':
         WriteExpression(infix);
         WriteExpression(postfix);
         break;
      }
}
```

The function ReadExpression will ask the user for an expression to be graphed, split it apart into tokens, and determine if it is syntactically correct. Next, the expression is converted into postfix form by the method we have already studied.

To graph the expression, the postfix form is evaluated for many different values of x, each differing from the last by a small increment, and the result plotted as a single point on the screen. How this is done varies from system to system; the Borland C version given later in the chapter is only illustrative of how it may be done.

The function ReadNewGraphLimits allows the user to select the domain of x values over which the graph will be plotted, the increment to use, and the range shown for the results of the expression evaluation. These values are kept within the structure plotdata.

*expression parameters*

In addition to the (independent) variable x used for plotting, the expression may contain further variables that we call *parameters* for the graph. For example, in the expression

$$a * \cos(x) + b * \sin(x),$$

a and b are parameters. The parameters will all retain fixed values while one graph is drawn, but these values can be changed from one graph to the next without making any other change in the expression. The function ReadNewParameters obtains values for all the parameters that appear in the expression.

The initialization within the main program establishes the definitions of the predefined tokens (such as the operators +, −, * amongst others, the operand x that will be used in the graphing, and perhaps some constants). The details will depend on our choice of data structures.

## 12.5.2 REPRESENTATION OF THE DATA

Our data-structure decisions concern how to store and retrieve the tokens used in Polish expressions and their evaluation. For each different token we must remember:

- Its name (as a string of characters), so that we can recognize it in the input expression;

- Its kind, one of operand, unary operator, binary operator, left parenthesis, or right parenthesis;

- For operators, its priority; for operands, its value.

It is reasonable to think of representing each token as a structure containing this information. One small difficulty arises: The same token may appear several times in an expression. If it is an operand, then we must be certain that it is given the same value each time. If we put the records themselves into the expressions, then when a value is assigned to an operand we must be sure that it is updated in all the records corresponding to that operand.

*lexicon*

We can avoid having to keep chains of references to a given variable by associating an integer code with each token and placing this code in the expression, rather than the full structure. We shall thus set up a *lexicon* for the tokens, which will be an array indexed by the integer codes, and which will hold the full records for the tokens. In this way, if $k$ is the code for a variable, then every appearance of $k$ in the expression will cause us to look in position $k$ of the lexicon for the corresponding value, and we are automatically assured of getting the same value each time.

Placing integer token codes rather than records in the expressions also has the advantage of saving some space, but space for tokens is unlikely to be a critical restraint for this project. The time required to evaluate the postfix expression at many different values of the argument x is more likely to prove expensive.

As the input expression is decoded, the program may find constants and new variables (parameters), which it will then add to the lexicon. These will all be classed as operands, but recall that, in the case of parameters, the user will be asked to give values before the expression is evaluated. Hence it is necessary to keep one more list, a list of the token codes that correspond to parameters.

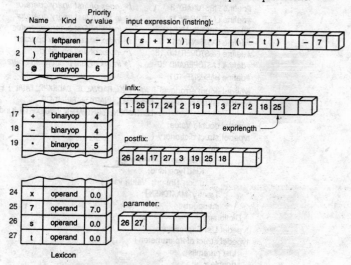

Figure 12.7. Data structures for program GraphExpression

All these data structures are illustrated in Figure 12.7, along with some of the data structures used in the principal functions.

The declarations include several other features that will be explained more fully later. Some of these, briefly, are:

- The expressions are declared as *lists* of token codes.
- Translation from infix to postfix uses a *stack* of token codes.
- Evaluation of the expression uses the recursive function we developed earlier.
- Given a token *code*, the lexicon provides information about the token. For parsing the input expression, however, we must start with a token *name* (a string of characters) and find the code. This task is done with a hash table called hashtable.
- Errors of different severity are processed differently.
- Sets of characters are used in determining the user's menu selections.

Here are all the declarations of constants, types, and variables required by the program, some of which will require further explanation later.

```
#define MAXPRIORITY 6        /* largest operator priority              */
#define MAXSTRING 101        /* maximum tokens in expression           */
#define MAXTOKEN 101         /* maximum distinct tokens                */
#define MAXNAME 7            /* number of characters in identifier     */
#define MAXLINE 100          /* maximum line length for an Expression  */
#define FIRSTUNARY 3         /* index of first unary operator          */
#define LASTUNARY 11         /* index of last unary operator           */
#define FIRSTBINARY 12       /* index of first binary operator         */
#define LASTBINARY 17        /* index of last binary operator          */
#define FIRSTOPERAND 18      /* index of first operand                 */
#define LASTOPERAND 20       /* index of last predefined operand       */
#define HASHSIZE 101

typedef enum errorlevel { WARNING, BADVALUE, BADEXPR, FATAL } ErrorLevel;
typedef enum kindtype { OPERAND, UNARYOP, BINARYOP,
                        LEFTPAREN, RIGHTPAREN, ENDEXPR } KindType;

typedef double Value;
typedef struct dictionary {
        struct {
            char name[MAXNAME];
            KindType kind;
            union {int pri; Value val; } info;
        } entry[MAXTOKEN];
        int count;
} Dictionary;
typedef List Expression;
typedef struct plotparameter {
    List paramlist;
    double x, y;
    double xlow, xhigh;
    double ylow, yhigh;
    double increment;
} PlotParameter;
```

We use one global variable to make the information available to the different parts of the program:

```
Dictionary lexicon;
```

### 12.5.3 INITIALIZATION AND AUXILIARY TASKS

The tasks of initializing all the variables are collected into one function, most of which needs no further explanation:

```
/* Initialize: */
void Initialize(Expression *infix, Expression *postfix, int hashtable[],
                PlotParameter *plotdata)

{
    SetupLexicon();
```

```
CreateList(infix);
CreateList(postfix);
CreateList( &plotdata->paramlist);
plotdata->x = plotdata->y = 0.;
plotdata->xlow = -10.;
plotdata->xhigh = 10.;
plotdata->ylow = -100.;
plotdata->yhigh = 100.;
plotdata->increment = .01;
CreateHashTable(hashtable);
FillHashTable(hashtable);
}
```

## 1. Predefined Tokens

The only task to be done by SetupLexicon is to place the names, kinds, priorities (for operators), and values (for operands) of all the predefined tokens into the lexicon. Hence the function consists only of a long series of assignment statements, which we omit. The complete list of predefined tokens used in this implementation is shown in Figure 12.8.

| Token | Name | Kind | Priority/Value | |
|-------|------|------|----------------|---|
| 0 | | ENDEXPR | | |
| 1 | ( | LEFTPAREN | | |
| 2 | ) | RIGHTPAREN | | |
| 3 | @ | UNARYOP | 6 | *negation* |
| 4 | abs | UNARYOP | 6 | |
| 5 | sqrt | UNARYOP | 6 | |
| 6 | exp | UNARYOP | 6 | |
| 7 | ln | UNARYOP | 6 | *natural logarithm* |
| 8 | log10 | UNARYOP | 6 | *base 10 logarithm* |
| 9 | sin | UNARYOP | 6 | |
| 10 | cos | UNARYOP | 6 | |
| 11 | tanh | UNARYOP | 6 | |
| 12 | + | BINARYOP | 4 | |
| 13 | – | BINARYOP | 4 | |
| 14 | * | BINARYOP | 5 | |
| 15 | / | BINARYOP | 5 | |
| 16 | % | BINARYOP | 5 | |
| 17 | ↑ | BINARYOP | 6 | |
| 18 | x | OPERAND | 0.00000 | |
| 19 | pi | OPERAND | 3.14159 | |
| 20 | e | OPERAND | 2.71828 | |

**Figure 12.8. Predefined tokens for GraphExpression**

Note that we can add operators that are not a standard part of a computer language (such as the base 2 logarithm lg) and constants such as *e* and *π*. The expressions in which we are interested in this section always have real numbers as their results. Hence we do not include any Boolean or set-valued operations. Several integer-valued operations are included, since integers can sensibly be regarded as real numbers.

### 2. Hash Table Processing

Next, we wish to set up the hash table used for indexing. Recall that, while the lexicon takes an index and returns a token name and information about the token, the hash table takes a token name and returns an index.

To set up the index in the hash table, we must first initialize the table to be empty:

```
/* CreateHashTable: initialize a hash table.
   Pre:   None.
   Post:  The hash table hashtable has been created and initialized to be empty. */
void CreateHashTable(int hashtable[ ])
{
   int i;
   for (i = 0; i < MAXTOKEN; i++)
       hashtable[i] = -1;
}
```

Our next task is to take all the tokens that have been defined in the lexicon and to insert each of them into the hash table. This task is accomplished by the following straightforward function:

```
/* FillHashTable: initialize a hash table.
   Pre:   hashtable has been created.
   Post:  All token codes from lexicon have been put into the table. */
void FillHashTable(int hashtable[ ])
{
   int i;
   for (i = 0; i <= LASTOPERAND; i++)
       hashtable[Hash(hashtable, lexicon.entry[i].name)] = i;
}
```

It is often the case that the performance of a hash function can be enhanced by taking into account the application for which it will be used. In our graphing program many of the tokens are single characters (some letters and some one-character operators). The hash function that we develop therefore gives special emphasis to the fact that many of the tokens are single characters:

```
/* Hash: find the place for a name in the hash table.
   Pre:   hashtable has been created and x is a token name.
   Post:  The function returns the location of x in hashtable if it is present, and otherwise
          the empty location where x may be inserted. */
```

```
int Hash(int hashtable[ ], char *x)
{
    int h = x[0] % HASHSIZE;
    while (1) {
        if (hashtable[h] == −1)
            break;                    /* Entry is empty.              */
        else if (strcmp(lexicon.entry[hashtable[h]].name, x) == 0)
            break;                    /* name in the hash table       */
        else {
            if (x[1] == '\0')
                h += 31;
            else
                h += x[1];
            h %= HASHSIZE;            /* Find another position.       */
        }
    }
    return abs(h);
}
```

### 3. Error Processing

To give the user more information and options, we supplement the standard Error routine into the following form:

```
/* ErrorInform: inform of an error and its severity.
   Pre:  level is a valid error level; msg is a message.
   Post: The message msg has been written to the screen with a message on the
         severity of the error. */
void ErrorInform(ErrorLevel level, char *msg)
{
    printf("%s\n", msg);
    switch(level) {
    case WARNING :
        printf("...program continues.\n");  break;
    case BADVALUE :
        printf("...bad value. Give new graphing limits.\n");  break;
    case BADEXPR :
        printf("...bad expression. Enter new expression.\n");  break;
    case FATAL :
        printf("...fatal error. Press Enter to terminate the program.\n");
        fflush(stdin);
        (void) getchar();
        RestoreScreen();
        exit(1);
    }
}
```

### 4. Expressions: Token Lists

We have already decided to treat expressions (both infix and postfix) as lists of (integer) token codes. Hence we may use the standard list operations. The function GetToken will remove token codes from its input list as it proceeds:

```
/* GetToken: get a new token.
   Pre:   expr is a valid expression.
   Post:  The first entry of the expression expr has been deleted and returned in token.
   Uses:  DeleteList. */

void GetToken(int *token, Expression *expr)
{
   DeleteList(0, token, expr);
}
```

Similarly, PutToken needs only to insert a token code at the end of its list, and EndExpression needs only to check whether or not its list is empty.

### 5. Properties of Tokens

For consistency with the functions developed earlier in this chapter, we shall use a function Kind to determine the kind corresponding to each token code; this function need only look in the lexicon to determine its result.

Similarly, we use a function Priority to look in the lexicon and return the priority of an operator. Both Kind and Priority will be left as exercises.

## 12.5.4 TRANSLATION OF THE EXPRESSION

In the next major section of the program, we must read an expression in ordinary (infix) form, check that it is syntactically correct, split it apart into tokens, and find their codes. As a sequence of tokens, the expression can then be converted to postfix form by the function written in Section 12.4, with only minor changes to conform with the declarations in this program.

### 1. Finding the Definitions of Tokens

As each token is split from the input string, we must find its code. This is an information retrieval problem: The name of the token is the key, and the integer code must be retrieved. In the expression there will usually be no more than a few dozen tokens, and it is quite arguable that the best way to retrieve the code is by sequential search through the lexicon. Sequential search would be easy to program, would require no further data structures, and the cost in time over more sophisticated methods would be negligible.

One of the objects of this project, however, is to illustrate larger applications, where the expense of sequential search may no longer be negligible. In a compiler, for example, there may be many hundreds of distinct symbols that must be recognized, and more sophisticated symbol tables must be used. A good choice is to use a hash table to make token names into integer codes. We call the hash table hashtable. In the hash table we shall store only codes, and use these to look in the lexicon to locate all the information about the token with a given name.

### 2. Decoding the Expression

Figure 12.8 includes both some tokens whose names are single special characters and some tokens whose names are words beginning with a letter. These latter may be any of unary or binary operators or operands. It is also possible to have tokens that are numbers, that is, which are made up of digits (and possibly a decimal point). Hence in splitting the input expression into tokens, we shall consider three cases, using three functions in the main loop,

ExtractWord    ExtractNumber    ExtractSymbol,

that will determine the name of the token and put its code into the output expression (still in infix at this stage).

*input format*    We must now establish conventions regarding the input format. Let us assume that the input expression is typed as one line, so that when we reach the end of the line, we have also reached the end of the input string. Let us use the following conventions concerning spaces: Blanks are ignored between tokens, but the occurrence of a blank terminates a token. If a token is a word, then it begins with a letter, which can be followed by letters or digits. Let us translate all upper-case letters to lower case, and use only lower case in comparisons. (Be sure that the predefined tokens are hashed as lower case only.) Let us truncate names to MAXNAME characters, where the symbolic constant MAXNAME is defined in expr.h.

*error checking*    It is in reading the input string that the greatest amount of error checking is needed to make sure that the syntax of the input expression is correct, and to make our program as robust as possible. This error checking will be done in the subsidiary functions.

With these provisions used to read in an expression, we obtain the following function:

```
/* ReadExpression: read an expression in infix form.
   Pre:  hashtable has been created and initialized with the predefined tokens found
         in the lexicon.
   Post: The expression infix has been read in and the tokens not found in the hashtable
         are added to the table.
   Uses: CreateList, */
Boolean ReadExpression(Expression *infix, int hashtable[ ],
                       PlotParameter *plotdata)
{
    Boolean valid;
    int h;                          /* Holds the hashtable value.           */
    int len, pos;
    char instring[MAXSTRING];
    CreateList(infix);
    fflush(stdin);
    printf("Please type (on one line) the expression to graph.\n");
    printf("Put blanks on each side of every token.\n");
    fgets(instring, MAXSTRING, stdin);
    len = strlen(instring);
    instring[len-1] = ' ';          /* sentinel for searches                */
    for (pos = 0; pos < len; ) {
        if (instring[pos] == ' ') {
            pos++;
            continue;
        } else if (isalpha(instring[pos]))
            pos = ExtractWord(instring, pos, &h, hashtable, plotdata);
        else if (isdigit(instring[pos]) || instring[pos] == '.')
            pos = ExtractNumber(instring, pos, &h);
        else pos = ExtractSymbol(instring, pos, &h, hashtable, infix);
        if (h == -1) {
            valid = FALSE;
            break;                   /* invalid token                        */
        } else {
            valid = TRUE;
            PutToken(h, infix);      /* h has the location in lexicon.       */
        }
    }
    if (valid)
        valid = ValidInfix(infix);
    if (!valid)
        ErrorInform(BADEXPR, "Expression invalid or too long.");
    PutToken(0, infix);              /* Mark the end of the expression.      */
    PutToken(0, &plotdata->paramlist);
    return valid;
}
```

### 3. Leading and Non-Leading Positions

The most important aspect of error checking that makes its first appearance in this routine is the Boolean-valued function Leading. To motivate the inclusion of this function, let us first consider a special case. Suppose that an expression is made up only from simple operands and binary operators, with no parentheses or unary operators. Then the only syntactically correct expressions are of the form

*operand    binaryop    operand    binaryop    ...    operand*

*leading positions*

where the first and last tokens are operands, and the two kinds of tokens alternate. It is illegal for two operands to be adjacent, or for two binary operators to be adjacent. In the leading position there must be an operand, as there must be after each operator, so we can consider these positions also as "leading," since the preceding operator must lead to an operand.

Now suppose that unary operators are to be inserted into the preceding expression. Any number of unary operators can be placed before any operand, but it is illegal to place a unary operator immediately before a binary operator. That is, unary operators that go on the left can appear exactly where operands are allowed, in leading positions but only there. On the other hand, the appearance of a unary operator leaves the position still as a "leading" position, since an operand must still appear before a binary operator becomes legal.

Let us now, finally, also allow parentheses in the expression. A bracketed sub-expression is treated as an operand and, therefore, can appear exactly where operands are legal. Hence left parentheses can appear exactly in leading positions and leave the position as leading, and right parentheses can appear only in nonleading positions and leave the position as nonleading.

All the possibilities are summarized in Figure 12.9.

|  | *Previous token any one of:* | *Legal tokens any one of:* |
|---|---|---|
| Leading position: | | |
| | start of expression | operand |
| | binary operator | unary operator |
| | unary operator | left parenthesis |
| | left parenthesis | |
| Nonleading position: | | |
| | operand | binary operator |
| | right parenthesis | right parenthesis |
| | | end of expression |

Figure 12.9. Tokens legal in leading and nonleading positions

These requirements are built into the following function that will be used in the subsidiary functions to check the syntax of the input.

```
/* Leading: TRUE if it is a leading position.
    Pre:   infix has been initialized.
    Post:  Returns TRUE if the token before position current in infix makes this a leading
           position, FALSE otherwise.
    Uses: Kind, RetrieveList. */

Boolean Leading(Expression *infix, int current)
{
    int tok;
    KindType kind;
    Boolean valid = FALSE;

    if (current == 0)
        valid = TRUE;

    else {
        RetrieveList(current − 1, &tok, infix);
        kind = Kind(tok);
        if (kind == LEFTPAREN || kind == UNARYOP || kind == BINARYOP)
            valid = TRUE;
    }
    return valid;
}
```

### 4. Unary and Binary Operators

The function ReadExpression contains a section of code that we can now explain. This concerns the two symbols '+' and '−', which can be either unary or binary operators. Fortunately, the function Leading will tell us which case occurs, since only a unary operator is legal in a leading position. We shall take no action for a unary '+', since it has no effect, and we replace a unary '−' by a private notation '@'. Note, however, that this change is peculiar to our program. It is certainly not standard notation.

### 5. Error Checking for Correct Syntax

Checking for proper kinds of tokens in leading and non-leading positions, together with determining that parentheses are properly balanced, is the task of the following function.

```
/* ValidInfix: verify that an infix expression is valid.
    Pre:   infix has been initialized.
    Post:  Returns TRUE if the expression is in valid infix form, FALSE otherwise.
    Uses: Kind, Leading, ListSize, RetrieveList. */
```

```
Boolean ValidInfix(Expression *infix)
{
    int i, tok;
    KindType kind;
    Boolean valid;
    int parencount = 0;

    for (i = 0; i < ListSize(infix); i++) {
        RetrieveList(i, &tok, infix);
        kind = Kind(tok);
        if (Leading(infix, i))
            if (kind == OPERAND || kind == UNARYOP || kind == LEFTPAREN)
                valid = TRUE;
            else
                valid = FALSE;
        else
            if (kind == BINARYOP || kind == RIGHTPAREN)
                valid = TRUE;
            else
                valid = FALSE;
        if (valid) {
            if (kind == LEFTPAREN)
                parencount++;
            else if (kind == RIGHTPAREN)
                if (--parencount < 0)
                    valid = FALSE;
        }
        if (!valid)
            break;
    }
    return valid;
}
```

### 6. Case: Token is a Word

We now turn to the three subsidiary functions for processing words, numbers and special symbols. The first of these must implement the decisions about the structure of words that we made earlier in this section. A word token can be any one of an operand, unary operator, or binary operator. The error checking must be adjusted accordingly. Or it may be that the word token does not yet appear in the lexicon, in which case it represents the first appearance of a new parameter, which must be entered accordingly into the lexicon and into the list of parameters.

These requirements translate into the following two functions. The first of these functions extracts a single word from the input string.

```
/* GetWord: get word from instring starting at pos.
   Pre:   instring has been initialized; pos is the position within instring starting the word
          to be extracted.
   Post:  The word has been extracted from instring and put in word.  The function
          returns the location after the word. */
int GetWord(char *instring, int pos, char *word)
{
   int i;
   char *pw = word;
   for (i = pos;  isalpha(instring[i]) || isdigit(instring[i]);  i++)
      *word++ = tolower(instring[i]);
   *word = '\0';
   if (i − pos > MAXNAME) {
      printf("Word %s was truncated.\n", pw);
      pw[MAXNAME] = '\0';
   }
   return i;                              /* Return next position in instring.        */
}
```

The second function inserts the word into the lexicon and the hash table.

```
/* ExtractWord: extract a word from instring.
   Pre:   instring has been initialized; pos is the position within instring starting the word
          to be processed.
   Post:  The word has been read from instring and pos points to next location (after the
          word). The word is inserted into the lexicon with hashtable holding the token's
          location in the lexicon.
   Uses: GetWord, ErrorInform, Hash. */
int ExtractWord(char *instring, int pos, int *h, int hashtable[ ],
           PlotParameter *plotdata)
{
   char word[MAXTOKEN];
   pos = GetWord(instring, pos, word);
   if ((*h = hashtable[Hash(hashtable, word)]) == −1)
      if (++lexicon.count >= MAXTOKEN) {
         ErrorInform(BADEXPR, "Too many distinct variables and constants.");
      } else {
         *h = hashtable[Hash(hashtable, word)] = lexicon.count;
         strcpy(lexicon.entry[lexicon.count].name, word);
         lexicon.entry[lexicon.count].kind = OPERAND;
         lexicon.entry[lexicon.count].info.val = 0.;
         PutToken(*h, &plotdata->paramlist);
      }
   return pos;
}
```

## 7. Case: Token is a Number

The treatment of numbers is generally similar to that of variables, but with two differences. One is that we must convert the number to binary so that we can use its value directly from the lexicon, rather than reading its value into a list of parameters. The other difference is that there is not necessarily a unique name for a number. If MAXNAME is large enough so that a string can hold as many digits as the precision of the machine, then unique names can be assigned, but if not, two different numbers might get the same name. To guard against this possibility, we shall regard every occurrence of a number as a newly defined token, and act accordingly. In converting the number from a character string into binary we use the function atof available in the C compiler library. We enter the number into the lexicon but we do not enter the number into the hash table.

```
/* ExtractNumber: extract a number from instring.
   Pre:  instring has been initialized; pos is the position within instring where the num-
         ber to be processed starts.
   Post: The number has been extracted from instring and put in the lexicon. The
         function returns the location after the number. */
int ExtractNumber(char *instring, int pos, int *h)
{
    if (++lexicon.count >= MAXTOKEN) {
        *h = -1;
        ErrorInform(BADEXPR, "Too many distinct variables and constants.");
    } else {
        *h = lexicon.count;
        lexicon.entry[lexicon.count].kind = OPERAND;
        strcpy(lexicon.entry[lexicon.count].name, "const");
        lexicon.entry[lexicon.count].info.val = atof(&instring[pos]);
        for (; isdigit(instring[pos]) || instring[pos] == '.'; pos++)
            ;
    }
    return pos;
}
```

## 8. Case: Token is a Special Symbol

The third subsidiary function treats the special symbols. Most of its work is simpler than the previous cases it need create no new tokens. If it fails to recognize a symbol, then an error occurs. The special symbols are all one character long, so counting positions in instring is easier.

```
/* ExtractSymbol: extract symbol from instring.
   Pre:  instring has been initialized; pos is the position within instring starting the
         symbol to be extracted.
   Post: The symbol has been read from instring and pos points to next location (after
         the symbol). The symbol is inserted into the lexicon with hashtable holding the
         token's location in the lexicon. */
```

```
int ExtractSymbol(char *instring, int pos, int *h, int hashtable[ ], Expression *infix)
{
    int i;
    char word[MAXTOKEN];
    for (i = 0; instring[pos] != ' '; i++, pos++)
        word[i] = instring[pos];
    word[i] = '\0';
    if ((*h = hashtable[Hash(hashtable, word)]) == -1) {
        ErrorInform(BADEXPR, "Unrecognized symbol in expression");
    } else {
        if (Leading(infix, ListSize(infix)))
            if (strcmp(word, "+") == 0)
                ;                               /* Do nothing with unary plus.        */
            else if (strcmp(word, "-") == 0)
                *h = hashtable[Hash(hashtable, "@")];
                                                /* special name for unary minus       */
    }
    return pos;
}
```

### 9. Translation into Postfix Form

At the conclusion of ReadExpression, the input expression has been converted into an infix sequence of tokens, in exactly the form needed by InfixtoPostfix as derived in Section 12.4. In fact, we now arrive at the key step of our algorithm and can apply the previous work without essential change; the only modifications needed in InfixtoPostfix are to adjust the declarations to those of this section.

When InfixtoPostfix has finished, the expression is a sequence of tokens in postfix form, and can be evaluated efficiently in the next stage. This efficiency, in fact, is important so that a graph can be drawn without undue delay, even though it requires evaluation of the expression for a great many different values.

## 12.5.5 EVALUATING THE EXPRESSION

### 1. Reading the Parameters

The first step in evaluating the expression is to establish values for the parameters, if any. This is done only once for each graph, provided the user does not wish only the default values of 0.0 for all parameters. The function ReadNewParameters is left as an exercise.

### 2. Postfix Evaluation

To evaluate the postfix expression, we again use a function developed in the first part of this chapter. We use the recursive version of EvaluatePostfix, again with no significant change. EvaluatePostfix requires subsidiary functions GetValue, DoUnary, and DoBinary, to which we now turn.

### 3. Evaluation of Operands

The first function need only look in the lexicon:

```
/* GetValue: get a value from lexicon[ ] for token.
   Pre:   token is a valid token code for an operand in the lexicon.
   Post:  The value of the operand is returned. */
Value GetValue(int token)
{
   if (Kind(token) != OPERAND)
      ErrorInform(FATAL, "Attempt to get value for nonoperand");
   return lexicon.entry[token].info.val;
}
```

## 4. Operators

Since we have integer codes for all the tokens, the application of operators can be done within a simple switch statement. We leave the one for unary operators as an exercise. For binary operators, we have the function below.

```
/* DoBinary: apply binary operator on x and y; return the result.
   Pre:   x and y are valid operand values; token is a token code of a binary operator in
          the lexicon.
   Post:  The operator pointed to by token in the lexicon has been performed. */
Value DoBinary(int token, Value x, Value y)
{
   switch(token) {
   case 12:                    /* binary plus                                    */
      return x + y;
   case 13:                    /* binary minus                                   */
      return x - y;
   case 14:                    /* times                                          */
      return x * y;
   case 15:                    /* divide                                         */
      if (y != (Value) 0)
         return x/y;
      else
         ErrorInform(FATAL, "Division by zero is not allowed.");
   case 16:                    /* modulus operator                               */
      if (y != (Value) 0)
         return fmod(x, y);
      else
         ErrorInform(FATAL, "Division by zero is not allowed.");
   case 17:                    /* x to the power y                               */
      if (x < 0. && y != (int) y)
         ErrorInform(FATAL, "pow() cannot handle x^y for x < 0 and fractional y.");
      return pow(x, y);
   default:
      printf("%d ", token);
      ErrorInform(FATAL, "is an invalid Binary token.");  break;
   }
}
```

Note that we can easily use the structure of this function to improve the error checking usually provided to the user by the operating system. The messages given for division by 0 will likely prove more helpful than something like

Floating point error,

which may be all that the system normally provides.

### 12.5.6 GRAPHING THE EXPRESSION

Now we come, finally, to the purpose of the entire program, graphing the expression on the computer screen. Graphics, unfortunately, are entirely system dependent, so what works on one machine may not necessarily work on another. In this section, we discuss only the requirements of Borland C.

The routine must determine what kind of graphics hardware is available, initialize it for graphics, and find the size of the screen in pixels. These tasks are done as follows in Borland C:

```
/* InitializeScreen: initialize screen to graphics mode.
   Pre:   None.
   Post:  The screen has been initialized to graphics mode and maximum size of the
          screen has been stored in the parameters.
   Uses: Uses Borland's graphics.h and graphic routines. */
void InitializeScreen(int *maxx, int *maxy)
{
    int errorcode, graphicdriver = DETECT, graphicmode;
    initgraph( &graphicdriver, &graphicmode, "");
    if ((errorcode = graphresult()) != grOk) {
        printf("Error is %d: %s\n", errorcode, grapherrormsg(errorcode));
        ErrorInform(FATAL, "Graphics error in InitializeScreen().");
    }
    *maxx = getmaxx();
    *maxy = getmaxy();
}
```

After the graph is drawn, text mode is restored by:

```
/* RestoreScreen: restore screen to text mode.
   Pre:   The output is in graphics mode.
   Post:  The screen has been restored to text mode.
   Uses: Uses Borland's graphics.h and graphic routine. */
void RestoreScreen(void)
{
    restorecrtmode();
}
```

Using the size of the screen in pixels, we can convert a single point in the user-specified range of $(x, y)$ values into a pixel location and graph it as follows:

```
/* GraphPoint: graph a point it is within screen range.
    Pre:   x and y are valid floating point numbers; maxx and maxy were calculated by
           the graphic routines.
    Post:  If the point x,y is within the range specified by the user then it is printed relative
           to maxx and maxy.
    Uses: Uses Borland's graphics.h and graphic routine. */
void GraphPoint(Value x, Value y, int maxx, int maxy, PlotParameter *plotdata)
{
    int ix, iy;
    if (x >= plotdata->xlow && x <= plotdata->xhigh &&
        y >= plotdata->ylow && y <= plotdata->yhigh) {
        ix = (x - plotdata->xlow) * maxx/(plotdata->xhigh - plotdata->xlow);
        iy = maxy -
             (y - plotdata->ylow) * maxy/(plotdata->yhigh - plotdata->ylow);
        putpixel(ix, iy, 3);
    }
}
```

This function is invoked by another that draws the graph by repeatedly evaluating the expression at x values separated by the variable increment, plotting a single point for each evaluation:

```
/* DrawGraph: use postfix expression to draw the graph.
    Pre:   postfix has been initialized. The plotting parameters in plotdata have been
           initialized.
    Post:  The expression postfix has been graphed.
    Uses: InitializeScreen, EvaluatePostfix, GraphPoint, RestoreScreen. */
void DrawGraph(Expression *postfix, PlotParameter *plotdata)
{
    Value x, y;
    int maxx, maxy;
    InitializeScreen( &maxx,  &maxy);
    for (x = plotdata->xlow;  x <= plotdata->xhigh;  x += plotdata->increment) {
        lexicon.entry [FIRSTOPERAND].info.val = x;
        y = EvaluatePostfix(postfix);
        GraphPoint(x, y, maxx, maxy, plotdata);
    }
    fflush(stdin);                    /* Discard any available input.          */
    (void) getchar();                 /* Wait for the user to press Enter.     */
    RestoreScreen();
    printf("Please enter the next command or h for Help.\n");
}
```

At this point, we have surveyed the entire project. There remain several subprograms that do not appear in the text, but these are all sufficiently straightforward that they can be left as a project.

**Exercises 12.5**  **E1.** State precisely what changes in the program are needed to add the base 2 logarithm function log( ) as an additional unary operator.

**E2.** Naïve users of this program might (if graphing a function involving money) write a dollar sign '$' within the expression. What will the present program do if this happens? What changes are needed so that the program will ignore a '$'?

**E3.** C or Pascal programmers might accidentally type a semicolon ';' at the end of the expression. What changes are needed so that a semicolon will be ignored at the end of the expression, but will be an error elsewhere?

**E4.** Explain what changes are needed to allow the program to accept either square brackets [ ... ] or curly brackets { ... } as well as round brackets ( ... ). The nesting must be done with the same kind of brackets; that is, an expression of the form ( ... [ ... ) ... ] is illegal, but forms like [ ... ( ... ) ... { ... } ... ] are permissible.

**Programming**  **P1.** Provide the missing subprograms and implement program GraphExpression
**Project 12.5**  on your computer.

## References for Further Study

The Polish notation is so natural and useful that one might expect its discovery to be hundreds of years ago. It may be surprising to note that it is a discovery of this century:

JAN ŁUKASIEWICZ, *Elementy Logiki Matematyczny*, Warsaw, 1929; English translation: *Elements of Mathematical Logic*, Pergamon Press, 1963.

The development of iterative algorithms to form and evaluate Polish expressions (usually postfix form) can be found in several data structures books, as well as more advanced books on compiler theory. The iterative algorithm for translating an expression from infix to postfix form appears to be due independently to E. W. DIJKSTRA and to C. L. HAMBLIN, and appears in

E. W. DIJKSTRA, "Making a Translator for ALGOL 60," *Automatic Programming Information* number 7 (May 1961); reprinted in *Annual Revue of Automatic Programming* 3 (1963), 347–356.

C. L. HAMBLIN, "Translation to and from Polish notation," *Computer Journal* 5 (1962), 210–213.

The recursive algorithm for evaluation of postfix expressions is derived, albeit from a rather different point of view, and for binary operators only, in

EDWARD M. REINGOLD, "A comment on the evaluation of Polish postfix expressions," *Computer Journal* 24 (1981), 288.

# A

# Mathematical Methods

**T**HE FIRST PART *of this appendix supplies several mathematical results used in algorithm analysis. The final two sections (Fibonacci and Catalan numbers) are optional topics for the mathematically inclined reader.*

## A.1 Sums of Powers of Integers

The following two formulas are useful in counting the steps executed by an algorithm.

**Theorem A.1**

$$1 + 2 + \cdots + n = \frac{n(n + 1)}{2}.$$

$$1^2 + 2^2 + \cdots + n^2 = \frac{n(n + 1)(2n + 1)}{6}.$$

**Proof**   The first identity has a simple and elegant proof. We let $S$ equal the sum on the left side, write it down twice (once in each direction), and add vertically:

$$
\begin{array}{ccccccccccc}
1 & + & 2 & + & 3 & + & \cdots & + & n-1 & + & n & = & S \\
n & + & n-1 & + & n-2 & + & \cdots & + & 2 & + & 1 & = & S \\
\hline
n+1 & + & n+1 & + & n+1 & + & \cdots & + & n+1 & + & n+1 & = & 2S
\end{array}
$$

There are $n$ columns on the left; hence $n(n + 1) = 2S$ and the formula follows.

The first identity also has the proof without words shown in Figure A.0.

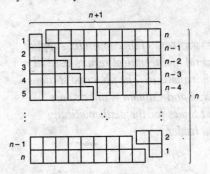

Figure A.1.  Geometrical proof for sum of integers

*proof by induction*

We shall use the method of ***mathematical induction*** to prove the second identity. This method requires that we start by establishing an initial case, called the ***induction base***, which for our formula is the case $n = 1$. In this case the formula becomes

$$1^2 = \frac{1(1 + 1)(2 + 1)}{6},$$

which is true, so the induction base is established. Next, using the formula for the case $n - 1$, we must establish it for case $n$. For case $n - 1$ we thus shall assume

$$1^2 + 2^2 + \cdots + (n - 1)^2 = \frac{(n - 1)n(2(n - 1) + 1)}{6}$$

It follows that

$$1^2 + 2^2 + \cdots + (n-1)^2 + n^2 = \frac{(n-1)n(2(n-1)+1)}{6} + n^2$$

$$= \frac{2n^3 - 3n^2 + n + 6n^2}{6}$$

$$= \frac{n(n+1)(2n+1)}{6},$$

which is the desired result, and the proof by induction is complete.

A convenient shorthand for a sum of the sort appearing in these identities is to use the capital Greek letter sigma

*summation notation*

$$\sum$$

in front of the typical summand, with the initial value of the index controlling the summation written below the sign, and the final value above. Thus the preceding identities can be written

$$\sum_{k=1}^{n} k = \frac{n(n+1)}{2}$$

and

$$\sum_{k=1}^{n} k^2 = \frac{n(n+1)(2n+1)}{6}.$$

Two other formulas are also useful, particularly in working with trees.

**Theorem A.2**

$$1 + 2 + 4 + \cdots + 2^{m-1} = 2^m - 1.$$

$$1 \times 1 + 2 \times 2 + 3 \times 4 + \cdots + m \times 2^{m-1} = (m-1) \times 2^m + 1.$$

*In summation notation these equations are*

$$\sum_{k=0}^{m-1} 2^k = 2^m - 1.$$

$$\sum_{k=1}^{m} k \times 2^{k-1} = (m-1) \times 2^m + 1.$$

**Proof**  The first formula will be proved in a more general form. We start with the following identity, which, for any value of $x \neq 1$, can be verified simply by multiplying both sides by $x - 1$:

$$\frac{x^m - 1}{x - 1} = 1 + x + x^2 + \cdots + x^{m-1}$$

for any $x \neq 1$. With $x = 2$ this expression becomes the first formula.

To establish the second formula we take the same expression in the case of $m + 1$ instead of $m$:

$$\frac{x^{m+1} - 1}{x - 1} = 1 + x + x^2 + \cdots + x^m$$

for any $x \neq 1$, and differentiate with respect to $x$:

$$\frac{(x-1)(m+1)x^m - (x^{m+1}-1)}{(x-1)^2} = 1 + 2x + 3x^2 + \cdots + mx^{m-1}$$

*end of proof*    for any $x \neq 1$. Setting $x = 2$ now gives the second formula.

Suppose that $|x| < 1$ in the preceding formulas. As $m$ becomes large, it follows that $x^m$ becomes small, that is

$$\lim_{m \to \infty} x^m = 0.$$

Taking the limit as $m \to \infty$ in the preceding equations gives

**Theorem A.3**    *If $|x| < 1$ then*

$$\sum_{k=0}^{\infty} x^k = \frac{1}{1-x}.$$

$$\sum_{k=1}^{\infty} kx^{k-1} = \frac{1}{(1-x)^2}.$$

## A.2 Logarithms

The primary reason for using logarithms is to turn multiplication and division into addition and subtraction, and exponentiation into multiplication. Before the advent of pocket calculators, logarithms were an indispensable tool for hand calculation: Witness the large tables of logarithms and the once ubiquitous slide rule. Even though we now have other methods for numerical calculation, the fundamental properties of logarithms give them importance that extends far beyond their use as computational tools.

The behavior of many phenomena, first of all, reflects an intrinsically logarithmic structure; that is, by using logarithms we find important relationships that are *physical* not otherwise obvious. Measuring the loudness of sound, for example, is logarith-
*measurements* mic: if one sound is 10 db. (decibels) louder than another, then the actual acoustic energy is 10 times as much. If the sound level in one room is 40 db. and it is 60 db. in another, then the human perception may be that the second room is half again as noisy as the first, but there is actually 100 times more sound energy in the second room. This phenomenon is why a single violin soloist can be heard above a full orchestra (when playing a different line), and yet the orchestra requires so many violins to maintain a proper balance of sound.

Earthquake intensity is also measured logarithmically: An increase of 1 on the RICHTER scale represents a ten-fold increase in energy released.

*large numbers*
Logarithms, secondly, provide a convenient way to handle very large numbers. The scientific notation, where a number is written as a small real number (often in the range from 1 to 10) times a power of 10, is really based on logarithms, since the power of 10 is essentially the logarithm of the number. Scientists who need to use very large numbers (like astronomers, nuclear physicists, and geologists) frequently speak of orders of magnitude, and thereby concentrate on the logarithm of the number.

A logarithmic graph, thirdly, is a very useful device for displaying the properties of a function over a much broader range than a linear graph. With a logarithmic graph, we can arrange to display detailed information on the function for small values of the argument and at the same time give an overall view for much larger values. Logarithmic graphs are especially appropriate when we wish to show percentage changes in a function.

## A.2.1 Definition of Logarithms

*base*
Logarithms are defined in terms of a real number $a > 1$, which is called the *base* of the logarithms. (It is also possible to define logarithms with base $a$ in the range $0 < a < 1$, but doing so would introduce needless complications into our discussion.) For any number $x > 0$, we define $\log_a x = y$ where $y$ is the real number such that $a^y = x$. The logarithm of a negative number, and the logarithm of 0, are not defined.

## A.2.2 Simple Properties

From the definition and from the properties of exponents we obtain

$$\log_a 1 = 0,$$
$$\log_a a = 1,$$
$$\log_a x < 0 \quad \text{for all } x \text{ such that } 0 < x < 1.$$
$$0 < \log_a x < 1 \quad \text{for all } x \text{ such that } 1 < x < a.$$
$$\log_a x > 1 \quad \text{for all } x \text{ such that } a < x.$$

The logarithm function has a graph like the one in Figure A.2.
*identities*
We also obtain the identities

$$\log_a(xy) = (\log_a x) + (\log_a y)$$
$$\log_a(x/y) = (\log_a x) - (\log_a y)$$
$$\log_a x^z = z \log_a x$$
$$\log_a a^z = z$$
$$a^{\log_a x} = x$$

that hold for any positive real numbers $x$ and $y$, and for any real number $z$.

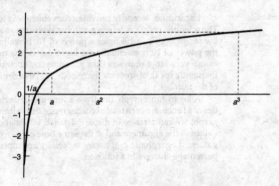

Figure A.2. Graph of the logarithm function

From the graph in Figure A.2 you will observe that the logarithm grows more and more slowly as $x$ increases. The graphs of positive powers of $x$ less than 1, such as the square root of $x$ or the cube root of $x$, also grow progressively more slowly, but never become as flat as the graph of the logarithm. In fact,

*As $x$ grows large, $\log x$ grows more slowly than $x^c$, for any $c > 0$.*

## A.2.3  CHOICE OF BASE

Any real number $a > 1$ can be chosen as the base of logarithms, but certain special choices appear much more frequently than others. For computation and for graphing, the base $a = 10$ is often used, and logarithms with base 10 are called *common logarithms*. In studying computer algorithms, however, base 10 appears infrequently, and we do not often use common logarithms. Instead, logarithms with base 2 appear the most frequently, and we therefore reserve the special symbol

*common logarithm*

$$\lg x$$

to denote a logarithm with base 2.

## A.2.4  NATURAL LOGARITHMS

In studying mathematical properties of logarithms, and in many problems where logarithms appear as part of the answer, the number that appears as the base is

$$e = 2.718281828459\ldots.$$

*natural logarithm*

Logarithms with base $e$ are called *natural logarithms*. In this book we always denote the natural logarithm of $x$ by

$$\ln x.$$

In many mathematics books, however, other bases than $e$ are rarely used, in which case the unqualified symbol $\log x$ usually denotes a natural logarithm. Figure A.3 shows the graph of logarithms with respect to the three bases 2, $e$, and 10.

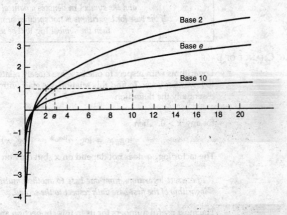

**Figure A.3. Logarithms with three bases**

The properties of logarithms that make $e$ the natural choice for the base are thoroughly developed as part of the calculus, but we can mention two of these properties without proof. First, the graph of $\ln x$ has the property that its slope at each point $x$ is $1/x$; that is, the derivative of $\ln x$ is $1/x$ for all real numbers $x > 0$. Second, the natural logarithm satisfies the infinite series

$$\ln(x + 1) = x - \frac{x^2}{2} + \frac{x^3}{3} - \frac{x^4}{4} + \cdots$$

for $-1 < x < 1$, but this series requires many terms to give a good approximation and therefore, is not useful directly for computation. It is much better to consider *exponential function* instead the exponential function that "undoes" the logarithm, and that satisfies the series

$$e^x = 1 + x + \frac{x^2}{2!} + \frac{x^3}{3!} + \cdots$$

for all real numbers $x$. This exponential function $e^x$ also has the important property that it is its own derivative.

### A.2.5 NOTATION

The notation just used for logarithms with different bases will be our standard. We thus summarize:

> **Conventions**
> *Unless stated otherwise, all logarithms will be taken with base 2.*
> *The symbol* lg *denotes a logarithm with base 2,*
> *and the symbol* ln *denotes a natural logarithm.*
> *If the base for logarithms is not specified or makes no difference,*
> *then the symbol* log *will be used.*

### A.2.6 Change of Base

Logarithms with respect to one base are closely related to logarithms with respect to any other base. To find this relation, we start with the following relation that is essentially the definition

$$x = a^{\log_a x}$$

for any $x > 0$. Then

$$\log_b x = \log_b a^{\log_a x} = (\log_a x)(\log_b a).$$

The factor $\log_b a$ does not depend on $x$, but only on the two bases. Therefore:

> *To convert logarithms from one base to another, multiply by a constant factor, the logarithm of the first base with respect to the second.*

*conversion factors*    The most useful numbers for us in this connection are

$$\lg e \approx 1.442695041,$$
$$\ln 2 \approx 0.693147181,$$
$$\ln 10 \approx 2.302585093,$$
$$\lg 1000 \approx 10.0$$

The last value is a consequence of the important approximation $2^{10} = 1024 \approx 10^3 = 1000$.

### A.2.7 Logarithmic Graphs

In a logarithmic scale the numbers are arranged as on a slide rule, with larger numbers closer together than smaller numbers. In this way, equal distances along the scale represent equal *ratios* rather than the equal *differences* represented on an ordinary linear scale. A logarithmic scale should be used when percentage change is important to measure, or when perception is logarithmic. Human perception of time, for example, sometimes seems to be nearly linear in the short term—what happened two days ago is twice as distant as what happened yesterday—but often seems more nearly logarithmic in the long term: We draw less distinction between one million years ago and two million years ago than we do between ten years ago and one hundred years ago.

*log-log graphs*    Graphs in which both the vertical and horizontal scales are logarithmic are called **log-log graphs**. In addition to phenomena where the perception is naturally logarithmic in both scales, log-log graphs are useful to display the behavior of a function over a very wide range. For small values, the graph records a detailed view of the function, and for large values a broad view of the function appears on the same graph. For searching and sorting algorithms, we wish to compare methods both for small problems and large problems; hence log-log graphs are appropriate. (See Figure A.4.)

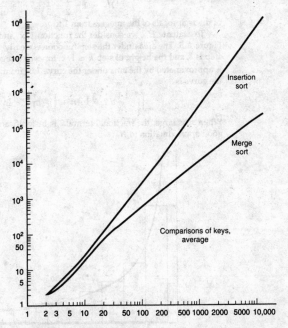

Figure A.4. **Log-log graph, comparisons, insertion and merge sorts**

One observation is worth noting: Any power of $x$ graphs as a straight line with a log-log scale. To prove this, we start with an arbitrary power function $y = x^n$, and take logarithms on both sides, obtaining

$$\log y = n \log x.$$

A log-log graph in $x$ and $y$ becomes a linear graph in $u = \log x$ and $v = \log y$, and the equation becomes $v = nu$ in terms of $u$ and $v$, which indeed graphs as a straight line.

## A.2.8 HARMONIC NUMBERS

As a final application of logarithms, we obtain an approximation to a sum that appears frequently in the analysis of algorithms, especially that of sorting methods. The $n^{th}$ *harmonic number* is defined to be the sum

$$H_n = 1 + \frac{1}{2} + \frac{1}{3} + \cdots + \frac{1}{n}$$

of the reciprocals of the integers from 1 to $n$.

To evaluate $H_n$, we consider the function $1/x$, and the relationship shown in Figure A.5. The area under the step function is clearly $H_n$, since the width of each step is 1, and the height of step $k$ is $1/k$, for each integer $k$ from 1 to $n$. This area is approximated by the area under the curve $1/x$ from $\frac{1}{2}$ to $n + \frac{1}{2}$. The area under the curve is

$$\int_{\frac{1}{2}}^{n+\frac{1}{2}} \frac{1}{x} dx = \ln(n + \tfrac{1}{2}) - \ln \tfrac{1}{2} \approx \ln n + 0.7.$$

When $n$ is large, the fractional term 0.7 is insignificant, and we obtain $\ln n$ as a good approximation to $H_n$.

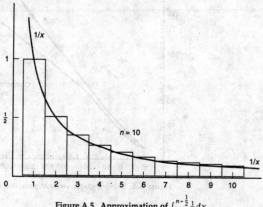

Figure A.5. Approximation of $\int_{\frac{1}{2}}^{n+\frac{1}{2}} \frac{1}{x} dx$

By refining this method of approximation by an integral, it is possible to obtain a very much closer approximation to $H_n$, if such is desired. Specifically,

**Theorem A.4**     *The harmonic number $H_n$, $n \geq 1$, satisfies*

$$H_n = \ln n + \gamma + \frac{1}{2n} - \frac{1}{12n^2} + \frac{1}{120n^4} - \epsilon,$$

*where $0 < \epsilon < 1/(252n^6)$, and $\gamma \approx 0.577215665$ is known as **Euler's constant**.*

# A.3 Permutations, Combinations, Factorials

## A.3.1 PERMUTATIONS

A *permutation* of objects is an ordering or arrangement of the objects in a row. If we begin with $n$ different objects, then we can choose any of the $n$ objects to be the first one in the arrangement. There are then $n - 1$ choices for the second object, and since these choices can be combined in all possible ways, the number of choices multiplies. Hence the first two objects may be chosen in $n(n - 1)$ ways. There remain $n - 2$ objects, any one of which may be chosen as the third in the arrangement. Continuing in this way, we see that the number of permutations of $n$ distinct objects is

*count of permutations*
$$n! = n \times (n - 1) \times (n - 2) \times \ldots \times 2 \times 1.$$

| Objects to permute: | a b c d | | | | | |
|---|---|---|---|---|---|---|
| *Choose a first:* | a b c d | a b d c | a c b d | a c d b | a d b c | a d c b |
| *Choose b first:* | b a c d | b a d c | b c a d | b c d a | b d a c | b d c a |
| *Choose c first:* | c a b d | c a d b | c b a d | c b d a | c d a b | c d b a |
| *Choose d first:* | d a b c | d a c b | d b a c | d b c a | d c a b | d c b a |

Figure A.6. Constructing permutations

Note that we have assumed that the objects are all distinct, that is, that we can tell each object from every other one. It is often easier to count configurations of distinct objects than when some are indistinguishable. The latter problem can sometimes be solved by temporarily labeling the objects so they are all distinct, then counting the configurations, and finally dividing by the number of ways in which the labeling could have been done. The special case in the next section is especially important.

## A.3.2 COMBINATIONS

A *combination* of $n$ objects taken $k$ at a time is a choice of $k$ objects out of the $n$, without regard for the order of selection. The number of such combinations is denoted either by

$$C(n, k) \quad \text{or by} \quad \binom{n}{k}.$$

We can calculate $C(n, k)$ by starting with the $n!$ permutations of $n$ objects and form a combination simply by selecting the first $k$ objects in the permutation. The order, however, in which these $k$ objects appear is ignored in determining a combination, so we must divide by the number $k!$ of ways to order the $k$ objects chosen. The order of the $n - k$ objects not chosen is also ignored, so we must also divide by $(n - k)!$. Hence:

*count of combinations*

$$C(n, k) = \frac{n!}{k!(n - k)!}$$

| Objects from which to choose: | | a b c d e f | | |
|---|---|---|---|---|
| a b c | a c d | a d f | b c f | c d e |
| a b d | a c e | a e f | b d e | c d f |
| a b e | a c f | b c d | b d f | c e f |
| a b f | a d e | b c e | b e f | d e f |

Figure A.7. Combinations of 6 objects, taken 3 at a time

*binomial coefficients*

The number of combinations $C(n, k)$ is called a ***binomial coefficient***, since it appears as the coefficient of $x^k y^{n-k}$ in the expansion of $(x + y)^n$. There are hundreds of different relationships and identities about various sums and products of binomial coefficients. The most important of these can be found in textbooks on elementary algebra and on combinatorics.

## A.3.3 FACTORIALS

We frequently use permutations and combinations in analyzing algorithms, and for these applications we must estimate the size of $n!$ for various values of $n$. An excellent approximation to $n!$ was obtained by JAMES STIRLING in the eighteenth century:

**Theorem A.5**

$$n! \approx \sqrt{2\pi n}\left(\frac{n}{e}\right)^n\left[1 + \frac{1}{12n} + O\left(\frac{1}{n^2}\right)\right].$$

*Stirling's approximation*

We usually use this approximation in logarithmic form instead:

**Corollary A.6**

$$\ln n! \approx (n + \tfrac{1}{2})\ln n - n + \tfrac{1}{2}\ln(2\pi) + \frac{1}{12n} + O\left(\frac{1}{n^2}\right).$$

Note that, as $n$ increases, the approximation to the logarithm becomes more and more accurate; that is, the difference approaches 0. The difference between the approximation directly to the factorial and $n!$ itself will not necessarily become small (that is, the difference need not go to 0), but the percentage error becomes arbitrarily small (the ratio goes to 1). KNUTH (Volume 1, page 111) gives refinements of Stirling's approximation that are even closer.

The complete proof of Stirling's approximation requires techniques from advanced calculus that would take us too far afield here. We can, however, use a bit of elementary calculus to illustrate the first step of the approximation. First, we take the natural logarithm of a factorial, noting that the logarithm of a product is the sum of the logarithms:

$$\ln n! = \ln(n \times (n-1) \times \cdots \times 1)$$
$$= \ln n + \ln(n-1) + \cdots + \ln 1$$
$$= \sum_{x=1}^{n} \ln x.$$

Next, we approximate the sum by an integral, as shown in Figure A.8.

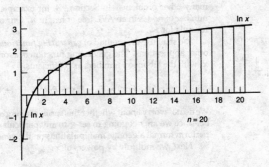

Figure A.8. Approximation of $\ln n!$ by $\int_{\frac{1}{2}}^{n+\frac{1}{2}} \ln x \, dx$

It is clear from the diagram that the area under the step function, which is exactly $\ln n!$, is approximately the same as the area under the curve, which is

$$\int_{\frac{1}{2}}^{n+\frac{1}{2}} \ln x \, dx = (x \ln x - x) \Big|_{\frac{1}{2}}^{n+\frac{1}{2}}$$
$$= (n + \tfrac{1}{2}) \ln(n + \tfrac{1}{2}) - n + \tfrac{1}{2} \ln 2.$$

For large values of $n$, the difference between $\ln n$ and $\ln(n + \tfrac{1}{2})$ is insignificant, and hence this approximation differs from Stirling's only by the constant difference between $\tfrac{1}{2} \ln 2$ (about 0.35) and $\tfrac{1}{2} \ln(2\pi)$ (about 0.919).

## A.4 Fibonacci Numbers

The Fibonacci numbers originated as an exercise in arithmetic proposed by LEONARDO FIBONACCI in 1202:

> *How many pairs of rabbits can be produced from a single pair in a year? We start with a single newly born pair; it takes one month for a pair to mature, after which they produce a new pair each month, and the rabbits never die.*

In month 1, we have only one pair. In month 2, we still have only one pair, but they are now mature. In month 3, they have reproduced, so we now have two pairs. And so it goes. The number $F_n$ of pairs of rabbits that we have in month $n$ satisfies

*recurrence relation*

$$F_0 = 0, \quad F_1 = 1, \quad \text{and} \quad F_n = F_{n-1} + F_{n-2} \quad \text{for} \quad n \geq 2.$$

This same sequence of numbers, called the *Fibonacci sequence*, appears in many other problems. In Section 9.4, for example, $F_n$ appears as the minimum number of nodes in an AVL tree of height $n$. Our object in this section is to find a formula for $F_n$.

*generating function*

We shall use the method of *generating functions*, which is important for many other applications. The generating function is a formal infinite series in a symbol $x$, with the Fibonacci numbers as coefficients:

$$F(x) = F_0 + F_1 x + F_2 x^2 + \cdots + F_n x^n + \cdots.$$

We do not worry about whether this series converges, or what the value of $x$ might be, since we are not going to set $x$ to any particular value. Instead, we shall only perform formal algebraic manipulations on the generating function.

Next, we multiply by powers of $x$:

$$
\begin{aligned}
F(x) &= F_0 + F_1 x + F_2 x^2 + \cdots + F_n \; x^n + \cdots \\
xF(x) &= \phantom{F_0 +} F_0 x + F_1 x^2 + \cdots + F_{n-1} x^n + \cdots \\
x^2 F(x) &= \phantom{F_0 + F_1 x +} F_0 x^2 + \cdots + F_{n-2} x^n + \cdots
\end{aligned}
$$

and subtract the second two equations from the first:

$$(1 - x - x^2)F(x) = F_0 + (F_1 - F_0)x = x,$$

since $F_0 = 0, F_1 = 1$, and $F_n = F_{n-1} + F_{n-2}$ for all $n \geq 2$. We therefore obtain

$$F(x) = \frac{x}{1 - x - x^2}.$$

The roots of $1 - x - x^2$ are $\frac{1}{2}(-1 \pm \sqrt{5})$. By the method of partial fractions we can thus rearrange the formula for $F(x)$ as:

*closed form*

$$F(x) = \frac{1}{\sqrt{5}} \left( \frac{1}{1 - \phi x} - \frac{1}{1 - \psi x} \right)$$

where

$$\phi = \tfrac{1}{2}(1 + \sqrt{5}) \text{ and } \psi = 1 - \phi = \tfrac{1}{2}(1 - \sqrt{5}).$$

(Check this equation for $F(x)$ by putting the two fractions on the right over a common denominator.)

The next step is to expand the fractions on the right side by dividing their denominators into 1:

$$F(x) = \frac{1}{\sqrt{5}}(1 + \phi x + \phi^2 x^2 + \cdots - 1 - \psi x - \psi^2 x^2 - \cdots).$$

The final step is to recall that the coefficients of $F(x)$ are the Fibonacci numbers, and therefore to equate the coefficients of each power of $x$ on both sides of this equation. We thus obtain

$$F_n = \frac{1}{\sqrt{5}}(\phi^n - \psi^n).$$

Approximate values for $\phi$ and $\psi$ are

$$\phi \approx 1.618034$$

and

$$\psi \approx -0.618034.$$

*golden mean*

This surprisingly simple answer to the values of the Fibonacci numbers is interesting in several ways. It is, first, not even immediately obvious why the right side should always be an integer. Second, $\psi$ is a negative number of sufficiently small absolute value that we always have $F_n = \phi^n/\sqrt{5}$ rounded to the nearest integer. Third, the number $\phi$ is itself interesting. It has been studied since the times of the ancient Greeks—it is often called the *golden mean*—and the ratio of $\phi$ to 1 is said to give the most pleasing shape of a rectangle. The Parthenon and many other ancient Greek buildings have sides with this ratio.

## A.5 Catalan Numbers

The purpose of this section is to count the binary trees with $n$ vertices. We shall accomplish this result via a slightly circuitous route, discovering along the way several other problems that have the same answer. The resulting numbers, called the *Catalan numbers*, are of considerable interest in that they appear in the answers to many apparently unrelated problems.

### A.5.1 THE MAIN RESULT

**Definition**    For $n \geq 0$, the $n^{th}$ *Catalan number* is defined to be

$$\text{Cat}(n) = \frac{C(2n, n)}{n + 1} = \frac{(2n)!}{(n + 1)!n!}.$$

**Theorem A.7**    *The number of distinct binary trees with $n$ vertices, $n \geq 0$, is the $n^{th}$ Catalan number* $\text{Cat}(n)$.

### A.5.2 THE PROOF BY ONE-TO-ONE CORRESPONDENCES

**1. Orchards**

Let us first recall the one-to-one correspondence from Theorem 10.1 (page 464) between the binary trees with $n$ vertices and the orchards with $n$ vertices. Hence to count binary trees, we may just as well count orchards.

**2. Well-Formed Sequences of Parentheses**

Second, let us consider the set of all well-formed sequences of $n$ left parentheses '(' and $n$ right parentheses ')'. A sequence is *well formed* means that, when scanned from left to right, the number of right parentheses encountered never exceeds the number of left parentheses. Thus '( ( ( ) ) )' and '( ) ( ) ( )' are well formed, but '( ) ) ( ( )' is not, nor is '( ( )', since the total numbers of left and right parentheses in the expression must be equal.

**Lemma A.8**    *There is a one-to-one correspondence between the orchards with $n$ vertices and the well-formed sequences of $n$ left parentheses and $n$ right parentheses, $n \geq 0$.*

*bracketed form*    To define this correspondence, we first recall that an orchard is either empty or is an ordered sequence of ordered trees. We define the *bracketed form* of an orchard to be the sequence of bracketed forms of its trees, written one after the next in the same order as the trees in the orchard. The bracketed form of the empty orchard is empty. We recall also that an ordered tree is defined to consist of its root vertex, together with an orchard of subtrees. We thus define the *bracketed form* of an ordered tree to consist of a left parenthesis '(' followed by the (name of the) root, followed by the bracketed form of the orchard of subtrees, and finally a right parenthesis ')'.

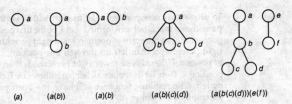

(a)          ((a)(b))          (a)(b)          (a(b)(c)(d))          (a(b(c)(d)))((e)(f))

Figure A.9. Bracketed form of orchards

The bracketed forms of several ordered trees and orchards appear in Figure A.9. It should be clear that the mutually recursive definitions we have given produce a unique bracketed form for any orchard and that the resulting sequence of parentheses is well formed. If, on the other hand, we begin with a well-formed sequence of parentheses, then the outermost pair(s) of parentheses correspond to the tree(s) of an orchard, and within such a pair of parentheses is the description of the corresponding tree in terms of its root and its orchard of subtrees. In this way, we have now obtained a one-to-one correspondence between the orchards with $n$ vertices and the well-formed sequences of $n$ left and $n$ right parentheses.

In counting orchards we are not concerned with the labels attached to the vertices, and hence we shall omit the labels and, with the correspondence we have outlined, we shall now count well-formed sequences of $n$ left and $n$ right parentheses with nothing else inside the parentheses.

### 3. Stack Permutations

Let us note that, by replacing each left parenthesis by $+1$ and each right parenthesis by $-1$, the well-formed sequences of parentheses correspond to sequences of $+1$ and $-1$ such that the partial sums from the left are always nonnegative, and the total sum is 0. If we think of each $+1$ as pushing an item onto a stack, and $-1$ as popping the stack, then the partial sums count the items on the stack at a given time. From this it can be shown that the number of stack permutations of $n$ objects (see Exercise E3 of Section 3.1, on page 89) is yet another problem for which the Catalan numbers provide the answer. Even more, if we start with an orchard and perform a complete traversal (walking around each branch and vertex in the orchard as though it were a decorative wall), counting $+1$ each time we go down a branch, and $-1$ each time we go up a branch (with $+1 - 1$ for each leaf), then we thereby essentially obtain the correspondence with well-formed sequences over again.

### 4. Arbitrary Sequences of Parentheses

Our final step is to count well-formed sequences of parentheses, but to do this we shall instead count the sequences that are *not* well formed, and subtract from the number of all possible sequences. We need a final one-to-one correspondence:

**Lemma A.9**      *The sequences of $n$ left and $n$ right parentheses that are not well formed correspond exactly to all sequences of $n - 1$ left parentheses and $n + 1$ right parentheses (in all possible orders).*

To prove this correspondence, let us start with a sequence of $n$ left and $n$ right parentheses that is not well formed. Let $k$ be the first position in which the sequence goes wrong, so the entry at position $k$ is a right parenthesis, and there is one more right parenthesis than left up through this position. Hence strictly to the right of position $k$ there is one fewer right parenthesis than left. Strictly to the right of position $k$, then, let us replace all left parentheses by right and all right parentheses by left. The resulting sequence will have $n-1$ left parentheses and $n+1$ right parentheses altogether.

Conversely, let us start with a sequence of $n-1$ left parentheses and $n+1$ right parentheses, and let $k$ be the first position where the number of right parentheses exceeds the number of left (such a position must exist, since there are more right than left parentheses altogether). Again let us exchange left for right and right for left parentheses in the remainder of the sequence (positions after $k$). We thereby obtain a sequence of $n$ left and $n$ right parentheses that is not well formed, and we have constructed the one-to-one correspondence as desired.

### 5. End of the Proof

With all these preliminary correspondences, our counting problem reduces to simple combinations. The number of sequences of $n-1$ left and $n+1$ right parentheses is the number of ways to choose the $n-1$ positions occupied by left parentheses from the $2n$ positions in the sequence, that is, the number is $C(2n, n-1)$. By Lemma A.9, this number is also the number of sequences of $n$ left and $n$ right parentheses that are not well formed. The number of all sequences of $n$ left and $n$ right parentheses is similarly $C(2n, n)$, so the number of well-formed sequences is

$$C(2n, n) - C(2n, n-1)$$

which is precisely the $n^{\text{th}}$ Catalan number.

Because of all the one-to-one correspondences, we also have:

**Corollary A.10**    *The number of well-formed sequences of $n$ left and $n$ right parentheses, the number of permutations of $n$ objects obtainable by a stack, the number of orchards with $n$ vertices, and the number of binary trees with $n$ vertices are all equal to the $n^{\text{th}}$ Catalan number* Cat$(n)$.

## A.5.3 History

Surprisingly, it was not for any of the preceding questions that Catalan numbers were first discovered, but rather for questions in geometry. Specifically, Cat$(n)$ provides the number of ways to divide a convex polygon with $n+2$ sides into triangles by drawing $n-1$ nonintersecting diagonals. (See Figure A.10.) This problem seems to have been proposed by L. Euler and solved by J. A. v. Segner in 1759. It was then solved again by E. Catalan in 1838. Sometimes, therefore, the resulting numbers are called the *Segner numbers*, but more often they are called *Catalan numbers*.

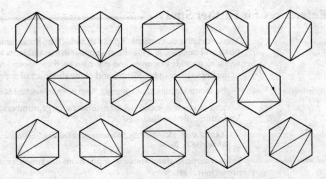

Figure A.10. Triangulations of a hexagon by diagonals

## A.5.4 NUMERICAL RESULTS

We conclude this section with some indications of the sizes of Catalan numbers. The first twenty values are given in Figure A.11.

For larger values of $n$, we can obtain an estimate on the size of the Catalan numbers by using Stirling's approximation. When it is applied to each of the three factorials, and the result is simplified, we obtain

$$\text{Cat}(n) \approx \frac{4^n}{(n+1)\sqrt{\pi n}}.$$

When compared with the exact values in Figure A.11, this estimate gives a good idea of the accuracy of Stirling's approximation. When $n = 10$, for example, the estimated value for the Catalan number is 17,007, compared to the exact value of 16,796.

| $n$ | $\text{Cat}(n)$ | $n$ | $\text{Cat}(n)$ |
| --- | --- | --- | --- |
| 0 | 1 | 10 | 16,796 |
| 1 | 1 | 11 | 58,786 |
| 2 | 2 | 12 | 208,012 |
| 3 | 5 | 13 | 742,900 |
| 4 | 14 | 14 | 2,674,440 |
| 5 | 42 | 15 | 9,694,845 |
| 6 | 132 | 16 | 35,357,670 |
| 7 | 429 | 17 | 129,644,790 |
| 8 | 1,430 | 18 | 477,638,700 |
| 9 | 4,862 | 19 | 1,767,263,190 |

Figure A.11. The first 20 Catalan numbers

# References for Further Study

More extensive discussions of proof by induction, the summation notation, sums of powers of integers, and logarithms appear in many algebra textbooks. These books will also provide examples and exercises on these topics. An excellent discussion of the importance of logarithms and of the subtle art of approximate calculation is

*logarithms*

N. DAVID MERMIN, "Logarithms!", *American Mathematical Monthly* 87 (1980), 1–7.

Several interesting examples of estimating large numbers and thinking of them logarithmically are discussed in

DOUGLAS R. HOFSTADTER, "Metamagical themas," *Scientific American* 246, no. 5 (May 1982), 20–34.

*harmonic numbers*

Several surprising and amusing applications of harmonic numbers are given in the nontechnical article

RALPH BOAS, "Snowfalls and elephants, pop bottles and $\pi$," *Two-Year College Mathematics Journal* 11 (1980), 82–89.

The detailed estimates for both harmonic numbers and factorials (Stirling's approximation) are quoted from KNUTH, Volume 1, pp. 108–111, where detailed proofs may be found. KNUTH, Volume 1, is also an excellent source for further information regarding permutations, combinations, and related topics.

The original reference for Stirling's approximation is

*factorials*

JAMES STIRLING, *Methodus Differentialis* (1730), p. 137.

*combinatorics*

The branch of mathematics concerned with the enumeration of various sets or classes of objects is called *combinatorics*. This science of counting can be introduced on a very simple level, or studied with great sophistication. Two elementary textbooks containing many further developments of the ideas introduced here are

GERALD BERMAN and K. D. FRYER, *Introduction to Combinatorics*, Academic Press, 1972.

ALAN TUCKER, *Applied Combinatorics*, John Wiley, New York, 1980.

*Fibonacci numbers*

The derivation of the Fibonacci numbers will appear in almost any book on combinatorics, as well as in KNUTH, Volume 1, pp. 78–86, who includes some interesting history as well as many related exercises. The appearance of Fibonacci numbers in nature is illustrated in

PETER STEVENS, *Patterns in Nature*, Little, Brown, Boston, 1974.

Many hundreds of other properties of Fibonacci numbers have been and continue to be found; these are often published in the research journal *Fibonacci Quarterly*.

*Catalan numbers*

A derivation of the Catalan numbers (applied to triangulations of convex polygons) appears in the first of the cited books on combinatorics (BERMAN and FRYER, pp. 230–232). KNUTH, Volume 1, pp. 385–406, enumerates several classes of trees, including the Catalan numbers applied to binary trees. A list of 46 references providing both history and applications of the Catalan numbers appears in

W. G. BROWN, "Historical note on a recurrent combinatorial problem," *American Mathematical Monthly* 72 (1965), 973–977.

The following article expounds many other applications of Catalan numbers:

MARTIN GARDNER, "Mathematical games" (regular column), *Scientific American* 234, no. 6 (June, 1976), 120–125.

The original references for the derivation of the Catalan numbers are:

J. A. v. SEGNER, "Enumeratio modorum, quibus figuræ planæ rectilinæ per diago-nales dividuntur in triangula," *Novi Commentarii Academiæ Scientiarum Imperialis Petropolitanæ* 7 (1758–1759), 203–209.

E. CATALAN, "Solution nouvelle de cette question: un polygone étant donné, de combien de manieres peut-on le partager en triangles au moyen de diagonales?", *Journal de Mathématiques Pures et Appliquées* 4 (1839), 91–94.

# B

# Removal of Recursion

*I*N SOME CONTEXTS (*like* FORTRAN 77
*and* COBOL) *it is not possible to use
recursion. This appendix discusses
methods for reformulating algorithms
to remove recursion. First comes a
general method that can always be used,
but is quite complicated and yields a
program whose structure may be obscure.
Next is a simpler transformation that,
although not universally applicable,
covers many important applications. This
transformation yields, as an example, an
efficient nonrecursive version of quicksort.
A nonrecursive version of mergesort is also
developed to illustrate other techniques for
recursion removal. Finally this appendix
studies threaded binary trees, which
provide all the capabilities of ordinary
binary trees without reference to recursion
or stacks.*

**NOTE**

Although the methods developed in this appendix can be used with any higher-level algorithmic language, they are most appropriate in contexts that do not allow recursion. When recursion is available, the techniques described here are unlikely to save enough computer time or space to prove worthwhile or to compensate for the additional programming effort that they demand. Although, for the sake of clarity, the sample programs are written in C, they are designed to facilitate translation into languages not allowing recursion.

*prerequisite*

Section 3.4 (Principles of Recursion) should be studied before consulting this appendix.

# B.1 General Methods for Removing Recursion

Recall from Section 3.4.2 that each call to a subprogram (recursive or not) requires that the subprogram have a storage area where it can keep its local variables, its calling parameters, and its return address (that is, the location of the statement following the one that made the call). In a recursive implementation, the storage areas for subprograms are kept in a stack. Without recursion, one permanent storage area is often reserved for each subprogram, so that an attempt to make a recursive call would change the values in the storage area, thereby destroying the ability of the outer call to complete its work and return properly.

To simulate recursion we must therefore eschew use of the local storage area reserved for the subprogram, and instead set up a stack, in which we shall keep all the local variables, calling parameters, and the return address for the function.

## B.1.1 PRELIMINARY ASSUMPTIONS

It is frequently true that stating a set of rules in the most general possible form requires so many complicated special cases that it obscures the principle ideas. Such is indeed true for recursion removal, so we shall instead develop the methods only for a special case and separately explain how the methods can be applied to all other categories of subprograms.

*direct and indirect recursion*

Recursion is said to be *direct* if a subprogram calls itself; it is *indirect* if there is a sequence of more than one subprogram call that eventually calls the first subprogram, such as when function *A* calls function *B*, which in turn calls *A*. We shall first assume that the recursion is direct, that is, we deal only with a single subprogram that calls itself.

For simplicity we shall, second, assume that we are dealing with a function with no return value (void). This is no real restriction, since any function can be turned into a void function by including one extra calling parameter that will be used to hold the output value. This output parameter is then used instead of the function value in the calling program.

*parameters*

We have used two kinds of parameters for functions: those called by value and those called by address (reference). Parameters called by value are copied into local variables within the function that are discarded when the function returns; parameters called by address exist in the calling program, so that the function refers to them there. The same observations are true of all other variables used by the function: they are either declared locally within the function or exist outside, globally to the function. Parameters and variables in the first category are created anew every time the function is started; hence, before recursion they must be pushed onto a stack so that they can be restored after the function returns. Parameters and variables of the second category must not be stacked, since every time the function changes them it is assumed that the global variables have been changed, and if they were restored to previous values the work of the function would be undone.

If the function has parameters called by address (arrays in C), then we shall assume that the actual parameters are exactly the same in every call to the function. This is again no real restriction, since we can introduce an additional global variable, say, t, and instead of writing P(x) and P(y) for two different calls to the function (where x, y, and t are arrays), we can write

$$copy \ x \ to \ t; \quad P(t); \quad copy \ t \ to \ x;$$

for one and

$$copy \ y \ to \ t; \quad P(t); \quad copy \ t \ to \ y;$$

for the other.

## B.1.2 GENERAL RULES

We now take $P$ to satisfy these assumptions; that is, $P$ is a directly recursive function for which the actual parameters called by address in $P$ are the same in every call to $P$. We can translate $P$ into a nonrecursive function by including instructions in $P$ to accomplish the following tasks. These steps involve insertion of statement labels and goto statements as well as other constructions that will make the result appear messy. At the moment, however, we are proceeding mechanically, essentially playing compiler, and doing these steps is the easiest way to go, given that the original function works properly. Afterward, we can clean and polish the function, making it into a form that will be easier to follow and be more efficient.

*initialization*

1. Declare a stack (or stacks) that will hold all local variables, parameters called by value, and flags to specify whence $P$ was called (if it calls itself from several places). As the first executed statement of $P$, initialize the stack(s) to be empty by setting the counter to 0. The stack(s) and the counter are to be treated as global variables, even though they are declared in $P$.

2. To enable each recursive call to start at the beginning of the original function $P$, the first executable statement of the original $P$ should have a label attached to it.

*recursive call*

The following steps should be done at each place inside $P$ where $P$ calls itself.

3. Make a new statement label $L_i$ (if this is the $i^{th}$ place where $P$ is called recursively) and attach the label to the first statement after the call to $P$ (so that a return can be made to this label).

4. Push the integer $i$ onto the stack. (This will convey on return that $P$ was called from the $i^{th}$ place.)

5. Push all local variables and parameters called by value onto the stack.

6. Set the dummy parameters called by value to the values given in the new call to $P$.

7. Replace the call to $P$ with a goto to the statement label at the start of $P$.

At the end of $P$ (or wherever $P$ returns to its calling program), the following steps should be done.

*return*

8. If the stack is empty then the recursion has finished; make a normal return.

9. Otherwise, pop the stack to restore the values of all local variables and parameters called by value.

10. Pop an integer $i$ from the stack and use this to go to the statement labeled $L_i$. In FORTRAN this can be done with a *computed goto* statement, in BASIC with an on ... goto, and in C with a switch statement.

By mechanically following the preceding steps we can remove direct recursion from any function.

## B.1.3 INDIRECT RECURSION

The case of indirect recursion requires slightly more work, but follows the same idea. Perhaps the conceptually simplest way (which avoids goto's from one function to another) is first to rename variables as needed to ensure that there are no conflicts of names of local variables or parameters between any of the mutually recursive functions, and then write them one after another, not as separate functions, but as sections of a longer one. The foregoing steps can then be carried through for each of the former functions, and the goto's used according to which function is calling which. Separate stacks can be used for different functions, or all the data can be kept on one stack, whichever is more convenient.

## B.1.4 TOWERS OF HANOI

As an illustration of the above method, let us write out a nonrecursive version of the program for the Towers of Hanoi, as it was developed in Section 3.2.4, to which you should compare the following program. This program is obtained as a straightforward application of the rules just formulated. You should compare the result with the original version.

```
/* Move: moves count disks from start to finish using temp for temporary storage */
/* nonrecursive version */
void Move(int count, int start, int finish, int temp)
{
    Stack stack;
    int return_address;          /* selects place to return after recursion       */
    stack.count = 0;             /* Initialize the stack.                          */
L0:                              /* marks the start of the original recursive function */
    if (count > 0) {
```
*first recursive call*
```
        Push(count, start, finish, temp, 1, &stack);
        count--;
        Swap( &finish, &temp);
        goto L0;
L1:                              /* marks the return from the first recursive call   */
        printf("Move a disk from %2d to %2d\n", start, finish);
```
*second recursive call*
```
        Push(count, start, finish, temp, 2, &stack);
        count--;
        Swap( &start, &temp);
        goto L0;
    }
L2:                              /* marks the return from the second recursive call  */
    if (stack.count > 0) {
        Pop( &count, &start, &finish, &temp, &return_address, &stack);
        switch (return_address) {
        case 1 :
            goto L1;
            break;
        case 2 :
            goto L2;
            break;
        }
    }
}
```

This version of function Move uses several auxiliary functions, as follows:

```
void Push(int count, int start, int finish, int temp, int address, Stack *stack)
{
    int i = stack->count;
    stack->entry[i].count = count;
    stack->entry[i].start = start;
    stack->entry[i].finish = finish;
    stack->entry[i].temp = temp;
    stack->entry[i].address = address;
    stack->count++;
}
```

```
void Pop(int *count, int *start, int *finish, int *temp,
    int *address, Stack *stack)
{
    int i = – – stack->count;
    *count = stack->entry[i].count;
    *start = stack->entry[i].start;
    *finish = stack->entry[i].finish;
    *temp = stack->entry[i].temp;
    *address = stack->entry[i].address;
}
void Swap(int *x, int *y)
{
    int tmp;
    tmp = *x;
    *x = *y;
    *y = tmp;
}
```

As you can see, a short and easy recursive function has turned into a complicated mess. The function even contains branches that jump from outside into the middle of the block controlled by an if statement, an occurrence that should always be regarded as very poor style, if not an actual error. Fortunately, much of the complication results only from the mechanical way in which the translation was done. We can now make several simplifications.

Note what happens when the function recursively returns from a call at the second place (return_address == 2). After the stack is popped it branches to statement L2, which does nothing except run down to pop the stack again. Thus what was popped off the stack the first time is lost, so that there was no need to push it on in the first place. In the original recursive function, the second recursive call to Move occurs at the end of the function. At the end of any function its local variables are discarded; thus there was no need to preserve all the local variables before the second recursive call to Move, since they will be discarded when it returns in any case.

*tail recursion*      This situation is ***tail recursion***, and from this example we see graphically the unnecessary work that tail recursion can induce. Before translating any program to nonrecursive form, we should be careful to remember Section 3.4.3 and remove the tail recursion.

## B.1.5 FURTHER SIMPLIFICATIONS

While we are considering simplifications, we can make a more general observation about local variables and parameters called by value. In a function being transformed to nonrecursive form, these will need to be pushed onto the stack before a recursive call only when they have both been set up before the call and will be used again after the call, with the assumption that they have unchanged values. Some variables may have been used only in sections of the function not involving recursive calls, so there is no need to preserve their values across a recursive call.

For example, the index variable of a for loop might be used to control loops either before or after a recursive call or even both before and after, but if the index variable is initialized when a loop starts after the call, there is no need to preserve it on the stack. On the other hand, if the recursive call is in the middle of a for loop, then the index variable must be stacked. By applying these principles we can simplify the resulting program and conserve stack space, and thereby perform optimizations of the program that a recursive compiler would likely not do, since it would probably preserve all local variables on the stack.

## B.2 Recursion Removal by Folding

### B.2.1 PROGRAM SCHEMATA

We can now further simplify our method for removing recursion: a function that includes a recursive call from only one place will not need to include flags to show where to return, since there is only one possibility. In many cases, we can also rearrange parts of the program to clarify it by removing goto statements.

After removal of the tail recursion, the second recursive version of the function Move for the Towers of Hanoi, as given in Section 3.4.3, is a program of the general schema:

*recursive schema*

```
void P(/* parameters */)              /* recursive version                       */
{
    /* local declarations to be inserted here */
    while (!termination) {
        Block A;          /* first part of program; empty for example  */
        P;                /* only recursive call to function itself     */
        Block B;          /* next part of program                       */
    }
    Block C;              /* final part of program; empty for our example */
}
```

Our general rules presented in the last section will translate this schema into the nonrecursive form:

*first nonrecursive schema*

```
void P(/* parameters */)              /* preliminary nonrecursive version         */
{
    /* local declarations to be inserted here */
    /* Declaration of stack goes here. */
    Set stack to be empty;
L0:
    while (!termination) {
        Block A;          /* first part of program                     */
        Push data onto stack and change parameters;
        goto L0;
```

```
L1 :
        Block B;                    /* next part of program          */
    }
    Block C;                        /* final part of program         */
    if (stack not empty) {
        Pop data from stack;
        goto L1;
    }
}
```

If we terminate the while loop after the line changing the parameters, then we can eliminate the goto L0. Doing this will require that when Block B is complete, we go back to the while statement. By moving the part of the schema that pops the stack to the front of Block B, we no longer need the other goto. On the first time through, the stack will be empty, so the popping section will be skipped. These steps can all be accomplished by enclosing the function in a statement

$$\text{do } \{ \quad \dots \quad \} \text{ while (stack not empty);}$$

We thus obtain:

*folded nonrecursive*
*schema*

```
void P(/* parameters */)          /* nonrecursive version          */
{
    /* local declarations to be inserted here */
    /* Declaration of stack goes here. */
    Set stack to be empty;
    do {
        if (stack not empty) {
            Pop data from stack;
            Block B;                /* next part of program          */
        }
        while (! termination) {
            Block A;                /* first part of program         */
            Push data onto stack and change parameters;
        }
        Block C;                    /* final part of program         */
    } while (stack not empty);
}
```

This rearrangement is essentially "folding" the loop around the recursive call. Thus the part coming after the recursive call now appears at the top of the program instead of the bottom.

### B.2.2 PROOF OF THE TRANSFORMATION

Since deriving the above rearrangement has required several steps, let us now pause to provide a formal verification that the changes we have made are correct.

**Theorem B.1**    *The recursive function P of the form given previously and the folded, nonrecursive version of P both accomplish exactly the same steps.*

To prove the theorem, we shall trace through the recursive and the folded non-recursive versions of $P$ and show that they perform exactly the same sequence of blocks $A$, $B$, and $C$. The remaining parts of both versions do only bookkeeping, so that if the same sequence of the blocks is done, then the same task will be accomplished. In tracing through the programs, it will help to note that there are two ways to call a recursive function: either from outside, or from within itself. We

*external and internal calls*

refer to these as ***external*** and ***internal*** calls, respectively. These two forms of call are indistinguishable for the recursive version, but are quite different for the non-recursive form. An external call starts at the beginning of the function and finishes at the end. An internal call starts after the data are pushed onto the stack and the parameters are changed and finishes when the line is reached that pops the stack.

*proof by induction: initial case*

We shall prove the theorem by using mathematical induction on the height of the recursion tree corresponding to a given call to $P$. The starting point is the case when $P$ is called with the termination condition already true, so that no recursion takes place (the height of the tree is 0). In this case the recursive version performs Block $C$ once, and nothing else is done. For the nonrecursive version we consider the two kinds of calls separately. If the call is external, then the stack is empty, so that the if statement does nothing, and the while statement also does nothing since the termination condition is assumed to be true. Thus only Block $C$ is done, and since the stack is empty, the function terminates. Now suppose that the call to $P$ is internal. Then $P$ has arrived at the line that pushes the stack (so it is not empty). Since the termination condition is true, the while loop now terminates, and Block $C$ is done. Since the stack is not empty, the do ... while loop next proceeds to the line that pops the stack, and this line corresponds to returning from the internal call. Thus in every case when the recursion tree has height 0, only Block $C$ is done once.

*induction step*

For the induction step we consider a call to $P$ where the recursion tree has height $k > 0$, and by induction we assume that all calls whose trees have height less than $k$ will translate correctly into nonrecursive form. Let $r$ be the number of times that the while loop iterates in the call to $P$ under consideration.

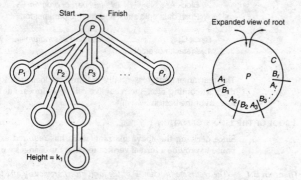

**Figure B.1. Traversal of a recursion tree**

This situation is illustrated in the sample recursion tree shown in Figure B.1. Each node in this tree should be considered as expanded to show the sequence of blocks being performed at each stage. The tree also, of course, shows when the stack will be pushed and popped: Consider traversing the tree by walking around it in a counterclockwise direction following each edge both down and up and going around each node. It is precisely as a branch is traversed going downward that the stack is pushed, and as we return up a branch the stack is popped.

The recursive version thus performs a sequence of blocks and calls:

$$A_1 \quad P_1 \quad B_1 \qquad A_2 \quad P_2 \quad B_2 \quad \ldots \quad A_r \quad P_r \quad B_r \quad C$$

where the subscripts specify only the iteration at which the block or call is done. The calls to $P$ denoted $P_1, P_2, \ldots, P_r$ all have recursion trees of heights strictly less than $k$ (at least one has height exactly $k - 1$), so by induction hypothesis the sequence of blocks embedded in these calls will be the same for the recursive and nonrecursive versions (provided that we can show that the sequence of outer blocks is the same, so that the calling parameters will be the same). In tracing through the nonrecursive function, we again consider the two kinds of calls separately.

*external call*    If the call is external, then the stack is initially empty, so the while loop begins iterating. First Block $A$ is done, and then an internal call to $P$ is started by pushing the stack. The corresponding return occurs when the stack is eventually popped and becomes empty again. The sequence of blocks and calls occurring in the meantime all correspond to the recursive call $P_1$, and by induction hypothesis correspond correctly to the recursive version. When the stack is popped and empty, then Block $B$ is done and we reach the while statement to begin the second iteration. The program thus continues, with each iteration starting with Block $A$, then an internal call, then Block $B$. After $r$ iterations the total sequence of blocks will have been the same as in the recursive version, and therefore the termination condition will become true for the first time, and so the while loop will be skipped. Block $C$ is then done, and since the stack is empty, the function terminates. Hence the total sequence of blocks is the same as in the recursive version.

*internal call*    Finally consider that the call (with tree of height $k$) is internal. The call then begins where the stack is pushed, so it then has $s > 0$ sets of data. Next Block $A$ is done, and another internal call instituted, that includes all steps until the stack is popped and again has exactly $s$ sets of data. Next Block $B$ is done, and the iterations continue as in the previous case, except that now the returns from internal calls that interest us are those leaving $s$ sets of data on the stack. After $r$ iterations the termination condition becomes true, so the while loop terminates, and Block $C$ is done. The stack has $s > 0$ entries, so the function now moves to the line that pops the stack, which constitutes the return from the internal call that we have been tracing. Thus in every case the sequence of blocks done is the same, and
*end of proof*    the proof of the theorem is complete.

## B.2.3 TOWERS OF HANOI: THE FINAL VERSION

With the method of folding that we have now developed, we can now write our final nonrecursive version of the program for the Towers of Hanoi, a version that is much clearer than the first nonrecursive one, although still not as natural as the recursive program.

```
/* Move: moves count disks from start to finish using temp for temporary storage */
/* folded nonrecursive version */
void Move(int count, int start, int finish, int temp)
{
    Stack stack;
    stack.count = 0;
    do {
        if (stack.count != 0) {
            Pop( &count, &start, &finish, &temp, &stack);
            printf("Move a disk from %2d to %2d\n", start, finish);
            count--;
            Swap( &start, &temp);
        }
        while (count > 0) {
            Push(count, start, finish, temp, &stack);
            count--;
            Swap( &finish, &temp);
        }
    } while (stack.count > 0);
}
```

**Exercises B.2**

**E1.** Remove the tail recursion from the algorithm for preorder traversal of a linked binary tree (Section 9.1.3). Show that the resulting program fits the schema of Theorem B.1, and thereby devise a nonrecursive algorithm, using a stack, that will traverse a binary tree in preorder.

**E2.** Repeat Exercise E1 for inorder traversal.

**E3.** Devise a nonrecursive algorithm, using one or more stacks, that will traverse a linked binary tree in postorder. Why is this project more complicated than the preceding two exercises?

**E4.** Consider a pair of mutually recursive functions P and Q that have the following schemata.

```
void P(void)
{
/* local declarations for P */
    while (!termP) {
        Block A;
        Q();
        Block B;
    }
    Block C;
}
```

```
void Q(void)
{
/* local declarations for Q */
    while (!termQ) {
        Block X;
        P();
        Block Y;
    }
    Block Z;
}
```

Assume that there are no conflicts of names between local variables or dummy parameters in P and in Q.

    **(a)** Write a nonrecursive function made up from the blocks in P and Q that will perform the same action as a call to P.

    **(b)** Prove that your translation is correct in a way similar to the proof of Theorem B.1.

**Programming Project B.2**

**P1.** Show that the Eight Queens program from Section 3.3 has the schema needed for Theorem B.1, and apply folding to remove the recursion. Run both the recursive and nonrecursive versions to see which is faster.

# B.3 Nonrecursive Quicksort

Because of its importance as an efficient sorting algorithm for contiguous lists, we shall devise a nonrecursive version of quicksort, as an application of the methods of the last section. Before proceeding, you should briefly review Section 7.8, from which we take all the notation.

    The first observation to make about the original recursive function Sort written for quicksort is that its second call is tail recursion, which can easily be removed. We thus obtain the following intermediate form.

*tail recursion removed*

```
/* Sort: removed tail recursion */
void Sort(List *list, int low, int high)
{
    int pivotloc;
    while (low < high) {
        pivotloc = Partition(list, low, high);
        Sort(list, low, pivotloc − 1);
        low = pivotloc + 1;
    }
}
```

This function is in precisely the form covered by Theorem B.1, so it can be folded to remove the recursive call. The only variables needed after the recursive call are low and pivotloc, so only these two variables need to be stacked.

    Before we proceed with the program transformation, let us note that, in doing the sorting, it really makes no difference which half of the list is sorted first. The calling parameters to be stacked mark the bounds of sublists yet to be sorted. It turns out that it is better to put the longer sublist on the stack and immediately sort the shorter one. The longer sublist along with the pivot will account for at least half of the items. Hence at each level of recursion, the number of items remaining to be sorted is reduced by half or more, and therefore the number of items on the stack is guaranteed to be no more than $\lg n$. In this way, even though quicksort has a worst-case running time that is $O(n^2)$, the extra space needed for its stack can be guaranteed not to exceed $O(\log n)$.

*stack space*

This decision to stack the larger sublist at each stage does not affect the application of folding, but only introduces an if statement at the appropriate point. We thus arrive at the following nonrecursive version of quicksort:

```
#define MAXSTACK 20              /* allows sorting up to 1,000,000 items         */

/* NRQuickSort: nonrecursive quicksort */

void NRQuickSort(List *list)
{
int low, high;                   /* bounds of list being sorted                  */
int pivotpos;
int lowstack[MAXSTACK];          /* Declare two arrays for the stack.            */
int highstack[MAXSTACK];
int nstack = 0;

    low = 0;
    high = list->count − 1;
    do {
      if (nstack > 0) {          /* Pop the stack.                               */
         nstack−−;
         low = lowstack[nstack];
         high = highstack[nstack];
      }
        while (low < high) {
           pivotpos = Partition(list, low, high)·
           /* Push larger sublist onto stack, and do smaller. */
           if (pivotpos − low < high − pivotpos) {
              /* Stack right sublist and do left. */
              if (nstack >= MAXSTACK)
                 Error("overflow");
              lowstack[nstack] = pivotpos + 1;
              highstack[nstack] = high;
              nstack++;
              high = pivotpos − 1;

           } else {
              /* Stack left sublist and do right. */
              if (nstack >= MAXSTACK)
                 Error("overflow");
              lowstack[nstack] = low;
              highstack[nstack] = pivotpos − 1;
              nstack++;
              low = pivotpos + 1;
           }
        }
    } while (nstack != 0);
}
```

# B.4 Stackless Recursion Removal: Mergesort

This section discusses point 5 of the guidelines for using recursion in Section 3.4.5; that is, the translation of a program into nonrecursive form by exploiting the regularity of its recursion tree, thereby avoiding the need to use a stack. The program we develop in this section is not likely to prove a great improvement over the recursive version, since the stack space saved is only $O(\lg n)$. It is primarily a matter of taste which version to use.

Mergesort is one of the most efficient sorting methods we have studied; it and heapsort are the only ones we considered for which the number of comparisons in the worst case, as well as in the average case, is $O(n \log n)$. Mergesort is therefore a good choice for large sorting problems when time constraints are critical. The recursion used in mergesort, however, may entail some overhead costs that can be avoided by rewriting mergesort in nonrecursive form.

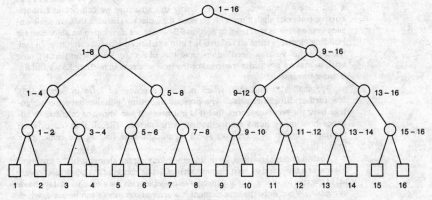

**Figure B.2.** Recursion tree for mergesort, $n = 16$

Let us begin by considering the tree of recursive calls that mergesort will make in sorting a list; this tree for $n = 16$ is drawn in Figure B.2. In the recursive formulation of mergesort, we begin at the root of the tree and divide the list in half. We then look at the left list (move to the left subtree) and repeat the division. Afterward, we look at the right sublist and move to the right subtree. In other words,

*Recursion in mergesort performs a preorder traversal of the tree.*

Now let us determine the order in which the merges are actually done. No sublists are actually merged until the list has been divided all the way down to sublists of one element each. The first two one-element sublists, represented as the leftmost two leaves in the tree, are then merged. Then the next two one-element sublists are merged, and afterward the resulting two-element sublists are merged into a four-element sublist. In this way the process continues building small sublists into larger ones. In fact,

> *The order in which the merges are actually done constitutes a postorder traversal of the tree.*

*traversal orders*

Translating mergesort into nonrecursive form amounts to rewriting the algorithm to perform a postorder traversal of the tree instead of a preorder traversal. We could, of course, use a stack to assist with the postorder traversal, but instead we shall take advantage of the fact that, when $n$ is a power of 2, the tree has a completely symmetric structure. Using this structure we can obtain a nonrecursive traversal algorithm with no need for a stack. The idea that we shall employ is the same as that used in Section 9.3, where we developed an algorithm for building elements from an ordered list into a balanced binary search tree. In fact, the algorithm we now need differs from that of Section 9.3 only in that we now wish to make a postorder traversal of the tree, whereas in Section 9.3 we did an inorder traversal.

We shall also find that, when $n$ is not a power of 2 (as in Section 9.3), few further difficulties arise. The present algorithm will also have the advantage over the recursive form, that it is not necessary to know or calculate in advance how many items are in the list being sorted. (Recall that our original recursive version of mergesort spent significant time finding the center of a linked list.)

To design our algorithm, let us imagine receiving the elements of the unsorted list one at a time, and as each element arrives, let us continue the postorder traversal of the tree by doing as many merges as possible with the elements that we have available. When only the first element has arrived, no merge can be done; when the second one comes, the first two sublists of size 1 will be merged. Element 3 does not induce any merges, but element 4 is first compared with element 3, and the resulting two-element sublist is then merged with the first two-element sublist. Continuing in this way, we see that element 5 does not induce any merge, element 6 induces only 1, element 7 none, and element 8 induces 3 merges. Further study of the tree will convince you that:

> *When mergesort processes the item in position $c$ of its input, then the number of times that sublists are merged before proceeding to the next element is exactly the highest power of 2 that divides $c$.*

In writing our algorithm we shall, as in Section 7.7, consider only a version sorting linked lists. In this way, we can use the same function presented in Section 7.7 to merge two sorted sublists, and we need not consider the auxiliary space or complicated algorithms needed to accomplish merging in contiguous lists.

As we progress through the tree, we shall find that at various stages several sublists will have been constructed that have not yet been merged with each other. We shall keep track of these sublists by using an auxiliary array of pointers. At any point in the process, there can be at most one such sublist corresponding to each level in the tree; hence the size of this array grows only logarithmically with the length of the list being sorted, and the amount of additional memory that it requires is inconsequential.

The main part of our algorithm can now be described completely: we shall traverse the linked list of input and use the function Power2(c) (taken from Section 9.3) to determine the number mergecount of times that sublists will be merged. We do these merges using the sublists whose headers are in the auxiliary array. After the appropriate merges are made, a pointer to the resulting sorted sublist is placed in location mergecount of the auxiliary array.

It now remains only for us to describe what must be done to complete the sort after the end of the input list is reached. If $n$ is an exact power of 2, then the list will be completely sorted at this point. Otherwise, it turns out that

*At the end of receiving input, the sorted sublists that must still be merged occupy precisely the same relative positions in the auxiliary array as those occupied by the nonzero digits in the representation of the counter c as a binary integer.*

*proof by induction*

We can prove this observation by mathematical induction. When $n = 1$ it is certainly true. In fact, when $n$ is any exact power of 2, $n = 2^k$, the first part of the algorithm will have merged all the items as received into a single sorted sublist, and the integer $n$ when written in binary has a single 1 in the digit position $k$ corresponding to the power of 2, and 0's elsewhere. Now consider the algorithm for an arbitrary value of $n$, and let $2^k$ be the largest power of 2 such that $2^k \le n$. The binary representation of $n$ contains a 1 in position $k$ (the count of digits starts at 0), which is its largest nonzero digit. The remaining digits form the binary representation of $m = n - 2^k$. When the first $2^k$ items have been received, the algorithm will have merged them into a single sublist, a pointer to which is in position $k$ of the auxiliary array, corresponding properly to the digit 1 in position $k$ of the binary representation of $n$. As the remaining $m$ items are processed, they will, by induction hypothesis, produce sublists with pointers in positions corresponding to 1's in the binary representation of $m$, which, as we have observed, is the

*end of proof*

same as the remaining positions in the binary representation of $n$. Hence the proof is complete.

With this background we can now produce a formal description of the algorithm. The notational conventions are those of Section 7.7.

```
#define MAXLOG 20                      /* allows over 1,000,000 entries in list      */
/* NRMergeSort: nonrecursive mergesort */
void NRMergeSort(List *list)
{
    ListNode *sublist[MAXLOG + 1];
    ListNode *p;                       /* first unsorted item from list             */
    ListNode *q;                       /* a (partial) merged list                   */
    int i;
    int c = 0;                         /* counter (index) of current item           */
    int mergecount;                    /* largest power of 2 dividing c             */
    int d;                             /* a digit in binary representation of c     */
    for (i = 0; i <= MAXLOG; i++)
        sublist[i] = NULL;
    p = list->head;
    while (p) {                        /* Traverse the unsorted list.               */
        c++;
        mergecount = Power2(c);
        q = p;
        p = p->next;
        q->next = NULL;                /* Split off q as a sublist of size 1.       */
        for (i = 1; i < mergecount; i++)
            q = Merge(q, sublist[i]);
        sublist[mergecount] = q;
    }
    /* At this point, the list has been traversed. The unmerged sublists correspond to
       the 1's in the binary representation of the counter c. Note that p == NULL at this
       point. */
    mergecount = 0;
    while (c != 0) {
        d = c % 2;                     /* d is a binary digit in c.                 */
        c /= 2;
        mergecount++;
        if (d != 0)
            if (p == NULL)             /* This only occurs for first nonzero d.     */
                p = sublist[mergecount];
            else
                p = Merge(p, sublist[mergecount]);
    }
    list->head = p;
}
```

---

**Exercise B.4**   **E1.** The algorithm for the Towers of Hanoi has a completely symmetric recursion tree. Design a nonrecursive program for this problem that uses no stacks, lists, or arrays.

**Programming**      **P1.** Run the nonrecursive mergesort of this section, and compare timings with
**Project B.4**      those of the recursive version of Section 7.7.

# B.5 Threaded Binary Trees

Because of the importance of linked binary trees, it is worthwhile to develop non-recursive algorithms to manipulate them, and to study the time and space requirements of these algorithms. We shall find that, by changing the NULL links in a binary tree to special links called *threads*, it is possible to perform traversals, insertions, and deletions without using either a stack or recursion.

## B.5.1 INTRODUCTION

First, let us note that the second recursive call in the ordinary recursive versions of both preorder and inorder traversal of a linked binary tree is tail recursion, and so can be removed easily, with no need to set up a stack. From now on we shall assume that this has been done, so that preorder and inorder traversal each involve only one recursive call. The situation with postorder traversal is more complicated, so we shall postpone its study to the end of the section.

*use of stack*        Removal of the remaining recursive call in preorder or inorder traversal does at first appear to require a stack. Let us see how many entries can possibly be on the stack. Since the functions use no local variables, the only value to be stacked is the calling parameter, which is a (simple, one-word) pointer variable, a pointer to the current position in the tree. After the pointer has been stacked, the algorithm moves to the left subtree as it calls itself. (Note that when the algorithm later moves to the right subtree it need only change the pointer, not push it onto the stack, since the tail recursion has been removed.) The pointers stop being stacked and the recursion terminates when a leaf is reached. Thus the total number of pointers that may appear on the stack is the number of left branches taken in a path from the root to a leaf of the tree, plus one more since a pointer to the leaf itself is stacked. The algorithms could easily be rewritten to avoid stacking this last pointer.

Since most binary trees are fairly bushy, the number of pointers on the stack is likely to be $O(\log n)$ if the tree has $n$ nodes. Since $\lg n$ is generally small in comparison to $n$, the space taken by the stack is usually small in comparison to the space needed for the nodes themselves. Thus if it is reasonable to assume that the tree is quite bushy, then it is probably not worth the effort to pursue sophisticated methods to save space, and either the recursive algorithms or their straightforward translation to nonrecursive form with a stack will likely be satisfactory.

*stack space*         It is, on the other hand, certainly possible that a binary tree will have few right branches and many left branches. In fact, the tree that is a chain moving to the left will put pointers to every one of its nodes onto the stack before working out of the recursion. Hence, if we wish to ensure that the traversal algorithms will never fail for want of space, we must be careful to reserve stack space for $n + 1$ pointers if there are $n$ nodes in the binary tree. (Keeping the recursion for the system to handle will, of course, not help at all, since the system must still find space for the stack, and will likely also use space for stacking return addresses, etc., and so will need more than $n + 1$ words of memory.) If we are working with a large binary tree that takes almost all the memory, then finding extra stack space can be a problem.

Whenever you run out of some resource, a good question to ask yourself is whether some of that same resource is being left unused elsewhere. In the current problem, the answer is *yes*. For all the leaves of any binary tree, both the left and right pointers are NULL, and often for some of the other nodes one of the pointers is NULL. In fact, the following easy observation shows that there are exactly enough NULL pointers in the tree to take care of the stack.

***Lemma B.2***    *A linked binary tree with n nodes, $n \geq 0$, has exactly $n + 1$ NULL links.*

***Proof***    We first note that each node of the tree contains two pointers, so there are $2n$ pointers altogether in a tree with $n$ nodes, plus one more in the header. There is exactly one pointer to each of the $n$ nodes of the tree (coming from the parent of each node except the root, and from the header to the root). Thus the number of NULL pointers is exactly

$$(2n + 1) - n = n + 1.$$

With this result, we could devise an algorithm to use the space occupied by NULL pointers and traverse the tree with no need for auxiliary space for a stack.

We shall not solve the problem this way, however, because of one danger in such a method. If the program should happen to crash in the middle of traversing the binary tree, having changed various pointers within the tree to reflect a (now-forgotten) current situation, it may later be difficult or impossible to recover the structure of the original tree. We might thereby lose all our data, with far more serious consequences than the original crash.

*goal*    What we want, then, is a way to set up the pointers within the binary tree permanently so that the NULL pointers will be replaced with information that will make it easy to traverse the tree (in either preorder or inorder) without setting up a stack or using recursion.

Let us see how far ordinary inorder traversal can go before it must pop the stack. It begins by moving left as many times as it can, while the left subtree is not empty. Then it visits the node and moves to the right subtree (if nonempty) and repeats the process, moving to the left again. Only when it has just visited a node and finds that its right subtree is empty must it pop the stack to see where to go next. In C we could write

```
p = root;                    /* pointer that moves through the tree        */
while (p) {
    while (p->left)
        p = p->left;
    Visit(p);
    p = p->right;
}
```

When this sequence of instructions is complete, we have p = NULL, and we must find some way to locate the next node under inorder traversal.

## B.5.2 THREADS

In a *right-threaded binary tree* each NULL right link is replaced by a special link to the successor of that node under inorder traversal, called a *right thread*. Using right threads we shall find it easy to do an inorder traversal of the tree, since we need only follow either an ordinary link or a thread to find the next node to visit. For later applications, we shall also find it useful to put *left threads* into the tree, which means to replace each NULL left link by a special link to the predecessor of the node under inorder traversal. The result is called a *fully threaded binary tree*. The word *fully* is omitted if there is no danger of confusion. Figure B.3 shows a threaded binary tree, where the threads are shown in color.

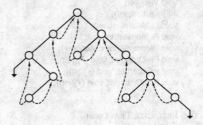

Figure B.3. A fully threaded binary tree

Note that two threads have been left as NULL in the diagram, the left thread from the first node under inorder traversal, and the right thread from the last node. We shall leave these two pointers as NULL. Another convention that is sometimes useful is to let these two nodes have threads pointing back to the root of the tree. This convention sometimes makes termination conditions slightly more complicated, but sometimes allows easier repetition of the full traversal of the tree, if that is desired.

*implementation*    In implementing threads in a programming language, we must have some way to determine whether each link is a true pointer to a nonempty subtree, or a thread to some node higher in the tree. With C structures, the usual way to do this would be to attach to each pointer a Boolean variable (that need only take one bit) that specifies if the pointer is a link or a thread.

In some environments, however, we can represent threads even more compactly. Nonrecursive traversal is most commonly used in nonrecursive languages, and in this case the nodes are usually represented as entries of arrays, and the pointers are indices (cursors) within the arrays. Thus true links are represented as positive integers, and the NULL link is usually represented as 0. We can then easily represent threads as negative integers, so that if a pointer variable $p$ is less than 0, then it is a thread to the node at $-p$.

For the remainder of this section we shall adopt this positive-negative convention, and use the implementation of linked lists with cursors in a workspace array that was developed in Section 5.5. This decision is implemented in the following declarations (tree.h), for which the constant MAX gives the size (in nodes) of the workspace ws.

```
#define MAXNODES 50
typedef int Key;
typedef struct node {
    Key key;
    /* Other information fields go here. */
    int left, right;
} Node;
extern Node ws[ ];          /* workspace for linked trees            */
extern int root;            /* root of the threaded binary search tree */
typedef enum action {GOLEFT, GORIGHT, VISITNODE} Action;
void Visit(int);
int Insert(int, int);
void LeftInsert(int, int);
void RightInsert(int, int);
void Parent(int, int *, Action *);
void PreOrder(int, void (*)(int));
void InOrder(int, void (*)(int));
void PostOrder(int, void (*)(int));
```

## B.5.3 INORDER AND PREORDER TRAVERSAL

First, let us see how easy it now is to traverse a threaded binary tree in inorder.

```
/* Inorder: inorder traversal of a threaded binary tree */
void Inorder(int p)
{
    if (p > 0)                  /* Find the first (leftmost) node for inorder traversal. */
        while (ws[p].left > 0)
            p = ws[p].left;
    while (p) {                 /* Now visit the node, and go to its successor.         */
        Visit(p);
        p = ws[p].right;
        if (p < 0)              /* If this is a thread link, it gives the successor.    */
            p = -p;
        else if (p > 0)         /* Otherwise, move as far left as possible.             */
            while (ws[p].left > 0)
                p = ws[p].left;
        /* If neither section is done, p == 0 and the traversal is done. */
    }
}
```

As you can see, this algorithm is somewhat longer than the original algorithm for inorder traversal. A direct translation of the original algorithm into nonrecursive form would be of comparable length and would, of course, require additional space for a stack that is not needed when we use threaded trees.

It is a surprising fact that preorder traversal of an inorder threaded tree is just as easy to write:

```
/* Preorder: preorder traversal of a threaded binary tree */
void Preorder(int p)
{
  while (p > 0) {
    Visit(p);
    if (ws[p].left > 0)
      p = ws[p].left;
    else if (ws[p].right > 0)
      p = ws[p].right;
    else {                      /* Otherwise, p is a leaf. We take its right thread,   */
      while (ws[p].right < 0)   /* which will return to a node already visited,        */
        p = -ws[p].right;       /* and move to the right again.                        */
      p = ws[p].right;
    }
  }
}
```

## B.5.4 INSERTION IN A THREADED TREE

To use threaded trees, we must be able to set them up. Thus we need an algorithm to add a node to the tree. We first consider the case where a node is added to the left of a node that previously had an empty left subtree. The other side is similar. Since the node we are considering has empty left subtree, its left link is a thread to its predecessor under inorder traversal, which will now become the predecessor of the new node being added. The successor of the new node will, of course, be the node to which it is attached on the left. This situation is illustrated in Figure B.4 and implemented in the following function.

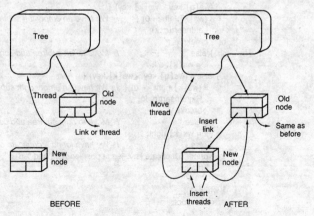

Figure B.4. Adding a node to a threaded binary tree

```
/* LeftInsert: inserts the node at q as the left subtree of the node at p */
void LeftInsert(int q, int p)
{
   if (ws[p].left > 0) {
      Error("non-empty left subtree");
   } else {
      ws[q].left = ws[p].left;
      ws[q].right = -p;
      ws[p].left = q;
   }
}
```

The general insertion algorithm for a threaded binary search tree can now be formulated like the nonrecursive insertion function developed in Section 9.2.3.

```
/* Insert:
    Pre:  q is a node to insert. root is a threaded tree.
    Post: q has been inserted and the root of the tree is returned. */
int Insert(int q, int root)
{
int k;
   if (root == 0) {                  /* Insert into an empty tree.                    */
      ws[q].left = 0;
      ws[q].right = 0;
      return q;
   } else {               /* Look for the place for the new key, starting at the root. */
      k = root;
      do {
         if (ws[q].key < ws[k].key) {
            if (ws[k].left <= 0) {    /* We have an empty left subtree, insert the node.  */
               LeftInsert(q, k);
               break;
            } else                    /* Move to left subtree and continue search.     */
               k = ws[k].left;
         } else if (ws[q].key > ws[k].key) {
            if (ws[k].right <= 0) {  /* We have an empty right subtree, insert the node. */
               RightInsert(q, k);
               break;
            } else                    /* Move to right subtree and continue search.    */
               k = ws[k].right;
         } else {                     /* We have found a duplicate of the new key.     */
            printf("Duplicate key: %d at positions %d and %d\n", ws[q].key, q, k);
            break;
         }
      } while (1);
      return root;
   }
}
```

As you can see, this algorithm is only a little more complicated than that required to add a node to an unthreaded tree. Similarly, an algorithm to delete a node (which is left as an exercise) is not much more difficult than before. It is only in the traversal algorithms where the additional cases lengthen the programs. Whether the saving of stack space is worth the programming time needed to use threads depends, as usual, on the circumstances. The differences in running time will usually be insignificant; it is only the saving in stack space that need be considered. Even this is lessened if the device of using negative indices to represent threads is not available.

Finally, we should mention the possibility of shared subtrees. In some applications a subtree of a binary tree is sometimes processed separately from other actions taken on the entire tree. With ordinary binary trees this can be done easily by setting the root of the subtree to the appropriate node of the larger tree. With threads, however, traversal of the smaller tree will fail to terminate properly, since after all nodes of the subtree have been traversed, there may still be a thread pointing to some successor node in the larger tree. Hence threads are often better avoided when processing complicated data structures with shared substructures.

## B.5.5 POSTORDER TRAVERSAL

Traversal of a threaded binary tree in postorder, using neither recursion nor stacks, is somewhat more complicated than the other traversal orders. The reason is that postorder traversal investigates each node several times. When a node is first reached, its left subtree is traversed. The traversal then returns to the node in order to traverse its right subtree. Only when it returns to the node the third time does it actually visit the node. Finally it must find the parent of the node to continue the traversal.

We can obtain an initial outline of an algorithm by following these steps. We shall use the enumerated type

```
typedef enum action {GOLEFT, GORIGHT, VISITNODE} Action;
```

to indicate the stage of processing the node in the following outline.

*outline*

```
void PostOrder(void)
{
    while (not all nodes have been visited)
        switch (nextaction) {
        case GOLEFT : Traverse the left subtree;
                Return to the node;
                nextaction = GORIGHT;  break;
        case GORIGHT : Traverse the right subtree;
                Return to the node;
                nextaction = VISITNODE;  break;
        case VISITNODE : Visit the node;
                Find the parent of the node;
                Set nextaction appropriately for the parent;  break;
        }
}
```

Note that this algorithm is written so that it performs three iterations for each node. In this way, at every point we need only know the value of nextaction to determine at what stage of the traversal we are. Had we written the three stages sequentially within a single iteration of the loop, then we would need to use recursion or a stack to determine our status after completing the traversal of a subtree.

Closer consideration, however, will show that even this outline does not yet succeed in avoiding the need for a stack. As we traverse a subtree, we shall continually change nextaction as we process each node of the subtree. Hence we must use some method to determine the previous value as we return to the original node. We shall first postpone this problem, however, by assuming the existence of an auxiliary function Parent that will determine the parent of a node and the new value of nextaction.

With these assumptions we arrive at the following function.

```
/* PostOrder: postorder traversal of binary tree with (inorder) threads */
void PostOrder(int p)
{
    Action_type nextaction;

    nextaction = GOLEFT;
    while (p)
        switch (nextaction) {

            /* Traverse the left subtree if it is nonempty. */
            case GOLEFT :
                if (ws[p].left > 0)
                    p = ws[p].left;
                else
                    nextaction = GORIGHT;
                break;

            /* Traverse the right subtree if it is nonempty. */
            case GORIGHT :
                if (ws[p].right > 0) {
                    p = ws[p].right;
                    nextaction = GOLEFT;
                } else
                    nextaction = VISITNODE;
                break;

            /* Visit the node and find its parent. */
            case VISITNODE :
                Visit(p);
                Parent(p, &p, &nextaction);
                break;
        }
}
```

Finally, we must solve the problem of locating the parent of a node and determining the proper value of the code, without resorting to stacks or recursion. The solution to this problem, fortunately, already appears in the outline obtained earlier. If we have just finished traversing a left subtree, then we should now set nextaction to GORIGHT; if we have traversed a right subtree, then nextaction becomes VISITNODE. We can determine which of these cases has occurred by using the threads, and at the same time we can find the node that is the parent node of the last one visited. If we are in a left subtree, then we find the parent by moving right as far as possible in the subtree, then take a right thread. If the left child of this node is the original one, then we know that we have found the parent and are in a left subtree. Otherwise, we must do the similar steps through left branches to find the parent. This process is illustrated in Figure B.5.

*finding the parent*

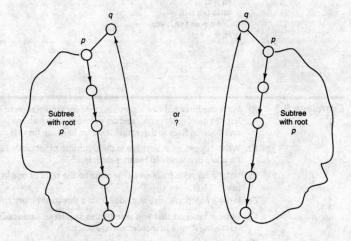

**Figure B.5. Finding the parent of a node in a threaded tree**

The translation of this method into a formal function is straightforward.

```
/* Parent: Finds the parent of node p, and sets q to the parent.  Returns nextac-
   tion = GORIGHT if p is the left child of q, and nextaction = VISITNODE if p is the right
   child of q. If p is the root, returns q = 0. */
void Parent(int p, int *q, Action *nextaction)
{
    *q = p;                        /* Locate the inorder successor of p; set it to q.    */
    while (*q > 0)
        *q = ws[*q].right;
    if (*q == 0)                   /* No successor: p cannot be a left child.            */
        *nextaction = VISITNODE;
    else if (ws[-*q].left == p) {  /* p is left child of -q.                             */
        *nextaction = GORIGHT;
        *q = -*q;
    } else
        *nextaction = VISITNODE;
/* If nextaction = GORIGHT, then we are finished. If nextaction = VISITNODE, find the par-
   ent as the inorder predecessor of subtree of p. */
    if (*nextaction == VISITNODE) {
        *q = p;
        while (*q > 0)
            *q = ws[*q].left;
        *q = -*q;
    }
}
```

---

**Exercises B.5**

E1. Write the threaded-tree algorithms in C for (a) insertion of a new node on the left, (b) inorder traversal, and (c) preorder traversal, using dynamic memory and Boolean flags to determine whether links are threads or real branches.

E2. What changes must be made in the algorithm of Section 9.2.2 in order to search for a key in a threaded binary search tree?

E3. Write a function to insert a new node on the right of one in a threaded binary tree.

E4. Write a function to delete a node from a threaded binary tree.

E5. Write a function that will insert threads into an unthreaded binary tree, by traversing it once in inorder, using a stack.

E6. Modify the function of Exercise E5 so that it uses no extra space for a stack, but the unused link space and threads already constructed instead.

E7. Write a function to insert a new node between two others in a threaded binary tree. That is, if p is a link to a node in the threaded tree, and p has nonempty left subtree, insert the new node (with q the pointer to it) as the left subtree of the one at p, with the left subtree of q being the former left subtree of p, and the right subtree of q being empty. Be sure to adjust all threads properly.

# References for Further Study

Some good ideas about techniques and procedures for the removal of recursion appear in

D. E. KNUTH, "Structured programming with goto statements", *Computing Surveys* 6 (1974), 261–302.

R. S. BIRD, "Notes on recursion elimination", *Communications of the ACM* 20 (1977), 434–439.

R. S. BIRD, "Improving programs by the introduction of recursion", *Communications of the ACM* 20 (1977), 856–863.

KNUTH (*op. cit.*, page 281) writes

There has been a good deal published about recursion elimination ...; but I'm amazed that very little of this is about "down to earth" problems. I have always felt that the transformation from recursion to iteration is one of the most fundamental concepts of computer science, and that a student should learn it at about the same time he is studying data structures.

A nonrecursive program using no stack is developed for the Towers of Hanoi in the paper

HELMUT PARTSCH and PETER PEPPER, "A family of rules for recursion removal," *Information Processing Letters* 5 (1976), 174–177.

Further papers on the Towers of Hanoi appear sporadically in the *SIGPLAN Notices* published by the A.C.M.

Presentation of nonrecursive versions of quicksort is a common topic, but so many slight variations are possible that few of the resulting programs are exactly the same. More extensive analysis is given in:

ROBERT SEDGEWICK, "The analysis of quicksort programs", *Acta Informatica* 7, (1976–77), 327–355.

Threaded binary trees constitute a standard topic in data structures, and will appear in most textbooks on data structures. Many of these books, however, leave the more complicated algorithms (such as postorder traversal) as exercises. The original reference for right-threaded binary trees is

A. J. PERLIS and C. THORNTON, "Symbol manipulation by threaded lists", *Communications of the ACM* 3 (1960), 195–204.

Fully threaded trees were independently discovered by

A. W. HOLT, "A mathematical and applied investigation of tree structures for syntactic analysis", Ph.D. dissertation (mathematics), University of Pennsylvania, 1963.

# C

# An Introduction to C

**T**HIS APPENDIX *presents a brief review of the C programming language, suitable for our needs in this book. For more details, consult a textbook on C.*

# C.1 Introduction

The following sections will give the reader a brief introduction to the C programming language. We have adhered to the American National Standards Institute (ANSI) standard definition of C (hereafter referred to as the ANSI C standard or just ANSI C). For those readers who are not familiar with C, we assume some previous experience with a similar high-level language such as Pascal and some rudimentary programming skills. Readers are advised to consult a textbook on C for a thorough treatment of the language. Several such books are listed in the references at the end of this appendix.

## C.1.1 OVERVIEW OF A C PROGRAM

A typical C program is made up of several functions which may be contained in one or more source files. Every C program must have a function named main which is where program execution always begins. Each source file is compiled separately, and then all are linked together to form the executable program. Quite often declarations or functions in one source file are referenced in another source file. In order for the compiler to be aware of the external references, "include" files are usually used. These will be covered in a later section.

# C.2 C Elements

## C.2.1 RESERVED WORDS

The following are *reserved words* in C:

| | | | |
|---|---|---|---|
| auto | double | int | struct |
| break | else | long | switch |
| case | enum | register | typedef |
| char | extern | return | union |
| const | float | short | unsigned |
| continue | for | signed | void |
| default | goto | sizeof | volatile |
| do | if | static | while |

These words serve a special purpose and may not be used as program identifiers. Two former reserved words, asm and fortran, may still be found in older programs but are now rarely used.

## C.2.2 CONSTANTS

Constants are program elements that do not change their value during the course of program execution. C has several different types of constants.

Integer constants are assumed to be decimal unless prefixed with a 0 (zero) to signify octal or 0X or 0x to signify hexadecimal. An integer constant may also be suffixed by u or U to specify that it is unsigned or l or L to specify that it is long.

Character constants are delimited by single quotes such as 'x'. There are several character constants that are used to specify certain special characters.

| | | | |
|---|---|---|---|
| newline | \n | backslash | \\ |
| horizontal tab | \t | single quote | \' |
| vertical tab | \v | double quote | \" |
| backspace | \b | audible alert | \a |
| carriage return | \r | octal number | \ooo |
| formfeed | \f | hex number | \xhh |

The octal and hex number escapes are used to specify the code of the desired character. For example, '\007' or '\x7' may be used to specify the ASCII bell character.

Floating point constants are decimal numbers with an optional signed integer exponent specified with either e or E. The number may also be suffixed by f, F, l or L to specify float or long double. If no suffix is given, the default is double.

String constants are a sequence of characters delimited by double quotes, for example, "this is a string". The double quotes are not part of the string itself. A string constant is actually represented internally as an array of characters terminated by the null character '\0'. String handling functions expect the null character to be present, signifying the end of the string.

Enumeration constants are those declared when defining an enumeration. For example, one that will be used throughout the book is

```
enum boolean { FALSE, TRUE };
```

This statement defines FALSE and TRUE to be enumeration constants with the values 0 and 1 respectively. Enumerations will be covered in more detail in a later section.

Symbolic constants are handled by the C preprocessor and are defined using the #define construct. It is a good programming practice to use symbolic constants where possible. This enables certain changes to be made with a minimal amount of effort. For instance,

```
#define MAXSIZE 20
```

defines the symbolic constant MAXSIZE to represent the value 20. MAXSIZE may now be used to define arrays, loop bounds, and such within the program. Now suppose the programmer decides to change this value to 100. Only one change is necessary; yet the change will be reflected throughout the program.

Finally, there is also the const qualifier that may be applied to any variable declaration to signify that its value cannot be modified. Hence, the following declares the floating point variable pi to be constant.

```
const float pi = 3.1416;
```

# C.3  Types and Declarations

C provides several built-in data types as well as the facilities for the programmer to define further types. Variables are declared using the following syntax:

type identifier_list;

where type is one of the types discussed below and the identifier_list contains one or more comma separated identifiers.

## C.3.1  BASIC TYPES

The basic types are char, int, float and double. A char is a single byte, which is capable of holding a single character. The character type may also be qualified with either signed or unsigned. The int type specifies an integer whose size depends on the particular machine. In addition to the signed and unsigned qualifiers, an int may also be short or long. The types float and double specify single-precision and double-precision floating point numbers respectively. The type qualifier long may be applied to double to specify extended-precision floating point. As with integers, the size of these numbers is also machine dependent. There is also a special type called void. It is usually used to declare a function that has no return value or takes no arguments.

## C.3.2  ARRAYS

C allows the declaration of multi-dimensional arrays using the following form:

type name[constant_expression]...

where type is the data type of the array elements, name is the array being declared and constant_expression is the size of the array. All arrays in C are indexed from 0 to constant_expression−1. The bracketed expression may be repeated to declare arrays with more than one dimension. For example, to declare a 5 by 5 integer matrix named Matrix_A one would use:

int Matrix_A[5][5];

Arrays will be discussed again when pointers are introduced.

## C.3.3  ENUMERATIONS

Enumerations provide a method of associating a constant set of values to a set of identifiers. Suppose a program was working with the days of the week. Rather than using the numbers 0 through 6 to represent Sunday through Saturday, the following could be used.

enum day {SUNDAY, MONDAY, TUESDAY, WEDNESDAY,
          THURSDAY, FRIDAY, SATURDAY};
enum day day_of_week;

The variable day_of_week may take on the values SUNDAY, MONDAY, and so on, which have more intuitive meanings than 0, 1, etc. The advantage of using enumerations over #define is that the values are generated automatically and the declarations of variables contain a little more information as to what values might be assigned. For instance, if the day of the week example had been done using:

```
#define SUNDAY 0
#define MONDAY 1
#define TUESDAY 2
#define WEDNESDAY 3
#define THURSDAY 4
#define FRIDAY 5
#define SATURDAY 6
```

The variable day_of_week would be declared as type int, imposing no restrictions on the integer values it could be assigned. (Note: most compilers do not restrict integer valued assignments to variables declared as enum.)

## C.3.4 STRUCTURES

The type declaration

$$\text{struct } tag \; \{ \ldots \}$$

in C establishes a type consisting of several *members* (also called *components*), each of which is itself of some (arbitrarily defined) type. The *tag* is optional and is called a *structure tag*. The use of a *tag* gives a name to the structure which can then be used in a subsequent declaration with the bracketed declaration list omitted. For example, we may define a type for a list of integers with the following declaration:

*declaration of list*

```
#define MAXLIST 200        /* maximum size of lists               */
struct list {
    int count;             /* how many elements are in the list   */
    int entry[MAXLIST];    /* the actual list of integers         */
};
```

Now when we want a list of integers we can use the following:

```
struct list List;
```

which declares List to be our desired list.

### 1. Accessing Structures

Individual parts of a C structure variable are referenced by giving first the name of the variable, then a period (.), then the member name as declared in the structure. Another method of access involves the arrow (->) operator. This is used when dereferencing a pointer to a structure. (We will discuss pointers in Section C.6.)

## C.3.5 UNIONS

Depending on the particular information stored in a structure, some of the members may sometimes not be used. If the data are of one kind, then one member may be

*example*

required, but if they are of another kind, a second member will be needed. Suppose, for example, that structures represent geometrical figures. If the figure is a circle, then we wish a member giving the *radius* of the circle. If it is a rectangle, then we wish the *height* and the *width* of the rectangle and whether or not it is a *square*. If it is a triangle, we wish the three *sides* and whether it is *equilateral*, *isosceles*, or *scalene*. For any of the figures we wish to have the *area* and the *circumference*. One way to set up the structure type for all these geometrical figures would be to have separate members for each of the desired attributes, but then, if the figure is a rectangle, the members giving the radius, sides of a square, and kind of triangle would all be meaningless. Similarly, if the figure is a circle or a triangle, several of the members would be undefined.

To avoid this difficulty, C provides *variant structures*, called *unions*, in which certain members are used only when the information in the structure is of a particular kind. Unions are similar to structures except that only one member is active at a time. It is up to the programmer to keep track of which member is currently being used. Thus, a union is a means to store any one of several types using a single variable. Unions are often combined with structures where one member in the structure is a union and another is used as a *tag* to determine which member of the union is in use.

All this will be clarified by returning to our geometrical example. The type specifying the kind of information in the structure is the enumerated type

```
enum shape { CIRCLE, RECTANGLE, TRIANGLE };
```

and the type specifying the kind of triangle is

```
enum triangle { EQUILATERAL, ISOSCELES, SCALENE };
```

The structure can then be declared as follows:

*geometry example*

```
struct figure {
        float area;                 /* This is the fixed part of the structure.    */
        float circumference;
        enum shape shape;           /* This is the tag.                            */
        union {
                float radius;       /* first variant for CIRCLE                    */
                struct {            /* second variant for RECTANGLE                */
                        float height;
                        float width;
                        enum boolean square;
                } rectangle;
                struct {            /* third variant for TRIANGLE                  */
                        float side1;
                        float side2;
                        float side3;
                        enum triangle kind;
                } triangle;
        } u;
}
```

*advantages of unions*   The first advantage of unions is that they clarify the logic of the program by showing exactly what information is required in each case. A second advantage is that they allow the system to save space when the program is compiled. Since only one of the union members is usable at any time for a particular union, the others members can be assigned to the same space by the compiler, and hence the total amount of space that needs to be set aside for the union is just the amount needed if the largest member is the one that occurs. This situation is illustrated in Figure C.1 for the example of structures describing geometrical shapes.

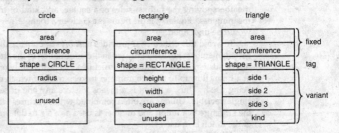

Figure C.1. Storage of unions

## C.3.6 TYPE DEFINITIONS WITH typedef

C provides a way of declaring new type names using the typedef construct. The basic syntax is

typedef data_type new_name;

where new_name is the new name given to the type data_type. (This is a simplified view of typedef, but it is sufficient for our purposes. A C textbook should be consulted for a complete explanation.) For instance, an earlier example declared a structure for a list of integers struct list. If we wanted to give a name to this, such as List, we could do so in the following manner:

typedef struct list List;

To declare a structure for a list of integers we may now use

List list;

instead of

struct list List;

(although both are equivalent).

We could also have defined the structure and the type at the same time by using

```
typedef struct list {
    int count;              /* how many elements are in the list        */
    int entry[MAXLIST];     /* the actual list of integers              */
} List;
```

# C.4 Operators

C has a large set of operators, and no attempt will be made to explain all of them here. The following chart lists the operators from highest to lowest precedence along with their associativity.

| Operators | Associativity |
|---|---|
| ( )   [ ]   -> | left to right |
| !   ~   ++   --   +   -   *   &   (*type*)   sizeof | right to left |
| *   /   % | left to right |
| +   - | left to right |
| ≪   ≫ | left to right |
| <   <=   >   >= | left to right |
| ==   != | left to right |
| & | left to right |
| ^ | left to right |
| \| | left to right |
| && | left to right |
| \|\| | left to right |
| ? : | right to left |
| =   +=   -=   *=   /=   %=   &=   ^=   \|=   ≪=   ≫= | right to left |
| , | left to right |

A few of the operators seem to have two different precedences. This is not the case. The & operator on the second line refers to the address of an object whereas the & operator on the eighth line is the bitwise AND. The * on the second line is the dereference operator and the * on the third line is multiplication. The + and - operators on the second line refer to the unary plus and minus as opposed to the binary plus and minus on the fourth line.

The ++ and -- operators are increment and decrement respectively. The ≪ and ≫ perform left shift and right shift operations. All the operators of the form *op* = are called assignment operators and provide a sort of shorthand. Expressions of the form

$$\text{variable = variable op value;}$$

may be replaced by

$$\text{variable op = value;}$$

The ternary operator ? : provides a conditional expression of the form

$$\text{expression1 ? expression2 : expression3}$$

where **expression1** is evaluated first followed by **expression2** or **expression3** depending on whether **expression1** evaluates to *true* (non-zero) or *false*. A C text should be consulted for a full treatment of all the operators.

# C.5 Control Flow Statements

In C, the semicolon is used as a statement terminator, not a separator as in Pascal. A *null* statement is signified by an isolated semicolon. For example, the following while loop reads characters until a newline is read. All the action is performed in the while expression so a loop body is not needed.

```
while ((ch = getchar( )) != '\n')
    /* null statement */;
```

A compound statement, or block, is a series of statements enclosed by braces, i.e.,

```
{
    statement1;
    statement2;
}
```

and is allowed wherever a single statement is valid. Variables may also be declared at the beginning of a block.

## C.5.1 IF – ELSE

The if statement has the following syntax,

```
                if (expression)
                    statement
                else
                    statement
```

with the else part being optional. If there are several nested if statements without a matching number of else clauses, each else is associated with the most recent previous if statement not containing an else.

## C.5.2 SWITCH

The switch statement is a multi-way branch based on a single expression.

```
switch (expression) {
case constant_expression : statements
case constant_expression : statements
/* as many cases as needed ... */
default : statements
}
```

If none of the cases satisfy the expression, the default part of the switch is executed. The default clause is optional and the switch statement will do nothing if none of the cases match (any side effects caused by the evaluation of the expression will still occur). The case and default clauses may be in any order.

One very important characteristic of the switch is that the cases *fall through*, that is, execution will continue to the following case unless explicit action is taken to leave the switch. That explicit action comes in the form of the break statement. When used anywhere in a switch statement (usually at the end of a case), the break will cause execution to continue after the switch.

## C.5.3 LOOPS

C provides several loops constructs, two of which test for loop termination at the top of the loop and one that tests at the bottom.

### 1. While

The while loop has the form:

```
while (expression)
    statement
```

where statement will be executed as long as expression evaluates to a non-zero value.

### 2. For

The for statement has the following syntax:

```
for (expression1; expression2; expression3)
    statement
```

All three expressions are optional; however, the semicolons are not. The for statement is equivalent to the following while loop:

```
expression1;
while (expression2) {
    statement
    expression3;
}
```

It is not uncommon for the comma operator to be used in expression1 and expression3 to allow multiple initializations and updates.

### 3. Do-while

The do ... while loop in C provides a loop that tests for loop termination at the end of the loop. Its syntax is

```
do
    statement
while (expression);
```

where statement will be executed at least once and then as long as expression remains *non*-zero thereafter.

## C.5.4 BREAK AND CONTINUE

The break statement will cause program execution to continue after the enclosing for, while, do, or switch statement. The continue statement will result in the next iteration of the enclosing for, while, or do loop to execute.

## C.5.5 GOTO

C does contain the goto statement but since its use is not looked upon with favor, it will not be discussed here.

# C.6 Pointers

A pointer is a variable that may contain the address of another variable. All variables in C, except variables of type register, have an address. The address is the location where the variable exists in memory. We use a * in front of a variable to declare the variable to be a pointer.

## C.6.1 POINTER TO A SIMPLE VARIABLE

We can declare a variable of type char by

```
char c = 'a';
```

and we can declare a pointer to something of type char by

```
char *p;
```

where p is the pointer. The * in front of p identifies it as a pointer, that is, a variable that may contain the address of another variable. In this case, p is a pointer to something of type char so p may contain the address of a variable of type char.

The pointer p has not been initialized yet so its current value is undefined—its value is whatever existed in the space reserved for p. To initialize the pointer we need to assign it an address. We can obtain the address of a simple variable by using the unary operator &:

```
p = &c;
```

Now p contains the address of the variable c. It is important that the type of the variable and the type of the pointer match. We will explain why when we discuss pointers to arrays.

To refer to a value that a pointer points to we need to *dereference* the pointer. In effect, we take the value in p, an address, and we go to that address to get the final value. Thus the following two statements print the same value:

```
printf("c is %c\n", c);
printf("c is %c\n", *p);
```

We can refer to the variable c by using its name or by using the pointer p that points to c. Consequently, we can change the value of c to be the representation for 'b' by using an assignment to c or indirectly (dereferencing) by using the pointer p:

```
p = &c;        /* initialize p               */
c = 'b';       /* assigns 'b' to c           */
*p = 'b';      /* assigns 'b' to c           */
```

### C.6.2 POINTER TO AN ARRAY

We can declare an array of characters and a pointer to character. For example,

```
char line[100], *p;
```

We may refer to the first two elements of line using

```
line[0] = 'a';
line[1] = 'b';
```

For each assignment the compiler will have to calculate the address: line plus offset zero, and line plus offset one. Another way to perform the above assignments is to use a pointer. First, we need to initialize the pointer p to point to the beginning of the array line:

```
p = &line[0];
```

Since an array name is a synonym for the array's starting address we can use

```
p = line;
```

Now we can perform the assignments

```
*p = 'a';    and    *(p + 1) = 'b';
```

The pointer p continues to point to the beginning of the array line. As an alternative, we could increment the pointer after each assignment

```
*p++ = 'a';
*p++ = 'b';
```

and the pointer p will be pointing to line[2] after the assignments.

When we use + 1 or the ++ operator with a pointer we are referring to the next element after the current element. If p points to the beginning of the array line (line[0]), then p++ moves the pointer to line[1]. Notice that when we increment the pointer we point to the next element of the array. In this case the pointer is of type char so when we increment it we point to the next byte which is the next character.

If we have a pointer to an int,

```
int numbers[10], *q = numbers;
```

then q points to numbers[0]. When we increment q we point to numbers[1] which could be two or four bytes away—depending on the hardware you are using an int could be two bytes or four bytes long.

We can add an integer expression to a pointer or we can subtract an integer expression from a pointer. We can also compare two pointers if they point to the same array, otherwise the comparison is not meaningful.

### C.6.3 ARRAY OF POINTERS

In C we can create arrays of variables of any type. Since a pointer is a variable that may contain the address of another variable it is feasible to create an array of pointers. Each element of such an array is a pointer. For example, the declaration

char *ap[3];

declares ap as an array of pointers to char. Each element of ap may point to the beginning of a character string. If we use malloc to allocate space for each string then each element of ap may point to some area in memory that contains the string. This situation is illustrated in Figure C.2.

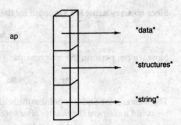

Figure C.2. Array of Pointers to Strings

On the other hand, the strings could be in some array line with each element of ap pointing to different parts of the array. See Figure C.3 for an example of such a situation.

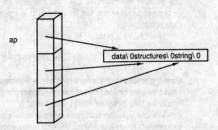

Figure C.3. Array of Pointers to Strings

### C.6.4 POINTER TO STRUCTURES

We can declare an array of structures and then use a pointer to point to the first element of the array. This is similar to the pointer to arrays we discussed before. For example,

```
struct example {
    char c;
    int i;
};
struct example ae[10], *p;
p = ae;
p->c = 'a';                    /* character in the first structure    */
p->i = 0;                      /* integer in the first structure      */
p++;                           /* make p point to ae[1]               */
p->c = 'b';                    /* character in the second structure   */
```

This example is illustrated in Figure C.4.

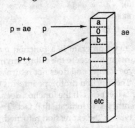

**Figure C.4. Pointer to Array of Structures**

The -> operator is used to dereference a pointer to a structure and access a member of that structure. The construction p->c is therefore equivalent to (*p).c.

An element of a structure can be a pointer to another structure of the same type. This is called a *self-referential* structure. For example,

```
struct selfref {
    char c;
    struct selfref *next;
};
struct selfref *p;
```

declares p as a pointer to a structure of type struct selfref. This could be a linked list (see Chapter 5) and p points to a structure in the list. To access the next element in the list we use

```
p = p->next;
```

since the structure contains the address of the next structure in the pointer next.

# C.7 Functions

In programming we normally break a task into separate functions because it is easier to deal with smaller tasks that may be independent of other parts of the program. A C program is normally a collection of functions. The main program, called main, is a function that may invoke other functions. The information we pass to a function is called an **argument**. The information the function receives is called a *parameter*.

The ANSI C standard allows the programmer to declare a *function prototype*, which is a concise way of describing the number and type of arguments a function expects and what the function .eturns. Take for example, the following code:

```
void f(int);
int main(void)
{
    int i = 3;
    f(i);
    return 0;
}
```

The main program is a function main that does not expect any arguments and returns an integer to the calling environment. The function f expects one argument of type integer and does not return anything to its calling function.

The function prototype informs the compiler of the number and type of arguments it expects. If the function does not expect any arguments then we use void, in parentheses, to indicate that fact. The type in front of the function name indicates the type of the expression returned. If the function does not return anything we use void as the return type.

## C.7.1 ARGUMENTS TO FUNCTIONS: CALL BY VALUE

C passes arguments to functions by value. That is, C makes a copy of the argument and passes the copy to the function: in effect it passes the value of the argument to the function. If the function modifies a parameter, the function is modifying only a copy of the original argument. Consider the function

```
void f(int j)
{
    j--;
    printf("j is %d\n", j);
}
```

f receives an integer, decrements it, prints its new value, and returns. If we invoke f with the argument i, say int i = 3;  f(i);  then the function receives a copy of i. When f decrements j it decrements a copy of the argument but not the argument itself. When the function returns, the value of i has not changed.

## C.7.2 ARGUMENTS TO FUNCTIONS: CALL BY REFERENCE

Often we want the function to have access to the original argument in the invoking function instead of its copy. In this case we pass the argument by reference; that is, we pass the address of the argument as a parameter for the function. Since the function has the address of the actual argument (not just a copy), it can change the value of this argument. For example, the function

```
void g(int *k)
{
    *k = 2;
}
```

expects a pointer to an integer variable. It then assigns 2 to the integer variable to which k points. As an example of invoking this function, consider the following code:

```
void g(int *);
int main(void)
{
    int i;
    g( &i);
    printf("i = %d\n", i);
    return 0;
}
```

This program passes the address of the variable i to g, the function receives a pointer to a variable in the invoking function (the address of i), and it modifies i. When the function g terminates, the main program has a modified variable i.

An exception to the pass by value rule in C is arrays. Arrays are always passed by reference.

```
int getline(char *, int);
...
int n;
char line[100];
n = getline(line, 100);
```

The above code fragment invokes a function getline that expects a pointer to a character and an integer. Since an array name is like an address we pass the array name, line, and an integer that indicates the size of the array. If the function modifies the first parameter it modifies the array in the invoking function.

## C.7.3 FUNCTION PROTOTYPES AND INCLUDE FILES

A *function prototype* is a declaration of a function type (what it returns) and the number and type of arguments, if any, that the function expects. Our earlier example,

void f(int);

is the function prototype for the function f. The function expects one argument of type int and it does not return anything as the function value; consequently it has the type void.

Standard library functions have their prototypes in the *.h files (where * denotes any name) available with your C compiler. Check your documentation to find out which *.h file applies to the library functions you are going to use. For example, the function strcpy has its prototype in string.h, so in order to let the compiler know what arguments strcpy expects and what it returns we include string.h in our program:

```
#include <string.h>
...
char buffer[100], line[100];
...
strcpy(line, buffer);
```

Standard *.h file names are enclosed in angle brackets<...>. Other *.h files that we create are in the current directory and their names are enclosed in double quotes. If we put the prototype for the function getline in a file called calls.h then the code fragment we used earlier could change to

```
#include "calls.h"
...
int n;
char line[100];
n = getline(line, 100);
```

## C.8 Pointers and Functions

We now discuss some common operations using pointers and functions.

### C.8.1 POINTER TO A FUNCTION

In C we can get the address of a function as well as that of variables. This allows us to pass a pointer to a function as an argument to another function. For example, we can write a function sort that invokes another function to perform the comparison of the elements being sorted. We can pass to sort the address of the function that will perform the comparisons. If we are sorting character strings we can use the standard library function strcmp and if we are sorting integers we can write our own numcmp function. The code fragment could look like

```
int strcmp(char *, char *);
int numcmp(char *, char *);
void sort(int (*fnc_ptr)(char *, char *));
void main(void)
{
   ...
   sort(strcmp);               /* Sort character strings.            */
   ...
   sort(numcmp);               /* Sort integers.                     */
}
```

sort expects one argument: a pointer to a function that expects two pointers to characters and returns an integer. Normally the integer returned is <0 when the first argument is less than the second, 0 when the arguments are equal, and > 0 when the first argument is greater than the second. The definition for less than, equal, and greater than depends on the application. The function sort will eventually invoke the function whose address we passed:

```
void sort(int (*f)(char *, char *))
{
   int condition;
   char *p, *q;
   /* p and q are initialized. */
   ...
   condition = (*f)(p, q);
   ...
   /* Take an action based on the condition. */
}
```

## C.8.2 FUNCTIONS THAT RETURN A POINTER

There are some standard library functions that return a pointer, such as strcpy(char *to, char *from), which copies the string from to the string to and returns a pointer to the beginning of the string to. The function prototype for strcpy appears in the standard include file string.h and looks like

```
char *strcpy(char *, char *);
```

The type char * in front of the function name indicates the type returned: strcpy returns a pointer to a character.

We can write our own functions that return pointers. Suppose we wrote a function MakeNode that allocates space for a node and returns a pointer to the allocated space. Each node is a structure defined as

```
typedef char Item;
typedef struct node {
       Item item;
       struct node *next;
} Node;
```

MakeNode expects an argument, invokes the standard library function malloc to allocate enough space for a node, copies the argument into the node, and returns a pointer to the node. The function looks like

```
/* MakeNode: make a new node and insert item. */
Node *MakeNode(Item item)
{
    Node *p;
    if ((p = (Node *)malloc(sizeof(Node))) != NULL)
        p->info = item;
    return p;
}
```

## C.8.3 POINTER TO A POINTER AS AN ARGUMENT

Whenever we want to modify an argument we pass it by reference. For example, we invoke a function f that modifies whatever the pointer p points to:

```
void f(char *);
void main(void)
{
    char c;
    f( &c);
}
void f(char *p)
{
    *p = 'a';
}
```

What if we want to modify the pointer itself, instead of what it points to? Then we have to pass the pointer by reference. We do that by passing the address of the pointer. What should the function expect? The function should expect the address of a variable that in this case is a pointer—a pointer to a pointer. The code fragment could look like

```
void g(char **);
void main(void)
{
    char line[100];
    char *p = line;       /* p points to line[0]      */
    g( &p);               /* p points to line[1]      */
}
void g(char **p)
{
    (*p)++;               /* Increment the pointer.   */
}
```

As you may suspect, there is a lot more about functions, about pointers, about C. This has been an introduction to some aspects of the language that we use in this book. As you write programs in C these constructs become familiar and you become proficient in the language and in data structures.

# References for Further Study

The programming language C was devised by DENNIS M. RITCHIE. The standard reference is

BRIAN W. KERNIGHAN and DENNIS M. RITCHIE, *The C Programming Language*, second edition, Prentice Hall, Englewood Cliffs, N.J., 1988, 272 pages.

This book contains many examples and exercises. For the solutions to the exercises in Kernighan and Ritchie, together with a chance to study C code, see

CLOVIS L. TONDO and SCOTT E. GIMPEL, *The C Answer Book*, second edition, Prentice Hall, Englewood Cliffs, N.J., 1989, 208 pages.

Two more references are

SAMUEL P. HARBISON and GUY L. STEELE JR., *C: A Reference Manual*, second edition, Prentice Hall, Englewood Cliffs, N.J., 1987, 404 pages.

NARAIN GEHANI, *C: An Advanced Introduction*, Computer Science Press, Rockville, Maryland, 1985, 332 pages.

Beginning and intermediate-level programmers may find the following books to be more readable.

THOMAS PLUM, *Learning to Program in C*, Prentice Hall, Englewood Cliffs, N.J., 1983.

ALLEN I. HOLUB, *The C Companion*, Prentice Hall, Englewood Cliffs, N.J., 1987, 284 pages.

# Index ▬▬▬▬▬▬▬▬▬▬

12. *Discrete Mathematical Structures 3rd ed.* 1996/**Bernard Kolman, Robert C. Busby, Sharon Ross**(离散数学结构 第 3 版 544 页)

13. *Computer graphics C Version 2nd ed.* 1997/**Donald Hearn, M. Pauline Baker**(计算机图形学 C 语言版 第 2 版 864 页 附彩插)

14. *Computer Networks and Internets* 1997/**Douglas E. Comer**(计算机网络与因特网 530 页 附光盘)

15. *A First Course in Database Systems* 1997/**Jeffrey D. Ullman, Jennifer Widom**(数据库系统基础教程 484 页)

16. *Digital Image Processing* 1996/**Kenneth R. Castleman**(数字图象处理 686 页)

17. *Business Data Communications 3rd ed.* 1998/**William Stallings, Richard Van Slyke**(事务数据通信 第 3 版 578 页)

18. *Software Architecture:* **Perspectives on an Emerging Discipline** 1996/**Mary Shaw, David Garlan**(软件体系结构 264 页)

19. *Digital Video Processing* 1995/**A. Murat Tekalp**(数字视频处理 548 页)

20. *IBM PC Assembly Language and Programming 4th ed.* 1998/**PETER ABEL**(*IBM PC* 汇编语言与程序设计 第 4 版 622 页)

21. *Operating Systems:* **Internals and Design Principles** 3rd ed. 1998/**William Stallings**(操作系统:精髓与设计原理 第 3 版 800 页)

22. *Programming Languages:* **Design and Implementation** 3rd ed. 1996/**Terrence W. Pratt, Marvin V. Zelkowitz**(程序设计语言:设计与实现 第 3 版 570 页)

23. *Computer System Architecture 3rd ed.* 1993/**M. Morris Mano**(计算机系统体系结构 第 3 版 542 页)

24. *Object-Oriented Systems Analysis and Design* 1996/**Ronald J. Norman**(面向对象系统分析与设计 456 页)

25. *Digital and Analog Communication Systems 5th ed.* 1997/**Leon W. Couch Ⅱ**(数字及模拟通信系统 第 5 版 776 页)

26. *Data Structures & Program Design in C 2nd ed.* 1997/**Robert Kruse, C. L. Tondo, Bruce Leung**(数据结构与程序设计 C 语言描述 692 页)

# 读者意见反馈卡

感谢您购买本书！本书系我社获美国 Prentice Hall 公司授权影印出版。Prentice Hall 公司是国际知名的教育图书出版公司，出版了许多技术含量高而风格独具的高校计算机类图书，成为美国以及全球高校采用率最高的教材，享誉全球教育界，Prentice Hall 公司为使本书更适应中国学生以及计算机业界人士对于英文原版参考书的实际需要，特别授予了联合影印版权，力求为中国计算机教育的发展及业界人士的自我提高尽一份力量。良好愿望的达成尚需广大读者的指导和帮助。在此，非常希望您能填妥下表，将读后感告诉我们，以便为您提供更优秀的图书。

**请附阁下资料**(或附名片，如您是教师或学生请特别注明您的专业/系别)

姓名：＿＿＿＿＿＿＿ 年龄：＿＿＿＿＿＿＿ 职务：＿＿＿＿＿＿＿＿＿＿

单位：＿＿＿＿＿＿＿＿＿＿＿＿＿＿＿＿＿＿＿＿＿＿＿＿＿＿＿＿＿＿＿

地址：＿＿＿＿＿＿＿＿＿＿＿＿＿＿＿ 邮编：＿＿＿＿＿＿＿＿＿＿＿

电话：＿＿＿＿＿ 传真：＿＿＿＿＿ 电子邮件：＿＿＿＿＿＿＿＿＿

1. 您获得此书的途径：
   ○校内书店　　　○校外书店　　　○商场　　　　○邮购
   ○学校教材科　　○其它：＿＿＿＿＿＿＿＿＿＿＿＿＿＿＿
2. 一般情况下，哪些因素影响您购买图书：
   ○封面(底)推荐　○作者及出版社　○封面设计及版式　○前言
   ○索引及目录　　○插图及表格　　○价格
   ○其它：＿＿＿＿＿＿＿＿＿＿＿＿＿＿＿＿＿＿＿＿＿＿
3. 您感兴趣的计算机类读物：
   ○网络与通信　　○Internet/WWW　○操作系统　　○数据库
   ○编程语言　　　○计算机游戏　　○文字处理　　○电子表格
   ○多媒体技术　　○软件工程　　　○其它：＿＿＿＿＿＿＿＿
4. 您最喜欢的计算机读物类型：
   ○原版教材或参考书　　　　　　○国内本版教材或参考书
   ○翻译版教材或参考书　　　　　○影印本教材或参考书
   ○原因：＿＿＿＿＿＿＿＿＿＿＿＿＿＿＿＿＿＿＿＿＿＿
5. 您认为国内计算机图书出版社实力最强的是哪三家？各有何特色？
   冠军：＿＿＿＿＿＿＿　特色：＿＿＿＿＿＿＿＿＿＿＿＿＿
   亚军：＿＿＿＿＿＿＿　特色：＿＿＿＿＿＿＿＿＿＿＿＿＿
   季军：＿＿＿＿＿＿＿　特色：＿＿＿＿＿＿＿＿＿＿＿＿＿
6. 您认为目前市场上比较短缺的图书有：
   ○＿＿＿＿＿＿＿　○＿＿＿＿＿＿＿　○＿＿＿＿＿＿＿
   ○＿＿＿＿＿＿＿　○＿＿＿＿＿＿＿　○＿＿＿＿＿＿＿

7. 您对清华大学出版社或西蒙与舒斯特公司有何建议和要求：
   ○ _____
   ○ _____

## 如果您是教师或学生,请您填写以下内容

8. 本学期正在开设的计算机类课程有：
   ○ _____ ○ _____
   ○ _____ ○ _____
   使用的教材为：
   ○ _____ 出版者：_____
   ○ _____ 出版者：_____
   ○ _____ 出版者：_____
   ○ _____ 出版者：_____

9. 是否正在采用或准备采用翻译版教材？
   ○ 是                    ○ 否
   如果是,书名：_____
   课程名：_____ 学生人数：_____
   出版者：_____ 原出版商：_____

10. 是否正在采用或准备采用影印版教材？
    ○ 是                   ○ 否
    如果是,书名：_____
    课程名：_____ 学生人数：_____
    出版者：_____ 原出版商：_____

11. 是否准备采用本书或本书的翻译版作为您的教材？
    本书：  ○ 是  ○ 否,  原因是：_____
    翻译版：○ 是  ○ 否,  原因是：_____

## 如有任何疑问或要求,请与我们联系：

Tsinghua Uinversity Press
清华大学出版社市场部
北京 100084
北京市海淀区清华园
清华大学校内
Tel：010 – 62781827
Fax：010 – 62770278

Simon & Schuster
BeijingOffice
西蒙与舒斯特北京代表处
北京 100086
北京市海淀区知春里 28 号
开源商务写字楼 102 房间
Fax：010 – 62615863
E-mail：ssbj@bupt.edu.cn